AF600275

Motif-Index
of
Folk-Literature

Vol. V

MOTIF-INDEX
OF
FOLK-LITERATURE

A Classification of Narrative Elements in Folktales, Ballads, Myths, Fables, Mediaeval Romances, Exempla, Fabliaux, Jest-Books, and Local Legends

REVISED AND ENLARGED EDITION BY

STITH THOMPSON
Indiana University

VOLUME FIVE
L-Z

INDIANA UNIVERSITY PRESS
BLOOMINGTON & INDIANAPOLIS

Indiana University Press gratefully acknowledges
the support of the L.J. and Mary C. Skaggs Foundation
in the republication of the six volumes of the
Motif-Index of Folk-Literature.

Manufactured in the United States of America

ISBN 0-253-33885-9

6 7 8 9 00 99 98 97

complete set ISBN 0-253-33887-5

L. REVERSAL OF FORTUNE

DETAILED SYNOPSIS

L. REVERSAL OF FORTUNE

L0—L99. Victorious youngest child.

L0. Victorious youngest child. *Fb "yngst" III 1132a; *Saintyves Perrault 128ff.; *Jacobs's list s.v. "Youngest best"; Breton: Sébillot Incidents s.v. "cadet"; French Canadian: Barbeau JAFL XXIX 13; India: Thompson-Balys.

Z200. Heroes.

L10. Victorious youngest son. *Types 326, 402, 471, 513, 550, 551, 554, 569, 570, 571, 577, 580, 610, 935, 1650. See also references under each of these type entries in FFC LXXIV. *Hdwb. d. Märchens I 186a; Malone PMLA XLIII 398f.; *A. Christensen Danske Studier (1916) 46ff.; Chauvin II 115 No. 88. — Irish myth: Cross; Icelandic: *Boberg; Spanish Exempla: Keller; Jewish: *Neuman; India: *Thompson-Balys; Chinese: Graham; Hawaii: Beckwith Myth 491; Tahiti: Henry Ancient Tahiti (Honolulu, 1928) 614; Tuamotu: Stimson MS (T-G. 3/403, 615); Easter Island: Métraux Ethnology 383; Polynesian: Dixon 41; N. A. Indian: *Thompson Tales 327 n. 185, (California): Gayton and Newman 74; Africa (Jaunde): Heepe 262, (Fang): Tessman 107, (Zanzibar): Bateman 155ff. No. 8, (Ekoi): Talbot 207, 259, 355, (Fjort): Dennett 65 No. 13, (Gold Coast): Barker and Sinclair 171 No. 34; Cape Verde Islands: Parsons MAFLS XV (1) 110f. No. 39.

D861.3. Magic object stolen by brothers. H912. Tasks assigned at suggestion of jealous brothers. H1242. Youngest brother alone succeeds on quest. H1471. Watch for devastating monster. Youngest alone successful. J22. Precepts of the lion to his sons. Only the younger keeps them and is successful. K308. Youngest brother surpasses elder as thief. K2211. Treacherous elder brother. L101. Unpromising hero (male Cinderella). Usually but not always the unpromising hero is also the youngest son. P11.2.1. King chosen by contest: prince finding greatest fault with his father. Youngest can find no fault and is chosen. R155.1. Youngest brother rescues his elder brothers. Z221. Eldest brother as hero.

L10.1. *Name of victorious youngest son.* Fb "Esben" I 256.

L10.1.1. *"Thirteen" as name of victorious youngest son.* (Youngest of thirteen brothers.) BP III 34; *Köhler-Bolte I 383; India: Thompson-Balys.

T596.2. Children named by numbers (1, 2, 3, etc.).

L10.2. *Abused son of younger co-wife becomes hero.* India: Thompson-Balys.

L11. *Fortunate youngest son.* Always has good luck. *Type 1650; BP II 69ff.; MacCulloch Childhood 365; India: *Thompson-Balys; Eskimo (Greenland): Rink 93, 281, 434, (Central Eskimo): Boas RBAE VI 630, (Ungava): Turner RBAE XI 265, (West Hudson Bay): Boas BAM XV 309, (Kodiak): Golder JAFL XVI 16.

L11.1. *Seal of humiliation put by youngest brother-in-law on the back of his rivals.* India: *Thompson-Balys.

Q472. Branding as punishment.

L12. *Favorite youngest son.* India: Thompson-Balys.

L13. *Compassionate youngest son.* Kind to people or animals: rewarded. *Types 513, 550, 551, 570, 571, 577, 610; Missouri French: Carrière; Jewish: Neuman; India: *Thompson-Balys; N. A. Indian (Klikitat): Jacobs U Wash II 10.

H486.2. Test of paternity: shooting at father's corpse. Q2. Kind and unkind. Churlish person disregards requests of old person (animal) and is punished. Courteous person (often youngest brother or sister) complies and is rewarded.

L13.1. *Youngest wife's son restores eyesight to blinded six wives of raja and reinstates his mother.* India: Thompson-Balys.

L21. *Stupid youngest son becomes clever.* Panzer Beowulf passim; N. A. Indian (Micmac, Shuswap): Thompson CColl II 416ff.

J1110. Clever persons.

L31. *Youngest brother helps elder.* Types 516, 550; Rösch FFC LXXVII 96; Missouri French: Carrière; Spanish: Espinosa Jr. No. 130; India: Thompson-Balys; Chinese: Graham.

K2211. Treacherous brother. Usually elder brother. R155.1. Youngest brother rescues his eldest brothers.

L32. *Only the youngest brother helps his sister perform dangerous task.* India: Thompson-Balys.

L41. *Younger brother given birthright of elder.* Jewish: *Neuman.

L50. Victorious youngest daughter. *Types 361, 425, 431, 440, 480, 510, 511, 707, 901, 923; **Cox Cinderella passim; *BP I 185; Nutt FL IV 133; Jacobs FL IV 269; Lang FL IV 413; Cox FL XVIII 191; *Roberts 110; Tegethoff 10; *MacCulloch Childhood 357; *Saintyves Perrault 113. — Missouri French: Carrière; Spanish: Boggs FFC XC 65 No. 471B*; Italian: Basile Pentamerone I Nos. 2, 8, II Nos. 2, 3, III No. 4, V No. 9, Rotunda; India: *Thompson-Balys; Chinese: Eberhard FFC CXX 248 No. 193; Indonesia: Dixon 210; N. A. Indian: *Thompson CColl II 382ff., 390, (Maliseet): Mechling GSCan IV No. 9, (Chinook): Boas BBAE XX 77ff. No. 4, (Kwakiutl): Boas and Hunt JE III 371, (Gros Ventre): Kroeber PaAM I 80ff. No. 19, (Wichita): Dorsey CI XXI No. 33.

K95. Finger-drying contest won by deception. Three daughters are to wet hands: the first to have hands dry is to be the first to marry. The youngest waves her hands, exclaiming, "I don't want a man!" She wins. M21. King Lear judgment. R157.1. Youngest sister rescues elder.

L51. *Favorite youngest daughter.* India: Thompson-Balys; Africa (Zulu): Callaway 85.

L52. *Abused youngest daughter.* *Types 425, 510, 511, 709; *Cox 492ff.; Böklen 78ff.; *Roberts 110; Tegethoff 10; Icelandic: Boberg; Italian Novella: Rotunda; India: *Thompson-Balys; Chinese: Eberhard FFC CXX 248 No. 193; Hawaii: Beckwith Myth 170 n. 5; Tuamotu: Stimson MS (z-G. 13/346). Most references to L50 apply to this motif.

L54. *Compassionate youngest daughter.* *Types 361, 431. See also most references to Q2.

Q2. Kind and unkind. Churlish person disregards requests of old person (animal) and is punished. Courteous person (often youngest brother or sister) complies and is rewarded.

L54.1. *Youngest daughter agrees to marry a monster;* later the sisters are jealous. *Type 425; India: Thompson-Balys; Korean: Zong in-Sob 199 No. 76.

D733. Loathly bridegroom. T216. Loathly bridegroom carried on back in basket by wife.

L55. *Stepdaughter heroine.* *Types 403, 425, 432, 450, 480, 510, 709; BP I 226; *Roberts 109; Lithuanian: Balys Index No. 481*; Missouri French: Carrière; Italian: Basile Pentamerone I No. 6.

L55.1. *Abused stepdaughter.* See references to L52 and L55. *Roberts 137; Missouri French: Carrière; Spanish: Espinosa Jr. Nos. 142—145; Greek: Grote I 103.

S31. Cruel stepmother.

L61. *Clever youngest daughter.* Type 923; Africa (Kaffir): Theal 123.

H592.1. "Love like Salt". Girl compares her love for her father to salt. Experience teaches him the value of salt. J1111. Clever girl.

L62. *Youngest daughter suspects impostor.* Elder have been deceived. N. A. Indian (Pawnee): Dorsey CI LIX 166 No. 44, (Kwakiut): Boas and Hunt JE X 196ff.; (Takelma): Sapir U Pa II (1) 64 No. 4, (Modoc): Curtin Myths of the Modocs (Boston, 1912) 27ff., (Yana): Curtin Creation Myths (Boston, 1898) 353ff.

K1900. Impostures.

L63. *Youngest daughter avoids seducer.* Elder sisters have been deceived. Type 883B; Italian: Basile Pentamerone III No. 4; India: Thompson-Balys.

K1300. Seduction.

L70. Youngest of group victorious.

L71. *Only the youngest of group of imprisoned women refuses to eat her newborn child.* India: *Thompson-Balys.

G72.2. Starving woman abandoned in cave eats newborn child.

L72. *Youngest animal in group overcomes adversary.* N. A. Indian (Klikitat): Jacobs U Wash II 7—9.

L100—L199. Unpromising hero (heroine).

L100. Unpromising hero (heroine). Irish myth: *Cross; India: *Thompson-Balys.

H1242.1. Unpromising hero succeeds in quest. J1111 Clever girl. J1113. Clever boy. K1815. Humble disguise. (Cap o' Rushes, Peau d' âne, Allerleirauh.) Usually in rough clothing. K1816. Disguise as menial. N170. The capriciousness of luck. S371. Abandoned daughter's son becomes hero. Z200. Heroes.

L101. *Unpromising hero* (male Cinderella). Usually, but not always, the unpromising hero is also the youngest son. *BP I 183ff.; *Rank Mythus v. d. Geburt d. Helden; *Cosquin Contes indiens 494ff.; Cox 437—462, 519; M. Bloomfield in Penzer VII x; *Hdwb. d. Märchens I 184b nn. 13ff.; Chauvin II 83 No. 9. — Icelandic: *Boberg; English: Wells 25 (The Tale of Gamelyn); Missouri French: Carrière; Italian Novella: Rotunda; Chinese: Eberhard FFC CXX 52 No. 32; Hawaii: Beckwith Myth 408; N. A. Indian: *Thompson Tales 327 n. 185; Africa (Fang): Trilles 251f.

L10. Victorious youngest son. L113.4. Peasant as hero.

L101.1. *Unpromising hero: aged man.* Irish myth: Cross; N. A. Indian (Zuñi): Benedict II 336.

L102. *Unpromising heroine.* Usually, but not always, the youngest daughter. See references to L50. *BP I 165ff.; **Cox passim; Irish myth: Cross; Breton: Sébillot Incidents s.v. "merle"; Missouri French:

Carrière; Italian Novella: *Rotunda; Tuamotu: Stimson MS (z-G. 13/346); N. A. Indian (Zuñi): Benedict II 336.

H561.1. Clever peasant girl asked riddles by king.

L103. *Unpromising hero given great powers by deity.* India: Thompson-Balys.

L110. Types of unpromising heroes (heroines).

N173. Disagreeable and disliked youth as favorite of fortune. N225. Man robbed and penniless entertained by wealthy widow and enriched.

L111. *Hero (heroine) of unpromising origin.* India: *Thompson-Balys; Chinese: Graham.

L111.1. *Exile returns and succeeds.* **A. Nutt FLR IV 1ff.; *Hibbard 111 n. 6; Boccaccio Decameron II No. 8 (Lee 39); v. Hahn Sagenwissenschaftliche Studien 341ff.; *Dickson 42 n. 42; Irish myth: *Cross; Missouri French: Carrière; Italian Novella: *Rotunda; India: *Thompson-Balys.

A516. Expulsion and return of culture hero. M373. Expulsion to avoid fulfillment of prophecy. P361.2. Faithful servant remains at home and fights for exiled hero. Q431. Punishment: banishment (exile). R131.11.2. King rescues abandoned child. S140. Cruel abandonments and exposures. S330. Circumstances of murder or exposure of children. S354. Exposed infant reared at strange king's court.

L111.1.1. *Banished youth becomes mighty king.* Icelandic: Völsunga saga ch. 1, Boberg.

L111.1.2. *Fugitive bull-calf returns when grown and defeats his father.* West Indies: Flowers 557—9.

L111.2. *Foundling hero.* *Dickson 144ff. n. 147; Hdwb. d. Märchens II 120b; Irish myth: Cross; Icelandic: *Boberg; Missouri French: Carrière; Italian Novella: *Rotunda; Tonga: Gifford 130; N. A. Indian: Lowie JAFL XXI 27.

L350. Mildness triumphs over violence. N861. Foundling helper. S350. Fate of abandoned child. T600. Care of children.

L111.2.1. *Future hero found in boat* (basket, bushes). Legends of Moses, Cyrus, Beowulf and others. *Usener Die Sintfluthsagen (Bonn, 1899) 80ff.; Hdwb. d. Märchens I s.v. "Aussetzung in Boot"; Icelandic: *Boberg; Missouri French: Carrière; Italian Novella: Rotunda; Jewish: *Neuman; India: Thompson-Balys; Japanese: Ikeda.

A511.2.1.1. Abandoned culture hero captured by use of net. S141. Exposure in boat. A person (usually a woman or child) set adrift in a boat (chest, basket, cask). T572.2.3. Hero an abortion thrown into the bushes. Z210.1. Lodge-Boy and Thrown-Away as joint adventurers.

L111.2.1.1. *Future heroine found in hollow tree* (calfshed, house "without door but only window and skylight"). Irish myth: *Cross.

L111.2.2. *Future hero found on shore.* Icelandic: *Boberg; Italian Novella: Rotunda; Tonga: Gifford 122.

L111.2.3. *Future hero found on top of a tree.* Chinese: Graham.

L111.2.4. *Future hero found in wolf den.* Irish myth: *Cross.

B535. Animal nourishes abandoned child.

L111.2.5. *Heroine found in harp.* Icelandic: Boberg.

L111.3. *Widow's son as hero.* *Jacobs's list s.v. "Widow's son"; *Krappe Balor 126ff.; Garnett FL III 265; Missouri French: Carrière; India: Thompson-Balys; Chinese: Graham.

L111.4. *Orphan hero.* Missouri French: Carrière; India: *Thompson-Balys; Chinese: Graham; New Hebrides: Codrington 283ff.; Buin: Wheeler No. 8; Tuamotu: Stimson MS (T-G. 3/818); Africa (Wakweli): Bender 81.

L111.4.1. *Orphan hero lives with grandmother.* Avenges slaughtered kin. N. A. Indian: Thompson Tales 320 n. 156 (most of the references).
Z211. Dreadnaughts.

L111.4.2. *Orphan heroine.* India: *Thompson-Balys; Africa (Mossi): Frobenius Atlantis VIII 274ff. No. 120.

L111.4.3. *Orphan brothers as heroes.* Chinese: Graham.

L111.4.4. *Mistreated orphan hero.* Eskimo (Greenland): Rink 93, Rasmussen I 123, 230, 238, II 34, 38, III 90, 295, (Cumberland Sound): Boas BAM XV 188, (West Hudson Bay): ibid. 309, (Ungava): Turner RBAE XI 265, (Central Eskimo): Boas RBAE VI 630.

L111.5. *Bastard hero.* Icelandic: Boberg; Buddhist myth: Malalasekera I 957; Africa (Nuba): Reinisch Sprachen von Nord-Ost-Africa (Wien, 1879) II 224ff. No. 9.
T640. Illegitimate children.

L111.6. *Anchorite's son as hero.* Icelandic: Boberg.

L111.7. *Future hero (heroine) raised by animal.* India: Thompson-Balys.
B535. Animal nurse.

L111.8. *Heroes sons of wife not favorite of king.* India: Thompson-Balys.

L111.8.1. *Heroine daughter of wife not favorite of king.* India: Thompson-Balys.

L111.9. *Hero of story neglected grandson of raja.* India: Thompson-Balys.

L111.10. *Unpromising fourth son succeeds.* Africa (Luba): DeClerq ZsKS IV 200.

L112. *Hero (heroine) of unpromising appearance.* Icelandic: *Boberg; India: *Thompson-Balys.
L145. Ugly preferred to pretty sister.

L112.1. *Monster as hero.* *Type 708; *BP II 236; Cosquin Lorraine II 224; India: Thompson-Balys.
F610. Remarkably strong man. (Strong John.) T550. Monstrous births.

L112.1.1. *Loathly man father of supernaturally born boy.* S. A. Indian (Chiriguano): Métraux MAFLS XL 159.

L112.2. *Very small hero.* Irish myth: Cross; Icelandic: Hrólfssaga Gautrekssonar passim; Spanish: Espinosa Jr. Nos. 133—135; Korean: Zong in-Sob 78 No. 44; Philippine: Fansler MAFLS XII 24.
F535.1. Thumbling. Person the size of a thumb.

L112.3. *Deformed child as hero.* Penzer I 184ff.

L112.3.1. *Hero with deformed head.* India: Thompson-Balys.

L112.4. *Dirty boy as hero.* Type 301; Missouri French: Carrière; Chinese: Graham; N. A. Indian: *Thompson Tales 327 n. 183.
D733. Loathly bridegroom.

L112.5. *"Burnt-belly" as hero.* N. A. Indian (Pawnee): Dorsey CI LIX Nos. 42, 44, 47, Grinnell 87ff., (Skidi Pawnee): Dorsey MAFLS VIII No. 9, (Arikara): Dorsey CI XVII Nos. 17—19, (Hidatsa): Curtis N. A. Indian IV 165.

L131. Hearth abode of unpromising hero (heroine).

L112.6. *"Scar-face" as hero.* N. A. Indian (Blackfoot): Grinnell Blackfoot Lodge Tales (New York, 1892) 93, McClintock Old North Trail (London, 1910) 491.

L112.7. *Skin-sore as hero.* Africa (Basuto): Kidd The Bull of the Kraal and the Heavenly Maidens (London, 1908) 51ff. No. 1.

L112.7.1. *Leper hero.* Tuamotu: Stimson MS (T-G. 3/45).

L112.8. *Lame child as hero.* India: *Thompson-Balys; Africa (Wakweli): Bender 79.

L112.9. *Ugly child becomes great poet.* Irish myth: *Cross.

L112.10. *One-armed hero.* India: Thompson-Balys.

L112.11. *Heroine born with pigeon's head.* Tonga: Gifford 31, 61—65.

L113. *Hero (heroine) of unpromising occupation.*

L113.1. *Menial hero.* Type 594*; *Cox xl, 437—446; Missouri French: Carrière; India: Thompson-Balys; N. A. Indian (Micmac): Rand 440 No. 85, (Zuñi): Parsons MAFL XXXI 245.

A181. God serves as menial on earth.

L113.1.0.1. *Heroine endures hardships with menial husband.* Rewarded by his success. BP I 443ff.; cf. Type 900; Cosquin Lorraine I 138ff.; Missouri French: Carrière; India: *Thompson-Balys; N. A. Indian: Thompson CColl 348ff., (Blackfoot): Wissler and Duvall PaAM II 81, (Wichita): Dorsey JAFL XVI 160ff., (Teton): Curtis N. A. Indian III 111, cf. Eskimo (Kodiak): Golder JAFL XVI 16.

D733. Loathly bridegroom.

L113.1.1. *Swineherd as hero.* (Cf. P412.2.) Hdwb. d. Märchens I 186b n. 109; Irish myth: *Cross:

L113.1.2. *Stable-boy as hero.* Breton: Sébillot Incidents s.v. "garçon"; Missouri French: Carrière.

K1816.8. Disguise as stable-boy.

L113.1.3. *Mad fisherman as hero.* Italian Novella: Rotunda.

L113.1.4. *Shepherd as hero.* Type 922; Jewish: *Neuman.

L113.1.5. *Goatherd as hero.* Icelandic: *Boberg.

L113.1.6. *Cowherd hero.* India: *Thompson-Balys; Icelandic: Boberg.

L113.1.6.1. *Cowherd's daughter (foster child) as heroine.* Irish myth: *Cross.

L113.1.7. *Slave as hero.* Jewish: Neuman.

L113.2. *Menial heroine.* Cox 1-121 passim; BP I 183; Missouri French: Carrière; Spanish: Espinosa Jr. No. 119; Italian Novella: Rotunda.

H151.6. Heroine in menial disguise discovered in her beautiful clothes: recognition follows. K1815. Humble disguise. K1816. Disguise as a menial.

L113.2.1. *Heroine has been goatherd.* Icelandic: Ragnars saga Lodbr. 127, 198, Boberg.

L113.3. *Poor weaver as hero.* India: *Thompson-Balys.

L113.4. *Peasant as hero.* Africa (Dschagga): Stamberg ZsES XXIII 296ff., (Ganda): Baskerville 1ff.

K1816.9. Disguise as peasant. N854. Peasant as helper. P15.1. Disguised king punished by peasant. Beaten because he does not get up early enough. P411. Peasant.

L113.5. *Woodcutter hero.* Africa (Nubian): Rochemonteix Quelques Contes Nubiens (Cairo, 1888) 48ff. No. 4, (Suaheli): Steere 13ff.

P458. Woodsman. Q410. Capital punishment. Z210. Brothers as heroes.

L113.6. *Smith as hero.* Icelandic: Þidriks saga I 73ff., 114—34 (Velent), Boberg.

A142. Smith of the gods. F451.3.4.2. Dwarfs as smiths. F531.6.10.1. Giant as smith. K1816.12. Disguise as smith. P447. Smith.

L113.7. *Quack-doctor as hero.* India: Thompson-Balys.

L113.8. *Barber becomes king.* India: Thompson-Balys.

L113.9. *Tailor as hero.* India: Thompson-Balys.

L113.10. *Flute player as hero.* India: Thompson-Balys.

L114. *Hero (heroine) of unpromising habits.* Icelandic: Boberg; India: Thompson-Balys.

L114.1. *Lazy hero.* *Type 675; *Fb "doven" IV 102b; *Chauvin VI 64 No. 233 n. 1, 202; Oesterley No. 91; Icelandic: *Boberg; Missouri French: Carrière; India: Thompson-Balys; Chinese: Graham; Hawaii: Beckwith Myth 416.

F583. Hero has lain motionless since birth. W111.1. Contest in laziness.

L114.2. *Spendthrift hero.* Type 969; Missouri French: Carrière; India: *Thompson-Balys.

N172. Prodigal as favorite of fortune.

L114.3. *Unruly hero.* Types 301, 650; Icelandic: *Boberg; India: Thompson-Balys; N. A. Indian (California): Gayton and Newman 95.

L114.4. *Cheater as hero.* India: Thompson-Balys.

L114.5. *Hero with disgusting habits.* Korean: Zong in-Sob 66 No. 36.

L115. *Successful foolish son.* India: *Thompson-Balys.

J1700. Fools. L21. Stupid youngest son becomes clever. N421. Lucky bargain.

L116. *Insane hero (heroine).* Irish myth: Cross (L125).

L121. *Stupid hero.* (Cf. Z253.) Icelandic: *Boberg; Missouri French: Carrière; Spanish: Espinosa Jr. No. 131; India: *Thompson-Balys.

L121.1. *Half-wit successful.* Eskimo (Kodiak): Golder JAFL XXII 23.

M301.9. Half-wit as prophet.

L122. *Unsophisticated hero.* *Dickson 128ff. nn. 94—99; Irish myth: *Cross; Jewish: Neuman.

J147. Child confined to keep him in ignorance of life. Useless. T371 The boy who had never seen a woman: the Satans. T617. Boy reared in ignorance of the world.

L123. *Pauper hero.* Jewish: *Neuman; India: *Thompson-Balys.

L123.1. *Penniless hero.* Loved by a courtisan, he proves later to be a great man. M. Bloomfield in Penzer VII xxiii.

L124. *Dumb hero.* Dickson 185; Irish myth: *Cross.

L124.1. *Child silent till seventh year.* Icelandic: *Boberg.

L124.1.1. *Famous poet does not speak until he is fourteen (four, seven) years old.* Irish myth: Cross.

L124.2. *Silent hero.* Icelandic: *Boberg.

L130. Abode of unpromising hero (heroine).

L131. *Hearth abode of unpromising hero (heroine).* *Cox 1—52, 87—121, 437—446, 493; *Fb "askefis" IV 17b; Saintyves Perrault 124ff.; *Cosquin Contes indiens 494ff.; Tupper and Ogle Walter Map 115; Icelandic: *Boberg; Spanish: Espinosa Jr. No. 119; Italian: Basile Pentamerone I No. 6; Chinese: Graham; N. A. Indian (Micmac): Michelson JAFL XXXVIII 45ff.

L112.5. "Burnt-belly" as hero. L112.6. "Scarface" as hero.

L131.1. *Ashes abode of unpromising hero.* India: Thompson-Balys; Chinese: Graham.

L132. *Pig-sty abode for unpromising hero (heroine).* *Type 314; Cox Nos. 1, 33, 77, 79, and passim; Chinese: Graham; N. A. Indian: Thompson CColl II 351.

Q485.1. Princess married to lowly hero must live in slave quarters.

L133. *Unpromising son leaves his home and goes into the world.* Icelandic: *Boberg.

F612.2. Strong hero kills playmates: sent from home.

L134. *Unpromising hero must live in hut.* India: Thompson-Balys.

L140. The unpromising surpasses the promising.

L141. *Stupid person surpasses clever.* Missouri French: Carrière; Chinese: Graham; West Indies: Flowers 559.

J1110. Clever persons. N170. The capriciousness of luck.

L141.1. *The stupid monk recovers the stolen flocks.* A nobleman steals the abbot's flocks, saying that the monks have no use for them since they eat no meat. The most learned of the monks tries to recover them, but without success. The most stupid is then sent. Asked to dinner, he eats till he can hold no more. He tells the nobleman that he ate as much as possible since he could take back with him only what he had in his stomach. The nobleman pleased with the reply returns the flocks. Pauli (ed. Bolte) No. 61; Alphabet No. 718; Mensa Philosophica No. 187.

L141.2. *Simpleton's naive answer to robbers makes them think he knows their secret.* They share their loot with him. Italian Novella: Rotunda.

K335.1. Robbers frightened from goods. N611.2. Criminal accidentally detected: "That is the first" — sleepy woman counting her yawns.

L141.3. *Hero stupid at games but fleet of foot.* Eskimo (West Hudson Bay): Boas BAM XV 214.

L141.4. *Inept child eventually surpasses others.* Tuamotu: Stimson MS (z-G. 3/1122).

L142. *Pupil surpasses master.* *Fb "mester" II 584a; Alphabet No. 38; Jewish: Neuman; India: Thompson-Balys.

L142.1. *Pupil surpasses thieves in stealing.* *Type 1525E; *BP III 393 n. 1.

K306. Thieves steal from each other.

L142.2. *Pupil surpasses magician.* *Type 325; Missouri French: Carrière; India: *Thompson-Balys.

D1711. Magician. D1711.0.1. Magician's apprentice. D1719.1. Contest in magic.

L142.3. *Son surpasses father in skill.* Jewish: *Neuman; India: Thompson-Balys.

L143. *Poor man surpasses rich.* *Types 676, 1535; *Hdwb. d. Märchens I 187b; Irish: Beal XXI 336, O'Suilleabhain 122; Spanish: Espinosa Jr. Nos. 181, 201; Chinese: Eberhard FFC CXX 256f.

Q1. Hospitality rewarded—opposite punished.

L143.1. *Poor girl chosen as wife in preference to rich.* India: Thompson-Balys.

L143.2. *Poor suitor makes good husband; rich suitor cruel.* Africa: Weeks Jungle 443f.

L144. *Ignorant surpasses learned man.*

L144.1. *Ignorant steward straightens his master's accounts.* The educated stewards have always cheated. The ignorant puts his belongings in one box, his master's in another. Both master and steward gain. Pauli (ed. Bolte) No. 355.

L144.2. *Farmer surpasses astronomer and doctor in predicting weather and choosing food.* Lithuanian: Balys Index No. 2448*; Russian: Andrejev No. 2132; Rumanian: Schullerus FFC LXXVIII No. 921 II*.

L145. *Ugly preferred to pretty sister.* Type (403_2); Breton: Sébillot Incidents s.v. "laide".

L112. Hero (heroine) of unpromising appearance.

L145.1. *Ugly sister helps pretty one.* *Type 711.

L146. *Neglected surpasses favorite child.*

L146.1. *Ape tries to flee with favorite child;* neglected child saves himself. The favorite child is killed through the mother's overanxiety. Wienert FFC LVI 62 (ET 253), 146 (ST 510); Halm Aesop No. 366.

L147. *Tardy surpasses punctual.*

L147.1. *Tardy bird alone succeeds at bird convocation.* Chauvin V 38 No. 365 n. 1.

B232. Parliament of birds. B571.2. Animal who arrives late performs tasks for man.

L148. *Slowness surpasses haste.*

L148.1. *If you hasten you will not get there.* In spite of the saint's advice the teamster hastens and breaks his wagon. Pauli (ed. Bolte) No. 255; Alphabet No. 324.

D1783.3. Faster one walks, longer the trail.

L151. *Peasant girl outwits prince.* Italian: Basile Pentamerone II No. 3.

H561.1. Clever peasant girl asked riddles by king. J1111. Clever girl. J1525. Poor girl outwits prince in fright contest.

L152. *Daughter succeeds on quest where son fails.* Africa (Rozwi): Posselt Fables of the Veld (Oxford, 1929) 30ff.

L154. *Scorning stops when it turns out that the scorned has saved the king by fighting alone against four.* Icelandic: *Boberg.

L155. *Disagreeable and disliked child surpasses the likeable one.* Italian Novella: Rotunda.

L156. *Unpromising hero kills those who scorn him.* Icelandic: *Boberg.

L156.1. *Lowly hero overcomes proud rivals.* Korean: Zong in-Sob 120 No. 58.

L160. Success of the unpromising hero (heroine). Irish: *Cross, O'Suilleabhain 27, Beal XXI 309; India: Thompson-Balys.

N225. Man robbed and penniless entertained by wealthy widow and enriched. N226. Wrecked man saved on coffer of jewels; becomes rich.

L161. *Lowly hero marries princess.* *Types 300, 301, 302, 303, 304, 306, 307, 308*, 314, 325, 329, 400, 434, 502, 506, 507, 508, 513, 514, 530, 545B, 552, 553, 559, 560, 561, 570, 571, 575, 577, 580, 590, 594*, 725, 853, 854, 930, 935; Child V 488 s.v. "marriages". — Missouri French: Carrière; Italian Novella: *Rotunda; India: *Thompson-Balys; Chinese: Graham; Japanese: Ikeda; Tahiti: Henry Ancient Tahiti (Honolulu, 1928) 614.

B535. Animal nurse. H335. Tasks assigned suitors. K1815. Humble disguise. M312.1. Prophecy: wealthy marriage for poor boy. P41. Princess cannot be married to someone of low-caste although he passes suitor test. Q499.7. Humiliating marriage as punishment. T55.1. Princess declares her love for lowly hero. T91.6.4. Princess falls in love with lowly boy. T121. Unequal marriage.

L161.1. *Marriage of poor boy and rich girl.* India: Thompson-Balys; Chinese: Graham; Korean: Zong in-Sob 81 No. 44; N. A. Indian (Zuñi): *Benedict II 336.

T121. Unequal marriage. T121.3.1. Princess marries lowly man.

L161.2. *Fool wins beautiful woman as wife.* Lithuanian: Balys Index No. 530B*; India: Thompson-Balys.

L161.3. *Mercenary soldier (exile) accepted lover of princess.* Irish myth: *Cross.

L162. *Lowly heroine marries prince (king).* *Types 310, 403, 428, 431, 440, 442, 450, 451, 501, 510, 511, 545A, 585, 652, 705, 706, 707, 708, 711, 870A, 873, 875, 883A, 887; Hibbard 190ff.; *Roberts 196. — Irish myth: *Cross; Missouri French: Carrière; Spanish: Espinosa II Nos. 107f., 154, Espinosa Jr. Nos. 80, 142; Italian: Basile Pentamerone III No. 5 and passim, *Rotunda; India: Cowell Jātaka I 27f., *Thompson-Balys; Buddhist myth: Malalasekera I 147, 423, II 103, 455, 1366; Japanese: Ikeda.

M312.1.1. Prophecy: wealthy marriage for poor girl. T67. Prince offered as prize. T121. Unequal marriage.

L165. *Lowly boy becomes king.* (Most references to L161 apply here). Jewish: *Neuman; India: *Thompson-Balys; Buddhist myth: Malalasekera I 51; Chinese: Eberhard FFC CXX 249; Tuamotu: Stimson MS (T-G. 3/45).

L175. *Lowly successful hero invites king and humbles him.* *Type 675; India: Thompson-Balys.

L175.1. *Lowly successful soldier invites general and humbles him.* Cheremis: Sebeok-Nyerges.

L176. *Despised boy wins race.* N. A. Indian: *Thompson Tales 327f. nn. 185f. (many references), (Zuñi): *Benedict II 336.

L177. *Despised boy wins gambling game.* N. A. Indian (Zuñi): Benedict II 336.

N1. Gamblers.

L200—L299. Modesty brings reward.

L200. Modesty brings reward.

J200. Choices. Q10. Deeds rewarded. Q61.1. The monk who did not ask for the position made abbot. He is given the bribe money paid by other ambitious monks.

L210. Modest choice best. Types 480, 580. See also references to L211 and L221. Scala Celi 26a No. 171; *Roberts 177, 198; Spanish: Espinosa Jr. Nos. 71, 74, 139, 191; Italian: Basile Pentamerone III No. 10; Icelandic: Boberg; Japanese: Ikeda; N. A. Indian (Zuñi): Benedict II 340; Africa: Werner African 196, 205; Cape Verde Islands: Parsons MAFLS XV (1) 277 No. 91; West Indies: Flowers 559.

C773.1. Tabu: making unreasonable requests. J2076. Absurdly modest wish.

L211. *Modest choice: three caskets type.* Objects from which choice is to be made are hidden in caskets (or the like). The worst looking casket proves to be the best choice. Type 480; *Cox 501ff.; Cosquin Lorraine No. 17; *Chauvin III 99 No. 4; *Crane Vitry 153 No. 47; *Oesterley No. 251; *Roberts 200; *Cosquin Contes indiens 527; Boccaccio Decameron X No. 1 (Lee 294); *Ward II 122; Herbert III 196; *Wesselski Märchen 213 No. 18; *Pauli (ed. Bolte) No. 836; *Fb "skål" III 352a. — North Carolina: Brown Collection I 633; Spanish Exempla: Keller; Italian Novella: *Rotunda; India: *Thompson-Balys; Chinese: Graham; Japanese: Anesaki 320; N. A. Indian (Arikara): Dorsey CI XVII No. 16, (Nez Percé): Spinden JAFL XXI 156, (Carib): Alexander Lat. Am. 264; Malay: V. Ronkel Catalogus der Maleische Handschriften te Batavia (Den Haag, 1909) 48; Africa (Angola): Chatelain 121 No. 10, 229 No. 41, (Benga): Nassau 225 No. 33.

A1335.3. Origin of death from unwise choice. Choice between two bundles, one containing tempting articles, the other everlasting life. D859.5 Magic object to be chosen from among identical worthless objects. H511.1. Three caskets. Princess offered to man who chooses correctly from three caskets . J260. Choice between worth and appearance. J1675.3. King's capriciousness censured: the ass in the stream. K476.1. Entrails substituted for meat. Prometheus divides the slain ox so that the bones and entrails seem to be the choicest part.

L212. *Choice among several gifts.* The worst horse, armor, or the like proves best. *Fb "hest" I 598b; Child II 444f., 450, 453f.; German: Grimm No. 57; Spanish: Espinosa Jr. Nos. 62, 64; Jewish: *Neuman; India: *Thompson-Balys; Chinese: Graham; N. A. Indian: Thompson CColl II 341, (Arikara): Dorsey CI XVII No. 16; West Indies: Flowers 559.

L212.1. *Saint, offered any gift from God, chooses (virginity and) wisdom.* Irish myth: *Cross.

L212.2. *Solomon, offered any gift from God, chooses wisdom.* Granted wisdom and wealth. Irish myth: Cross.

L212.3. *Hero prefers fame to long life.* Irish myth: Cross.

L212.3.1. *"Fame (honor) is more enduring than life."* Irish myth: *Cross.

L212.4. *Modest choice proves good* (simple unique privilege). Girl offered reward of five villages chooses rather to be only one on certain night to be allowed to have light in her house and to keep all animals who enter as hers. All kinds of livestock come. India: Thompson-Balys.

L213. *Poor girl chosen rather than the rich.* Treasure follows. Chauvin III 103 No. 13; Spanish Exempla: Keller.

L213.1. *Modest choice best: wife chosen from crowd of women* — only one poorly dressed. Chinese: Graham.

L213.2. *Choice of ugliest girl as bride.* Chinese: Graham.

L214. *Old chosen rather than new.* Fortunate choice. Africa (Basuto): Jacottet 142 No. 20.

L215. *Unpromising magic object chosen.* Hero refuses to take one that cries out "take me!" Roberts 204; Tonga: Beckwith Myth 25, Gifford 20; Africa (Benga): Nassau 114 No. 11; Jamaica: *Beckwith MAFLS XVII 269 No. 81.

C811.1. Tabu: heeding persuasive voice of magic drum. Not to pick up drum that says "take me". C811.2. Tabu: heeding magic yam that says not to take it up.

L216. *Poor game proves rich.* N. A. Indian (California): Gayton and Newman 83.

L217. *Accustomed rags preferred to new garments.* A Brahmin returns home to find a palace instead of a cottage; he recognizes his wife only after she throws off her jewels and ornaments to stand before him in her old rags. India: Thompson-Balys.

L217.1. *Former poverty chosen over new riches.* Weaver laments loss of water vessel. Offered many new, but prefers old and modest life. India: Thompson-Balys.

J300. Present values chosen.

L220. Modest request best. *Cox 480; *BP II 232; *MacCulloch Childhood 191; N. A. Indian: *Thompson Tales 276 n. 18a.

A575. Departed deity grants requests to visitors. Q3. Moderate request rewarded; immoderate punished.

L221. *Modest request: present from the journey.* Asked what her father shall bring her as a present, the heroine chooses a modest gift. It is usually a flower but sometimes does not turn out to be such a simple gift after all (golden cloak, golden apple). *Type 425; *Fb "rose" III 80a, "guldæble" I 515b, "guldrok" I 514b; *Hdwb. d. Märchens I 206b; Tegethoff 11; Italian Basile Pentamerone II No. 8; India: Thompson-Balys.

J1805.2.1. Daughter says "Sobur" (wait) to her father when he asks what to bring from the journey: father finds Prince Sobur.

L221.1. *Present from the journey: what you first see.* Hdwb. d. Märchens I 606a nn. 80—89.

S241. Child unwittingly promised: "first thing you meet."

L222. *Modest choice: parting gift.* Small gift with blessing preferred to large gift with parent's curse. *Köhler-Bolte I 188; BP I 214 n. 1; Gunkel Das Märchen im alten Testament (Tübingen, 1921) 100f.; Campbell Tales I 220 No. 13; Lang English Fairy Tales 136 No. 23;

Gipsy: Aichele Zigeunermärchen 289 No. 69; Jewish: Neuman; Cape Verde Islands: Parsons MAFLS XV (1) 110, 122.

J229.3. Choice: a big piece of cake with my curse or a small piece with my blessing. N782. Mother's parting gift to adventuring sons: the two loaves of bread, one for hunger; one for overeating.

L222.1. *Modest choice for parting gift—money or counsels.* Counsels chosen. Jewish: bin Gorion Born Judas III 100, 304.

J21. Counsels proved wise by experience. J163.4. Good counsels bought. J171. Proverbial wisdom: counsels.

L222.2. *Modest parting gift best—meat or bones.* Bones thrown to pursuing dogs delay them and allow escape; not so with meat. India: Thompson-Balys.

R231. Obstacle flight—Atalanta type. Objects are thrown back which the pursuer stops to pick up while the fugitives escape.

L222.3. *Modest choice for parting gift: when offered money man takes magic stick.* Chinese: Graham.

L222.4. *Modest choice of parting gift: magic iron measure chosen.* Korean: Zong in-Sob 27 No. 12.

L225. *Hero refuses reward.* Rides away without it. *Types 300, 303; Italian: Basile Pentamerone I No. 7; Icelandic: Boberg.

B11.11. Fight with dragon. R222. Unknown knight.

L250. Modest business plans best.

L251. *Beggar with small bag surpasses the one with the large.* Latter refuses all but large donations; gets none. Pauli (ed. Bolte) No. 607; *Crane Vitry 168 No. 77; Alphabet No. 607.

L290. Modesty brings reward—miscellaneous.

L291. *Prosperity forever or for a day?* King asks prince whether he has secret of prosperity forever or a day. Prince says "forever" and is captured. Later his wife, asked same question, says "for a day" and is honored. India: Thompson-Balys.

L300—L399. Triumph of the weak.

L300. Triumph of the weak. Chauvin II 204 No. 59; Irish myth: Cross.

B771.2. Animal tamed by holiness of saint. K1815. Humble disguise. (Cap o' Rushes, Peau d'âne, Allerleirauh.) Usually in rough clothing. K1815.1.1. Pious pilgrim dies unknown in his father's house. K1816. Disguise as a menial. N170. The capriciousness of luck.

L301. *Hermes distributes wit.* Gives everyone the same measure of wit, so that the smaller are more clever than the large. Wienert FFC LVI 35; Halm Aesop No. 150.

L310. Weak overcomes strong in conflict.

L311. *Weak (small) hero overcomes large fighter.* *Type 328; A. Stender-Petersen Acta Jutlandica VI (1934) 166ff.; Irish myth: Cross; English: Child II 35ff.; Icelandic: *Boberg; Spanish Exempla: Keller; Italian Novella: Rotunda; Japanese: Anesaki 311; Jewish: Neuman, I Samuel 17:23 (David and Goliath); N. A. Indian (Southern Paiute, Shivwits): Lowie JAFL XXXVII 150 No. 17; Guatamala Indian (Quiché): Alexander Lat. Am. 168ff.; Tuamotu: Beckwith Myth 476.

G510. Ogre killed or captured.

L311.1. *Sick hero overcomes antagonist.* Italian Novella: Rotunda.

L311.2. *Poorly-armed hero overcomes well-armed by strategy.* India: Thompson-Balys.

L311.3. *Poor prince overcomes king.* India: Thompson-Balys.

L311.4. *Little innocent girl is able to drive giant out of land.* India: Thompson-Balys.

G500. Ogre defeated.

L311.5. *Small boy overcomes enraged gorilla.* Africa: Stanley 281ff.

L312. *Little strong man defeats giant in race.* Eskimo (Labrador): Hawkes GSCan XIV 150.

L315. *Small animal overcomes large.* *BP II 437.

L315.1. *Bird flies into large animal's ear and kills him.* *Type 228; *BP II 437; Japanese: Ikeda; Indonesia: DeVries's list No. 115.

L315.1.1. *Mouse runs into buffalo's ear and overcomes him.* Africa (Congo): Weeks Jungle 393f.

L315.2. *Mouse torments bull who cannot catch him.* Wienert FFC LVI 48 (ET 74), 113 (ST 236).

L315.3. *Fox burns tree in which eagle has nest.* Revenges theft of cub. Herbert III 12; *Crane Vitry 194 No. 144.

L315.4. *Mother ape burns bear.* Revenges theft of her young. *Crane Vitry 194 No. 143.

L315.5. *Lark causes elephant to fall over precipice.* Chauvin II 81 No. 1; India: Thompson-Balys; Buddhist myth: Malalasekera II 771; Japanese: Ikeda.

K891.5. Dupe induced to jump over precipice.

L315.5.1. *Elephant killed by mouse who runs up open end of trunk to head* and there smears poison over his brain. India: Thompson-Balys; Africa (Congo): Weeks Jungle 393f.

L315.6. *Insects worry large animal to despair or death.* Wienert FFC LVI *48 (ET 76), 120 (ST 301); Spanish: Espinosa Jr. Nos. 187, 209; Japanese: Ikeda; Indonesia: DeVries's list Nos. 132, 137.

L478. Gnats having overcome lion are in turn killed by spider.

L315.7. *Dungbeetle keeps destroying eagle's eggs.* Eagle at last goes to the sky and lays eggs in Zeus's lap. The dungbeetle causes Zeus to shake his apron and break the eggs. Wienert FFC LVI *51 (ET 106), 77 (ET 432), 113 (ST 237), 114 (ST 249); Halm Aesop No. 7.

L315.8. *Fish pricks monster with fins and defeats him.* India: Thompson-Balys.

L315.9. *Falcon attacks eagle repeatedly and defeats him.* Spanish Exempla: Keller.

L315.10. *Mice overcome camel.* India: Thompson-Balys.

L315.11. *Lizard defeats leopard.* India: Thompson-Balys.

L315.12. *Rabbit slays rhinoceros.* India: Thompson-Balys.

L315.13. *Hedgehog defeats tiger by jumping into tiger's mouth and tormenting him.* India: Thompson-Balys.

L315.14. *Ants overcome serpent.* Africa (Congo): Weeks Jungle 386.

L315.15. *Small animals dupe larger into trap.* Africa (Bankon): Ittman 85, (Wachaga): Gutmann 190, (Cameroon): Lederbogen 19.

K730. Victim trapped.

L316. *Offended rats gnaw saddle girths of king's horses so that he is defeated in battle.* India: Thompson-Balys.

L318. *Mice win war with woodcutters.* India: Thompson-Balys.

L330. Easy escape of weak (small).

J832. Reeds bend before wind (flood). Save themselves, while oak is uprooted. J1662. The cat's only trick. She saves herself in a tree. The fox, who knows a hundred tricks, is captured.

L331. *Little fishes escape from the net.* The large are caught. *Type 253; *BP III 355; Wienert FFC LVI 66 (ET 299), 113 (ST 240); Halm Aesop No. 26.

L332. *Mice escape into their holes; weasels cannot follow them.* Wienert FFC LVI 48 (ET 65), *113 (ST 241); Halm Aesop No. 291.

L333. *Hummingbird can see fowler's net; eagle is caught in spite of his boasts of good eyesight.* *Pauli (ed. Bolte) No. 290; Rumanian: Schullerus FFC LXXVIII No. 254*.

L350. Mildness triumphs over violence.

L350.1. *Mildness triumphs over violence: queen advises husband to use kindness to enemies.* This wins them over where war failed. Spanish Exempla: Keller.

L350.2. *Saint uses kind words to pagan priest who has just smitten a Christian.* This causes pagan to repent. Conversion follows. Spanish Exempla: Keller.

L351. *Contest of wind and sun.* Sun by warmth causes traveler to remove coat, while wind by violent blowing causes him to pull it closer around him. Wienert FFC LVI 43 (ET 7), 80 (ET 457), 136 (ST 419); Halm Aesop No. 82; Lithuanian: Balys Index No. 3900; Estonian: Loorits Grundzüge I 381ff.; Russian: Andrejev No. 298*; Indonesia: DeVries's list Nos. 95, 140. Cf. Halm No. 414.

A287.0.1. Rain god and wind god brought back in order to make livable weather. Have been banished by sun god. H1562.14. Mighty-of-his-mouth and mighty-of-his hands decide to live together to test strength. Strength of mind is winner.

L351.1. *Contest between wind (rain) and sun.* Rain also tries unsuccessfully like wind. India: Thompson-Balys.

L351.2. *Sun cursed by man for its burning rays, wind for its hot breath, but moon is blessed for its soft, cool, and beautiful light.* India: Thompson-Balys.

L353. *Mild brother triumphs over warlike.* Survives him and inherits property. Africa (Fang): Tessman 191ff.

L361. *Priest who gives mild penances succeeds where others fail.* Scala Celi 48a No. 272; Alphabet No. 183; Herbert III 505, 570; Spanish Exempla: Keller.

L363. *Goldsmith gives money to one who addressed him as friend* (the goldsmith had no friends because he has cheated everybody.) India: Thompson-Balys.

Q41. Politeness rewarded.

L390. Triumph of the weak-miscellaneous.

H592.1. "Love like Salt". Girl compares her love for her father to salt. Experience teaches him the value of salt.

L391. *Needle kills an elk.* Slips into his stomach. Type 90.

L391.1. *Reed pricks and drives away dog that urinates on it.* Spanish Exempla: Keller.

L392. *Mouse stronger than wall, wind, mountain.* *DeCock Volkssage 31ff.; BP I 148 n. 2; Wesselski Mönchslatein 82 No. 75; Chauvin II 97 No. 55; Archiv f. d. Studium d. neueren Sprachen LXXXI 265; Germania II 481; Basset RTP VII 394ff.; Basset Contes Berbères 95f; *Bødker Exempler 297 No. 60. — Spanish: Keller, Espinosa III Nos. 275—277; Jewish: Neuman; India: Thompson-Balys; Japanese: Ikeda.

H631. Riddle: what is the strongest? Z42. Stronger and strongest.

L392.1. *Mosquitoes sting King Pharaoh and show they are stronger than the man who cannot escape them.* Spanish Exempla: Keller.

L393. *Only love to offer.* Bride asks suitors what they have to offer her. Poor youth who has nothing but love to offer gets her. India: Thompson-Balys.

H310. Suitor tests.

L394. *Slow flying swan lasts longer than speedy crow in flying.* India: Thompson-Balys.

L395. *Frog, tortoise, fish each tell of how long they expect to live.* Frog alone does not expect to live to a hundred and ten years and alone escapes fisherman's net. India: Thompson-Balys.

L400—L499. Pride brought low.

L400. Pride brought low. Jewish: *Neuman.

A2232.1. Camel asks for horns: punishment, short ears. A2232.8. Dogs' embassy to Zeus chased forth; dogs seek ambassador: why dogs look at one another under tail. C450. Tabu: boasting. C770. Tabu: overweening pride. H1215. Quest assigned because of hero's boast. J950. Presumption of the lowly. J1476. The proud hide humbled. A hide is in the river. River: "What is your name?" — Hide: "Hard hide". — River: "Hunt another name; I'll soon soften you." J2061.2. Air-castle: pail of milk to be sold. J2272.1. Chanticleer believes that his crowing makes the sun rise. Disappointed when it rises without his aid. J2273.1. Bird thinks sky will fall if he does not support it. Q331. Pride punished.

L410. Proud ruler (deity) humbled.

L410.1. *Proud king humbled:* realizes that pomp, possessions, power are all of short duration. Spanish Exempla: Keller.

L410.2. *King, defeated in battle, obliged to flee without money.* India: Thompson-Balys.

L410.3. *Boasting king insulted by crow dropping filth on him.* India: Thompson-Balys.

L410.4. *Defeated king must be peddler or beggar.* India: *Thompson-Balys.

L410.5. *King overthrown and made servant.* India: *Thompson-Balys.

L410.6. *Ruler enslaved.* India: *Thompson-Balys.

L410.7. *Queen forced to become a courtesan.* India: Thompson-Balys.

L411. *Proud king displaced by angel.* (King in the bath.) While the king is in the bath (or hunting) an angel in his form takes his place. The king is repulsed on all sides until he repents of his haughtiness. *Type 757; **Varnhagen Ein indisches Märchen auf seine Wanderung durch die asiatischen und europäischen Literaturen (Berlin, 1882); Chauvin II 161 No. 51; *Wesselski Märchen 237 No. 49; Hibbard 58ff.; *Herbert III 202; *Oesterley No. 59; *Andraea Anglia Beiblatt XIII 302; *von der Hagen III cxv; bin Gorion Born Judas III 47ff., 299f.; *Goebel Jüdische Motive im Märchenhafte Erzählungsgut (Gleiwitz, 1932) 89ff. — Italian Novella: *Rotunda; Icelandic: Boberg; India: *Thompson-Balys.

D45.1. Kings exchange forms and kingdoms for a year. D2012.1. King in the bath: years of experience in a moment. This illusion takes place when the king puts his head under water. K1934.1. Impostor (magician, demon) takes the place of the king.

L412. *Rich man made poor to punish pride.* He boasts that God has no power to make him poor. While he is at church, his property burns and he returns home poor. Type 836; Irish: Beal XXI 336, O'Suilleabhain 122; Jewish: bin Gorion Born Judas II 249; India: Thompson-Balys.

L412.1. *Woman casts ring into sea boasting that it is as impossible for her to become poor as for the ring to be found.* Ring is found in fish: she becomes poor. W. Jones Finger-Ring Lore (London, 1898) 440; Finnish-Swedish: Wessman 19 No. 178.

B548.2.1. Fish recovers ring from sea.

L413. *Proud inscriptions sole remains of powerful king.* *Chauvin V 33 No. 16; Spanish Exempla: Keller. Cf. Shelley's "Ozymandias".

L414. *King vainly forbids tide to rise.* (Canute.) Herbert III 62; Spanish Exempla: Keller.

J910. Humility of the great. J1930. Absurd disregard of natural laws. N101.1. Inexorable fate: no day without sorrow. A king, who has made decree against sorrow on a certain day is blinded by a swallow in his sleep.

L414.1. *King vainly attempts to measure the height of the sky and the depth of the sea.* Lithuanian: Balys Index No. 920A*.

L415. *God punishes David for his pride in the number of his subjects.* An angel is sent to kill his people. Desists only when David repents. Italian Novella: Rotunda.

L416. *King commanded to wear enemy's shoes on his shoulders as sign of submission.* Irish myth: Cross.

L416.1. *Proud king humbled when imprisoned by enemies.* Spanish Exempla: Keller.

L417. *God finds that his statue sells at low price.* He prices it in a statue shop and finds that his price is lower than other gods. Wienert FFC LVI 80 (ET 455), 94 (ST 77); Halm Aesop No. 137.

L418. *King shown he is less powerful than God.* In spite of all his plans, his servant recovers the lost (exchanged) treasure. Type 841.

L419. *Proud ruler (deity) humbled—miscellaneous.*

L419.1. *Goose boasts superiority to mushroom.* Both served up at same meal. India: Thompson-Balys.

L419.2. *King (prince) becomes beggar.* Jewish: Neuman; India: *Thompson-Balys.

L420. Overweening ambition punished. Chinese: Graham.

A724.1. Charioteer of the sun. A2232. Animal characteristics: punishment for immoderate request. Dissatisfied animal finds that when his request is granted he is worse off than before. A2723.1. Discontented pine-tree: cause of pine needles. C770. Tabu: overweening pride. C771. Tabu: building too large a structure. J510. Prudence in ambition. Q338. Immoderate request punished.

L420.0.1. *Overweening ambition punished.* Man sets self up as a god. Spanish Exempla: Keller.

L421. *Attempt to fly to heaven punished.* Car supported by eagles. Persian: Carnoy 336.

F1021.2.1. Flight so high that sun melts glue of artificial wings. K1041. Borrowed feathers. Dupe lets himself be carried aloft by bird and dropped.

L421.1. *Attempt to climb to heaven punished.* India: Thompson-Balys.

L423. *Peter acts as God for a day: tires of bargain.* A girl takes her goat to pasture and leaves him: "My God care for you!" Peter must run everywhere after the goat. *Dh II 188.

L424. *Man who has never known unhappiness or want is swallowed up by earth with all his household.* Spanish Exempla: Keller.

Q552.2.3. Earth swallowings as punishment.

L425. *Dream (prophecy) of future greatness causes banishment* (imprisonment). *Type 671, 725; *BP I 322ff., 324; Japanese: Ikeda.

L427. *Poor man aspires to high office: made a cook.* India: Thompson-Balys.

L430. Arrogance repaid. Icelandic: *Boberg.

L431. *Arrogant mistress repaid in kind by her lover.* *Type 900; *BP I 443ff.; **Philippson König Drosselbart FFC L; Krappe Études ital. II 141ff.; *Gigas "Et eventyrs vandring" Litteratur og Historie (København, 1902); *Fb "bejler" IV 31b; Icelandic: Boberg; West Indies: Flowers 560.

K1600. Deceiver falls into own trap.

L431.1. *Haughty mistress makes extravagant demands of lover: repaid.* (Glove and the Lion.) *Shearin MLN XXVI 113; *Buchanan Modern Language Review IV 183 n. 1; Krappe MLN XXXIV 16; Italian Novella: *Rotunda; N. A. Indian: *Thompson Tales 349 n. 256.

H933.1. Princess throws handkerchief high in tree; asks hero to get it.

L431.2. *Scorned lover poses as rich man and cheats his scornful mistress.* Boccaccio Decameron VIII No. 10 (Lee 266); Italian Novella: *Rotunda.

K1667. Unjust banker deceived into delivering deposits by making him expect even larger.

L431.3. *Sneering princess is impregnated by magic.* Italian Novella: Rotunda.

T513. Conception from wish.

L432. *Impoverished husband begs from wife's new husband.* He has formerly refused this man charity. *Chauvin II 174 No. 16, VIII 180 No. 212; *Wesselski Hodscha Nasreddin I 263 N. 232; *Basset 1001 Contes II 305.

H152.2. Impoverished husband in service of wife recognized. V432. Man beggars self by charity.

L432.1. *Cruel brothers brought to beg charity from abused sister.* India: *Thompson-Balys.

L432.2. *Impoverished father begs from daughter he has banished: recognized.* India: Thompson-Balys.

H151. Attention drawn and recognition follows. M21. King Lear Judgment.

L432.2.1. *Impoverished father begs from his prosperous daughter whom he has made to marry a poor man.* Chinese: Graham.

L432.3. *Impoverished husband begs from wife he has formerly expelled.* Chinese: Graham.

L432.4. *Impoverished youngest brother comes to elders in search of work.* India: Thompson-Balys.

L434. *Arrogant farmer allows none to ride his precious horse without permission.* He kills the man who does it, but is in revenge deprived of most of his goods. Icelandic: Hrafnkels saga Freysgods ch. 2ff. (ed. F. S. Cawley) (Cambridge, Mass., 1932).

L435. *Self-righteousness punished.*

Q280. Unkindness punished.

L435.1. *Self-righteous hermit must do penance.* He has said of a condemned man that he deserves his punishment. *Types 756A, 756B; BP III 463ff.; *Andrejev FFC LXIX 160ff., 250ff.; Wesselski Mönchslatein 21 No. 16; Alphabet No. 206; Irish: O'Suilleabhain 99, Beal XXI 332; Spanish: Espinosa II Nos 79f.

Q553.2. Punishment: angel ceases to appear to self-righteous hermit. T412.1. Mother guilty of incest with son forgiven by Pope (Virgin Mary).

L435.1.1. *Self-righteous monk rebuked by abbot.* Abbot tells him to search his own heart to see if he is free of sin before attacking others. Spanish Exempla: Keller.

L435.2. *Self-righteous woman punished.* She has passed judgment on a girl who has a bastard. Köhler-Bolte I 147f., *578, 581.

L435.2.1. *Woman with three hundred sixty-five children. Punished for self-righteous condemnation of unchaste girl.* *Taylor Notes and Queries No. 251 (Feb., 1923) 96; *K. Nyrop Grevinden med de 365 Børn (København, 1909); Zs. f. Vksk. XIX 469; Child II 67f., IV 463b.; *Köhler Lais der Marie de France[2] xc; *DeCock Volkssage 9ff.

T586.1. Many children at a birth. T587.1. Birth of twins an indication of unfaithfulness in wife. Z72. Formulas based on the year.

L435.3. *Self-righteous tailor in heaven expelled.* Throws God's footstool at an old woman thief on earth. *Type 800; BP I 342; Wesselski Bebel I 126 No. 19.

F1037.1. Footstool thrown from heaven. Q312.1. Punishment for finding fault with God's works in heaven.

L435.4. *The beggar on the cross in place of Christ.* Is made to leave the cross for his impatience concerning the sinners. Lithuanian: Balys Index No. 800A*.

L450. Proud animal less fortunate than humble.

J230. Choice: real and apparent values.

L451. *Wild animal finds his liberty better than tame animal's ease.*

J211.2. Town mouse and country mouse. Latter prefers poverty with safety.

L451.1. *Tame bird and wild bird.* The tame bird tells the wild one to look about him. He is shot. Type 245; Japanese: Ikeda.

L451.2. *Wild ass envies tame ass until he sees his burdens.* Wienert FFC LVI 59 (ST 198), 124 (ST 328); Halm Aesop No. 321.

L451.3. *Wolf prefers liberty and hunger to dog's servitude and plenty.* *Type 201; Crane Vitry 221 No. 217; Wienert FFC LVI 61 (ET 238), 124 (ST 326); Halm Aesop No. 278; Jacobs Aesop 206 No. 28; Pauli (ed. Bolte) No. 433; Scala Celi 76b No. 435; Italian Novella: Rotunda; Spanish Exempla: Keller.

L451.4. *Parrot prefers cold wet nest in freedom to luxury in royal palace.* India: Thompson-Balys.

L452. *Ass is jealous of the horse until he learns better.*

J212.1. Ass envies horse in fine trappings. Horse killed in battle; ass content.

L452.1. *Ass jealous of horse, but sees horse later working in a mill.* *Chauvin III 50 No. 2; Wienert FFC LVI *56 (ET 171), 94 (ST 78).

L452.2. *Ass jealous of war-horse until he sees him wounded.* Wienert FFC LVI 58 (ET 191), 124 (ST 327); Halm Aesop No. 328; Spanish Exempla: Keller.

L453. *Mule carrying corn escapes while one carrying gold is robbed.* Wienert FFC LVI 56 (ET 169), 94 (ST 75).

L455. *Lean dogs envy arena-dog his fatness.* Later see their error. Wienert FFC LVI 56 (ET 169), 94 (ST 75).

L456. *Calf pities draft ox: is taken to slaughter, ox spared.* Wienert FFC LVI 61 (ET 230), 57 (ET 185), *92 (ST 44), 124 (ST 331); Halm Aesop No. 113.

L460. Pride brought low—miscellaneous.

L461. *Stag scorns his legs but is proud of his horns.* Caught by his horns in trees. *Type 77; Wienert FFC LVI 65 (ET 285), 140 (ST 465); Halm Aesop No. 128; *Crane Vitry 254 No. 274; Herbert III 23; Jacobs Aesop 206 No. 25.

L462. *Fox destroys nest of bird who boasts of nest's warmth.* India: Thompson-Balys.

L465. *The mule's double ancestry.* When well fed says, "My mother was a thoroughbred horse." Later, hard worked, says, "My father was a miserable ass." Wienert FFC LVI 64 (ET 275), 94 (ST 80); Halm Aesop No. 157.

J954.1. Mule as descendant of king's war horse. Fails to mention his mother.

L471. *The man scorns the storm: killed by it.* Type 933*.

L472. *Zeus smites Capaneus while he is climbing a ladder.* Greek: Frazer Apollodorus I 367 n. 3.

Q552.1. Death by thunderbolt as punishment.

L473. *Pride or wealth of man brought low by actions of gods.* India: Thompson-Balys.

L475. *Oil lamp blown out: had thought that it outshone stars.* Wienert FFC LVI 75 (ET 409), 93 (ST 64); Halm Aesop No. 285.

L476. *Jackal singing about his deeds falls down from tree* and is eaten by alligator. India: Thompson-Balys.

L478. *Gnats having overcome lion are in turn killed by spider.* Wienert FFC LVI 48 (ET 75), 92 (ST 57); Halm Aesop No. 234.

L315.6. Insects worry large animal to despair or death.

L482. *Men too prosperous (happy): things are made more difficult.*

A1330. Beginnings of trouble for man. A1346. Man to earn bread by sweat of his brow.

L482.1. *Men are too rich: greedy gods created to impoverish them.* India: Thompson-Balys.

L482.1.1. *Men are too rich: gold sent below ground.* India: Thompson-Balys.

A1100. Establishment of natural order.

L482.2. *Men are too rich: weeds created to spoil their harvests.* India: Thompson-Balys.

L482.3. *Men are too proud: snakes created.* India: Thompson-Balys.

L482.4. *Men are fearless: tiger made to frighten them.* India: Thompson-Balys.

A1815. Creation of tiger.

L482.5. *Men enjoy themselves too much: disease created.* India: Thompson-Balys.

A1330. Beginnings of trouble for man. A1337.0.6. Disease to prevent man enjoying self too much.

M. ORDAINING THE FUTURE

DETAILED SYNOPSIS

M. ORDAINING THE FUTURE

M0—M99. Judgments and decrees.

M0. Judgments and decrees.

A530. Culture hero establishes law and order. A611. Fiat creation. Universe is created at command of creator. A1100. Establishment of natural order. A1300. Ordering of human life. D1318.1.1. Stone bursts as sign of unjust judgment. D1318.2.1. Laughing fish reveals unjust judgment. D1765. Magic results produced by command. M400. Curses.

M1. *Senseless judicial decisions.* *Chauvin VIII 203 No. 245.

J1700. Fools.

M2. *Inhuman decisions of king.* Fansler MAFLS XII 137; Jewish: Neuman.

M2.1. *Inhuman decision of king: sends man's sons to certain death and then murders man.* Spanish Exempla: Keller.

M4. *Deity settles disputes between races.* Africa (Fang): Trilles 142.

M10. Irrevocable judgments.

A196.2. Decree of the gods irrevocable. M203. King's promise irrevocable. M415. Irrevocable curse. P10. Kings. P421. Judge. Q115.1. Reward: any boon that may be asked—king's wife demanded.

M11. *Irrevocable judgment causes judge to suffer first.* Has decreed that no one enter a meeting armed. He forgets to remove his sword. Kills himself. Pauli (ed. Bolte) No. 353; Spanish Exempla: Keller; Italian Novella: Rotunda.

K1681. Originator of death first sufferer.

M12. *Irrevocable sentence carried out even when innocence is proved.* A knight condemned for murdering his comrade is met by the latter on the way to the gallows. A centurion leads them to the emperor, who condemns all three to death: first because he has been sentenced; second for causing by his absence the conviction of his comrade; third for delay in the execution. Oesterley No. 140; Herbert III 208.

M13. *Sentence applied to king's own son.* Those caught in adultery are to have eyes put out. When king's son is found guilty he insists on the punishment. He finally compromises by having one of his own and one of his son's eyes put out. *Pauli (ed. Bolte) No. 226; Spanish Exempla: Keller; Italian Novella: *Rotunda.

Q241. Adultery punished. Q451.7. Blinding as punishment.

M13.1. *Ruler has son beheaded for rape.* Italian Novella: Rotunda.

T471. Rape.

M13.2. *Captain hangs own son for violating order not to enter enemy city.* Italian Novella: Rotunda.

M13.3. *Gardener made king by minister decides against him in law case and returns lands to plaintiff.* India: Thompson-Balys.

M14. *Irrevocable judgment of king upheld.* King leaves laws that must be kept until his death. Years later he has his bones sent back to that land to let people know that he is dead and they are free. Spanish Exempla: Keller.

M20. Short-sighted judgments.

M21. *King Lear judgment.* A king flattered by his elder daughters and angered by the seeming indifference, though real love, of the youngest, banishes the youngest and favors the elder daughters. Type 510; BP II 47, III 305; *Cox Nos. 208—226; *Hartland FLJ IV 308; *Oesterley No. 273; Herbert III 201; India: *Thompsón-Balys; Chinese: Eberhard FFC CXX 183 No. 124.

H592.1. "Love like salt". Girl compares her love for her father to salt. Experience teaches him the value of salt. L50. Victorious youngest daughter. L432.2. Impoverished father begs from daughter he has banished. Recognized. Q431.3. Banishment because of disobedience.

M50. Other judgments and decrees.

M51. *Decree that hero must wed only a virgin.* English: Wells 22 (Sir Beues of Hamtoun).

M133. Vow: man will love only a virgin.

M55. *Judgment: pardon given if hero produces the lady about whom he has boasted.* English: Wells 132 (Sir Launfal).

C31.5. Tabu: boasting of supernatural wife. H915. Tasks assigned because of girl's (boy's) own foolish boast. H1215. Quest assigned because of hero's boast.

M56. *Judgment: thief to be pardoned if he can steal king's treasure without being caught.* India: Thompson-Balys.

K301. Master thief. Man undertakes to steal various closely guarded things. Succeeds by cleverness.

M90. Judgments and decrees—miscellaneous motifs.

M91. *Virgin Mary reverses judgments of church.* *Ward II 638 No. 5, 651 No. 4, 668 No. 15, 682 No. 21, 704 No. 42, 722 No. 30 and passim; Irish: Beal XXI 315, O'Suilleabhain 41.

V250. The Virgin Mary.

M92. *Decision left to first person to arrive.* Type 613; Hdwb. d. Märchens I 604b n. 31ff.; Irish: O'Suilleabhain 118, Beal XXI 335; India: *Thompson-Balys.

K451.1. Unjust umpire decides a religious dispute. His confederate thus wins an absurd wager. K451.2. The wager that sheep are hogs. A trickster wagers with a sheep driver that the sheep he is driving are hogs. The next man to overtake them will act as umpire. The trickster's confederate now arrives and declares that they are hogs. K455.7. Greatest liar to get his supper free. Each lie is corroborated by a confederate who poses as a newly arrived stranger. N125.4. Districts named from first person met in each.

M93. *Deity grants woman two sons, one to be wise and ugly and the other a fool and handsome.* Buddhist myth: Malalasekera II 964.

M100—M199. Vows and oaths.

M100. Vows and oaths. *Penzer X 355 s.v. "vow"; *Hdwb. d. Abergl. II 659ff.; *Encyc. Rel. Ethics IX 430ff.; Estonian: Loorits Grundzüge I 198ff.; Missouri French: Carrière; Jewish: *Neuman.

B279.2. Attitudes of animals toward oath. C68. Tabu: neglecting to fulfill vow made to god. D1273.5. Magic oath. E451.3. Ghost laid when vow is fulfilled. H251.1. Bocca della Verità. Person swearing oath places hand in mouth of image. If oath is false the hand is bitten off. H251.2. Stone of truth. When one stands on it he must utter truth.

H253. Oaths before gods as test of truth. J1169.4. The ass beheaded. King vows to sacrifice first thing he meets. It is a miller driving an ass. Miller pleads that the ass preceded him. They behead the ass. K236.2. Drinking only after a bargain. A woman having thus sworn keeps buying and selling the same mule many times a day. S241. Jephthah's vow. V113.0.2. Vow to visit a sacred shrine. V470. Clerical vows.

M101. *Punishment for broken oaths.* Kristensen Danske Sagn VI (1) (1900) 33ff., (1936) 18ff.; Jewish: *Neuman.

Q263. Lying (perjury) punished.

M101.1. *False swearer not allowed to approach altar.* Pauli (ed. Bolte) No. 485.

M101.2. *Broken oaths cause of maimed people.* Pauli (ed. Bolte) No. 487.

M101.3. *Death as punishment for broken oath.* Irish myth: *Cross.

C94.2. Tabu: false and profane swearing of oath. C920. Death for breaking tabu.

M101.3.1. *Death caused by elements (exposure, drowning, etc.) as punishment for broken oath.* Irish myth: *Cross.

M119.1. Swearing by the elements.

M101.3.2. *Man offers to sacrifice bangles if he is given a son;* when he takes bangles back, son dies. India: Thompson-Balys.

M101.4. *Broken oath causes girl's hand to wither.* (Cf. D2062.) Spanish Exempla: Keller.

M101.5. *Punishment for broken oath: loss of the inheritance of earth or heaven.* Irish myth: Cross.

M105. *Equivocal oaths.* Icelandic: Boberg.

J1161.3. Trespasser's defense: standing on his own land. K1513. The wife's equivocal oath. K2310. Deception by equivocation. K2312. Oath literally obeyed.

M106. *Escape from vengeance caused by broken oaths.* India: Thompson-Balys.

M107. *Vow fulfilled in next existence.* Buddhist myth: Malalasekera II 1221.

M108. *Violators of oaths.*

M108.1. *Babylonians do not keep their oaths.* Jewish: *Neuman.

M110. Taking of vows and oaths.

M110.1. *Swearing while one knows that his oath is rendered valueless.* India: Thompson-Balys.

M110.2. *Oath is valid only when decreed in presence of ten.* Jewish: *Neuman.

M110.3. *Oath uttered by pious when in danger of succumbing to temptation.* Jewish: *Neuman.

M111. *Oaths taken over severed pieces of horse.* Pieces are then buried. Greek: Fox 25.

M112. *Oath taken on ring.* Hdwb. d. Abergl. II 67; Brumer Deutsche Rechtsgeschichte I 258; Icelandic: *Boberg.

M113. *Oath taken on arms.* Irish myth: *Cross.

M113.1. *Oath taken on sword.* Scottish: Campbell-McKay No. 20; Icelandic: Herrmann Saxo II 197; Jewish: Neuman.

M114. *Oath taken on sacred object.* Jewish: Neuman; Icelandic: *Boberg.

M114.1. *Oath on sacred book.*

M114.1.1. *Oath by Tora.* Jewish: *Neuman.

M114.2. *Oath taken on holy stone.* (Cf. M119.5.) Icelandic: Boberg.

M114.3. *Vows taken on holy swine.* Icelandic: Boberg.
V1.8.4. Swine (hog) worship.

M114.4. *Swearing on sacred relics.* Irish myth: *Cross.

M114.5. *Taking oath on cowdung.* India: Thompson-Balys.

M114.6. *Oath by touching sacred thread.* India: Thompson-Balys.

M115. *Only one oath binding.* It must be by so and so or else it is worthless. Italian: Basile Pentamerone IV Nos. 6, 8, V No. 4.

M115.1. *Three-fold oath.* India: Thompson-Balys.

M115.1.1. *Oath so heavy it dries up stream;* oath so great it splits the rock in twain; oath so violent it makes the tree wither. India: Thompson-Balys.

M116. *Oath taken on hand of saint.* Irish myth: Cross.

M116.0.1. *Swearing on hand of king.* Irish myth: Cross.

M116.1. *Swearing by saint's bachall.* Irish myth: Cross.

M116.2. *Swearing by saint's bell.* Irish myth: Cross.

M117. *Vow to perform certain act unless cataclysm occurs.* Irish myth: *Cross.

M118. *Swearing on a skull.* Irish myth: Cross.

M119. *Taking of vows and oaths—miscellaneous.*

M119.1. *Swearing by the elements: sun, moon, stars, wind.* Irish myth: *Cross; Greek: Argonautica III 689, Odyssey V 185.
M101.3.1. Death caused by elements (exposure, drowning, etc.) as punishment for broken oath.

M119.1.1. *Oath by River Styx.* Greek: Grote I 56f.

M119.2. *Swearing by (clan) gods.* Irish myth: *Cross.
A415. Clan gods.

M119.3. *Vows taken as an old Norse custom at the festival of Yule.* Icelandic: Cleasby and Vigfússon Icel.-Eng. Dict. (1874) 853 s.v. "heitstrenging"; Lagerholm 18, *Boberg.

M119.4. *Vows taken by placing one's foot on a certain post in the hall.* Icelandic: *Boberg.

M119.5. *Swearing on a stone.* (Cf. M114.2.) Irish myth: Cross.

M119.6. *Swearing by "the Seven Things which they serve."* Irish myth: *Cross.

M119.7. *Oath by placing hand on genitals.* Irish myth: Cross; Jewish: *Neuman.

M119.8. *Oath taken by the life of a person.* Jewish: Neuman.

M119.8.1. *Swearing by one's father and mother.* India: Thompson-Balys.

M119.8.2. *Swearing by life of father.* Jewish: *Neuman.

M120. Vows concerning personal appearance.
C720. Tabu: attending toilet needs.

M121. *Vow not to shave or cut hair until a certain time.* *BP II 431ff.; A. Bugge "Harald Haarfagres løfte" Edda VII 166; Helm Altgermanische Religionsgeschichte I 301; Eitrem Opferritus und Voropfer (Skrifter Vidensk. Selsk. i Oslo No. 1, 1914) 400; Frazer Golden Bough III 194; Kruyt Het Animisme 33; FFC LXXXIII xxiv. — Irish: O'Suilleabhain 24, 45, Beal XXI 307, 316; Icelandic: *Boberg; Swiss: Jegerlehner Oberwallis 308 No. 39; Spanish: Boggs FFC XC 53 No. 400B*; Greek: Roscher Lexikon s.v. "Achilleus"; Jewish: *Neuman.

M122. *Vow: woman not to bind hair till enemy is conquered.* Alphabet No. 529.

M125. *Vow not to change clothes till a certain time.* Spanish: Boggs FFC XC 53 No. 400B*.

M126. *Vow not to wash till a certain time.* Greek: Iliad XXIII 49.

M130. Vows concerning sex. (Cf. M151.2, M152.)

M131. *Vow of chastity.* Penzer I 67; Wesselski Mönchslatein 142 No. 117; Irish myth: *Cross; Missouri French: Carrière; Greek: *Grote I 162f.
C110. Tabu: sexual intercourse. T131. Marriage restrictions. T300. Chastity and celibacy.

M132. *Vow of virginity.* Penzer III 40.

M133. *Vow: man will love only a virgin.* Malone PMLA XLIII 427.
M51. Decree that hero must wed only a virgin.

M134. *Prince vows to marry no woman unless he can beat her daily.* India: *Thompson-Balys.

M135. *Vow never to remarry.* Irish myth: *Cross; India: *Thompson-Balys.
M255. Deathbed promise concerning the second wife. Promises his dying wife that he will not marry unless the bride meets the specifications the dying wife imposes. T211. Faithfulness to marriage in death.

M136. *Vow not to marry till iron shoes wear out.* Köhler-Bolte Zs. f. Vksk. VI 71 (to Gonzenbach No. 32); *Roberts 137.
H1125. Task: traveling till iron shoes are worn out. M202.1. Promise to be fulfilled when iron shoes wear out.

M137. *Vow never to be jealous of one's wife.* Wells 64 (The Avowynge of King Arthur, etc.); Irish myth: *Cross.
T257. Jealous wife or husband.

M137.1. *Woman requires husband free from jealousy.* Irish myth: *Cross.

M138. *Vow to marry first person performing certain act.* India: Thompson-Balys.
D1812.5.0.7. Divination from first person (thing) met. H0. Identity tests.

M138.1. *Vow to marry off two daughters to first two men father looks at on the following morning.* India: Thompson-Balys.
T62. Princess to marry first man who asks for her.

M141. *Vow never to strive against a woman.* Irish myth: Cross.

M142. *Vow never to carry a woman.* Irish myth: Cross.

M145. *Vow to wed no man who cannot perform certain feat.*
H335. Tasks assigned suitors.

M145.1. *Vow to wed no man who fears to saddle and mount a lion.* India: Thompson-Balys.

M146. *Vow to marry a certain woman.* Icelandic: *Boberg.
T61. Betrothal.

M146.1. *Vow to marry queen of fairies and not to eat or drink inside kingdom until this is done.* India: Thompson-Balys.

M146.2. *Boy vows to marry none but girl born under the same circumstances as he.* India: Thompson-Balys.

M146.3. *Vow that magically conceived children shall marry* (or be friends). India: Thompson-Balys.
T69.2. Parents affiance children without their knowledge.

M146.4. *Brother and sister arrange marriage of their unborn children to each other.* India: Thompson-Balys.

M146.5. *Vow to marry none but daughter of certain man.* Jewish: *Neuman.

M146.7. *Vow of enemy chief to marry princess of besieged city.* Jewish: Neuman.

M149. *Vows concerning sex—miscellaneous.*

M149.1. *Lovers vow to marry only each other.* Icelandic: *Boberg.

M149.2. *Vow to die rather than marry unwelcome suitor.* Icelandic: *Boberg.
R111.1.9. Princess rescued by undesired suitor. T326. Suicide to save virginity.

M149.3. *Vow to kill more successful rival.* Icelandic: *Boberg.
H335.4.3. Suitor task: to kill all earlier suitors. T92.10. Rival in love killed.

M149.4. *Quarreling prince and princess vow that if they are married he will desert her on the wedding day* and she will make him eat boiled rice and thin broth for six months. It so happens. India: Thompson-Balys.

M149.5. *Oath to marry daughters only into family with bridegroom for each daughter.* India: Thompson-Balys.

M149.6. *Vow to get stubborn girl half-married only.* India: Thompson-Balys.

M149.7. *Vow only to marry daughter to the man who kills snake by her house.* Icelandic: *Boberg.

M150. Other vows and oaths.

M151. *Vow not to eat before hearing of adventure.* Sir Gawayne and the Green Knight § 5; Irish myth: *Cross; India: Thompson-Balys.

C231. Tabu: eating before certain time. C287. Tabu: consuming feast without discovering new wonder. P14.6. King's (prince's) sulking chamber. W213.1. Host requires deed of bravery before feast is eaten.

M151.1. *Vow not to eat before learning secret.* India: Thompson-Balys.

N440. Valuable secrets learned.

M151.2. *Vow not to marry until quest is concluded.* Irish myth: Cross.

M151.2.1. *Vow not to reign and to starve to death unless picture's original is found.* India: Thompson-Balys.

T11.2. Love through sight of picture.

M151.3. *Vow not to take food or drink until manner of father's death is learned.* Irish myth: Cross.

M151.4. *Vow not to take food or drink until enemy is killed.* Irish myth: Cross; Jewish: Neuman.

M151.5. *Vow not to eat or sleep until certain event is brought to pass.* Irish myth: Cross.

C231. Tabu: eating before certain time. C761.4.1. Tabu: staying two nights in one place until certain event is brought to pass.

M151.5.1. *Vow not to eat, drink, or move from position until dead anchorite comes himself to accept necklace.* India: Thompson-Balys.

M151.6. *Vow not to eat or drink before knowing if king is alive.* Icelandic: Boberg.

M151.7. *Heroine will not laugh till arrival of destined hero.* (Cf. H341.) Irish myth: Cross.

M151.8. *Vow not to eat until lost son is found.* India: Thompson-Balys.

H1385. Quest for lost persons.

M151.9. *Vow not to see friends until quest is completed.* English romance: Malory XI 12.

M152. *Vow not to go to bed with wife till enemy is killed.* Icelandic: Boberg.

M152.1. *Vow not to kiss anybody until father is revenged.* Icelandic: Boberg.

M161.2. Vow to revenge (king, friends, father) or die.

M152.2. *Vow not to sit on father's high-seat until he is revenged.* Icelandic: Boberg.

M155. *Vow to perform act of prowess.* Icelandic: *Boberg.

H1220. Quests voluntarily undertaken. T11.2. Love through sight of picture.

M155.1. *Vow to kill wild boar alone at night.* Wells 64 (The Avowynge of King Arthur, etc.).

M155.2. *Vow to find vanished sister.* Icelandic: *Boberg.

M155.3. *Vow never to flee from fire or weapon.* Icelandic: Boberg.

M156. *Vow to watch at frightful place all night.* Wells 64 (The Avowynge of King Arthur).

H1410. Fear test: staying in frightful place.

M157. *Vow to ride the forest all night and slay all comers.* Wells 64 (The Avowynge of King Arthur, etc.).

M158. *Vow never to refuse food to any man.* Wells 64 (The Avowynge of King Arthur); Icelandic: Boberg.

C871. Tabu: refusing a request.

M161. *Vow never to flee in fear of death.* Irish myth: *Cross.

M161.1. *Vow to attack (kill) the enemy or die.* Icelandic: *Boberg.

M161.2. *Vow to revenge (king, friends, father) or die.* English: Malory XX 10; Icelandic: *Boberg.

M152.1. Vow not to kiss anybody until father is revenged. M152.2. Vow not to sit on father's high-seat until he is revenged. P273.1.1. Foster brothers avenge each other.

M161.3. *Vow to live and die with the king.* Icelandic: *Boberg.

M161.4. *Vow rather to die (on a spear) than to accept grace.* (Cf. M165.) Hdwb. d. Märchens II s.v. "Gnade ausbitten"; Icelandic: Ragnars saga Lodbr. 139-41, *Boberg.

M161.5. *Rather die than go in the enemy's service.* Icelandic: Boberg.

R74. Defeated warriors go into the conqueror's service.

M161.6. *Rather die in battle than in bed.* Icelandic: cf. MacCulloch Eddic 305ff., *Boberg.

P16.3. King killed when old.

M162. *Vow not to be killed by a single opponent.* Irish myth: Cross.

M163. *Vow never to make a nocturnal assault.* Irish myth: Cross.

M164. *Bard vows that none of his profession will make a request of any man.* Irish myth: Cross.

M165. *Vow to ask nobody for peace, grace.* (Cf. M161.4.) Icelandic: Boberg.

M166. *Other vows about fighting.*

M166.1. *Vow never to give more than one blow in a fight* and never to beat a fallen enemy nor take his weapons. Icelandic: Boberg.

M166.2. *Vow rather to be cut in pieces than permit oneself to be bound.* Icelandic: Boberg.

M166.3. *Vow to kill anyone who touches his beard.* India: Thompson-Balys.

M166.4. *Vow: never to fight with brother.* Buddhist myth: Malalasekera II 1019.

M166.5. *Oath not to fight relatives of king.* English romance: Malory X 44.

M167. *Vow to serve only the most generous of all kings.* Icelandic: *Boberg.

M168. *Vow not to devastate country or take revenge after release.* Icelandic: Boberg.

Q151. Life spared as reward.

M168.1. *Vow not to deceive the man who spared one's life.* Icelandic: Boberg.

M171. *Vow never to accept a man who does not know any sport.* Icelandic: Boberg.

M172. *Vow not to touch certain thing.*
C500. Tabu: touching.

M172.1. *Vow never to touch money and to give what anyone begs for.* India: Thompson-Balys.

M172.2. *Vow not to touch certain tree.* Later cannot cross bridge made of this wood. India: Thompson-Balys.
K134.1. Horse which will not go over trees.

M175. *Pledge to say but a single phrase.* In carrying out this agreement the men innocently confess a crime. *Types 360, 1697; BP II 561ff.; Wesselski Mönchslatein 37 No. 44; India: *Thompson-Balys.
C495.2.2. "We three" — "For gold" — "That is right": phrases of foreign language. Three travelers know each one phrase of foreign language. They incriminate themselves. J1141.13. Witness always to answer "No." J1255. Answering only "yes" and "no." J2511.2. Numskulls make silence wager. Arrested as thieves. N610. Accidental discovery of crime.

M177. *Vow to change religion.*

M177.1. *Vow to become a Christian.*
V331. Conversion to Christianity.

M177.1.1. *King swears to become Christian if he wins battle.* Spanish Exempla: Keller.

M177.1.2. *Oath not to be christened until he has fought in seven battles for Jesus.* English romance: Malory X 47.

M177.2. *Prince vows that he will always be servant of a goddess (Kali).* India: Thompson-Balys.

M182. *Vow not to enter any house before reaching one's own.* Icelandic: Boberg.

M183. *Religious vows.* (Cf. M177.)
V0. Religion.

M183.1. *Vow to build shrine.* India: Thompson-Balys.

M183.2. *Vow to bathe in the Ganges.* India: Thompson-Balys.

M183.3. *Vow to find Holy Grail before returning to Round Table.* English romance: Malory XIII 7.

M183.4. *Vow to become monk should he escape execution.* Buddhist myth: Malalasekera II 817.

M184. *Vow if queen bears another girl she and child will both be killed.* India: Thompson-Balys.

M184.1. *Vow that no daughter born to chief's wife will be allowed to live until she bears a son.* Hawaii: Beckwith Myth 526.

M185. *Vow to abide by laws.* Jewish: *Neuman.

M186. *Vow never to pass over demarcation line into other's property.* Jewish: *Neuman.

M187. *Oath to abide by results of lot drawing.* Jewish: *Neuman.

M188. *Oath not to mention what has been seen.* Jewish: *Neuman.
C420. Tabu: uttering secrets.

M192. *Vow to put to death every king that comes his way unless engaged in marrying a lady at the time he sees them.* India: Thompson-Balys.

M193. *Vow to destroy kingdom by austerities.* India: Thompson-Balys.

M200—M299. Bargains and promises.

M200. **Bargains and promises.** India: Thompson-Balys.
B312.2. Helpful animals obtained by exchange. D837. Magic object acquired through foolish bargain. D851. Magic object acquired through exchange. D871. Magic object traded away. E342. Dead return to fulfill bargain. J2080. Foolish bargains. K100. Deceptive bargains. K236.2. Drinking only after a bargain. A woman having thus sworn keeps buying and selling the same mule many times a day. K1357. Lover's gift regained. The husband appears before payment can be made. K1358. Girl shows herself naked in return for youth's dancing hogs. K1361. Beggar buys right to sleep before girl's door, etc. N421. Lucky bargain. P273.2.1. Promise of marriage to king's daughter induces warrior to fight foster brother. P525. Contracts. S223. Childless couple promise child to the devil if they may only have one. T61.2. Parting lovers pledge not to marry for seven years.

M201. *Making of bargains and promises.*
H1561.1. Tests of valor: tournament. P311.1. Combatants become sworn brethren.

M201.0.1. *Bargain with God (by holy man).* Irish myth: Cross; Jewish: *Neuman.

M201.0.1.1. *Covenant between Israel and God.* Jewish: *Neuman.

M201.0.2. *Covenant between heathen and Israelites.* Jewish: Neuman.

M201.1. *Blood covenant.* Contract written (or signed) with blood. Hdwb. d. Abergl. II 272ff., 1026; *Wilken Verspreide Geschriften I 539ff.; *W. Robertson Smith Religion of the Semites[3] 270ff.; *Penzer I 98 n.; *Fb "skrive"; "blod" IV 47b; ** H. C. Turmbull The Blood Covenant (London, 1887). — Breton: Sébillot Incidents s.v. "sang", "pacte"; Jewish: *Neuman; India: Thompson-Balys.
D1273.0.1. Charm written in blood has magic power.

M201.1.1. *Blood of contractors mixed to seal bargain.* Irish myth: *Cross; Africa (Ekoi): Talbot 268.
P312. Blood-brotherhood. Friends take oath of brotherhood by means of mixing their blood.

M201.1.2. *Pact with devil signed in blood.* (Theophilus.) (Cf. M211.) Type 756B; *Andrejev FFC LXIX 64; Scala Celi 9a, 135b Nos 58, 749; Wünsche Teufel 55f.; England, U.S.: Baughman; Irish: Beal XXI 310—312, O'Suilleabhain 33f.; Spanish Exempla: Keller; Argentina: Jijena Sanchez 80.
M210. Bargain with devil.

M201.2. *Covenant confirmed by eating together.* Hdwb. d. Abergl. II 272ff.; U.S.: Baughman; Africa (Fang): Nassau 242 No. 9.

M201.3. *Spitting of all parties into vessel to seal bargain.* Icelandic: MacCulloch Eddic 53; England: Baughman.
A1211.3.1. Being made from spittle of the gods.

M201.4. *Covenant between saints confirmed by cutting off their thumbs.* Irish myth: Cross.

S160. Mutilations.

M201.5. *Covenant confirmed by marriage.* Icelandic: *Boberg.

M201.6. *Covenant confirmed by hostages.* Icelandic: *Boberg.

P271.4. Living king's or nobleman's son as foster son of father's friend.

M202. *Fulfilling of bargain or promise.*

P557.2. Pledge with enemy to be kept.

M202.0.1. *Bargain or promise to be fulfilled at all hazards.* English romance: Malory VIII 30; Irish myth: *Cross.

C650. The one compulsory thing. C871. Tabu: refusing a request.

M202.1. *Promise to be fulfilled when iron shoes wear out.* *Cox Cinderella 508.

H1125. Task: traveling till iron shoes are worn out. M136. Vow not to marry till iron shoes wear out.

M202.1. *Prisoner would be set free only after he has used up a pair of harmed shoes.* Krappe Philological Quarterly XI (1932) 87f.

M202.2. *Man keeps word to return to enemy if his mission to his people fails.* Spanish Exempla: Keller.

M203. *King's promise irrevocable.* Basil Pentamerone I No. 5; Irish myth: *Cross; Missouri French: Carrière; Spanish Exempla: Keller; India: Thompson-Balys; West Indies: Flowers 560.

M10. Irrevocable judgments. P10. Kings. Q115. Reward: any wish that may be asked. Q152. City saved from disaster as reward.

M203.1. *King punishes one of his men who robs someone to whom the king has given safe conduct.* Spanish Exempla: Keller.

M203.2. *King kills self to carry out own promise.* India: Thompson-Balys.

M203.3. *King sells self and family into slavery to keep promise.* India: Thompson-Balys.

M204. *Demanding of promised boon postponed.*

M204.1. *Demanding of promised boon postponed until an auspicious moment.* Granted anything he may ask, the recipient waits to announce his choice. English romance: Malory VIII 15; India: Thompson-Balys.

Q115. Reward: any boon that may be asked.

M205. *Breaking of bargains or promises.* India: Thompson-Balys; West Indies: Flowers 561.

H1241.1. Hero returning from successful quest sent upon another. K231.3. Refusal to make sacrifice after need is past. K2111.3. Friar refuses to keep promise after enjoying woman. M256. Promises to dying man broken.

M205.0.1. *Promise kept in deed but not in spirit.* English romance: Malory X 38.

M205.1. *Animal punishes broken promise.*

M205.1.1. *Turtle carrying man through water upsets him because of a broken promise.* Chinese: Werner 367.

B551. Fish carries man across water. K1042. Water bird carrying dupe to sea shakes him off.

M205.1.1.1. *Fish (whale) carrying man through water shakes him off when man strikes him with coconut.* Tahiti: Beckwith Myth 252; Tuamotu: Stimson MS (T-G. 3/600).

K952.1. Ungrateful river passenger. R245. Whale boat.

M205.1.2. *Cat witness to betrothal punishes violator.* Kills the man's son when he has married a different woman. Hebrew: *bin Gorion Born Judas[2] I 368.

M205.2. *Curse as punishment for broken promise.* Irish myth: *Cross.

Q556. Curse as punishment.

M205.3. *A man who breaks his oath to a woman cannot be king with right.* Icelandic: Boberg.

M205.4. *King breaks promise to care for man's family.* Is caught trying to steal his money. India: Thompson-Balys.

M206. *Promise made merely as a matter of form not binding.*

M206.1. *Host offers to send his guest a cask of the wine he has praised.* Later refuses to send it as it was merely a "verba honoris". Pauli (ed. Bolte) No. 308.

M207. *Land grants (bargains).* Irish myth: *Cross.

M208. *Price set on one's head.* Icelandic: *Boberg.

M210. Bargain with devil. Types 310, 313A, 316, 360, 400, 425C, 441, 500, 502, 706, 710, 756B, 810—812, 1170—1199; BP II 164, 329f., 427, 561ff., III 12; *Andrejev FFC LXIX 222ff.; *Fb "djævel" IV 99a, "blod" IV 47b. — England, U.S.: Baughman; Missouri French: Carrière; Italian Novella: *Rotunda; Jewish: *Neuman; India: *Thompson-Balys; West Indies: Flowers 562.

B620.1. Daughter promised to animal suitor. C758.1. Monster born because of hasty wish of parents. E511.1.2. Flying Dutchman sails because of pact with devil. E756.2. Soul won from devil in card game. F613.1. Strong man's labor contract: blow at end of year. Blow sends his master to sky. F613.4. Strong man serves ogre as punishment for stealing food. G303. The devil. H543.1. Devil held off from person by answering his riddles. H932. Tasks assigned to devil (ogre). K170.1. Deceptive partnership between man and ogre. K172. Anger bargain. The trickster makes a bargain with his master that the first to become angry must submit to punishment. He thereupon heaps abuses on his master till the latter breaks out in anger and must take his punishment. K210. Devil cheated of his promised soul. The man saves it through deceit. M201.1.2. Pact with devil signed in blood.

M211. *Man sells soul to devil.* (Faust, Theophilus.) Types 330, 360, 361, 756B, 810, 812, 1170-1199; *BP II 164, 427, 561ff., III 12; *Andrejev FFC LXIX 46, 50, 223, 227 n.; Lidzbarski Am Urds-Brunnen IV 59 n. 1; Scala Celi 9a, 112a, 135b Nos. 58, 625, 749; *Pauli (ed. Bolte) No. 667; *Fb "sjæl" III 215a; Faligan RTP V 1; Alphabet Nos. 50, 467; *Ludorff Anglia VII 60ff.; *Loomis White Magic 112f.; *K. Bittner Die Faustsage im russischen Schrifttum (Reichenberg. i. B. [Prager Deutsche Studien No. 37], 1925); *Krappe Bulletin Hispanique XXXIX 34. — Lithuanian: Balys Index No. 3400, Legends No. 757; Spanish: Boggs FFC XC 49, 67 Nos. 330, 510, Espinosa Jr. Nos. 70-74, 83f.; Italian Novella: Rotunda; Argentina: Jijena Sanchez 74; N. A. Indian (Wampanoag): Knight JAFL XXXVIII 134, (Salinan): Mason U Cal X 196.

G303.22. The devil helps people. H1273.1. Quest to devil in hell for return of contract. K551.1. Respite from death granted until prayer is finished. It lasts till rescue comes. K1955.6. The sham physician and the devil in partnership. The devil is to enter the girl and the physician will collect reward for driving the devil out. S211. Child sold (promised) to devil (ogre). S221.2. Youth sells himself to an ogre in settlement of a gambling debt. S240. Children unwittingly promised (sold). S251. Virgin Mary rescues child promised to the devil. V264.1. Virgin Mary brings man a pact he signed with the devil and frees the man from devil's power.

M211.1. *Man unwittingly sells soul to devil.* He jestingly offers to sell his soul. Devil in disguise buys it. *Pauli (ed. Bolte) No. 280; *Wesselski Märchen 245 No. 55.

M211.1.1. *Man goes to well at midnight on Old Christmas to see water turned into wine.* Just as it turns into wine the devil takes him, or injures him. England, U.S.: *Baughman.

M211.2. *Man sells soul to devil in return for devil's building house* (barn, etc.). Wünsche Teufel 29-56 passim.

G303.9.1. The devil as a builder.

M211.3. *Man bequeaths soul to devil.* U.S.: Baughman; Italian Novella: Rotunda.

M211.4. *Jews must repay devil's help by giving tribute of persons each year.* Lithuanian: Balys Index No. 1867D*.

E752.2. Soul carried off by demon (devil). G303.9.5.7. Devil carries a Jew to hell. R11.2.1. Devil carries off wicked people. V360. Christian traditions concerning Jews.

M211.5. *Formulas for selling one's soul to devil.* England: Baughman.

M211.6. *Man sells soul to devil for visit home in boat that sails through sky.* U.S.: Baughman.

M211.7. *Man sells soul to devil for magic power to escape capture.* Canada: Baughman.

M211.8. *Man sells soul to devil for devil's doing one specific job.* England, Wales: *Baughman.

M211.9. *Person sells soul to devil in return for the granting of wishes.* England: Baughman.

M212. *Devil agrees to help man with robberies.*

M212.1. *Devil as helper of robber refuses to let women's ornaments be stolen.* They are his own weapons. Pauli (ed. Bolte) No. 86.

M212.2. *Devil at gallows repudiates his bargain with robber.* Ring turns to rope. The judge cannot find a rope and is about to release the thief because of the miracle. But the ring in the box presented by the devil as a bribe turns out to be a rope. The man is hanged. *Krappe Archivum Romanicum VII 470ff.; *Wesselski Märchen 244 No. 54; Spanish Exempla: Keller.

J1130. Cleverness in the law court. K210. The devil cheated of his promised soul. The man saves it through deceit.

M213. *Devil as substitute for day laborer at mowing.* He mows with a magic sickle. The evil overseer tries to keep up with him and dies of overexhaustion. Type 820.

M214. *Devil to help gambler in exchange for one task yearly.* Spanish: Boggs FFC XC 55 No. 408A*.

N6.1. Luck in gambling from compact with devil.

M215. *With his whole heart: devil carries off judge.* The devil refuses to take anything not offered him with the whole heart. He hears the judge (advocate) cursed for fraud with such sincerity that he carries him off. *Type 1186; **Taylor PMLA XXXVI 35ff., also in Bryan and

Dempster Sources and Analogues of Chaucer's Canterbury Tales 269-74; *Herbert III 592; *Fb "ridefoged" III 53b; *Pauli (ed. Bolte) Nos. 81, 807; *Robinson Complete Works of Geoffrey Chaucer (Cambridge, Mass., 1933) 809 (Friar's Tale).

C12.2. Oath: "May the devil take me if ..." Devil does. G303.22.11. Devil as advocate of falsely condemned man. M432. Curse: to be carried off by evil spirit.

M216. *Devil bargains to help man become priest.* He must not later exorcise him from people. Spanish: Boggs FFC XC 50 No. 332.

M216.1. *The devil helps man study for priesthood.* For this, he must promise the devil his soul. Having become a great priest, the man finds means to save himself. Lithuanian: Balys Index No. 3266, Legends Nos. 400ff.

K218.3. Devil cheated when his victim becomes a priest.

M216.2. *The devil makes the herdsman's son a priest in return for a whistle.* After quarreling with the devil, who asked to repair the whistle during Mass, the priest forgets all he learned and does not know how to hold Mass. Is beaten. Lithuanian: Balys Index No. 3269, Legends Nos. 413f.

M217. *Devil bargains to help man win woman.* *Loomis White Magic 113; Alphabet No. 64; Spanish: Boggs FFC XC 66 No. 508A*, Keller; Italian Novella: *Rotunda. Cf. Cosquin Etudes 545ff. (sale of self to magician).

T331.5. Anchorite saved by miracle. V345. Dove flies out of man's mouth.

M217.1. *Servant makes pact with devil denying Christ to secure nobleman's daughter.* Spanish Exempla: Keller.

M218. *Contract with the devil destroyed.* Dh I 140; Alphabet Nos. 64, 467; Irish: Beal XXI 311, O'Suilleabhain 33.

H1273.1. Quest to devil in hell for return of contract. K210. Devil cheated of his promised soul.

M218.1. *Pacts with the devil, sealed in blood, made ineffective by a saint.* *Loomis White Magic 75.

M219. *Other devil contract motifs.*

M219.1. *Bargain with the devil for an heir.* Irish myth: *Cross.

S223. Childless couple promise child to the devil if they may only have one.

M219.2. *Devil fetches man contracted to him.*

M219.2.1. *Devil appears in great storm, takes away soul of person contracted to him.* (Cf. D2141.0.4, D2141.0.5, Q550.1.) England, U.S.: *Baughman.

M219.2.2. *Devil flays corpse of person contracted to him.* (Cf. Q457.2.) England: Baughman.

M219.2.3. *Man contracted to the devil responds to call by voice:* "The hour has come but not the man." England, Scotland: *Baughman.

D1311.11.1. River says "The time has come but not the man."

M219.2.4. *Devil carries off hunt-loving priest.* (Cf. G303.17.2.4.) England: *Baughman.

M219.2.5. *Body of devil's disciple is removed from coffin by devil.* England, U.S.: *Baughman.

M219.2.6. *Devil puts body of convert on a sea monster which takes it away.* U.S.: Baughman.

M219.3. *Familiars guard and protect those who have pact with the devil.* Argentina: Jijena Sanchez 80.

M219.4. *Familiar devours whoever does not keep pact with devil.* Argentina: Jijena Sanchez 82.

M220. Other bargains.

D1853. Immortality exchanged. Wounded Centaur immortal but cannot be cured. He gives away his immortality to Prometheus and is thus allowed to die. E165. Resuscitation of wife by husband giving up half his remaining life. (Sometimes vice versa.) H1239.1. Prince agrees to marry a servant girl if she will help him on a quest. J1161.2. Literal pleading frees man from pound of flesh contract. Contract does not give the right to shed blood. Impossible, therefore, to carry out. K944. Deceptive agreement to kill wives (children). Trickster shams the murder; dupe kills his. S210. Children sold or promised. S220. Reasons for promise (sale) of child.

M221. *Beheading bargain.* Giant allows hero to cut off his head; he will cut off hero's later. **Kittredge Gawain and the Green Knight; Irish myth: *Cross.

F531.1.2.3. Giant's self-returning head.

M221.1. *Hag offers to run race with men on condition that the one left behind shall be beheaded.* Marvelous runner beheads hag. Irish myth: Cross.

M222. *Man umpires dispute in exchange for guarantee of safety.* Disputants, bear and tiger, agree not to eat him. India: Thompson-Balys.

J685.1. Man, lion, and bear in pit. K579.5. Respite while captor acts as umpire between captives.

M223. *Blind promise (rash boon).* Person grants wish before hearing it. English romance: Malory X 22; Irish myth: *Cross.

N2.0.1. Play for unnamed stakes. P319.7. Friendship without refusal. Q115. Reward: any boon that may be asked.

M223.1. *Person who never refuses a request.* Irish myth: Cross.

C871. Tabu: refusing a request.

M225. *Eyes exchanged for food.* A starving man lets himself be blinded in return for food. *Type 613; *BP II 468ff.; **Christiansen FFC XXIV 46, 54; *Fb "øje" III 1166b; Missouri French: Carrière; India: Thompson-Balys.

E781.2. Eyes bought back and replaced.

M225.1. *Horse, clothes, and members of rider's body exchanged for food.* India: Thompson-Balys.

M226. *In return for magic shirt from girl hero is to stay in Ireland for three years.* In return he claims her as wife. Icelandic: Boberg.

M231. *Free keep in inn exchanged for good story.* *Fb "kro" II 303a.

M232. *Prince to give up life in exchange for learning a secret.* Malone PMLA XLIII 405, 413.

M233. *Three deformed witches invited to wedding in exchange for help.* *Type 501; BP I 109; **Von Sydow Två Spinnsagor.

G201.1. Three witches (hags) deformed from much spinning. J51. Sight of deformed witches causes man to release wife from spinning duty. N825.3. Old woman helper.

M234. *Life spared in return for life-long service.* Irish myth: *Cross.

H542. Death sentence escaped by propounding riddle king (judge) cannot solve. H924. Tasks assigned prisoner so that he may escape punishment. K613. Prisoner released on promise of life-long allegiance.

M234.1. *Life spared in return for poetic mead.* Icelandic: MacCulloch Eddic 53.

A154.2. Theft of magic mead by Odin.

M234.2. *Life spared for bringing a dreaded enemy without weapon.* Icelandic: MacCulloch Eddic 83 f. (Thor and Loki).

M234.3. *Life bought for gold.* Icelandic: Boberg.

M234.4. *Life bought with promise of reparations and healing of enemy.* Icelandic: Boberg.

M235. *Bargain: woman rides naked through streets to obtain freedom for citizens.* Godiva. Liebrecht 104; Hartland FL I 207.

C312.1.2. Tabu: looking at nude woman riding through town.

M236. *Peace bought for husband.* Icelandic: MacCulloch Eddic 103, *Boberg.

M237. *Bargain to save face.* Irish myth: Cross.

M237.1. *Opponents agree not to fight and are thus undefeated.* Irish myth: *Cross.

M241. *Bargain: to divide all winnings.*

J1621. Sharing his wounds. K187. Strokes shared.

M241.1. *Dividing the winnings: half of the bride demanded.* When the hero shows that he is willing to carry out the bargain, his helper relents. *Type 505—508; *BP III 490; Köhler-Bolte I 11, 444; *Liljeblad Tobiasgeschichte; English: Wells 160 (Sir Amadace); India: Thompson-Balys.

J1171.2. Solomon's judgment: the divided bride.

M241.2. *Dividing the winnings: presents (favors) from man's own wife.* After the agreement to divide all winnings the first man receives favors (presents, kisses) from the second's wife. He faithfully delivers them. *Type 1364; Wesselski Märchen 187 No. 2; English: Wells 55 (Sir Gawayne and the Green Knight).

M242. *Bargains and promises between mortals and supernatural beings.* (Cf. M221, M222, M223.) Irish myth: *Cross.

F252.1.0.1. Mortal rules fairyland jointly with fairy king. F327. Family carried away to fairyland as part of bargain.

M242.1. *Mortal fosters fairy child to prevent destruction of crops.* Irish myth: *Cross.

F369.5. Fairies destroy crops. F393. Fairy visits among mortals.

M242.2. *Contract between hungry god and untouchable:* to give gods food it they will eat from his hands. India: Thompson-Balys.

M242.3. *Ogre released in return for his magic girdle.* Tuamotu: Stimson MS (Z-G. 13/152, 221, 1314).

M244. *Bargains between men and animals.*

M244.1. *Bargain with king of mice.* India: Thompson-Balys.

B241.2.5. King of mice.

M244.2. *Captured bird promises to deliver fifteen birds in exchange for freedom.* Africa (Cameroon): Lederbogen 73.

M246. *Covenant of friendship.*

P312. Blood-brotherhood. Friends take oath of brotherhood by means of mixing their blood.

M246.1. *Covenant of friendship between animals.*

A2493. Friendship between the animals.

M246.1.1. *Covenant of friendship between elephant and jackal.* India: Thompson-Balys.

M246.1.2. *Covenant of friendship between louse and crow.* India: Thompson-Balys.

M246.2. *Covenant of friendship: no matter how poor son of one is, daughter of other will accept him as groom.* India: Thompson-Balys.

M246.3. *Covenant of friendship: to secure brides for each other.* India: Thompson-Balys.

M250. Promises connected with death.

E374.1. Return of the dead to keep promise. K2065.1. Woman has sick husband: "Would that death take me in his stead!"

M251. *Dying man's promise will be kept.* Fb "love" II 452a.

D1715. Magic power of dying man's words. J154. Wise words of dying father. J155.6. Wise words of dying woman (queen). M411.3. Dying man's curse. P17.3. Dying king names successor. P401. Son insists on following father's trade. This has been kept secret at request of dying father who was unsuccessful. Son learns from mother.

M252. *Promise of dying man to bring news of other world.* (Or two friends agree that the first to die shall bring news.) *Type 470; Swiss: Jegerlehner Oberwallis 305 No. 6, 323 Nos. 112, 113, 329 Nos. 31, 33; Irish: Beal XXI 331f., O'Suilleabhain 99—102, *Cross; Jewish: bin Gorion Born Judas VI 123, 311.

M253. *Friends in life and death.* In pursuance of the pledge, the living follows the other to the world of the dead. *Type 470; Pauli (ed. Bolte) No. 561; **MacKay The Double Invitation; Jewish: Neuman.

M254. *Promise to be buried with wife if she dies first.* *Type 612; *BP I 128.

M255. *Deathbed promise concerning the second wife.* Promises his dying wife that he will not marry unless the bride meets the specifications the dying wife imposes. *Type 510B; *Cox 53—79 passim; DeVries Studien over Færösche Balladen 133; Icelandic: Boberg; Danish: Grundtvig No. 135.

H363. Deceased wife marriage test. Man will marry woman meeting certain specifications prescribed by his deceased wife. J155.6. Wise words of dying woman (queen). M135. Vow never to remarry.

M256. *Promise to dying man broken.*

M205. Breaking of bargains and promises.

M256.1. *Sons break promise to have masses for father's soul.* "If he is in Hell it will do him no good; if he is in Heaven he won't need it; and if he is in Purgatory he can purge himself." Italian Novella: Rotunda.

V40. Mass.

M257. *Dying monster's request and promise.* Hero is to drink his blood, suck his eyes and brains, and give his heart to his loved one to eat. He will become marvelously strong and his wife will have three sons and four daughters with great powers. Köhler-Bolte I 117; Gascon: Bladé I 3, 181; India: Thompson-Balys.

D1335.2.1. Blood as magic strengthening drink.

M257.1. *Dying hero's request and promise to disciples.* India: Thompson-Balys.

M257.2. *Murdered person's request and promise.* India: Thompson-Balys.

M258. *Promise to dying man sacred.* Icelandic: *Boberg.

M258.1. *Promise to dying father leads to adventures.* Type 884; *BP II 56ff.

M258.2. *Promise to dying father not to wed woman of certain tribe.* Jewish: *Neuman.

M258.3. *Promise to dying father to bury him in his homeland.* Jewish: *Neuman.

M260. Other promises.

M261. *Chaste woman promises herself to her lover when the rocks leave the coast.* (They are moved by magic.) Robinson Complete Works of Geoffrey Chaucer (Cambridge, Mass., 1933) 826 (Franklin's Tale); **Dempster and Tatlock in Bryan and Dempster Sources and Analogues of Chaucer's Canterbury Tales 333—56; Irish myth: Cross; cf. Type 976.

D2136.1. Rocks moved by magic. H1552.1. Which was most generous — husband, robber, or lover? Woman has promised her lover to go to him on her wedding night. Husband lets her go. On way she meets robbers and tells her story. Robbers take her to her lover. She tells what has happened. Lover returns her immediately to her husband. K1350. Woman persuaded (or wooed) by trick. Z61. Never. Various ways of expressing this idea. When black sheep turn white, when a dry branch sprouts, etc.

M261.1. *Chaste woman promises herself to her lover when he can make a garden bloom in winter.* (Cf. H352.) Italian Novella: Rotunda.

D961.1. Garden produced by magic. H1023.3. Task: bringing berries (fruit, roses) in winter.

M261.1.1. *Raja to marry girl when cut mango branch blooms.* India: Thompson-Balys.

M261.2. *Princess promises to embrace her teacher on her wedding day.* Teacher has only been testing her promise. India: Thompson-Balys.

M262. *Person promises to have but one consort if he is cured.* Irish myth: Cross.

M263. *Retreat in return for cessation of attack.* Host agrees to march back a day's journey if warrior will cease his feats of arms upon them until a certain battle in the future. Irish myth: Cross.

M266. *Man promises to build church if he is saved at sea.* Danish: Kristensen Danske Sagn III (1895) 145ff., (1931) 107ff.; Estonian: Aarne FFC XXV 134 No. 85; Italian Novella: Rotunda; West Indies: Flowers 562.

K231.3. Refusal to make sacrifice after need is past. In distress a person promises a sacrifice to a god (saint) but disregards the promise when the danger passes.

M267. *Promise to give another one's wife for a day.* India: *Thompson-Balys.

T161. Jus primae noctis. Overlord claims right of sleeping the first night with subject's wife.

M268. *Marriage promised to save life.* India: *Thompson-Balys.

M271. *Sons agree to meet at father's grave after they have been out in world for one year to learn trade.* Chinese: Graham.

M272. *Supernatural woman promises to return if she gives birth to a boy.* Chinese: Graham.

T645.2. "Keep it if it is a girl; send it to me if it is a boy."

M290. Bargains and promises—miscellaneous.

M291. *Trickster undertakes impossible bargains and collects his part.* Trusts that in the year he is given either he or the other will die. Chauvin VIII 117ff. No. 101 n. 1.

J2050. Absurd short-sightedness. K551.11. Ten-year respite given captive while he undertakes to teach elephant (ass) to speak.

M292. *Wife undertakes man's penances for him:* also to go to heaven for him? He has a dream and when he sees that she also goes to heaven for him he decides against the bargain. *Pauli (ed. Bolte) No. 287.

D1855.2. Death postponed if substitute can be found. J1545. Wife outwits her husband.

M293. *Covenant: one nation not to wrest city from inhabitants without their consent.* Jewish: *Neuman.

M294. *Divine promise not to destroy sinful city if righteous live there.* Jewish: Neuman.

M295. *Bargain to keep secret.*

M295.1. *Tiger lets man go on condition he does not tell what he has overheard.* India: Thompson-Balys.

C425. Tabu: revealing knowledge of animal languages.

M296. *Two men in love agree to have nothing to do with the girl without the other's consent.* Hawaii: Beckwith Myth 153.

M300—M399. Prophecies.

M300. Prophecies. *Encyc. Rel. Ethics s.v. "Divination"; Irish: *Cross, Beal XXI 326, 334f.; Schott Weissagen und Erfüllung im deutschen Volksmärchen (München, 1936).

A463. God of fate. A463.1. The Fates. Goddesses who preside over the fates of men. A1501. Tribal customs established by diviner (man who sees future). C401.2. Tabu: speaking during seven days of danger. As result of prophecy of seven days of danger, an injunction of silence during this period. D1317. Magic object warns of danger. D1812.3.3. Future revealed in dream. T12. Love through prophecy that prince shall marry the fairest.

M300.1. *Prophecy by Jesus that certain people shall live "till coming of Patrick."* So it was. Irish myth: Cross.

M300.2. *Unconscious prophecy.* Jewish: *Neuman.

M300.3. *Prophetic gift received from another prophet.* Jewish: Neuman.

M300.4. *Suppression of prophecy.* Jewish: Neuman.

M301. *Prophets.* **E. Bass Die merkmale der israelitischen Prophetie nach der traditionellen Auffassung des Talmud (Berlin, 1917); *Hdwb. d. Abergl. IX Nachträge 66—100; Icelandic: *Boberg; Irish myth: *Cross; Jewish: *Neuman.

A178. God as prophet. A471. God of prophecy. B81.7.1. Mermaid prophesies. B140. Prophetic animal. B143. Prophetic bird. B150. Oracular animals. B521. Animal warns of fatal danger. D1810.0.2. Magic knowledge of magician. D1812. Magic power of prophecy. D1814.1. Advice from magician (fortune-teller, etc.) D1825.1. Second sight. Power to see future happenings. F312. Fairy presides at child's birth. Sometimes the Norns, the Fates, etc. F315. Fairy predicts birth of child. F316. Fairy lays curse on child. F451.3.3.7. Dwarfs predict. H1233.3.3. Quest accomplished with aid of prophet (sage). J154. Wise words of dying father. Counsel proved wise by experience. N847. Prophet as helper.

M301.0.1. *Prophet destined never to be believed.* Greek: Fox 179 (Cassandra); India: Thompson-Balys.

M301.0.2. *Prophet speaks six nights each year.* Irish myth: Cross.

M301.1. *Wild man as prophet.* Dickson 121 n. 68.

F567. Wild man.

M301.2. *Old woman as prophet.* *Pauli (ed. Bolte) No. 624; Icelandic: *Boberg.

N825.3. Old woman helper.

M301.2.1. *Enraged old woman prophesies for youth.* He has accidentally knocked her over (broken water pot, etc.). Type 516; *Cosquin Études 555; *Köhler in Gonzenbach I 209ff.; *BP IV 189; *Penzer Pentamerone of Basile (London, 1932) I 11; Penzer Ocean V 171; Rösch FFC LXXVII 100; Icelandic: *Boberg.

M411.5. Old woman's curse . N825.3. Old woman helper. S375. Old woman's maledictions inform abandoned hero of his parentage and future.

M301.2.2. *Old Woman, "völva", prophesies at child's birth.* Icelandic: *Boberg.

F312. Fairy presides at child's birth. M301.5.1. Anchorite prophesies at childbirth. M301.12. Three fates "norns" prophesy at child's birth. M311. Prophecy: future greatness of unborn child.

M301.3. *Druids as prophets.* Irish: Plummer clxii, *Cross.

D1711.4. Druid as magician. D1812.3.3.0.1. Druid interprets prophetic dream. M364.7.1. Coming of saint prophesied by druid.

M301.4. *Prophecies from old man who writes in a book.* *Cosquin Études 448ff.

M301.5. *Saints (holy men) as prophets.* *Loomis White Magic 71; Irish myth: *Cross; Jewish: *Neuman.

M312.5. Prophecy: child will build religious edifice. V223. Saints have miraculous knowledge.

M301.5.1. *Anchorite prophesies at childbirth.* Icelandic: Boberg.

F312. Fairy presides at child's birth. M311. Prophecy: future greatness of unborn child.

M301.5.2. *Cuchulinn prophesies birth of 50 women.* Shall be loyal folk to God. Irish myth: Cross.

M301.6. *Fairies as prophets.* Irish myth: *Cross.

D1810.0.4. Magic knowledge of fairies. F302.7. Fairy mistress prophesies mortal lover's fate in battle. F315. Fairy predicts birth of child. F317. Fairy predicts future greatness of (new-born) child.

M301.6.1. *Banshees as portents of misfortune.* Irish myth: *Cross.

M301.7. *Biblical worthy as prophet.* Jewish: *Neuman.

M301.7.1. *Moses as prophet.* Irish myth: Cross.

M301.7.2. *David as prophet.* Jewish: *Neuman.

M301.7.3. *Abraham as prophet.* Jewish: *Neuman.

M301.8. *Personification prophesies.* Irish myth: Cross.
V515. Allegorical visions. Z116. Sovereignty personified.

M301.9. *Half-wit as prophet.* Irish myth: *Cross; Jewish: Neuman.
L116. Insane hero (heroine).

M301.9.1. *Fool (entertainer) as prophet.* Irish myth: *Cross.

M301.10. *Angels as prophets.* (Cf. V230.) Irish myth: *Cross; Icelandic: Boberg; Jewish: Neuman.
D1810.0.6. Magic knowledge of angels. M311.2. Prophecy: child born at certain time will build religious edifice.

M301.11. *Spirit as prophet.* (Cf. F400.) Irish myth: *Cross.

M301.12. *Three fates, "norns", prophesy at child's birth.* Icelandic: Corpus Poeticum Boreale I 131, FFC LXXIII xxxvii, *Boberg.
F312. Fairy presides at child's birth. H41.6. Prophecy for newborn princesses: the one who takes gold in the mouth will be married to a prince, the one who takes hawkweed to a peasant. M301.2.2. Old woman, "volva", prophesies at child's birth. M301.5.1. Anchorite prophesies at childbirth. M311. Prophecy: future greatness of unborn child.

M301.13. *Icelandic guardian spirits, "spádísar", prophesy victory.* Icelandic: *Boberg.
M356.1. Prophecies concerning outcome of war.

M301.14. *Summoned dead prophesies.* Icelandic: Herrmann Saxo II 98, *Boberg.
E389.1. Ghost summoned in order to talk to it. E545. The dead speak.

M301.15. *Mountain in human shape prophesies whole family's death.* Icelandic: Boberg.
F316.2. Fairy's curse partially overcome by her own amendment after being appeased. F755.1. Speaking mountain. M460. Curses on families.

M301.16. *Gods prophesy both good and evil about hero's fate.* Icelandic: *Boberg.

M301.17. *King as prophet.* Irish myth: *Cross.

M301.17.1. *King in will foretells that daughters of his son shall be fruitful.* Irish myth: Cross.

M301.18. *Poet as prophet.* Irish myth: *Cross.

M301.19. *Smith as prophet.* Irish myth: Cross.

M301.20. *Child as prophet.* Jewish: *Neuman.
T585. Precocious infant.

M301.21. *Sibyl as prophet.* Writes on leaves blown about by winds. (Cf. M302.8.) Greek: *Grote I 307.
J166.1. Sibylline books bought at great price.

M302. *Means of prophesying.* Irish myth: Cross.

D1311. Magic object used for divination. D1812.3. Means of learning future. D1812.5. Future learned through omens.

M302.1. *Prophesying through knowledge of animal languages.* Type 516; Rösch FFC LXXVII 116; Greek: Frazer Apollodorus I 87 n. 3.

B216. Knowledge of animal languages. Person understands them. N451. Secrets overheard from animal (demon) conversation.

M302.2. *Man's fate written on his skull.* *Penzer VII 24 n. 1; India: *Thompson-Balys.

N120. Determination of luck or fate.

M302.2.1. *Fate written on the head.* India: Thompson-Balys.

M302.2.2. *Man's destiny read in his face.* Korean: Zong in-Sob 73 No. 40.

M302.3. *Descent into hell to learn future.* Vergil Aeneid Book 6; Icelandic: MacCulloch Eddic 127.

F81. Descent to lower world of dead (Hell, Hades).

M302.4. *Horoscope taken by means of stars.* *Prato RTP IV 178; *Wesselofsky Romania VI (1877) 161ff.; *Patch Fortuna 76—78 and notes; Dickson 33 n. 15; Fb "lykkestjærne" II 477, "stjærne" III 577b; *Hdwb. d. Abergl. VIII 461ff., IX N. 596—762; *Loomis White Magic 52. — Irish: Cross, Beal XXI 313; Icelandic: *Boberg; Italian Novella: *Rotunda; Jewish: *Neuman; Chinese: Graham.

P481. Astrologers. T54. Choosing bride by horoscope.

M302.4.1. *Astrology forbidden.* Jewish: *Neuman.

M302.5. *Tasks assigned so as to learn future.* India: Thompson-Balys.

H940. Assignment of tasks—miscellaneous.

M302.6. *Prophecy inscribed on well.* India: Thompson-Balys.

M302.7. *Prophecy through dreams.* Jewish: *Neuman.

D1812.3.3. Future revealed in dream.

M302.8. *Prophecy from book.* (Cf. M301.21.) Jewish: Neuman, Gaster Thespis 348.

M303. *Prophecy by reading palm.* Italian Novella: Rotunda.

M304. *Prophecy from enigmatical laugh.* (Cf. N456.) Irish myth: *Cross.

M305. *Ambiguous oracle.* Dickson 132 n. 108; Frazer Apollodorus I 285 n. 4; Gaster Oldest Stories 205; Irish myth: Cross; Jewish: *Neuman.

K981. Fatal deception: changed message from oracle. K2310. Deception by equivocation. M341.3.1. Prophecy: death in Jerusalem. Dies in Jerusalem Chamber. N122.0.1. The choice of roads. At parting of three roads are equivocal inscriptions tells what will happen if each is chosen.

M306. *Enigmatical prophecy.* Irish myth: *Cross.

H580. Enigmatic statements. Apparently senseless remarks (or acts) interpreted figuratively prove wise.

M306.1. *Enigmatical prophecy: what thou sowest thou shalt not reap, etc.* (Thou shalt have children and they shall not die, etc.) Jewish: Neuman, Gaster Exempla 217 No. 144, Gaster Oldest Stories 205.

M306.2. *Two sons: one a purse cutter and the other a killer.* Wife tells husband that they will make a purse designer of one, and a butcher of the other. Spanish: Childers.

N121. Fate decided before birth.

M306.3. *Enigmatical prophecy: princess will wed physician, fisherman and prince all in one.* Man puts on the guise of all three, one on top of another. India: Thompson-Balys.

M306.4. *Enigmatical prophecy: "He that is to kill you shall grow up in Braja* (a place). India: Thompson-Balys.

M341.2.15. Prophecy: death at hands of man bearing a certain name.

M306.5. *Enigmatical prophecy: "He who will kill your child is not here, but in the village."* Africa (Fang): Tessman 187.

M310. Favorable prophecies. Irish myth: *Cross.

M310.1. *Prophecy: future greatness and fame.* Irish myth: *Cross; Icelandic: *Boberg.

M310.1.1. *Prophecy: preeminence of man's descendants.* Irish myth: Cross; Jewish: Neuman.

M310.1.1.1. *Prophecy of preeminence to descendants of man provided they do the will of saint to be born.* Irish myth: Cross.

M311. *Prophecy: future greatness of unborn child.* (Cf. M301.2.2, M301.5.1, M301.12, M359.3, M371.1.) Gaster Exempla 229 No. 242 (Moses); Wells 103 (Alliterative Alexander Fragment); Loomis White Magic 16f.; Irish myth: *Cross; Danish: Grundtvig No. 42; Icelandic: Boberg; Spanish Exempla: Keller; Greek: Frazer Apollodorus I 24 n. 1 (Zeus and Mitis), Roscher Lexikon s.v. "Achilleus"; India: *Thompson-Balys.

F312. Fairy presides at child's birth. N121. Fate decided before birth. N200. The good gifts of fortune. Z254. Destined hero.

M311.0.1. *Heroic career prophesied for (new-born) child.* Irish myth: *Cross; India: *Thompson-Balys.

F317. Fairy predicts future greatness of (new-born) child. N127. The auspicious day. T589.8. Woman strives to delay birth until auspicious day.

M311.0.2. *Prophecy: birth of hero at certain time* (in certain place). Irish myth: *Cross.

D1812.5.2.8. The auspicious day. T589.8. Woman strives to delay birth until auspicious day.

M311.0.2.1. *Prophecy: conception of hero at certain time.* Irish myth: *Cross.

M311.0.3. *Prophecy: child to be born.* India: Thompson-Balys.

N451. Secrets overheard from animal (demon) conversation.

M311.0.3.1. *Prophecy: child to be born to childless couple.* India: Thompson-Balys.

M311.0.3.2. *Prophecy that if raja should take one more queen he will have a son.* India: Thompson-Balys.

M311.0.4. *Heavenly voices proclaim birth of future child hero.* Jewish: Neuman.

M311.1. *Prophecy: king's grandson will dethrone him.* Irish: MacCulloch Celtic 167, *Cross; Babylonian: Spence 157.

A525.2. Culture hero slays his grandfather. E765.4.3. Father will die when daughter bears son. M343.2. Prophecy: murder by grandson. P17. Succession to the throne. S11.4.1. Jealous father vows to kill his daughter's suitors. T97. Father opposed to daughter's marriage.

M311.2. *Prophecy: child born at certain time will build religious edifice.* (Cf. M312.5.) Irish myth: Cross.

M311.3. *Prophecy: unborn child to be a saint.* Loomis White Magic 17f.; Irish: *Cross, Beal XXI 327, O'Suilleabhain 74.

M364.7. Coming (birth) of saint prophesied.

M311.4. *Prophecy: unborn child to become king.* (Cf. M314.) Irish myth: *Cross.

M311.5. *Unborn child will become nation's deliverer.* Jewish: Neuman.

M311.6. *Prophecy: unborn child will be prophet.* Jewish: *Neuman.

M312. *Prophecy of future greatness for youth.* *Types 461, 517, 725, 930; *BP I 322; English romance: Malory XI 4; Jewish: *Neuman; India: *Thompson-Balys; Buddhist myth: Malalasekera II 531; Korean: Zong in-Sob 72 No. 39, 209 No. 98.

B147.3.1.2. Bees leave honey on lips of infant to show future greatness. N200. The good gifts of fortune.

M312.0.1. *Dream of future greatness.* *Type 725; *BP I 324; Cox 500; MacCulloch Childhood 354; Irish myth: Cross; Jewish: *Neuman; India: *Thompson-Balys.

D1812.3.3. Future revealed in dream.

M312.0.2. *Prophecy of future greatness given by animals.* *Type 517; *BP I 322; Spanish Exempla: Keller.

B140. Prophetic animal.

M312.0.3. *Prophecy of future greatness if boy lives to be eighteen.* Italian Novella: Rotunda.

M341.1. Prophecy: death at certain time.

M312.0.4. *Mother's symbolic dream (vision) about the greatness of her unborn child.* Loomis: White Magic 18f; Icelandic: *Boberg.

M312.0.4.1. *The dream about a tree which sprouts enormously,* indicates the birth of a hero (saint). Loomis White Magic 19.

M312.0.5. *Prophecy: son will tie father to a horse's leg and strike him fifty blows.* India: Thompson-Balys.

M312.1. *Prophecy: wealthy marriage for poor boy.* *Types 461, 930; **Aarne FFC XXIII; **Tille Zs. f. Vksk. XXVIII 22; India: Thompson-Balys.

H931. Tasks assigned in order to get rid of hero. H1211. Quest assigned in order to get rid of hero. H1510. Tests of power to survive. Vain attempts to kill hero. L161. Lowly hero marries princess. M372. Confinement in tower to avoid fulfillment of prophecy. T22.2. Predestined wife. T91.5.1. Rich girl in love with poor boy.

M312.1.1. *Prophecy: wealthy marriage for poor girl.* *BP I 288; *Aarne FFC XXIII 110.

L162. Lowly heroine marries prince (king). M436. Curse: prince to fall in love with witch's daughter. T22.1. Lovers mated before birth. Fate compels their union as soon as they meet.

M312.2. *Prophecy: parents will humble themselves before their son.* (Vaticinium.) *Type 517; *BP I 324; Köhler-Bolte I 145, 430; *Wesselski Märchen 221 No. 35; Campbell Sages cxii; Jewish: *Neuman; India: Thompson-Balys.

N682. Prophecy of future greatness fulfilled when hero returns home unknown. Parents serve him. T91.5.1. Rich girl in love with poor boy.

M312.2.1. *Prophecy: son to be more powerful than father.* Greek: Grote I 173

M312.2.2. *Prophecy: youngest brother to rule over his brethren.* Jewish: *Neuman.

M312.3. *Eater of magic bird-heart will become rich* (or king). *Type 567; *BP III 3; **Aarne MSFO XXV 176; Chauvin VI 170; India: *Thompson-Balys; Buddhist myth: Malalasekera II 1138; Indonesia: DeVries's list No. 190.

B113.1. Treasure-producing bird-heart. Brings riches when eaten. D1015.1.1. Magic bird heart. D1561.1.1. Magic bird-heart (when eaten) brings man to kingship.

M312.3.1. *Eater of magic fish will have power to spit up treasure.* India: Thompson-Balys.

M312.3.2. *Whoever eats outside of fruit will become a king and whoever eats the seed will drop gems from his mouth every time he laughs.* India: Thompson-Balys.

M312.4. *Prophecy: superb beauty for girl.* Type 709; Africa (Thonga): Junod II 266ff., (Ekoi): Talbot 401.

M312.5. *Prophecy: child will build religious edifice.* (Cf. M311.2.) Irish myth: Cross.

M301.5. Saints (holy men) as prophets.

M312.6. *Prophecy: boys to be fathers of saints.* Irish myth: Cross.

M312.7. *Prophecy of luck for outcast child.* Buddhist myth: Malalasekera I 828.

S301. Children abandoned.

M312.8. *Prophecy: man will make sun and moon stand still.* Jewish: *Neuman.

M312.9. *Prophecy: no people or king will be able to stand up against hero.* Jewish: *Neuman.

M313. *Man transformed into swine will regain his human form after third marriage.* Italian Novella: Rotunda.

D136. Transformation: man to swine. D791. Disenchantment possible under unique conditions.

M314. *Prophecy: man (child) will become king.* (Cf. M311.4.) Irish myth: *Cross; Jewish: *Neuman; India: *Thompson-Balys.

M395. Prophesied son of certain name will become king; all sons given the name. W215.3. Long life sacrificed that descendants may be kings as prophesied.

M314.0.1. *Prophecy: girl will be queen.* Buddhist myth: Malalasekera II 539

M314.1. *Prophecy: son who catches certain fawn will become king.* Irish myth: *Cross.

B731.7.2. Fawn with golden lustre. H1154. Task: capturing animals.

M314.2. *Prophecy: king will be succeeded by the son whom he shall see next.* Sends for elder son, who delays and is preceded by younger son. Elder son is slain next day; younger son becomes king. Irish myth: Cross.

M314.3. *Prophecy: younger son will succeed to throne.* Irish myth: Cross.

M314.4. *Prophecy of future empire for fugitive hero.* Greek: *Grote I 307.

M315. *Prophecy: man will eat magic salmon and gain knowledge.* Irish myth: *Cross.

B162.1. Supernatural knowledge from eating magic fish. D1811.1.1. Thumb of knowledge.

M316. *Prophecy: strength to be gained when milk is drunk from hero's skull.* Irish myth: Cross.

F866.4. Cup made of skulls. Q491.5. Skull used as drinking cup.

M317. *Prophecy: race will never be without an illustrious woman.* Irish myth: Cross.

M318. *Prophecy: no snakes in Ireland.* Irish myth: *Cross.

A2434.2.3. Why there are no snakes in Ireland.

M318.1. *Prophecy: no snakes in Israel.* Jewish: *Neuman.

M321. *Prophecy: long life.* Irish myth: *Cross; Icelandic: Boberg.

M321.1. *Blessing of saint to descend from generation to generation.* Irish myth: *Cross.

M322. *Prophecy: person will avenge his own death.* Irish myth: *Cross.

M323. *Prophecy: victory against great odds.* Irish myth: Cross; Buddhist myth: Malalasekera I 183.

M324. *Prophecy: future Golden Age.* Irish myth: Cross; Jewish: Neuman.

A1101.1. Golden Age.

M325. *Prophecy: glory and prosperity for a people.* Greek: Aeschylus Eumenides 920; Jewish: *Neuman.

M326. *Prophecy: future success as hunter.* Eskimo (West Hudson Bay): Boas BAM XV 343.

M331. *Princess to marry prince.* India: Thompson-Balys.

M340. Unfavorable prophecies.

F312. Fairy presides at child's birth. F316. Fairy lays curse on child. F989.10. Animals distribute parts of man's body in accordance with prophecy. F1041.8.8. Madness from hearing prophetic voice from air. K2115.3. Prophecy of ogre-child so that pregnant woman will be killed. M358.1. Evil predictions concerning journeys.

M340.1. *Prophecy of grief fulfilled by death of relative* (friend, etc.). Irish myth: *Cross.

M340.2. *Forced prophecies are unfavorable.* Icelandic: *Boberg.

M340.3. *Prophecy of general misfortune to newborn child.* India: *Thompson-Balys.

M340.4. *Bridegroom to meet with disaster if he rides a certain elephant which comes to meet him.* India: Thompson-Balys.

M340.5. *Prediction of danger.* Africa (Bankon): Ittman 95.

M340.6. *Prophecy of great misfortune.* Korean: Zong in-Sob 73 No. 40.

M341. *Death prophesied.* Penzer IV 175f.; Ward II 620 No. 24; Alphabet Nos. 266, 305; Irish: *Cross, Beal XXI 333; Icelandic: *Boberg; Italian Novella: Rotunda; India: *Thompson-Balys.

D1812.5.1. Bad omens. E489.4. Man's spirit in land of dead prophesies his own future death. E765.1. Life bound up with light (flame). E765.2. Life bound up with that of animal. E765.3. Life bound up with object. E765.4. Life bound up with external even. Death to come when certain thing happens.

M341.0.1. *Saint prophesies that certain man will have a warning of coming death.* Irish myth: *Cross.

M341.0.2. *All forty of man's sons to die at once.* India: Thompson-Balys.

M341.0.3. *Prophecy of death not to come true if baby is married to girl of twelve years.* India: Thompson-Balys.

M341.1. *Prophecy: death at (before, within) certain time.* Irish: Beal XXI 313, O'Suilleabhain 37, *Cross; Spanish Exempla: Keller; Jewish: Neuman; India: *Thompson-Balys; Japanese: Ikeda.

A487.0.1. Death kills only those whose time it is to die. M358.1.1. Prophecy: death on journey. N250. Persistent bad luck. N300. Unlucky accidents.

M341.1.1. *Prophecy: death on wedding day.* Type 333*; India: *Thompson-Balys.

M341.1.1.1. *Prophecy: death within year after marriage.* India: Thompson-Balys.

M341.1.1.2. *Prophecy: death on seventh day of marriage.* India: Thompson-Balys.

M341.1.1.3. *Prophecy of death upon daughter's marriage.* Greek: *Grote I 146.

M341.1.1.4. *Prophecy: death on entrance to the marriage chamber.* Moreno Esdras (N389).

M341.1.2. *Prophecy: early death.* Irish myth: *Cross; India: Thompson-Balys.

M341.1.2.1. *Prophecy: death of king* (before the morrow). Irish myth: *Cross; India: Thompson-Balys.

M341.1.2.2. *Prophecy of death on twelfth day after birth.* India: *Thompson-Balys.

M341.1.2.3. *Prophecy: death within two months.* Africa (Wakweli): Bender 103.

M341.1.2.4. *Prophecy: death in three years and three months.* India: Thompson-Balys.

M341.1.2.5. *Prophecy of only seven days' life for baby.* Buddhist myth: Malalasekera I 285, 507.

M341.1.3. *Prophecy: death before certain age.*

C315.2.2.1. Tabu: looking at sun before prince becomes 14 years old.

M341.1.3.1. *Prophecy: child shall hang before fifteen years.* Fb "hænge" I 731b.

M341.1.3.2. *Prophecy: death before eighteen years.* Italian Novella: Rotunda.

M341.1.4. *Prophecy: death at certain age.*

M341.1.4.1. *Prophecy: death at sixteen.* India: *Thompson-Balys.

M341.1.4.2. *Prophecy: danger to threatened newborn boy at his eighteenth year.* India: Thompson-Balys.

M341.1.4.3. *Prophecy: death when twenty-five years old.* Spanish: Boggs FFC XC 62 No. 449*.

M341.1.4.3.1. *Prophecy: death on twenty-first birthday.* India: Thompson-Balys.

M341.1.4.4. *Prophecy: man shall hang himself when he is thirty years old.* Italian Novella: Rotunda.

J21.15. "If you wish to hang yourself, do so by the stone which I point out."

M341.1.4.5. *Prophecy: death at sixty.* India: Thompson-Balys.

M341.1.5. *Prophecy: death within certain period.* Icelandic: Boberg.

M341.1.5.1. *Prophecy: death in ten years.* Icelandic: Boberg.

M341.1.5.2. *Prophecy that hero will not live another eighteen years.* Icelandic: Boberg.

M341.1.6. *Prophecy: death after certain time.* Korean: Zong in-Sob 49 No. 29.

M341.1.6.1. *Prophecy: death after three life spans.* Icelandic: Boberg.

M341.1.6.2. *Prophecy: death after two life spans.* Icelandic: *Boberg.

M341.1.6.3. *Prophecy: death after three-year dominion.* Jewish: *Neuman.

M341.1.7. *Prophecy: death at birth of child.* India: *Thompson-Balys.

M341.1.7.1. *Death at sight of son before twelve years.* India: *Thompson-Balys.

M341.2. *Prophecy: death by particular instrument.* In spite of all precautions the prophecy is fulfilled. *Basset 1001 Contes II 209; *Krappe Scandinavian Studies 16 (1942) 20—35; Irish myth: *Cross; India: Thompson-Balys; Japanese: Ikeda.

M377. Sword that is to kill one is weighted and sunk so as to avoid the prophecy. Q582.5. Man boasts he fears saint no more than hornless sheep: killed by hornless sheep.

M341.2.0.1. *Prophecy: death by particular weapon.* Irish myth: *Cross.

Z312. Unique deadly weapon.

M341.2.1. *Prophecy: death by mistletoe.* *Frazer Golden Bough X—XI (Balder the Beautiful); Icelandic: *Boberg.

K863. Shooting game: blind man's arrow aimed.

M341.2.2. *Prophecy: death by storm.* *Type 932*.

M341.2.3. *Prophecy: death by drowning.* Irish myth: Cross; Japanese: Ikeda.

M341.2.3.1. *Death by drowning: man strangles to death* on drinking water. Irish: Beal XXI 328, O'Suilleabhain 87; Estonian: Aarne FFC XXV 136 No. 95; India: Thompson-Balys.

M341.3.3. Prophecy: drowning in particular stream.

M341.2.4. *Prophecy: three-fold death.* Child to die from hunger, fire, and water. It so happens. *Jackson The Motive of the Threefold Death in the Story of Suibhne Geilt (Essays and Studies Presented to Eoin MacNeill 535—550); Irish myth: *Cross; Estonian: Aarne FFC XXV 136 No. 96; Spanish Exempla: Keller.

C927.3. Burning and drowning as punishment for breaking a tabu.

M341.2.5. *Prophecy: death by horse's head.* Man is killed in that way. **Taylor MPh XIX 93ff.; Krappe PSASS XVII (1942—43) 20ff.; Icelandic: Boberg.

M341.2.6. *Prophecy: death by wolf.* Killed by a wolf claw (or by a cat transformed to wolf). Type 333*; Lithuanian: Balys Index No. 166*; Estonian: Aarne FFC XXV 136 No. 94.

M341.2.7. *Prophecy: death by fire.* India: Thompson-Balys; Africa (Benga): Nassau 107 No. 9.

M341.2.7.1. *Prophecy: sinners to be burnt by fire on Doomsday.* Irish myth: Cross.

A1002. Doomsday. Q414. Punishment: burning alive. Q560. Punishment in hell.

M341.2.8. *Prophecy: death by poison.* Greek: Fox 108 (Pelias and Aeson).

M341.2.9. *Prophecy: death from hands of man with one sandal.* Greek: *Frazer Apollodorus I 94 n. 1 (Jason); India: Thompson-Balys.

M341.2.10. *Prophecy: death from bite of stone lion.* Man killed by scorpion concealed in the statue. *Pauli (ed. Bolte) No. 827; Icelandic: *Boberg; India: Thompson-Balys.

K1125. Dupe tries to dig up alleged treasure buried in ant hill: bitten by snake and killed. M370. Vain attempts to escape fulfillment of prophecy.

M341.2.10.1. *Prophecy: death by tiger.* Tiger-shaped cake becomes tiger and kills man in spite of all precautions. India: Thompson-Balys.

M341.2.10.2. *Prophecy: death from tiger.* Tiger picture comes to life and kills man. India: *Thompson-Balys; Korean: Zong in-Sob 51 No. 30, 58 No. 33.

M341.2.11. *Prophecy: death by lightning.* Lithuanian: Balys Index No. 932*; Estonian: Aarne FFC XXV No. 932*; Russian: Andrejev No. 932*; Spanish: Boggs FFC XC 62 No. 449*.

M341.2.12. *Prophecy: death through future husband.* Greek: Frazer Apollodorus II 157 n. 4.

M341.2.13. *Prophecy: death through spindle wound.* *Type 410; *BP I 434.

D1364.17. Spindle causes magic sleep. F316. Fairy lays curse on child.

M341.2.14. *Prophecy: death by means of bone.* Italian: Basile Pentamerone II No. 8, III No. 3, V No. 5.

M341.2.15. *Prophecy: death at hands of man bearing a certain name.* Russian: Afanasief "Tale of Prince Arta" (Moscow, 1897) 149 (cited in von Sydow Fåvne 45).

M306.4. Enigmatical prophecy: "He that is to kill you shall grow up in Braja [a place]."

M341.2.16. *Prophecy: death from thorns in rice.* India: Thompson-Balys.

M341.2.17. *Prophecy: king to be slain by certain spear unless it is given when demanded.* Irish myth: *Cross.

C650. The one compulsory thing.

M341.2.18. *Prophecy: death in battle.* Irish myth: *Cross.

M356.1.1. Prophecy: loss of battle (combat).

M341.2.18.1. *Hero kept from going to battle lest he be slain.* Irish myth: *Cross.

M341.2.19. *Prophecy: death at hands of certain person.* Irish myth: *Cross; India: *Thompson-Balys.

M341.2.20. *Prophecy: wholesale slaughter to be inflicted by colossal wheel rolling over Europe.* Irish myth: *Cross.

M341.2.21. *Prophecy: death from snakebite.* India: *Thompson-Balys.

M341.2.21.1. *Prophecy (through dream): death from cobra.* India: Thompson-Balys.

M341.2.22. *Prophecy: death by calf.* Icelandic: Boberg.

M341.2.23. *Prophecy: death by hanging.* Irish: O'Suilleabhain 107; Icelandic: *Boberg.

M341.1.3.1. Prophecy: child shall hang before fifteen years. M341.1.4.4. Prophecy: man shall hang himself when he is thirty years old.

M341.2.24. *Prophecy: death by alligator (crocodile).* India: *Thompson-Balys.

M341.2.25. *Prophecy: man to be swallowed up by earth at the foot of his stairs.* Buddhist myth: Malalasekera II 1220.

M341.2.26. *Prophecy: king's son to die for lack of water.* Buddhist myth: Malalasekera I 598.

M341.3. *Prophecy: death in particular place.* Irish myth: *Cross; Icelandic: Boberg.

M341.3.1. *Prophecy: death in Jerusalem.* Man dies in Jerusalem Chamber. **R. Meyer Gerbertsagnet 89ff.; *Liebrecht Zur Volkskunde 48; Graf Nuova Anthologia (1890) 239; *Fb "lys" II 483b; Alphabet No. 50.

K2310. Deception by equivocation. M305. Ambiguous oracle.

M341.3.2. *Prophecy: death between Erin and Alba.* Man dies between two hills so named. Irish myth: *Cross.

M341.3.3. *Prophecy: drowning in particular stream.* Irish myth: Cross.

M341.2.3. Prophecy: death by drowning.

M341.3.4. *Prophecy: death on seashore.* India: *Thompson-Balys.

M341.4. *Prophecy: criminal going to death predicts that his judge (king, prince) shall soon meet him.* *Pauli (ed. Bolte) Nos. 130, 833, 834.

M341.5. *Prophecy: either youth or mother will die.* Prato RTP IV 178.

M341.6. *Prophecy: person foretells own death.* Irish myth: *Cross.

M342. *Prophecy of downfall of kingdom.* Bødker Exempler 301 No. 68; Irish myth: *Cross; English: Wells 61 (Awntyrs off Arthure at the Terne Wathelyne); Spanish Exempla: Keller; India: *Thompson-Balys.

M342.1. *Prophecy of downfall of king* (prince). Irish myth: *Cross.

M342.2. *Prophecy: son-to-be to destroy lineage.* Buddhist myth: Malalasekera I 108.

M343. *Parricide prophecy.* In spite of all attempts to thwart the fates, the child kills his father. *Type 931; *Krappe Balor 11 n. 37; *Baum PMLA XXXI 481; Krappe Neuphilologische Mitteilungen XXIV 11ff.; Saintyves Saints Successeurs 268—70; Chauvin VI 36 No. 206; Irish myth: *Cross; Greek: Fox 33, 48f., 63, Grote I 6, 9, 85, 206, 243, 263, 466; Jewish: Neuman, bin Gorion Born Judas[2] I 166, 372; India: Thompson-Balys; Buddhist myth: Malalasekera I 34, 698, II 286, 924; N. A. Indian: Thompson CColl II 414.

A525.2. Culture hero slays his grandfather. E765.4.1. Father will die when daughter marries. H931. Tasks assigned in order to get rid of hero. H1510. Tests of power to survive. Vain attempts to kill hero. M375.2. Slaughter of children to prevent fulfillment of parricide prophecy. N101.2. Inexorable fate. N323. Parricide prophecy unwittingly fulfilled. N730. Accidental reunion of families. P233. Father and son. Q211.1. Parricide punished. S11.3.4. Cruel father, who learns that he is to be killed by his son, puts to death all children born to him. S22. Parricide.

M343.0.1. *Parricide prophecy: king's successors will be parricides.* Irish myth: Cross.

M343.0.2. *Prophecy: mother will be killed by children.* S. A. Indian (Kaigua): Métraux RMLP XXXIII 139.

M343.1. *Prophecy: murder by son-in-law.* *Krappe Balor 11 n. 37; Greek: Fox 119 (Pelops).

M343.2. *Prophecy: murder by grandson.* Greek: Fox 33 (Perseus).

A525.2. Culture hero (god) slays his grandfather. M311.1. Prophecy: King's grandson will dethrone him.

M343.3. *Prophecy: murder by nephew.* Irish myth: *Cross; Buddhist myth: Malalasekera I 428.

M343.4. *Prophecy: wicked couple to be killed by own child.* Irish myth: Cross.

M343.5. *Prophecy: death at hands of parents.* Africa (Fang): Tessman 134f.

M344. *Mother-incest prophecy.* In spite of all precautions the youth marries his mother. *Type 931; *Cosquin Etudes 451; Hibbard 276; *Baum PMLA XXXI 481; Irish myth: *Cross; Greek: Fox 49 (Oedipus); India: Thompson-Balys.

N365. Incest unwittingly committed. N383.3. Mother dies of fright when she learns that she was about to commit incest with her son. P231. Mother and son. T412. Mother-son incest.

M344.1. *Father-daughter incest prophecy.* Greek: Fox 120 (Thyestes); India: Thompson-Balys.

M345. *Prophecy: daughter shall commit murder and incest* and be sentenced to death. Type 728*.

M345.1. *Prophecy: girl shall have a hundred lovers, shall marry her servant and die from spider's bite.* This happens. *Basset 1001 Contes II 208. Cf. Gaster Exempla 246 No. 341; Chauvin VIII 104 No. 80.

M345.1.1. *Prophecy: woman will have many lovers.* India: Thompson-Balys.

M345.2. *Prophecy: man will deceive many women.* India: Thompson-Balys.

M346. *Prophecy: child to be abducted at certain time.* Hdwb. d. Märchens I 546b nn. 109—126; Italian: Basile Pentamerone IV No. 6.

M432. Curse: to be carried off by evil spirit.

M348. *Murderer warned by God's voice that murder will be avenged.* *BP II 535 n. 1; *Wesselski Mönchslatein 88 No. 76; Irish: Beal XXI 336, O'Suilleabhain 123; Lithuanian: Balys Index No. 787*; Spanish: Espinosa Jr. No. 205.

F442.1. Mysterious voice announces death of Pan. F966. Voices from heaven. N271. Murder will out.

M351. *Prophecy that youth shall abandon his religion and become Christian.* (Baarlam and Josaphat.) *Cosquin Etudes 27ff.; Ward II 111ff.; Spanish Exempla: Keller.

V331. Conversion to Christianity.

M352. *Prophecy of particular perils to prince on wedding journey.* *Type 516; *Rösch FFC LXXVII 114; India: *Thompson-Balys.

R169.4.1. Rescue of bride from mysterious perils by hidden faithful servant. T137. Customs following wedding. T175. Magic perils threaten bridal couple.

M353. *Prediction by bird that girl will have dead husband.* (She disenchants him from magic sleep.) *Cosquin Contes indiens 108ff.; India: Thompson-Balys.

B143. Prophetic bird. D700. Person disenchanted.

M354. *Prophecy that child will have external soul.* India: Thompson-Balys.

M354.1. *Prophecy of rebirth as monkey.* Buddhist myth: Malalasekera II 847.

M355. *Prophecy: unborn child to be blind, deformed, sickly, etc.* Irish myth: Cross.

M356. *Prophecies concerning destiny of country.* Irish myth: *Cross.

M356.1. *Prophecies concerning outcome of war.* Irish myth: *Cross; Icelandic: Boberg.

M356.1.1. *Prophecy: loss of battle (combat).* Irish myth: *Cross; Jewish: *Neuman.

M341.2.18. Prophecy: death in battle.

M356.1.2. *Prophecies concerning fate of heroes in battle.* (Cf. M341.2.18.) Irish myth: *Cross; Jewish: Neuman.

F302.7. Fairy mistress prophesies mortal lover's fate in battle.

M356.1.3. *Prophecy: first side to slay in battle will be defeated.* Irish myth: Cross.

M356.1.4. *Prophecy: destruction of fortress.* Irish myth: Cross.

M356.2. *Prophecy of a plague consisting of "a flame of fire" which shall destroy three-fourths of the population of Ireland.* Plague can be prevented by fasting, etc. Irish myth: Cross.

M356.3. *Prophecy: unborn (new-born) child (girl) to bring evil upon land.* Irish myth: *Cross.

M356.4. *Prophecy: evil to come to country.* Irish: O'Suilleabhain 88; Jewish: *Neuman.

M356.5. *Prophecy: end of Round Table for Arthur's knights.* English romance: Malory XI 2.

M357. *Prophecy: world catastrophe.* Irish myth: *Cross; Jewish: *Neuman; Buddhist myth: Malalasekera I 501.

A1000. World catastrophe.

M357.1. *Prophecy: fiery bolt from a dragon to kill world population.* Irish myth: *Cross.

B11.2.11. Fire-breathing dragon.

M358. *Prophecies connected with journeys.* Irish myth: *Cross.

M361. Fated hero. Only certain hero will succeed in exploit.

M358.1. *Evil predictions concerning journeys.* Irish myth: *Cross.

M340. Unfavorable prophecies.

M358.1.1. *Prophecy: death on journey.* (Cf. M341.1.) Irish myth: *Cross.

M358.2. *Journey to otherworld foretold.* Irish myth: *Cross.

F370. Visit to fairyland.

M359. *Unfavorable prophecies — miscellaneous.* Irish myth: Cross; Jewish: Neuman.

M359.1. *Prophecy: weapons with which man is killed will recount deed to his son.* Irish myth: Cross.

D1318.16. Speaking earth reveals murder.

M359.2. *Prophecy: prince's marriage to common woman.* India: Thompson-Balys.

M436. Curse: prince to fall in love with witch's daughter.

M359.3. *Prophecy: unborn child to kill enemy in revenge.* Irish myth: Cross.

M311. Prophecy: future greatness of unborn child. N121. Fate decided before birth.

M359.4. *Prophecy: torture "with varied tortures."* Irish myth: Cross.

M359.5. *Prophecy: poverty from birth.* India: *Thompson-Balys.

M359.6. *Prophecy: all flocks will perish and family die.* India: Thompson-Balys.

M359.7. *Prophecy: rich man will have a son but the son will marry a poor girl.* Chinese: Graham.

M359.8. *Deluge prophesied.* Chinese: Graham.

M359.9. *Prophecy of famine.* Chinese: Graham.

M359.10. *Thievery a predestined lot.* India: Thompson-Balys.

M360. Other prophecies.

D791.1.1. Disenchantment at end of seven years. D1960.2. King asleep in mountain. Will awake one day to succor his people. P11.0.1. Prophecy that brother who first kisses saint will be king.

M361. *Fated hero.* Only certain hero will succeed in exploit. Dickson 132 n. 108; Irish myth: *Cross; Icelandic: Sturlaugs saga Starfsama; India: Thompson-Balys.

M358. Prophecies connected with journeys.

M361.1. *Prophecy: certain hero to achieve Holy Grail.* English romance: Malory XIV 2.

M362. *Prophecy: death of ruler to insure victory.* Spanish Exempla: Keller; Italian Novella: Rotunda.

P711.9. Patriotism: king learning that nation will triumph whose king dies in battle, allows self to be killed.

M363. *Coming of religious leader prophesied.* (Cf. M300.1.)

M363.1. *Coming of Christ (Christianity) prophesied.* Irish myth: *Cross.

V211. Christ.

M363.1.1. *Coming of Antichrist prophesied.* Irish myth: Cross.

M363.2. *Prophecy: coming of Messiah.* Jewish: *Neuman.

M363.2.1. *Prophecy: woman to be ancestress of David and the Messiah.* Jewish: *Neuman.

M364. *Various prophecies connected with saints (or holy men).* Irish myth: *Cross; Jewish: *Neuman.

V220. Saints.

M364.1. *Prophecy: saint's monastery will be persecuted.* Irish myth: Cross.

M364.1.1. *Prophecy: founding of church at certain place by saint.* Irish myth: Cross.

M364.2. *Prophecy: remission of tax through endeavor of saint.* Irish myth: Cross.

M364.3. *Prophecy: saint will succeed in conversion.* Irish myth: Cross.

M364.3.1. *Prophecy: sinners going to heaven are to be numbered by hairs in saint's chasuble.* Irish myth: Cross.

M364.3.2. *Prophecy: great numbers (three) to be saved through virtue of saint.* Irish myth: *Cross.

M364.4. *Place of saint's resurrection prophesied.* Irish myth: Cross.

E0. Resuscitation.

M364.4.1. *Saint's resurrection to take place where chariot breaks down.* Irish myth: Cross.

M364.5. *Prophecy: vicinity in which saint lost tooth will be deserted by heathen.* Irish myth: Cross.

M364.6. *Prophecy: rainbow will appear at saint's death.* Irish myth: Cross.

F960.1. Extraordinary nature phenomena at death of holy person.

M364.7. *Coming (birth) of saint prophesied.* (Cf. M363.1.2.) Loomis White Magic 17; Irish myth: *Cross.

M311.3. Prophecy: unborn child to be a saint. V222.0.1. Birth of saint predicted by visions of miracles.

M364.7.1. *Coming of saint prophesied by druids.* Irish myth: *Cross.

M301.3. Druids as prophets.

M364.7.2. *Coming of saint (Christianity) prophesied by heathen.* Irish myth: *Cross.

M364.7.3. *Bishop foretells birth of saint.* Irish myth: *Cross.

M364.7.4. *Prophecy: unborn child shall be nun.* Irish myth: Cross.

M364.8. *Prophecy: miraculous removal of saint's bones.* Irish myth: *Cross.

M364.8.1. *Saint foretells desecration of his bones.* Irish myth: Cross.

M364.9. *Hero prophesies that one-half of the churches in Ireland shall be named for Ciaran.* Irish myth: Cross.

M364.10. *Destruction and rebuilding of church foreseen by saint.* Irish myth: Cross.

M364.11. *Everyone buried in saint's soil shall go to heaven.* Irish myth: Cross.

M365. *Prophecy: eternal peace in an early death or long troublesome life.* (Cf. M369.7.) Greek: Roscher Lexikon s.v. "Achilleus".

M365.1. *Prophecy: hero may win fame but die early.* Chooses fame. Irish myth: *Cross.

J200. Choices.

M365.2. *Son to be brave and wise but not to remain and cause mother to weep.* India: Thompson-Balys.

M365.3. *Prophecy: girl will be perfect in love but will die in a desert* overcome by separation from her love. India: Thompson-Balys.

M366. *Prophecy: hero may win lady's love but die early.* Chooses this rather than long life without her. Icelandic: Volsunga saga 53.

J300. Present values chosen.

M367. *Prophecy: immunity from certain types of death.*

M367.1. *Immunity from wet or dry, steel or wood, sword or javelin, by day or by night.* Man killed at edge of sea, at twilight, with force of sea and thunderbolt. India: Thompson-Balys; Hindu: Keith 133.

D1840. Magic invulnerability. H1050. Paradoxical tasks.

M368. *Prophecy: punishment for misappropriàtion of property.* Italian Novella: Rotunda.

Q270. Misdeeds concerning property punished.

M369. *Miscellaneous prophecies.* Irish myth: Cross.

M369.1. *Prophecies that person will tell three (two) falsehoods before death.* Irish myth: *Cross.

M369.2. *Prophecies concerning love and marriage.* Irish myth: Cross.

T0. Love

M369.2.1. *Future husband (wife) foretold.* Irish myth: Cross; Jewish: Neuman; India: *Thompson-Balys.

M369.2.1.1. *Prophecy of king taking a cruel stepmother to her sons after her death* enacted before eyes of dying queen by sparrow family living in tree by palace window. India: Thompson-Balys.

J133. Animal gives wise example to man.

M369.2.1.2. *Prophecy: princess will marry a bastard.* Jewish: *Neuman.

M369.2.2. *Prophecy: lovers not destined to meet in life will never part after death.* Irish myth: *Cross.

M369.2.3. *Prophecy: marriage when one is twelve years old.* India: Thompson-Balys.

M369.2.4. *Prophecy: if the raja marries certain girl he will prosper.* India: Thompson-Balys.

M369.2.5. *Prophecy: descendant of mistress shall serve that of handmaid.* Irish myth: Cross.

M369.3. *Prophecy that certain person will fight particular battle.* Irish myth: Cross.

M369.4. *Names of future kings foretold.* Irish myth: Cross.

M369.4.1. *Prophecy that bird will become king.* India: Thompson-Balys.

M369.5. *Prophecies concerning invasion and conquest.* Irish myth: *Cross; Jewish: Neuman.

M369.5.1. *Signs before destruction of Jerusalem.* Irish myth: Cross.

M369.6. *Time and place of landing of returning heroes prophesied.* Irish myth: Cross.

M369.7. *Prophecy about birth of children.* (Cf. M365.) Jewish: *Neuman.

M369.7.1. *Prophecy: birth of twins.* India: Thompson-Balys.

M369.7.2. *Prophecy about birth of heir.* Jewish: Neuman.

M369.7.3. *Prophecy: sex of unborn child.* Jewish: *Neuman.

M369.8. *Prophecies about children born at the same time.* India: *Thompson-Balys.

B311. Congenital helpful animal.

M369.9. *Prophecy: king will have head pounded by strange queen.* Due to peculiar set of circumstances this happens. India: Thompson-Balys.

M369.10. *Prophecy: boy to be great hunter.* India: Thompson-Balys.

M370. Vain attempts to escape fulfillment of prophecy. (Cf. M341.2.10, M343, M344.) *Type 930; **Aarne FFC XXIII 110ff.; *BP IV 116 n. 10; *Fb "rig" III 55a; *Cosquin Études 27ff.; Irish myth: *Cross; Greek: Grote I 85; Jewish: *Neuman; India: *Thompson-Balys; Buddhist myth: Malalasekera I 109, 428, 598, II 1220; Chinese: Eberhard FFC CXX 202 No. 149; Africa (Wakweli): Bender 103.

N101. Inexorable fate. N130. Changing of luck or fate.

M370.1. *Prophecy of death fulfilled.* Lithuanian: Balys Index No. 932A*; Russian: Andrejev No. 932I*; Rumanian: Schullerus FFC LXXVII No. 932*; India: Thompson-Balys.

M370.1.1. *Prophecy wittingly fulfilled by wazir that he will murder the raja,* but unwittingly causes his own death twelve years hence. India: Thompson-Balys.

M371. *Exposure of infant to avoid fulfillment of prophecy.* *Type 930; **Aarne FFC XXIII 56, 91; *Encyc. Religion and Ethics s.v. "Abandonment and exposure"; *Krappe Revue de l'Histoire des Religions CVII (1933) 126ff.; Icelandic: Boberg; Jewish: Neuman, bin Gorion Born Judas[2] I 165, 372; Greek: Fox 5, 118; India: Thompson-Balys.

S310. Reasons for abandonment of children.

M371.0.1. *Abandonment in forest to avoid fulfillment of prophecy.* India: *Thompson-Balys.

S143. Children abandoned in forest.

M371.0.2. *Father throws boy of boy-girl twin birth into river to avoid evil effects of twin birth.* Africa (Fang): Tessman 91.

T587.1. Birth of twins an indication of unfaithfulness in wife.

M371.1. *Exposure (murder) of child to avoid fulfillment of prophecy of future greatness.* Parent fears that the child will overcome him. Irish: MacCulloch Celtic 167; Icelandic: De la Saussaye 142; Italian Novella: *Rotunda; Greek: Fox 6f.; India: Thompson-Balys.

A516. Expulsion and return of culture hero. A511.7. Culture hero reared in seclusion. L111.1. Exile returns and succeeds. M311. Prophecy: future greatness of unborn child. Q431. Punishment: banishment (exile). S350.2. Child driven out (exposed) brought up in secret.

M371.2. *Exposure of child to prevent fulfillment of parricide prophecy.* *Type 931; Irish myth: *Cross; Greek: Fox 48 (Oedipus); India: Thompson-Balys.

M371.3. *Murder of child to prevent fulfillment of prophecy of ruin she will bring upon kingdom.* India: Thompson-Balys.

M372. *Confinement in tower to avoid fulfillment of prophecy.* Type 932*; Köhler in Gonzenbach II 222; *Wesselski Mönchslatein 91 No. 77; Chauvin V 253 No. 150, VIII 105 No. 80; Irish myth: *Cross; Russian: Andrejev No. 932*; Spanish Exempla: Keller; Italian Novella: *Rotunda, Basile Pentamerone III No. 3, IV No. 6; Jewish: Neuman.

E765.4.3. Father will die when daughter bears son. F772.2.1. Brazen tower. J147. Child confined to keep him in ignorance of life. Useless. M312.1. Prophecy: wealthy marriage for poor boy. M343. Parricide prophecy. M311.1. Prophecy: king's grandson will dethrone him. R41.2. Captivity in tower. T50.1. Girl carefully guarded from suitors. T381. Imprisoned virgin to prevent knowledge of men (marriage, impregnation). Usually kept in a tower.

M372.1. *Confinement in iron house below surface of earth to avoid fulfillment of prophecy.* India: Thompson-Balys.

M373. *Expulsion to avoid fulfillment of prophecy.* *Types 517, 671, 725; Köhler-Bolte I 145; *BP I 322ff.; Cox 500; MacCulloch Childhood 354; India: *Thompson-Balys; Indonesia: DeVries's list No. 204.

L111.1. Exile returns and succeeds. Q431. Punishment: banishment (exile).

M375. *Slaughter of innocents to avoid fulfillment of prophecy.* *Hartland Perseus I 14; Irish myth: *Cross; Spanish Exempla: Keller.

K515. Children hidden to avoid their execution (death). S310. Reasons for abandonment of children.

M375.1. *All male children killed for fear that they will overcome parent.* Africa (Zulu): Callaway 41.

F565.1.2. All male children killed by Amazons.

M375.2. *Slaughter of children to prevent fulfillment of parricide prophecy.* Irish myth: Cross; India: Thompson-Balys; Hindu: Keith 171.

K514. Disguise as girl to avoid execution. M343. Parricide prophecy.

M375.3. *Child mutilated to avoid fulfillment of prophecy.* Irish myth: Cross.

S160. Mutilations.

M375.4. *Wooers slain to avoid fulfillment of prophecy.* Irish myth: Cross.

M376. *God swallows his pregnant wife to prevent birth of son whom he fears.* Greek: *Frazer Apollodorus I 24 n. 1.

M376.1. *Exposure of pregnant woman to avoid fulfillment of prophecy concerning future child.* India: *Thompson-Balys.

M376.2. *Murder of pregnant woman to avoid fulfillment of prophecy.* Irish myth: Cross; India: Thompson-Balys.

M376.3. *Children swallowed one after the other as they are born for fear one of them will overcome father.* Greek: Grote I 6.

M376.4. *Delivery of child fated to rule retarded in order to avoid fulfillment of prophecy.* Greek: Grote I 88.

M377. *Sword that is to kill one is weighted and sunk so as to avoid the prophecy.* (Cf. M341.2.) Icelandic: Boberg.

M377.1. *Stone that is to kill one powdered and thrown into distant sea.* Irish myth: Cross.

M381. *Man whose death has been prophesied takes refuge in church,* but is accidentally slain through window by arrow directed at stag. Irish myth: Cross.

M382. *Futile moving to avoid death.* Man told by Death he will die where he stands sells everything and moves to another town. He goes for a ride on a mare which runs away with him and throws him on the spot he so dreads, killing him. India: Thompson-Balys.

M390. *Prophecies—miscellaneous motifs.* Irish myth: Cross.

M391. *Fulfillment of prophecy.*

M391.1. *Fulfillment of prophecy successfully avoided.* India: Thompson-Balys.

M391.1.1. *Prophecy of misfortune for prince avoided successfully in one respect.* India: Thompson-Balys.

M391.2. *Wandering skull fulfills prophecy.* India: *Thompson-Balys.

M392. *Queen dies from fright from evil prophecy.* Icelandic: *Boberg.

M393. *Favorable prophecies: blessings, beatitudes.*

M393.1. *Child pronounces blessing according to which countries are to be filled with what they are later famous for.* India. Thompson-Balys.

M394. *Hero's coming prophesied.* Irish myth: Cross.

B143.0.8.1. Crows announce coming of hero to otherworld.

M395. *Prophecy: son of certain name will become king;* all sons given the name. Irish myth: *Cross.

M314. Prophecy: man (child) will become king.

M396. *Prophecy: meeting will take place only after death.* Irish myth: Cross.

M397. *Prophecy: hunters will encounter certain wild boar.* Irish myth: Cross.

M398. *Futility of weather prophecies.* Irish: O'Suilleabhain 72, 110.

M400—M499. Curses.

M400. Curses. *Encyc. Rel. Ethics s.v. "Cursing and Blessing"; Icelandic: *Boberg; Irish: *Cross, Beal XXI 326, 328, O'Suilleabhain 73, 88; Estonian: Loorits Grundzüge I 205ff.; Jewish: *Neuman; India: Thompson-Balys.

A1330. Beginning of troubles for man. A1614.1. Negroes as curse on Ham for laughing at Noah's nakedness. A2230. Animal characteristics as punishment. C94.1.1. The cursed dancers. C494. Tabu: cursing. C987. Curse as punishment for breaking tabu. D1761. Magic results produced by wishing. D1792. Magic results from curse. D1870. Magic hideousness. D2060. Death or bodily injury by magic. D2071. Evil Eye. Bewitching by means of a glance. D2081. Land made magically sterile. D2176. Exorcising by magic. D2192. Work of day magically overthrown at night. N591. Curse on treasure. Q2. Kind and unkind. Q556. Curse as punishment.

M401. *Cursing match* (flyting). Irish myth: *Cross.

M402. *Satire*. Irish myth: *Cross.

A1464.3. Origin of satire. D1273. Magic formula (charm). D1275. Magic song. D1318.12.1.1. Poet's spell causes ale vessels to burst when mother's request for ale is refused. D1402.15. Magic poem (satire) causes king to waste away. D1403.1. Magic poem (satire) raises blotches on face. D1445.3. Saint's chant kills animal. D1445.4. Magic poem (satire) kills animals. D1563.2.3. Magic poem (satire) makes land sterile. D1799.3. Magic results from special rituals. P427.4. Poet (druid) as satirist. Q265.2. Punishment for undeserved satire. Q265.2.1. Blotches on face of satirist as punishment for wrongful satire. Q451.4.6. Tongue cut out as punishment for satire. Q499.4. Satirizing as punishment for refusing to grant request. Q499.4.1. Satirizing as punishment for breaking treaty. Q556.7.1. Curse (satire) for enforced hospitality. Q558.8. Mysterious death as punishment for wrongful satire. V229.6.1. Saint limits powers of satirist.

M402.1. *Woman satirist*. Irish myth: *Cross.

M402.1.1. *Woman satirists punished in hell*. Irish myth: *Cross.

M402.2. *No one to go security for a satirist*. Irish myth: *Cross.

M403. *Curse of everlasting terror*. Buddhist myth: Malalasekera I 318.

M404. *Unintentional curse or blessing takes effect*. Jewish: *Neuman.

M410. Pronouncement of curses. Icelandic: Herrmann Saxo II 119.

D1766.5.1. Masses used along with other magic for cursing. D2175. cursing by magic.

M411. *Deliverer of curse*. India: Thompson-Balys.

F316. Fairy lays curse on child. G269.4. Curse by witch.

M411.0.1. *Curse by oneself*. The person in despair curses himself to sink with palace into the earth. Lithuanian: Balys Historical; India: Thompson-Balys.

F941.1. Castle (palace) sinks into earth.

M411.1. *Curse by parent*. Penzer IV 230 n. 2; Irish myth: *Cross; Lithuanian: Balys Index No. 3591; Spanish Exempla: Keller; Greek: Fox 50 (Oedipus), Grote I 247; India: Thompson-Balys.

S223.2. Mother curses her unborn child.

M411.1.1. *Curse by stepmother*. (Cf. S31.) Icelandic: *Boberg; Modern Icelandic: Rittershaus 34, 48, 50, 58, 66, 161, Sveinsson FFC LXXXIII xxviii ff.

G205. Witch stepmother. P18.1. After highly mourned wife's death the king marries another who turns out to be an evil witch.

M411.1.2. *Curse by foster mother*. Italian Novella: Rotunda.

M411.2. *Beggar's curse.* Beggar is refused request. "May your bread turn to stones!" *Kittredge Witchcraft 132, 452 n. 52; England: Baughman; Spanish: Espinosa Jr. No. 183; India: *Thompson-Balys.

A2231.1.1. Discourteous answer: why cow (horse) is always eating.

M411.3. *Dying man's curse.* Icelandic: *Boberg; Greek: Aeschylus Agamemnon 235.

D1715. Magic power of dying man's words. M251. Dying man's promise will be kept.

M411.4. *Man pursued by hatred of the gods.* Irish: MacCulloch Celtic 74ff., *Cross; Greek: Grote I 147; India: *Thompson-Balys.

A180. Gods in relation to mortals.

M411.4.1. *Curse by a god.* Icelandic: *Boberg.

M411.5. *Old woman's curse (satire).* Irish myth: *Cross; Icelandic: *Boberg; Spanish: Espinosa Jr. No. 106; Italian: Basile Pentamerone Int.

M301.2.1. Enraged old woman prophesies for youth. N825.3 Old woman helper. S375. Old woman's maledictions inform abandoned hero of his parentage and future.

M411.6. *Druid's curse.* Irish myth: *Cross.

D1711.4. Druid as magician.

M411.6.1. *Druid's curse makes land sterile.* Irish myth: *Cross.

M411.7. *Curse by spirit.* Irish myth: Cross.

F402.1. Deeds of evil spirits.

M411.8. *Saint's (prophet's) curse.* *Loomis White Magic 100f.; Irish myth: *Cross; Jewish: *Neuman; India: Thompson-Balys.

D1713. Magic power of hermit (saint).

M411.8.1. *Saints curse by ringing bells against offender.* Irish myth: *Cross.

M411.8.2. *Hermit curses men who kill his pet bear and all the men die.* Spanish Exempla: Keller.

M411.8.3. *Curses on places because of offensive answer to saint.* Irish myth: Cross.

M411.8.4. *Animals cursed by saint.* (Cf. M471.) *Loomis White Magic 100f.

M411.8.5. *Saint curses books hidden by inhospitable host:* no man shall read them. Irish myth: *Cross.

M411.9. *Giantess lays a curse on the one on earth who eventually hears her.* Icelandic: Boberg.

M411.10. *Curse by berserk, giant (ogre).* Icelandic: Boberg; India: Thompson-Balys.

M411.11. *Curse by girl in revenge of the murdering of her foster father.* Icelandic: Boberg.

M411.11.1. *Curse by amazon,* "skjaldmær". (Cf. F565.) Icelandic: Boberg.

M411.12. *Curse by witch.* (Cf. G269.4.) Icelandic: *Boberg; India: Thompson-Balys.

M411.13. *Curse by thrall.* Icelandic: *Boberg.

M411.14. *Curse by priest.* French Canadian: Sister Marie Ursule.

M411.14.1. *Priest curses sinner: even his grave shall not rest.* The grave rolls like a wave. U.S.: Baughman.

M411.14.2. *Curse by anchorite.* India: Thompson-Balys.

M411.14.3. *Brahmin's curse.* India: Thompson-Balys.

M411.15. *Curse by monk.* French Canadian: Sister Marie Ursule.

M411.16. *Fairy lays curse on village.* Cheremis: Sebeok-Nyerges.

M411.17. *Curse by king.* Irish myth: *Cross.

M411.18. *Curse by poet.* Irish myth: *Cross.

D1810.0.11. Magic knowledge of poet. P19.3. King subject to satire by poets. P427.4. Poet (druid) as satirist.

M411.19. *Curse by animal.*

M411.19.1. *Curse by wounded animal.* India: *Thompson-Balys.

M411.19.2. *Ox curses ungrateful man.* Buddhist myth: Malalasekera I 812.

M411.20. *Curse by spouse.* India: Thompson-Balys; Jewish: Neuman.

M411.21. *Curse by disguised deity.* India: Thompson-Balys.

M411.22. *Curse by head of religious order.* England: *Baughman.

M411.23. *Curse by other wronged man or woman.* England, U.S.: *Baughman.

M411.24. *Curse on city by sage.* India: Thompson-Balys.

M412. *Time of giving curse.*

M412.1. *Curse given at birth of child.* *Type 410; *BP I 434; Köhler-Bolte Zs. f. Vksk. VI 70 (to Gonzenbach No. 28); Irish myth: Cross; Icelandic: *Boberg.

M412.2. *Curse given on wedding night.* Icelandic: Boberg.

M413. *Place of giving curse.*

M413.1. *Curse given from a height.* Will fall with full effect on objects at which it is aimed. Irish: Plummer clxxiv, Cross; Italian Novella: Rotunda.

M414. *Recipient of curse.*

M414.1. *God cursed.* Jewish: *Neuman.

M414.2. *Goddess cursed.* Irish myth: Cross.

M414.3. *Saint cursed.* Irish myth: *Cross.

M414.4. *Four year old girl cursed.* Icelandic: Boberg.

M414.5. *King cursed.* Irish myth: *Cross; Jewish: Neuman.

M414.6. *Poet cursed.* Irish myth: *Cross.

M414.7. *Hostages cursed.* Irish myth: Cross.

M414.8. *Animals cursed.*

M414.8.1. *Mice (rats, cats) cursed.* Irish myth: *Cross.

M414.8.2. *Pigs cursed.* Irish myth: Cross.

M414.8.3. *Serpent cursed.* Jewish: *Neuman.

M414.8.4. *Birds cursed.* Irish myth: Cross.

M414.9. *Curse on wife's lover.* India: Thompson-Balys.

M414.10. *Thief cursed.* Jewish: *Neuman.

M414.11. *Man who betrays secrets cursed.* Jewish: Neuman.

M414.12. *Earth cursed.* Jewish: Neuman.

M414.13. *Curse on a deity.*

M414.13.1. *Curse: god to live life of a cat for twelve full years in house of huntsman on earth.* India: Thompson-Balys.

M415. *Irrevocable curse.* Penzer VI 103 n. 1, 162 n. 1; Irish myth: Cross; India: Thompson-Balys.

M10. Irrevocable judgments.

M416. *Curse given to negate good wish.* Odin gives man life three times the normal; Thor ordains that in each he is to commit crime. Odin gives him the choicest weapons; Thor denies him landed property, etc. Icelandic: MacCulloch Eddic 73.

F316.1. Fairy's curse partially overcome by another fairy's amendment.

M416.1. *Curse: appetite of twelve men.* Given with the gift of twelve men's strength. Hartland Science 144.

F610. Remarkably strong man.

M416.2. *Curse: eternal life without eternal youth.* Greek: Fox 246 (Tithonus).

D1850.1. Immortality useless without eternal youth.

M418. *Method of cursing.*

M418.1. *Curse by "building a fire of stones" in fireplace.* The person who removes the stones is cursed. U.S.: Baughman.

M420. Enduring and overcoming curses.

F316.1. Fairy's curse partially overcome by another fairy's amendment.
M438.4. Curse: hero has to remain as dead till the curser dies.

M421. *Release from curse with birth of child.* Penzer VIII 59 n. 2.

M422. *Curse transferred to another person or thing.* Irish: Plummer clxxiii, *Cross, Beal XXI 326, O'Suilleabhain 73.

M423. *Curse removed when victims reform.* Italian Novella: Rotunda.

M425. *Curse changed by God into blessing.* Jewish: Neuman.

M427. *Curse on everybody* on *earth who listens to the fatal mentioning of trolls' names, is evaded by person in cave, because he is in the earth.* Icelandic: *Boberg.

M428. *Curse mitigated by deity when superhuman task is performed.* India: Thompson-Balys.

M429. *Miscellaneous ways to overcome curses.* (Cf. D2071.1.)

M429.1. *Release from curse by burning vomit.* French Canadian: Sister Marie Ursule.

M429.2. *Release from curse by putting pins around horse's heart and then boiling it.* French Canadian: Sister Marie Ursule.

M429.3. *Release from curse by burning animal in straw pile.* French Canadian: Sister Marie Ursule.

M429.4. *Release from curse by heating the colter of the plow in the stove.* French Canadian: Sister Marie Ursule.

M429.5. *Release from curse by pricking louse and hanging it on wall.* French Canadian: Sister Marie Ursule.

M429.6. *Release from curse by putting a five cent piece in the churn.* French Canadian: Sister Marie Ursule.

M429.7. *Release from curse by putting a piece of silver in the gun.* French Canadian: Sister Marie Ursule.

M430. Curses on persons. Irish myth: *Cross.

D521. Transformation through wish. D521.1. Transformation through thoughtless wish of parent. D525. Transformation through curse. D565.1 Midas's golden touch. D1792. Magic results from curse. D2021.1. Dumbness as curse. D2004.1. Curse of forgetfulness. D2061.2.4. Death by cursing. D2072.2. Magic paralysis by curse.

M431. *Curse: bodily injury.* Lagerholm 106—107; Irish myth: Cross.

D2064. Magic sickness.

M431.1. *Curse: loss of eye.* *Type 1331; *BP II 219 n. 1; Irish myth: *Cross; and notes to J2074.

D2062.2. Bli. ng by curse. J2074. Twice the wish to the enemy. (The covetous and the envious). A can have a wish, but B will get twice the wish. A wishes that he may lose an eye, so that B may be blind.

M431.2. *Curse: toads from mouth* *Type 403; *Roberts 208; *BP I 99ff.; *Fb "tudse" III 889a; India: *Thompson-Balys.

D1454.2. Treasure falls from mouth. Q2. Kind and unkind.

M431.3. *Curse: fire to burn hands and feet.* Pauli (ed. Bolte) No. 440.

M431.4. *Curse: arm to fall off.* Irish: Plummer clxxiv, Cross.

M431.4.1. *Curse: hand of person cursed to drop off.* U.S.: Baughman.

M431.5. *Curse: wound not to heal.* Irish myth: Cross; Icelandic: Boberg.

D2161.4.10.2. Wound healed only by person who gave it.

M431.6. *Wicked stepmother cursed to have fire lit under her.* Icelandic: Boberg.

M431.7. *Curse: leprosy.* India: Thompson-Balys; Buddhist myth: Malalasekera II 1050.

M431.8. *Curse of sterility on wife of enemy.* India: Thompson-Balys.

M431.9. *Curse: head to split in seven pieces.* Buddhist myth: Malalasekera II 279.

M431.10. *Curse: to be plagued by nightmares.* Buddhist myth: Malalasekera II 925.

M432. *Curse: to be carried off by evil spirit.* Pauli (ed. Bolte) No. 456; Hdwb. d. Märchens I 547a nn. 127—139.

M215. With his whole heart: devil carries off judge. M346. Prophecy: child to be abducted at certain time.

M433. *Endless sleep given Endymion.* Greek: Fox 245.

D1962.1. Magic sleep through curse.

M434. *Curse: to be swallowed by a siren.* Italian Novella: Rotunda.

B81.10. Mermaid swallows man. F910. Extraordinary swallowing.

M435. *Curse: not to taste food from own table.* Food always seized by harpies. Greek: Fox 111.

M436. *Curse: prince to fall in love with witch's daughter.* Italian: Basile Pentamerone II No. 7.

M312.1.1. Prophecy: wealthy marriage for poor girl. M359.2. Prophecy: prince's marriage to common woman. T22.2. Predestined wife.

M437. *Curse: monstrous birth.*

Q552.5. Monstrous births as punishment for girl's pride. T550. Monstrous births.

M437.1. *Curse: "What I carry may you carry; what you carry may I carry."* Cat thus causes ungrateful pregnant woman to bear cats and herself to bear twin girls. India: Thompson-Balys.

Q281.3. Woman eats flesh and leaves cat only bones of fish cat has caught for them. T554. Woman gives birth to animal.

M437.2. *Jealous sisters curse the child one of them may have by the god Thor,* so that it never will grow nor thrive. Icelandic: *Boberg.

F321.1. Changeling. Fairy steals child from cradle and leaves fairy substitute. Changeling is usually mature and only seems to be a child.

M438. *Curse: humiliation.* Irish myth: Cross.

C929.1. "Shame and disgrace" threatened for refusing love of forthputting woman. D2063. Magic discomfort. Q470. Humiliating punishments.

M438.1. *Curse: man (poet) to kiss a leper.* Irish myth: *Cross.

M438.2. *Curse: hero not to be able to stand the sight of blood.* Icelandic: *Boberg.

M438.3. *Girl bewitched so that no man will remain faithful to her.* Icelandic: Boberg.

M438.4. *Curse: hero to remain as dead till the curser dies.* Icelandic: *Boberg.

M438.5. *Dying father condemns weak son to be servant of his brothers.* Irish myth: Cross.

M441. *Curse: failure in all undertakings.* India: *Thompson-Balys.

M441.1. *Curse: man's sword will fail in danger.* Icelandic: Boberg.

M441.1.1. *Curse: when brothers' swords bite the very best, they will all be killed by a single man.* Icelandic: Boberg.

M442. *Curse: deformity.* Irish myth: Cross.

M442.1. *Curse: descendants to be unshapely.* Irish myth: *Cross.

M460. Curses on families.

M442.2. *Curse: she-wolf to carry off man's genitals.* Irish myth: *Cross.

M443. *Curse: privation.* Irish myth: Cross.

M443.1. *Curse: lack of food, shelter, good company.* Irish myth: Cross; Icelandic: *Boberg.

M444. *Curse of childlessness.*

M444.1. *Curse laid on unborn child; it is stillborn.* India: Thompson-Balys.

M445. *Giant cursed: may neither heaven nor earth receive him.* Irish myth: Cross.

M446. *Curse: undertaking dangerous quest.* Icelandic: *Boberg.

M446.1. *Curse: undertaking dangerous revenge of father.* Icelandic: Boberg.

M448. *Curse: to sink into the earth.* Tupper and Ogle Walter Map 91; India: Thompson-Balys; Eskimo (Central Eskimo): Boas RBAE VI 585.

F942.1. Ground opens and swallows up person. Q552.2.3. Earth swallows as punishment.

M448.1. *Curse: ground shall swallow children.* India: Thompson-Balys.

M451. *Curse: death.* England, U.S.: *Baughman; Jewish: Neuman; Chinese: Eberhard FFC CXX 126.

D2161.2.4. Death by cursing.

M451.1. *Death by suicide.* England, Wales: *Baughman.

M451.2. *Death by drowning.* England, U.S.: *Baughman.

M452. *Curse: insanity.* U.S., Wales: Baughman.

M453. *Curse: corpse to be put in three different places after person's death.* India: Thompson-Balys.

K2321. Corpse set up to frighten people.

M454. *Curse: change of sex.* India: *Thompson-Balys.

E605.1. Reincarnation with change of sex.

M455. *Curse: restlessness.* (Cf. K1837.4.) Irish myth: *Cross; Icelandic: Lagerholm lxi—ii.

M455.1. *Hero cursed to restlessness (except on boat or in tent), till he sees girl.* (Cf. D1900.) Icelandic: *Boberg.

M455.2. *Curse: not to be able to love the same woman more than twelve months.* Icelandic: Boberg.

M455.3. *Thrall cursed to sit on chest and yell and never have rest.* Icelandic: Lagerholm 99—100, *Boberg.

M455.4. *Curse: couple to wander until new seat of race is pointed out.* India: Thompson-Balys.

M458. *Curse of petrifaction.* India: Thompson-Balys.

M459. *Miscellaneous curses on persons.*

M459.1. *Curse: woman will not travel far.* French Canadian: Sister Marie Ursule.

M460. Curses on families. Irish: Plummer clxxiv, *Cross; England, Wales, U.S.: Baughman; Icelandic: *Boberg; Greek: Fox 120 (Tantalus), Grote I 244f. (Oedipus); Jewish: Neuman; Buddhist myth: Malalasekera I 108.

F316.2. Fairy's curse partially overcome by her own amendment after being appeased. F755.1. Speaking mountain. M301.15. Mountain in human shape prophesies whole family's death. M442.1. Curse: descendants to be unshapely.

M460.1. *Curse: children will be sick.* French Canadian: Sister Marie Ursule.

M461. *Curse: descendants of nine robbers never to exceed nine.* Irish: Cross, Plummer clxxiv.

M461.1. *Curse on village: descendants never to exceed certain number.* (Cf. M475.) Cheremis: Sebeok-Nyerges.

M462. *Curse: race to lose sovereignty.* Irish myth: *Cross; U.S.: Baughman.

M463. *Curse on tribe (district).* Irish myth: *Cross; Jewish: Neuman; India: Thompson-Balys.

M464. *Curse of a woman against her caste:* they should remain unclothed and untaught. India: Thompson-Balys.

M470. Curses on objects or animals.

F451.5.2.13. Dwarfs curse weapons and treasures which they are forced to give or which the receiver does not appreciate. N591. Curse on treasure.

M471. *Curses on animals.* (Cf. M411.8.4.) U.S.: Baughman.

M471.1. *Curse: cow will give red milk.* French Canadian: Sister Marie Ursule.

M471.1.1. *Curse: milk will not turn to butter.* French Canadian: Sister Marie Ursule.

M471.2. *Cursing to make pigs lean.* Irish myth: Cross; French Canadian: Sister Marie Ursule.

M471.3. *Curse: horses will die.* French Canadian: Sister Marie Ursule.

M471.3.1. *Curse: horse will be lame.* French Canadian: Sister Marie Ursule.

M474. *Curse on land.* U.S.: *Baughman.

M475. *Curse on a city.* (Cf. M461.1.) Irish myth: *Cross (M430.0.1).

M475.1. *Curse on a city: never to grow.* North Carolina: Brown Collection I 691.

M476. *Curse on river.* Irish myth: Cross.

M476.1. *Curse on river or sea: no fish in it from that day.* Irish myth: *Cross.

M477. *Curse on lake.*

M477.1. *Curse on lake: fire from lake will burn the forest around it.* Icelandic: Boberg.

M490. Curses—miscellaneous.

M491. *Presence of cursed person brings disaster to land.* Greek: Fox 50, 55.

M493. *Whomsoever demons curse is blessed, and vice versa.* Irish myth: Cross.

N. CHANCE AND FATE

DETAILED SYNOPSIS

N0—N99. Wagers and gambling
- N0. Wagers and gambling
- N10. Wagers on wives, husbands, or servants
- N50. Other wagers
- N90. Wagers and gambling—miscellaneous

N100—N299. The ways of luck and fate
- N100—N169. Nature of luck and fate
  - N100. Nature of luck and fate
  - N110. Luck and fate personified
  - N120. Determination of luck or fate
  - N130. Changing of luck or fate
  - N140. Nature of luck and fate—miscellaneous motifs
  - N170. The capriciousness of luck
  - N200. The good gifts of fortune
  - N250. Persistent bad luck
  - N270. Crime inevitably comes to light

N300—N399. Unlucky accidents
- N300. Unlucky accidents
- N310. Accidental separations
- N320. Person unwittingly killed
- N330. Accidental killing or death
- N340. Hasty killing or condemnation
- N350. Accidental loss of property
- N360. Man unwittingly commits crime
- N380. Other unlucky accidents

N400—N699. *Lucky accidents*

N410—N439. Lucky business ventures

N440—N499. Valuable secrets learned
- N440. Valuable secrets learned
- N450. Secrets overheard

N500—N599. Treasure trove
- N500. Treasure trove
- N510. Where treasure is found
- N530. Discovery of treasure
- N550. Unearthing hidden treasure
- N570. Guardian of treasure
- N590. Treasure trove—miscellaneous motifs

N600—N699. Other lucky accidents
- N610. Accidental discovery of crime
- N620. Accidental success in hunting or fishing
- N630. Accidental acquisition of treasure or money
- N640. Accidental healing

N650. Life saved by accident
N680. Lucky accidents—miscellaneous

N700—N799. Accidental encounters
N700. Accidental encounters
N710. Accidental meeting of hero and heroine
N730. Accidental reunion of families
N760. Other accidental encounters
N770. Experiences leading to adventures

N800—N899. Helpers
N800. Helpers
N810. Supernatural helpers
N820. Human helpers

N. CHANCE AND FATE

N0—N99. Wagers and gambling.

N0. **Wagers and gambling.** *Penzer II 232 n., VII 72 n. 2; Paton Encyc. Rel. and Ethics s.v. "Gambling"; *Fb "kort" II 278; Jewish: *Neuman.

A482. God of gambling (luck). H942. Task assigned as result of lost wager. J2511. The silence wager. K92. Gambling contest won by deception. K455.7. Greatest liar to get his supper free. Wager. Each lie is corroborated by a confederate, who poses as a newly arrived stranger. K1545. Wives wager as to who can best fool her husband. K2378.1. Person allowed to win first game so that he will play further for high stakes. Q381. Punishment for gambling. X416. Parson preaches so that half the congregation weeps and half laughs. Has clothes torn in the back. Those that see this laugh. He wins the wager.

N1. *Gamblers.* Spanish: Espinosa Jr. Nos. 70—73, 210; Missouri French: Carrière; Jewish: *Neuman.

D1407. Magic object helps gambler win. F679.7. Skillful gambler always wins. Whatever he earns in day he spends immediately. G11.13. Gambling cannibal. G101. Giant gambler as ogre. H588.5. Father's counsel: if you want to gamble, then gamble with experienced gamblers. (If you see how wretched professional gamblers are you will not want to gamble.) J1115.1. Clever gambler. L177. Despised boy wins gambling game. M214. Devil to help gambler in exchange for one task yearly. N221. Man granted power of winning at cards. S221.1. Bankrupt father sells his daughters in marriage to animals. (Sometimes to pay gambling debt.) S221.2. Youth sells himself to an ogre in settlement of a gambling debt.

N1.0.1. *Gambling caused by possession of men by evil demons.* India: Thompson-Balys.

N1.1. *Hero makes fortune through gambling.* Scotch: Campbell Tales II 253, 271.

N1.2. *Conquering gambler.* Bankrupt gambler gets supernatural power and wins back his fortune. N. A. Indian: *Thompson Tales 354 n. 276, (Zuñi): Benedict II 342, (Klikitat): Jacobs U Wash II 5.

N1.2.1. *The miracle of broken die at gambling saves man.* Krappe Hispanic Review XIV (1946) 164ff.

N1.2.2. *Dice made from bones from graveyard.* India: *Thompson-Balys.

D1278. Ghoulish charm. Charm made from parts of corpse or things associated with corpse. D1407. Magic object helps gambler win.

N1.3. *Betting contest between two kings.* Philippine: Fansler MAFLS XII 8.

N2. *Extraordinary stakes at gambling.* Irish myth: Cross.

N2.0.1. *Play for unnamed stakes.* Irish myth: *Cross; Scottish: Campbell-McKay Nos. 1, 17.

K100. Deceptive bargain. M223. Blind promise.

N2.0.2. *Stakes not claimed by winner, who insists on another game.* Scottish: Campbell-McKay No. 17.

N2.1. *Own body as stake: to be taken as slave.* Missouri French: Carrière; India: *Thompson-Balys; Buddhist myth: Malalasekera II 882; N. A. Indian: *Thompson Tales 354 n. 277.

N2.2. *Lives wagered.* *Fb "spille" III 487b; Icelandic: *Boberg; India: *Thompson-Balys; Burmese: Scott Indo-Chinese 323; Hawaii: Beckwith Myth 111, 459; N. A. Indian: *Thompson Tales 354 n. 277; Africa (Fjort): Dennett 71 No. 15.

N2.3. *Bodily members wagered.*

N2.3.1. *Head wagered.* India: *Thompson-Balys.

N2.3.2. *Hand wagered.* To be cut off. Penzer II 232n.

N2.3.2.1. *Hands and feet wagered.* India: Thompson-Balys.

N2.3.3. *Eyes wagered.* *Type 613; Christiansen FFC XXIV 48ff., 55; India: *Thompson-Balys; N. A. Indian (California): Gayton and Newman 82.

K451.1. Unjust umpire decides a religious dispute. His confederate thus wins an absurd wager. N61. Wager that falsehood is better than truth. Left to unjust umpire, so that falsehood wins.

N2.3.4. *Nose wagered.* India: Thompson-Balys.

N2.3.5. *Intestines wagered.* Africa (Wute): Sieber 212f.

N2.4. *Helpful animals lost in wager.* India: Thompson-Balys.

N2.5. *Whole kingdom (all property) as wager.* *Fb "spille" III 487b, "konge" II 264b; Icelandic: Boberg; India: *Thompson-Balys; Hawaii: Beckwith Myth 429.

K285. To keep first thing touched. Wealth (or woman) is on platform. First thing touched is ladder leading up.

N2.5.1. *Right of succession to the throne lost in gambling.* India: Thompson-Balys.

N2.5.2. *Half kingdom as wager.* India: Thompson-Balys.

Q112. Half of kingdom as reward.

N2.6. *Wife as wager.* *Fb "spille" III 487b; Irish myth: *Cross; India: *Thompson-Balys; Chinese: Eberhard FFC CXX 216 No. 165; N. A. Indian: *Thompson Tales 354 n. 276.

Q115.1. Reward: any boon that may be asked — king's wife demanded. T200. Married life.

N2.6.1. *Sister as wager.* India: *Thompson-Balys.

N2.6.2. *Daughter as wager.* India: *Thompson-Balys.

T68. Princess offered as prize.

N2.6.3. *Damsel as wager.* India: Thompson-Balys.

N2.7. *Love wagered in game.* Danish: Grundtvig No. 238; Italian Novella: Rotunda.

N3. *Supernatural adversary in gambling (witch or giant).* Norse: Boberg.

N3.1. *Gambling with a god.* India: Thompson-Balys; N. A. Indian (Zuñi) *Benedict II 338.

N4. *Devil as gambler.* Fb "kort" II 279a, "klör" II 204; Alphabet No.

450; Scala Celi 110b, 111a Nos. 615, 616; Irish: O'Suilleabhain 33, 36, Beal XXI 311, 313; Missouri French: Carrière.

E756.2. Soul won from devil in card game. G303.4.5.3.1. Devil detected by his hoofs. While playing cards the devil drops a card on the floor and his partners notice his monstrous feet.

N4.0.1. *Devil cheated at card playing.* Fb "fanden" I 267b.

N4.1. *Devil makes wager with builder of Cologne Cathedral.* Wünsche 83f.

N4.2. *Playing game of chance (or skill) with uncanny being.* Irish myth: *Cross.

N5. *Card-playing parson.* The parson plays cards all Saturday night, goes to sleep at church, and calls out the names of the cards. Type 1839A; Lithuanian: Balys Index No. 1785E*. Cf. Type 1839B.

N71. Wager: to begin sermon with illustration from card-playing. Card-playing parson wins the wager. N410. Jokes on parsons.

N6. *Luck in gambling.*

D1407. Magic object helps gambler win. H512. Guessing with life as wager. N131.1. Luck changing after cohabitation.

N6.1. *Luck in gambling from compact with devil.* Scala Celi 24a No. 154; Spanish: Boggs FFC XC 55 No. 408A*, Espinosa Jr. Nos. 70—73.

M214. Devil to help gambler in exchange for one task yearly.

N6.2. *Cuckold loses luck.* A man's wife is deceived in order that he may lose in gambling. N. A. Indian (California): Gayton and Newman 81.

K1501. Cuckold. Husband deceived by adulterous wife. N131. Acts performed for changing luck.

N6.3. *Saint helps gambler.* Icelandic: Boberg.

N7. *Trained rat upsets pieces in gambling game:* trained (or transformed) cat chases it away. India: *Thompson-Balys.

J1908.1. The cat and the candle. J1908.2. Cat transformed to maiden runs after mouse. K264.2. Deceptive wager: cat to carry lantern into room (has been specially trained).

N8. *Gambler's attention distracted by women.* India: *Thompson-Balys.

T26. Attention distracted by sight of beloved.

N9. *Wagers and gambling—miscellaneous.*

N9.1. *Gambler loses everything.* (Cf. N2.5.) India: *Thompson-Balys.

N10. Wagers on wives, husbands, or servants.

J1545. Wife outwits her husband.

N11. *Wager on wife's complacency.* Though the man has foolishly bargained everything away, she praises him and he wins the wager. Type 1415; *BP II 199; *Hdwb. d. Märchens I 187 n. 131.

H474. Complacent wife agrees with all of husband's absurd statements. J2081.1. Foolish bargain: horse for cow, cow for hog, etc. Finally nothing is left. N421. Lucky bargain.

N12. *Wager on the most obedient wife.* The husband tames his shrewish wife so that he wins the wager. *Type 901; *Wesselski Märchen 216 No. 24; von der Hagen I lxxxii; *Köhler-Bolte I 137; Shakespeare's "The Taming of the Shrew"; N. A. Indian (Zuñi): Boas JAFL XXXV 76.

H386. Bride test: obedience. T251.2. Taming the shrew. By outdoing his wife in shrewishness the husband renders her obedient. W31. Obedience.

N12.1. *Wager: raja's daughter will bring servant dinner in field.* Merchant ignorant that she is his wife. India: *Thompson-Balys.

N13. *Husbands wager that they will be able to do what wives tell them to do.* One is told to drown himself: loses wager. England: Baughman.

N15. *Chastity wager.* A man makes a wager on his wife's chastity. In spite of unsuccessful attempts to seduce her and of false proofs presented, he wins the wager. *Type 882; *Köhler-Bolte I 211f., 375, 581; **G. Paris Romania XXXII 481ff.; *von der Hagen III lxxxiii; Boccaccio Decameron II No. 9 (Lee 42); Shakespeare's "Cymbeline"; *Child V 500 s.v. "wager". — Irish myth: Cross; Welsh: MacCulloch Celtic 110; England: Baughman; Italian Novella: *Rotunda; Jewish: bin Gorion Born Judas[2] I 276ff., III 109, 304; India: *Thompson-Balys; Philippine: Fansler MAFLS XII 62, 253ff.

K1210. Humiliated or baffled lovers. K1342.0.1. Man carried into woman's room hidden in basket. K1512.1. Cut-off finger proves wife's chastity. K2112.1. False tokens of woman's unfaithfulness. T337. Woman wagers that she can seduce anchorite.

N15.1. *Chastity wager: woman succumbs.* Buddhist myth: Malalasekera I 51.

N15.2. *Wager on nun's chastity.* Buddhist myth: Malalasekera II 996.

N16. *Wagers on unborn children.*

N16.1. *Wager on sex of unborn child.* India: Thompson-Balys.

N16.2. *Fathers whose unborn children are affianced wager as to mastery in the house.* (Cf. N12.) India: Thompson-Balys.

N25. *Wager on truthfulness of servant.* The servant is sent to a neighbor's where he is made drunk and is seduced by the neighbor's wife. He tells the master all. *Type 889; Wesselski Märchen 200; Wesselski Mönchslatein I No. 1; Fb "lyve" II 491a, "sandhed" III 157b; Italian Novella: Rotunda .

H1556. Tests of fidelity. P361. Faithful servant.

N50. Other wagers.

K52. Contest in seeing sunrise first. K96. Writing contest won by deception.

N51. *Wager: who can call three tree names first.* The bear names different varieties of the same tree, so that the fox wins the wager. *Type 7; Dh I 193; Krohn Bär (Wolf) und Fuchs (JSFO VI) 65ff.; Fb "træ" III 867b; N. A. Indian (San Carlos Apache): cf. Goddard PaAM XXIV 24.

N51.1. *Wager about tree names: learned and common names.* Brahmin gives learned names but servant's common names are confirmed by illiterate peasants. India: Thompson-Balys.

N53. *Wager: it is an auspicious day.* In spite of all misfortunes wagerer insists that he is right. (Cf. N127.) India: Thompson-Balys.

N55. *Shooting contest on wager.* *Type 592; *BP II 490ff.; Spanish: Espinosa III 153.

K31. Shooting contest won by deception.

N55.1. *Loser of shooting wager to go naked into thorns for bird.* *Type 592; *BP II 490ff.

N56. *Wager: woman to turn somersault in middle of public square.* It is performed not exactly in the center of the square; hence she loses. India: Thompson-Balys.

N61. *Wager that falsehood is better than truth.* Left to unjust umpire, so that falsehood wins. *Type 613; *BP II 468ff.; **Christiansen FFC XXIV 47; Chauvin V 11 No. 8, 13 No. 9, 14 No. 158; *Pauli (ed. Bolte) No. 489; India: *Thompson-Balys; N. A. Indian: Thompson CColl II 395.

K451.1. Unjust umpire decides a religious dispute. His confederate thus wins an absurd wager. M92. Decision left to first person to arrive. N2.3.3. Eyes wagered.

N63. *Wager: more doctors than men of other professions.* The trickster feigns toothache. Everyone suggests remedies. He takes down their names as doctors and wins the wager. *Wesselski Gonnella 110 No. 11; Italian Novella: *Rotunda.

N66. *Wager: fortune made from capital or from working at vocation.* Test: money given to workman is stolen or lost; lead for his work given him is lent to fisherman who rewards him with a fish in which is a diamond. *Chauvin VI 32 No. 202.

N211.1. Lost ring found in fish.

N67. *Wager: woman can be forced to give alms.* Trickster announces that only those who have deceived their husbands are exempt. Italian Novella: Rotunda.

J1182.1. To be beaten by deceiver of husband.

N71. *Wager: to begin sermon with illustration from card-playing.* Card-playing parson wins the wager. Type 1839B.

H603. Symbolic interpretation of playing cards. N5. Card-playing parson. X410. Jokes on parsons.

N72. *Wager on second marvelous object.* First object has proved to be ordinary. King induced to make large wager that second is ordinary. He loses. India: *Thompson-Balys.

J2415. Foolish imitation of lucky man. Because one man has had good luck a numskull imitates and thinks he will have equal luck. He is disappointed.

N73. *Wager: whose hunger is it more difficult to appease—that of man or that of beast?* When nuts are strewn before master's well-fed guests, they snatch and eat them. Herdsman wins wager. Lithuanian: Balys Index No. 1545*.

N75. *Wager: to swallow egg with one gulp.* Tricksters give numskull egg with chick in it. Fool hears chick peep as he starts to swallow his egg, but he says that the chick peeped too late. Spanish: Childers.

N77. *Wager: bullock to defeat elephant.* Elephant is frightened and flees. India: Thompson-Balys.

K1710. Ogre (large animal) overawed.

N78. *Ghoulish wager won.* England: *Baughman.

N90. Wagers and gambling—miscellaneous.

N91. *Purchase of box without knowledge of its contents.* *Chauvin VI 17 No. 189 n. 2.

N92. *Wager to win or lose according to whether jackal howls or ass brays before game is finished.* India: Thompson-Balys.

N94. *Father hides wealth to keep son from gambling it away.* India: Thompson-Balys.

N100—N299. The ways of luck and fate.

N100—N169. NATURE OF LUCK AND FATE

N100. Nature of luck and fate. Penzer V 182f.; *Köhler Aufsätze 99ff.; *Patch Fortuna 78; Irish myth: Cross.

N101. *Inexorable fate.* *Cosquin Contes Indiens 126f.; Hdwb. d. Märchens II 63 s.v. Fatalismus; Icelandic: *Boberg; India: *Thompson-Balys.

D1311.11.1. River says, "The time has come but not the man." Man thus induced to drown himself. M302.4. Horoscope taken by means of stars. M370. Vain attempts to escape fulfillment of prophecy. N733.2. Brother unwittingly kills half brother in fight.

N101.1. *Inexorable fate: no day without sorrow.* A king, who has made decree against sorrow on a certain day is blinded by a swallow in his sleep. Pauli (ed. Bolte) No. 481.

L414. King vainly forbids tide to rise.

N101.2. *Inexorable fate: death from violating tabus.* (Cf. C920.) Irish myth: *Cross.

N101.3. *Man cannot die: snake will not bite him though it is provoked by him.* (Cf. N146.) Buddhist myth: Malalasekera II 1030.

N101.4. *Man fated to become king becomes so despite fact he breaks his tooth in which his luck resides.* (Cf. N113.2.2.) Buddhist myth: Malalasekera I 860.

N102. *Fortune comes to deserving and undeserving.* Jewish: Neuman.

N110. Luck and fate personified.

A463. God of fate.

N111. *Fortuna.* Luck (fate) thought of as a goddess. **Patch Fortuna; *Penzer I 106f., 135, II 49, 116, III 24, 74, 298, VI 42, 72, 105 n. 1, 124, 156, 159, VII 70, VIII 87; Frazer Pausanias III 424; India: *Thompson-Balys.

A463.1. The Fates. A473.1. Goddess of wealth. A482. God of gambling (luck). C50.1. Tabu: offending goddess of fortune. H1263. Quest to god for fortune. H1281. Quest to Fortune to seek fortune. H1376.3.1. Quest for the anger of God. Z110. Abstractions personified. Z111.5. Death (fate) assumes various forms to destroy men. Z134. Fortune personified.

N111.1. *Dwelling place of Fortuna.*

N111.1.1. *Home of Fortuna in other world.* Patch PMLA XXXIII 630.

F132.2. Dwelling of Fortune on lofty mountain.

N111.1.2. *Home of Fortuna on island (in otherworld).* *Köhler-Bolte II 412f.; *Patch Fortuna 129ff.; Hartland Science 199.

N111.2. *Appearance of Fortuna.*

N111.2.1. *Fortuna blind.* *Patch Fortuna 44 n. 2.

N111.2.1.1. *Fortune has one eye, watches over everybody.* India: Thompson-Balys.

N111.2.2. *Fortuna with two faces.* *Patch Fortuna 43 nn. 3, 4.

N111.2.3. *Fortuna half white, half black.* *Patch Fortuna 43 n. 4.

N111.3. *Fortune's wheel.* **Patch Fortuna 147ff.; *Köhler-Bolte II 66; Irish: O'Suilleabhain 122, Beal XXI 336; Jewish: *Neuman.

N111.3.1. *Fortune's wheel turned by dead king in mountain.* Armenian: Ananikian 34.

D1960.2. King asleep in mountain.

N111.3.2. *Fortune with pair of scales in his hands weighs man's balance.* India: Thompson-Balys.

N111.4. *Fortune's dealings with men.*

N111.4.1. *Man thanks earth for saving his life;* had he fallen into well he would have blamed Fortune. Wienert FFC LVI 81 (ET 470), 125 (ST 341); Halm Aesop No. 316; Italian Novella: Rotunda.

N111.5. *Giant is clerk to God of Destiny and measures out mortals' spans of existence.* India: Thompson-Balys.

N112. *Bad luck personified.*

N112.1. *Bad luck put into a sack.* Köhler-Bolte I 258.

N113. *Good luck personified.*

N113.1. *Good fortune resides in an object.* Buddhist myth: Malalasekera II 1138.

N113.1.1. *Casket with Good Luck in it given to men by Zeus.* Wienert FFC LVI 36; *Babrius No. 58.

A1400. Acquisition of human culture. C321. Tabu: looking into box.

N113.2. *Personification of Good Luck lives in man's forehead.* India: Thompson-Balys.

N113.2.1. *Lucky right hand.* Gaster Thespis 174.

N113.2.2. *Man's luck resides in his tooth.* (Cf. N101.4.) Buddhist myth: Malalasekera I 860.

N113.3. *Personification of Good Luck leaves palace since king is destined to die that night.* India: Thompson-Balys.

N113.4. *Luck can be found in certain place.* India: Thompson-Balys.

N114. *Fortune as an old woman.* India: Thompson-Balys.

N115. *Book of fate.* India: *Thompson-Balys; Gaster Thespis 348.

N118. *Issues left to fate (luck).*

N118.1. *Ship's course left to the winds that it might be carried where fate wills it.* India: Thompson-Balys.

N119. *Luck and fate personified—miscellaneous.*

N119.1. *Dog tries to catch its fate in its own tail.* India: Thompson-Balys.

N119.2. *Buffalo's fate in bamboo growing from head.* India: Thompson-Balys.

N119.3. *Ill-omened face of king; harbinger of evil.* India: Thompson-Balys.

N120. Determination of luck or fate.

G303.10.7. Devil gives luck with hunting and fishing. M302.2. Man's fate written on his skull. M302.4. Horoscope taken by means of stars. S262.3. Sacrificial victim chosen by lot. T589.4. Birth with veil brings luck.

N121. *Fate decided before birth.* Irish myth: *Cross; Jewish: *Neuman; India: Thompson-Balys.

A189.7. Deity ascertains destiny of newborn babe and inscribes it upon its forehead. M306.2. Two sons: one a purse cutter, the other a killer. M311. Prophecy: future greatness of unborn child. M359.3. Prophecy: unborn child to kill enemy in revenge.

N121.1. *Child born with objects that indicate fate.* Cheremis: Sebeok-Nyerges.

N121.1.1. *Spirit of new-born child in uniform.* God has determined fates of everyone. Type 934*; Lithuanian: Balys Index No. 934C*; Livonian: Loorits FFC LXVI No. 934I.

N121.1.2. *New-born child with a weapon and a game animal: fated to be hunter.* Cheremis: Sebeok-Nyerges.

N121.2. *Death forestalls evil fates.* Mother shown what would have been the evil fates of her children if they had not died. BP III 472ff.; Irish: Beal XXI 336, O'Suilleabhain 120.

N121.3. *Newborn girl fated to be a courtesan.* India: Thompson-Balys.

T450.1. Wife born to be prostitute.

N121.4. *Seventh daughter predestined to be magician.* (Cf. Z71.5.) Argentina: Jijena Sanchez 54, 64; Spain: ibid. 69; Portugal: ibid. 70.

N122. *Lucky or unlucky places.*

N122.0.1. *The choice of roads.* At parting of three roads are equivocal inscriptions telling what will happen if each is chosen. Brothers each choose a different road. Köhler-Bolte I 537ff.; India: Thompson-Balys.

H1236. Perilous path traversed on quest. J266. Choice between short and dangerous or long and sure way. K2310. Deception by equivocation. M305. Ambiguous oracle.

N122.1. *Unlucky places.* Jewish: *Neuman.

N125. *Choices by chance.*

N125.1. *He upon whom feather (wisp) falls to be king's fool.* Irish myth: Cross.

N125.2. *Luck determined by whether a crooked-necked demigod is looking at one.* India: Thompson-Balys.

N125.3. *King to be victorious as long as he rides muzzled gelding.* Irish myth: Cross.

N125.4. *Districts named from first person met in each.* Irish myth: Cross.

D526. Transformation through greeting: first creature to be greeted will be transformed. D1812.5.0.7. Divination from first person (thing) met. M92. Decision left to first person to arrive. T62. Princess to marry first man who asks for her. T456. Bed partner to receive payment from first man she meets in the morning.

N126. *Lots cast to determine luck or fate.* Irish myth: Cross; Icelandic: *Boberg; Jewish: *Neuman.

S262.3. Sacrificial victim chosen by lot.

N126.1. *Lots cast to determine who shall undertake adventure.* Irish myth: Cross.

N770. Experiences leading to adventures.

N126.2. *Lots cast to determine father of illegitimate child.* Irish myth: *Cross.

H480. Father tests. T640. Illegitimate children.

N127. *The auspicious (lucky) day (days).* (Cf. N53.) Irish myth: *Cross; Jewish: *Neuman.

D1812.5.0.16. Prognostications for year from winds blowing on January 1.

N127.0.1. *Different kinds of luck attending persons born on the several days of the week.* Irish myth: *Cross.

N127.1. *Tuesday as auspicious day.* Irish myth: *Cross.

N127.2. *Wednesday as auspicious (inauspicious) day.* Irish myth: *Cross.

N127.3. *Thursday as lucky day.* Irish myth: Cross.

N127.4. *Friday as auspicious day.* Irish myth: *Cross.

N128. *Unlucky days ("cross-days").* Irish myth: *Cross.

C751. Tabu: doing thing at certain time.

N128.0.1. *Days of the week on which certain tragic deaths occurred.* Irish myth: *Cross.

N128.1. *National disasters occur always at the same date.* Jewish: Neuman.

N128.2. *Monday and Wednesday as unlucky days.* Jewish: Neuman.

N130. Changing of luck or fate.

K2371.2. Gods tricked into help in escaping one's fate. M370. Vain attempts to escape fulfillment of prophecy.

N131. *Acts performed for changing luck.* *Fb "lykke" II 474f.

B147. Animal of ill-omen. C424. Tabu: speaking of good luck. C493.1. Tabu: wishing good luck. C933. Luck in hunting lost for breaking tabu. D1812.5. Future learned through omens. F302.5.3. Man loses luck when he leaves fairy wife for mortal. F348.2. Cup given by fairy not to be broken. Bad luck will follow. F348.3. Fairy gift not to leave possession of mortal's family. Bad luck will follow.

N131.1. *Luck changing after cohabitation.* Icelandic: Bósasaga 23, Hrólfs saga Kraka 96ff.

T453. Getting advice from a woman in bed.

N131.2. *Turning right-handwise in certain place brings luck.* Irish myth: Cross.

D1272. Magic circle. D1791. Magic power by circumambulation.

N131.3. *Spilling salt brings bad luck.*

N131.3.1. *Judas Iscariot spills salt at the Last Supper.* England: Baughman.

N131.4. *Luck changing after change of name.* Jewish: *Neuman.

N131.5. *Luck changing after change of place.* Jewish: *Neuman.

N134. *Persons effect change of luck.* Irish myth: Cross.

P427.0.2. Person assailed by druid loses treasure.

N134.1. *Persons bring bad luck.* Jewish: *Neuman.

N134.1.1. *Unlucky to have man in house while cloth is being dyed.* Irish myth: Cross.

N134.1.2. *Wife brings bad luck to the husband's family.* India: Thompson-Balys.

N134.1.3. *Persons lose luck as punishment.* India: Thompson-Balys.
Q553. Divine favor withdrawn as punishment.

N134.1.4. *Spirit of adversity brings bad luck to house.* India: Thompson-Balys.

N134.1.5. *Passenger brings bad luck to ship.* Cast overboard. Jonah. (Cf. S264.1.)

N135. *Objects effect change of luck.* India: Thompson-Balys.
D1409.1. Magic object brings evil (bad luck) upon person. D1561.1.2. Magic ring brings good luck. D1561.1.3. Horseshoe brings good luck. D1561.1.6. Food left on magic stone brings good luck thereafter. Z148. Yellow a lucky color.

N135.1. *Thirteen as unlucky number.* **Böklen Die "unglückezahl" Dreizehn (Leipzig, 1913); Hdwb. d. Abergl. s.v. "Zahlen" B 13; *Fb "tretten"; **Kyriakiodos To Dysoionon tou Arithmou 13 (Athens, 1953).
D1273.1. Magic numbers. Z71.9. Formulistic number: thirteen.

N135.2. *Possession of money brings luck.* Nothing escapes a mouse as long as she has in her hole a purse of money. Chauvin II 94 No. 45; Bødker Exempler 291 No. 49.

N135.2.1. *Discovery of treasure brings luck.* Chinese: Graham.

N135.3. *The luck-bringing shirt.* The king is to become lucky when he puts on the shirt of a lucky man. The only man who says that he is lucky has no shirt. *Type 844; **Köhler Aufsätze 119ff.; H. C. Andersen's "Lykkens Galocher"; Edwin Markham's "The Shoes of Fortune."
H1195. Task: having a shirt made by a woman free from trouble and worry. J347.4. Rich merchant is poorer in happiness than poor man. J1081.1. King buys spendthrift's bed. It must have been an extraordinary bed to permit a man with so many debts to sleep on it.

N135.3.1. *Feast for those who have not known sorrow.* Dying Alexander's letter to his mother orders such a feast. No one comes. *Köhler-Bolte I 579; Köhler Aufsätze 130.
H1394. Quest for person who has not known sorrow.

N135.4. *Lucky marks on body.* India: Thompson-Balys.

N136. *The judge's bad-luck bringing boots.* The wealthy merchant becomes a beggar, due to the judge's boots he acquired through exchange (theft). Lithuanian: Balys Index No. 2447*.

N137. *Philosopher conquers evil fate.* India: Thompson-Balys.

N140. Nature of luck and fate—miscellaneous motifs.

N141. *Luck or intelligence?* Dispute as to which is the more powerful. Man with intelligence remains poor (is brought into court). Saved by mere luck. *Type 945; BP III 53f.; Tille FFC XXXIV 254; Jewish: bin Gorion Born Judas[2] IV 47, 128, 276, 281; India: *Thompson-Balys.

N141.1. *Which is more important, learning or wit?* India: Thompson-Balys.

N141.2. *Which is more powerful, wealth or wisdom?* India: *Thompson-Balys.

N141.3. *Which is more beautiful, nymph of Luck or of Ill-Luck* (Luck when coming, Ill-Luck when going). India: Thompson-Balys.

N141.4. *Weaver married by Wealth to a princess to show Wisdom that he is the more powerful.* India: Thompson-Balys.

N142. *Destiny better than work, show, or speculation.* A peasant makes a little by his work; a nobleman more by his outward show; a merchant still more by speculation; but a prince most of all by his destiny. Chauvin II 109 No. 72; Bødker Exempler 305 No. 76; Spanish Exempla: Keller.

N143. *Luck only with money that is earned honestly.* Icelandic: Boberg.

N145. *Cast-out princess prospers because of Good Luck.* India: *Thompson-Balys.

N146. *Man not fated to die cannot be killed.* (Cf. N101.3.) Jewish: *Neuman.

N170. The capriciousness of luck. Icelandic: *Boberg; Jewish: Neuman; India: Thompson-Balys.

J52. King observes retaliation among animals: becomes just. Dog breaks fox's foot; man breaks dog's; horse breaks man's leg; horse steps in hole and breaks his. J2415. Foolish imitation of lucky man. L100. Unpromising hero (heroine). L140. The unpromising surpasses the promising.

N171. *Unprotected son makes fortune; protected son has bad luck.* Type 935*.

N730. Accidental reunion of families.

N172. *Prodigal as favorite of fortune.* *Type 935; Irish: Beal XXI 305, O'Suilleabhain 14.

L114.2. Spendthrift hero. P233.8. Prodigal son returns.

N172.1. *Prodigal son favored over faithful son.* Spanish Exempla: Keller.

N173. *Disagreeable and disliked youth as favorite of Fortune.* Italian Novella: Rotunda.

L110. Types of unpromising heroes (heroines).

N174. *Careful builder outside when storm comes is killed;* careless builder saved. Spanish Exempla: Keller; Africa (Angola): Chatelain 247 No. 58.

J741.1. Bear build house of wood; fox of ice. N253. Safety in shadow of wall. After many misfortunes the man is apparently safe. The wall falls on him.

N177. *Beggar escapes from fire.* Refused hospitality, he must sleep outdoors. The house burns down. *Pauli (ed. Bolte) No. 479; Jewish: Neuman.

N178. *Loss of eye saves man from execution.* Man to be buried with king. Gets off because he lacks an eye. *Wesselski Märchen 230; Pauli (ed. Bolte) No. 480.

P16.4. Persons buried with dead king.

N178.1. *Broken leg saves man from fatal fight.* King has ordered that he be killed in a fight. He breaks his leg and cannot take part. Meantime the king learns of his innocence. Chauvin II 152 No. 18; Spanish Exempla: Keller.

N178.2. *Man chosen for execution because he is fat.* India: *Thompson-Balys.

J2233. Logically absurd defenses.

N178.3. *King's counselor expelled from a court thereby escapes accompanying the king,* who is killed by robbers. India: Thompson-Balys.

N178.4. *Only crippled cow not driven away by robbers.* India: Thompson-Balys.

N181. *Fortunes of the rich man and of the poor man.* The Fortune of the rich brother tells the poor brother to seek his luck under a bush. The poor man goes there and Fortune tells him to become a merchant. He becomes rich. Type 735; India: Thompson-Balys.

N182. *Snake turns to gold in answer to dream.* Woman tells dream of pot of gold. Robbers overhear but finding only snake in pot turn it loose on woman's bed. It turns to gold. India: Thompson-Balys.

D420. Transformation: animal to object.

N183. *Money lost twice: recovered third time.* Type 935**; Lithuanian: Balys Index No. 946*; Spanish: Boggs FFC XC 114 No. 945A*.

N185. *Fugitive woman burdened with child saved; childless woman killed.* Estonian: Aarne FFC XXV 136 No. 92.

N186. *Man who derided another's faith in the stars becomes respected astrologer.* (Cf. P481.) Italian Novella: Rotunda.

N187. *Hero fails to meet the man he seeks, though they are close to one another.* Icelandic: Sterka 436, Boberg.

N200. The good gifts of fortune.

K511. Uriah letter changed. K1612. Message of death fatal to sender. M311. Prophecy: future greatness of unborn child. M312. Prophecy of future greatness for poor youth. M370. Vain attempts to escape fulfillment of prophecy. N400. Lucky accident.

N201. *Wish for exalted husband realized.* Girls make wish that they may marry king (prince, etc.). It so happens. *Type 707; *BP II 380ff., 393; Italian Novella: Rotunda; India: Thompson-Balys; N. A. Indian: Thompson CColl II 388.

C15. Wish for supernatural husband realized. C15.1. Wish for star-husband realized. C26. Wish for animal husband realized. N455.4. King overhears girl's boast as to what she should do as queen. Marries her. N711. King (prince) accidentally finds maiden and marries her.

N202. *Wishes for good fortune realized.* Jewish: *Neuman; India: *Thompson-Balys; Buddhist myth: Malalasekera I 87, 420, II 824.

D1761. Magic results produced by wishing.

N202.1. *Wish realized that all women should fall in love with man at sight.* Buddhist myth: Malalasekera I 724.

F112.1. Man on Island of Fair Women overcome by loving women.

N203. *Lucky person.* Icelandic: *Boberg; Jewish: *Neuman; India: *Thompson-Balys.

L11. Fortunate youngest son.

N211. *Lost object returns to its owner.*

N211.1. *Lost ring found in fish. (Polycrates.)* *Pauli (ed. Bolte) No. 635; *Wesselski Mönchslatein 188 No. 146; *Chauvin V 17 No. 10, 141 No. 68, VI 32 No. 202; Fb "ring" IV 328b; Toldo VIII 40; Saintyves "L'Anneau de Polycrate" Revue de l'histoire des religions (1912) 1—32; *Loomis White Magic 121. — Irish: Plummer clxxxiv, *Cross;

Norwegian: Solheim Register 20; Italian Novella: Rotunda; Jewish: *Neuman, *Gaster Exempla 210 No. 118, *bin Gorion Born Judas[2] II 106, 344, III 51, 55, 300; India: *Thompson-Balys; Japanese: Ikeda; Korean: Zong in-Sob 29; Philippine: Fansler MAFLS XII 7; Africa (Gold Coast): Barker and Sinclair 133.

A2275.5.4. Dolphins seek King Solomon's ring. B107.1. Fish with ingot of gold inside it. B548.2.1. Fish recovers ring from sea. H75.3. Recognition by hair found in a fish which has swallowed it. N66. Wager: fortune made from capital or from working at vocation. Test: money given to workman is stolen or lost; lead for his work given him is lent to fisherman who rewards him with a fish in which is a diamond. N529.2. Pearl found in fish's stomach. X1154.1. Lie: fisherman catches fish with amazing contents.

N211.1.0.1. *Lost articles found in interior of fish through virtue of saint.* Irish myth: Cross.

N211.1.1. *Lost pin found in fish.* Irish myth: Cross.

N211.1.2. *Key (to fetters) found in fish.* Irish myth: *Cross.

N211.1.3. *Lost sword found in fish.* Icelandic: Boberg.

N211.1.4. *Lost trinket found in fish.* Irish myth: Cross.

N211.1.5. *Brooch lost by saint found in fish.* Irish myth: Cross.

N211.2. *Unavailing attempt to get rid of slippers;* they always return. *Chauvin VI 130 No. 283.

N211.3. *Angel helps to find lost pin.* Irish myth: Cross.

V232. Angel as helper.

N212. *Money cannot be kept from where it is destined to go.* Miser told that his hoard is to go to poor man. He hides it in a trunk and throws it into the sea but it drifts to the house of the poor man, who tries in vain to restore it to its owner. *Type 745; *Chauvin II 129 No. 137; *Herbert III 234, 377 No. 61, 447; *Oesterley No. 109, Lithuanian: Balys Index No. 934B*; Russian: Andrejev No. 834B*; West Indies: Flowers 563.

D1602.11. Self returning magic coin.

N212.1. *Husband's magic gift returns to him.* Wife gives husband's magic gift (fruit) to lover, who presents it to a dancing girl, who sells it back to the husband. India: *Thompson-Balys.

N213. *Man fated to be rich.* Buddhist myth: Malalasekera I 828, 931.

N215. *Child borne off by tiger, which is caught by griffin,* which is killed by lioness, which rears child with her whelps. English: Wells 118 (Octavian); India: Thompson-Balys.

B535. Animal nurse. Animal nourishes abandoned child. N251. Man pursued by misfortune.

N221. *Man granted power of winning at cards.* Irish: Beal XXI 329, O'Suilleabhain 90; Spanish: Boggs FFC XC 45, 52 Nos. 313, 345, Espinosa II Nos. 122ff., 168—171, Espinosa Jr. Nos. 70—73, 210.

F679.7. Skillful gambler always wins. Whatever he earns in day he spends immediately. N1. Gamblers.

N222. *First objects picked up bring fortune.* India: Thompson-Balys.

H507.1. Princess offered to man who can defeat her in repartee. N400. Lucky accident.

N223. *Man must have drinking horn; stumble reveals one as he departs on search.* Irish myth: Cross.

N224. *Man finds treasure he refused as gift.* Irish myth: Cross.

N225. *Man robbed and penniless entertained by wealthy widow and enriched.* Boccaccio Decameron II No. 2 (Lee 25); Italian Novella: *Rotunda.

L160. Success of an unpromising hero (heroine).

N226. *Wrecked man saved on coffer of jewels; becomes rich.* Boccaccio Decameron II No. 4 (Lee 30); Italian Novella: *Rotunda.

L160. Success of unpromising hero (heroine).

N227. *Man who is impoverished is given high post by princess in disguise.* Marries her. (Cf. N251.3.) Italian Novella: Rotunda.

K1812.8. Incognito queen (princess). T121. Unequal marriage.

N228. *Leopard tied in bag in water floats to shore and finds a mate.* Grateful to trickster who has tied him up. India: *Thompson-Balys.

N231. *The fourteen lucky daughters.* The husband leaves his wife, who has given birth to fourteen girls, thinking he is persecuted by bad luck because of failure to have a son. On the seashore, the girls find precious stones. The wife, now prosperous, finds her husband among beggars. Lithuanian: Balys Index No. 1668*.

N234. *Boast of poor boy made good by fate:* he boasts to elder brothers he will build a palace on a certain spot; accidentally comes on treasure trove and makes good his boast. India: Thompson-Balys.

N530. Discovery of treasure.

N250. **Persistent bad luck.** *Fb "ulykke" III 973a; Jewish: Neuman; India: *Thompson-Balys.

M341.1. Prophecy: death at certain time. N351. Money unwittingly given away. Unlucky man given a loaf which is filled with gold exchanges it for another loaf. N591. Curse on treasure. Finder or owner to have bad luck.

N250.1. *Bad luck follows man who shoots stork.* *Fb "stork" III 592b.

C92.1.4. Tabu: killing stork as sacred being. C841.1. Tabu: killing stork. C933. Luck in hunting lost for breaking tabu. D1311.11.1. River says, "The time has come but not the man." Man thus induced to drown himself.

N250.2. *Persecution by bad luck.* Wishing to escape it, the luckless couple build themselves a new home. Scarcely do they establish themselves in the new home, when bad luck addresses them from the hearth: "I have already waited for you here three days." Lithuanian: Balys Index No. 735B*.

N250.3. *Persecution by a god so that will of deity can be followed.* India: Thompson-Balys.

N250.4. *Bad luck banished and freed.* The poor man in some way banishes his bad luck and becomes prosperous. Out of envy his rich brother sets it free; it then follows him. Lithuanian: Balys Index No. 735A*; Russian: Andrejev No. 735 I*.

A482.1. Goddess of ill-luck. Z133. Poverty personified.

N251. *Person pursued by misfortune.* (Placidas, Eustacius.) His goods are destroyed, his wife carried off by a ship captain and his children by animals. *Type 938; Herbert III 241; *Oesterley No. 110; *Bolte Zs. f. Vksk. XXVIII 154f.; Alphabet No. 311; *Hibbard 3ff.; Boccaccio Decameron II Nos. 6, 8 (Lee 34, 39); *Loomis White Magic 112; **Gerould PMLA XIX 335ff.; Dickson 100 n. 7. — Irish: *Cross, O'Suilleabhain 42, Beal XXI 315; Italian Novella: *Rotunda; Jewish: *Neuman, bin

Gorion Born Judas[2] I 374; India: *Thompson-Balys; Buddhist myth: Malalasekera II 113, 793; West Indies: Flowers 564.

N215. Child borne off by tiger, which is caught by griffin, which is killed by lioness, who rears child with her whelps. N730. Accidental reunion of families. S451. Outcast wife at last united with husband and children.

N251.1. *Man captured by pirates is maimed, crippled, blinded.* He is patient through it all. Finally he is elected ruler by his dead master's subjects. Italian Novella: Rotunda.

N251.2. *Man who aspires to greater wealth loses all.* When he is about to be rewarded by king the latter dies. Italian Novella: Rotunda.

N251.3. *Man who loses fortune marries widow of his rich master.* (Cf. N227.) Italian Novella: Rotunda.

N251.4. *Travelers pursued by misfortune.* Italian Novella: Rotunda.

N251.5. *Fortune of the lucky wife.* A luckless man becomes successful in all his undertakings when he marries a lucky woman and lives by her luck. Lithuanian: Balys Index No. 737B*.

N251.6. *The luckless son and his envious father.* Seeing a luck-bringing animal at his son's house, the wizard father orders it to be destroyed, but the grandchildren eat of its meat and become fortunate. Lithuanian: Balys Index No. 738*.

Z134. Fortune personified.

N251.7. *Misfortune pursues farmer.* U.S.: *Baughman.

N252. *Messengers announce successive misfortunes.* Spanish Exempla: Keller; Greek: Aeschylus Agamemnon line 860; Jewish: Neuman. Cf. story of Job.

N252.1. *Messengers announce successive misfortunes to warrior as he sets out for war.* Tells of death of father, mother, brother, and sister, but he refuses to turn back. Finnish: Kalevala rune 36.

N253. *Safety in shadow of wall.* After many misfortunes the man is apparently safe. The wall falls on him. *Type 947; *BP III 289f.; Bødker Exempler 277 No. 18; Spanish Exempla: Keller.

N174. Careful builder outside when storm comes is killed: careless builder saved.

N255. *Escape from one misfortune into worse.*

R210. Escapes.

N255.1. *Stag escapes from hunters to be eaten by lion.* Wienert FFC LVI *49, 55 (ET 86, 152), 116, 136 (ST 261, 417); Halm Aesop No. 129, 252.

N255.2. *Ass gets progressively worse masters.* Finally the farmer beats him living and will not spare his hide when he is dead. Wienert FFC LVI 77 (ET 435), 109 (ST 214, 390); Halm Aesop No. 329.

J229.8.1. Weaver prefers master with one hedgehog.

N255.3. *Halcyon builds nest on sea-cliff to escape land hazards.* Tempest blows nest away. Wienert FFC LVI *63 (ET 266), 140 (ST 462); Halm Aesop No. 29.

N255.4. *Fugitive slave takes refuge in mill house, where he must work harder than ever.* Wienert FFC LVI *83 (ET 499), 116 (ST 260); Halm Aesop No. 121.

N255.5. *Daw fleeing from captivity caught in trees by thread around foot.* Starves. Wienert FFC LVI 63 (ET 265), 116 (ST 259); Halm Aesop No. 202.

N255.6. *Old man burns self with gunpowder, and then burns himself worse when he pours hot water over his body.* India: Thompson-Balys.

N256. *Unlucky classes.*

N256.1. *Goldsmith unlucky.* India: Thompson-Balys.

N258. *Train of troubles from lost horseshoe nail.* Master tries to go on in spite of the loss. *BP III 335ff.

Z45. The horseshoe nail.

N261. *Train of troubles from sparrow's vengeance.* A man runs over the dog, friend of the sparrow. Through the sparrow's vengeance the man loses his horse, his property, and finally his life. *Type 248; *BP I 515; Jamaica: Beckwith MAFLS XVII 254 No. 34.

B857. Animal avenges injury. Q211.6. Killing an animal revenged. Q401. Chain of punishments.

N261.1. *Train of troubles for seven brothers for having destroyed bird's nest.* India: Thompson-Balys.

N264. *Whether man begs all day or for an hour he gets only a small basket of grain.* India: *Thompson-Balys.

N265. *Person brings bad luck to others.*

N265.1. *Girl brings ill luck and death to everyone she comes in contact with.* India: Thompson-Balys.

N270. Crime inevitably comes to light. Irish: Beal XXI 336, O'Suilleabhain 119; India: Thompson-Balys.

B131.2. Bird reveals treachery. B133.2. Horse reveals treachery. D1318. Magic object reveals guilt. E231. Return from dead to reveal murder. E613.0.1. Reincarnation of murdered child as bird. H252. Act of truth. Q210. Crimes punished.

N271. *Murder will out.* Missouri French: Carrière; Spanish: Espinosa Jr. Nos. 202—209; Jewish: *Neuman; India: *Thompson-Balys.

D1318.7.0.1. Speaking flesh reveals murder. D1817.0.3. Magic detection of murder. E613.0.1. Reincarnation of murdered child as bird. E632. Reincarnation as musical instrument. The Singing Bone. A musical instrument from the bone of a murdered person, or from a tree growing from the grave, speaks and tells of the crime. F961.1.1. Sun refuses to shine when murder is done. K1686. Tail sticking from ground betrays killing of calf. M348. Murderer warned by God's voice that murder will be avenged. Q211. Murder punished. Q211.0.1. God revenges murder after thirty years. T575.1.1.1. Child in mother's womb reveals murder.

N271.1. *The sun brings all to light.* The murderer repeats as he sees the rays of the sun, the last words of the dying man, thus betraying the crime. *Type 960; *BP II 531; *Hdwb. d. Märchens I 98b, *Zachariae Kleine Schriften 134; *Basset 1001 Contes II 381.

N271.1.1. *Moon brings murder to light.* (Like N271.1.) BP II 532.

N271.2. *Murder revealed by unusual names of boys.* The dying man leaves message to name his sons "O God" and "O king" (or the like). This arouses the king's curiosity and brings the murder to light. BP II 336, 535; Spanish: Boggs FFC XC 116 No. 960.

N271.3. *The Cranes of Ibycus.* Murdered man calls on cranes, the only witnesses of the murder, to avenge him. The cranes follow the murderer and point him out. *BP II 532; *Amalfi Zs. f. Vksk. VI 115ff.; *Zachariae ibid. IX 336; Scala Celi 100b No. 539; Hertz Abhandlungen 334; Köhler-Bolte II 563; Chauvin II 123, VII 146; *Krappe Bulletin Hispanique XXXIX 27. — England: Baughman; Spanish: Espinosa Jr. No. 209; Jewish: *Neuman.

B131.1. Bird reveals murder.

N271.3.1. *Ravens pursue murderer who has killed two children.* England: Baughman.

N271.4. *Murder discovered through knowledge of bird languages.* Birds point out the murder. *Type 781.

Q211.4. Murder of children punished.

N271.5. *Murderer through miracle suspected of theft;* murder thus discovered. Type 761*.

N271.6. *Murder revealed by child.*

E613.0.1. Reincarnation of murdered child as bird. G61.1. Child recognizes relative's flesh when it is served to be eaten.

N271.6.1. *Child's song reveals murder.* Africa (Bantu): Torrend Specimens of Bantu Folk-lore from Northern Rhodesia (New York, 1921) 9ff. No. 1, 14ff. No. 2.

K435. Child's song incriminates thief.

N271.7. *Murder discovered on digging foundations of house.* House burns. Diggers discover body. Italian Novella: *Rotunda.

N271.8. *Murderer traced through victim's ring.* Italian Novella: Rotunda.

N271.9. *Tree follows murderer.* Scotland: Baughman.

N271.10. *Ship will sink if murderer is aboard.* England: Baughman.

N271.11. *Murder will out: murderers quarrel under influence of drink and reveal crime.* Buddhist myth: Malalasekera II 1216.

J2136.5.2. Talkative thief caught.

N275. *Criminal confesses because he thinks himself accused.* *BP II 534, 412; India: *Thompson-Balys.

J1141. Confession obtained by a ruse. N611.1. Criminal accidentally detected: "that is the first."

N275.1. *Criminal confesses because of misunderstood animal cries.* BP II 534, 412; Pauli (ed. Bolte) No. 66.

J1811. Animal cries misunderstood.

N275.2. *Criminal confesses because of misunderstanding of a dialect.* BP II 534, 412.

J1802. Words in a foreign language thought to be insults.

N275.3. *Detection by accidental remark.* Wife misunderstands husband's remark and confesses. Cent Nouvelles Nouvelles No. 32.

N275.4. *Thief imagines that group of people in street are talking and laughing at him; he confesses.* U.S.: Baughman.

N275.5. *Criminal in church mistakes words of service as accusation.* (Cf. Type 1833.)

N275.5.1. *Sheep thief confesses when preacher says, "All we like sheep have gone astray."* U.S.: Baughman.

N277. *Oxen bear dead usurer to gallows to be buried.* They are allowed to go where they will. Pauli (ed. Bolte) No. 197.

B151.1.1. Horses determine road to be taken. B151.1.1.2.1. Ass carries usurer's body to the gallows instead of to the church. He has been denied burial in the church. Q273. Usury punished. X510. Jokes concerning usurers.

N278. *Supernatural voice points out criminal.* Pauli (ed. Bolte) No. 352; *Wesselski Mönchslatein 182 No. 140.

N300—N399. Unlucky accidents.

N300. Unlucky accidents. Norwegian: Solheim Register 21.

D860. Loss of magic object. J2093. Treasure given away or sold for trifle. J2173.4. Deer lost through premature celebration. J2661. Bungling fool has succession of accidents. K675.1. Paramour unwittingly drinks sleeping potion (opiate). K1685. The treasure-finders who murder one another. M341.1. Prophecy: death at certain time. N551.1. Only weak-minded person may unearth a treasure. T35.0.1. Lover late at rendezvous: detained by incessant talker. X1110.1. The unlucky hunt.

N310. Accidental separations. Missouri French: Carrière.

N352. Bird carries off ring which lover has taken from sleeping mistress's finger. He searches for the ring and becomes separated from her.

N311. *Separation of persons caused by looking for water.* *M. Bloomfield in Penzer VII xxiv ff.; India: *Thompson-Balys.

N312. *Separation of twins through being carried off by beast.* Dickson 107.

R13. Abduction by animal. S314. Twins (triplets) exposed.

N313. *Child follows bird and loses its mother.* Tobler Epiphanie der Seele 71.

N314. *Persons fall asleep on rock, which magically shoots upward.* N. A. Indian (California): Gayton and Newman 76.

N315. *Separation by being on different banks of stream.* India: *Thompson-Balys.

N316. *Separation in jungle (forest).* India: *Thompson-Balys.

S143. Abandonment in forest.

N317. *Separation of family by shipwreck.* India: Thompson-Balys; Icelandic: Boberg.

N318. *Accidental separation of lovers.*

N318.1. *Man, thinking it an enemy, flees as sweetheart comes after him in pursuit.* India: Thompson-Balys.

K1573. Trickster sends his master running after the paramour. Though the master does not know of the adultery, the lover is thoroughly frightened. K2137. The priest's guest and the eaten chickens. K2338. Wife to drive away parasite priest.

N318.2. *Princess accidentally elopes with wrong man.* India: Thompson-Balys.

K1371.1. Lover steals bride from wedding with unwelcome suitor. R225. Elopement.

N320. Person unwittingly killed.

A2275.6. Son accidentally kills father, who returns to life as cuckoo and tells people how to sow grain. N733.2. Brother unwittingly kills half brother in fight.

N320.1. *Man unwittingly causes death of daughter.* English romance: Malory III 15.

N321. *Son returning home after long absence unwittingly killed by parents.* (Cf. N338.3.) Type 939*; Lithuanian: Balys Index No. 939*; Livonian: Loorits FFC LXVI No. 939[1].

J21.2. "Do not act when angry": counsel proved wise by experience. Man returns home and sees someone sleeping with his wife. Though he thinks it is a paramour, he restrains himself and finds that it is a newborn son. N730. Accidental reunion of families.

N322. *Eavesdropping person unwittingly killed.* Icelandic: *Boberg. Cf. death of Polonius in Shakespeare's "Hamlet".

N322.1. *Eavesdropping man in disguise as devil killed unwittingly by daughter's lover.* Swiss: Jegerlehner Oberwallis 305 No. 4.

K1663. Spying parent jolted in basket. K1810. Deception by disguise.

N322.2. *Eavesdropping wife hidden in bushes killed unwittingly by husband.* Greek: Fox 72 (Prokris).

N323. *Parricide prophecy unwittingly fulfilled.* *Type 931; *Krappe Balor 13 n. 45; Greek: *Grote I 206; India: Thompson-Balys. See all references to M343 (Parricide prophecy).

N324. *Man unwittingly kills prince.* Exiled. *Boje 120f.

N324.1. *Transformed prince unwittingly killed.* Irish myth: Cross.

N325. *Unwitting murder because of insane illusion.*

K1870. Illusions.

N325.1. *Man kills son thinking that he is cutting a branch.* Greek: Frazer Apollodorus I 329 n. 1.

N325.2. *Women, driven mad, devour their infants' flesh.* Greek: Frazer Apollodorus I 331 n. 4.

G61. Relative's flesh eaten unwittingly.

N325.3. *Mother kills son thinking him a wild beast.* Greek: Frazer Apollodorus I 331 n. 3.

N330. Accidental killing or death. Irish myth: Cross.

D1812.5.1.23. Man killed by accident when ship is pushed into the sea taken as an evil omen. F363.1. Fairies, directed by druid, bring about death of king by causing fish-bone to stick in his throat. F901.1. Extraordinary threefold death. K1600. Deceiver falls into own trap. M341.2.3.1. Prophecy: death by drowning. Forgotten uncovered well to rise and drown household. T71.1. Accidental death fate of woman scorned in love.

N331. *Things accidentally fall and kill person.*

N331.1. *Dagger in wall above bed falls and kills girl.* Has been placed there by her lover. Indonesia: DeVries's list No. 219.

N331.1.1. *Knife accidentally strikes girl's throat and kills her.* India: *Thompson-Balys.

N331.1.2. *Prince's arrow accidentally grazes breast of merchant's wife.* India: Thompson-Balys.

N331.1.3. *Bride lets dagger fall and kill husband.* India: Thompson-Balys.

N331.2. *Bread accidentally dropped from tree on bear's nose kills bear.* Type 2006*.

N331.2.1. *Man hidden in tree so frightened of lioness he drops his sword and kills her.* India: *Thompson-Balys.

K335.1.1. Object falls on robbers from tree. N622. Game killed by jumping on it from above. N696. Fugitive in tree urinates from fright: pursuers think it rain and leave.

N332. *Accidental poisoning.*

K1613. Poisoner poisoned with his own poison.

N332.1. *Man accidentally fed bread which his father has poisoned.* The wicked man puts poison in the bread he gives a beggar. The beggar gives his loaf to the son. Type 837; *DeVries Tijdschrift voor Nederlandsche Taal- en Letterkunde XLVII 63ff.; India: *Thompson-Balys.

K527.1. Poisoned food (drink) fed to animal instead of intended victim. K1685. The treasure-finders who murder one another.

N332.1.1. *Poisoned bath prepared for another accidentally used by hero.* India: Thompson-Balys.

N332.2. *Horse accidentally poisoned instead of master.* An attempt is made to give the hero a poisoned cup. He is on horseback and spurs his horse away to avoid the cup. The poison is spilled and enters the horse's ear and kills him. *Type 851; *BP I 189; Spanish: Espinosa Jr. No. 131.

K527.1. Poisoned food (drink) fed to animal instead of to intended victim.

N332.2.1. *Elephant on rampage accidentally poisoned instead of man. Man claims having killed elephant.* India: Thompson-Balys.

N332.3. *Serpent carried by bird lets poison drop into milk and poisons drinkers.* *Chauvin VIII 60 No. 25; *Krappe Balor 184 n. 12; Spanish Exempla: Keller; Jewish: Neuman, bin Gorion Born Judas III 96; India: Thompson-Balys.

N332.3.1. *Head of killed snake bites and kills king.* India: Thompson-Balys.

N332.3.2. *Snake in jug bites would-be thief.* India: *Thompson-Balys.

N332.4. *Boy accidentally drinks "poison" intended for his stepbrother.* Doctor had substituted sleeping potion for the requested poison. Italian Novella: *Rotunda.

K1613.3. Poisoner's own son takes the beverage intended for stepbrother. K1856. Sleeping potion substituted for poison. K2111 Potiphar's wife. S31. Cruel stepmother. T418. Lustful stepmother.

N332.4.1. *Youth accidentally takes the poison he intended for his father.* Italian Novella: Rotunda.

N332.5. *Woman unwittingly poisons her son.* Mistakes poison for medicine. Italian Novella: Rotunda.

N332.6. *Man eats food which is mysteriously poisoned.* S. A. Indian (Chiriguano): Métraux RMLP XXXIII 177; Jewish: *Neuman; Buddhist myth: Malalasekera II 511.

N332.7. *Hidden fruit accidentally poisoned by snake.* India: Thompson-Balys.

N333. *Aiming at fly has fatal results.*

K946. Bird flies on head of dupe's child. Dupe strikes at bird and kills child.

N333.1. *Person killed by hitting fly on his face.* Italian Novella: Rotunda; India: *Thompson-Balys; Japanese: Ikeda; Indonesia: DeVries's list No. 285. Cf. Type 1586.

J1193.1. Killing the fly on the judge's nose. The judge has told the boy that he should kill a fly wherever he sees one. J1833. Numskull thinks the bishop's snoring is his death rattle. He strikes at a fly on the bishop's nose.

N333.1.1. *To give child a slap to stop its crying, numskull kills it.* India: *Thompson-Balys.

J1911. Nature of a baby misunderstood.

N333.2. *Man accidentally killed by bear trying to chase away flies.* *Chauvin II 118 Nos. 99, 100; India: Thompson-Balys.

N334. *Accidental fatal ending of game or joke.*

J1919.5.1. Ignorant bride castrates groom when jokingly told to do so.

N334.1. *Children play hog-killing: one killed.* *Type 2401; *BP I 202; Wesselski Archiv Orientálni II 431; England, U.S.: Baughman.

K850. Fatal deceptive game.

N334.2. *Hanging in game or jest accidentally proves fatal.* Wesselski Theorie 18; Fb "hænge" I 731b; Danish: Christensen DF XLVII 200 No. 36; Icelandic: Boberg; Lithuanian: Balys Index No. 3309, Legends Nos. 605—609; Estonian: Aarne FFC XXV 122 Nos. 40, 41.

J2130. Foolish disregard of personal danger. K852. Deceptive game: hanging each other. Dupe really hanged.

N334.3. *Practical joker asks doctor to castrate him.* Doctor insists on the operation. Italian Novella: *Rotunda.

N335. *Unexpected death at hands of an animal.*

N335.1. *Bird hunter killed by adder just as he is shooting bird.* Wienert FFC LVI 65 (ET 295), 207 (ST 197); Halm Aesop No. 171; India: Thompson-Balys.

N335.2. *Blood bath causes woman to be carried off by bird.* A pregnant woman demands a bath of blood: husband substitutes a bath of red dye. A Garuda bird attracted by the dye carries her off. Penzer I 97; Dunlop-Liebrecht 135.

B56. Garuda-bird. Lower part man, upper part bird. T571. Unreasonable demands of pregnant women.

N335.2.1. *Sick queen lying under red satin carried off by bird who thinks it is red meat.* India: Thompson-Balys.

N335.3. *Death by rebounding bow.* Ants gnaw a bowstring, so that the bow rebounds and cuts off head of man who is leaning on it. *Bloomfield in Penzer VII xx ff.

J514.2. Wolf tries to eat bowstring.

N335.4. *Accidental death from flying splinter of bone.* Bone being gnawed by animal lets splinter fly and kills young animals. Africa (Larusa): Fokken "Erzählungen und Märchen der Larusa" ZsKS VII 82ff. No. 1, (Wachaga): Gutmann 87ff. No. 44, (Masai): Fuchs Sagen, Mythen und Sitten der Masai (Jena, 1910) 50ff., (Uganda): Rowling The Tales of Sir Apolo: Uganda Folklore and Proverbs (London, n.d.) 47ff., (Congo): Stanley My Dark Companions and their Strange Stories (New York, 1906) 161ff., Casati Ten Years in Equatoria and the Return with Emin Pasha (New York, 1891) II 45f.

N335.5. *Hound strikes unique vulnerable spot.* Irish myth: Cross.
Z310. Unique vulnerability.

N335.6. *Series of accidental animal killings.*
X1110. The wonderful hunt.

N335.6.1. *Attacking animal is killed by another in ambush.* India: Thompson-Balys.

N335.7. *Tortoise lands on elephant's back so that elephant's back is broken.* India: Thompson-Balys.

N336. *Accidental death through dream.* Man dodging blow in dream hits his head against wall and kills himself. Alphabet No. 285.
F1068. Realistic dream.

N337. *Accidental death through misdirected weapon.* Irish myth: *Cross; Greek: Frazer Apollodorus II 63 n. 2; Buddhist myth: Malalasekera II 715; Africa (Fang): Tessman 135, (Congo): Grenfell 820.
Q582.7. Boy who threw stones at clerics killed by thrown stone.

N337.1. *Blind poet unintentionally kills friend.* Irish myth: *Cross.

N337.2. *Hero, while measuring wild boar, accidentally wounded mortally by bristle.* Irish myth: *Cross.

N337.3. *Axe thrown at one animal misses but kills another.* India: Thompson-Balys.

N338. *Death as result of mistaken identity: wrong person killed.* Irish myth: *Cross.
K1611. Substituted caps cause ogre to kill his own children. K1840. Deception by substitution.

N338.1. *Saint changes places with charioteer; latter is killed.* Irish myth: Cross.
N650. Life saved by accident.

N338.2. *Fool (person) disguised as (supposed) king killed.* Irish myth: *Cross.
K1810. Deception by disguise.

N338.3. *Son killed because mistaken for someone else.* (Cf. N321.) Icelandic: Boberg; Italian Novella: Rotunda (N366); Greek: Grote I 242; Jewish: Neuman; Philippine (Tinguian): Cole 98.
N731.2. Father-son combat. Neither knows who other is.

N338.3.1. *Father orders unrecognized son thrown into sea.* Hawaii: Beckwith Myth 480.

N339. *Accidental death—miscellaneous.*

N339.1. *Man falls into jar of honey and is drowned.* Chases a mouse. Greek: Frazer Apollodorus I 310 n. 2.

N339.2. *Flies caught in honey.* Death from greed. Wienert FFC LVI 61 (ET 242), 146 (ST 512); Halm Aesop No. 293.

N339.3. *Foxes crowd into house and are suffocated.* Eskimo (Koryak): *Jochelson JE VI 363.

N339.4. *Groom killed by lightning on wedding night.* Italian Novella: Rotunda.
T80. Tragic love.

N339.5. *Uxorious king is burned to death while taking an alcohol bath.* Italian Novella: Rotunda.

Q550. Miraculous punishments.

N339.6. *Man forgets to wear magic gown and is killed.* Irish myth: *Cross.

D1344.8. Saint's cowl renders invulnerable.

N339.7. *Army drowned by unnoticed incoming tide.* Irish myth: *Cross.

N339.8. *Accidental death from fall on own weapon* (shield). Irish myth: *Cross; Icelandic: Boberg.

N339.8.1. *Accidental death of father from fall into the fire when taking down weapons for his son.* Icelandic: Boberg.

N339.9. *Girl abducted by fairy left on shore, where she is accidentally drowned.* Irish myth: *Cross.

F324. Girl abducted by fairy.

N339.10. *Youth gazing at own image reflected in water falls and drowns.* Irish myth: Cross.

N339.11. *Girl lets down her sari for hero to climb up by but, when he is halfway up, sari breaks and he is killed.* India: Thompson-Balys.

N339.12. *Prefect, cursed by bishop, dies of fish-bone stuck in his throat.* Irish myth: Cross.

N339.13. *Accidental death by striking head against lintel of door.* Irish myth: Cross.

N339.14. *Wife throwing husband's corpse into river (according to custom) is caught by corpse's arm and drowned.* India: Thompson-Balys.

N384.2. Death in the graveyard: person's clothing is caught; he thinks something awful is holding him and dies of fright.

N339.15. *Thief crushed to death by fallen fragments of wall he has bored.* India: *Thompson-Balys.

Q582. Fitting death as punishment.

N339.16. *King mortally wounded on killed enemy's tooth.* Icelandic: Boberg.

N339.17. *Bottle wherein jinn is imprisoned inadvertently opened and jinn escapes to kill his captor.* India: Thompson-Balys.

D2177.1. Demon enclosed in bottle. R181. Demon enclosed in bottle released.

N340. Hasty killing or condemnation (mistake).

B331.1. Faithful falcon killed through misunderstanding. F1041.16.9. Chief beheads sentinel who does not recognize him. J21.2. "Do not act when angry": counsel proved wise by experience. J571. Avoid hasty judgment. K2110.1. Calumniated wife. K2152. Unresponsive corpse. M175. Pledge to say but a single phrase. In carrying out this agreement the men innocently confess a crime. S411. Misunderstood wife banished by husband. S461. Tale bearer unjustly drowned for lack of proof of accusation.

N340.1. *Suicide in remorse over hasty condemnation.* Irish myth: Cross.

N340.2. *King hastily has 7,000 people put to death for stoning his judges to death.* Spanish Exempla: Keller.

N340.3. *Woman wrongly condemned for drunkeness when seen to take one drink.* Spanish Exempla: Keller.

N341. *Misunderstood message causes messenger to be killed (accused).* BP II 366.

N342. *Hasty condemnation of man who accidentally becomes suspected of crime.* India: Thompson-Balys.

N342.1. *Faithful servant guarding master's wife from danger falsely condemned for betraying his master.* *Type 516; *BP I 42ff.; *Rösch FFC LXXVII 129; Italian: Basile Pentamerone IV No. 9; India: *Thompson-Balys; Korean: Zong in-Sob 155ff. No. 68.

R169.4.1. Rescue of bride from mysterious perils by hidden faithful servant. T175. Magic perils threaten bridal couple.

N342.1.1. *Faithful son guarding his father from monster falsely accused by stepmother.* India: Thompson-Balys.

K2111. Potiphar's wife.

N342.2. *Stumbling over bloody corpse brings accusation of murder.* Man gets blood on himself. *Chauvin V 136 No. 64.

K2155.1. Blood smeared on innocent person brings accusation of murder.

N342.3. *Jealous and overhasty man kills his rescuing twin brother.* *Type 303; Italian: Basile Pentamerone I No. 7; India: Thompson-Balys.

N342.4. *False accusation overheard causes hasty killing.* Irish myth: Cross.

N342.5. *Angry brother kills husband, thinking latter had killed wife (sister) and baby.* Heptameron No. 23.

N342.6. *Woman mistakenly accused of cannibalism.* She is seen biting off finger of corpse to get its ring. India: *Thompson-Balys.

N343. *Lover kills self believing his mistress dead.* She has been frightened away by a lion. (Pyramus and Thisbe.) Köhler-Bolte I 4; Irish myth: *Cross; Italian Novella: Rotunda; Greek: Fox 201, **G. Hart Ursprung und Verbreitung der Pyramus und Thisbe-Sage (1889); *C. de Boer Pyramus et Thisbé (Amsterdam, 1911).

K1087.1. Message falsified to bring about death of lovers. T37.1. Despairing lover at lady's tomb takes poison. T80. Tragic love.

N343.1. *Mistress kills self, believing her lover dead.* Irish myth: *Cross; Italian Novella: Rotunda; India: *Thompson-Balys.

N343.2.1. *Wife dies, believing husband dead.* Irish myth: Cross.

N343.3. *Woman feigns death to meet exiled lover.* It leads to his death. Lover hears of her supposed death, returns and submits to execution. Italian Novella: Rotunda.

K1538. Death feigned to meet paramour.

N343.4. *Lover commits suicide on finding beloved dead.* Heptameron No. 70.

N344. *Father kills self believing that son is dead.* The son forgets to spread white sails, the prearranged signal of his safety. (Told also of lovers.) *Schoepperle II 437f.; Greek: Frazer Apollodorus II 137 n. 4.

Z140.1. Color of flag (sails) on ship to indicate good or bad news.

N344.1. *Wrong sign put out leads to boys' leaving home.* They are to be informed by a sign if a sister is born. *Type 451; BP I 70ff.; Italian: Basile Pentamerone IV No. 8.

T595. Sign hung out informing brothers whether mother has borne boy or girl.

N344.2. *Father causes death of innocent son, believing him guilty of adultery with father's wife.* Irish myth: *Cross; Icelandic: Boberg.

N345. *The falcon of Sir Federigo.* An impoverished suitor has only a falcon to catch birds with. His lady's sick son wants the falcon and she goes to ask for it. The suitor serves dinner for her—his falcon. When she makes her request it is too late. *Bédier Fabliaux 153f.; Boccaccio Decameron V No. 9 (*Lee 170); Italian Novella: *Rotunda.

J1826. The falcon not as good as represented.

N346. *Pigeon hastily kills his mate for stealing wheat.* It has merely dried out and no longer fills the nest. When the dampness later swells the wheat, he sees his mistake and kills himself in remorse. Chauvin II 104 No. 66; Bødker Exempler 302 No. 69; Spanish Exempla: Keller; India: Thompson-Balys.

N347. *Innocent man accidentally suspected of crime.* (Cf. N342.2.) India: *Thompson-Balys.

N347.1. *Clerk who enters tavern arrested with others for murder.* Scala Celi 59a No. 326; Chauvin IX 19; Spanish Exempla: Keller; Icelandic: Boberg.

K2150. Innocent made to appear guilty. V465. Clerical vices.

N347.2. *Saint who entered house of ill fame to reform inmates accused of going with evil intent.* Spanish Exempla: Keller.

N347.3. *Boy is hanged for cattle theft; the strayed cattle are discovered later.* U.S.: Baughman.

N347.4. *Man having purchased stolen ornament unwittingly presents it to owner as gift;* is thrown into jail as thief. India: Thompson-Balys.

N347.5. *Poor man presented rich robe by emperor is locked up as a thief.* India: Thompson-Balys.

N347.6. *Man falsely accused commits suicide.* India: Thompson-Balys.

N347.7. *Greedy disciple decides to remain in city despite learned teacher's warning* and is condemned to take the place of a thief. India: Thompson-Balys.

N348. *Jealous husband kills innocent wife.* Suspicions aroused when villain leaves his handkerchief in her room. (Othello.) Italian Novella: Rotunda.

N349. *Hasty killing or condemnation—miscellaneous.* Irish myth: Cross.

N349.1. *Warriors erroneously slay allies in night battle.* Irish myth: *Cross.

N349.2. *Father kills his son in battle rage.* Icelandic: Boberg.

J675.1. Son slays father in order not to be slain himself. N731.2. Father-son combat. Neither knows who the other is.

N349.3. *King, seeing eldest son leaving room, decides that he is a rakshasa.* India: Thompson-Balys.

N350. Accidental loss of property.

N351. *Money (treasure) unwittingly given away.* Unlucky man given a loaf which is filled with gold exchanges it for another loaf. *Type 841; *Pauli (ed. Bolte) Nos. 326, 327; Spanish: Espinosa Jr. No. 185; Italian Novella: Rotunda; Icelandic: Boberg; India: *Thompson-Balys; Chinese: Graham; Japanese: Ikeda; N. A. Indian (Pochulata): Boas JAFL XXV 223.

L410. Proud ruler (deity) humbled. N250. Persistent bad luck.

N351.1. *Boy's servant takes pearl to his wife instead of to merchant;* she throws it away. India: Thompson-Balys.

N351.2. *Beggar accidentally overlooks money put into his way.* India: *Thompson-Balys.

N352. *Bird carries off ring which lover has taken from sleeping mistress's finger.* He searches for the ring and becomes separated from her. *Penzer IV 192 n. 1; *von der Hagen I cxxxiii; *Köhler-Bolte II 351; Italian Novella: Rotunda; India: Thompson-Balys.

N310. Accidental separations. B522.2. Kite steals jewels and thus saves condemned man. Innocent man in possession of stolen jewels, is about to be apprehended. Kite carries off the jewels and saves him.

N352.1. *Bird carries off jeweled veil with which girl had covered sleeping lover's face.* Lover pursues bird and becomes separated from the girl. Italian Novella: Rotunda.

N352.2. *Jewel (garment) carried off by bird from bather.* Clothes have been left on bank of stream. India: *Thompson-Balys.

D865. Magic jewel carried off by bird. N527. Treasure (money) carried by bird to nest.

N352.3. *Serpent steals jewels: person falsely accused of theft.* (Cf. N347.) India: Thompson-Balys.

N360. Man unwittingly commits crime. U.S.: Baughman.

N361. *Sacred animal unwittingly killed.*

N361.1. *Brahmin unwittingly kills calf.* India: Thompson-Balys.

C92.1.2. Tabu: killing sacred calf. Q211.6. Killing an animal revenged.

N362. *King (prince) unwittingly killed.* Africa (Fulah): Frobenius Atlantis VI 182ff. No. 4.

N365. *Incest unwittingly committed.*

N681.3. Incest accidentally averted. N730. Accidental reunion of families. T410. Incest.

N365.1. *Boy unwittingly commits incest with his mother.* See all references to M344. Heptameron No. 30; Spanish: Boggs FFC XC 117 No. 983; Italian Novella: *Rotunda; Minehassa (Celebes): Dixon 158.

M344. Mother-incest prophecy. N383.3. Mother dies of fright when she learns that she was about to commit incest with her son. N681.3.1. Man about to consummate marriage with own mother when he is identified by plaque. T412. Mother-son incest.

N365.1.1. *Man unwittingly falls in love with his own mother.* India: *Thompson-Balys.

N365.2. *Unwitting father-daughter incest.* Irish myth: *Cross; Icelandic: *Boberg; Greek: Fox 198 (Myrrha); Tuamotu: Stimson MS (z-G. 13/116).

T411. Father-daughter incest.

N365.2.1. *Father unwittingly falls in love with daughter.* India: *Thompson-Balys.

N365.3. *Unwitting brother-sister incest.* Irish myth: *Cross; Welsh: MacCulloch Celtic 201; Italian Novella: *Rotunda; India: Thompson-Balys; Tuamotu: Stimson MS (T-G. 3/59); Hawaii: Beckwith Myth 516.

H310.2. Brother unwittingly qualifies as bridegroom of sister in test. T415. Brother-sister incest. T471.1. Man unwittingly ravishes his own sister.

N365.3.1. *Brother and sister unwittingly in love with each other.* India: *Thompson-Balys.

N365.3.2. *Boy says, "Whoever eats this mushroom is my wife."* His own sister eats it and he runs away. India: *Thompson-Balys.

N365.4. *Man unwittingly lies with mother-in-law.* Italian Novella: Rotunda.

N367. *Daughter unwittingly turns her own parents out of doors.* India: Thompson-Balys.

N380. Other unlucky accidents.

N381. *Drop of honey causes chain of accidents.* Hunter drops honey in a grocery; weasel eats honey; cat chases weasel; dog chases cat; grocer kills dog: all the cause of a bloody feud between villages. *Taylor JAFL XLVI 87 No. 2036; BP II 104 n. 2; *Wesselski Hessische Blätter f. Vksk XXXII 21; Chauvin VIII 41 No. 9; Spanish Exempla: Keller.

Z20. Cumulative tales.

N381.1. *Ant pinching frog causes chain of accidents.* India: *Thompson-Balys.

N382. *Fugitive slave takes wrong road and is caught.* Wienert FFC LVI 85 (ET 518), 116 (ST 264).

N383. *Man falls dead from sudden realization.*

F1041. Extraordinary physical reactions of persons. K2320. Deception by frightening.

N383.1. *Man falls dead when he realizes that he has been riding over frozen sea.* *Bolte Zs. f. Vksk. XVIII 91.

N383.2. *Man falls dead when he realizes that he has eaten bread from flour used for abscess plaster.* Chauvin VIII 38 No. 6; Spanish Exempla: Keller.

N383.3. *Mother dies of fright when she learns that she was about to commit incest with her son.* He has disguised himself to test her chastity. *Krappe Balor 181ff.; Alphabet No. 710 (Secundus).

M334. Mother-incest prophecy. N365.1. Boy unwittingly commits incest with his mother. T312. Saint's daughter dies when wooed. T412. Mother-son incest.

N384. *Death from fright.* (Cf. N383.3.) Italian Novella: Rotunda; Eskimo

(Greenland): Rink 228, 439, 452, Rasmussen I 148, II 334, III 61, 97, Holm 26.

F1041.1. Death from broken heart. F1041.1.5. Death from excessive joy. F1041.1.11. Death from fear. J955.4. Old simpleton resolves to become a Senator. Dies of fright when told he is wanted as an archer. J2600. Cowardly fool. K2320. Deception by frightening. N334. Death from being frightened in game or joke. T81. Death from love.

N384.0.1. *Madness from fright.* U.S.: *Baughman.

N384.0.1.1. *The cadaver arm.* Medical students (or student nurses or hospital employees) play trick on one of their number by suspending a cadaver arm or leg from the light cord in the person's room (sometimes the object is placed in the person's bed). Some circumstance keeps them from being on hand to observe the person's reaction; the next day they remember the joke and go to the victim's room to investigate. They have to break down the door. They find the victim sitting on the bed—her hair is snow white—and she is gnawing on the cadaver arm. U.S.: *Baughman.

N384.1. *Mouse frightens man to death.* Type 167*.

J2614. Fools frightened by stirring of an animal. K2320. Deception by frightening.

N384.2. *Death in the graveyard; person's clothing is caught;* the person thinks something awful is holding him; he dies of fright. Ireland, England, U.S.: Baughman.

H1416. Test: spending night by grave. J2625. Coward is frightened when clothing catches on thistle. N339.14. Wife throwing husband's corpse into river (according to custom) is caught by corpse's arm and drowned.

N384.3. *Wicked stepmother falls into the fire because of fright.* (Cf. M431.6.) Icelandic: Boberg.

N384.4. *Fraternity initiate dies of fright.* U.S.: *Baughman.

N384.5. *Queen dies from fright because of evil prophecy.* Icelandic: Boberg.

N384.6. *Sham magician causes simpleton's death.* Is frightened to death by the impersonation of demons. Italian Novella: Rotunda.

N384.7. *Sham execution proves fatal.* Jester condemned to die on block. Pail of water used instead of axe. He dies. Italian Novella: *Rotunda.

N384.8. *Priest frightens boy by tying girl's corpse to bell-rope.* In revenge the boy puts the body in the priest's bed. Priest flees. Dies from injuries. Italian Novella: Rotunda.

K2151. The corpse handed around.

N384.9. *Lover frightens mistress as a joke.* She dies from the shock. Italian Novella: Rotunda.

N384.10. *Man playing ghost killed.* Meaning to frighten son, father plays devil or a ghost. Son kills him. Lithuanian: Balys Index No. 3443, Legends Nos. 861ff.

N384.11. *Joker playing dead killed.* Lithuanian: Balys Index No. 3443A, Legends Nos. 864f.

N384.12. *Woman playing dead to spy on husband killed.* Lithuanian: Balys Legends No. 866.

H1556.1. Test of fidelity by feigning death.

N384.13. *Brothers fall dead at sight of long lost brother whom they sold into captivity.* (Cf. N733.) Jewish: *Neuman.

N385. *Unintentional injuries bring unfortunate consequences.* (Sometimes the injuries are mere breeches of tabu.) *Penzer II 147, VII 92 n. 1.

N385.1. *Person has successive misfortunes while making plans because he forgets to say, "If God wills."* (Cf. G224.1, J1217.1.) Irish myth: *Cross; Lithuanian: Balys Index No. 848*.

N386. *Lover's wound breaks while he is in bed with mistress.* He bleeds to death (or is discovered because of the blood). Schoepperle I 222; von der Hagen I cxxvii; Italian Novella: Rotunda.

N386.1. *Lover's spur catches in sheet when he tries to escape.* Uncovers mistress. Heptameron No. 62.

N386.2. *Man pinned in bed by weapon caught in quilt.* Irish myth: Cross.

N387. *Feud starts over trifle.*

N387.1. *Quarrel over dog starts the Guelph-Ghibelline feud.* Italian Novella: Rotunda.

N388. *Blind men accidentally hurt each other.* (Trying to kill pig, or the like.) Herbert III 71.

K1081. Blind men duped into fighting. N333. Aiming at fly has fatal results. U170. Behavior of the blind.

N391. *Lover who is detained away beyond stipulated time returns to find fiancée married.* Italian Novella: *Rotunda.

N681. Husband (lover) arrives home just as wife (mistress) is to marry another. T86. Lovers buried in same grave.

N391.0.1. *Hospitality enforced on hero keeps him overlong from home;* meantime wife abducted. Chinese: Graham.

N391.1. *Mistress expecting lover accidentally exchanges places with her maidservant.* Italian Novella: Rotunda (also K1856).

K1223. Mistress deceives lover with a substitute. K1843. Wife deceives husband with substituted bedmate.

N392. *Robber attempting to steal cow at night seizes thieving tiger.* Great fight in stable. India: *Thompson-Balys.

J2132.4. Numskull rides on tiger's back. Dragged to his death (or is injured). J2172.2.1. Wolf almost locked up in the stable by the shepherd. N691.1. Numskull's outcry overawes tiger who is carrying him on his back. Tiger thinks that words are the name of the "demon" riding him.

N392.1. *Escaping prisoner falls by accident onto tiger's back and is carried away.* Korean: Zong in-Sob 175 No. 75.

N392.2. *Woman errs on to the road-of-the-tiger: carried off.* S. A. Indian (Chiriguano): Métraux RMLP XXXIII 161.

N394. *Delay in bringing pardon allows deserved execution.* Messenger, ignorant of contents of message, stops to view culprit's execution. Italian Novella: Rotunda.

N394.1. *Sign of prisoner's reprieve changed by wind.* A flag to be flown in certain way, but wind catches it just at the wrong moment so that prisoner is executed. Korean: Zong in-Sob 61 No. 34.

N395. *Man blinded trying to heal girl.* Powders blow into his one good eye. Italian Novella: *Rotunda.

N396. *The sleeping guard.* Watchman falls asleep as enemy approaches. Irish myth: Cross.

N397. *Accidental self-injury.* Irish myth: Cross.

S160.1. Self-mutilation.

N398. *Mistake in interpreting prophecy (oracle) brings misfortune.* India: Thompson-Balys.

M305. Ambiguous oracle.

N399. *Additional unlucky accidents.*

N399.1. *Shipwrecked man lands on deadly enemy's territory and is attacked.* Icelandic: Boberg.

N399.2. *Man's inordinate laughter brings unfortunate results.* India: Thompson-Balys.

N399.3. *Man discovers he is married to wer-tiger.* India: Thompson-Balys.

D112.2. Transformation of man to tiger. T110. Unusual marriage.

N400—N699. LUCKY ACCIDENTS

N400. Lucky accident.

D1812.2.3. Power of prophecy from accidental drinking of water from magic fountain. H507.1.0.1. Princess defeated in repartee by means of objects accidentally picked up. H565. Riddle propounded from chance experience. K1951.2. Runaway cavalry hero. K1955.3. Sham physician predicts the sex of the unborn child. "From one side it looks like a boy, from the other a girl." The woman bears twins and the husband pays the doctor. N200. The good gifts of fortune. N222. First objects picked up bring fortune.

N410—N439. Lucky business ventures.

N410. Lucky business venture.

J2415.1. The two presents to the king: the beet and the horse. A farmer takes an extraordinary beet as present to the king and receives a large reward.

N411. *Object unknown in a country sold for a fortune.*

N411.1. *Whittington's cat.* A cat in a mouse-infested land without cats sold for a fortune. *Types 1650, 1651; *BP II 69ff.; *Fb "kat" II 108, IV 255b, "mus" II 632a; *Brueyre RTP III 36; Italian Novella: Rotunda.

B582.1.1. Animal wins wife for his master (Puss in Boots). F708.1. Country without cats. J2101. Getting rid of the cat. In a land in which cats are not known, one is bought at a great price.

N411.1.1. *Cat as sole inheritance.* *Types 1650, 1651, 545AB; *BP I 325, II 69ff., III 487; Missouri French: Carrière; Italian: Basile Pentamerone II No. 4.

B312.3. Helpful animal bequeathed to hero.

N411.2. *Sickle sold for fortune in land without sickles.* *Types 1650, 1202; *BP II 69ff., 72 n. 1.

J1865. Sickle punished by drowning. In a land where the sickle is not known the new sickle cuts off the head of a man. It is drowned. J2196.

Grain shot down with guns. People unacquainted with the sickle. J2514. Sickle bought at great cost given back. In a land where the sickle is not known the new sickle cuts off the head of a man and is thereupon given back to the original owner.

N411.2.1. *Sickle as only inheritance.* *Type 1650; *BP II 69ff.

N411.3. *Fortune from informing foreign king of use of saddle, bridle, and stirrups.* *Chauvin VII 19 No. 373D n. 2.

N411.4. *Salt in saltless land sold for fortune.* Russian: Andrejev No. 1651*; India: Thompson-Balys.

N411.5. *Sandalwood merchant sells his product at high price in land lacking sandalwood.* Spanish Exempla: Keller.

N412. *Fortune from trifling sum sent abroad with merchant.* *Chauvin VI 65 No. 233 n. 1.

N415. *King's example makes merchant wealthy.* The king buys shoes for a high price and then has all his dinner guests buy them. Estonian: Aarne FFC XXV 137 No. 100.

N421. *Lucky bargain.* *Types 571, 1415; Missouri French: Carrière.

D837. Magic object acquired through foolish bargain. J2080. Foolish bargain. K251.1. The eaten grain and the cock as damages. M200. Bargains and promises. N11. Wager on wife's complacency. Though the man has foolishly bargained everything away, she praises him and he wins the wager.

N421.1. *Progressive lucky bargains.* (Opposite of J2081.) *Type 1415; BP II 199ff.; India: *Thompson-Balys; Africa: Werner African 219f.; American Negro (Georgia): Harris Friends 176 No. 24.

Z41.4.3. Lending and repaying: progressively worse (or better) bargain.

N425. *Abducted princess wishes that she were with rejected suitor; discovers that she is.* Icelandic: Boberg.

N455.4. King overhears girl's boast as to what she should do as queen. Marries her.

N426. *Poor man carries unwittingly in his water jar a large scorpion which brings him fortune.* India: Thompson-Balys.

N440—N499. Valuable secrets learned.

N440. Valuable secrets learned. Missouri French: Carrière.

A33.3.1. Bee as God's spy overhears devil's secret. C420. Tabu: uttering secrets. D1316.5. Magic speaking reed (tree) betrays secret. D1610.34. Fiddle made from wood to which secret has been confided reveals it. E451.1.1. Corpse cannot be laid until after he has confided the secret of magic charms. G275.5. Witch forced to divulge her secret powers. H13. Recognition by overheard conversation with animals or objects. H1243. Riches the reward of questions solved on quests. H1292. Answers found in otherworld to questions propounded on the way. J21.22. Do not tell a secret to a woman. J155.2. King has amours with great men's wives so as to learn secrets from them. J229.5. Choice between bad master, bad official, or bad neighbor. J1582. Base money in the offering. K1165. Secret learned by intoxicating dupe. K2213.4. Betrayal of husband's secret by his wife. M151.1. Vow not to eat before learning secret. T252.3. Wife threatens husband with death if he will not tell secret.

N450. Secrets overheard. *Chauvin V 13, 293, VIII 61 No. 26; French Canadian: Barbeau JAFL XXIX 23; India: Thompson-Balys.

N451. *Secrets overheard from animal (demon) conversation.* *Types 516, 517, 670, 673; BP I 42ff., 131f.; **Aarne FFC XV; **Rösch FFC LXXVII 102, 114; Penzer I 48, III 60; Icelandic: Corpus Poeticum Boreale I 131, 144, Boberg; Italian Novella: Rotunda,-Basile Pentamerone IV No. 9; Greek: Grote I 105; Jewish: Neuman; India: *Thompson-Balys; Buddhist myth: Malalasekera II 1138; Chinese: Graham; Japanese: Ikeda; Korean: Zong in-Sob 150, 155.

B211. Animal uses human speech. B216. Knowledge of animal languages. B235. Secrets discussed in animal meeting. N471. Foolish attempt of second man to overhear secrets (from animals, demons, etc.). N537. Speaking bird tells where treasure is buried.

N451.1. *Secrets of animals (demons) accidentally overheard from tree (bridge) hiding place.* *Type 613; BP II 468ff., *481; **Christiansen FFC XXIV 60ff.; *Fb "bjørn" IV 43a, "ravn" III 22b, "bro", IV 62n; Lithuanian: Balys Index No. 3296, Legends No. 527; French Canadian: Barbeau JAFL XXIX 16, 23; Missouri French: Carrière; India: *Thompson-Balys.

G661.1. Ogre's secret overheard from tree. H963. Tasks performed by means of secrets overheard from tree.

N452. *Secret remedy overheard in conversation of animals (witches).* *Types 432, 613, 613*; BP II 261ff.; **Christiansen FFC XXIV 77, 81, 123; Lithuanian: Balys Legends No. 527; Italian: Basile Pentamerone II No. 2; India: *Thompson-Balys, Panchatantra III 11 (tr. Ryder) 346; Chinese: Graham; Japanese: Ikeda; Korean: Zong in-Sob 150; Buriat: Holmberg Siberian 427; S. A. Indian (Chincha): Alexander Lat. Am. 230.

B513. Remedy learned from overhearing animal meeting. D1244. Magic salve (ointment). H963. Tasks performed by means of secrets overheard from tree.

N452.1. *Remedy for lack of water in certain place overheard in conversation of animals (demons).* *Type 613; **Christiansen FFC XXIV 86ff.; Lithuanian: Balys Legends No. 527.

N452.1.1. *Reason for withering of tree overheard in conversation of animals (demons).* Type *613; **Christiansen FFC XXV 89ff.

H1292.2. Question (propounded on quest): Why does not a certain tree flourish?

N452.2. *Secret remedy revealed by departing animal.* House spirit (or bird) leaves saying, "If you knew what valerian is good for, the people would not die so fast." **A. Martin "Die Pestage vom Vogel, der Bimbanelle und Baldrian als Heilmittel verkundet im Vogelsberg" Volk. u. Scholle IX No. 1.

N537. Speaking bird tells where treasure is buried.

N453. *Man transformed as ant, learns secret of freeing princess.* French Canadian: Sister Marie Ursule.

N454. *Conversation of objects overheard.*

D1610. Magic speaking objects.

N454.1. *Speaking bed-legs overheard.* India: *Thompson-Balys.

N617. Impostor accidentally gives king talking bed which reveals his identity.

N454.2. *King overhears conversation of lamps.* India: *Thompson-Balys.

N455. *Overheard (human) conversation.* *Dickson 29 n. 1; Missouri French: Carrière; Jewish: Neuman; Japanese: Ikeda.

N455.1. *Overheard boast about hidden money brings about robbery.* Type 1577*; India: *Thompson-Balys.

J2356. Fool's talking causes himself and companions to be robbed. K1081.5. Trickster steals blind man's money.

N455.2. *Robbers' plans overheard: owner warned.* Swiss: Jegerlehner

Oberwallis 325 No. 8; Missouri French: Carrière; India: *Thompson-Balys.

K420. Thief loses goods or is detected.

N455.2.1. *Robbers' secret overheard and later used in court against them.* Spanish Exempla: Keller.

N455.3. *Secret formula for opening treasure mountain overheard from robbers* (Open Sesame). *Type 676; *BP III 137ff.; Missouri French: Carrière; Spanish: Espinosa Jr. No. 144; India: Thompson-Balys; Hawaii: Beckwith Myth 339.

D1552.2. Mountain opens to magic formula. F721.4. Underground treasure chambers. K439.10. Hidden person sees robbers concealing their treasure and takes it. N471. Foolish attempt of second man to overhear secrets (from animals, demons, etc.). He is punished. N512. Treasure in underground chamber (cavern).

N455.4. *King overhears girl's boast as to what she should do as queen.* Marries her. *Type 707; BP II 380ff., *393; India: *Thompson-Balys; N. A. Indian: Thompson CColl II 388.

H71.1. Star on forehead as sign of royalty. H71.7. Child born with chain around neck: sign of royalty. N201. Wish for exalted husband realized. N425. Abducted princess wishes that she were with rejected suitor: discovers that she is. N711. King (prince) accidentally finds maiden and marries her. T30. Lovers' meeting.

N455.5. *Secret remedies learned from green-clad woman.* Italian: Basile Pentamerone IV No. 2.

F233.1. Green fairy.

N455.6. *Husband learns of wife's fidelity through conversation overheard.* Irish myth: Cross.

T210. Faithfulness in marriage.

N455.7. *Secret about prince's father learned by eavesdropper from his mother's talking to him.* Icelandic: Boberg.

N455.8. *Friend lingering in the kitchen learns of friend's distress and helps him.* Icelandic: Göngu-Hrólfs saga 307, Boberg.

M253. Friends in life and death. In pursuance of the pledge, the living follows the other to the world of the dead.

N455.9. *Location of sought object learned from overheard conversation.* Korean: Zong in-Sob 69; Tonga: Gifford 54.

N455.10. *By hiding, stupid son overhears conversation and claims magic power for bamboo cup.* Chinese: Graham.

L115. Successful foolish son.

N455.11. *Servant overhearing conversation realizes the misery of his employment.* India: Thompson-Balys.

N455.12. *Men hear father threaten to marry daughters to first comers.* India: Thompson-Balys.

T62. Princess to marry first man who asks her.

N456. *Enigmatical smile (laugh) reveals secret knowledge.* *Type 670; **Aarne FFC XV 31ff.; Wesselski Mönchslatein 93 No. 153; Wesselski Archiv Orientálni I 82; Krappe Revue Celtique XLVIII 401ff.; *Schoepperle I 198 n. 1; *Penzer I 46 n. 2; Irish myth: *Cross; Icelandic: Corpus Poeticum Boreale I 358; India: *Thompson-Balys.

B81.7.1. Mermaid prophesies. B217. Animal language learned. C425. Tabu: revealing knowledge of animal languages. D1318.2.1. Laughing fish reveals unjust judgment. D1639.4. Statue laughs and reveals crime. J1149.5. Detection of guilt by smile. M304. Prophecy from enigmatical laugh. S261.1. Child as foundation sacrifice smiles and wins freedom. T252.3. Wife threatens husband with death if he will not tell secrets. U15. Fool laughs at absurdities he sees about him.

N465. *Secret physical peculiarity discovered by barber.* (Midas.) See all references to F511.2.2. and D1316.5. Alphabet No. 268; Irish myth: *Cross; Rumanian: Schullerus FFC LXXVIII No. 886 I*.

D1316.5. Magic speaking reed (tree) betrays secret. D2161.4.19.1. Barber begins to recover after he reveals raja's secret. F511.2.2. Person with ass's (horse's) ears. Midas. P446. Barber.

N465.0.1. *Secret physical blemish revealed by beaten handmaid.* Irish myth: Cross.

N465.1. *Secret of person's sleeplessness discovered by trickery.* Irish myth: Cross.

N466. *Daughter lousing mother weeps and reveals secret.* Chinese: Graham.

K874. Deception by pretended lousing.

N467. *King in disguise to learn secrets of his subjects.* India: *Thompson-Balys.

K1812. King in disguise. P10. Kings.

N468. *Newborn babe reveals secret; then becomes silent.* India: Thompson-Balys.

T585.2. Child speaks at birth.

N471. *Foolish attempt of second man to overhear secrets* (from animals, demons etc.). He is punished. *Types 461, 503, 613, 676; *BP II 468ff., III 137ff., 324ff.; *Aarne FFC XXIII 169; *Christiansen FFC XXIV 103ff.; *Hdwb. d. Märchens I 230b s.v. "Belauschen von Dämonen". — Missouri French: Carrière; Spanish: Espinosa Jr. No. 117; India: Thompson-Balys; Japanese: Ikeda, Mitford 191; Korean: Zong in-Sob 151 No. 66; Indonesia: Dixon 216; N. A. Indian (Pochulata): Boas JAFL XXV 223; Africa (Yoruba): Ellis 249ff. No. 2.

D1552.2. Mountain opens to magic formula. F331. Mortal wins fairies' gratitude by joining in their sport. F342.1. Fairy gold. Fairies give coals (wood, earth) that turns to gold. G661.1. Ogre's secret overheard from tree. J2415. Foolish imitation of lucky man. Because one man has had good luck a numskull imitates and thinks he will have equally good luck. He is disappointed. K1026. Dupe imitates trickster's thefts and is caught. N451. Secrets overheard from animal conversation. N455.3. Secret formula for opening mountain overheard from robbers. Q3. Moderate request rewarded; immoderate punished.

N475. *Secret name overheard by eavesdropper.* *Type 500; *Clodd Tom-Tit-Tot; *Polivka Zs. f. Vksk. X 254ff.; *Von Sydow Två Spinnsagor; Icelandic: Boberg; Japanese: Ikeda; Jamaica: *Beckwith MAFLS XVII 247 No. 23, 267 No. 75, 279 Nos. 92, 93; West Indies: Flowers 564.

C432.1. Guessing name of supernatural creature gives power over him. H521. Test: guessing unknown propounder's name. K1844.3. Groom deceives bride with substituted bedmate and hides self in order to learn the secret she has promised to tell.

N475.1. *Secret age overheard by eavesdropper.* Man masking as cuckoo in tree causes the surprised ogre to disclose secret. BP I 497.

K216.2.1. Guessing name of devil's secret plant. K1691. The woman as cuckoo on the tree shot down.

N475.2. *Secret reason why hero does not want to eat the food of the foreign king overheard by eavesdropper.* Icelandic: Boberg.

N476. *Secret of unique vulnerability disclosed.*

K975.2. Secret of external soul learned by deception. K2213.4.1. Secret of vulnerability disclosed by hero's wife.

N476.1. *Secret of vulnerability voluntarily disclosed.* India: *Thompson-Balys.

Z311. Achilles heel.

N476.2. *Man vulnerable only in armpits shot as he stretches his arms.* India: Thompson-Balys.

N476.3. *Secret unique means of killing ogre overheard from children.* Chinese: Graham.

N478. *Secret wealth betrayed by money left in borrowed money-scales.* *Type 676; *BP III 137ff.; *Fb "skjæppe" III 275b; Spanish: Boggs FFC XC 70 No. 545C*; Missouri French: Carrière; India: *Thompson-Balys; Philippine: Fansler MAFLS XII 336, 338; Africa (Ekoi): Talbot 389.

K1954.1. Helpful cat borrows measure for his master's money. The master thus gains a reputation for wealth.

N478.1. *Secret meat-eating betrayed by grease on mouth.* Africa (Larusa): Fokken ZsKS VII 82ff. No. 1, (Masai): Hollis The Masai (Oxford, 1905) 212ff., (Mossi): Frobenius Atlantis VIII 239ff.

N481. *Secret escapes with man's blood.* Irish myth: Cross.

N482. *Secret learned by torture.*

N482.1. *Secret learned by burning hand.* *Cosquin Contes indiens 397ff.

S112. Burning to death.

N484. *Giant unwittingly reveals span of life to dwarf, who is thus emboldened to attack him.* India: Thompson-Balys.

N500—N599. Treasure trove.

N500. Treasure trove. **Norlind Skattsägner (bibliography 67f.); **Kittredge Witchcraft 204ff., 516ff.; *Fb "skat" III 234ff.; *Wehrhan 80f.; RTP XIV 71, 568, XVIII 418, XIX 306; *S. Hirschberg Schatzglaube und Totenglaube (Breslau, 1934); **Hurley WF X 197—216. — Danish: Kristensen Danske Sagn III (1895) 419ff., (1931) 293ff., A. Olrik Nordisk Aandsliv (Copenhagen, 1907) 8—87; Norwegian: Solheim Register 20; Irish myth: *Cross; Livonian: Loorits FFC LXVI 69ff. Nos. 199—221; German: **Winter Die deutsche Schatzsage; Missouri French: Carrière; U.S. (Texas): *Dobie Coronado's Children; Chinese: Graham.

B11.2.8. Tail of dragon (full of treasure). D1450. Magic object furnishes treasure. D1552.2. Open sesame. F721.4. Underground treasure chambers. H1292.2. Question (propounded on quest): Why does not a certain tree flourish? Answer: Gold is hidden under it. K1685. The treasure-finders who murder one another. V13. Sacrifice made when treasure is found.

N510. Where treasure is found. Chinese: Graham.

H588.7. Father's counsel: find treasure within a foot of the ground. (Sons dig everywhere and thus loosen soil of vineyard, which becomes fruitful.) H1292.2. Question (propounded on quest): Why does not a certain tree flourish? Answer: Gold is hidden under it. J21.15. "If you wish to hang yourself, do so by the stone which I point out": counsel proved wise by experience. Father has left money which will fall out when the spendthrift son goes to hang himself in despair. J1852.1. Numskull sells cow to bird. When he comes for his money the bird flies to a trash pile, where the fool finds a treasure. J1853.1.1. Money from the broken statue. Fool sells goods to a statue and when it will not pay him knocks it to pieces. He finds a treasure inside. N211.1. Lost ring found in fish.

N511. *Treasure in ground.* Irish myth: *Cross; Icelandic: Boberg; U.S.: Baughman; Chinese: Graham.

N511.1. *Treasure buried by men.* Irish myth: *Cross; North Carolina: Brown Collection I 692; Danish: Kristensen Danske Sagn III (1895) 425ff., (1931) 297ff.; Icelandic: *Boberg; Jewish: Neuman.

N511.1.0.1. *Treasure buried by dying man.* Estonian: Aarne FFC XXV 128 No. 63; Finnish: Aarne FFC XXXIII 5 No. 63.

N511.1.0.2. *Sword hidden by old man.* Herrmann Saxo II 306.

N511.1.1. *Treasure buried in graves.* *Winter 11; Icelandic: *Boberg; Chinese: Graham.

N531.4. Grateful king advises merchant in dream to take treasure in his grave mound. N538. Treasure pointed out by supernatural creature.

N511.1.2. *Treasure buried in ancient settlements.* *Winter 16.

N511.1.3. *Treasure buried in extraordinary topographical formations.* *Winter 27.

N511.1.4. *Buried treasure wanders from place to place.* Indicated by a light. (Cf. N532.) *Winter 30.

N511.1.5. *Treasure buried in woodshed.* Type 935***.

N511.1.6. *Treasure in cellar of ruined house.* Italian: Basile Pentamerone I No. 7.

N511.1.6.1. *Treasure found in ruined wall.* Cheremis: Sebeok-Nyerges; Italian Novella: Rotunda.

N511.1.7. *Treasure hidden by retreating army.* Lithuanian: Balys Index No. 3740.

N511.1.8. *Treasure buried in chest, cask, kettle, or cannon barrel.* (Cf. N525.) U.S.: *Baughman.

N511.1.9. *Treasure buried under tree.* U.S.: Baughman; India: *Thompson-Balys.

N511.1.10. *Treasure buried under flower.* U.S.: Baughman.

N511.1.11. *Treasure buried on top of mountain.* U.S.: Baughman.

N511.1.12. *Treasure buried on island.* Canada, U.S.: *Baughman.

N511.1.13. *Treasure buried under stump.* U.S.: Baughman; Cheremis: Sebeok-Nyerges.

N511.2. *Natural underground treasure.* *Winter 35; Icelandic: Boberg.

N511.3. *Treasure placed in ground by supernatural beings.*

N511.3.1. *Treasure of mountain spirit.* *Winter 36.

D812.11. Magic object received from giant. D838.6. Magic object stolen from giant. D845.1. Magic object found in giant's cave. F531.6.7. Giant's treasure. F460. Mountain-spirits. F752. Mountain of treasure. G610. Theft from ogre. N538.2. Treasure from defeated giant. N570. Guardian of treasure.

N511.3.2. *Treasure placed in old fortifications by supernatural beings.* *Winter 38.

N511.4. *Treasure found in snake hole.* India: Thompson-Balys.

B11.6.2. Dragon guards treasure. N570. Guardian of treasure.

N511.6. *Treasure under stone.* A. F. Schmidt DF XXXIX 106ff.

N512. *Treasure in underground chamber (cavern).* *Type 676; *Winter 23; *Hartland Science 174, 176, 189; Irish myth: *Cross; U.S.: Baughman; Icelandic: Boberg; Missouri French: Carrière; Jewish: *Neuman; Chinese: Graham, Eberhard FFC CXX 39f., 221; Japanese: Ikeda; West Indies: Flowers 564.

F721.4. Underground treasure chambers. N455.3. Secret formula for opening treasure mountain overheard from robbers (Open Sesame).

N513. *Treasure hidden under the water.* *Winter 19; *Fb "skat" III 235a; Danish: Kristensen Danske Sagn III (1895) 442ff., (1931) 305ff.; Icelandic: *Boberg.

N513.1. *Man jumps into the sea, river or waterfall with his treasure.* Icelandic: Boberg.

N511.1. Treasure buried by men. N570. Guardian of treasure. R317. Well (spring) as refuge.

N513.2. *Sword hidden under water.* Icelandic: *Boberg.

N513.3. *Treasure hidden in spring.* U.S.: Baughman.

N513.4. *Treasure hidden in river.* U.S.: *Baughman.

N513.5. *Treasure buried in sunken ship.* U.S.: *Baughman.

N513.6. *Queen's jewel-box thrown into tank floats to top during first week of new moon;* light or large jewel on top reveals it to passersby. It disappears when someone tries to get it. India: Thompson-Balys.

N514. *Treasure hidden in religious shrine.* *Winter 14.

N514.1. *Treasure hidden in sanctuary.* Icelandic: Boberg.

N514.2. *Treasure in temple.* Jewish: Neuman.

N516. *Treasure at end of rainbow.* *Fb "regenbue" III 31b, "skat" III 235a; African: Werner African 234.

A791. Origin of the rainbow. F152.1.1. Rainbow bridge to otherworld.

N517. *Treasure hidden in building.*

N517.1. *Treasure hidden in secret room in house.* England, U.S.: *Baughman.

N517.2. *Treasure hidden within wall (under floor) of house.* Irish myth: Cross.

N518. *Gold found, concealed in bricks and successfully secured.* Lithuanian: Balys Index No. 1669*.

N521. *Treasure left in stick. It accidentally falls apart.* *Chauvin II 129 No. 137; Icelandic: *Boberg; Estonian: Aarne FFC XXV 129 No. 67.

J1161.4. Money in the stick. Before swearing, the cheater hands a stick containing the stolen money to the man he has stolen it from. He then swears that he has repaid it. K333.4. Blind beggar overheard telling that his money is kept in a stick. Thief exchanges sticks.

N522. *Treasure hidden in pillow under dead man's head.* Estonian: Aarne FFC XXV 129 No. 66; Lithuanian: Balys Index No. 3622; Finnish: Aarne FFC XXXIII 45 No. 66.

N523. *Treasure hidden in a stone.* India: Thompson-Balys.

N524. *Treasure found in beggar's hat.* Italian Novella: *Rotunda.

N524.1. *Money found in the dead beggar's coat.* Lithuanian: Balys Index No. 842*; Russian: Andrejev No. 842 I.

N525. *Treasure found in chest (kettle, cask).* (Cf. N511.1.8.) Type 968*; *Fb "skat" III 236b; Icelandic: Boberg; Finnish-Swedish: Wessman 78 Nos. 652—656; Italian Novella: Rotunda; India: Thompson-Balys.

N526. *Treasure found in bundle of rags.* Italian Novella: Rotunda.

N527. *Treasure (money) carried by bird to nest.* English: Wells 114 (Sir Isumbras); Lithuanian: Balys Index No. 937*.

N352.3. Jewel (garment) carried off by bird from bather. Clothes have been left on bank of stream.

N527.1. *Diamond in meat carried to eagle's nest.* *Chauvin VII 11 No. 373B n. 1.

N527.2. *Talisman found in bird's stomach.* India: Thompson-Balys.

N528. *Treasure found in hollow of tree.* Cheremis: Sebeok-Nyerges.

N529. *Where treasure is found—miscellaneous.* Irish myth: Cross.

N529.1. *Lump of gold appears in Arabia at Christ's birth.* Irish myth: Cross.

N529.2. *Pearl found in fish.* Jewish: *Neuman; India: Thompson-Balys.

N211.1. Lost ring found in fish.

N530. Discovery of treasure. *Fb "skat" III 235a; India: Thompson-Balys; Chinese: Graham.

B153. Dog's barking indicates hidden treasure. B562.1. Animal shows man treasure.

N531. *Treasure discovered through dream.* Type 834*; Scotland, England, U.S.: Baughman; North Carolina: Brown Collection I 693; Icelandic: *Boberg; Danish: Kristensen Danske Sagn III (1895) 481ff., (1931) 323ff.; Jewish: bin Gorion Born Judas V 18; India: *Thompson-Balys; Chinese: Graham; Africa (Fjort): Dennett 39 No. 5; West Indies: Flowers 564.

D1812.3.3. Future revealed in dream. J157. Wisdom (knowledge) from dream. X31. The dream of marking the treasure. A man dreams that he finds treasure and that he marks the spot with his excrements. Only the latter part of the dream is true.

N531.1. *Dream of treasure on the bridge.* A man dreams that if he goes to a distant city he will find treasure on a certain bridge. Finding no treasure, he tells his dream to a man who says that he too has dreamed of treasure at a certain place. He describes the place, which is the first man's home. When the latter returns home he finds the treasure. *Type 1645; **Bolte Zs. f. Vksk. XIX 289ff.; *Wesselski Mönchslatein 120 No. 101; *Hauffen Zs. f. Vksk. X 432; *Tille in Veckenstedt's Zs. f. Vksk. III 132ff.; DeCock RTP XV 294; *Fb "skat" III 235a, "bro" IV 62b; *Chauvin VI 94 No. 258; Lithuanian: Balys Index No. 3636; Japanese: Ikeda.

N531.2. *Dream brings treasure: trade vineyards with neighbor.* A treasure is found in the new vineyard. Pauli (ed. Bolte) No. 328.

N531.3. *Dream of treasure bought.* Treasure has been seen by man's soul absent in sleep in form of a fly. The purchaser of the dream finds the treasure. Lithuanian: Balys Index No. 3520; Persian: Lorimer Persian Tales 311 No. 49; Japanese: Ikeda.

N531.4. *Grateful king advises merchant in dream to take treasure from his grave mound.* Icelandic: ASB 14 p. 76 n., *Boberg.

N531.5. *Man dreams of large jars full of wealth, which he can get if he will sacrifice his wife for the getting.* India: Thompson-Balys.

N532. *Light indicates hidden treasure.* (Cf. N511.1.4.) *Fb "lys" II 480b; *Norlind 34ff., 57; England, U.S.: Baughman; North Carolina: Brown Collection I 691, 694; Icelandic: *Boberg; Danish: Kristensen Danske Sagn III (1895) 419ff., (1931) 293ff.; Lithuanian: Balys Index No. 3632.

N532.1. *Half-moon close to the earth indicates hidden treasure.* Icelandic: Boberg.

N533. *Treasure discovered by magic object.*

D1314.2. Magic wand locates hidden treasure. D1314.3. Saint's bachall discovers gold. D1314.5. Hand of glory indicates location of treasure. D1331.3.1. Salve causes magic sight and blindness: put on left eye causes one to see all treasures of earth; on the right, makes blind.

N533.1. *Treasure discovered by clairvoyant vase.* (Cf. D1323.2.) *Chauvin V 259 No. 154.

N533.2. *Treasure found by clairvoyant mirror.* (Cf. D1323.1.) *Winter 83.

N533.3. *Treasure discovered by hand of unborn child.* Finnish-Swedish: Wessman 7 No. 645.

D1361.8. Heart of unborn child renders person invisible. D1500.1.6.1. Corpse's hand as remedy.

N533.4. *Consecrated wine used to discover treasure.* Finnish-Swedish: Wessman 77 No. 649.

V34. Miraculous workings of the Host.

N533.5. *Men find mines of copper, silver, gold and iron where balls fall.* India: Thompson-Balys.

N534. *Treasure discovered by accident.* Irish myth: Cross; Finnish-Swedish: Wessman 78 Nos. 652—656; India: *Thompson-Balys; Chinese: Graham; West Indies: Flowers 565.

J1852.1. Numskull sells cow to bird. When he comes for his money the bird flies to a trash pile, where the fool finds a treasure.

N534.1. *Stumble reveals depository of treasure.* Irish myth: Cross.

N534.2. *Gold hoard found by cow stepping into hole.* India: Thompson-Balys.

N534.3. *Saint sticks crozier into sod and finds pound of gold.* Irish myth: Cross.

N534.4. *Information about treasure received from overheard conversation.* India: *Thompson-Balys.

N455. Secrets from overheard (human) conversation.

N534.5. *Poor boy accidentally finds deserted city with treasure.* India: Thompson-Balys.

N534.6. *Treasure found by man when he obeys call of nature.* India: Thompson-Balys.

K1956.1. Sham wise man gives purgative and helps find a lost horse. His pills get the credit.

N534.7. *Man digging stones in the pavement finds a chest of treasure.* India: Thompson-Balys.

N534.7.1. *Men digging hole to plant rose-tree find treasure.* India: Thompson-Balys.

N534.8. *Jewel found accidentally on a bought donkey's neck.* Jewish: *Neuman.

N535. *Treasure indicated by statue (stone) with inscription, "Dig here".* *Spargo Virgil the Necromancer 363 n. 3; *Fb "skat" III 235a; *Oesterley No. 107; Danish: Blinkenberg Danske Studier (1928) 97ff.; Spanish Exempla: Keller; India: *Thompson-Balys.

D1620.1.5. Magic statue of archer. J1853.1.1. Money from the broken statue. Fool sells goods to a statue and when it will not pay him knocks it to pieces. He finds a treasure inside.

N535.1. *Treasure indicated by stone cross on the ground.* Spanish Exempla: Keller.

N536. *Treasure pointed out by angels.* Irish myth: Cross; Jewish: Neuman, bin Gorion Born Judas[2] I 188, 374.

V232. Angel as helper.

N537. *Speaking bird tells where treasure is buried.* Italian Novella: Rotunda; Jewish: Neuman, *bin Gorion Born Judas IV 29, 275; India: Thompson-Balys.

N451. Secrets overheard from animal (demon) conversation.

N538. *Treasure pointed out by supernatural creature (fairy, etc.).* Finnish-Swedish: Wessman 75 No. 60; India: Thompson-Balys; Buddhist myth: Malalasekera I 299, 624f., II 979.

E545.12. Ghost directs man to hidden treasure. F451.5.1.9. Dwarfs direct mortals to treasure.

N538.1. *Treasure pointed out by soul which has left body for this purpose.* Spanish Exempla: Keller.

N538.2. *Treasure from defeated giant.* (Cf. F531.6.7, G610, D838.6.) Icelandic: *Boberg.

F531.6.7. Giant's treasure. N511.3.1. Treasure of mountain spirit.

N541. *Treasure reveals itself only at certain times.*

N541.1. *Treasure reveals itself only on Christmas at midnight (or Christmas Eve).* Swiss: Jegerlehner Oberwallis 294—308 passim; Lithuanian: Balys Index No. 3611.

N541.2. *Treasure reveals itself once a century.* Swiss: Jegerlehner Oberwallis 295 No. 21.

N541.3. *Treasure found on Hallowe'en.* Irish myth: Cross.

N541.4. *Treasure discovered at the Nativity of Christ.* Irish myth: Cross.

N542. *Special conditions for finding treasure.* Finnish-Swedish: Wessman 77 Nos. 642—644, 648; Japanese: Ikeda.

N542.1. *Treasure found if one goes with one-night old colt on to one-night old ice.* Finnish: Aarne FFC XXXIII 45 No. 65**.

N542.2. *Treasure to be found when three-legged cat shrieks over the burial place.* Estonian: Aarne FFC XXV 129 No. 69.

N543. *Certain person to find treasure.* Lithuanian: Balys Index Nos. 3612, 3616, 3620.

N591. Curse on treasure.

N543.0.1. *Only particular persons see hidden treasure in its true form;* others see it as coal, serpents, scorpions, etc. India: Thompson-Balys.

N543.1. *Treasure to be found by hand that hid it.* Finnish-Swedish: Wessman 77 Nos. 638, 639; Finnish: Aarne FFC XXXIII 45 No. 64; Lithuanian: Balys Index No. 3611; Estonian: Aarne FFC XXV 128 No. 64.

N543.2. *Treasure to be found by man who plows with cock and harrows with hen.* North Carolina: Brown Collection I 693; Finnish: Aarne FFC XXXIII 45 No. 65; Lithuanian: Balys Index No. 3615; Estonian: Aarne FFC XXV 129 No. 65.

N543.3. *Treasure to be found by man who marries original owner's daughter.* Estonian: Aarne FFC XXV 129 No. 68.

N545. *Man in despair digging own grave finds treasure.* Jewish: bin Gorion Born Judas[2] I 288, 378.

N545.1. *Man in despair preparing to hang himself finds treasure in the tree* (beam). Lithuanian: Balys Index No. 3623; Italian Novella: *Rotunda.

J21.15. Father has left money which will fall out when spendthrift son goes to hang himself.

N545.2. *Man ready to kill self hears voice directing him to buried fortune.* India: Thompson-Balys.

N547. *Understanding of animal languages leads to discovery of a treasure.* India: Thompson-Balys; Chinese: Eberhard FFC CXX 42.

B216. Knowledge of animal languages. B562.1. Animal shows treasure.

N549. *Discovery of treasure—miscellaneous.*

N549.1. *Four pots of rupees magically appear on horns of buffaloes stuck in pond, and poor owner becomes rich.* India: Thompson-Balys.

N550. Unearthing hidden treasure. Irish myth: *Cross; Japanese: Ikeda.

E415.1.2. Return from dead to uncover secretly buried treasure. E451.5. Ghost laid when treasure is unearthed. F451.6.9. Dwarfs dig for treasure. H1181. Task: raising a buried treasure.

N550.1. *Continual failure to find or unearth hidden treasure.* Texas: Dobie Coronado's Children passim.

N551. *Who may unearth a treasure.*

N551.1. *Only weak-minded person may unearth a treasure.* Fb "sær" III 723b.

N551.2. *Treasure may be unearthed only by man who on the spot has sexual relations with a woman in the manner of dogs.* Cheremis: Sebeok-Nyerges.

N552. *Treasure opens itself.*

D1552. Mountains or rocks open and close.

N552.1. *Treasure opens itself for destined hero.* Icelandic: Boberg.

N553. *Tabus in effect while treasure is being unearthed.*

N553.1. *Tabu: incontinence while treasure is being raised.* Winter 77.

C110. Tabu: sexual intercourse.

N553.2. *Unlucky encounter causes treasure-seekers to talk and thus lose treasure.* *Fb "skat" III 236b; Finnish-Swedish: Wessman 78f. Nos. 659, 664—672; Danish: Kristensen Danske Sagn III (1895) 439ff., 447ff., (1931) 304ff., 307ff.; North Carolina: Brown Collection I 692f.

C401.3. Tabu: speaking while searching for treasure.

N553.3. *Treasure finders must not take all of money.* Fb "penge" II 803a.

N553.4. *Tabu: looking around while raising treasure.* Finnish-Swedish: Wessman 78, 80 Nos. 658, 668.

C332. Tabu: looking around.

N553.5. *Tabu: fear of threatening animals while treasure is being raised.* Finnish-Swedish: Wessman 76 No. 636.

H1400. Fear test.

N554. *Ceremonies and prayers used at unearthing of treasure.* *Winter 77.

N554.1. *Sacrifices at unearthing of treasure.* Finnish-Swedish: Wessman 76f. Nos. 637, 646.

N555. *Time favorable for unearthing treasure.* *Winter 69.

N555.1. *Between midnight and cockcrow best time for unearthing treasure.* Fb "midnat" II 587.

N555.2. *Treasure nearest to surface at full of moon.* North Carolina: Brown Collection I 695.

N556. *Treasure-finders always frightened away.* North Carolina: Brown Collection I 692; Lithuanian: Balys Index No. 3642; India: Thompson-Balys.

N557. *Treasure disappears after being uncovered.* U.S.: Baughman.

N558. *Raised treasure turns into charcoal (shavings).* If one takes it along it will turn back into gold. *Norlind 56; Finnish-Swedish: Wessman 75f. Nos. 631—634; West Indies: Flowers 565.

C967. Valuable object turns worthless for breaking tabu. F342.1. Fairy gold. Fairies give coals (wood, earth) that turns to gold. F348.0.1. Fairy gift disappears or is turned to something worthless when tabu is broken. F451.5.1.4. Dwarf's gold. Seemingly worthless gift given by dwarfs turns to gold. F531.5.6.1. Giant's magic gifts return to original form in hands of men.

N561. *Electric shock scares away treasure diggers.* Scotland: Baughman.

N562. *Treasure removes itself from time to time.* North Carolina: Brown Collection I 695.

D1641. Object removes itself.

N562.1. *Treasure having removed itself eventually returns.* North Carolina: Brown Collection I 695.

N563. *Treasure seekers find hole from which treasure has recently been removed.* (Often they have delayed searching for one reason or another, arrive too late.) U.S.: *Baughman.

N564. *Magic illusion prevents men from raising treasure.* Danish: Kristensen Danske Sagn III (1895) 447ff., (1931) 307ff.

N570. Guardian of treasure. *Fb "skat" III 235b, 236a; *Winter 41; *Norlind 69ff.; Finnish-Swedish: Wessman 73ff. Nos. 623—629.

B11.6.2. Dragon guards treasure. B576.2. Animals guard treasure. N511.4. Treasure found in snake hole.

N571. *Devil (demon) as guardian of treasure.* *Fb "skat" III 235b, "djævel" IV 99b; *Kittredge Witchcraft 204f., 517 n. 8; *Penzer III 133n.; *Winter 41; U.S.: Baughman; Icelandic: *Boberg; Swiss: Jegerlehner Oberwallis 16 No. 9; India: *Thompson-Balys; Buddhist myth: Malalasekera II 678.

G302. Demons. Malevolent creatures. G303. Devil.

N571.1. *Ogre's son guardian of treasure trove.* India: Thompson-Balys.

N572. *Woman as guardian of treasure.*

N572.1. *"White woman" as guardian of treasure.* *Norlind 69ff.; *Winter 47.

E425.1.1. Revenant as lady in white.

N572.2. *Swan maidens as guardians of treasure.* *Norlind 71f.

D361.1. Swan maiden.

N572.3. *Girl with ghostly treasure in boat.* Lithuanian: Balys Index No. 3631.

N573. *Sleeping king in mountain as guardian of treasure.* *Norlind 4ff.; Hartland Science 207.

D1960.2. King asleep in mountain.

N574. *Dwarf as guardian of treasure.* *Winter 58.

F451. Dwarf as underground spirit.

N575. *Griffin as guardian of treasure.* (Cf. B42.) Penzer I 104.

N576. *Ghosts prevent men from raising treasure.* U.S.: Baughman; North Carolina: Brown Collection I 693; Finnish-Swedish: Wessman 4 No. 30; Lithuanian: Balys Index No. 3642; Italian: Basile Pentamerone I No. 7; West Indies: Flowers 565.

N576.1. *Voice of ghost scares away treasure seekers.* Canada, England, U.S.: *Baughman.

N576.2. *Ghostly lights frighten treasure seekers.* England, U.S.: *Baughman.

N576.3. *Ghost of treasure's human owner as guardian.* Icelandic: *Boberg.

N577. *Blind man carrying lame man as guardians of treasure.* Irish myth: *Cross; Jewish: Neuman.

N886. Blind man carries lame man.

N581. *Treasure guarded by magic object.* (Cf. D1560.)

N581.1. *Treasure guarded by magic millstone.* U.S.: Baughman.

N582. *Serpent guards treasure.* India: Thompson-Balys.

B11.6.2. Dragon guards treasure. B576.2. Animal guards treasure.

N583. *Angel as guardian of treasure.* Jewish: Neuman.

N590. Treasure trove—miscellaneous motifs.

N591. *Curse on treasure. Finder or owner to have bad luck.* *Fb "skat" III 234b, 235b; Icelandic: *Boberg; N. A. Indian (Wampanoag): Knight JAFL XXXVIII 134; Africa (Ekoi): Talbot 185.

D2141.0.2. Storm from calling up spirits to help find buried treasure. E451.5. Ghost laid when treasure is unearthed. M470. Curses on objects. N250. Persistent bad luck.

N591. *Treasure from striking animal or person and disenchanting him.* Lithuanian: Balys Index No. 3627f.

D712.3. Disenchantment by striking.

N595. *Helper in hiding treasure killed in order that nobody may ever find it.* Icelandic: Boberg.

N596. *Discovery of rich mine.*

N596.1. *Rich mine discovered through dream.* (Cf. N531.) U.S.: *Baughman.

N596.2. *Rich mine discovered by accidental breaking off of rock.* U.S.: Baughman.

N597. *Discovery of underground oil pools.*

N597.1. *Pools of underground oil discovered through dreams.* (Cf. N531.) U.S.: Baughman.

N600—N699. Other lucky accidents.

N610. Accidental discovery of crime.

J1141. Confession obtained by a ruse. N270. Crime inevitably comes to light.

N611. *Criminal accidentally detected: "that is the first."* India: *Thompson-Balys.

J1895. Woman thinks calf's bleating has accused her. J2671.2.1. Fool's talking to himself thought to be inappropriate greetings. K1155. Casual words uttered by dupe used to cheat him of his property. M175 Pledge to say but a single phrase. In carrying out this agreement the men innocently confess a crime. N275.3. Detection by accidental remark. Wife misunderstands husband's remark and confesses.

N611.1. *Criminal accidentally detected: "that is the first" — sham wise man.* The sham wise man employed to detect theft is feasted. As the servants enter with food he remarks to his wife, "That is the first" (course). (Or allowed to feast for three days remarks at end of first day "That is the first.") The servants, thinking they are detected, confess. *Type 1641; BP II 401ff., *409; *Pauli (ed. Bolte) No. 818; *Penzer III 75f.; India: *Thompson-Balys; Indonesia: DeVries's list No. 302.

K1956. Sham wise man. N275. Criminal confesses because he thinks himself accused.

N611.1.1. *Name of criminal accidentally spoken out* (identical with ordinary word in speech). India: *Thompson-Balys.

N611.2. *Criminal accidentally detected: "That is the first" — sleepy woman counting her yawns.* Robber hearing her flees. (Cf. N612.) *BP II 412; U.S.: Baughman.

K335.1. Robbers frightened from goods. L141.2. Simpleton's naive answer to robbers makes them think he knows their secret.

N611.3. *Numskull bridegroom unwittingly sings out phrases that thieves mistake to mean he has detected them.* India: Thompson-Balys.

N611.4. *Thief hears owner of house singing "Bore and throw out the earth" and thinks himself detected.* Offers owner money to purchase his silence. India: Thompson-Balys.

N612. *Numskull talks to himself and frightens robbers away.* *Wesselski Hodscha Nasreddin II 211 No. 428, *215 No. 446; India: *Thompson-Balys.

J2671.2.1. Fool's talking to himself thought to be inappropriate greetings. K335.1.0.1. Frightened robber leaves his coat behind.

N612.1. *Man scolds his ass and frightens robber away.* While the man is absent from his ass the robber steals the man's coat. The ass brays and the man scolds him. The robber thinking he is discovered flees and leaves the coat. Wesselski Hodscha Nasreddin I 224 No. 62.

N613. *Numskull bribed to keep silent in elephant sale when he manifests interest, though utterly ignorant.* India: Thompson-Balys.

N614. *Cane as evidence of robbery.* A man believing that he has killed a robber forgets his cane. Later finds it in robber's house. Type 961*; Lithuanian: Balys Index No. 961*; Russian: Andrejev No. 961*.

N615. *Murder revealed to thieves climbing into bank.* Type 951B.

N617. *Impostor accidentally gives king talking bed which reveals his identity.* India: Thompson-Balys.

D1610.17. Speaking bed. N454.1. Speaking bed legs overheard.

N618. *Officer comes accidentally to the same building where the fugitive sleeps.* Jewish: Neuman.

N620. Accidental success in hunting or fishing.

X1110. Lie: the wonderful hunt.

N621. *Lucky shot with arrow — foot and ear of deer.* Deer is scratching ear. *Fischer-Bolte 203ff.; *Wesselski Märchen 226 No. 38; Japanese: Ikeda.

F661. Skillful marksman. F679.5.3. Man kills many tigers with one arrow. X1120. Lie: the great marksman.

N621.1. *Arrow accidentally makes shot for which prize is given.* India: Thompson-Balys.

N622. *Game killed by jumping on it from above.* Icelandic: Boberg.

N331.2.1. Man hidden in tree so frightened of lioness he drops his sword and kills her.

N622.1. *Tortoise jumps from tree and breaks rhinoceros's back.* India: Thompson-Balys.

N623. *Lucky cast of spear (weapon).* Irish myth: Cross.

N623.1. *Lucky cast of spear — animal's mouth pinned shut.* Irish myth: Cross.

N623.2. *Lucky cast of ball: boy throws ball into mouth of hostile hound.* Ball carries out entrails. Irish myth: *Cross.

N623.3. *Lucky cast of ball made of human brains — ball sticks in head of enemy.* Irish myth: *Cross.

N623.4. *Lucky cast from sling slays hostile queen.* Irish myth: *Cross.

N624. *Man falls into well and accidentally kills cobra: rewarded.* India: Thompson-Balys.

N625. *Fish jumps into boat of disheartened fisherman.* Wienert FFC LVI 67 (ET 311), 141 (ST 472); Halm Aesop No. 24.

N626. *Ass falls into water and catches fish in his ear.* Pauli (ed. Bolte) No. 744.

N627. *Destructive elephant eats poison man has prepared for himself.* Man rewarded. India: *Thompson-Balys.

K527.1. Poisoned food (drink) fed to animal instead of to intended victim. Animal perishes. K1787. Man falsely claims to have killed elephant with his flat hand.

N630. Accidental acquisition of treasure or money.

F585.4. Treasure struck from hand of phantom. K335.1.1. Door falls on robbers from tree.

N633. *The early pupil finds the gold.* An innkeeper hears that education makes one rich and enters school. He is scolded for coming late. He comes very early and in twilight finds a purse of gold. Type 1645*; Lithuanian: Balys Index No. 1665*; Russian: Andrejev No. 1665*; Livonian: Loorits FFC LXVI No. 1645[1].

N635. *The triple tax.* A poet is given by the king the right to demand a coin of the first hunchback he meets, from the first man of a certain name, and from the first man of a certain city. He sees a hunchback and demands the coin. A quarrel arises in which it appears that the hunchback also has the required name and residence. With each revelation the poet demands a new coin. *Type 1661; *Wesselski Hodscha Nasreddin II 194 No. 382; *Basset 1001 Contes I 521; Herbert III 87f., 249, 329, 509, 671; *Chauvin IX 19 No. 5; *Pauli (ed. Bolte) No. 285; Alphabet No. 234; Spanish Exempla: Keller; Icelandic: Boberg.

J2225. Three reasons for not giving alms.

N640. Accidental healing. India: Thompson-Balys.

N641. *Patient laughs so at foolish diagnosis of sham physician that his abscess breaks and he gets well.* She has been told to examine the floor around the patient's bed for signs of what he has been eating. She finds the patient surrounded with pillows: he has eaten too many pillows. *Wesselski Mönchslatein 19 No. 13, Theorie 163.

J2412.4. Imitation of diagnosis by observation: ass's flesh. K1955. Sham physician.

N641.1. *Patient laughs at monkey and cures himself.* Monkey takes medicine and cuts capers as result. Nouvelles Récréations No. 89.

N641.2. *Frog removed from queen's nose by telling such interesting story that she gives quick breath and dislodges him.* India: Thompson-Balys.

N642. *Insane man accidentally cured by blow on head.* Pauli (ed. Bolte) No. 36.

N642.1. *Blind and deaf cure each other by blow on head.* India: Thompson-Balys.

N643. *Stinging of buttocks as cure for cough.* Patient applies stinging medicine and makes himself sore. He represses his cough to keep from hurting his hindquarters and is finally cured. India: Thompson-Balys.

N644. *Cure by fall which causes bleeding.* Irish myth: Cross.

N645. *Lost memory recovered in battle.* Irish myth: Cross.

N646. *Man thinks to end life by drinking poisonous water, but it cures him.* India: Thompson-Balys.

N647. *Thorn accidentally removed from cobra's throat by woman's finger.* Grateful cobra. India: Thompson-Balys.

B381. Thorn removed from lion's paw. In gratitude the lion later rewards the man. B388. Cobra grateful for cure of ulcer.

N648. *King accidentally cured by doctor's ruse and excuses pretended inability to cure him.* India: Thompson-Balys.

N650. Life saved by accident.

H215. Magic manifestation at execution proves innocence. N338.1. Saint changes places with charioteer; latter is killed.

N651. *Pet swan saves self by singing death song.* Master about to mistake the swan in the dark for the goose that is to be slaughtered. Wienert FFC LVI 71 (ET 359), 143 (ST 487); Halm Aesop Nos. 215, 216.

B752.1. Swan song.

N652. *Nut falls and wakes man about to be bitten by snake.* Spanish: Boggs FFC XC 38 No. 285B*, Espinosa Jr. No. 57.

N653. *Child falls from cliff; uninjured.* Irish myth: Cross.

Q559.9. Saints miraculously cause child to fall over cliff as punishment for mother's washing clothes in holy well.

N654. *Hero catches spear hurled at him and kills serpent with it.* Irish myth: Cross.

N655. *Waves break caul of abandoned child.* He is rescued. Irish myth: Cross.

R130. Rescue of abandoned or lost persons.

N656. *Angry man strikes king just in time to save his life.* India: *Thompson-Balys.

N657. *Warriors discover in the last moment that it is their own chief they are about to murder by burning.* Icelandic: Boberg.

K955. Murder by burning.

N658. *Husband arrives home just in time to save wife and her father from being burned to death in their home.* Icelandic: Boberg.

R151. Husband rescues wife.

N659. *Life saved by accident—miscellaneous.*

N659.1. *Poisoned cakes intended for man by his wife eaten by thieves:* booty left to man. India: Thompson-Balys.

N659.2. *Youth accidentally absent when entire family is wiped out.* Greek: Grote I 106.

N660. Accidental escapes. Irish myth: Cross.

K500. Escapes by deception. R210. Escapes.

N661. *Sleeping king abducted by fairies wakes when his foot touches water.* They free him. Irish myth: *Cross.

F320. Fairies carry people away to fairyland.

N662. *Storm blows down tree and frees marooned tortoise.* Africa (Nyang): Ittman 53.

N680. Lucky accidents—miscellaneous.

H575. Accidental discovery of answer to riddle. T415.3. Lovers reared as brother and sister learn to their joy that they are not related.

N680.1. *Lucky fool.* India: Thompson-Balys.

J1700. Fools. K1951.1. Boastful fly-killer: "seven at a blow." N691.1. Numskull's outcry overawes tiger.

N680.2. *Series of lucky successes.* India: Thompson-Balys.

N681. *Husband (lover) arrives home just as wife (mistress) is to marry another.* *Types 301, 400, 665; **Splettstösser Der heimkehrende Gatte und sein Weib in der Weltliteratur; *Chauvin V 108 No. 40; **Rajna Romania VI 359ff.; *Bolte Zs. f. Vksk. XII 59, XXVIII 74 n. 2; *BP II 318ff., 335ff., IV 168 n. 6; *Huet RTP XXXII 97, 145; *Oesterley No. 193; Deutschbein I 3, 187; Herrmann Saxo II 84f.; *Boje 105, 116; *Child V 488 s.v. "marriage"; Boccaccio Decameron X No. 9 (Lee 343); Herbert III 193; *Dickson 141, 221 n. 15; Malone PMLA XLIII 432; *Köhler-Bolte I 117, 584. — Icelandic: *Boberg; Norwegian: Solheim Register 21; Lithuanian: Balys Index No. 509*; Livonian: Loorits FFC LXVI No. 974[1]; Russian: Andrejev No. 891*; Missouri French: Carrière; French Canadian: Barbeau JAFL XXIX 18; Spanish: Boggs FFC XC 84, 107 Nos. 750A, 896, Espinosa II Nos. 133—135, Espinosa Jr. Nos. 63, 68; Italian Novella: *Rotunda; India: *Thompson-Balys; Indonesia: v. Ronkel Catologus der Maleische Handschriften 263; N. A. Indian: *Thompson CColl 323ff., 334ff.; Jamaica: Beckwith MAFLS XVII 278 No. 90.

H80. Identification by tokens. H151.2. Attention drawn by helpful animal's theft of food from wedding table: recognition follows. K1550. Husband outwits adulteress and paramour. K1551. Husband returns home secretly and spies on adulteress and lovers. K1816.0.3.1. Hero in menial disguise at heroine's wedding. N391. Lover is detained away beyond stipulated time. Returns to find sweetheart married. N730. Accidental reunion of families. N741. Unexpected meeting of husband and wife. T150. Happenings at weddings. T151. Year's respite for unwelcome marriage. T200. Married life.

N681.0.1. *Return home to one's own funeral.* Icelandic: Herrmann Saxo II 250, Boberg.

N681.1. *Wife finds lost husband just as he is to marry another.* Type 425; Tegethoff 52; Italian Novella: Rotunda.

N681.2. *Ruler makes ready to abandon barren wife and marry another.* He remains with her when he learns that she is with child. Italian Novella: Rotunda.

N681.3. *Incest accidentally averted.*

H0. Identity tests—recognition. N365. Incest unwittingly committed. T410. Incest.

N681.3.1. *Man about to consummate marriage with own mother;* accidentally prevented. Italian Novella: Rotunda; India: *Thompson-Balys.

N681.3.2. *Man in love with his own sister accidentally learns her identity.* Italian Novella: Rotunda.

N681.4. *Son returns on day his mother is to be married to another (though her husband still lives).* India: Thompson-Balys.

N682. *Prophecy of future greatness fulfilled when hero returns home unknown.* Parents serve him. *Type 517.

M312.2. Prophecy: parents will humble themselves before their son.

N683. *Stranger accidentally chosen king.* Picked up by sacred elephant. *Cosquin Contes indiens 320 n. 4; India: *Thompson-Balys; Buddhist myth: Malalasekera II 68.

H171. Animal indicates election of ruler. H171.1. King selected by elephant's bowing to him. P11.1. Choice of kings by divine will. P17.1. First man to arrive after king's death to be heir. T63. Princess's husband selected by elephant bowing to him.

N684. *Naked soldier becomes general.* Stripped for bathing he takes his place as guard when the king unexpectedly arrives. King invites him to come naked to the castle, where he is chosen as husband by a general's daughter. Type 1670*; Russian: Andrejev No. 1670*.

L161. Lowly hero marries princess.

N685. *Fool passes as wise man by remaining silent.* Pauli (ed. Bolte) No. 32; Spanish Exempla: Keller.

J580. Wisdom of caution. J2350. Talkative fool. K1956.5. Sham wise man stays alone feigning study. Really is killing flies.

N686. *Hero's (heroine's) identity established as he (she) is on the point of being executed.* Italian Novella: *Rotunda.

N731. Unexpected meeting of father and son. R175. Rescue at the stake.

N687. *Hero unwittingly helps fee's sons: rewarded.* Italian: Basile Pentamerone I No. 3.

F347. Fairy adviser. N810. Supernatural helpers.

N688. *What is in the dish: "Poor Crab".* A sham wise man named Crab is put to a test of his powers of divination. He is to tell what is in a covered dish (crabs). In despair he says, "Poor Crab!" and is given credit for knowing. *Type 1641; *BP II 401ff., 409; Louisiana French: Fortier MAFLS II 116; India: *Thompson-Balys; Indonesia: DeVries's list No. 302; Philippine: Fansler MAFLS XII 7f., 144; American Negro (Georgia): Harris Friends 24ff. No. 3; Cape Verde Islands: Parsons MAFLS XV (1) 182 No. 62.

K1956. Sham wise man.

N688.1. *Doctor know-all accidentally saves raja.* Roof caves in after he has dragged raja out with the intention of killing him and putting an end to all of his questions. India: Thompson-Balys.

N691. *Objects accidentally picked up used to overawe ogress.* India: Thompson-Balys; East Africa: Rattray Some Folk-Lore Stories and Songs in Chinvanja (London, 1907) 149ff. No. 24.

G570. Ogre overawed. H507.1.0.1. Princess defeated in repartee by means of objects accidentally picked up. K1710. Ogre (large animal) overawed.

N691.1. *Numskull's outcry overawes tiger who is carrying him on his back.* Tiger thinks that words are the name of the "demon" riding him. India: Thompson-Balys.

K1710. Ogre (large animal) overawed. K1951.2. Runaway cavalry-hero. K2320. Deception by frightening. N392. Robber attempting to steal cow at night seizes thieving tiger. Great fight in stable.

N691.1.1. *Hero attempting to escape from tiger plays music and tiger follows.* People marvel and give him money and he is rewarded with princess's hand. Korean: Zong in-Sob 149 No. 65.

N691.1.2. *Stupid man grabs tiger in the dark, ties it up, and saddles it, believing it to be a horse.* It happens to be the tiger for whose capture a reward has been offered. India: Thompson-Balys.

N692. *Person reported lost joins unwittingly in search for himself.*

N692.1. *Missing girl reveals identity and saves man condemned for kidnapping her.* Buddhist myth: Malalasekera II 817.

N693. *Man sent away from battlefield to deliver message the only survivor of battle.* Jewish: *Neuman.

N694. *Apparently dead woman revives as she is being prepared for burial.* Cf. Type 990. Italian Novella: Rotunda.

E0. Resuscitation. T37. Lover finds lady in tomb apparently dead. She revives and marries him.

N694.1. *Apparently dead woman revives when dropped.* Had swallowed a bone. Lover exhumes her. Stumbles as he carries her. She revives and later marries him. Italian Novella: Rotunda.

E21. Resuscitation by withdrawal of wounding instrument.

N695. *Passengers on a boat are terrorized by a cutthroat.* He turns courteous and leaves them unharmed. Italian Novella: Rotunda.

N696. *Fugitive in tree urinates from fright: pursuers think it rain and leave.* India: Thompson-Balys.

J1818. Urination of bull thought to be bleeding. K335.1.1. Object falls on robbers from tree. K500. Escape from death or danger by deception. N331.2.1. Man hidden in tree so frightened of lioness he drops his sword and kills her.

N696.1. *Man falls out of tree and frightens tiger away.* India: Thompson-Balys.

N696.2. *Grinding stones carried by men seeking refuge in tree-top fall, killing their enemies below.* India: Thompson-Balys.

K335.1.1. Objects fall on robbers from tree.

N698. *Hawk carries off necklace from bathing queen and drops it by lucky girl, who gets reward.* India: Thompson-Balys.

B522.2. Kite steals jewels and thus saves condemned man. N352. Bird carries off ring which lover has taken from sleeping mistress's finger. He searches for the ring and becomes separated from her.

N699. *Other lucky accidents.*

N699.1. *Father and brother accidentally return home just as they are most needed in fight.* Icelandic: Boberg.

N699.2. *King's son comes home just at his father's funeral, when the heritage has to be divided.* Icelandic: Boberg.

N699.3. *Companions arrive as hero is about to be killed.* Irish myth: Cross.

N699.4. *Orphan gets wife because swollen creek prevents marriage to someone else.* Chinese: Graham.

N699.5. *Boy while cutting trees comes to one which happens to be bound up with the life of an ogre.* Ogre bribes him with large fortune not to cut tree. India: Thompson-Balys.

E711.2. Soul in plant.

N699.6. *Overheard wish is realized.* India: *Thompson-Balys.

N700—N799. Accidental encounters.

N700. Accidental encounters.

K1812.18. Fallen king in disguise recognized by former ally and helped. T456. Bed-partner to receive payment from first man she meets in the morning. It so happens: she marries the man and he makes her wealthy.

N710. Accidental meeting of hero and heroine.

T30. Lovers' meeting. T62. Princess to marry first man who asks for her.

N711. *King (prince) accidentally finds maiden and marries her.* *Types 403, 451, 705, 709; *BP I 99ff., 295ff.; Irish myth: *Cross; Icelandic: Boberg; Spanish: Espinosa II Nos. 99—103, Espinosa Jr. Nos. 80, 115; Italian: Basile Pentamerone I No. 8; India: *Thompson-Balys.

N455.4. King overhears girl's boast as to what she should do as queen. Marries her. T91.6.3.1. Prince falls in love with merchant's daughter exposed in jungle.

N711.1. *King (prince) finds maiden in woods (tree) and marries her.* *Types 450, 706, 710; Irish myth: Cross; Icelandic: *Boberg; Missouri French: Carrière; French Canadian: Sister Marie Ursule; India: *Thompson-Balys.

F562.2. Residence in a tree. F811.10.1. Hollow tree as residence for hero. N771. King (prince) lost on hunt has adventures. R311. Tree refuge.

N711.2. *Hero finds maiden in (magic) castle.* *Types 304, 400, 408, 410, 590; Irish myth: *Cross; India: *Thompson-Balys.

N711.3. *Hero finds maiden in (magic) garden.* *Types 550, 551, 706; Spanish: Espinosa Jr. No. 106; India: Thompson-Balys.

T645. Paramour leaves token with girl to give their son.

N711.4. *Prince sees maiden at church and is enamored.* *Types 510AB; Missouri French: Carrière; Spanish: Espinosa III Nos. 111f., Espinosa Jr. No. 119.

T381.1. Guarded maiden first seen by hero in church.

N711.4.1. *Lovers meet at temple.* India: *Thompson-Balys.

N711.5. *Prince (king) finds girl floating on water in basket: marries her.* Hertel Zs. f. Vksk. XIX 83ff.; Penzer II 5; Italian: Basile Pentamerone III No. 2; India: Thompson-Balys.

N711.6. *Prince sees heroine at ball and is enamored.* *Type 510AB; Missouri French: Carrière; Spanish: Espinosa II 107—112, 154; Espinosa Jr. Nos. 123f.; India: Thompson-Balys.

R221. Heroine's threefold flight from ball.

N712. *Prince first sees heroine as she comes forth from her hiding-box.* She has concealed herself until the favorable moment. *Cox 489; India: Thompson-Balys.

N831.1. Mysterious housekeeper.

N712.1. *Princess concealed in trunk and sent to beggar, who marries her.* India: Thompson-Balys.

N713. *King marries girl who finds lost object of his.*

N713.1. *Princess catches raja's golden bird; he trails it to her palace.* India: Thompson-Balys.

N713.2. *King marries girl who finds his lost ring.* India: Thompson-Balys.

N715. *Lovers first see each other on shores of lake.* M. Bloomfield in Penzer VII xxiii; India: Thompson-Balys.

N715.1. *Hero finds maiden at fountain (well, river).* Irish myth: *Cross; Jewish: Neuman.

N716. *Lover sees beloved first while she is bathing.* II Samuel ch. 11; India: *Thompson-Balys.

K1335. Seduction (or wooing) by stealing clothes of bathing girl. T16. Man falls in love with woman he sees bathing.

N716.1. *Man stumbles on bathing maiden.* Mono-Alu: Wheeler Nos. 8, 9, 31, 48.

N718. *Accidental meeting with the son of the only person who can overcome curse on hero.* Icelandic: Boberg.

N721. *Runaway horse carries bride to her lover.* Bridegroom unwittingly hires a horse belonging to his rival for his bride to ride to the wedding. A storm arises and the horse carries her to his master. *Bédier Fabliaux 119, 473.

N723. *Girl sees man as he lies sleeping by wayside.* India: Thompson-Balys.

N724. *Hunter accidentally discovers beautiful girl being secretly reared in a cave.* Africa (Pangwe): Tessman 366.

N730. Accidental reunion of families. *Chauvin VI 167ff. No. 327E; Boccaccio Decameron II Nos. 6, 8 (Lee 34, 39); Irish myth: *Cross; Missouri French: Carrière; Italian Novella: *Rotunda; Jewish: Neuman; India: *Thompson-Balys; Buddhist myth: Malalasekera II 947.

H0. Identity tests. Recognition. H90. Identification by ornaments. H110. Identification by cloth or clothing. H151.8. Husband attracted by wife's power of healing: recognition follows. N251. Man pursued by misfortune. (Placidas, Eustacius.) His goods are destroyed, his wife carried off by a ship captain, and his children by animals. He finally recovers them all. R131. Exposed or abandoned child rescued. R150. Rescuers. S145. Abandonment on an island. S433. Cast-off wife abandoned on island. T96. Lovers reunited after many adventures.

N731. *Unexpected meeting of father and son.* Irish myth: *Cross; Missouri French: Carrière; Italian Novella: *Rotunda; Jewish: Neuman; India: Thompson-Balys.

D1810.8.2.5. Raja told in a dream the stranger he seeks to destroy is his own son. H1216. Mother sends son to find unknown father. H1381.2. Quest for unknown father.

N731.1. *Unknown son returns to father's court.* Irish myth: Cross; Greek: Fox 119 (Paris).

N731.1.1. *King unknowingly adopts his own lost son.* India: Thompson-Balys.

N731.2. *Father-son combat.* Neither knows who the other is. (Sohrab and Rustem.) **Potter Sohrab and Rustem; Deutschbein I 232ff.; Potter FL XV 216ff.; Rank Inzest-Motif 164ff.; Hibbard 227 n. 5; *Köhler-Bolte II 256ff.; L. Wolff Hessische Blätter f. Volksk. XXXIX 54—63. — Irish: *Cross, MacCulloch Celtic 145, 169 (Cuchulainn, Fionn), Thurneysen 403ff.; English: Wells 135 (Sir Degare); Icelandic: *Boberg; Greek: Fox 140 (Telegonos and Odysseus); Arabian: Burton Nights VII 89 n.; Persian: Carnoy 332; Chinese: Werner Myths 315—319, Coyajee JPASB XXIV 179; Philippine: Dixon 235; Hawaii: Beckwith Myth 508.

A515.5. Culture hero fights with (encounters) son without recognizing him. C436. Tabu: disclosing own identity. A supernatural person must not tell who he is. D1317.6.1. Sword bursts in son's hand when he is about to kill his father. H151.10. Combat of unknown brothers brings about recognition. J675.1. Son slays father in order not to be slain himself. K1094.1. God persuades hero to substitute a false bride for his father, which results in a fight where the son kills the father. N338.3. Father kills son taking him for another. N349.2. Father kills his son in battle rage. N767. Unwitting combat between sons of friends. P205. Refusal to fight relatives. P233. Father and son.

N731.2.1. *Hero fights with friend of father and then reveals himself.* English: Wells 17 (Reinbrun, Gy son of Warwike).

N731.2.2. *Undesired combat between sworn (blood) brothers (foster brothers).* Irish myth: *Cross.

N731.3. *Father unexpectedly meets abandoned son and reinstates him.* Irish myth: Cross.

S350. Fate of abandoned child.

N731.4. *At execution block condemned man discovered to be king's unknown son.* India: Thompson-Balys.

N732. *Accidental meeting of father and daughter.* Missouri French: Carrière.

N732.1. *Father unwittingly buys daughter who has been sold into slavery.* Greek: Frazer Apollodorus I 389 n. 1 (Tisiphone).

R153.5. Father rescues abducted daughter.

N732.2. *Deserted daughter's good fortune discovered by accident.* N. A. Indian: *Thompson Tales 348 n. 251.

N732.2.1. *Daughter's good fortune accidentally discovered by father who has become a beggar.* Chinese: Graham.

N732.3. *Parents accidentally meet daughter who has survived their attempts to drown her.* Italian Novella: Rotunda.

R131. Exposed or abandoned child rescued. S10. Cruel parents. S140. Cruel abandonment and exposures.

N733. *Accidental meeting of brothers.* Irish myth: *Cross; Icelandic: *Boberg; Jewish: Neuman.

H1233.2.2. Quest accomplished with aid of brother in disguise. K867. Fatal duel: brother kills brother in pretended game. K2211. Treacherous brother. Usually elder brother. P251. Brothers.

N733.1. *Brothers unwittingly fight each other.* (Cf. N731.2.2.) Dickson 100, 109, 153; Icelandic: Boberg; Tuamotu: Stimson MS (z-G. 13/317).

H151.10. Combat of unknown brothers brings about recognition. P205. Refusal to fight relatives. P251. Brothers. P314. Combat of disguised friends.

N733.2. *Brother unwittingly kills half brother in fight.* Icelandic: Boberg.

N320. Person unwittingly killed.

N733.3. *Joseph and his brethren.* Elder brothers unwittingly come to maltreated youngest in great need. Eventual recognition. India: Thompson-Balys.

N733.4. *Two returning brothers unwittingly purchase bird, which is transformed youngest brother, as present intended for him.* India: Thompson-Balys.

N733.5. *Brothers accidentally reunited when wedding of one to a king's daughter is celebrated* and neighboring rulers are invited. India: Thompson-Balys.

N734. *Accidental meeting of brother and sister.* Irish myth: Cross.

N734.1. *Slaves ordered married discover they are brother and sister.* Irish myth: Cross.

T415.4. Two lovers give each other up when they learn that they are brother and sister.

N734.2. *Saint prays with woman; learns she is his sister.* Irish myth: Cross.

N735. *Accidental meeting of mother and son.* Irish myth: *Cross; Jewish: Neuman; India: Thompson-Balys; Chinese: Graham.

N735.1. *Begging ascetics beg alms of their own mother.* Buddhist myth: Malalasekera II 511.

N736. *Accidental meeting of mother and daughter.* India: Thompson-Balys.

N737. *Accidental reunion of lovers.* Italian Novella: *Rotunda.

T30. Lovers' meeting.

N738. *Accidental meeting of nephew and uncle.* Hero takes refuge unwittingly at his uncle's court. *Dickson 143 n. 143; Icelandic: *Boberg.

P293. Uncle. P297. Nephew. R331. Hero takes refuge at king's court.

N738.1. *Uncle and nephew unwittingly about to kill one another.* Icelandic: Boberg.

N741. *Unexpected meeting of husband and wife.* Irish myth: *Cross; Missouri French: Carrière; Spanish: Espinosa II Nos. 99—103; India: *Thompson-Balys.

H151.8. Husband attracted by wife's power of healing: recognition follows. H152.3. Abandoned wife recognized among workers. N681. Husband (lover) arrives home just as wife (mistress) is to marry another. T298. Reconciliation of a separated couple.

N741.1. *Concealed wife.* Unknown wife supernaturally conceals herself until the favorable moment to come forward. Italian: Crane 340; Greek: Garnett II 18; Hindu: Rouse FL V 85.

N741.2. *Husband and wife become separated in shipwreck.* Wife unexpectedly meets husband on street. They are reunited. Italian Novella: Rotunda.

N741.3. *Slandered queen chances to be in Rome at the same time as her estranged husband.* Reconciled by the Pope. Italian Novella: Rotunda.

N741.3.1. *Calumniated wife is forced to flee.* (Cf. K2210.) Reunited by chance after many years at Emperor's court. Italian Novella: Rotunda.

N741.4. *Husband and wife reunited after long separation and tedious quest.* India: Thompson-Balys.

N741.5. *Maiden found in magic garden; prince's wife in former life.* India: Thompson-Balys.

N743. *Accidental meeting of sisters.* India: Thompson-Balys.

N745. *Accidental meeting of seeker of exiled prince with prince at meal.* Messenger in pilgrim garb invites unknown prince to eat with him. Recognition. *Boje 85.

N746. *Accidental meeting of cousins.* Icelandic: Þorsteins saga Vík. 446, Boberg.

N760. Other accidental encounters.

N761. *Unexpected encounter in oasis.* Malone PMLA XLIII 398.

N762. *Person accidentally met unexpectedly knows the other's name.* Icelandic: *Boberg.

N763. *Hero captured by man he has formerly rescued: rewarded.* *Type 953; Scottish: Campbell-McKay No. 25.

N764. *Unexpected meeting with wild man.* (Cf. F567.) Dickson 122 n. 72; Missouri French: Carrière.

N765. *Meeting with robber band.* Dickson 68 n. 14.

K1916. Robber bridegroom. N884. Robbers help. P475. Robber. Q53. Reward for rescue. Q111.3. Riches as reward for help against robbers. Q451.2. Laming as punishment.

N766. *Unwitting adultery with blood-brother's wife.* *Type 1364; Wesselski Märchen 187 No. 2.

N767. *Unwitting combat between sons of friends.* Recognition and reconciliation. (Cf. N731.2.) Greek: Fox 128 (Glaukos and Diomedes).

N768. *Abandoned children accidentally discovered by villainess.* India: Thompson-Balys.

N770. Experiences leading to adventures.

D1313.1. Magic ball indicates road. H1226.2. Pursuit of magic arrow leads to adventures. N126.1. Lots cast to determine who shall undertake adventure.

N770.0.1. *Feast as occasion for the beginning of adventures or the arrival of questers.* Irish myth: *Cross.

N771. *King (prince) lost on hunt has adventures.* *BP I 432 n. 2; *Köhler-Bolte II 408ff.; Dickson 93, 123 n. 75; Malone PMLA XLIII 398; Irish myth: *Cross; Icelandic: *Boberg; Italian: Basile Pentamerone I No. 8, V No. 5; India: *Thompson-Balys.

D659.10. Transformation to lure hunters to certain place. G405. Man in hunt falls into ogre's (witch's) power. H1222. Prince a-hunting enters on quest. K1812.1. Incognito king helped by humble man. Gives reward. N711.1. King (prince) finds maiden in woods (tree) and marries her.

N771.1. *King on hunt is taken prisoner.* Icelandic: þidriks saga II 120—40.

N771.2. *Girls going in the wood for nuts have adventures.* Icelandic: *Boberg.

N772. *Parting at crossroads to go on adventures.* *Type 303; *Ranke FFC CXIV (motif B2); India: Thompson-Balys; Chinese: Graham.

N773. *Adventure from following animal to cave (lower world).* *Type 301; Irish myth: *Cross; Spanish: Boggs FFC XC 66 No. 508 A*, Espinosa Jr. No. 67; Indonesia: DeVries's list No. 163; N. A. Indian (California): Gayton and Newman 74.

D102.1. Transformation: demon to animal. F92. Pit entrance to lower world. F102. Accidental arrival in lower world.

N773.1. *Adventure from following ogre to cave.* India: Thompson-Balys.

N773.2. *Adventure from returning for forgotten* comb. India: Thompson-Balys.

N774. *Adventures from pursuing enchanted animal (hind, boar, bird).* (Guiding Beast.) Types 710 (Grimm No. 3), 425; *Tegethoff 14; **Pschmadt Die Sage von der verfolgten Hinde (Greifswald, 1911); Dickson 53f.; Clouston Tales I 215; *Fb "hjort" I 625a; Hibbard 244 (Chevalere Assigne). — Irish myth: *Cross; Icelandic: Lagerholm

25—26, Sveinsson FFC LXXXIII xxxiii, *Boberg; Italian: Basile Pentamerone I No. 9, *Rotunda; India: *Thompson-Balys; New Britain: Dixon 140.

B151.1.1. Horses determine road to be taken. B151.2.0.2. Birds show way to otherworld. B172.6. Magic birds lure hunters to certain places. D102.1. Transformation: demon to animal. F989.15. Hunt for extraordinary (magic) animal. G211. Witch in animal form. G402.1. Pursuit of bird leads to ogre's house. H1331.2. Quest for marvelous boar pig).

N774.1. *Adventure from pursuing thieving birds.* Type 610; India: Thompson-Balys.

N774.2. *Adventures from seeking (lost) domestic beast (bull).* Type 511; Icelandic: Boberg; India: Thompson-Balys.

N774.3. *Adventures from pursuing animal (not magic).* India: *Thompson-Balys.

N774.3.1. *Runaway ox leads pursuer to burial place of Adam and Eve.* Jewish: *Neuman.

N775. *Race with fairies leads to adventures.* Irish myth: Cross.

N776. *Light seen from tree lodging place at night leads to adventures.* *Type 130, 327; *Aarne FFC XI 111; BP I 115ff.; Missouri French: Carrière; Japanese: Ikeda.

F1045. Night spent in tree. R311. Tree refuge.

N776.1. *Climbing tree to look around leads to adventures.* India: *Thompson-Balys; Chinese: Graham.

N776.2. *Adventures from trying to strangle oneself in tree.* India: Thompson-Balys.

N776.3. *Adventures from having slept beneath tree.* India: *Thompson-Balys.

N777. *Dropped ball (basket) leads to adventures when recovery is attempted.* Italian: Basile Pentamerone III No. 10 (Type 440).

D1313.1.1. Magic ball of thread indicates road. Rolls ahead.

N777.1. *Adventures encountered in running after cotton being blown away by wind.* Type 480; *Roberts 130; India: Thompson-Balys.

N777.2. *Bucket dropped into well leads to adventures.* Type 480; *Roberts 125.

N777.3. *Flax dropped into well leads to adventures.* Type 480; *Roberts 125.

N777.4. *Spindle dropped into well leads to adventures.* Type 480; *Roberts 125.

N778. *Taking refuge in a grave leads to adventure.* Italian Novella: *Rotunda.

N781. *Hero embarks in rudderless boat.* Köhler-Bolte I 189; *Schoepperle Tristan and Isolt II 370ff.; Irish myth: *Cross.

N782. *Mother's parting gift to adventuring son: the two loaves of bread. One for hunger, one for overeating.* India: Thompson-Balys.

L222. Modest choice: parting gift.

N783. *Broken vessel (calabash, etc.) to be mended leads to adventure.* Africa (Guinea Coast): Trautmann La Litterature à la Côte des

Esclaves (Paris, 1927), West Africa: Travélé Proverbes et contes Bambara (Paris, 1923) 205ff., No. 66, Frobenius Atlantis VIII 274ff. No. 120.

N784. *Shouting after bathing: adventures follow.* N. A. Indian (California): Gayton and Newman 88.

N785. *Adventures from seeking water.* Irish myth: *Cross; Icelandic: Boberg.

N311. Separation of persons caused by looking for water.

N785.1. *Man hunting honey encounters lost maiden, returns her to her parents.* Africa (Fang): Tessman 121.

N786. *Anchor catching in oratory of submarine monastery leads to adventures.* Irish myth: Cross.

F133.3. Submarine monastery.

N788. *Incidents when wife takes food to husband in field or forest.* India: Thompson-Balys.

N791. *Adventures from pursuing object carried off by river.* Type 480; Roberts 129.

N792. *Adventures from pursuing objects carried off by bird.* Type 480; Roberts 130.

N800—N899. Helpers.

N800. Helpers.

B300. Helpful animal. B400. Helpful domestic beast. B571. Animals perform tasks for man. D671.0.1. Fugitive transformed by helper to escape detection. D810. Magic object a gift. D1421.1. Magic object summons genie. E323.4. Advice from dead mother. E341. The grateful dead. F601.1. Extraordinary companions perform hero's tasks. H970. Help in performing tasks. H1233.6. Animals help hero on quest. H1235. Succession of helpers on quest. K2036. Helper steals object obtained at end of quest. R150. Rescuers. V232. Angel as helper. V252. Virgin Mary defends innocent accused.

N801. *Helper grateful for being bought from slavery.* Type 516; Rosch FFC LXXVII 97.

N810. Supernatural helpers. Irish myth: *Cross; Missouri French: Carrière; Spanish: Espinosa II Nos. 111f., Espinosa Jr. Nos. 117, 138, 140, 149, 202—204; Jewish: *Neuman; India: *Thompson-Balys.

A172. Gods intervene in battle. A528. Culture hero has supernatural helpers. B53.1. Drowning man rescued by siren. B313.1. Helpful animal reincarnation of parent. C311.1.5. Tabu: observing supernatural helper. D812. Magic object received from supernatural being. D825.1. Magic object received from cat-woman; i.e., woman transformed intermittently to cat. D842. Magic object found on mother's grave. D2121.5. Magic journey: man carried by spirit or devil. F451.5.1. Helpful dwarfs. F460.4.2. Helpful mountain-men. F481.2. Cobolds furnish supplies to their masters. G284. Witch as helper. G303.22. The devil helps people. G303.22.11. Devil as advocate of falsely condemned man H970. Help in performing tasks. H972. Tasks accomplished with help of grateful dead. H984. Tasks performed with help of saint. M212. Devil agrees to help man with robberies. M214. Devil to help gambler in exchange for one task yearly. M216. Devil bargains to help man become priest. M217. Devil bargains to help man win woman. N687. Hero unwittingly helps fée's sons: rewarded. T53.1. Incognito prophet as matchmaker.

N810.1. *Invisible guardians.* Hindu: Tawney I 193, 544; Icelandic: *Boberg.

E748. The soul as a guardian spirit. F494.1. Guardian spirit of land. N110. Luck and fate personified.

N810.2. *Helper's beard and eyebrows cut.* Only after hero has performed this service is help forthcoming. *BP II 392.

N810.3. *Hero's divine father as helper.* India: Thompson-Balys.

N810.4. *Supernatural helper comes from sky.* Korean: Zong in-Sob 65 No. 35.

N810.5. *Supernatural person disguised as servant as helper.* Irish myth: *Cross.

N810.6. *Saint disguised (as poor man) as helper.* Irish myth: Cross.

N811. *Supernatural godfather.* A king chooses as the godfather of his son the first man he meets. The godfather proves to be supernatural. *Type 652; *BP I 377ff., II 121ff., III 18.

D1725.1. Death as godfather. F451.5.1.1. Dwarf as godfather. F460.4.7. Mountain-man as godfather. K557. Death cheated by moving bed. The man has chosen Death as his godfather. P296.1. Godfather. S224. Child promised to devil for acting as godfather.

N812. *Giant or ogre as helper.* *Types 531, 709; Böklen 84ff.; BP III 18ff.; Malone PMLA XLIII 412; Irish myth: *Cross; Missouri French: Carrière; India: *Thompson-Balys; Eskimo (Bering Strait): Nelson RBAE XVIII 471; Africa (Zulu): Callaway 44, (Benga): Nassau 208ff.

D812.11. Magic object received from giant. D845.2. Magic object found in giant's cave. D1421.4. Magic object summons giant. F460.4.2. Helpful mountain-men. F531.5.1. Giant friendly to man. F531.5.7.1.2. Giantess daughter of giant and abducted maiden (therefore helps hero). F531.6.1.2. Giant is transformed man. G284. Witch as helper. G303.22. The devil helps people. G513.1. Grateful ogre resuscitates his benefactor. G514.0.1. Demon must bring treasure to those who have released him. G530. Ogre's relative aids hero. G671. Wild man released from captivity aids hero.

N812.0.1. *Giant's help secured by feeding him.* *Type 531; BP III 18ff.

N812.1. *Wise giant as foster father of hero.* Icelandic: Olrik Sakses Oldhistorie I (1892) 40ff., *Boberg.

F531.6.17.7. Giants are wise. P271. Foster father. P271.5. Foster father as constant helper. P272. Foster mother

N812.2. *Giantess as foster mother and helper of hero.* Iclandic: *Boberg.

N812.3. *Grateful giantess as helper.* Icelandic: *Boberg.

N812.4. *Giantess helps the man she loves.* Icelandic: *Boberg.

G530.2. Help from ogre's daughter or son. T91.1. Giant's daughter loves hero.

N812.5. *Monster grateful to hero for being spared becomes helpful.* India: *Thompson-Balys.

N812.6. *Ogre magically produces water for caravan.* Buddhist myth: Malalasekera I 15.

N812.7. *Chief with three supernatural ogre helpers.* Marquesas: Handy 76.

N813. *Helpful genie (spirit).* *Types 561, 562; *Aarne MSFO XXV 3—82; *BP II 535ff., 547ff.; *Fischer-Bolte 215. — Missouri French: Carrière; India: *Thompson-Balys; Buddhist myth: Malalasekera II 1302; Chinese: Eberhard FFC CXX 182; Philippine (Tinguian): Cole 67, 140, 142; Samoa: Beckwith Myth 438, 442; Easter Island: Métraux Ethnology 319, 369, 375; Tuamotu: Stimson MS (z-G. 3/1007, 13/174, 221), Henry Ancient Tahiti (Honolulu, 1928) 520f., Beckwith Myth

450; S. A. Indian (Mura): Métraux MAFLS XL 36; Africa (Fang): Tessman 194.

D812.5. Magic object received from genie. D1421.1. Magic object summons genie. F403.2. Spirits help mortal. Familiar spirits. F450.1. Helpful underground spirit. H973. Tasks performed by helpful forest spirits.

N814. *Helpful angel.* Hdwb. d. Märchens I 535b; Irish myth: Cross; Jewish: *Neuman; India: Thompson-Balys.

V232.1. Angel as helper in battle.

N814.1. *Man carried through air by angel.* Icelandic: Boberg; Jewish: bin Gorion Born Judas I 117, 374.

N815. *Fairy as helper.* Irish myth: *Cross; Icelandic: *Boberg; India: *Thompson-Balys.

D1421.1.6. Magic ring summons genie. F302.3.2.1. Fairy offers aid to man if he will marry her. F302.9. Fairy mistress rescues hero from battle. F311.1. Fairy godmother. Attendant good fairy. F312.1. Fairies bestow supernatural gifts at birth of child. F312.2. Fairies control destinies of a mortal. F330. Grateful fairies. F340. Gifts from fairies. F347. Fairy adviser. F420.5.1. Kind water-spirits. H973.1. Tasks performed by fairies. H1233.4.1. Fairies as helpers on quest.

N815.0.1. *Helpful tree-spirit.* (Cf. F441.2.) India: Thompson-Balys; Buddhist myth: Malalasekera I 534.

N815.0.2. *Helpful water-spirit.* (Cf. F420.) India: Thompson-Balys.

N815.0.2.1. *Gift of gold bracelet from river goddess.* (Cf. A425.1.) India: Thompson-Balys.

N815.1. *Fairy nurse as helper.* Irish myth: Cross.

F371. Human being reared in fairyland.

N816. *Santa Claus as bringer of Christmas gifts.* *Hoffman-Krayer Zs. f. Vksk. XXV 121 nn. 7—9.

N817. *Deity as helper.* Greek: Iliad and Odyssey passim; India: *Thompson-Balys; Buddhist myth: Malalasekera I 840, II 504.

A172. Gods intervene in battle. A180. Gods in relation to mortals. A536. Demigods fight as allies of mortals. K1811. Gods (saints) in disguise visit mortals.

N817.0.1. *God as helper.* Irish myth: *Cross; Jewish: *Neuman; Hawaii: Beckwith Myth 22, 111, 174.

N817.0.2. *Goddess as helper.* Greek: Grote I 54; Buddhist myth: Malalasekera II 979.

N817.1. *Gods discuss means of settling dispute among girl's suitors.* Venus has girl make her own choice. Italian Novella: Rotunda.

N818. *Sky as helper.* Africa (Thonga): Junod 266ff.

N818.1. *Sun as helper.* India: Thompson-Balys.

N819. *Supernatural helpers—miscellaneous.*

N819.1. *Immortal as helper.* Chinese: Graham.

N819.2. *Transformed person as helper.* Chinese: Graham.

N819.2.1. *Transformed mother as helper.* Chinese: Graham.

N819.3. *Helpful vital heads.* India: Thompson-Balys.

E783. Vital head.

N819.3.1. *Helpful speaking skull.* India: Thompson-Balys.

D1610. Magic speaking objects.

N819.4. *Supernatural medicine-man as helper.* S. A. Indian (Tupenamba): Métraux RMLP XXXIII 168.

N820. Human helpers.

H1235. Succession of helpers on quest. K1812.18. Fallen king in disguise recognized by former ally and helped. P361. Faithful servant. R131. Exposed or abandoned child rescued.

N821. *Help from little man.* *Types 513B, 570; *BP III 267ff.

F535. Pygmies. Remarkably small men.

N822. *Lame boy (girl) as helper.* Africa (Ekoi): Talbot 35, 58, 248, 280.

N825. *Old person as helper.* Spanish: Espinosa II Nos. 99—103, 119—121, 126—132.

F571.2. Sending to the elder. Old person refers enquirer to his father, who refers to his father, and so on for several generations. H1233.1. Old person as helper on quest. H1235. Succession of helpers on quest. One helper sends to another, who sends to another, etc.

N825.1. *Childless old couple adopt hero.* Malone: PMLA XLIII 399.

N825.2. *Old man helper.* *Types 307, 329, 480, 512*; *BP III 365ff., 534ff.; *Chauvin VI 109 No. 273 n. 1; Roberts 150. — Irish myth: Cross; Missouri French: Carrière; Spanish: Espinosa II Nos. 75, 99—103, 138f.; India: *Thompson-Balys; Chinese: Graham; Japanese: Ikeda; Tuamotu: Stimson MS (z-G. 13/174); Hawaii: Beckwith Myth 461; N. A. Indian (Seneca): Curtin-Hewitt RBAE XXXII 88 No. 4; Africa (Kaffir): Theal 83.

D822. Magic object received from old man.

N825.3. *Old woman helper.* *Types 316, 400, 480, 707; *BP II 380ff., 466; *Cosquin Etudes 563; Hdwb. d. Märchens I s.v. "Alte im Walde"; Roberts 150. — Irish myth: *Cross; Icelandic: *Boberg; Finnish: Kalevala rune 7; Breton: Sébillot Incidents s.v. "vieille"; Missouri French: Carrière; Italian: Basile Pentamerone V No. 9, Rotunda; Spanish: Espinosa II Nos. 99—103, 126—132, Espinosa Jr. Nos. 107, 109; India: *Thompson-Balys; Korean: Zong in-Sob 63, 166; Polynesia (general): Beckwith Myth chapt. 17 passim; Hawaii: ibid. 257—264, 491; Tahiti: ibid. 251; Tonga: Gifford 156; Maori: Dixon 59; Eskimo (Greenland): Rasmussen II 162; N. A. Indian: *Thompson Tales 327 n. 180; Africa: Werner African 233, (Ekoi): Talbot 18, 207, 235, 364, (Basuto): Jacottet 118 No. 17, 142 No. 20, 204 No. 30, 226 No. 33, (Kaffir): Theal 48ff., 82, 145, (Zanzibar): Bateman 128 No. 7, (Angola): Chatelain 47 No. 1, 57 No. 2, 93 No. 5, (Zulu): Callaway 217.

D821. Magic object received from old woman. G530.5. Help from old woman in ogre's house. H971.1. Tasks performed with help of old woman. H1233.1.1. Old woman helps on quest. M301.2. Old woman as prophet. M411.5. Old woman's curse. P361.5. Abandoned maiden helped by her faithful nurse.

N825.3.1. *Help from old beggar woman.* *Hdwb. d. Märchens I 248b; BP III 206 (Grimm No. 150.)

N825.3.2. *Old woman by spring as helper.* *Type 480; Roberts 151; Italian: Basile Pentamerone IV No. 7.

N825.3.3. *Help from grandmother.* N. A. Indian (California): Gayton and Newman 69.

P292. Grandmother. S351.1. Abandoned child cared for by grandmother.

N826. *Help from beggar.* (Cf. N825.3.1.) *Type 531; Fb "tigger" III 794b; India: Thompson-Balys.

N827. *Child as helper*. (Cf. N832.) Spanish: Boggs FFC XC 105 No. 860; Chinese: Graham; Korean: Zong in-Sob 47.

T66.2. Grateful little boys help hero win girl.

N828. *Wise woman as helper*. Italian: Basile Pentamerone V No. 3.

N831. *Girl as helper*. Types 311, 313; Dickson 52f.; Tobler Epiphanie der Seele 71; Missouri French: Carrière; India: *Thompson-Balys.

D825. Magic object received from maiden. G530.2. Help from ogre's daughter (or son). G535. Ogre's captive princess hero's helper. K781. Castle captured with assistance of owner's daughter. She loves the attacker. R162. Rescue by captor's daughter (wife, mother). T30. Lovers' meeting.

N831.1. *Mysterious housekeeper*. Men find their house mysteriously put in order. Discover that it is done by a girl (frequently an animal transformed into a girl). *Type 709; **Böklen Sneewittchenstudien 89ff.; MacCulloch Childhood 261; *BP I 450ff.; Hatt Asiatic Influences 96—102. — Breton: Sébillot Incidents s.v. "menage"; Missouri French: Carrière; Spanish: Espinosa Jr. Nos. 71—74, 81, Espinosa II No. 114, Boggs FFC XC 48 No. 327D*; Italian: Basile Pentamerone IV No. 6; India: *Thompson-Balys; Chinese: Graham; Korean: Zong in-Sob 30; Indonesia: DeVries's list No. 152, Dixon 218; New Britain, Philippine, Melanesia: Dixon 110 n. 25, 224 nn. 27, 28; Philippine (Tinguian): Cole 34; Eskimo (Kodiak): Golder JAFL XVI 88, (West Hudson Bay): Boas BAM XV 223; N. A. Indian: *Thompson Tales 335 n. 207; S. A. Indian: *Jijena Sanchez 23, (Surinam): Alexander Lat. Am. 274; Africa (Ekoi): Talbot 134, 136, (Basuto): Jacottet 110 No. 16, (Kaffir): Theal 74, (Congo): Weeks 215 No. 11, (Zulu): Callaway 124.

B537. Animals adopt mysterious housekeeper. B651.1. Marriage to fox in human form. K1911.3.5. True bride reinstated by acting as mysterious housekeeper. N712. Prince first sees heroine as she comes forth from her hiding-box. She has concealed herself until the favorable moment.

N831.1.1. *Mysterious housekeeper is fairy mistress*. Irish myth: *Cross.

N832. *Boy as helper*. (Cf. N827). Cheremis: Sebeok-Nyerges.

N832.1. *Boy as mysterious housekeeper for buffalo herd*. (Cf. H831.1.) India: *Thompson-Balys.

N831.1. Mysterious housekeeper.

N832.2. *Sons as helpers*. Type 551; Icelandic: Boberg.

N835. *Wealthy (powerful) man as helper*. French Canadian: Barbeau JAFL XXIX 14.

N836. *King as helper*. Spanish Exempla: Keller.

K1812.1. Incognito king helped by humble man. K1812.1.1. Incognito king is asked by humble man to aid him. K1812.12. Incognito king comes to the aid of an enemy who has refused to vilify him. P10. Kings.

N836.1. *King adopts hero (heroine)*. English: Wells 8 (King Horn), 11 (Horn Childe and Maiden Rimnild), 17 (Reinbrun, Gy sone of Warwike), 20 (William of Palerne), 115 (Sir Eglamour of Artois), 117 (Sir Torrent of Portyngale); Icelandic: Boberg; India: *Thompson-Balys.

R131.11.2. King rescues abandoned child. R331. Hero takes refuge at king's court. S354. Exposed child reared at strange king's court (Joseph, Oedipus). T670. Adoption of children.

N836.2. *Each of four kings does something to save dying falcon*. Italian Novella: Rotunda.

N836.3. *King helps princes in exile to avenge their father and take their homeland back.* Icelandic: Boberg.

N837. *Queen as helper.* Icelandic: Boberg; India: Thompson-Balys; Africa (Zulu): Callaway 239.

N838. *Hero (culture hero) as helper.* Irish myth: *Cross.

N841. *Shepherd as helper.* Spanish: Boggs FFC XC 54 No. 405A*, Espinosa Jr. No. 215; Chinese: Graham.

P412. Shepherd. R131.3. Herdsman rescues abandoned child.

N842. *Cook as helper.*

N842.1. *Cook as foster father.* Arabian: Burton I 226.

P271. Foster father.

N843. *Hermit as helper.* Irish myth: Cross; Icelandic: Boberg; English: Wells 66 (Ywain and Gawain); Spanish: Boggs FFC XC 70 No. 535, Espinosa Jr. Nos. 129, 139; India: *Thompson-Balys; Hindu: Tawney I 486, II 146.

P426.2. Hermit. R131.10. Hermit rescues abandoned child. R169.2. Boys rescued from beasts by hermit.

N844. *Dervish as helper.* Malone PMLA XLIII 400.

N844.1. *Sadhu as helper.* India: *Thompson-Balys.

N844.2. *Fakir as helper.* India: *Thompson-Balys.

N845. *Magician as helper.* Dickson 121 n. 64; Lithuanian: Balys Index No. 3669, Legends No. 621; India: *Thompson-Balys; Tuamotu: Stimson MS (z-G. 3/1386, 13/203, 317).

D1711. Magician. P271.1. Magician as foster father.

N846. *Cleric as helper.*

N846.1. *Palmer as helper.* Dickson 63.

R131.13. Palmer rescues abandoned child.

N846.2. *Priest as helper.* Tuamotu: Stimson MS (z-G. 3/1174).

N847. *Prophet as helper.* Moreno Esdras (N829); Irish myth: Cross; Jewish: Neuman.

N848. *Saint (pious man) as helper.* Irish myth: *Cross; Icelandic: *Boberg; Jewish: Neuman; India: *Thompson-Balys.

R165. Rescue by saint. V220. Saints. V221.6. Saint sustains man on gallows.

N848.0.1. *Holy man as helper.* India: Thompson-Balys.

N848.1. *Hero ransoms maltreated picture of a saint.* As reward he gets help from the grateful saint. Lithuanian: Balys Index No. 506C*.

E341.1. Dead grateful for having corpse ransomed. H984. Tasks performed with help of saint.

N848.2. *A wise man (saint, brahmin) recognizes that a man unwittingly carries a venomous serpent in his proviant sack and warns him.* Krappe Moyen Âge (1937) No. 4.

N851. *Merchant as helper.* Malone PMLA XLIII 409; India: Thompson-Balys.

P431. Merchant. R131.7. Merchant rescues abandoned child.

N852. *Soldier as helper.* Cheremis: Sebeok-Nyerges.

N854. *Peasant as helper.* Icelandic: Ásmundar saga Kappabana 472, Boberg.

K1816.9. Disguise as peasant. L113.4. Peasant as hero. P15.1. Disguised king punished by peasant. Beaten because he does not get up early enough. (King Alfred and the cakes.) P411. Peasant.

N854.1. *Peasant as foster father.* Icelandic: Boberg.

N855. *Helpful smith.* Missouri French: Carrière.

P447. Smith. R131.8.4. Smith rescues abandoned child.

N855.1. *Smith as foster father.* *Von Sydow Sigurds strid med Fåvne 19ff.; Icelandic: Boberg.

N856. *Helpful forester.* English: Wells 96 (Chevalere Assigne).

N856.1. *Forester as foster father.* *Type 652; BP II 121ff., *122; Icelandic: Boberg.

N856.2. *Cowherd as foster father.* Irish myth: Cross.

N857. *Enemy's servant as helper.* Italian Novella: Rotunda.

N861. *Foundling helper.* Type 516; Rösch FFC LXXVII 96; Icelandic: Boberg.

L111.2. Foundling hero.

N863. *Slave (swineherd) as helper of princess.* Icelandic: *Boberg.

H38.3. Slave recognized by his conversation, habits and character. K2251. Treacherous slave. P170. Slaves. Q285.4. Slave-driving punished.

N864. *Leper as helper.* Irish myth: *Cross.

N884. *Robber as helper.* West Africa: Nassau Fetischism in West Africa (London, 1904) No. 2.

N884.1. *Robber helps king.* *Type 952; *BP III 450ff.; India: Thompson-Balys.

K1812.2.1. Incognito king joins robbers. K1916. Robber bridegroom. N765. Meeting with robber band. P475. Robber. Q53. Reward for rescue. Q111.3. Riches as reward for help against robbers.

N886. *Blind man carries lame man.* They thus combine and are able to get along. *Type 519; *Wesselski Arlotto II 255 n. 1; Herbert III 192; Oesterley No. 71; Scala Celi 23b No. 151. — Irish: Mac Culloch Celtic 68, *Cross; Jewish: *Neuman; India: *Thompson-Balys; Philippine: Fansler MAFLS XII 53; N. A. Indian (Navaho): Alexander N. Am. 174.

N577. Blind man carrying lame man as guardians of treasure. S162. Mutilation: cutting off legs (feet). T125.2. Blind girl marries lame man.

N886.1. *Hunchback leads blind man.* India: Thompson-Balys.

P. SOCIETY

DETAILED SYNOPSIS

P0—P99. Royalty and nobility
- P0. Royalty and nobility
- P10. Kings
- P20. Queens
- P30. Princes
- P40. Princesses
- P50. Noblemen (knights)
- P60. Noble (gentle) ladies
- P90. Royalty and nobility—miscellaneous

P100—P199. Other social orders
- P110. Royal ministers
- P120. Church dignitaries
- P150. Rich men
- P160. Beggars
- P170. Slaves
- P190. Other social orders—miscellaneous

P200—P299. The family
- P200. The family
- P210. Husband and wife
- P230. Parents and children
- P250. Brothers and sisters
- P260. Relations by law
- P270. Foster relatives
- P280. Steprelatives
- P290. Other relatives

P300—P399. Other social relationships
- P310. Friendship
- P320. Hospitality
- P340. Teacher and pupil
- P360. Master and servant

P400—P499. Trades and professions
- P400. Trades and professions
- P410. Laborers
- P420. Learned professions
- P430. Financiers and merchants
- P440. Artisans
- P460. Other trades and professions

P500—P599. Government
- P500. Government
- P510. Law courts
- P550. Military affairs

P600—P699. Customs
- P600. Customs.

P700—P799. Society—miscellaneous motifs
- P710. Nations

P. SOCIETY

A546. Culture hero establishes social system. A1470. Beginning of social relationships. A1650. Origin of different classes—social and professional. C550. Class tabu.

P0—P99. Royalty and nobility.

P0. Royalty and nobility.

D1900.1. Favor with royalty induced by magic. H41. Recognition of royalty by personal characteristics or traits. H71. Marks of royalty. H1567.1.1. Test of leadership. H1574. Tests of social position.

P3. *Issue of marriage of brother and sister of highest chiefly rank is a god.* Hawaii: Beckwith Myth 521.

P10. Kings. Jewish: *Neuman.

A1653. Origin of kings (from god[s]). B240. King of animals. C501. Tabu: contact with things belonging to a king. C563. Tabus of kings. C938. Rulers of inferior character after tabu is broken. D45.1. Kings exchange forms and kingdoms for a year. D1654.11. Paper in hand which none but king can remove. D1960.2. King asleep in mountain. D2012.1. King in the bath: years of experience in a moment. F402.2.1. King of demons (Asmodeus). F571.6. King so old that he cannot get on horseback without help. H38.1. Disguised king recognized by habitual speech. H171. Animal or object indicates election of ruler. H508.1. King propounds questions to his sons to determine successor. H561.2. King and abbot. H561.6. King and peasant vie in riddling questions and answers. H583. Clever youth (maiden) answers king's inquiry in riddles. H711.1. How much am I (the king) worth? H921. King assigns tasks to his unknown son. H1311.1. King seeks one richer (more magnificent) than himself. H1381.3.1.1. Quest for bride for king. J215.1.2. King refuses to exile gossipers. J811.3. King honors poet and critic. J816.1.1. King brought to sense of duty by philosopher. J816.3. King brought to sense of duty by woman's words. J913. King has earthen vessels placed on table when he eats. J1081.1. King buys spendthrift's bed. J1284.2. "Cease being king." J1371. The account book of mistakes. J1675. Clever dealing with a king. J1675.3. King's capriciousness censured. J2415.1. Two presents to the king. K929.3. Ruler promises minister that he will not kill him "on any day of his life." K1812. King in disguise. M2. Inhuman decisions of king. M203. King's promise irrevocable. N467. King in disguise to learn secrets of his subjects. N836. King as helper. Q91.3. King rewards poem. Q286.2. Priest will not bury the dead unless paid in advance. Ruler has him buried alive with the corpse. T64. King seeks bride only because counsellors insist. U11.2. He who steals much is called king. W11.2.1. Emperor thinks day lost when he gives no gifts . W11.12.1. King rewards knight with large sum of money. W181.2. King kills architect after completion of great building.

P10.1. *Special place where occur births of royalty.* Hawaii: Beckwith Myth 376.

P11. *Choice of kings.* India: Thompson-Balys.

B236. Animal parliament elects king. B242.1. Various birds as king of birds. H41. Recognition of royalty by personal characteristics or traits. H41.9. Seat in which only fated king can sit. H71. Marks of royalty. H1567. Test of leadership. H1574.2. Fruitfulness of nature as proof of kingly right. H1574.3. King chosen by test.

P11.0.1. *Prophecy that brother who first kisses saint will be king.* Irish myth: Cross.

P11.0.2. *Choice of king of trees.*

P11.0.2.1. *Bramble chosen king of trees.* Herbert III 34; Hebrew: Judges 9: 8—15.

P11.1. *Choice of kings by divine will.* *Egerton JAOS XXXIII 158; Krappe Revue Hispanique LVI (1922) 5—24; *Penzer V 175ff.; *Chauvin VI 75 No. 239; India: Thompson-Balys.

H31.1. Recognition by unique ability to dislodge sword. H171. Animal or object indicates election of ruler. N683. Stranger accidentally chosen king. Picked up by sacred elephant.

P11.1.1. *Kings chosen by lot.* *Chauvin VI 75 No. 239; Africa (Swahili): Steere 141.

P11.2. *Winner of contest to be king.* *Pauli (ed. Bolte) No. 269; Jewish: *Neuman; India: Thompson-Balys.

H1561.5. Test of valor worthy for kingship: taking possession of royal insignia placed between two ferocious lions.

P11.2.1. *King chosen by contest: princes finding greatest fault with their father.* Youngest can find no fault and is chosen. Type 924**.

P11.2.2. *King chosen by contest.* Irish myth: Cross.

P11.2.2.1. *The one of two giant brothers who performs the greatest feat and procures the wildest dog elected as king.* Icelandic: Boberg.

P11.2.3. *The one of two giant brothers who gets the most skillful princess elected as king.* Icelandic: Boberg.

P11.3. *Owner of magic object chosen as king.* India: Thompson-Balys.

P11.4. *King chosen on basis of strength and exploits.* Irish myth: Cross; Spanish Exempla: Keller.

P11.4.1. *He who can open palace door to be king.* India: Thompson-Balys.

P11.4.2. *Amasser of largest fortune to be king.* India: Thompson-Balys.

P11.5. *He who can fill out a certain wide seat chosen as king.* Icelandic: Boberg.

H41.9. Siege Perilous.

P11.6. *Inauguration of king as espousal to goddess.* Irish myth: *Cross.

P12. *Character of kings.*

G11.7. Cannibalistic king.

P12.1. *Hunting a madness of kings.* Penzer II 127; Irish myth: *Cross; Icelandic: Boberg; India: Thompson-Balys.

P12.2. *Injustice deadliest of monarch's sins.* Penzer I 124 n. 1.

P12.2.1. *Tyrannical king.* Jewish: *Neuman; India: Thompson-Balys.

P12.3. *Usurper imposes burdensome taxes.* Dickson 175 n. 39.

P12.4. *King who intends rape killed.* Attackers flee into exile. Irish myth: Cross.

Q210.1. Criminal intent punished.

P12.5. *Good king never retreats in battle.* Irish myth: *Cross.

P12.5.0.1. *Dead king carried into battle in his war-chariot.* Irish myth: Cross.

P12.5.1. *King in battle hides in ditch, with earth piled around him.* Irish myth: *Cross.

P12.6. *Just king brings good fortune upon people.* Irish myth: *Cross.

P12.6.1. *Four duties of king to subjects:* devotion, protection of subjects, justice, and increase of his kingdom. India: Thompson-Balys.

P12.7. *Clever king knows everything in advance.* Icelandic: Boberg.

P12.8. *King banishes nobleman whose castle he wants.* Icelandic: *Boberg.

P12.9. *Nobility of character a mark of kings.* Kings overcomes passion for beautiful captives and sends them back untouched to their people. Spanish Exempla: Keller.

P12.10. *King is superior to all in strength, beauty, largeness, etc.,* and usually has victory. Icelandic: *Boberg; Jewish: *Neuman.

P12.11. *Uxorious king neglects duties.* India: Thompson-Balys.

P12.12. *King avenges lack of homage.* India: Thompson-Balys.

P12.13. *King quick to anger.* India: Thompson-Balys.

P12.13.1. *King to be seen after anger cools.* India: Thompson-Balys.

P12.14. *Modesty of king.* Jewish: *Neuman.

P13. *Customs connected with kings.* Irish myth: *Cross.

C563. Tabus of kings. H31. Recognition by unique ability. J221.1. King overlooks wife's unfaithfulness rather than to cause troubles of state. J634.1. King to avoid possible assassination singes his beard rather than have a barber shave him. J1675.2. Clever ways of breaking bad news to a king, who will kill bearer of bad tidings. M203. King's promise irrevocable. T281.2. Sex hospitality given to king.

P13.0.1. *Privileges of under-king.* Irish myth: Cross.

P13.0.2. *Duties of under-king's retainers.* Irish myth: Cross.

P13.1. *King cannot judge without crown.* Fb "konge" II 264b.

P13.2. *Mismanagement of king's treasury a mortal offense.* Fb "penge" II 803a.

P13.3. *Royal purple (golden diadem) worn as sign of royalty.* Irish myth: Cross.

P13.3.1. *Kingly insignia worn only on field of battle.* Irish myth: Cross.

P13.3.2. *Ring can make or unmake a king.* India: Thompson-Balys.

P13.4. *King must marry.* Irish myth: Cross.

P13.5. *Crowning of kings.* Icelandic: *Boberg; Buddhist myth: Malalasekera I 986.

P13.5.1. *Anointing of kings.* Jewish: *Neuman.

P13.6. *Custom to appoint a king by day and slay him at night.* India: Thompson-Balys.

P13.7. *Royal anniversaries.* Jewish: *Neuman.

P13.8. *King must never be present at funeral.* Jewish: *Neuman.

P13.9. *Royal perquisites.*

P13.9.1. *King has first choice in booty.* Jewish: Neuman.

P13.9.2. *Fifth of the land's production belongs to king.* Jewish: *Neuman.

P14. *Particular practices of kings.*

W154.21. Workers (builder) killed when they finish a secret building or grave for a king with the purpose of preventing pillage.

P14.1. *Prisoners released as celebration of king's success.* *Chauvin VI 101 No. 269 n. 2; Babylonian: Spence 59.

P14.2. *King will not permit a one-eyed man in his presence.* *Chauvin V 160 No. 84 n. 1.

P14.3. *King playing chess when important news arrives.* *Dickson 233 n. 30; Icelandic: *Boberg.

P14.4. *King orders all gold brought to him.* Wesselski Archiv Orientální I 77.

K447. Contraband gold discovered when king offers large price for gold.

P14.5. *King never touches earth: carried always by slaves.* Africa (Upoto): Einstein 121.

C520. Tabu: touching ground.

P14.6. *King's (prince's) sulking chamber.* He sulks here until his wishes are carried out. India: *Thompson-Balys.

H1212.3. King (prince, etc.) sulks until quest is accomplished. M151. Vow not to eat before hearing of adventure.

P14.7. *None permitted to enter hall of king unless he possesses an art.* Irish myth: Cross.

P14.8. *King does not want men who are unable to engage in any sport.* Icelandic: Örvar-Odds saga 142—43.

P337. King demands work, sport or entertainment from winter guests.

P14.8.1. *King asks all newcomers what they can do and expects a prompt answer.* Icelandic: *Boberg.

P14.9. *Law that nobody may give the king bad tidings.* Icelandic: *Boberg.

J1675.2. Clever ways of breaking bad news to king. P522. Laws.

P14.10. *Kings have seat on hills.* Icelandic: *Boberg; India: Thompson-Balys.

P14.11. *King angry at hero who rides straight into the castle without permission.* Icelandic: Völsunga saga ch. 28 (26).

P14.12. *King has his own gifts stolen back for him.* India: Thompson-Balys.

P14.13. *King gives his own wife as reward.* India: Thompson-Balys.

T281. Sex hospitality.

P14.14. *King requires everyone who comes before him to tell a story.* Irish myth: Cross.

C564.1. Tabu: chief being in ale-house when there is no story-telling.

P14.15. *King has champion to enforce respect.* Irish myth: Cross.

P14.15.1. *Old, wise counsellor of court.* Irish myth: Cross.

P14.15.2. *Court messenger.* Irish myth: Cross.

P14.16. *Threefold division of king's day:* one third dedicated to watching boys at play; one third to playing fidehell (chess?); one third to drinking. Irish myth: Cross.

P14.17. *King's stronghold on island.* Irish myth: Cross.

P14.18. *King orders man whose neck the rope will fit to be executed.* India: Thompson-Balys.

J2233. Logically absurd defenses.

P14.19. *King goes in disguise at night to observe his subjects.* India: *Thompson-Balys; Buddhist myth: Malalasekera I 424, 908.

K1812. King is disguised.

P14.20. *Tom-tom beater to spread the news of kingship.* India: *Thompson-Balys.

P14.21. *King shows himself in public only one day a year.* Jewish: *Neuman.

P14.22. *King keeps lions as pets and a lion-tamer at his palace.* Jewish: Neuman.

P14.23. *King does not eat much during years of famine in order not to forget the hungry.* Jewish: *Neuman.

P15. *Adventures of kings.*

R3. King imprisons another king's embassy.

P15.1. *Disguised king punished by peasant.* Beaten because he does not get up early enough. (King Alfred and the cakes.) *BP III 451 n. 1.

K521.4.1.2. Man in danger of life dressed by hostess as woman and set to baking. K1816.9. Disguise as peasant. L113.4. Peasant as hero. N854. Peasant as helper.

P15.1.1. *Disguised king taught courtesy by peasant.* English: Wells 94 (The Taill of Rauf Coilyear).

K1812.1. Incognito king helped by humble man. Gives reward.

P15.1.2. *King pardons person who has made mistake of addressing one of his courtiers as king.* Spanish Exempla: Keller.

P15.2. *King demands subject's wife for himself.* India: Thompson-Balys; Chinese: Graham.

H931. Prince envious of hero's wife assigns hero tasks. R10.1. Princess (maiden) abducted. T11. Falling in love with person never seen. T11.1.1. Beauty of woman reported to king causes quest for her as his bride. T161. Jus primae noctis.

P15.2.1. *King carries off subject's wife and makes her his own.* India: Thompson-Balys.

P15.3. *King loses his kingdom to impostor.* (Cf. K1934.1.) Jewish: Neuman.

P15.4. *King is cursed by disguised dwarf-smiths whose work he criticised.* Icelandic: Ásmundar saga Kappabana 466.

P15.5. *King frees man sent by rival king to kill him.* He sees bravery in the would-be assassin. Spanish Exempla: Keller.

P15.6. *King descends to bottom of sea in glass barrel to study ways of fishes.* Spanish Exempla: Keller.

P15.7. *King himself works at brick building so that subjects cannot complain of enforced labor.* Jewish: *Neuman.

P15.8. *Subjects drive their ruler away after he has made them do forced labor.* India: Thompson-Balys.

P16. *End of king's reign.*

J711.3. King for a year provides for future. P236.4. Son deposes father and usurps throne. Q281.2. Ungrateful ruler is deposed. S11.3.5. Cruel king slays brother and brother's son. S22.1. Parricide to obtain kingship. S71.1. Cruel uncle poisons nephew king. S73.1.1. Fratricide in order to gain control of kingship.

P16.1. *King (prince) retires from the world* (becomes hermit, swineherd). *Chauvin VI 194 No. 363; Irish myth: Cross; Icelandic: *Boberg.

J1634. To follow the king. Q520. Penances.

P16.1.1. *King on retiring orders funeral obsequies given him.* Chauvin VIII 115 No. 98.

P16.1.2. *King learning of queen's adultery abdicates.* India: Thompson-Balys.

K1500. Deception connected with adultery. T230. Faithlessness in marriage. T300. Chastity and celibacy.

P16.1.3. *The higher the office held in this world, the heavier the judgment of God:* Cuchulinn's reason for abjuring kingship. Irish myth: Cross.

P16.1.4. *Father abdicates in favor of son.* India: Thompson-Balys.

P16.2. *King must resign if maimed* (disfigured). Irish: MacCulloch Celtic 25, Cross.

C563.2. Tabu: king having physical blemish.

P16.2.1. *King must resign if he begets natural son.* Icelandic: *Boberg.

P16.3. *King killed when old.* Hawaii: Beckwith 409f.; Tonga: Gifford 31.

M161.6. Rather die in battle than in bed. S140.1. Abandonment of aged.

P16.3.0.1. *King commits suicide.* Irish myth: Cross.

P16.3.1. *Old king attacked.* Icelandic: *Boberg.

P16.3.1.1. *Attempt to kill old king by suffocating him in bathroom.* Icelandic: Boberg.

S113.2.2. Suffocating in bathroom.

P16.3.2. *King too old to fight goes himself into his grave mound.* Icelandic: Boberg.

P16.4. *Persons buried with dead king.* *Wesselski Märchen 230; Icelandic: Corpus Poeticum Boreale I 303, *Boberg.

N178. Loss of eye saves man from execution. Man to be buried with king. Gets off because he lacks an eye. R212.1. Man buried alive with king escapes from the tomb. V67.4. Men buried with dead chief.

P16.4.1. *Suttee.* Wife burned with dead king. *Penzer IV 255 ff., 264; **Zachariae Zs. f. Vksk. XIV 198ff., 302ff., 395ff., XV 74ff.; Chauvin VII 20; Mansikka FFC XLIII 330ff.; Hert Die Indogermanen II 440, 490ff.; Grimm Deutsche Rechtsalterthümer I 622; Hoops' Reallexikon IV 556ff.; Schreuer Zs. f. Vgl. Rechtswissenschaft XXXIV 19ff. — Icelandic: *Boberg; Slavic: Máchal 233; India: *Thompson-Balys; Melanesia: Codrington 288ff.; Africa: Frobenius Atlantis VII 106, 227.

A1545.5.1. Origin of custom of wife self-sacrifice. H479.1. Widow prepared for suttee can lift by little finger heavy stone by temple. Q414.6. Woman cast on husband's funeral pyre as punishment. S123.2. Burial of living husband or wife with dead spouse. S260.1. Human sacrifice. T211.2.1. Wife throws herself on husband's funeral pyre. V61.2. Dead burned on pyre.

P16.5. *Shavings of spear which killed king cast into cataract.* Irish myth: Cross.

P16.6. *Kings worshipped after their death.* Icelandic: *Boberg.

P16.7. *King slain by "his own household" in revenge for deposing his father.* Irish myth: Cross.

P16.8. *Land where every raja dies;* if he rules for a day he dies that night; if he rules for a night, he dies that day. India: Thompson-Balys.

P16.9. *King's coffin sunk into river.* Jewish: *Neuman.

P17. *Succession to the throne.* Missouri French: Carrière.

M311.1. Prophecy: king's grandson will dethrone him. M314. Prophecies concerning succession to throne. M395. Prophecy: son of certain name will become king: all sons given the name. P11. Choice of kings. S22.1. Parricide to obtain kingship. S73.1.1. Fratricide in order to gain control of kingdom.

P17.0.1. *No sons left to rule after father.* Lawmaker's sons slain in rebellion against him. Irish myth: Cross.

P236. Undutiful children.

P17.0.2. *Son succeeds father as king.* Icelandic: *Boberg.

P17.0.2.1. *At son's wedding king names him as successor.* Icelandic: Boberg.

P17.0.3. *Vengeance for destruction of fairy-mound pursues king's descendants.* Irish myth: Cross.

P17.1. *First man to arrive after king's death to be heir.* (Cf. N683.) Hdwb. d. Märchens I 605a n. 62; India: *Thompson-Balys.

P17.2. *Queen chosen to live rather than king so that she can bear an heir to the throne.* Serpents alleged to tell by their death which shall die first: male serpent predicts king's death; female, queen's. King has male serpent killed. BP IV 139; Gesta Romanorum No. 92.

J210. Choice between evils. P253.3. Brother chosen rather than husband or son.

P17.3. *Dying king names successor.* Icelandic: Boberg.

D1715. Magic power of dying man's words. J154. Wise words of dying father. J155.6. Wise words of dying woman (queen). M251. Dying man's promise will be kept. M258. Promise to dying man sacred.

P17.3.1. *Second-born son declared as successor because message about the birth of first son was slower traveling.* Emperor will not change proclamation. India: Thompson-Balys.

M203. King's promise irrevocable.

P17.4. *Kingship rotates among brothers.* Irish myth: Cross.

P17.5. *Brothers rule jointly.* Irish myth: Cross; Icelandic: Boberg.

P17.6. *Succession by mother-right.* Irish myth: Cross.

P17.7. *Succession will fall to line that has been wronged.* Irish myth: Cross.

P17.8. *Kingship given to younger brother.* (Cf. P17.10.) Irish myth: Cross; Icelandic: Boberg; Jewish: Neuman.

P17.9. *Natural son succeeds to the throne.* Irish myth: Cross.
P233.4. Natural son preferred to legitimate.

P17.9.1. *Natural son is refused kingship and half heritage.* Icelandic: Hervarar saga 86—88, Boberg.

P17.10. *Three sons each get a kingship, but the youngest the most important in the home country.* (Cf. P17.8.) Icelandic: Boberg.

P17.11. *Slayer of king marries widow and inherits kingdom.* Icelandic: *Boberg.

P17.12. *King to be succeeded by whoever can carry his dead body a certain distance.* Irish myth: Cross.

P17.13. *What the princes most desire: king asks each of three sons separately.* Answers: to study, to make pilgrimages, to build a great kingdom. Last chosen. India: Thompson-Balys.

P18. *Marriage of kings.* Irish myth: Cross.
T131.7. King may not marry girl who has been wife of another. T381.0.1. Girl intended for marriage with king cloistered.

P18.1. *After highly mourned wife's death the king marries another who turns out to be an evil witch.* Icelandic: *Boberg.
G205. Witch stepmother. M411.1.1. Curse by stepmother.

P18.2. *Limited number of wives for polygamous king.* Jewish: *Neuman.

P19. *Other motifs connected with kings.* Irish myth: Cross.

P19.1. *King's presence necessary for army's victory.* English romance: Malory passim.

P19.2. *King may have any woman as paramour if he makes her a settlement.* Irish myth: Cross.

P19.2.1. *King abducts woman to be his paramour.* Irish myth: Cross.
R10. Abduction.

P19.3. *King must procure whatever visiting poets ask, or suffer from their satire.* Irish myth: Cross.

P19.4. *Kingly powers (rights).* Irish myth: Cross.
C563. Tabus of kings.

P19.4.0.1. *King's wand (rod).* Irish myth: Cross.

P19.4.1. *King may judge against all save one of highest rank in religion or learning.* Irish myth: Cross.

P19.5. *King raised from dead (by saint).* Irish myth: Cross.

P20. Queens. Irish myth: Cross.

F322.2. Man (king) rescues his wife from fairyland. F402.2.2. Queen of demons. H540.2. Queen propounds riddles. K1812.8. Incognito queen (princess). K2213.11. Treacherous queen tricks king into bestowing kingdom for a year upon her son by a former marriage. K2246.0.1. Treacherous princess (queen). K778.2. Amazonian woman (queen) disguised as leper seduces and binds enemies one by one. N837. Queen as helper. Q56.3. Queen rewards love of man of low lineage by making him an ambassador. Q211.4.1. Queen expelled for poisoning stepson. T55. Forthputting woman. T146. Polyandry. T146.2. Woman (queen) requires thirty men. T148. Matriarchy. T249.2. Husband and wife (king and queen) each unfaithful to the other.

P20.1. *Clever queen.* Icelandic: *Boberg.

P21. *Queen intervenes for condemned courtiers.* *Chauvin II 104 No. 65.

P21.1. *Queen as intercessor with king.* Greek: Odyssey VI 313; Jewish: Neuman; India: Thompson-Balys.

P22. *Queen marries murderer of her fiancé.* Italian Novella: Rotunda.

P17.11. Slayer of king marries widow and inherits kingdom. T231. The faithless widow.

P22.1. *Queen leaves country with her son,* having killed her husband in revenge for his killing of her father and brother. Icelandic: *Boberg.

P211. Wife chooses father's side in feud. Must choose between husband and father. P231.4. Mother kills sons who lack courage to help her revenge her father and brothers, and are likely to betray the plot.

P23. *Queen persuades king to make war without cause that her sons may have territory.* Irish myth: Cross.

P23.1. *Queen persuades husband to riot against his superior.* Icelandic: Boberg.

P23.2. *Queen persuades husband to claim her father's kingdom after his death.* Icelandic: Boberg.

P23.3. *Queen persuades husband to avenge her father.* Icelandic: Boberg

P23.4. *Queen offers son to be killed in order to spur to fight and avenge her first husband.* (Cf. S12.3.) Icelandic: Boberg.

P24. *Queen must pay tribute to victorious queen to the amount paid by king to victorious king.* Irish myth: Cross.

P531. Taxation and payment of fines or tribute.

P25. *Queen meddles in state affairs.* India: Thompson-Balys.

P26. *Captured queen commits suicide.* (Cf. P16.3.0.1.) Irish myth: Cross; India: Thompson-Balys.

P26.1. *Queen commits suicide, as her husband vanquishes and kills her father and her brother.* Icelandic: Boberg.

P234. Father and daughter. P250. Brothers and sisters.

P27. *Grief at queen's death.* Icelandic: *Boberg.

P27.1. *King sits mourning on his wife's grave mound.* Icelandic: *Boberg.

P27.2. *King mourns so much at wife's death that he goes on piracy, (every summer afterward).* Icelandic: *Boberg.

P27.3. *King calls daughter in second marriage by the name of his first queen.* Icelandic: Boberg.

P28. *Marriage of queen.*

P28.1. *Chieftainess of such rank that none of her countrymen can woo her.* Maori: Clark 2.

P29. *Queens—miscellaneous.*

P29.1. *No king to rule who is not husband of certain queen.* Irish myth: Cross.

P29.2. *Queen commits adultery with husband's foster son.* Irish myth: Cross.

P29.3. *Queen (princess) pours liquor for battle champions.* Irish myth: Cross.

P30. Princes. Irish myth: Cross.

D93. Transformation: prince to old man. H1239.1. Prince agrees to marry a servant girl if she will help him on a quest. H1574.3.1. Prince surpasses brothers by salvaging anvil from burning smithy. K1812.11. Incognito prince sold into slavery. K1952. Sham prince (nobleman). K2246. Treacherous prince. L162. Lowly heroine marries prince. M395. Prophecy: son of certain name will become king: all sons given the name. N324. Man unwittingly kills prince. P173. Captive king's sons made slaves. R71. Captive prince joins captor out of gratitude for his freedom. S21.2. Prince takes kingdom from his father and has his eyes put out. S110.4. Prince resolves to drive relatives from his domain. Kills many. T10.1. Sluggish prince reformed by falling in love. T281.2. Sex hospitality given to prince.

P30.1. *King's sons called kings.* Icelandic: Boberg.

P31. *Prince must learn a trade.* (Cf. P51.) *Chauvin VI 74 No. 239.

P31.1. *Princes as smiths.* Irish myth: Cross.

P32. *Friendship of prince and commoner.* India: Thompson-Balys.

P32.1. *All children born in realm on same day as chief's son are brought to palace to be the boy's companions.* Hawaii: Beckwith Myth 441.

P34. *Prince imprisoned as hostage for safety from king.* Irish myth: Cross.

P35. *Unknown prince chosen chief of children in play.* *Type 920; *DeVries FFC LXXIII 40ff.

H41.5. Unknown prince shows his kingly qualities in dealing with his playmates. J123. Wisdom of child decides lawsuit. K1921.1. Son of the king and of the smith exchanged.

P36. *Dispossessed prince taunted by usurper's son.* West Africa: Frobenius Atlantis VI 182ff. No. 4.

T646. Illegitimate child taunted by playmates.

P37. *Birth rites confer royalty on infant prince.* Easter Island: Métraux Ethnology 59.

P38. *Prince forfeits father's and God's blessing if he fails to claim throne.* English romance: Malory I 4.

P40. Princesses.

C196. Tabu: asking for king's daughter in marriage. C312.2.1. Tabu: looking at princess on public appearance. C567. Tabus of princesses. C567.1. Tabu: eloping with king's daughter. C940.1. Princess's secret sickness from breaking tabu. D2064.2. Sickness of princess dependent on witch's fire. D2064.4. Magic sickness because of evil eye. H41.1. Princess on the pea. H162. Recognition of disguised princess by bee lighting on her. H311. Inspection test for suitors. Suitors for princess's hand must present themselves for public inspection. H316. Suitor test: apple thrown indicates princess's choice. H322. Suitor test: finding princess. H324. Suitor test: choosing princess from others identically clad. H331.5.1. Race with princess for her hand. H341. Suitor test: making princess laugh. H342. Suitor test: outwitting princess. H343. Suitor test: bringing dumb princess to speak. H344. Suitor test: entering princess's chamber. H345. Suitor test: overcoming princess in strength. H346. Princess given to man who can heal her. H347. Suitor test: to consort with princess. H507.1. Princess offered to man who can defeat her in repartee. H511. Princess offered to correct guesser. H525. Test: guessing princess's birthmarks. H551. Princess offered to man who can out-riddle her. H933. Princess sets hero tasks. H1301.1.2. Quest for far-off princess. K425. King's daughter put into brothel to catch thief. K1612.1. Person sends wrong man to sleep with king's daughter (princess). K1915.2. Through power of saint, man is caused to assume lover's form and sleep with princess. K2034.1. King's daughter secretly pledged to many to win their aid. R111.1.1. Rescue of princess from ogre. T50.2. King loves his daughter so much that he does not want to marry her to anybody. T55.1.1. Princess declares love for courtier.

P41. *Princess cannot be married to someone of low caste, though he passes suitor test.* India: Thompson-Balys.

H310. Suitor tests. L161. Lowly hero marries princess. T121. Unequal marriage.

P41.1. *Great warrior destroyed by king when he asks for princess in marriage.* India: Thompson-Balys.

P50. Noblemen (knights).

E501.2.1. Knights in wild hunt. H38.1. Disguised king (noble) recognized by habitual speech. H1574.1. Tests for noble blood. K3.2. Young knight substitutes for old suitor in tournament. K1816.10.1. Nobleman disguised as cobbler woos woodcutter's daughter. K2126. Knight falsely accused of sedition. P322.1. Nobleman insists that man fleeing from prison accept his hospitality. Q54.2. Captive knight free for having kept his word. Q81.1. Nobleman's perseverance gains him coveted place on reserved bench. U34. Nobleman murders one of the people. W11.5.3. Wronged knight conquers enemy and pardons him. W11.7. Nobleman's generosity enables impoverished lover to entertain his lady. W11.7.1. Nobleman in poverty offers wife to ruler.

P50.0.1. *King and vassals: obligations of vassals to king.* Irish myth: Cross.

P50.0.1.1. *King demands open gate to vassals' castle (city).* Irish myth: Cross.

P50.1. *Earl.* Icelandic: *Boberg.

P50.1.1. *Earl's name preferred to king's.* Icelandic: Boberg.

P50.2. *Marshall.*

K2245. Treacherous marshall.

P51. *Noble person saves self from difficulties by knowledge of a trade.* (Cf. P31.) Chauvin VIII 111 No. 90.

P52. *Knight jousts with all comers.* (Cf. P561.) English romance: Malory passim.

P52.1. *Knight's duty to perform as lady bids.* English romance: Malory VI 5.

P55. *Wild man of noble birth.* (Cf. F567.) Dickson 135 n. 117; Irish myth: Cross.

P60. Noble (gentle) ladies.

E501.2.2. Ladies in wild hunt.

P61. *Noble woman given to foreigners on condition that thereafter their land be held by female right.* Irish myth: Cross.

P90. Royalty and nobility—miscellaneous.

P92. *Bathing pool reserved for royalty.* Tahiti: Henry Ancient Tahiti (Honolulu, 1928) 608.

P93. *Certain foods, ornaments, feathers, etc. reserved for royalty.* Hawaii: Beckwith Myth 376.

P94. *Garment must be removed in presence of certain high chiefs.* Hawaii: Beckwith Myth 376.

P95. *Impossible to refuse the request of a troubled nobleman.* Greek: Odyssey IV 653.

P100—P199. Other social orders.

P110. Royal ministers. Missouri French: Carrière.

C402.1. Tabu: king speaking before his druids speak. H561.5. King and minister. King propounds riddles and questions to his clever minister. K1231.2. Ambassador asks queen to lie with him. K1839.7. Disguise as foreign ambassador. R169.7. Royal minister rescues abandoned queen(s).

P111. *Banished minister found indispensable and recalled.* *Chauvin VI 38 No. 207 n. 5; India: Thompson-Balys.

H561.5. King and clever minister. J151.1. Wisdom of hidden old man saves kingdom. K2101. Falsely accused minister reinstates himself by his cleverness.

P116. *Minister acts as stepping-stone in midst of flame-filled trench so that king can step across from one side to the other.* India: Thompson-Balys.

P120. Church dignitaries. Irish myth: Cross.

B252. Animal churchmen. D1311.12.1. Bell sounds to indicate pope. H561.2. King and abbot. K1826. Disguise as churchman. K1961. Sham churchman. P19.4.1. King may judge against all save one of highest rank in religion or learning. P426. Clergy. Q556.12.1. Thievish abbot to be eaten by wolves: curse by saint. V450. Religious orders. W16. Bishop exchanges places with prisoner so that he may return to his mother. X410. Jokes on parsons.

P150. Rich men. Irish myth: Cross; Missouri French: Carrière.

B113.1. Treasure-producing bird-heart. K1603. Rich man falls into sacrificial grave prepared for others. K2015. Child adopted by rich man in order to get rid of him. L143. Poor man surpasses rich. L162. Lowly heroine marries prince (king). M312.1. Prophecy: wealthy marriage for poor boy. M312.3. Eater of magic bird-heart will become rich (or king). Q272.1. Devil carries off rich man. Q491.4. Toads and snakes devour corpse of rich man in his grave.

P151. *Man so rich that people prefer the dung from his mules over king's gold and silver.* Jewish: Neuman.

P160. Beggars. Irish myth: Cross; Missouri French: Carrière; Jewish: Neuman.

X530. Jokes on beggars.

P161. *Beggars' many children.* *Wesselski Bebel II 131 No. 97, 136 No. 107.

P162. *Lepers.* Irish myth: Cross; Jewish: Neuman.

P162.1. *Naked leper.* Irish myth: Cross.

P163. *Beggar rewarded by king for poem (song).* India: *Thompson-Balys.

P170. Slaves. Irish myth: Cross.

A1657. Origin of slaves. C561.1. Tabu: slave going near fetish. C563.4. Tabu: king settling quarrel among thralls. H38.3. Slave recognized by his conversation, habits and character. K2251. Treacherous slave. N801. Helper grateful for being bought from slavery. N863. Slave (swineherd) as helper of princess. P523.3. Slave may not bring suit. Q285.4. Slave-driving punished. Q437. Criminal's wife and children sold into slavery. Q482.1.1. Second wife (slave) must serve as menial. Q482.2.1. Queen forced to do menial service rescued by son. Q558.7. Slave-driver mysteriously stricken dead. R40. Places and conditions of captivity. R61. Person sold into slavery. R111.1.6. Princess ransomed from slavery. S113.1.1. Slaves killed by hanging. S210.1. Child sold into slavery. T121.6. Man marries his bondmaid.

P170.0.1. *Female slaves.* (Cf. P173.1.) Irish myth: Cross.

P170.0.1.1. *Female slaves as medium of exchange (unit of value).* Irish myth: Cross.

P171. *Branding person makes him one's slave for life.* Wesselski Hodscha Nasreddin II 198 No. 391.

P171.1. *Slave's ear bored.* Jewish: *Neuman.

P171.2. *Bond woman with rope girding her loins.* Jewish: Neuman.

P172. *Requirement that slaves given as tribute should not know Irish.* Irish myth: Cross.

P532. Payment of tax (tribute).

P173. *Captive king's sons made slaves.* Irish myth: Cross; Jewish: Neuman.

P173.1. *Captive king's daughter as slave.* Icelandic: Boberg.

P173.2. *Killed enemy's son as slave.* Icelandic: Boberg.

P173.3. *Captives from battle sold as slaves.* Icelandic: *Boberg.

P173.4. *Futile attempt to get rid of man by selling him to merchants as slave.* Icelandic: Boberg.

P174. *Children of slave and free person become slaves.* Hawaii: Beckwith Myth 300.

P175. *Slave killed.* Icelandic: *Boberg.

P175.1. *Slave hanged.* Icelandic: *Boberg.

P176. *Murder by slaves.* Icelandic: Boberg.

P177. *Origin of thralls.* Icelandic: Boberg.

P178. *Slaves freed.* Icelandic: *Boberg.

P178.1. *Knocking out a slave's tooth entitles him to freedom.* Jewish: Neuman.

P178.2. *Slaves released after definite term.* Jewish: Neuman (seven years).

P190. Other social orders—miscellaneous. Irish myth: Cross.

P191. *Social status of foreigners.* Irish myth: Cross.

P523.1. Foreigners may not bring suit. P524.2. Foreigners may not act as security.

P192. *Madmen (fools, professional fools).* Irish myth: Cross.

J1700. Fools. P523.2. Madman may not bring suit. P525.1. Contract made by madman void.

P192.1. *Professional fool.* Irish myth: Cross.

P192.2. *Fool as clever judge.* Irish myth: Cross.

P192.3. *Fool can walk on water.* Irish myth: Cross.

P192.4. *Fool can live under water.* Irish myth: Cross.

P192.5. *Fool makes friends with birds and beasts.* Irish myth: Cross.

P192.6. *Customary to shave heads of demented so that they may be recognized as such.* Irish myth: Cross.

P192.7. *Fool recognized by lump on his forehead.* Irish myth: Cross.

P200—P299. The family.

P200. The family.

A1570. Origin of regulations within the family. E220. Dead relative's malevolent return. E320. Dead relative's friendly return. G61. Relative's flesh eaten unwittingly. H175. Recognition by "force of nature". Unknown member of family immediately and magically recognized. J390. Choices: kind strangers, unkind relatives. K2210. Treacherous relatives. N730. Accidental reunion of families. P525.3. The nearest to blood of slain man must avenge his death. Q211.0.2. Enormity of kin murder. S0. Cruel relatives. V53. Prayers of family comfort prisoner. V451. First-born son and one of every ten born thereafter given to Church.

P201. *Inherent enmity between members of a family.* Dickson 100 n. 5.

P201.1. *Feud between two branches of family.* Irish myth: Cross.

P202. *Person reproached for having no relatives.* Irish myth: Cross; Koryak: *Jochelson JE VI 372.

P203. *Game with ancestors' bones.* A boy interrupts a game played with the bones of his father or other murdered relative. N. A. Indian: Kroeber JAFL XXI 225.

F839.1. Gnawed bone as weapon. S139.2.2.4. Parts of corpses used in sport.

P205. *Refusal to fight relatives.* Hindu: Tawney I 175; Icelandic: Boberg.

H1558.8. Friends refuse to fight against each other. N731.2. Father-son combat. Neither knows who the other is. N733.1. Brothers unwittingly fight each other.

P210. Husband and wife.

A736.1.4. Sun and moon married. A762.1. Star-husband. Star takes mortal maiden as wife. A1270. Primeval human pair. A1555.2. Origin of custom of purchasing wives. C31. Tabu: offending supernatural wife. D662. Transformation to cure inconstant husband. D861.5. Magic object stolen by hero's wife. D1976.2. Future wife met during magic sleep. E165. Resuscitation of wife by husband giving up half his remaining life. (Sometimes vice versa.) E221. Dead spouse's malevolent return. E321. Dead husband's friendly return. E322. Dead wife's friendly return. F322.2. Man rescues his wife from fairyland. H151.8. Husband attracted by wife's power of healing. H363. Deceased wife's marriage test. H422. Test for true husbands. H425. Tests for cuckolds. H460. Wife tests. H492.1. Husband refuses to murder his wife for high honors; wife agrees to murder husband. H592.1.1. "Love like wind in hot sun". Husband offended but later learns wife's meaning. H916. Tasks imposed because of wife's foolish boast. H922. Departing husband assigns his wife tasks. H934. Wife assigns husband tasks. H1187. Task left by departing husband for wife to accomplish. H1212. Quest assigned because of feigned illness. H1312.1. Quest for three persons as stupid as his wife. H1385.3. Quest for vanished wife (mistress). J1540. Retorts between husband and wife. J1545. Wife outwits her husband. J2301. Gullible husbands. K1500. Deceptions connected with adultery. K2213. Treacherous wife. N741. Unexpected meeting of husband and wife. P253.3. Brother chosen rather than husband or son. P525.2. Contract made by woman without her husband void. Q211.3. Uxorcide punished. Q482.1.1. Second wife must serve as menial. R151. Husband rescues wife. R227.2. Flight from hated husband. S410. Persecuted wife. T141.2. Wives exchanged. T147. Annual marriages. T145. Polygamous marriage. T146. Polyandry. T200. Married life. T250. Characteristics of wives and husbands.

P211. *Wife chooses father's side in feud.* Must choose between husband and father. S. A. Indian (Carib): Alexander Lat. Am. 266.

P22.1. Queen leaves the country with her son, having killed her husband in revenge for his killing of her father and brother.

P211.1. *Wife chooses father rather than husband or son.* (Cf. P253.3.) Only one can be saved; he alone is irreplacable. Spanish: Childers.

P211.2. *Mother kills husband for murdering their daughter.* Africa (Kamerun): Mansfield 228.

P212. *Wife more merciful than blood relations.* They refuse to ransom condemned man; wife does so. Child II 349f., III 516, IV 481, V 231ff., 296.

P213. *Husband more merciful than blood relations.* They refuse to ransom condemned woman; husband does so. Child II 346—53, III 511, IV 481f., V 231ff., 296.

P214. *Wife drinks blood of slain husband.* Irish myth: Cross.

T231. The faithless widow.

P214.1. *Wife commits suicide (dies) on death of husband.* (Cf. P16.4.1.) Irish myth: Cross.

P216. *Wife only one able to persuade her husband.* Icelandic: Boberg.

P230. Parents and children. Hdwb. d. Märchens I 527a s.v. "Eltern und Kinder"; Spanish Exempla: Keller.

A401. Mother earth. The earth is conceived of as the mother of all things. A625. World parents. Sky-father and earth-mother as parents of the universe. A745.1. Moon born from first couple. A1277.1. First parents devour offspring. A1575. Origin of relation of mother and children. D444.2. Transformation: meat to toad. Punishment for ungrateful son. E324. Dead child's friendly return to parents. E613.0.1. Reincarnation of murdered child as bird. E765.4.3.1. Father and mother will die same day as daughter. G71. Unnatural children eat parent. G72. Unnatural parents eat children. H151.3. Recognition when parents come to son (priest, pope) to be confessed. H151.9. Abandoned child joins parents in game: recognition follows. H491.1. In large family father unwilling but mother willing to sell children. H637.1. What is hardest? — Parent's heart (said by child being sacrificed). H1381.1. Quest for unknown parents. J154. Wise words of dying father. K2213.11. Treacherous queen tricks king into bestowing kingdom for a year upon her son by former marriage. K2214.1. Treacherous daughter. K2214. Treacherous children. M343. Parricide prophecy. M344. Mother-incest prophecy. M371.1. Exposure (murder) of child to avoid fulfillment of prophecy. M411.1. Curse by parent. Q65. Filial duty rewarded. Q211.4. Murder of children punished. Q211.1. Parricide punished. Q281.1. Ungrateful children punished. Q431.9.2. Exile as punishment for parricide. Q553.4.1. Child taken from parents because they have ceased to think of God. R153. Parent rescues child. S20. Cruel children. S210. Children sold or promised. S223. Childless couple promise child to the devil if they may only have one. S300. Abandoned or murdered children. S322.2.1. Mother exposes child for fear of jealous co-wife. S351. Abandoned child cared for by mother secretly. T600. Care of children.

P230.1. *Mother prefers son, father daughter.* Icelandic: *Boberg.

P230.2. *Mother dislikes her children in forced marriage.* Icelandic: Boberg.

P230.3. *Queen dislikes son who is unlike her and loves a poor girl:* plots against him. Icelandic: Boberg.

P231. *Mother and son.*

D688. Transformed mother suckles child. D815.1. Magic object received from mother. D842.1. Magic object found on mother's grave. H633.3. What is sweetest? — Mother's breast. H652.2. What is softest? — Mother's bosom. H662. Riddle: what is dearer than gold? — Mother love. H1216. Mother sends son to find unknown father. K2384. Man tricked to be one's sworn brother in order to secure his help against his mother. L111.3. Widow's son as hero. M344. Mother-incest prophecy. P282.2. Stepmother mourns her stepsons' death, not her own son's. R154.1. Son rescues mother. T412. Mother-son incest. W28.1. Woman drinks poison that son may be king. W28.2. Woman sacrifices life for son's honor.

P231.1. *Boy sickens from grief at mother's death.* Irish myth: Cross.

F1041. Extraordinary physical reactions of persons.

P231.2. *Son warns mother.* (Hamlet.) Icelandic: *Boberg.

P231.3. *Mother-love.* Icelandic: *Boberg.

P231.4. *Mother kills sons who lack courage to help her revenge her father and brothers, and are likely to betray the plot.* Icelandic: Boberg.

P231.5. *Mother reveals fact that son is offspring of supernatural father.* Irish myth: Cross.

P231.6. *Mother (eagle) casts out dull, stupid changeling;* rears bold, energetic son. Irish myth: Cross.

P231.7. *Mother commits suicide when son wants to marry foreigner according to foreign rites.* Chinese: Eberhard FFC CXX 267.

P232. *Mother and daughter.*

H914. Tasks assigned because of mother's foolish boasting. S322.2. Jealous mother casts daughter forth.

P232.1. *Wicked mother and her sons do everything to prevent daughter's marriage with beloved.* Icelandic: Boberg.

P232.2. *Mother lets daughter unwittingly marry own father in order to avenge his raping.* Icelandic: Boberg.

N365.2. Unwitting father-daughter incest.

P233. *Father and son.* Irish myth: Cross; Spanish Exempla: Keller.

D815.2. Magic object received from father. D1317.6.1. Sword bursts in son's hand when he is about to kill his father. F1041.9.1.1. Man keeps to his bed, mourning over drowned son. H151.11. Hero is served at table by his unknown son: recognition of his wife follows. H480. Father tests. H1210.1. Quest assigned by father. H1216. Mother sends son to find unknown father. H1381.2. Quest for unknown father. H1462. Vigil for dead father. J122. Naïve remark of child: "You forgot to strike mother." J675.1. Son slays father in order not to be slain himself. M258.1. Promise to dying father leads to adventures. M343. Parricide prophecy. N731. Unexpected meeting of father and son. N731.2. Father-son combat. R54. Hero locked up while his father is murdered. R153.3. Father rescues son(s). S11. Cruel father. T131.1.2. Father's consent to son's (daughter's) marriage necessary.

P233.1. *Son as pledge for father who has committed murder.* Irish myth: Cross.

P233.2. *Young hero rebuked by his father.* Icelandic: *Boberg.

P233.2.1. *Father drives away bad son whom the mother prefers.* Icelandic: Boberg.

P233.3. *Berserks scold their father who apparently without reason called their adversary invincible.* Icelandic: Boberg.

P233.3.1. *Hero's son by giantess scorns his father's feebleness: still it is the son who is slain.* Icelandic: Boberg.

P233.4. *Natural son preferred to legitimate.* Icelandic: Boberg.

P233.5. *Oldest son responsible to father for welfare of others.* Jewish: Neuman.

P233.6. *Son avenges father.* English romance: Malory X 21, 34, 36; Icelandic: *Boberg; Jewish: Neuman; India: Thompson-Balys; Africa: Bouveignes 163.

P233.7. *Son must threaten father before he will recognize him as son,* even though he brings ring from his mother. Icelandic: *Boberg.

T645. Paramour leaves token with girl to give their son.

P233.8. *Prodigal son returns.* India: Thompson-Balys.

N172. Prodigal as favorite of fortune.

P233.9. *Son chastizes father for scorning mother.* India: Thompson-Balys.

P233.10. *Father in vision reproves son about to succumb to temptation.* Jewish: Neuman.

P233.11. *Birthright transferred by father from the oldest son to another.* (Cf. P251.7.) Jewish: Neuman.

P234. *Father and daughter.* Irish myth: Cross; Spanish Exempla: Keller.

H592.1. "Love like salt." Girl compares her love for her father to salt. Experience teaches him the value of salt. H807. Formerly I was daughter, now I am mother, etc. K2214.1. Treacherous daughter. S11.7. Jealous father vows to kill daughter's suitors. T97. Father opposed to daughter's marriage. T411. Father-daughter incest. T411.1. Lecherous father. Unnatural father wants to marry his daughter (Manekine).

P234.1. *Daughter marries her husband's slayer in order to save her old father from war.* Icelandic: Boberg.

P234.2. *Father and daughter die at same time.* Icelandic: Boberg.

P236. *Undutiful children.* Irish myth: Cross.

P17.0.1. No son to rule after his father. Lawmaker's sons slain in rebellion against him. Q281.1. Ungrateful children punished. S20. Cruel children.

P236.1. *Folly of father's giving all property to children before his death.* They abandon him. *Oesterley No. 273; Spanish: Boggs FFC XC 116 No. 980A. Cf. Shakespeare's King Lear.

J705. Safe provision for life not to be lightly surrendered.

P236.2. *Supposed chest of gold induces children to care for aged father.* They think that the chest of stones contains the inheritance. *Pauli (ed. Bolte) No. 435; Scala Celi 98b No. 528; Dunlop-Wilson II 185f.; von der Hagen II lviii No. 49; Hdwb. d. Abergl. IV 1290. — Lithuanian: Balys Index No. 2452*; Spanish: Boggs FFC XC 116 No. 980A; Italian Novella: *Rotunda; Palestine: Schmidt-Kahle Volkserzählungen aus Palästina II No. 123; India: *Thompson-Balys; Indonesia: Jeynball Catalogus Maleische en Sundaneesche Hss. 173, ibid. Supplement Catalogus Javaansche en Madoereesche Hss. 22.

K476.2. False articles used to produce credit. K1667. Unjust banker deceived into delivering deposits by making him expect even larger.

P236.3. *Not daring to curse father directly, son does so indirectly.* Nouvelles Récréations No. 50.

P236.4. *Son deposes father and usurps throne.* Irish myth: Cross.

P236.5. *Undutiful children ridicule father while he is drunk and naked.* Spanish Exempla: Keller.

P236.6. *Undutiful son overawes his father by threats.* India: Thompson-Balys.

P236.7. *Undutiful son taught lesson showing his mother has suffered from him.* India: Thompson-Balys.

P237. *Daughters flogged by parents.* Child I 192, II 435, V237a.

Q458. Flogging as punishment.

P241. *Parents descend to hell instead of sons.* Irish: O'Suilleabhain 53.

P241.1. *Pious children save their parents from hell.* Jewish: Neuman.

P242. *Children punished for fathers' sins.* Jewish: Neuman.

P250. Brothers and sisters.

A515.1. Culture heroes brothers. A515.1.1. Twin culture heroes. A736.1. Sun sister and moon brother. A736.1.2. Sun brother and moon sister. A1273. Twin first parents. D815.4. Magic object received from sister. K2211. Treacherous brother. Usually elder brother. K2212. Treacherous sister. Usually elder sister.

P250.1. *Elder children to protect younger.* Breton: Sébillot Incidents s.v. "aînés".

P251. *Brothers.* *Penzer III 272 n. 1; Irish myth: Cross; Spanish Exempla: Keller.

D861.3. Magic object stolen by brothers. G551.3. Rescue of children from ogre by brother. H151.10. Combat of unknown brothers brings about recognition. H255. Test: which of twins is elder. H912. Tasks assigned at suggestion of jealous brothers. K867. Fatal duel: brother kills brother in pretended game. K2211. Treacherous brother. N733. Accidental meeting of brother. N733.1. Brothers unwittingly fight each other. Q211.9. Fratricide punished. Z210. Brothers as heroes.

P251.1. *Friend unfaithful but brother faithful.* Brought to test by actions at apparent death of hero. India: Thompson-Balys.

H466. Feigned death to test wife's faithfulness. P310. Friendship.

P251.2. *Warrior will not fight where his brother was slain.* Place considered defiled. Irish myth: Cross.

P251.3. *Brothers follow each other in exile.* Icelandic: *Boberg.

P251.3.1. *Brothers strive to avenge each other.* Icelandic: *Boberg.

P251.4. *Brothers scorn brother's wise counsel.* Icelandic: *Boberg.

J21. Counsels proved wise by experience.

P251.4.1. *Brothers kill brother because they fail to understand his wise answer.* Icelandic: Boberg.

P251.5. *Two brothers.* Type 303; Icelandic: *Boberg.

F610.3.3.1. Two berserk-brothers.

P251.5.1. *Two brothers follow and help each other on piracy, etc.* Icelandic: *Boberg.

P251.5.2. *Two brothers are confusingly like each other.* Icelandic: *Boberg.

P251.5.3. *Hostile brothers.* Icelandic: *Boberg; Jewish: *Neuman.

S73.1. Fratricide.

P251.5.4. *Two brothers as contrasts.* Hdwb. d. Märchens II "Formel"; Icelandic: *Boberg.

P251.5.5. *Brother unjustly imprisoned by brother.* Irish myth: Cross.

P251.5.6. *Man's descendants shall serve those of his brother.* Irish myth: Cross.

P251.6. *Several brothers.*

P251.6.1. *Three brothers.* Types 654, 655; Icelandic: *Boberg.

P251.6.2. *Four brothers.* Types 653, 655.

P251.6.3. *Six or seven brothers.* Type 451.

P251.6.4. *Eight brothers.* Icelandic: Boberg.

P251.6.5. *Nine brothers.* Icelandic: *Boberg.

P251.6.6. *Eleven brothers.* Type 451; Icelandic: Boberg.

P251.6.7. *Twelve brothers.* Type 451.

F610.3.4.1. Fighting with twelve berserks.

P251.7. *Older brother has birthright, entitling him to a double share.* (Cf. P233.11.) Jewish: *Neuman.

P251.8. *Repudiation of relationship of birth between man and his bad brother.* Africa (Wakweli): Bender 92f.

P252. *Sisters.*

G73. Girls eat their sister. G551.2. Rescue of sister from ogre by another sister. K2212. Treacherous sister.

P252.1. *Two sisters.* Type 480, 711, 426.

P252.1.1. *Sister kills sister.* Irish myth: Cross; Icelandic: Boberg.

P252.2. *Three sisters.* Types 311—12, 510, 511.

P252.3. *Seven sisters.* Icelandic: *Boberg.

P252.4. *Eight sisters.* Icelandic: Boberg.

P252.5. *Nine sisters.* Icelandic: *Boberg.

P252.6. *Ten sisters.* Icelandic: *Boberg.

P252.7. *Eighteen sisters kill one another.* Icelandic: Boberg.

T92.8. Sisters in love with same man.

P253. *Sister and brother.* Type 450; Irish myth: Cross; Spanish Exempla: Keller.

Q458.2.1. Brother flogs unchaste sister to death. T415. Brother-sister incest.

P253.0.1. *Sister's son.* Irish myth: Cross.

P253.0.2. *One sister and two brothers.* Icelandic: *Boberg.

P253.0.3. *One sister and three (four) brothers.* Icelandic: *Boberg.

P253.0.4. *One sister and ten brothers.* Icelandic: Boberg.

P253.0.5. *One sister and six (seven, eleven, twelve) brothers.* Type 451.

P253.1. *Brother about to drink blood of seemingly guilty sister.* Köhler-Bolte Zs. f. Vksk. VI 61.

Q243. Incontinence punished. Q450. Cruel punishment.

P253.2. *Sister faithful to transformed brother.* *Types 450, 451; Child I 315f.

P253.2.1. *Brother faithful to persecuted sister.* East Africa: Zuure L'Ame du Murundi (Paris, 1932) 331ff. No. 2.

P253.3. *Brother chosen rather than husband or son.* Only one can be saved; he alone is irreplacable. Chauvin II 190 No. 2; Tawney Journal of Philology XII 121; Aly Volksmärchen bei Herodot 35, 109; Philippine: Fansler MAFLS XII 257 No. 31.

P211.1. Wife chooses father rather than husband or son.

P253.4. *Girl comes to brother's aid when he is attacked.* She slays the assailant and is eventually acquitted. Italian Novella: Rotunda.

P253.5. *Sister avenges brother's death.* India: Thompson-Balys; Icelandic: *Boberg.

P253.6. *Sister warns brothers.* Icelandic: *Boberg.

P253.7. *Brothers persecute sister's lover and are in return killed by him.* Icelandic: Boberg.

P253.8. *Clever sister saves life of brother.* Irish myth: Cross.

P253.9. *Woman dies of sorrow for death of brother.* Irish myth: Cross.

J253.10. *Great love of brothers for sister.* India: Thompson-Balys.

P260. Relations by law.

P261. *Father-in-law.* India: Thompson-Balys.

D815.5. Magic object received from father-in-law. H331.4.1. Suitors contest with bride's father in shooting. H331.5.2. Suitor contest: race with bride's father. H384.1. Bride test: kindness — father-in-law disguised as beggar. K959.2.2. Man kills son-in-law and his children while they sleep. S52. Cruel father-in-law.

P262. *Mother-in-law.* Irish myth: Cross.

S51. Cruel mother-in-law. T417.1. Mother-in-law seduces son-in-law.

P262.1. *Bad relations between mother-in-law and daughter-in-law.* India: Thompson-Balys.

P263. *Brother-in-law.* (Cf. K2211.1.)

P263.1. *Widower marries wife's sister.* Jewish: *Neuman.

P264. *Sister-in-law.* (Cf. K2212.2.)

P265. *Son-in-law.*

P265.1. *Idle sons-in-law driven away by gradually reducing their food.* India: Thompson-Balys.

P270. Foster relatives. Irish myth: Cross.
R131. Exposed or abandoned child rescued. T670 Adoption of children.

P270.1. *Foster parents fined for blemish on child.* Irish myth: Cross.

P270.2. *Peasant and his wife as foster parents of exposed king's son.* Icelandic: *Boberg.

P270.3. *Parents kill son for slaying their foster son.* Irish myth: Cross.

P271. *Foster father.* **C. Schubert Der Pflegesohn (Nourri) im Heldenepos (Marburg, 1906); Irish myth: Cross; Missouri French: Carrière.
D815.7. Magic object received from foster parents. F1041.16.7. King is about to kill foster son because of his evil explanations of a dream. N812.1. Wise giant as foster father of hero. N842.1. Cook as foster father. N855.1. Smith as foster father. N856.1. Forester as foster father.

P271.1. *Magician as foster father.* (Cf. N845.) English romance: Malory, Book 1; Icelandic: Boberg.

P271.2. *Fisherman as foster father.* Icelandic: Boberg.

P271.3. *Dwarf as foster father.* (Cf. F451.5.1.) Icelandic: MacCulloch Eddic 267, *Boberg.

P271.4. *Living king's or nobleman's son as foster son of father's friend:* considered an honor for the foster father. Weinhold Altnordisches Leben (1856) 285ff.; Icelandic: *Boberg.
M201.6. Covenant confirmed by hostages. P281.1. Stepfather as foster father. P293.1. Mother's brother as foster father.

P271.5. *Foster father as constant helper.* Icelandic: *Boberg.
N812. Giant or ogre as helper.

P271.6. *Foster children return foster father's love:* avenge him, etc. Icelandic: *Boberg.

P271.7. *King's son named after his father's foster father.* Icelandic: Boberg.

P271.8. *Thor slays his foster father and takes himself the realm of Thrace.* Icelandic: Snorra Edda Prol. III, MacCulloch Eddic. 314.

P272. *Foster mother.* Irish myth: Cross; Missouri French: Carrière.
D815.7.1. Magic object received from girl's foster mother. D2074.2.4.1. Foster mother summoned by saying her name. M411.1.2. Curse by foster mother.

P272.1. *Witch foster mother.* Icelandic: *Boberg.

P272.2. *Foster mother as helper.* (See all items under P272.) Icelandic: *Boberg.

P272.3. *Former mistress as sons' foster mother.* Icelandic: Bosa saga 6ff.

P273. *Foster brother.* *Valtýr Gudmundsson "Fóstbræðralag" in þrjár Ritgjörðir (Kaupmannahöfn, 1892) 29—55; Irish myth: Cross; Icelandic: *Boberg.
P311. Sworn brethren.

P273.1. *Faithful foster brother.* *Type 516; *BP I 46; *Rosch FFC LXXVII 96; Irish myth: Cross; Icelandic: *Boberg.

P273.1.1. *Foster brothers avenge each other.* Icelandic: *Boberg.
M161.2. Vow to avenge (king, friends, father) or die.

P273.1.2. *King's son begs pardon for treacherous foster brother.* Icelandic: *Boberg.

P273.1.3. *Foster brother as constant adviser.* Icelandic: *Boberg.

P273.2. *Faithless foster brother.*

K1766.1. False boasting of having killed foster brother makes his men follow the boasting. K1931.1.1. Impostor tries to push foster brother into water. K2211.2. Treacherous foster brother.

P273.2.1. *Promise of marriage to king's daughter induces warrior to fight foster brother.* Irish myth: Cross.

P273.2.2. *Earl's son seduces foster brother's sister and betrays himself.* Icelandic: *Boberg.

P273.2.3. *King's son falsely accuses foster brother of attempt to seduce his sister.* Icelandic: Lagerholm 161—63, introd. lxxviii, *Boberg.

P273.2.4. *Magic writing makes foster brothers enemies.* Icelandic: *Boberg.

D1266.1. Magic writings.

P273.3. *Unable to hit man himself, enemy kills his foster brother.* Icelandic: Boberg.

P273.4. *Children of Tuatha Dé Danann fostered by Milesians.* Irish myth: Cross.

P274. *Foster sister.*

P274.1. *Love between foster sister and foster brother.* Icelandic: Herrmann Saxo II 80, *Boberg.

P275. *Foster son.* Irish myth: Cross.

P275.1. *Foster son commits adultery with foster father's wife.* Irish myth: Cross.

P280. Steprelatives.

P281. *Stepfather.*

S32. Cruel stepfather. T418.1. Lustful stepfather.

P281.1. *Stepfather as foster father.* Icelandic: Boberg.

P293.1. Mother's brother as foster father.

P281.2. *Stepfather murdered.* Icelandic: Boberg.

P282. *Stepmother.* Irish myth: Cross; Missouri French: Carrière.

K2111.1. Woman makes vain overtures to stepson and accuses him of murder. Q65.1. Supplying food to ungrateful stepmother rewarded. Q151.2. Death passes by man who has fed his stepmother. S31 Cruel stepmother. T418. Lustful stepmother.

P282.1. *Realm ruled by stepmother, while king is absent.* Icelandic: Boberg.

P282.2. *Stepmother mourns her stepsons' death, not her own son's.* Icelandic: Boberg.

P282.3. *Stepmother in love with stepson.* (Cf. T418.) Irish myth: Cross; Greek: Euripides Hippolytus; Chinese-Persian: *Coyajee JPASB XXIV 192.

P282.3.1. *Love of stepmother who has killed her husband refused.* Icelandic: *Boberg.

P283. *Stepbrother.*
K2125.3. Man falsely accused of murdering his stepbrother.

P283.1. *Stepbrothers kill devastating monsters.* India: Thompson-Balys.
B11.11. Fight with dragon. Z210. Brothers as heroes.

P284. *Stepsister.* (Cf. K2212.1.) Icelandic: Boberg; Missouri French: Carrière.

P290. Other relatives.

P291. *Grandfather.* Irish myth: Cross; Missouri French: Carrière.
K1812.14. Lecherous prince disguises as merchant in order to kill his grandchildren. S42. Cruel grandfather.

P291.1. *Grandfather as foster father.* Icelandic: *Boberg.

P292. *Grandmother.* Missouri French: Carrière.
A31. Creator's grandmother. G303.11.4. The devil's grandmother. K2011. Wolf poses as "grandmother" and kills child. S41. Cruel grandmother. S351.1. Abandoned child cared for by grandmother.

P292.1. *Grandmother as foster mother.* Icelandic: Boberg.

P293. *Uncle.* **W. O. Farnsworth Uncle and Nephew in the Old French Chansons de Geste (New York, 1913); Irish myth: Cross.
A711.1. Sun and moon as uncle and nephew who ascended to the sky. H1556.4.4. Old uncle tests nephew's fidelity by sleeping with his beloved. K2125.5. Man falsely accuses nephew of murder. K2133. Wicked counselor accuses king's nephews of attempting to seduce the queen so that he kills them. N738. Accidental meeting of nephew and uncle. S71. Cruel uncle.

P293.1. *Mother's brother as foster father.* Icelandic: *Boberg.

P293.2. *Mother's brother as helper.* Icelandic: *Boberg.

P293.2.1. *Children take after their mother's brothers.* Jewish: *Neuman.

P293.3. *Hero killed in fighting with father's brother.* Icelandic: Boberg.

P293.4. *Young prince sent to his father's mother's brother.* Icelandic: Boberg.

P293.5. *Father's brother avenged.* Icelandic: Boberg.

P294. *Aunt.* *Rivers "The Father's Sister in Oceania" FL XXI 42.

P294.1. *Paternal aunt as aid.* N. A. Indian (California): Gayton and Newman 82.

P295. *Cousins.*
N746. Accidental meeting of cousins.

P296. *Godparents.*
Q242.1. Cohabitation of godfather and godmother punished.

P296.1. *Godfather.* Hdwb. d. Abergl. III 803; Missouri French: Carrière. See also N811 and all references and cross-references.

P296.2. *Godmother.*
F311.1. Fairy godmother.

P297. *Nephew.* *F. B. Gummere The Sister's Son (Oxford, 1901); C. H.

Bell The Sister's Son in the Mediaeval German Epic (Berkeley, 1922); Irish myth: Cross.

N738. Accidental meeting of nephew and uncle. Hero takes refuge unwittingly at his uncle's court.

P298. *Niece.*

P300—P399. Other social relationships.

P310. Friendship. *Type 516; *BP I 46; **Rosch FFC LXXVII 96; India: *Thompson-Balys.

A2493. Friendships between the animals. E165.1. One man prays either to keep friend from death or for both to die. H1558. Tests of friendship. J496. Choice of friend over mistress. K2131.3. Woman destroys men's friendship by pretending to whisper to one. K2297. Treacherous friend. S268. Child sacrificed to provide blood for cure of friend. T511.0.1. Queen and maidservant conceive from eating same food. Their sons are like brothers.

P310.1. *Friends want to divide good and evil.* Icelandic: *Boberg.

P310.2. *Friends avenge each other.* Icelandic: *Boberg.

P310.3. *Dying hero sends greetings to friends.* Icelandic: Boberg.

P310.4. *Friends want their children to be friends too.* Icelandic: *Boberg.

P310.4.1. *Dying man asks friends to let his son inherit his friendship together with his father's weapons.* Icelandic: þidriks saga II 358, Boberg.

P310.4.2. *Friends' children become enemies.* Icelandic: *Boberg.

P310.5. *Defeated enemy turns true friend.* (Cf. P311.1.) Icelandic: Lagerholm 108ff., *Boberg.

P310.6. *One friend dies shortly after the other.* Icelandic: Boberg.

P310.7. *Man wins wife for his friend.* India: Thompson-Balys.

T51. Wooing by emissary.

P310.8. *Friendship possible only between equals.* India: Thompson-Balys.

P310.9. *Friends given the power of reading each other's secret thoughts.* India: Thompson-Balys.

P311. *Sworn brethren.* Friends take an oath of lasting brotherhood. *Type 516; Rösch FFC LXXVII 98; *Hibbard 68 n. 7, 145 n. 3; Child IV 146f.; Wesselski Märchen 187 No. 2; *Krappe Bulletin Hispanique XXXIX 17; *Abeles "Die Bürgschaft als Motif in der jüdischen Literatur" Monatsch. f. Geschichte u. Wissenschaft der Juden LX 213ff., 263ff. — English: Wells 158 (Amis and Amiloun); Icelandic: Olrik Sakses Oldhistorie I (1892) 59ff., *Boberg; Italian Novella: *Rotunda; Jewish: *Neuman, bin Gorion Born Judas [2] IV 14, 20, 274; India: Thompson-Balys; Korean: Zong in-Sob 63 No. 35.

A515.1.2. Sworn brothers as culture heroes. A1599.12. Origin of covenanted friendships. K2384. Man tricked to be one's sworn brother in order to secure his help against his mother. P273. Foster brother.

P311.0.1. *Friends exchange names.* Irish myth: Cross.

P311.1. *Combatants become sworn brethren.* Dickson 123 n. 73; Icelandic: *Boberg; Italian Novella: *Rotunda.

M201. Making of bargains and promises. P310.5. Defeated enemy turns true friend.

P311.2. *Flower-friendship.* Friends take oath of brotherhood by exchanging flowers. India: Thompson-Balys.

P311.3. *Human sons of animal companions go together on adventures.* Africa (Lamba): Doke MAFLS XX 14 No. 11.

P311.4. *Friends born at same moment.* India: Thompson-Balys.

B311. Congenital helpful animal. T511.0.1. Queen and maidservant conceive from eating same food.

P311.5. *Covenant of friendship.* Irish myth: Cross.

P311.6. *Ceremonial friendship.* India: Thompson-Balys.

P311.7. *Saints exchange bachalls as mark of affection.* Irish myth: Cross.

P311.7.1. *Saints exchange bells.* Irish myth: Cross.

P311.8. *Friendship between a prince and common man.* India: *Thompson-Balys.

P312. *Blood-brotherhood.* Friends take oath of brotherhood by means of mixing their blood. *Type 1364; **Encyc. Rel. Ethics II 717a, 857ff.; **H. C. Trumbull The Blood Covenant (London, 1887); *Chauvin VII 20 No. 373D; *Hibbard 145 n. 3; Fb "blod" IV 46b; Nitze MPh IX 291; DeVries Acta Philologica Scandinavica III 106; *Basset RTP VI 577—XXV 438 passim; *Julian Revue d'Ethnographie et de Trad. Pop. II 1ff.; **H. Tegnæus Blood-Brothers (Stockholm, 1952). — Irish myth: Cross: Icelandic: *Boberg; Tuamotu: Stimson MS (z-G 13/203); Africa: Stanley 274.

A515.3. Culture hero has blood brother. C165. Tabu: marriage with person whose blood one has drunk. M201.1.1. Blood of contractors mixed to seal bargain. T61.1. Betrothal by lovers' drinking each other's blood.

P312.0.1. *Saint makes blood covenant with animals.* (Cf. B279.) Irish myth: Cross.

P312.1. *Drinking mixture of blood, milk, and wine as pledge of covenant.* Irish myth: Cross.

P312.2. *Sworn brethren and blood brethren avenge each other.* Icelandic: *Boberg.

P312.3. *Surviving blood brother to watch three nights in grave-mound.* Icelandic: Egils saga ok Ásm., Lagerholm 28 (cf. introd. xxiv—xxix).

P313. *Milk-brotherhood.* Friends bound in brotherhood through partaking of milk from the same woman. *Cosquin Études 247ff.; Wiedemann Am Urquell III 259ff.

T671. Adoption by suckling.

P313.1. *Friendship starts at babyhood: two babies exchanged.* Jewish: *Neuman.

P314. *Combat of disguised friends.* Brown Iwain 17 and passim.

N731.2. Father-son combat. N733.1. Brothers unwittingly fight each other.

P315. *Friends offer to die for each other.* (Bürgschaft.) Each falsely confesses crime so as to save the other. Neither guilty. Often combined with P325. **Abeles "Die Bürgschaft als Motif in der jüdischen Literatur" Monatschr. f. Geschichte u. Wissenschaft der Juden LX 213ff., 263ff.; **K. Kelling Das Bürgschaftsmotiv in der französischen Literatur (Leipzig diss., 1915); *Chauvin III 124 No. 113, V 215f., VIII 194ff., IX 16f.; *Hdwb. d. Märchens I 350a s.v. "Bürgschaft"; Köhler-Bolte II 557, 580f.; Gaster Exempla Nos. 362, 419; Basset 1001 Contes II 293ff.; Boccaccio Decameron X No. 8 (*Lee 330); Fischer Zs. f. deutsche Morgenländische Ges. LXXII 290; Bolte Zs. f. Vksk. XXI 193 n. 4, 194; Scala Celi 10a, 11b Nos. 62, 68; bin Gorion Born Judas IV 20, 274; Alphabet Nos. 53, 57. — Spanish Exempla: Keller; Italian Novella: *Rotunda.

J1180. Clever means of avoiding legal punishment.

P315.1. *Competition in friendship: prisoner and jailor.* Officer in charge of prison offers to let his friend escape, though his own life will be forfeited. The friend refuses; tells officer to let king think he has escaped and if the king demands his life the officer can produce the prisoner. King hears of the generosity and forgives the prisoner. Chauvin V I No. 1.

P315.2. *Friend gives false witness to set free his accused friend.* Africa (Wakweli): Bender 99f.

P316. *Friend sacrifices his life for the other.* Buddhist myth: Malalasekera II 1369.

P316.1. *Man knowing of murder plot against his friend disguises and is killed in his place.* (Cf. P361.1.) Scala Celi 9b No. 61; Spanish Exempla: Keller.

P317. *Refusal to believe that a friend has spoken ill of one.* Alphabet No. 220; Spanish Exempla: Keller.

P317.1. *Refusal to believe that a friend will harm one.* Alexander drinks cup said to have been poisoned by his friend. Spanish Exempla: Keller.

P318. *Man refuses to follow friend in wicked conduct.* Scala Celi 11a No. 66; Alphabet No. 56; Italian Novella: Rotunda.

P319. *Deeds of friendship—miscellaneous.*

P319.1. *Two friends captured by Moors have money to ransom only one.* The ransomed one returns home, gets money and buys the other's freedom. Italian Novella: Rotunda.

P319.2. *Man who has counseled friend in assassination asks to be killed on the other's body.* Italian Novella: Rotunda.

P319.3. *Friend's intercession saves man from execution.* Italian Novella: Rotunda.

P319.4. *The sacred partnership.* Man is abducted by pirates and kept in slavery forty years. Upon his return his friend divides his earnings with him. Italian Novella: *Rotunda.

P319.5. *Hands of friends extend through sides of tombs and clasp in death.* Irish myth: Cross.

P319.6. *Successful rival gives his lady to unsuccessful friend.* Italian Novella: *Rotunda.

P319.7. *"Friendship without refusal."* Friends bind themselves each to grant every desire of the other. Irish myth: Cross.

C871. Tabu: refusing a request. M202.0.1. Bargain or promise to be fulfilled at all hazards. M223. Blind promise (rash boon). Q115. Reward: any boon that may be asked. W11.15. Generous person refuses no man anything.

P319.8. *Danger of one saint voluntarily incurred by another.* Irish myth: Cross.

P320. Hospitality. Relation of host and guest. Irish myth: Cross.

A547. Culture hero dispenses food and hospitality. A1598. Origin of customs of hospitality. C874. Tabu: breaking up revelry before its end. C282. Tabu: refusing a feast. C616. Tabu: feasting visitors at certain place. C901.1.4. Tabu imposed by host. D2105.5. Saint causes fish to come out of lake to satisfy guests for whom he has no food. F151.0.1. Hospitable host entertains adventurer on way to otherworld. F361.1.2. Fairy takes revenge for not being offered food (drink). H509.1. Guest of convent given choice of nuns. H1564. Test of hospitality. J21.9.1. Guest stays so long that host gives him black bread instead of white. J1183. Execution escaped by invoking laws of hospitality. J1341. Retort from underfed servant. J1561. Inhospitality repaid. J1563. Treatment of difficult guests. K532.3. Hospitality to retainers as payment of tax (tribute). K1812.4. Incognito king is given hospitality by fisherman. K2326.1. Hosts frighten guest by disguising as ghosts. K2294. Treacherous host. M158. Vow never to refuse food to any man. P634. Feasts. Q42.1.3. Excessive hospitality causes chieftian to become poor. Q45. Hospitality rewarded. Q111.2. Riches as reward for hospitality. Q292. Inhospitality punished. Q292.3. Abuse of hospitality punished. Q556.7. Curse for inhospitality. T281. Sex hospitality. T331.2. Knight unsuccessfully tempted by host's wife. W12. Hospitality as a virtue. W151.2.2. Hospitable man impoverished by greedy guests. W158. Inhospitality.

P320.1. *Hospitality for a whole winter.* Icelandic: Lagerholm 10 n., *Boberg.

H1219.7. Quest assigned as payment for hospitality.

P320.2. *Hospitality for (three) years.* Irish myth: Cross.

P321. *Salt of hospitality.* Eating a man's salt creates mutual obligation. *Chauvin VI 196 No. 368.

P322. *Guest given refuge.* Murderer of a man's father takes refuge in his house and is saved by him. *Chauvin II 198 No. 31.

H1558.1. Test of friendship: the half-friend.

P322.1. *Nobleman forces escaping prisoner to accept his hospitality.* Intercedes for his pardon. Italian Novella: Rotunda.

P322.2. *Guest in disguise or under false name.* (Cf. K1831.) *Boberg.

P322.3. *Refugee entertained in holy place* (church, monastery, etc.) Irish myth: Cross.

P323. *Hosts refrain from telling guest of death in household.* Wesselski Archiv Orientální II 431; Greek: Euripides Alcestis.

P324. *Host greets guest with gifts.* English romance: Malory passim; Icelandic: Boberg.

P324.1. *Host treats guest with food and everything possible.* Icelandic: *Boberg.

P324.2. *Guests fed before being questioned.* Greek: Odyssey III 70 and passim.

P324.3. *Guests' life inviolable.* Greek: Odyssey XIV 403 and passim.

P325. *Host surrenders his wife to his guest.* The guest unwittingly falls in love with the wife. The host, on being informed, out of pure generosity repudiates the wife and has her marry the guest. (Often joined with P315.) Chauvin V 136 No. 64; also references to P315; Spanish Exempla: Keller.

H509.1. Guest of convent given choice of nuns. T281. Sex hospitality.

P325.1. *Guest begets son with his host's daughter.* Icelandic: *Boberg.

P326. *If host does not return, the house shall belong to the guest.* So declares the host as he departs on a mission for the guest. *Chauvin V 209 No. 120 n. 1; Japanese: Ikeda.

P327. *Barmecide feast.* Host places imaginary feast before guest, who accepts it in the same spirit. Guest's courtesy is rewarded by real feast. *Chauvin V 163 No. 86; Arabian: Burton Nights I 317.

K445. The emperor's new clothes. K1870. Illusions.

P328. *Strangers entertained by family to whose hitching-ring they happen to tie their horses.* Thus confusion avoided as to where strangers are to be entertained. Italian: L. de Francia Novellino (Torino, 1930), Rotunda.

P331. *Refusal to receive preferred help until series of stories has been told.* Scottish: Campbell-McKay No. 5.

J1185. Execution escaped by story-telling. Z10. Formulistic framework for tales.

P332. *Selfish guest expels host.* Porcupine asks rabbit for hospitality. When rabbit complains of being pricked, porcupine tells him to leave if he does not like it. Italian Novella: Rotunda.

P334. *Shabby hospitality forces guests to leave.* Italian Novella: Rotunda (P329).

P334.1. *Guests accused of greediness.* India: Thompson-Balys.

P336. *Poor person makes great effort to entertain guests.*

P336.1. *Poor host and his wife kill themselves because they are unable to entertain expected guests.* India: Thompson-Balys.

P336.2. *Wife scolds husband's hospitality, as he really has nothing to give.* Icelandic: Boberg.

P336.3. *Poor peasant closes the eyes in order not to see guest eat: later suicide.* Icelandic: Boberg.

P337. *King demands work, sport or entertainment from winter guests.* Icelandic: *Boberg.

P320.1. Hospitality for a whole winter.

P337.1. *Christian king makes baptism a condition for hospitality during the winter.* Icelandic: Boberg.

P338. *Sitting in a circle of feasts.* Irish myth: Cross.

P340. Teacher and pupil. Irish myth: Cross.

K1594. Student extends his course so as to enjoy the professor's wife. K1692. Teacher instructs pupil in the art of love: cuckolded. T481.4. Wife seduces husband's pupil. V246.2. Angel as saint's teacher.

P340.0.1. *Druids as teachers.* Irish myth: Cross.

P341. *Teacher dies of pride over success of pupil.* Alphabet No. 341.

P342. *Student enters competition with his master.* Italian Novella: Rotunda.

P342.1. *Student challenges his fencing master.* Is overcome by the latter's tricks. Italian Novella: *Rotunda.

P343. *Teacher threatens to curse pupils if they disobey.* Irish myth: Cross.

P360. Master and servant. **Hdwb. d. Märchens I 389ff.

F615.3. Strong hero overawes master. H38.2.3. Recognition of maidservant substitute bride by her habitual conversation. H919.1. Tasks assigned at suggestion of treacherous servants. J955.2. Servant plays at being emperor. J955.3. Servant asks master for arms of knighthood. J2464. The servant to improve on master's statements. K1465. Blinded slave's revenge.

P361. *Faithful servant.* *Types 516; *BP I 46; **Rösch FFC LXXVII 95f.; **Hdwb. d. Märchens I 389 (and cross references there given); Icelandic: *Boberg; Spanish Exempla: Keller; Jewish: *Neuman; India: Thompson-Balys; Korean: Zong in-Sob 154ff. No. 68.

F875. Iron bands around heart to keep it from breaking. When master is disenchanted, the bands around heart of faithful servant snap one by one. H1556. Tests of fidelity. K512.2.2. Compassionate executioner: substituted child. The servant charged with sending the hero to executioners sends his own child instead. N25. Wager on truthfulness of servant. N342.1. Faithful servant guarding master's wife from danger falsely condemned. R169.4. Hero rescued by servant. T133.1. Faithful servant accompanies bride to new home.

P361.1. *Faithful servant dies for his master.* Puts on his master's clothes so as to be slain in his place. (Cf. P316.) Alphabet No. 327; Japanese: Ikeda.

F1041.1.3.2. Servant grieves over master's death. Kills wife and himself. K1810. Deception by disguise.

P361.1.1. *Faithful servant kills his master's murderer and is killed in turn.* Italian Novella: Rotunda.

P361.1.2. *Faithful servant wants to follow on dangerous quest, where he alone is killed.* Icelandic: Boberg.

P361.1.3. *Hero's charioteer faithful to master till death.* Irish myth: Cross.

P361.2. *Faithful servant remains at home and fights for exiled hero.* *Boje 82ff.

L111.1. Exile returns and succeeds.

P361.3. *Faithful servant sacrifices sons to save life of king.* Sons resuscitated and servant enriched. Penzer IV 177f., VI 272f.; India: Thompson-Balys.

S268. Child sacrificed to provide blood for cure of friend. T211.1. Wife dies so that husband's death may be postponed.

P361.4. *Faithful nurse tries to save tyrant's daughter by exposing her own in her place.* Italian Novella: Rotunda.

K1840. Deception by substitution. S300. Abandoned or murdered children.

P361.5. *Abandoned maiden helped by her faithful nurse.* India: Thompson-Balys.

N825.3. Old woman helper. R131. Exposed or abandoned child rescued. S350. Fate of abandoned child.

P361.6. *Faithful servant dies avenging master's death.* Irish myth: Cross.

P361.7. *Captain will not betray king's secret.* He refuses to betray where recruits are being raised. Spanish: Childers.

P361.8. *Faithful servant undergoes torture for sake of his master.* Spanish Exempla: Keller.

P361.9. *Crow lets itself be caught so as to save king of crows.* India: Thompson-Balys.

P362. *Faithful servant entrusted with care and education of crown prince.* India: *Thompson-Balys.

P365. *Faithless servant.* *Hdwb. d. Märchens I 391; Italian Novella: *Rotunda.

H919.1. Tasks assigned at suggestion of treacherous servants. K1353.2. Faithless servant tells mistress that master has ordered him to kill her. K1356. Seduction by falsely accusing woman's husband of infidelity. K2250. Treacherous servants and workmen.

P365.1. *Faithless men-servants corrupt the maids in the household.* Pauli (ed. Bolte) No. 209; Italian Novella: Rotunda.

P365.2. *Servant planning to possess his master's goods.* Has already possessed his wife. Pauli (ed. Bolte) No. 613.

P366. *Master demands that servant tell him of his faults as well as of his good qualities.* Pauli (ed. Bolte) No. 42.

P400—P499. Trades and professions.

P400. Trades and professions. **Sébillot Légendes et Curiosités des Métiers (Paris, n.d.); Jewish: Neuman.

J1115. Clever professions.

P401. *Son insists on following father's trade.* This has been kept secret at request of dying father who was unsuccessful. Son learns from mother. *Cosquin Contes indiens 395ff.

J154. Wise words of dying father. M258. Promise to dying man sacred.

P410. Laborers.

L113.5. Woodcutter hero.

P411. *Peasant.* **Hdwb. d. Märchens I 184a.

F365.3. Fairies occupy peasant's house. F460.4.4.2. Mountain-men chain captive peasant. F460.4.4.5. Mountain-folk steal from peasant. F460.4.5. Mountain-men borrow from peasant. H38.2.2. Peasant boy masking as prince betrays self by his answers. H561.1. Clever peasant girl asked riddles by king. H561.6. King and peasant vie in riddling questions and answers. J1705.1. Stupid peasant. K1816.9. Disguise as peasant. L113.4. Peasant as hero. N854. Peasant as helper. P15.1. Disguised king punished by peasant. R131.6. Peasant rescues abandoned child.

P411.1. *Peasant refuses to sell possessions to king.* (Miller of Sanssouci.) Swiss: Jegerlehner Oberwallis 309 No. 13.

P411.1.1. *Peasant and his wife in hut near castle as contrasts to king and queen.* Icelandic: Lagerholm lvi, *Boberg.

P411.2. *Peasant is cutting wood in front of his house as guests arrive.* Icelandic: *Boberg.

P411.3. *Wounded hero finds shelter and is cured in peasant's house.* Icelandic: *Boberg.

P411.4. *Hero stays overnight in peasant's house, to which he accident-*

ally comes, and where he gets advice and direction. (Cf. H1232.4.) Icelandic: *Boberg.

P412. *Shepherd.*

A453. Shepherd-god. A1952. Creation of hoopoe. Transformed shepherd. A1957.1. Woodpecker from devil's herdsman transformed. A1965.2. Bittern from transformed shepherd. A2005. Origin of insects: God throws sand on lazy shepherds. N841. Shepherd as helper. R131.3.1. Shepherd rescues abandoned child.

P412.1. *Shepherd as hero.* *Type 300.

P412.1.1. *Life of shepherd proper preparation for ruler.* Jewish: Neuman.

P412.2. *Swineherd.* (Cf. L113.1.1.) Irish myth: Cross.

P412.3. *Hero as rabbit-herd.* Type 570.

P413. *Ferryman.*

P413.1. *Eternal ferryman.* Always transports passengers and when the ruler is in danger takes his place. (Cf. Q25.) Cosquin Lorraine I 215.

P413.1.1. *Ferryman puts oar into king's hand and he must remain ferryman.* *Type 461; Japanese: Ikeda.

P414. *Hunter.* Types 246, 304; Von Sydow Våra folksagor (1941) 39.

P415. *Collier.* (Cf. K2262.)

P415.1. *Hero as collier.* Icelandic: Þidriks saga I 308f., Boberg.

P420. Learned professions.

X350. Jokes on teachers. X370. Jokes on scholars.

P421. *Judge.* Irish myth: Cross; Icelandic: *Boberg.

J167. Wisdom from continual reminder of foolishness in the past. Unjust judge skinned and his skin stretched over a footstool kept in the presence of judges, so as to remind them to be just. J1192. The bribed judge. J1212. Judge put out of countenance. J1280. Repartee with judge. M0. Judgments. M10. Irrevocable judgments. Q265.1. Bribed false judge punished. X331. Jokes on magistrates.

P421.1. *Jackals as judges.* India: Thompson-Balys.

P422. *Lawyer.* Hdwb. d. Abergl. I 202.

X310. Jokes on lawyers.

P422.1. *Lawyers punished in hell.* Alphabet Nos. 42, 43.

Q469.5. Punishment: choking with smoke. This given a lawyer who has "sold smoke", i.e., idle words.

P422.1.1. *Tongue of dead lawyer found to be lacking.* Scala Celi 7b No. 44; Etienne de Bourbon No. 440.

P424. *Physician.* Penzer X 263a s.v. "Physician"; Irish myth: Cross.

A144. Physician of the gods. A454. God of healing. A1594.1. Establishment of doctor's fees. F668. Skillful surgeon. K1955. Sham physician. P427.5. Druid as physician. X372. Jokes on doctors.

P424.1. *Physician hides eyes as he passes graveyard.* He does not want to see those who have died from his medicine. *Wesselski Hodscha Nasreddin I 259 No. 204.

P424.2. *Doctor who can cure can also poison.* This reflection brings the doctor under the king's suspicion. *Chauvin V 276 No. 156.

P424.3. *Physician killed for fatal diagnosis.* Irish myth: Cross.

P424.3.1. *"Skillful" physician compelled to help carry away the bier of his dead patient.* India: Thompson-Balys.

P424.4. *Fairy as physician.* Irish myth: Cross.

P424.5. *Female physician.* Irish myth: Cross.

P425. *Scribe.*

P425.1. *Scribe who cannot read his own writing.* India: Thompson-Balys.

P426. *Clergy.*

F531.5.8.2. Giants exorcised by clergy. J1260. Repartee based on church or clergy. K1961. Sham churchman. P551.3. Clerics exempted from military service. V294. The Pope. V450. Religious orders.

P426.0.1. *In fear of clerics pagans flee into fairy mounds.* Irish myth: Cross.

P426.1. *Parson (priest).* Jewish: Neuman (P426.1, V452).

K1961.1. Sham parson (priest). Q286.2. Priest will not bury dead unless paid in advance. Ruler has him buried alive with the corpse. V5.2. Negligent priests buried under bags filled with words omitted from service. X410. Jokes on parsons.

P426.1.1. *First of animals and fruits belong to priest.* Jewish: Neuman.

P426.2. *Hermit.* Hdwb. d. Märchens I 507b; Irish myth: Cross; Spanish: Espinosa II No. 75, Espinosa Jr. No. 186.

J225.0.1. Angel and hermit. J485. Three sins of the hermit. K1837.3. Repentant nurse disguises as hermit. N843. Hermit as helper. Q34. Reward for austerities of hermit. R131.10. Hermit rescues abandoned child. T330. Anchorites under temptation.

P426.3. *Monks.* Irish myth: Cross.

P426.3.1. *Untrained monk becomes skillful wright (smith) through power of saint.* Irish myth: Cross.

P426.3.2. *Monks as converted druids.* Irish myth: Cross.

P425.3.3. *Woman disguised as monk enters monastery.* Irish myth: Cross.

P427. *Druid (poet, learned man).* Irish myth: Cross; Icelandic: MacCulloch Eddic 311.

A611.1. Druids as creators. A974.1. Certain stones are druids transformed by power of saint. B242.1.2.1. Wren as "druid of the birds." C10.1. Druidism forbidden. C402.1. Tabu: king speaking before his druids speak. C901.1.2. Tabu imposed by druid. D1814.1. Advice from magician (fortune-teller, etc.). F394.1.1. Druids direct fairies.

P427.0.1. *Druid inspires great respect and fear.* Irish myth: Cross.

P427.0.2. *Person assailed by druid loses treasure.* Irish myth: Cross.

N134. Persons effect change of luck.

P427.0.3. *Women druids.* Irish myth: Cross.

P427.0.4. *Simon Magus as druid.* Irish myth: Cross.

P427.1. *Druid performs sacrifices.* Irish myth: Cross.

P427.1.1. *Druids perform human sacrifice.* Irish myth: Cross.

P427.1.2. *Druids as priests.* Irish myth: Cross.

P427.1.3. *Druidic (heathen) baptism.* Irish myth: Cross.

P427.1.4. *Druidic tonsure.* Irish myth: Cross.

P427.2. *Druid as emissary of peace.* Irish myth: Cross.

P427.3. *Advice (instruction) from druid.* Irish myth: Cross.

P427.4. *Poet (druid) as satirist.* (Cf. M402.) Irish myth: Cross.

P427.4.1. *Fear of druidic lampoon as activating power.* Irish myth: Cross.

P427.5. *Druid as physician.* (Cf. P424.) Irish myth: Cross.

P427.5.1. *Wounded soldiers healed by bath in pool of milk through power of druid.* Irish myth: Cross.

P427.6. *Druid as judge.* Irish myth: Cross.

P427.7. *Poet.* Irish myth: Cross; Icelandic: *Boberg.

A1464.1. Acquisition of poetry. C872. Tabu: refusing requests of poets. F996. Waters react to words of poet. P19.3. King must procure whatever visiting poets ask, or suffer from their satire. P524.1. Poet may not act as security.

P427.7.1. *Extemporaneous composition by poets.* Irish myth: Cross.

P427.7.2. *Extensive repertory of poets.* Irish myth: Cross.

C568.1. Tabus: poets to be ignorant of national literature.

P427.7.2.1. *Difficult language used by poets.* Irish myth: Cross.

P427.7.2.1.1. *Poets and fools closely allied.* Irish myth: Cross.

P427.7.3. *Blind poets.* Irish myth: Cross.

P427.7.4. *Women poets.* Irish myth: Cross.

P427.7.5. *Bard.* Irish myth: Cross.

P427.7.6. *Poet's rod.* Irish myth: Cross.

P427.7.7. *Poet as judge.* Irish myth: Cross.

P427.7.8. *Poet rewarded for poem.* Irish myth: Cross; Icelandic: *Boberg.

P427.7.9. *Poets banished.* Irish myth: Cross.

P427.7.9.1. *Excessive demands of poets.* Irish myth: Cross.

P427.7.10. *Rivaling poets.* Icelandic: *Boberg.

P427.8. *Druids as rath-builders.* Irish myth: Cross.

A538. Culture hero builds raths.

P427.9. *Druids (poets) boil spell.* Irish myth: Cross.

P428. *Musician.* Icelandic: Boberg.

Q223.9.2. Musician flogged for eating a kid on Friday (day of fast).

P428.1. *Harper.* Irish myth: Cross; Jewish: Neuman.

A1461.2.1. Origin of harp. K1817.3. Disguise as harper.

P429. *Miscellaneous learned professions.*

P429.1. *Astronomers.* Jewish: *Neuman.

P430. Financiers and merchants.

P431. *Merchant.* Jewish: *Neuman.

K1817.4. Disguise as merchant. K2249.4. Treacherous merchant. N851. Merchant as helper. Q274.2. Devil suffocates swindling merchant. R131.7. Merchant rescues abandoned child.

P431.1. *Merchants as spreaders of news.* *Dickson 174 n. 35.

P435. *Usurer.*

B151.1.1.2.1. Ass carries usurer's body to the gallows instead of to the church. E411.4. Usurer cannot rest in grave. N277. Oxen bear dead usurer to gallows to be buried. Q273. Usury punished. Q558.3. Usurer boasts that God did not get him during the plague. W154.1.1. Usurer's ingratitude toward servant. X510. Jokes concerning usurers.

P435.1. *Wealthy usurer prays that the sons of the rich will become mad.* That will benefit his business. His own sons lose their minds. Italian Novella: Rotunda.

P435.2. *Usurer stops lending money.* He does so, not because it is wrong, but because he is losing money. Italian Novella: Rotunda.

P440. Artisans. Jewish: *Neuman.

P441. *Tailor.* *Fb "skrædder"; *Chauvin IX 29 No. 18; *Sébillot Métiers No. 7; *Feilberg Dania I 165ff., III 184ff.; Paludan Danske Studier (1925) 19ff.; Missouri French: Carrière.

F662. Skillful tailor. H38.2.1. Tailor married to princess betrays trade. K1951.1. Boastful fly-killer: "seven at a blow". A tailor who has killed seven flies writes on a placard: "Seven at a blow." He is received as a great warrior. X220. Jokes about tailors.

P441.1. *Tailor occupies God's throne for a day.* *Type 800; *BP I 342.

K2371.1. Heaven entered by a trick.

P441.2. *Tailoring only trade devil cannot learn.* He fails to knot thread because it would make sign of the cross. Scotch: Campbell Superstitions 304.

G303.16.3.4. Devil made to disappear by making sign of the cross.

P441.3. *Tailor punished in hell.* Irish myth: Cross.

P441.4. *Busy tailor asks soldier to mount watch in his place.* Missouri French: Carrière 177f. No. 36, 261 No. 59.

P442. *Baker.* *Sébillot Métiers Nos. 2, 3; *Nyrop Dania VIII 174ff.

P442.1. *Baker and devil walking together.* Breton: Sébillot Incidents s.v. "boulanger".

P443. *Miller.* Type 461 (Danish); Von Sydow Våra folksagor (1941) 38; *Sébillot Métiers No. 1; Missouri French: Carrière; Spanish: Espinosa Jr. Nos. 137, 141, 198.

A677.2. Miller of hell. R131.2. Miller rescues abandoned child. X210. Jokes about millers.

P443.0.1. *Water-miller.* Icelandic: Boberg.

P443.1. *Why millers are thieves.* Flemish: DeMeyer FFC XXXVII 84 No. 27e.

P444. *Cabinet-maker.* *Sébillot Métiers No. 14.

P444.1. *Brave soldier and timid cabinet-maker as companions.* German: Grimm No. 130a; BP III 67.

P445. *Weaver.* Sébillot Métiers No. 6.

H1022.1. Task: weaving cloth from two threads. L113.3. Poor weaver as hero.

P445.1. *Why weavers are the most unhappy of men.* They gave a nail for the Crucifixion. Flemish: DeMeyer FFC XXXVII 84 No. 27C.

A2231.2. Animal characteristics: punishment for hostility at crucifixion.

P445.2. *Why weavers have patience.* Flemish: DeMeyer FFC XXXVII 84 No. 27d.

P446. *Barber.* Sébillot Métiers No. 11; Penzer III 100 n. 1.

F665. Skillful barber. J21.1. Barber hired to cut king's throat. J625. Barber makes heavy demands of customer while he has the razor at the latter's throat. K1825.3. Disguise as barber. N465. Secret physical peculiarity discovered by barber.

P446.1. *Barbers as bunglers of plans.* Chauvin V 154ff. Nos. 78ff. and n. 1.

P446.2. *Barbers cunning and greedy.* India: Thompson-Balys.

P447. *Smith.* *Sébillot Métiers Nos. 17, 18; *Hdwb. d. Abergl. IX Nachträge 257—67; Andree (1878) 153; *Nyrop Dania IX 186ff.; Von Sydow Våra folksagor (1941) 39ff. — Irish myth: Cross; Icelandic: *Boberg; Missouri French: Carrière; Jewish: *Neuman.

A142. Smith of the gods. A1447. Origin of metal-working. A1861.2. Christ and the smith. D853. Magic object forged by smith to order. F343.3. Fairy smith gives knight a magic sword. F451.3.4.2. Dwarfs as smiths. F663. Skillful smith. H312.4. Successful suitor must have whitest hands. Blacksmith qualifies because of frequent washing of hands. J1161.7. Ruler forbids smith to reveal solution of riddle. K1816.12. Disguise as smith. L113.6. Smith as hero. N855. Helpful smith. R131.8.4. Smith rescues abandoned child.

P447.0.1. *Smith from Lochlann* (Scandinavia, otherworld [?]) Irish myth: Cross.

P447.1. *Smith as grandfather of king.* Irish myth: Cross.

P447.2. *Smith as rath-builder.* Irish myth: Cross.

P447.3. *Smith as lord of hall of hospitality.* Irish myth: Cross.

P447.4. *Smith punished in hell.* Irish myth: Cross.

P447.5. *Smith honored by king as indispensable.* Invited to festival. England: *Baughman.

P447.6. *Rivaling smiths.* Icelandic: Boberg.

P447.7. *Goldsmith as lover.* Icelandic: Boberg.

F556.2. Voice changed by work of silversmith.

P447.8. *Covetous goldsmith.* India: Thompson-Balys.

W100. Unfavorable traits of character.

P448. *Butcher.* Sébillot Métiers No. 4.

P451. *Spinner.* Sébillot Métiers No. 5; *Von Sydow Spinnsagor.

G201.1. Three witches (hags) deformed from much spinning. G282. Witches punish lazy spinning women. H1092. Task: spinning impossible amount in one night. J51. Sight of deformed witches causes man to release wife from spinning duty.

P452. *Dressmaker (milliner, etc.).* Type 326; German Grimm No. 4; *Hdwb. d. Abergl. IX Nachträge 269f.; Sébillot Métiers No. 8.

P453. *Shoemaker.* **C. Nyrop Dania VIII 195ff.; *Sébillot Métiers No. 10; Irish myth: Cross; Spanish: Espinosa Jr. Nos. 151, 155—157, 185.

F346.1. Fairies make shoes for shoemaker. K1816.10. Disguise as cobbler. X240. Jokes about cobblers.

P453.1. *Why shoemakers are indolent.* A shoemaker spits at Christ on way to be crucified. Christ tells him, "A poor slobbering fellow thou shalt be, and all shoemakers after thee, for what thou has done to me." (Cf. A2231.2, P445.1.) England; Baughman.

P454. *Hatter.* Sébillot Métiers No. 10 pp. 52ff.

P455. *Mason (bricklayer).* Sébillot Métiers No. 12.

P456. *Carpenter.* Sébillot Métiers No. 13; Panchatantra (tr. Ryder) 62ff., 89ff., 260ff.; Irish myth: Cross; Jewish: Neuman.

A143. Carpenter (wright) of the gods. A1445.2. Origin of carpentry.

P457. *House-painter.* Sébillot Métiers No. 15.

P458. *Woodsman.* Types 327, 700; Köhler Aufsätze 49; Sébillot Métiers No. 16; Missouri French: Carrière.

E501.1.4. Forester as wild huntsman. L113.5. Woodcutter hero. N856. Forester as helper.

P459. *Other artisans.*

P459.1. *Printer.* Sébillot Métiers No. 19.

P460. Other trades and professions.

P461. *Soldier.* *Hdwb. d. Abergl. IX Nachträge 485ff.; Missouri French: Carrière.

E501.2.6. Soldiers in wild hunt.

P461.1. *Soldier who has had both hands severed fights with his teeth until he is killed.* Italian Novella: Rotunda.

P461.2. *Soldier dies happy on learning of enemy's rout.* Italian Novella: Rotunda.

P461.3. *Soldier is ordered to set fire to enemy's armada.* Is caught and sawed in two. Italian Novella: Rotunda.

Q469.8. Punishment: sawing in twain.

P461.4. *Woman instructs in art of arms.* (Cf. F565.1.) Irish myth: Cross.

P471. *Actor.*

P471.1. *Actors banished along with vagabonds.* Pauli (ed. Bolte) No. 537.

P475. *Robber.* Irish myth: Cross; Missouri French: Carrière; Jewish: *Neuman.

K300—K499. Thefts and cheats. K301. Master thief. K1054. Robber persuaded to climb down moonbeam. K1812.2.1. Incognito king joins robbers. K1916. Robber bridegroom. N765. Meeting with robber band. N884. Robber's help. Q111.3. Riches as reward for help against robbers.

P475.1. *Twelve robbers.* Fb III 132a "røver".

P475.2. *Robbers defeated and killed.* Icelandic: *Boberg.

K420. Thief loses his goods or is detected.

P481. *Astrologer.* Penzer X 77a s.v. "Astrologer"; Jewish: *Neuman; India: Thompson-Balys.

D1712. Soothsayer. J2133.8. Stargazer falls in well. K1964. Sham astrologer. M302.4. Horoscope taken by means of stars. N186. Man who derided another's faith in the stars becomes a respected astrologer.

P482. *Painter (artist).*

P482.1. *Devil pulls painter from chair.* Scala Celi 120b No. 660.

P483. *Juggler (conjurer).* Irish myth: Cross.

P485. *Philosopher.*

P485.1. *Treacherous philosophers.* India: Thompson-Balys.

P500—P599. Government.

P500. Government.

A1580. Origin of laws. A1582. Origin of government. B220. Animal kingdom (or community). B230. Parliament of animals. F252. Government of fairies. F402.2. Government of demons. P10. Kings. T148. Matriarchy.

P510. Law courts. *E. v. Künssberg Rechtliche Volkskunde (Halle, 1936); **Spargo Juridicial Folklore in England (Durham N.C., 1944); Irish myth: Cross.

A464. God of justice. B270. Animals in legal relations. D1318. Magic object reveals guilt. D1318.2.1. Laughing fish reveals unjust judgment. D1406. Magic object helps win in law court. H220. Ordeals. J1130. Cleverness in law court—general. P14.1. Prisoners released as celebration of king's success. P19.4.1. King may judge against all save one of highest rank in religion or learning. Q200. Deeds punished. Q400. Kinds of punishment. T647. Illegal to care for illegitimate child.

P511. *Criminal allowed to choose his method of execution.* *Wesselski Märchen 199.

K558. Man allowed to pick out tree to be hanged on. Cannot find one.

P511.1. *Chooses to die of old age.* Criminal given choice of deaths. (Cf. J1181.) Hdwb. d. Märchens s.v. "Friedrich der Grosse" n. 58.

P511.2. *Man condemned to lose his eye is allowed to choose the instrument.* Herbert III 71; Hervieux IV 310 No. 117; Spanish Exempla: Keller.

P512. *Condemned woman may be freed by marrying a rogue.* *Fb "gifte" I 432; Zs. f. Vksk. XXIII 108, XXV 286, XXVII 236; Sehreuer Zs. f. vgl. Rechtswiss. XXXIV 201; Blätter f. pommersche Volkskunde VII 63.

H542. Death sentence escaped by propounding riddle king (judge) cannot solve. H924. Tasks assigned prisoner so that he may escape punishment. J1181. Execution escaped by use of special permissions granted the condemned. T110. Unusual marriage.

P512.1. *Release from execution at a woman's request (by marriage to her).* *Taylor JAFL LX 185.

P513. *Criminal may fight against odds rather than be judicially executed.* Child IV 497a.

H218. Trial by combat.

P515. *Pardoning of criminal comes too late.* Icelandic: Boberg.

P516. *Youngest of judges first to give decision.* Jewish: *Neuman.

P517. *Crime less serious if committed at request of a lady.* English romance: Malory VII 18.

P518. *Cities of refuge.* Jewish: *Neuman.

P521. *Complacent judge disregards the confession.* He has put the criminal to torture without success. When he releases him, the criminal says, "In a moment I should have confessed all." The judge lets him go nevertheless. Wesselski Hodscha Nasreddin I 266 No. 247.

P522. *Laws.*

P522.1. *Lex talionis.* One life for one life. Equal number must be given up by each feuding side. (Cf. P535.) Irish myth: Cross (P548.2); India: Thompson-Balys; New Guinea: Ker 61.

P522.1.1. *A nose for a nose.* India: Thompson-Balys.
Q451.5. Nose cut off as punishment.

P523. *Bringing suit in law courts.* Irish myth: Cross.

P523.1. *Foreigner may not bring suit.* (Cf. P191.) Irish myth: Cross.

P523.2. *Madman may not bring suit.* Irish myth: Cross.

P523.2.1. *Fool not to be punished for his crime.* Irish myth: Cross.

P523.3. *Slave may not bring suit.* (Cf. P170.) Irish myth: Cross.

P524. *Legal security.* Irish myth: Cross.

P524.1. *Poet may not act as security.* (Cf. P427.) Irish myth: Cross.

P524.2. *Foreigner may not act as security.* (Cf. P191.) Irish myth: Cross.

P525. *Contracts.* Irish myth: Cross.
M200. Bargains and promises.

P525.0.1. *"It is a debt if it is promised."* Irish myth: Cross.

P525.1. *Contract made by madman void.* (Cf. P192.) Irish myth: Cross.

P525.2. *Contract made by woman without her husband void.* Irish myth: Cross.

P525.3. *He nearest to blood of slain man must avenge his death.* Irish myth: Cross.

P526. *Legal principles.*

P526.1. *"To every cow belongs its calf,"* a legal principle applied to question of ownership of copy of manuscript. Irish myth: Cross.

P526.2. *"To every son belongs his mother":* in case of suspected illegitimacy, child is not guilty. Irish myth: Cross.

P531. *Taxation and payment of fines or tribute.* Irish myth: *Cross.
H928. Tasks imposed as tribute. P24. Queen must pay tribute to victorious queen to the amount paid by king to victorious king.

P531.1. *Tribe failing to attend yearly feast to send gift as sign of submission.* Irish myth: Cross.

P531.1.1. *Tribute required of conquered foreigners.* Irish myth: Cross.

P531.2. *Tax on treasure trove.* (Cf. N500.) Irish myth: Cross.

P532. *Payment of tax (tribute).* Irish myth: *Cross.

P533. *Feudal tribute.* Specified interchange of aid and gifts. Irish myth: Cross.

P533.1. *Hostages.* Irish myth: Cross.

P533.1.1. *Boys as hostages.* Irish myth: Cross.

P535. *Éric fines (imposed for personal injury, etc.).* (Cf. P522.1.) Irish myth: *Cross.

P536. *Punishment for failure to pay tax.* Irish myth: Cross.

P536.1. *Nose cut off for failure to pay tax.* (Cf. Q451.5.) Irish myth: Cross.

P537. *Payment of stipend.* Irish myth: Cross.

P541. *Law-making.* Irish myth: Cross.

P541.1. *Heptads. Laws made in groups of seven.* (Cf. Z71.5.) Irish myth: Cross.

P541.2. *Laws made at yearly feast.* Irish myth: Cross.

P541.2.1. *Laws made at feast every seven years.* Irish myth: Cross.

P548. *Miscellaneous legal customs.* Irish myth: Cross.

P550. Military affairs. *Hdwb. d. Abergl. IX Nachträge 181—254; Jewish: Neuman.

A485. God of war. B184.2.1.2. Magic soldier-producing cow. B260. Animal warfare. C845. Tabus concerning war. D1475. Magic object furnishes soldiers. K2350. Military strategy. P14.1. Prisoners released in celebration of victory.

P551. *Army.*

A1596. Origin of army. E502. The Sleeping Army. H1022.2.1. Task: clothing an army from one hank of flax. P29.3. Queen pours for battle champions.

P551.0.1. *Band of professional warriors.* Irish myth: Cross; Icelandic: *Boberg.

A1658. Origin of professional warriors.

P551.1. *Army of young men.* Old men excluded. *Chauvin VII 84 No. 373bis.

P551.2. *Soldiers chained (tied) together to prevent flight from battle.* Irish myth: Cross.

P551.3. *Clerics exempted from military service.* Irish myth: Cross.

P551.4. *Hero drives retreating warriors back into battle.* Irish myth: Cross.

P551.5. *Boy corps.* Irish myth: Cross.

P551.6. *Law requiring military service of women revoked through influence of saint.* Irish myth: Cross.

P551.7. *Conflicts with the recruting officers.* Lithuanian: Balys Index No. 3743.

P551.8. *Retainers not required to go to battle under overlord except for pay.* Irish myth: Cross.

P551.8.1. *Only 700 subjects of under-king required to serve under overlord on any one hosting.* Irish myth: Cross.

P551.9. *"Battle seeds"* (semen bellicosum). Irish myth: Cross.

P552. *Battle formations.* Irish myth: Cross.

P552.1. *Battle-pen. Warriors fight in circle around leader.* Irish myth: Cross.

P552.2. *Superior troops distributed throughout army to prevent their soldierly qualities from being too obvious.* Irish myth: Cross.

P552.3. *Phalanx.* Irish myth: Cross.

P552.3.1. *Roof of shields.* Testudo. Irish myth: Cross.

P552.4. *War-machines.* Irish myth: Cross.

P552.5. *Haircut as preparation for war.* Maori: Beckwith Myth 250.

P553. *Weapons.* Irish myth: Cross; Jewish: Neuman.

P553.1. *Poisoned weapons.* Irish myth: Cross.

P554. *Battle-cairn.* Losses reckoned by number of stones remaining in pile after each survivor has removed one. Irish myth: Cross.

A989.4. Pile of stones (cairn) marks site of battle.

P555. *Defeat in battle.* Irish myth: Cross; Jewish: *Neuman.

P555.1. *Submission indicated by defeated lying with conqueror's sword between teeth.* Irish myth: Cross.

P555.2. *Corpses of dead foes dismembered.* Tupper and Ogle Walter Map 93.

P555.2.1. *Heads of fallen enemies piled up after battle.* Irish myth: Cross.

P555.2.1.1. *"Publication of slaying."* Heads of slain enemies displayed. Irish myth: Cross; *Icelandic: Boberg.

P555.2.1.2. *Jawbone cut from slain opponent.* Hawaii: Beckwith Myth 422.

P555.3. *Gate of captured town (castle) to be widened until overlord's spear can pass through crosswise.* Irish myth: Cross.

P556. *Challenge to battle.* Irish myth: Cross; Jewish: Neuman.

P556.1. *Challenge by turning left side of shield toward enemy.* Irish myth: Cross.

P556.2. *Challenge to battle by hurling javelin skyward.* Virgil Aeneid IX 53.

P557. *Military customs.* Irish myth: Cross.

P557.1. *Warrior not entitled to ransom if captured without arms.* Irish myth: Cross.

P557.2. *Pledge with enemy to be kept.* Irish myth: Cross.

P557.3. *Stones erected where enemy falls.* Irish myth: Cross.

P557.4. *Customs concerning single combat.* Irish myth: Cross.

P557.4.1. *First to reach field of combat has choice of weapons.* Irish myth: Cross.

P557.4.2. *Warrior who begins combat has right to desist.* Irish myth: Cross.

P557.4.3. *Choice of weapons alternates each succeeding day.* Irish myth: Cross.

P557.4.4. *"Men's truth"* (fir fer). Challenger to single combat must submit to same conditions as person challenged. Irish myth: Cross.

P557.4.4.1. *Warrior engaged in combat with one-armed opponent allows one hand to be bound to his side.* Irish myth: Cross.

P557.5. *Warrior disgraced by slaying of those under his protection.* Irish myth: Cross.

P557.6. *Warrior dies with face toward foe.* Irish myth: Cross.

P557.7. *Divorce given to wives before leaving for battle.* Jewish: Neuman.

P561. *Tournaments.* **R. C. Clephan The Tournament (London. 1919); *O. Mueller Turnier und Kampf in den altfrz. Artusromanen (Erfurt, 1907); Jewish: Neuman.

H331.2. Suitor contest: tournament. H1561.1. Tests of valor: tournament. P52. Knight jousts with all comers. R222. Unknown knight. Three days' tournament.

P561.1. *King is persuaded to rescind ban on tournaments.* Italian Novella: Rotunda.

P561.2. *Tournament: to avenge death of king.* India: Thompson-Balys.

P600—P699. Customs.

P600. Customs.[1] Jewish: *Neuman.

A545. Culture hero establishes customs. A1500. Origins of customs. C650.1. Customs connected with unique compulsion. P13. Customs connected with kings. P14.1. Prisoners released in celebration of victory. P52. Knight jousts with all comers. S110.1. Old people killed in famine. S140.1. Abandonment of the aged.

P611. *Women meet when bathing.* Icelandic: Snorra Edda Skaldsk. XLI (Nibel), *Boberg; India: Thompson-Balys.

P612. *Trumpet blown before house of one sentenced to death.* *Crane Vitry 151 No. 42; Spanish Exempla: Keller.

P613. *Charon's fee: putting coin in dead person's mouth to pay for ferry across Styx.* Italian Novella: *Rotunda.

A672.1.1. Charon exacts fee to carry souls across Styx. E431.11. Coin placed in mouth of dead to prevent return.

P616. *Newcomers forced to pass the night with ruling princess.* Given sleeping potion. Goods confiscated for failure to consummate marriage. Italian Novella: Rotunda.

K675. Sleeping potion given to man who is to pass the night with a girl.

P617. *People weep when child is born.* They sing and laugh at burials. Italian Novella: Rotunda.

X1505. Topsy-turvy land.

P621. *Bridle goes with horse when horse is bought.* *Wesselski Märchen 245f. No. 55.

[1] Except in so far as customs enter narratives, they are not in the scope of this work.

P622. *Servant must keep horns and hide of his cattle that are slain.* Wesselski Märchen 200.

P623. *Fasting (as a means of distraint).* Irish myth: Cross.

B253.3. Fox fasts as penance. C200. Tabu: eating (general).

P623.0.1. *Fasting against God.* Irish myth: Cross.

P623.0.1.1. *Clerics fast against God for revelation.* Irish myth: Cross.

D1810.9. Magic knowledge from God.

P623.0.2. *Fasting against the Devil.* Irish myth: Cross.

P623.0.3. *Fasting against fairies.* Irish myth: Cross.

P623.0.4. *Fasting against saints.* Irish myth: Cross.

P623.0.5. *Fasting by saints causes tree worshipped by pagans to fall.* Irish myth: Cross.

P623.0.6. *Fasting to enforce saint's dues.* Irish myth: Cross.

P623.0.7. *Calves not let to cows during fast.* Irish myth: Cross.

P631. *Strangers to be given precedence over man at home.* Duke permits visiting duke to go through narrow path first. This sets custom. Pauli (ed. Bolte) No. 515.

P632. *Customs concerning recognition of rank.* Irish myth: Cross.

A1539.1. Origin of seating arrangements in royal hall. C550. Class tabu. C853. Tabus concerning entry into assembly. C878. Tabu concerning clothing.

P632.1. *Couches provided for men of high rank.* Irish myth: Cross.

P632.2. *Cuts of meat distributed according to rank.* Irish myth: Cross.

P632.2.1. *"The champion's portion."* The choicest portion assigned to the bravest at feasts. Irish myth: Cross.

H1395. Heroes seek judgment as to which is greatest (is to receive "champion's portion"). H1568.1. Test of championship.

P632.3. *Rank among children recognized by quality of appointments and food.* Irish myth: Cross.

P632.4. *Color worn signifies rank.* Irish myth: Cross.

P632.4.1. *Precedence shown by position of shield (flag).* Irish myth: Cross.

P632.5. *Long hair prized by Irish heroes.* Irish myth: Cross.

C722. Tabu: cutting hair.

P633. *Young not to precede old.* Irish myth: Cross.

P634. *Feasts.* Irish myth: Cross.

C282. Tabu: refusing a feast.

P634.0.1. *Customs connected with eating and food.* Jewish: Neuman.

P634.1. *Feast (hospitality) endures for three days and three nights.* Irish myth: Cross.

P634.2. *Feast (hospitality) endures for seven days and seven nights.* Irish myth: Cross.

P541.2.1. Laws made at feast every seven years.

P641. *Injured husband will not kill a naked man.* Child V 489 s.v. "naked".

K1500. Deceptions connected with adultery.

P642. *Only the brave to wear beards.* Irish myth: Cross.

C565. Tabus of bearded men.

P643. *With only opponent's arms.* Hero goes to encounter unarmed except for the arms he wrests from his opponent. Irish myth: Cross.

P644. *Hero unwilling to answer questions before he is dressed.* Icelandic: Boberg.

P651. *Customs concerning bells.*

P651.1. *Bells hung at every corner of ship.* Child IV 462a.

P651.2. *Bells on horse's mane.* Child I 323, II 183—191, 344, IV 410, 413.

P651.3. *Bells rung backward as alarm.* Child III 26.

P661. *Hut for invalid to prevent noxious odor.* *Schoepperle 367ff.

P665. *Custom: boasting of sexual prowess.* India: Thompson-Balys.

P671. *Woman veils self as expression of surprise.* Chauvin V 149 No. 73 n. 1.

P672. *Pulling a man's beard as an insult.* E. Hinojosa Homenaje a Menéndez y Pelayo I 568ff.; R. Menéndez Pidal Cantar del Mio Cid II 498; Italian Novella: *Rotunda.

Q497. Beard shaved as punishment for murder. S327.2. Baby ordered killed because it pulls beard of father (raja).

P672.1. *Fur made of beards of conquered kings.* Welsh: MacCulloch Celtic 185.

H1273.2. Quest for three hairs from devil's beard.

P672.2. *Cutting off a man's (woman's) hair as an insult.* Irish myth: Cross; Icelandic: Boberg.

C722. Tabu: cutting hair.

P672.3. *Rubbing shaved head of hero with cow dung as insult.* Irish myth: Cross.

P672.4. *Insult: lighting lamp with king's moustache.* India: Thompson-Balys.

P673. *Footwashing as sign of reconciliation.* India: Thompson-Balys.

P674. *Old person commits suicide when strength fails.* Irish myth: Cross.

S140.1. Aged people abandoned.

P675. *Touching head as sign of acceptance of bargain.* India: Thompson-Balys.

P676. *Feet (legs) seized in supplication.* Greek: Iliad XXII 337 and passim; India: Thompson-Balys.

P677. *Customs connected with dueling.*

P677.1. *Duel: shooting and catching arrows in turn.* India: Thompson-Balys.

P678. *Pulling out hair as sign of grief.* Jewish: Moreno Esdras (P673.1).

P678.1. *Tearing garments as sign of grief.* Jewish: *Neuman.

P681. *Mourning customs.* Jewish: *Neuman.

P682. *Greeting customs.* Jewish: *Neuman.

P682.1. *Greeting in God's name.* Jewish: Neuman.

P682.2. *Voyagers have right to ask landsman first question.* Marquesas: Handy 56, 72.

P700—P799. Society—miscellaneous motifs.

P710. Nations.

P711. *Patriotism.* Irish myth: Cross; Spanish Exempla: Keller.

A536.1. Culture hero (saint) defends Ireland against foreign invaders. V61.3.0.1. Hero buried in armor, standing with face toward land of enemies. W34. Loyalty.

P711.1. *Wolves of his own country dearer than dogs of another.* Pauli (ed. Bolte) No. 420.

P711.2. *Mother of invalided soldier says of his limping: "Every step will remind you of your virtue."* Italian Novella: Rotunda.

P711.3. *Common citizen saves the honor of his country.* Gives his own funds. Italian Novella: Rotunda.

P711.4. *Scipio plunges into burning pit to save Rome from destruction.* Italian Novella: Rotunda.

P711.5. *Roman undertakes to kill Hannibal.* Kills another by mistake. Burns off his hand for having failed. Italian Novella: Rotunda.

P711.6. *National unity preserved by expulsion of all foreign elements.* Jewish: Moreno Esdras, Neuman.

P711.7. *Aristotle rises from sick bed to rush into battle for his country.* Spanish Exempla: Keller.

P711.8. *Aversion to burial in foreign soil.* Irish myth: Cross; Jewish: Neuman.

P711.9. *Patriotism: king learning that nation will triumph whose king dies in battle, allows self to be killed.* Spanish Exempla: Keller.

M362. Prophecy: death of ruler to insure victory.

P715. *Particular nations* (races).

A1600. Distribution and differentiation of peoples. X600. Humor concerning races or nations.

P715.1. *Jews.* **Goebel Jüdische Motive in märchenhafte Erzählungsgut (Gleiwitz, 1932) 281—288; Jewish: *Neuman.

A1681.2. Why Jews do not eat pork. V266. Virgin Mary converts a Jew to Christianity. V360. Christian traditions concerning Jews. X610. Jokes concerning Jews.

P720. Population. Irish myth: Cross.

P721. *Diseases (plague) invoked to combat overpopulation.* Irish myth: Cross.

Q. REWARDS AND PUNISHMENTS

DETAILED SYNOPSIS

Q. REWARDS AND PUNISHMENTS

Q0. Rewards and punishments. Irish myth: Cross; Jewish: *Neuman.

A693. Intermediate future world. Residence for those whose good and evil deeds exactly counterbalance. E752. Lost souls. Q172. Reward: admission to heaven. V520. Salvation.

Q1. *Hospitality rewarded—opposite punished.* Irish myth: *Cross.

C282. Tabu: refusing a feast.

Q1.1. *Gods (saints) in disguise reward hospitality and punish inhospitality.* Usually the hospitable person is poor, the inhospitable rich. *Types 750AB, 751, 750*; *BP II 210, III 206; Aarne FFC XXIII 46; *Dh II 117; *Fb "Sankt Peder" III 164b, "rig" III 55a. — Spanish: Espinosa II No. 86, III Nos. 168—171, Espinosa Jr. No. 181; India: *Thompson-Balys; Buddhist myth: Malalasekera II 656; Japanese: Ikeda.

A180. Gods in relation to mortals. K1811. Gods (saints) in disguise visit mortals. L143. Poor man surpasses rich. Q42.3. Generosity to saint (god) in disguise rewarded. Q45. Hospitality rewarded. Q141. Reward: man's cows magically multiply. Q286.1. Uncharitableness to holy person punished. Q292.1. Inhospitality to saint (god) punished. V200. Sacred persons.

Q2. *Kind and unkind.* Churlish person disregards requests of old person (animal) and is punished. Courteous person (often youngest brother or sister) complies and is rewarded. *Types 361, 403, 431, 440, 480, 513, 550, 551, 554, 570, 571, 577, 610, 620, 707, 750**, 287**; *BP I 86, 99, 207, 503, II 21, 39, 380, 394, 427, III 84, 267, 276; **Roberts; *Cox Cinderella 481; MacCulloch Childhood 61; *Saintyves Perrault 10. — Irish: O'Suilleabhain 18; French Canadian: Barbeau JAFL XXIX 15; Missouri French: Carrière; Spanish: Boggs FFC XC 75 No. 594, Espinosa II No. 86, III Nos. 141—143, 153, Espinosa Jr. Nos. 117, 183, 202—204; Italian: Basile Pentamerone III No. 10, IV No. 7, V No. 2; India: *Thompson-Balys; Chinese: Graham; Japanese: Anesaki 318f., Ikeda; Korean: Zong in-Sob 32 No. 15, 46 No. 27; Indonesia: DeVries's list No. 172, Dixon 210; Tuamotu: Stimson MS (z-G. 13/167); N. A. Indian: *Thompson CColl II 383, 386ff., 432, *Thompson Tales 276 n. 18b, (California): Gayton and Newman 95; Africa: Werner African 138ff., 204, 208, 210, (Gold Coast): Barker and Sinclair 89 No. 16, (Benga): Nassau 213 No. 23, (Ekoi): Talbot 237, 280, (Kaffir): Theal 48, 52, (Basuto): Jacottet 140, 146, 224, (Yoruba): Ellis 244 No. 1, (Fjort): Dennett 121f., (Ibo, Nigeria): Basden 282, (Duala): Lederbogen JAS IV 70, Märchen 84; Cape Verde Islands: Parsons MAFLS XV (1) 125 No. 44.

D1454.1.2. Jewels from hair. D1454.2. Treasure falls from mouth. D1454.3. Treasure from spittle. D1663.6. Magic tree gives money to good—poisonous animals to bad brother. D1870. Magic hideousness. H1242. Youngest brother alone succeeds on quest. J2415. Foolish imitation of lucky man. L13. Compassionate youngest son. Kind to people or animals: rewarded. L54. Compassionate youngest daughter. M431.2. Curse: toads from mouth. Q41. Politeness rewarded. R246. Crane-bridge. Fugitives are helped across a stream by a crane who lets them cross on his leg. The pursuer is either refused assistance or drowned by the crane.

Q3. *Moderate request rewarded; immoderate punished.* India: Thompson-Balys; Japanese: Ikeda; West Indies: Flowers 566.

A2232.3. Beetle makes immoderate request; ant modest: inverse awards. D2172.2. Magic gift: power to continue all day what one starts. One woman measures linen; another throws water on pig. J2415. Foolish imitation of lucky man. Because one man has had good luck a numskull imitates and thinks he will have equal luck. He is disappointed. L220. Modest request best. N471. Foolish attempt of second man to overhear secrets (from animals, demons, etc.).

Q3.1. *Woodsman and the gold axe.* A woodsman lets his axe fall into the water. Hermes comes to his rescue. Takes out a gold axe but the woodsman says that it is not his. The same with a silver axe. Finally he is given his own axe and rewarded for his modest choice. His companion tries this plan and loses his axe. Wienert FFC LVI 79* (ET 449), 139 (ST 444); Halm Aesop No. 308; Lithuanian: Balys Index No. 729*; Chinese: Eberhard FFC CXX 34 No. 20; Japanese: Ikeda.

F420.5.1.7.4. Water-spirit returns to the woodchopper a silver axe in place of the one he has lost.

Q3.2. *Lion divides slain bullock.* The thief who demands half of the bullock driven off; the traveler who modestly withdraws invited to take half. Wienert FFC LVI 70 (ET 342), 140 (ST 459).

Q4. *Humble rewarded, haughty punished.* Irish myth: *Cross.

Q66. Humility rewarded. Q151.5. Humble man miraculously saved from drowning. Q331. Pride punished. Q552.19.5. Miraculous drowning as punishment for haughtiness.

Q5. *Laziness punished; industry rewarded.*

Q5.1. *Lazy jackal punished; industrious pig rewarded.* India: Thompson-Balys.

Q5.2. *Lazy owl punished; industrious hummingbird rewarded.* Africa (Wute): Sieber 200.

Q6. *Good thoughts rewarded, bad punished.* Chinese: Eberhard FFC CXX 186f.

Q6.1. *Foolishness brings a man to death, quiet calm to fortune.* Africa (Wakweli): Bender 92f.

Q7. *Deity descends and makes king and wronged subject change places.* Buddhist myth: Malalasekera II 425.

Q10—Q99. Deeds rewarded.

Q10. Deeds rewarded.

B320. Reward of helpful animal. B350. Grateful animals. K231.2. Reward for accomplishment of task deceptively withheld. L200. Modesty brings reward. W15. Woman shelters murderer of her son out of charity. W27. Gratitude. W31. Obedience.

Q20. Piety rewarded. Irish: *Cross, O'Suilleabhain 120, Beal XXI 336; Spanish Exempla: Keller; Jewish: *Neuman; India: *Thompson-Balys; Buddhist myth: Malalasekera II 1153; Hawaii: Beckwith Myth 70.

A185.11. God rewards mortal for pious act. A2221. Animal characteristic reward for pious act. A2711. Plant blessed for pious act. K3.2.1. Supernatural substitute in tournament for pious warrior. Q112.0.1.1. Kingdom as reward for piety. Q113.3. High position as reward for piety. Q116.1. Favorable decree as reward for helping holy person. Q147. Supernatural manifestations at death of pious person. Q156. Victory as reward for piety. Q157. Escape of hostages miraculously prevented as reward for piety. Q170. Religious rewards. V. Religion.

Q20.1. *Reward for service of god, hero, or ascetic for a period.* India: Thompson-Balys.

Q20.2. *Fulfillment of precepts rewarded.* Jewish: *Neuman.

Q21. *Reward for religious sacrifice.* India: *Thompson-Balys; Buddhist myth: Malalasekera I 427.

Q223.3. Neglect to sacrifice punished. V10. Religious sacrifices.

Q21.1. *Old woman gives her only cow believing she would receive a hundred in return from God.* A bishop hearing of her faith sends her a hundred cows. Spanish Exempla: Keller.

J1262.5. 100 for 1. K366.1.1. Cow makes a hundred-fold return.

Q22. *Reward for faith.* India: *Thompson-Balys.

Q23. *Reward for securing converts.* India: Thompson-Balys.

Q25. *Reward for carrying Christ across a stream.* Christ is in the form of a child. (St. Christopher.) *Type 768; Dh II 266; Legenda Aurea (ed. Graesse) 432; *Schwickert Zs. f. Vksk. NF III 14—26; Klapper Erzählungen des Mittelalters 111 No. 101; *Loomis White Magic 114.

K1811. Gods (saints) in disguise visit mortals. P413.1. Eternal ferryman. V211. Christ.

Q25.1. *Boy risks life to carry leper across stream.* Leper is Christ in disguise. Irish myth: Cross.

Q26. *Keeping fast rewarded.* India: Thompson-Balys.

Q27. *Reward for faith: boy doomed to die saved (miraculously).* India: Thompson-Balys.

Q28. *Reward for religious pilgrimage.* Chinese: Eberhard FFC CXX 188 No. 28.

Q32. *Reward for offering food to crucifix (Madonna).* BP III 474ff.

Q33. *Reward for saying of prayers.* (Cf. V50.) Ward II 621 No. 30; Scala Celi 136b No. 760; Jewish: *Neuman; India: *Thompson-Balys.

Q34. *Reward for austerities of hermit.* (Cf. Q144.1.) The further he must carry water, the greater his heavenly reward. Scala Celi 15a No. 84; Oesterley No. 80; *A. E. Schönbach Die Legende von Engel und Waldbruder (Wien, 1901); India: *Thompson-Balys.

Q35. *Reward for writing hymn.* (Cf. Q172.5.) Irish myth: Cross.

Q36. *Reward for repentance.* (Cf. Q174.1.) Irish myth: Cross; Jewish: *Neuman.

Q36.1. *Reward for confession of sins.* Jewish: *Neuman.

Q37. *Reward for carrying out dead man's request.* Chinese: Graham.

Q38. *Reward for attendance on holy man.* (Cf. Q116.1.) Jewish: Neuman; Chinese: Eberhard FFC CXX 83, 158, 163f.

Q39. *Piety rewarded—miscellaneous.*

Q39.1. *Asceticism rewarded.* (Cf. V462.) Buddhist myth: Malalasekera I 500, II 750.

Q40. **Kindness rewarded.** *Chauvin VI 109 No. 274 n. 2; Irish: Beal XXI 304; Missouri French: Carrière; Greek: Fox 200 (Phaon); Buddhist myth: Malalasekera I 362; Chinese: Graham, Eberhard FFC CXX 132 No. 87; Africa (Bankon): Ittman 83, (Bulu): Krug 109, (Duala): Lederbogen JAS IV 71.

Q41. *Politeness rewarded.* *Roberts 173; Icelandic: Boberg; Breton: Sébillot Incidents s.v. "politesse"; Missouri French: Carrière; Spanish: Espinosa III No. 152, Espinosa Jr. Nos. 117, 130, 183; Italian: Basile Pentamerone IV Nos. 7, 8.

L363. Goldsmith gives money to one who addresses him as his friend (the goldsmith had no friends because he cheated everybody). Q2. Kind and unkind.

Q41.1. *Ogre appeased by being called uncle (aunt, etc.).* India: Thompson-Balys.

K347. Cozening. Trickster's claim of relationship causes owner to relax vigilance.

Q41.2. *Reward for cleansing loathsome person.* Cleansing eyelids, bathing, lousing etc. *Roberts 168; Type 480; Africa (Chaga): Gutmann 132ff. No. 83, (Alo): Pratt-Chadwick and Lamprey The Alo Man (New York, 1927) 17ff., (Batanga): Nassau JAFL XXVIII 45ff. No. 16, (Bulu): Krug JAFL XXV 113 No. 9, (Bambara): Travélé 205ff. No. 66, (Hausa): Equilbecq Contes indigènes III 291ff., Tremearne Hausa Superstitions and Customs (London, 1913) 424ff. No. 93.

D583. Transformation by lousing. D733. Loathly bridegroom.

Q42. *Generosity rewarded.* *Chauvin V 14 No. 68; *Penzer VIII 130ff.; Irish myth: Cross; Breton: Sébillot Incidents s.v. "charité"; Spanish: Keller, Espinosa III No. 152, Espinosa Jr. Nos. 202—204, 210; India: *Thompson-Balys; Buddhist myth: Malalasekera II 897, 904, 934, 988; Tahiti: Beckwith Myth 38.

Q151.1. Charitable man's death postponed. Q172.2. Man admitted to heaven for single act of charity. V410. Charity rewarded. W11. Generosity.

Q42.1. *Spendthrift knight.* Divides his last penny. He is later helped by the grateful person. *Types 508, 592, 665; BP II 490ff., Scala Celi 81b No. 467; *Hibbard 73, 79; Alphabet No. 291; Japanese: Anesaki 320.

E341.1. Dead grateful for having corpse ransomed. W131.1. Profligate wastes entire fortune before beginning his own adventures.

Q42.1.1. *Child divides last loaf with fairy (witch, etc.).* Rewarded. Hdwb. d. Märchens I 396b; *Roberts 150, 169.

Q42.1.1.1. *Reward for giving last loaf.* Chinese: Graham.

Q42.1.2. *Man who divides his food with beggar is later freed from captivity by him.* Italian Novella: Rotunda.

R110. Rescue of captive.

Q42.1.3. *Excessive hospitality causes chieftain to become poor.* Irish myth: *Cross.

Q42.2. *Reward for providing coffins for poor.* Chinese: Werner 384.

Q42.3. *Generosity to saint (god) in disguise rewarded.* (Cf. Q1, Q45.1.) Alphabet Nos. 297, 344, 365; Scala Celi 39b No. 222; Irish: Beal XXI 304, 325, O'Suilleabhain 2, 68; Spanish: Keller, Espinosa II No. 86, III Nos. 168—171, Espinosa Jr. Nos. 83—85, 181f., 210; India: *Thompson-Balys; Buddhist myth: Malalasekera I 485; Chinese: Graham.

Q42.4. *Man frees slave (incognito prince):* rewarded when slave becomes king. Italian Novella: *Rotunda.

K1812.11. Incognito king (prince) sold into slavery.

Q42.4.1. *Slave freed as reward for killing enemy's two slaves,* and given as much land as he can cultivate in three days. Icelandic: *Boberg.

Q42.5. *Reward for generosity to king's buffoon.* Ruler rewards herald who is generous to his buffoon. Italian Novella: Rotunda.

Q42.6. *Reward for tearing out eye when demanded.* Irish myth: Cross.

Q161. Sight restored as reward.

Q42.7. *Reward for remitting tribute.* (Cf. Q172.7.) Irish myth: Cross.

Q42.8. *Saint gives a man all his credit for good deeds so that the man may go to heaven.* Saint is then rewarded with even greater credit. (Cf. Q172.) Spanish Exempla: Keller.

Q42.9. *Cobbler gives new pair of shoes to poor boy* and says: "You can pay me when you become archbishop." Generously rewarded many years later. India: Thompson-Balys.

Q43. *Reward for giving counsel.* Irish myth: Cross.

B392. Hero divides spoil for animals. Q111.5. Giant gives gold, silver and weapon as reward for good advice. Q113.1. Appointment to earldom as reward for good advice. Q114.0.1. Gifts made to advisor.

Q44. *Reward for almsgiving.* Scala Celi 81b, 83a Nos. 465, 472; Alphabet 298, 302; Crane Vitry 175 No. 96; Spanish: Keller, Espinosa II No. 86, Espinosa Jr. No. 200; Jewish: Neuman; India: Thompson-Balys; Buddhist myth: Malalasekera I 134, 342, II 1091, 1366; Japanese: Ikeda.

Q44.1. *Reward to almsgiving monk given in form of restored honor and position.* Spanish Exempla: Keller.

Q44.2. *Man pardoned for short accounts* when it is learned that he has given the money to the poor as alms. Spanish Exempla: Keller.

Q44.3. *One rupee given away for charity incidentally brings back ten rupees.* India: Thompson-Balys.

K366.1.1. Cow makes a hundred-fold return.

Q45. *Hospitality rewarded.* Scala Celi 51b, 81b, 83b, 104b, 152b, 158a, 164b Nos. 290, 466, 477, 569, 839, 884, 926; Alphabet No. 368; Irish myth: *Cross; Swiss: Jegerlehner Overwallis 323 No. 95; Spanish: Espinosa III No. 152, Espinosa Jr. Nos. 181f.; Italian Novella: *Rotunda; India: Thompson-Balys; Buddhist myth: Malalasekera II 455, 989; Africa (Loango): Pechuël-Loesche 110, (Kaffir): Kidd 251 No. 13, (Ekoi): Talbot 208.

A2222. Animal characteristics reward for hospitality. B391. Animal grateful for food. K1812.4. Incognito king is given hospitality by fisherman. P320. Hospitality. Relation of host and guest. Q1. Hospitality rewarded—opposite punished. Q111.2. Riches as reward for hospitality. Q152.1. Hospitality of a citizen saves a city from destruction. Q292. Inhospitality punished.

Q45.1. *Angels entertained unawares.* Hospitality to disguised saint (angel, god) rewarded. (Cf. Q42.3.) *Dh II 133ff.; *bin Gorion Born Judas[2] I 366; Scala Celi 39b, 81b Nos. 221, 464, 468; Alphabet Nos. 167, 365, 439; Herbert III 392; Literary treatment: Lowell "Vision of Sir Launfal". — Irish: Cross, O'Suilleabhain 90; Lithuanian: Balys Index No. 752B*; Spanish: Keller, Espinosa Jr. Nos. 181f.; Greek: Pauly-Wissowa s.v. "Baukis"; India: *Thompson-Balys; Buddhist myth: Malalasekera II 35; Japanese: Anesaki 251f.; N. A. Indian (Maliseet): Mechling JAFL XXVI 219ff.; Africa (Konnoh): Willans 140.

K1811.Gods (saints) in disguise visit mortals. Q145.1. Miraculously long life as reward. V235. Mortal visited by angel. W11.4.1. Brahman steals to feed guests (deities).

Q45.1.1. *Three Nephites give blessings as reward for hospitality.* (Mormon tradition.) **H. Lee, The Three Nephites: the Substance and Significance of the Legend in Folklore (Albuquerque, New Mexico, 1949).

Q45.1.2. *King refuses to invite Patrick to feast.* Poor man kills only cow and uses his only measure of meal to entertain Patrick. Patrick blesses his wife and son. Irish myth: Cross.

Q45.1.3. *Hospitality to saint repaid:* neither he nor his posterity will ever be hurt by venomous creatures. *Loomis White Magic 131.

Q45.2. *Hospitality to devil repaid.* *Type 821A; Christiansen Norske Eventyr 105.

Q45.2.1. *Man saves the unrecognized devil from thunder and is generously rewarded.* Estonian, Swedish, and Lithuanian: *Balys Tautosakos Darbai VI 27—31; Cheremis: Sebeok-Nyerges.

A162.3. Combat between thundergod and devil. K1177. Dupe deceived concerning thunder.

Q45.3. *Hospitality to ascetic rewarded.* Buddhist myth: Malalasekera II 221, 604, 656, 775.

Q45.3.1. *Hospitality to monk rewarded.* Buddhist myth: Malalasekera I 819.

Q45.4. *Revenge given up as reward for hospitality.* (Cf. Q151.6.) Icelandic: *Boberg.

Q45.5. *Hospitality repaid by attack on devastating enemy.* Icelandic: Boberg.

Q45.6. *Hospitality repaid by magic procuring of provisions.* Icelandic: *Boberg.

Q46. *Reward for protecting fugitive.*

Q46.1. *Reward for protecting holy fugitive.* Lithuanian: Balys Index No. 3104, Legends Nos. 198—206; Greek: Frazer Apollodorus II 280 n. 1.

D2157.2. Magic quick growth of crops. Reward for helping holy fugitive. Q135. Wine as reward. Twelve jars of honey-sweet wine as reward for protection. R220. Flights.

Q47. *Kindness to orphans repaid by dead parents.* Jewish: Neuman; Africa (Ekoi): Talbot 99.

E341. The grateful dead.

Q51. *Kindness to animals rewarded.* Jewish: *Neuman; Chinese: Eberhard FFC CXX 83, Africa (Wakweli): Bender 87f., (Wute): Sieber 197, (Fang): Tessman 196.

B350. Grateful animals.

Q51.1. *Knight covers foal with his coat to protect it from storm.* English: Wells 60 (Sire Gawene and the Carle of Carelyle).

Q51.2. *Reward for kindness to tiger.* India: Thompson-Balys.

Q53. *Reward for rescue.* Icelandic: *Boberg; Jewish: Neuman; India: Thompson-Balys; Japanese: Ikeda.

B360. Animals grateful for rescue from peril of death. J1522. Rebuke to the stingy. King Cresus gives soldier small reward for saving his life. Q111.3. Riches as reward for help against robbers. R100. Rescues.

Q53.1. *Disguised king rewards rescuer from robbers.* (Cf. K1812.) *BP III 450ff.

Q53.2. *Magic shirt and information about sought robbers as reward for rescue of poor fisherman.* Icelandic: Boberg.

Q53.2.1. *Plenty of fishes as reward for rescue.* Icelandic: Boberg.

Q53.3. *Maiden queen offers her hand as reward for rescuing her town.* Icelandic: Boberg.

T68.1. Princess offered as prize to rescuer.

Q53.3.1. *Maiden gives her hand and riches to man who rescues her from trap.* Africa (Loango): Pechuël-Loesche 109.

Q54. *Uprightness rewarded.* (Cf. Q151.7.)

Q54.1. *Ruler tries in vain to intimidate judge.* Rewards him with high post. Italian Novella: Rotunda.

Q54.2. *Captive knight freed for having kept his word.* Is allowed to leave to collect ransom (or marry fiancée). When he returns his captor frees him (or raises ransom). Italian Novella: *Rotunda.

Q55. *Reward for sparing life when in animal form.* Hartland Science 51; India: Thompson-Balys.

B371.1. Lion spares mouse: mouse grateful. D100. Transformation: man to animal.

Q56. *Love rewarded.*

T215. Faithfulness of married couple in misfortune.

Q56.1. *Ruler rewards man's love for his captive wife with riches and freedom.* Italian Novella: Rotunda.

Q56.2. *Ruler rewards captives' love for each other.* Sets them free and enriches them. Italian Novella: Rotunda.

Q56.3. *Queen rewards love of man of low lineage by making him an ambassador.* Italian Novella: Rotunda.

Q57. *Attendance on the sick rewarded.* Africa (Duala): Lederbogen JAS IV 66, Märchen 83.

Q57.1. *Reward for shielding Mary in childbirth from gaze of onlookers.* Irish: O'Suilleabhain 5.

Q60. Other good qualities rewarded.

Q61. *Self-abnegation rewarded.* (Cf. L200.) Irish myth: Cross; Spanish Exempla: Keller; Jewish: Neuman.

Q61.1. *Monk who did not ask for position made abbot.* He is given the bribe money paid by other ambitious monks. Wesselski Mönchslatein 124 No. 107; India: Thompson-Balys.

Q61.2. *Devil spares abbot because of humility.* Scala Celi 104b No. 570.

Q62. *Reward for ability to keep secrets.* Type 480; *Roberts 159; Africa (Ekoi): Talbot 178.

C420. Tabu: uttering secrets.

Q64. *Patience rewarded.* (Cf. W26.) Jewish: Neuman.

Q65. *Filial duty rewarded.* Jewish: *Neuman; Chinese: Graham; Tonga: Gifford 34.

Q65.1. *Supplying food to ungrateful stepmother rewarded.* (Cf. Q151.2.) Africa (Gold Coast): Barker and Sinclair 129 No. 23.

Q66. *Humility rewarded.* Irish myth: Cross; Jewish: *Neuman.

Q4. Humble rewarded, haughty punished. Q151.5. Humble man miraculously saved from drowning.

Q66.1. *Humility before saint (god) in disguise rewarded.* Irish myth: Cross.

K1811. Gods (saints) in disguise visit mortals. Q45.1. Angels entertained unawares. Q142. Magic treasure as reward for humility.

Q67. *Kingly duty rewarded.* Irish myth: Cross.

Q153. Nature benign and fruitful during reign of good king.

Q68. *Integrity rewarded.* Irish myth: Cross.

Q145.2. Miraculously long life as reward for integrity.

Q68.1. *Truth-speaking rewarded.* Jewish: *Neuman.

Q68.2. *Honesty rewarded.* Finnish-Swedish: Hackman FFC VI No. 940*; Lithuanian: Balys Index No. 941*; Chinese: Graham.

Q72. *Loyalty rewarded.* Jewish: Neuman.

Q72.1. *Reward for loyalty to king.* India: Thompson-Balys.

Q80. Rewards for other causes.

Q81. *Reward for perseverance.* Penzer II 97.

Q81.1. *Nobleman's perseverance wins him coveted place on reserved bench.* Elected upon the death of one of its occupants. Italian Novella: Rotunda.

Q82. *Reward for fearlessness.* Reward given by devil or ghost. *Type 326; Penzer VII 120 n. 2; Irish myth: *Cross; Icelandic: Boberg; India: Thompson-Balys; Japanese: Ikeda.

E465. Revenant rewards its conqueror. H1400. Fear test.

Q82.1. *Snake helps girl who permits it to wind itself around her body.* Africa (Rozwi): Posselt Fables of the Veld (London, 1929) 39ff., (Thonga): Junod 248ff., Berthoud ZsES XXI 154f. No. 10.

H1400. Fear test. A person is put to various tests in order to make him show fear.

Q82.2. *Ferocious animal (lion, tiger, etc.) rewards man who does not fear it.* Africa (Congo): Christaller Handbuch der Duala-Sprache (Basel, 1892) 68ff.

Q83. *Reward for marital fidelity.* (Cf. Q87.) Jewish: Moreno Esdras, Neuman.

H492. Test of faithfulness of husband and wife. T210. Faithfulness in marriage.

Q83.1. *Reward for wife's fidelity.* India: Thompson-Balys; Buddhist myth: Malalasekera I 845.

Q84. *Reward for stoic endurance of pain.* Irish myth: Cross.

Q154.1. Descendants of man who endured pain without crying out not to meet violent deaths.

Q85. *Reward for asking proper questions.* Irish myth: *Cross; Welsh: MacCulloch Celtic 203.

C651. The one compulsory question.

Q86. *Reward for industry.* Hdwb. d. Märchens II 66a; India: *Thompson-Balys; West Indies: Flowers 567.

Q86.1. *Reward to ant for industry.* Ant has food all winter because she keeps it safe and dry by airing it in the sun. Spanish Exempla: Keller.

Q87. *Reward for preservation of chastity.* Irish myth: Cross; Jewish: Neuman, Moreno Esdras.

Q87.1. *Ruler marries maiden who has repulsed his advances.* Italian Novella: Rotunda.

Q87.1.1. *Spurned ruler has the maiden marry highest ranking knight.* Italian Novella: *Rotunda.

Q87.1.2. *Married woman spurns king's offer of marriage.* King honors her husband. Italian Novella: Rotunda.

Q87.1.3. *Spurned suitor is offered girl by her mother.* He rewards her refusal by a gift of money. Italian Novella: Rotunda.

Q87.2. *Courtier rewarded for resisting princess's advances.* When her father learns of the affair he rewards the courtier and has him marry his daughter. Italian Novella: *Rotunda.

T31.1. Lover's meeting: hero in service of lady's father.

Q87.3. *Reward for long-suffering nun: made abbess of convent.* Heptameron No. 22.

Q88. *Reward for proficiency.*

Q88.1. *Fra Lippo Lippi is freed by Moors because of his greatness as a painter.* Italian Novella: Rotunda.

Q88.2. *Princess kisses ugly poet while he sleeps.* Kisses not the ugly face but the divine mouth. Italian Novella: *Rotunda.

Q91. *Reward for cleverness.*

H500. Test of cleverness or ability.

Q91.1. *Princess given in marriage to clever thief.* Italian Novella: Rotunda.

K301. Master thief. T68. Princess offered as prize. T121. Unequal marriage.

Q91.2. *King rewards scullion for bon-mot.* Makes him a valet. Italian Novella: Rotunda.

Q91.3. *King rewards poem.* (Cf. Q112.0.1.2, Q411.10.1.) Icelandic: *Boberg; India: Thompson-Balys.

Q91.4. *Answer rewarded with gold ring; message rewarded with purse with silver.* Icelandic: Boberg.

Q93. *Reward for supernatural help.*

Q93.1. *Reward for bringing rain.* Chinese: Graham.

Q93.2. *Reward for resuscitating dead.* (Cf. E0.) Chinese: Graham.

Q94. *Reward for cure.* India: Thompson-Balys.

D1505. Magic object cures blindness. D2161.3.1. Blindness magically cured. F952. Blindness miraculously cured. H346. Princess given to man who can heal her. H1292.4. Question (propounded on quest):

how can the prince be cured? T67.2. Marriage to prince as reward for curing him.

Q95. *Reward for musician.*

Q95.1. *Reward for flute-playing.* Chinese: Eberhard FFC CXX 70.

Q100—Q199. Nature of rewards.

Q100. Nature of rewards.

A2220. Animal characteristics as reward. A2632. Origin of plant as reward. A2710. Plant characteristics as reward. H1244. Forgiveness the reward of successful quest.

Q101. *Reward fitting to deed.* Jewish: *Neuman.

Q580. Punishment fitted to crime.

Q101.1. *Reward like deed: liberal and munificent girl blessed with riches and prosperity.* India: Thompson-Balys.

Q110. Material rewards.

H1596.1. Golden apple as prize in beauty contest.

Q111. *Riches as reward.* *Roberts 190; Irish myth: *Cross; Spanish: Espinosa Jr. Nos. 132, 181; Jewish; Neuman; Chinese: Graham; Africa (Wakweli): Bender 88.

Q111.1. *Hero made business partner of rich man.* English: Wells 175 (The Childe of Bristowe).

Q111.2. *Riches as reward (for hospitality).* (Cf. Q45.) Irish myth: Cross.

Q111.3. *Riches as reward for help against robbers.* Icelandic: Boberg.

K1916. Robber bridegroom. N765. Meeting with robber band. N884. Robber's help. P475. Robber. Q53. Reward for rescue.

Q111.4. *Gold ring as reward.* (Cf. Q91.3, Q91.4.) Icelandic: *Boberg.

Q111.5. *Giant gives gold, silver and weapon as reward for good advice.* (Cf. Q113.1, Q114.) Icelandic: Örvar-Odds saga 124—125.

Q111.6. *Treasure as reward.* Chinese: Graham.

Q111.7. *Jewels as reward.* Jewish: Neuman; India: *Thompson-Balys; Chinese: Graham.

Q111.8. *Large quantity of land as reward.* India: *Thompson-Balys.

Q112. *Half of kingdom as reward.* *Types 575, 653; *BP II 131ff., III 45ff.; Christiansen FFC XXIV 99; *Fb "prins og prinsesse" II 876; Icelandic: Egils saga einhenda ok Ásmundar Berserkjabana (FAS III) 366 (one-third of kingdom), Boberg; French Canadian: Barbeau JAFL XXIX 19; Spanish: Espinosa III No. 50; Jewish: Neuman; India: *Thompson-Balys; N. A. Indian (Micmac): Rand 427 No. 80; Africa (Yoruba): Ellis 264.

H335. Tasks assigned suitors. Bride as prize for accomplishment. N2.5. Whole kingdom (all property) as wager. N2.5.2. Half kingdom as wager. T68. Princess offered as prize.

Q112.0.1. *Kingdom as reward.* Irish myth: Cross; Jewish: *Neuman; India: *Thompson-Balys.

Q112.0.1.1. *Kingdom as reward for piety.* (Cf. Q20.) Irish myth: Cross; Jewish: Neuman.

Q112.0.1.2. *Kingdom as reward for poem.* (Cf. Q91.3.) Icelandic: Boberg.

Q112.0.1.3. *Kingdom as reward for finding abducted princess.* Icelandic: Boberg.

Q112.0.2. *Half of property as reward.* India: Thompson-Balys.

Q112.0.3. *Two thirds of kingdom as reward for finding abducted princesses.* Icelandic: Boberg.

Q112.0.4. *One third of kingdom and the king's daughter as reward for getting victory-stone during the night.* Icelandic: Boberg.

Q112.0.5. *Kingdom and hand of princess as reward for virtuous life.* Spanish Exempla: Keller.

Q112.0.6. *Dominion over world as reward.* Jewish: *Neuman.

Q112.0.7. *Reward: royal line of descendants.* Jewish: *Neuman.

Q112.1. *Chieftainship as reward.* Tuamotu: Stimson MS (z-G. 3/1142, 13/174, 420); Africa (Ganda): Baskerville 1ff., (Hausa): Mischlich 164ff. No. 22, (Bondei): Woodward FL XXXVI 367ff. No. 12.

Q112.2. *Reward: sovereignty for hour (day).* India: *Thompson-Balys.

Q112.3. *Reward: seat next to king.* India: Thompson-Balys.

Q113. *Knighthood as reward.* English: Wells 94 (The Taill of Rauf Coilyear); and very frequently in mediaeval romances.

Q113.0.1. *High honors as reward.* Chinese: Graham.

Q113.1. *Appointment to earldom as reward for good advice.* (Cf. Q43, Q111.5.) Icelandic: *Boberg.

Q113.2. *Appointment as page as reward.* Icelandic: *Boberg.

Q113.3. *High position as reward for piety.* (Cf. Q20.) Jewish: Neuman.

Q113.4. *Appointment to priesthood as reward.*

Q113.4.1. *Institution of priests and Levites as reward for observance of Sabbath.* Jewish: Neuman.

Q114. *Gifts as reward.* (Cf. Q111.5.) Irish myth: Cross.

Q114.0.1. *Gifts made to advisor.* (Cf. Q43.). Irish myth: Cross.

Q114.1. *Precious knife and belt as gift on unknown helper's spearshaft outside his tent.* Icelandic: Göngu-Hrólfs saga 346.

Q114.2. *Gifts as rewards for gifts.* Icelandic: *Boberg.

Q114.3. *Sword as reward.* Icelandic: *Boberg.

Q115. *Reward: any boon that may be asked.* *Schoepperle II 420ff., 528—541; Malone PMLA XLIII 413; Irish myth: *Cross; India: *Thompson-Balys; Buddhist myth: Malalasekera II 946, 1153.

C871. Tabu: refusing a request. F341. Fairies give fulfillment of wishes. J2071. Three foolish wishes. K175. Deceptive bargain: three wishes. M202.0.1. Bargain or promise to be fulfilled at all hazards. M204.1. Demanding of promised boon postponed. M223. Blind promise (rash boon). N2.0.1. Play for unnamed stakes. P319.7. Friendship without refusal.

Q115.1. *Reward: any boon that may be asked—king's wife demanded.* *Schoepperle II 420ff., 528ff.; *Krappe Revue Celtique XLVIII

(1931) 94; Cross and Nitze Lancelot and Guenevere (Chicago, 1930) 31ff.; Irish myth: *Cross; India: Thompson-Balys.

M10. Irrevocable judgments. N2.6. Wife as wager.

Q115.2. *King promises daughter she may marry anyone she desires.* India: *Thompson-Balys.

Q115.3. *Reward: any boon that may be asked—man asks only for son.* India: Thompson-Balys.

Q116. *Favorable decree as reward.* Irish myth: Cross; Icelandic: Boberg; Jewish: *Neuman.

Q116.1. *Favorable decree as reward for helping holy person.* (Cf. Q38.) Irish myth: Cross.

Q121. *Freedom as reward.*

Q121.1. *Slaves freed as reward.* Icelandic: Boberg.

Q135. *Wine as reward.* Twelve jars of honey-sweet wine as reward for protection. (Cf. Q46.1.) Greek: Frazer Apollodorus II 280 n. 1.

Q140. Miraculous or magic rewards.

A575. Departed deity grants requests to visitors. B217.3. Animal languages learned from ghost (spirits). B500. Magic power from animals. D810. Magic object a gift. D1720. Acquisition of magic powers. D1810.1. Magic knowledge from queen of otherworld. D1811.2. Magic wisdom received from supernatural being. D1812.1.1. Power of prophecy from fairy. D1815.0.1. Gift of tongues received from ghosts. D1846.2. Invulnerability bestowed by many-headed monster. D1903. Power of inducing love given by animals. D1983.1. Invisibility conferred by a god.

Q141. *Reward: man's cows magically multiply.* (Cf. Q1.) Type 750B; Spanish: Espinosa Jr. No. 181; Japanese: Ikeda.

Q141.1. *Monks' who always shared with the poor receive supplies of flour or bread.* Spanish Exempla: Keller.

Q141.2. *Plentiful game animals (fish) as reward.* Africa (Wakweli): Bender 37; S. A. Indian (Toba): Métraux MAFLS XL 27f.

Q142. *Magic treasure as reward for humility.* (Cf. Q66.1.) Irish myth: Cross.

Q143. *Superior rebirth as reward.* India: *Thompson-Balys; Buddhist myth: Malalasekera I 155, 167, 427, 1157, II 604, 671, 775, 904.

Q144. *Reward: hearing voice of God.*

Q144.1. *Hermit as reward for austerities hears voice of God.* (Cf. Q34.) Spanish Exempla: Keller.

Q145. *Miraculously long life as reward.* (Cf. Q151.) Greek: Fox 158 (Sarpedon); Jewish: Gaster Exempla 222 No. 179, *Neuman, Moreno Esdras (Q151.6).

Q145.0.1. *Reward: happiness during last year of life.* Jewish: *Neuman.

Q145.1. *Miraculously long life as reward for hospitality.* (Cf. Q45.1.) Irish myth: *Cross.

Q145.1.1. *Health as reward for drink.* Icelandic: Boberg.

Q145.2. *Miraculously long life as reward for integrity.* (Cf. Q68.) Irish myth: Cross.

Q146. *Reward: end of plague.* (Cf. Q552.10.) India: Thompson-Balys.

Q147. *Supernatural manifestations at death of pious person.* Irish: Cross, Beal XXI 317, O'Suilleabhain 46; Finnish-Swedish: Wessman 1 Nos. 1—3; Spanish: Espinosa Jr. No. 186.

F960.2. Extraordinary nature phenomena at death of holy person. F965.2. Sun darkened at death of holy person. Q20. Piety rewarded.

Q147.1. *Body of saint miraculously rolls over to make room in his grave for pious man.* Spanish Exempla: Keller.

Q147.2. *Pope who has warred on wicked nobles refused burial in church.* Magic wind blows doors open to show he has right to be buried there. Spanish Exempla: Keller.

Q147.3. *Death by kiss from God.* Jewish: Neuman.

Q149. *Miraculous or magic reward—miscellaneous.*

Q149.1. *Color (of animal) as reward for pious act.* Irish myth: Cross.

Q150. Immunity from disaster as reward.

A2221.2.4. Swallows lift Christ's crown of thorns from his brow: why their nests are not destroyed. Q171. Immunity from punishment for sin as reward.

Q150.1. *Rescue from deluge as reward.* Jewish: Moreno Esdras, *Neuman; Chinese: Eberhard FFC CXX 81f.

Q150.1.1. *Lot and family rewarded by being saved from destruction of city.* (Cf. Q152.) Spanish Exempla: Keller; Jewish: *Neuman.

Q150.2. *Loss of all evil and corruption as reward.* Jewish: Moreno Esdras (Q151.9).

Q151. *Life spared as reward.*

Q151.1. *Charitable man's death postponed.* (Cf. Q42, Q145.) Pauli (ed. Bolte) No. 337.

Q151.2. *Death passes by man who fed his stepmother.* (Cf. Q65.1.) Africa (Gold Coast): Barker and Sinclair 129 No. 23.

Q151.3. *Hospitable person saved from death.* (Cf. Q45.1.) Dh II 134ff.

Q151.4. *Faithful old dog threatened with death proves his worth and is spared.* BP I 425 n. 1, III 74 n. 2.

Q151.5. *Humble man miraculously saved from drowning.* (Cf. Q4.) Irish myth: Cross.

Q151.6. *Life spared as reward for hospitality.* (Cf. Q45.4.) Icelandic: Boberg.

Q151.7. *Life spared as reward for uprightness.* (Cf. Q54.) PMLA XLVI 1004; Icelandic: *Boberg.

Q151.8. *Life spared as reward for bravery and constancy.* Centurion tells his enemies to kill him rather than attempt to win him. Spanish Exempla: Keller.

Q151.9. *Resurrection as reward.* Jewish: Moreno Esdras (Q151.5); Chinese: Eberhard FFC CXX 188 No. 128.

Q151.10. *Honest brahman spared by tiger.* (Cf. Q68.) India: Thompson-Balys.

Q151.11. *Man saved from lions as reward.* Jewish: *Neuman.

Q151.12. *Pot of boiling oil thrown at compassionate woman does not harm her.* Buddhist myth: Malalasekera I 362.

Q151.13. *Women rewarded with their lives for excellent dancing.* Tuamotu: Stimson MS (z-G. 3/1260).

Q152. *City saved from disaster as reward.* Jewish: *Neuman; Chinese: Graham; Hawaii: Beckwith Myth 63, 70.

M10. Irrevocable judgments. M203. King's promise irrevocable.

Q152.1. *Hospitality of a citizen saves a city from destruction.* (Cf. Q45.) Alphabet No. 368.

Q153. *Nature benign and fruitful during reign of good king.* (Cf. Q67.) Irish myth: *Cross; Icelandic: *Boberg.

A1101.1.1. Reign of peace and justice (under certain king). H1574.2. Fruitfulness of nature as proof of kingly right. Q176. God gives "peace and favorable weather" as consequence of enactment of good law. Q552.3. Failure of crops during reign of wicked king.

Q153.1. *Cows white-headed during reign of good king.* Irish myth: *Cross.

A2411.1.6.4. Color of cow. B184.2.0.1. Magic white cow. B731.4.1. Cow with white ears. F980. Extraordinary occurrences concerning animals.

Q154. *Immunity from death by violence as reward.* Irish myth: Cross.

Q154.1. *Descendants of man who endured pain without crying out not to meet violent deaths.* (Cf. Q84.) Irish myth: *Cross.

Q156. *Victory as reward for piety.* (Cf. Q20.) Irish myth: Cross.

Q157. *Escape of hostages miraculously prevented as reward for piety.* (Cf. Q20.) Irish myth: *Cross.

Q161. *Healing as reward.*

Q161.1. *Sight restored as reward.* (Cf. F952, Q42.6.) Irish myth: *Cross.

Q161.2. *Healing of disease as reward.* Chinese: Eberhard FFC CXX 188 No. 128.

Q161.3. *Hunchback healed as reward for kindness.* (Cf. Q40.) Africa (Bulu): Krug 109.

Q162. *Invulnerability as reward for pious act.* Irish myth: Cross.

Q170. Religious rewards. *Krappe Bulletin Hispanique XXXIX 23; Jewish: *Neuman.

Q171. *Immunity from punishment for sin as reward.* Spanish Exempla: Keller; Jewish: *Neuman.

V254.1. Saying of "Aves" obliterates sin.

Q171.1. *Forgiveness of sin for acts of charity.* Alphabet No. 296; Irish: Beal XXI 332, O'Suilleabhain 101.

Q171.1.1. *Husband forgiven for having killed jealous wife:* builds monastery and becomes monk in it. Heptameron No. 70.

Q520.1. Murderer does penance.

Q172. *Reward: admission to heaven.* Irish myth: *Cross; Spanish Exempla: Keller; Jewish: *Neuman; India: *Thompson-Balys.

A661. Heaven. A1095. The Messianic Age. E754. Saved souls. E755. Destination of the soul. D1588. Magic object assures going to heaven. K2371.1. Heaven entered by a trick. Q42.8. Saint gives a man all his credit for goods so that the man may go to heaven. Q291.1. St. Peter's mother dropped from heaven because of hard-heartedness. V311.3. Given choice between life and heaven, person chooses latter. V520. Salvation.

Q172.0.1. *Fairy minstrel asks admission to heaven as reward for playing for saint.* (Cf. F262.3.) Irish myth: Cross.

Q172.0.2. *Rewards in heaven.* Icelandic: Boberg.

Q172.1. *Child taken to heaven: offers food to crucifix.* BP III 474ff.; Reinhard PMLA XL 93; Irish: O'Suilleabhain 105, Beal XXI 333; Lithuanian: Balys Index No. 3727; Spanish: Boggs FFC XC 90 No. 767*.

Q172.2. *Man admitted to heaven for single act of charity.* Herbert III 328 No. 9; Irish: Beal XXI 330; Spanish: Keller, Espinosa Jr. No. 182; Jewish: Neuman.

Q172.2.1. *The rich man's trial in heaven.* A piece of bread given to a beggar is placed on the scales. Lithuanian: Balys Index No. 802A*; Prussian: Plenzat 46.

Q172.3. *Man admitted to heaven as reward for penance.* (Cf. Q520.) *Type 756B; *BP III 463; **Andrejev FFC LXIX 154; English: Wells 114 (Sir Isumbras); Spanish Exempla: Keller.

Q172.4. *Palace being built in heaven for pious king.* India: Thompson-Balys.

Q172.4.1. *Rooms in heaven are prepared for good man in heaven.* The dead miser asks the living man to give him at least one of them. Lithuanian: Balys Index No. 804A*.

Q172.5. *Numerous sinners to go to heaven as reward for man's writing hymn.* (Cf. Q35.) Irish myth: Cross.

Q172.6. *Heaven as reward for renouncement of long life.* Irish myth: *Cross.

E755.0.1. Resurrected boys choose to return to heaven.

Q172.7. *Man admitted to heaven for remitting tribute.* (Cf. Q42.7.) Irish myth: Cross.

Q172.8. *Mother of saint admitted to heaven.* Irish myth: Cross.

Q172.8.1. *Saint goes to heaven every Thursday.* Irish myth: *Cross.

Q172.9. *Deification as reward.* Tahiti: Beckwith Myth 38.

Q173. *Saint made judge of doom for men of Ireland (as reward).* Irish myth: *Cross.

Q174. *Reward: release from hell.* Irish myth: Cross.

Q560. Punishments in hell.

Q174.1. *Release from hell as reward for repentance* (Cf. Q36.) Irish myth: *Cross.

Q174.1.1. *Saint's requests for releasing souls from hell.* (Cf. Q20.) Irish myth: *Cross.

Q174.1.1.1. *Saint requests that on Doomsday he may bring out of hell, for every hair of his chasuble, seven condemned souls.* Irish myth: Cross.

Q174.1.1.2. *God grants to saint the boon that no one buried in any of his churches shall go to hell.* Irish myth: Cross.

Q174.1.1.3. *God grants to saint the boon that two persons are to be rescued from hell by him "to the end of the world."* Irish myth: Cross.

Q174.1.1.4. *Saint requests that any person appealing to him at death shall escape hell.* Irish myth: *Cross.

Q175. *Reward: holy person to be buried and resurrected in one place.* Irish myth: Cross.

Q176. *God gives "peace and favorable weather" in consequence of enactment of good law.* (Cf. Q153.) Irish myth: Cross.

Q190. Rewards — miscellaneous.

Q191. *Family line of good man rewarded.* Irish myth: Cross; Jewish: *Neuman.

Q192. *Child given as reward for prayer.* Jewish: Moreno Esdras, *Neuman.

T580. Childbirth.

Q193. *Crowns and palms as reward.* Jewish: Moreno Esdras (Q191).

Q195. *Blessings.* India: Thompson-Balys.

Q200—Q399. Deeds punished.

Q200. Deeds punished. **Encyc. Rel. Ethics s.v. "Crimes and punishments"; *DeCock Volkssage passim; Irish myth: Cross; Jewish: *Neuman.

A1018. Flood as punishment. C900—C999. Punishment for breaking tabu. E511.1. Reason for Flying Dutchman's punishment. P510. Law courts. T75.1. Scorn of unloved suitor punished. W133.1. Prince penalizes cursing although he himself curses.

Q210. Crimes punished. Irish myth: Cross; Norwegian: Solheim Register 21.

Q210.1. *Criminal intent punished.* (Cf. Q211.8, Q261.1, Q451.7.0.2.4.) Irish myth: Cross.

P12.4. King who intends rape killed. Attackers flee into exile.

Q211. *Murder punished.* (Cf. Q411.6, Q413.4, Q414.0.12, Q416.0.2, Q417.1, Q421.0.4, Q424.0.1, Q431.1, Q431.9, Q450.1.1, Q451.1.4, Q451.2.3, Q451.4.5, Q451.7.4, Q469.6, Q469.12, Q491.6, Q497, Q511, Q511.1, Q512.0.1, Q520.1, Q545, Q551.3.3, Q551.8.3, Q552.3.0.2, Q556.2, Q556.10, Q558.9, Q582.3.) Irish: Beal XXI 336, O'Suilleabhain 124; Icelandic: MacCulloch Eddic 319f.; Spanish: Keller, Espinosa Jr. Nos. 202, 205—09; Jewish: *Neuman; India: *Thompson-Balys; Buddhist myth: Malalasekera II 267; Chinese: Eberhard FFC CXX 38 No. 25; Tuamotu: Stimson MS (z-G. 3/818, 1353, 13/127); Eskimo (Cumberland Sound): Boas

BAM XV 168, (Greenland): Rasmussen III 76, 111, 294; S. A. Indian (Chiriguano): Métraux RMLP XXXIII 156, 163.

A1581.1. Origin of penalty for murder. A2631.1. Punishment for first murder: thistles, etc. B131.1. Bird reveals murder. B181.7. Magic horse avenges hero's death. B591. Animal avenges murder. E231. Return from dead to reveal murder. E411.1. Murderer cannot rest in grave. E632. Musical instrument made from the bones of a murdered person. H1219.2. Quest assigned as punishment for murder. M348. Murderer warned by God's voice that murder will be avenged. N271. Murder will out. P522.1. Lex talionis. W155.4. Hardhearted man refuses reprieve for father's murderers.

Q211.0.1. *God revenges murder after thirty years.* *Wesselski Märchen 200; *BP II 535 n. 1.

Q211.0.2. *Enormity of kin murder.* Irish myth: *Cross.

Q211.0.3. *Emperor punished for his many murders.* He is carried to hell. Spanish Exempla: Keller.

Q211.1. *Parricide punished.* (Cf. Q552.2.3.3, Q552.3.1.1, Q553.3.3.) *Types 756B, 761*; *Andrejev FFC LXIX 239; Irish myth: *Cross; Finnish-Swedish: Wessman 19 No. 185.

E501.3.3. Wild huntsman wanders because of parricide. S22. Parricide.

Q211.2. *Matricide punished.* Greek: Frazer Apollodorus I 383 n. 3, Aeschylus Eumenides.

Q211.3. *Uxoricide punished.* (Cf. Q414.0.1, Q416.0.2.1, Q596.1.) Italian Novella: *Rotunda; Koryak, American Indian: *Jochelson JE VI 378; Africa (Bankon): Ittman 98.

Q211.4. *Murder of children punished.* (Cf. Q418.2, Q455.1, Q553.5.) *Types 781, 832; Irish: O'Suilleabhain 31, Beal XXI 310; Spanish: Espinosa Jr. Nos. 148f.; Greek: Grote I 160; Jewish: *Neuman; Tuamotu: Stimson MS (T-G. 3/15).

N271.4. Murder discovered through knowledge of bird languages. Birds point out the murder.

Q211.4.1. *Queen expelled for poisoning stepson.* Icelandic: Boberg.

Q211.4.2. *Woman murders son's wives.* (Cf. Q426.1.) Africa (Wakweli): Bender 86.

Q211.5. *Suicide punished.* (Cf. Q503.1.)

E411.1.1. Suicide cannot rest in grave. E501.3.2. Wild huntsman wanders because of suicide.

Q211.6. *Killing an animal revenged.* (Cf. Q231, Q424.1, Q582.4.)

B857. Animal avenges injury. N261. Train of troubles for sparrow's vengeance. A man runs over the dog, friend of the sparrow. Through the sparrow's vengeance the man loses his horse, his property, and finally his life. N361. Sacred animal unwittingly killed.

Q211.6.1. *Punishment for flaying live calf.* Fb "kalv" II 79a.

Q211.6.2. *Punishment for killing sacred whale.* Polynesia: *Beckwith Myth 504f.

Q211.7. *Punishment for splitting head and eating man's brains.* Greek: Frazer Apollodorus I 369 n. 4 (Tydeus).

Q211.8. *Punishment for desire to murder.* (Cf. Q210.1, Q469.4, Q552.19.2.) Irish myth: Cross; Jewish: Neuman; Eskimo (Smith Sound): Kroeber JAFL XII 177, (Greenland): Rink 157, 222, 469, Holm 47, (Cumberland Sound): Boas BAM XV 62.

R153.2.1. Father hides children from murderous mother. After many years they come forth and she dies of fright.

Q211.8.1. *Wounded king exacts fine from those intending to slay him.* Irish myth: Cross.

Q211.9. *Fratricide punished.* (Cf. Q411, Q414.0.13.) Irish myth: *Cross; Icelandic: Boberg; Italian Novella: Rotunda.

Q211.9.1. *God punishes murder of brother-in-law by having murderer's male heirs die.* (Cf. Q558.) Heptameron No. 40.

Q211.9.2. *Punishment for killing foster brother.* Irish myth: Cross.

Q211.10. *Punishment for murder of co-wife.* Africa (Bankon): Ittman 100.

Q211.11. *Punishment for wholesale massacre of tribe.* India: Thompson-Balys; Buddhist myth: Malalasekera II 877.

Q211.12. *Murder of parents punished by member of family.* Tuamotu: Stimson MS (T-G. 3/818); Easter Island: Métraux Ethnology 385; Tonga: Gifford 53; Maori: Beckwith Myth 474.

Q211.13. *Slave killed who killed enemy at owner's order.* Icelandic: Boberg.

Q212. *Theft punished.* (Cf. Q221.8, Q413.1, Q428.2, Q431.15, Q451.0.4, Q451.1.1, Q451.2.2, Q451.4.1, Q451.5.2, Q451.6.2, Q451.7.0.2.2, Q458.0.3, Q458.2.2, Q467.2, Q469.10.2, Q520.2, Q551.2.3.ff., Q551.6.4, Q551.7.2, Q552.4, Q552.6, Q552.19.3, Q554.1, Q558.6, Q559.10, Q597.3.) *Bloomfield Am. Journ. Philology XLIV 227, *Penzer V 61 n. 1, 143 n., VI 19; *Loomis White Magic 98. — Swiss: Jegerlehner Oberwallis 325 No. 1; Spanish: Boggs FFC XC 96 No. 1, Keller; Jewish: *Neuman; India: *Thompson-Balys; Easter Island: Métraux Ethnology 378; Hawaii: Beckwith Myth 122; Philippine (Tinguian): Cole 195; Africa (Cameroon): Mansfield 225, (Luba): DeClerq Zs. f. KS IV 222, (Ekoi): Talbot 233; West Indies: Flowers 567.

A920.1.3. Lake bursts forth to drown thief. A1115.2. Why the sea is salt. Magic salt mill is stolen by sea-captain, who takes it aboard and orders it to grind. It will stop only for its master; ship sinks and mill keeps grinding salt. A1346.1. Man must work as punishment for theft of fire. C91. Tabu: stealing from spirits. D881.1. Recovery of magic object by use of magic apples. These apples cause horns to grow. E501.18.1.2. Wild hunt harmful to thieves. S11.3.3.1. Father kills son for stealing.

Q212.1. *Theft from dwarf (witch) revenged.* *Hoffmann-Krayer Zs. f. Vksk. XXV 117.

F451.5.2.6. Dwarfs punish. G200. Witch.

Q212.2. *Grave-robbing punished.* Estonian: Aarne FFC XXV 116 No. 17.

Q552.2.2. Grave sinks so that grave-robbers cannot get out.

Q212.3. *Punishment of theft: origin of sweating.* India: Thompson-Balys.

Q212.4. *Stolen animal's meat impossible to cook.* *Loomis White Magic 101f.

D471.8.1. Stolen chickens by cooking turned to stones.

Q213. *Abduction punished.* (Cf. Q411.8, Q595.2, R10.) Irish myth: Cross; India: Thompson-Balys.

Q215. *Cannibalism punished.* India: Thompson-Balys; Eskimo (Greenland): Holm 91.

Q217. *Treason punished.* Buddhist myth: Malalasekera II 597.

Q220. Impiety punished. (Cf. Q457.2, Q458.0.5, Q467.2, Q552.2.3.1.2,

Q552.2.3.2.2, Q558.11, Q558.12, Q558.17, Q559.4, Q559.5.) Irish: *Cross, Beal XXI 317, 331, 335; Spanish Exempla: Keller; Jewish: *Neuman; India: *Thompson-Balys.

A920.1.8. Lake bursts forth to drown impious people. A1650.1. The various children of Eve. Eve hides children when God visits her. They become inferior peoples. A1861.1. Monkeys from children hidden by Eve when God visited her. A2231. Animal characteristics: punishment for impiety. C50. Tabu: offending the gods. C94.1.1. The cursed dancers. Dancers rude to holy man (Jesus) cursed and must keep dancing till Judgment Day. C631. Tabu: breaking the sabbath. E606.1. Reincarnation as punishment for sin. V245.1. Angel scourges mortal for disobedience to God.

Q220.1. *Devil plagues impious people.* Finnish-Swedish: Wessman 13 No. 113; Lithuanian: Balys Legends Nos. 719—43, 825f.; West Indies: Flowers 567.

Q220.1.1. *Devil takes shape of old woman to punish impious nuns.* Introduces them to three youths disguised as girls and brings about nuns' seduction. Nuns are stoned to death. Italian Novella: Rotunda.

G303.3.1.12.1. Devil in form of woman lures women. K1321.4. Men disguised as women enter convent and seduce impious nuns. Q422. Punishment: stoning to death. T330. Anchorites under temptation. V465.1.2. Incontinent nun.

Q221. *Personal offences against gods punished.* (Cf. Q551.3.4.2, Q552.14.0.1.).

A180. Gods in relation to mortals. C51.1.6. Tabu: discontinuing use of a church. C51.2. Tabu: stealing from god or saint. C51.3. Tabu: revealing name of god. C51.5. Tabu: imitating god. C53. Tabu: refusing credit to god. C312.1.1. Tabu: man looking at nude goddess. C431. Tabu: uttering name of god (or gods). V233.1. Angel of death spares mother who is suckling children. As punishment angel must serve as sexton.

Q221.1. *Discourtesy to god punished.* (Cf. Q327.) Irish: Beal XXI 336, O'Suilleabhain 125; Spanish Exempla: Keller; Greek: Grote I 32; India: *Thompson-Balys; Hawaii: Beckwith Myth 132, *190, 233; Easter Island: Métraux Ethnology 141; Society Islands: Henry Ancient Tahiti (Honolulu, 1928) 382; West Indies: Flowers 567.

A1650.1. The various children of Eve. A1715.2. Animals from men transformed for discourtesy to God (Jesus). A1861.1. Monkeys from children hidden by Eve when God visited her. A2231.1. Animal characteristics: punishment for discourteous answer to God (saint). D475.2.3. Transformation: money to leaves.

Q221.1.1. *Discourtesy to messengers of the Gods punished.* Jewish: Moreno Esdras, Neuman.

Q221.2. *Punishment for opposition to Christ at crucifixion.* (Cf. Q556.1.)

A2231.2. Animal characteristics: punishment for hostility at crucifixion. A2721.2. Plant cursed for disservice at crucifixion. J1616. St. Peter not guiltless. Soldiers are admitted neither to hell nor to heaven. They remind Peter of his denial of Christ. He admits them. V211. Christ.

Q221.3. *Blasphemy punished.* (Cf. Q551.1.8, Q558.4.) *Loomis White Magic 98f.; Spanish: Keller, Espinosa Jr. No. 190; Jewish: *Neuman.

Q221.4. *Seaman who defies God shipwrecked.* England: Baughman; Finnish-Swedish: Wessman 18 No. 174.

Q502.1. The Wandering Jew.

Q221.4.1. *Dam builder remarks that God Almighty could not sweep completed dam away.* The whole structure gives away, disappears. U.S.: Baughman.

Q221.4.2. *Man vows to recover loose boat or go to hell trying.* He goes to hell. U.S.: Baughman.

Q221.4.3. *Party of horsemen detained by bad weather vow to reach town whether God will or no.* The earth swallows them up. (Cf. Q552.2.3.) England: Baughman.

Q221.5. *Disobedience to God punished.* Jewish: Moreno Esdras (Q229).

Q221.6. *Lack of trust in God punished.* India: Thompson-Balys.

Q221.7. *Doubt of veracity of goddess' statement punished.* India: Thompson-Balys.

Q221.8. *Theft from water-deity punished.* India: Thompson-Balys.

Q222. *Punishment for desecration of holy places (images, etc.)* (Cf. Q411.11, Q415.7, Q431.13, Q491.1.2, Q499.3, Q551.6.5, Q551.8.2, Q552.17, Q556.6, Q557.7, Q558.5, Q558.14, Q558.17, Q558.18, Q559.9.) Irish: *Cross, O'Suilleabhain 114; Spanish: Espinosa Jr. No. 190; Greek (Herodotus): Classical Philology XXXIX (1944) 179f.; Jewish: Neuman.

C51.1. Tabu: profaning shrine. C93. Tabu: trespassing sacred precinct. E501.3.8. Wild huntsman wanders for disturbing church service. V100. Religious edifices and objects.

Q222.0.1. *Stone in church sheds blood to foretell coming plunder of church.* Irish myth: Cross.

Q222.0.2. *Miraculous flow of blood from desecrated building or object.* Irish myth: Cross.

Q222.1. *Punishment for desecration of host.* Irish: O'Suilleabhain No. 190; England: Baughman; Heptameron No. 33.

C55.3. Bee-master puts consecrated host into beehive. Has success with his bees. When he dies, his spirit haunts the place.

Q222.1.1. *Renegade priest punished by death for allowing heathen to defile the host.* A knight slays the priest. Spanish Exempla: Keller.

Q222.2. *Punishment for heaping indignities upon crucifix.* Spanish Exempla: Keller.

Q222.3. *Foul portrayal of Jesus on the Cross brings punishment to the artist and the man responsible.* Spanish Exempla: Keller.

Q222.4. *Magic storm as punishment for profaning of temple.* Icelandic: Boberg.

Q222.5. *Punishment for desecrating church* (shrine, idol). Spanish Exempla: Keller.

Q222.5.1. *Stones fall in churchyard, punish desecrators of church.* England: Baughman.

Q222.5.2. *Magic storm as punishment for desecrating of temple.* Icelandic: *Boberg.

D905. Magic storm. D2141. Storm produced by magic.

Q222.5.3. *Bold woman who danced naked in church is stricken with leprosy.* *Loomis White Magic 97.

Q222.5.4. *Thieves who attempt to steal from churches or shrines are miraculously rendered powerless to get out, and walk in a circle.* *Loomis White Magic 97f., 98.

Q222.5.5. *Desecrated church burned by burning straw carried by sparrow.* (This is done through power of saint.) Irish myth: Cross; England, Wales, Scotland: Baughman.

Q222.5.6. *Hand stuck for beating an idol.* India: Thompson-Balys.

Q551.2. Punishment: animal skin growns on man's back.

Q222.6. *Punishment for desecration of holy temple utensils.* Jewish: Neuman.

Q223. *Punishment for neglect of services to gods (God).* (Cf. Q523.7, Q554.2, Q557.7, Q559.4.) Spanish Exempla: Keller; India: *Thompson-Balys.

V5.2. Negligent priests buried under bags filled with words omitted from service.

Q223.1. *Neglect to pray punished.* Köhler-Bolte I 148; Lithuanian: Balys Index No. 3361, Legends Nos. 691f.; Swiss: Jegerlehner Oberwallis 280 No. 47.

Q553.4.1. Child taken from parents because they have ceased to think of God.

Q223.2. *Neglect to thank gods punished.* Greek: Fox 59.

Q223.3. *Neglect to sacrifice punished.* Alphabet No. 782; Greek: Frazer Apollodorus I 305 n. 3; Jewish: Neuman; India: Thompson-Balys.

C57.1.1. Tabu: fraudulent sacrifice. C57.1. Tabu: neglect of sacrifice to deity. K231.3. Refusal to make sacrifice after need is past. Q21. Reward for religious sacrifice. V10. Religious sacrifices.

Q223.4. *Neglect to hear confessional punished.* Scala Celi 47a No. 263; Alphabet No. 175; Spanish Exempla: Keller.

V22. Condemnation because of death without confession.

Q223.4.1. *Priest joins devils after death because he lets woman die without confession.* Scala Celi 161b No. 916.

Q223.5. *Neglect to attend church punished.* U.S.: Baughman; Finnish-Swedish: Wessman 18 No. 167.

Q223.6. *Failure to observe holiness of Sabbath punished.* (Cf. Q551.2.2, Q552.14.1.) *Loomis White Magic 99f.; Irish myth: *Cross; England, Scotland, U.S.: *Baughman; Lithuanian: Balys Index No. 3375, Legends Nos. 719—45; Jewish: *Neuman; India: Thompson-Balys.

A751.1.1. Man in the moon as punishment for burning brush on Sunday. C631. Tabu: breaking the Sabbath. E501.3.6. Wild huntsman wanders for hunting on Sunday.

Q223.7. *Punishment for neglect of mass.* Irish: O'Suilleabhains 98.

Q223.7.1. *Virgin Mary appears to lady who neglected to hear mass.* Woman awakens from trance to find piece of taper the Virgin took from her. Spanish Exempla: Keller.

Q223.8. *Failure to do penance punished.* Monk fails and becomes ill. Spanish Exempla: Keller.

Q223.9. *Neglect to fast punished.* Jewish: Neuman.

Q223.9.1. *Neglect to fast punished by sight of dragon ready to carry man off to hell.* Spanish Exempla: Keller.

Q223.9.2. *Musician flogged for eating a kid on Friday (day of fast).* (Cf. Q458.) Icelandic: Boberg.

Q223.10. *Neglect to study scriptures punished.*

Q223.10.1. *Neglect to study Tora punished.* Jewish: Neuman

Q223.11. *Failure to circumcise child punished.* Jewish: Neuman.

Q223.12. *Failure to finish period of mourning punished.* Philippine (Tinguian): Cole 180.

Q223.13. *Neglect of clerical duties punished.* Irish myth: Cross.

Q223.13.1. *Monk neglecting to prostrate self at canonical hours expelled from monastery by saint and dies on seventh day.* Irish myth: Cross.

Q223.13.2. *Punishment (fine) for not giving benediction on finished work.* Irish myth: Cross.

Q223.14. *Punishment for failure to give customary offering to gods.* Marquesas: Handy 81, Métraux Ethnology 329.

Q224. *Punishment for betraying confessional.* (Cf. Q414.0.9.) *Dickson 46 n. 55; *Pauli (ed. Bolte) No. 302; *Krappe "La fille de l'homme riche" Byzantion XVII (1944—45) 339—346; Irish: Beal XXI 334.

K443.8. Priest induced to betray secrets of confessional. V20. Confession of sins. V468. Priest bribed into betraying the confessional.

Q225. *Punishment for scoffing at religious teachings.* (Cf. Q415.8, Q458.0.5, Q551.10.1, Q552.7, Q552.8, Q552.13.1.2, Q553.1, Q554.3, Q554.4, Q555.1, Q558.1.) Finnish-Swedish: Wessman 18 Nos. 171—173; Spanish Exempla: Keller; Jewish: Neuman.

E501.18.1.1. Wild hunt harmful to mockers.

Q225.1. *Heresy punished.* (Cf. Q414.0.8, Q469.7, Q559.11.) Spanish Exempla: Keller.

Q225.2. *Punishment for denying pagan gods.* (Cf. Q413.6.)

Q225.3. *Punishment for doubting Buddha's religion.* Buddhist myth: Malalasekera I 479.

Q226. *Punishment for leaving holy orders.* (Cf. Q520.5, Q551.3.4.3.)

V475. Renunciation of clerical vows.

Q226.1. *Hermit leaving his cell to become robber falls and breaks his neck.* He has seen a penitent robber's soul borne to heaven and resolves therefore to be a robber. *Crane Vitry 166 No. 72; Kittredge Englische Studien XIX 177; *Herbert III 60. Cf. Type 756B.

L435.1. Self-righteous hermit must do penance.

Q226.2. *Mutinous clerics expelled in shapes of swine.* (Cf. Q551.3.2.) Irish myth: *Cross.

D136. Transformation: man to swine. D661. Transformation as punishment.

Q227. *Punishment for opposition to holy person.* (Cf. Q286.1, Q421.2, Q428.3, Q451.3.3, Q451.7.0.2.1, Q457.4, Q494.1, Q551.2.1, Q551.6.2, Q551.7.1, Q551.8.4, Q551.9.1, Q552.1.0.1.1, Q552.1.4, Q552.2.0.1.1, Q552.2.3.1.1, Q552.2.3.1.3, Q552.2.3.2.1, Q552.2.3.2.3, Q552.13.1.1, Q552.13.2.1, Q552.13.2.2, Q552.13.3, Q552.15, Q552.16, Q552.18.1, Q552.18.2, Q552.19.1, Q556.4, Q556.5, Q557.6, Q558.13, Q559.5, Q559.7, Q571.1, Q572.3, Q575, Q576.1, Q582.7, Q591, Q595.1.) *Loomis White Magic 98, 101f.; Irish: *Cross, O'Suilleabhain 82f., Beal XXI 328; Icelandic: *Boberg; Jewish: *Neuman; India: *Thompson-Balys; Buddhist myth: Malalasekera II 59, 1249.

A2231.7. Animal harmful to holy person cursed. C94. Tabu: rudeness to sacred person or thing. D661.2. Transformation as punishment for denouncing saint. T331.6. Saint flogs woman who tempts him.

Q227.1. *Punishment for slaying king under holy protection.* Irish myth: Cross.

Q227.1.1. *Punishment for imprisoning person under holy protection.* Irish myth: Cross.

Q227.2. *Punishment for looking at saint's corpse.* Irish myth: *Cross.

Q227.3. *Saint (hero) drives chariot over person who displeases him.* Irish myth: *Cross.

Q228. *Punishment for trying to harm sacred animal.* Glutton tries to kill a pig dedicated to St. Anthony. The pig turns upon him and tramples him severely. Italian Novella: Rotunda.

B811. Sacred animals. V1.8. Animal worship. W125. Gluttony.

Q231. *Brahmin punished for killing animal.* India: Thompson-Balys.

Q211.6. Killing an animal revenged.

Q232. *Punishment for change of religious faith.*

Q232.1. *Pagan punished by fellows for conversion to Christianity.* Irish myth: Cross.

Q501.7.1. Salt food without drink as punishment for man who accepted Christianity.

Q232.2. *Punishment of Jew for apostacy.* Jewish: Neuman.

Q232.2.1. *Punishment for leaving Palestine.* Jewish: Neuman.

Q233. *Punishment for yielding to temptation by the devil.* (Cf. Q582.2.) Irish myth: Cross.

Q235. *Cursing punished.*

Q235.1. *Man put in moon for cursing God.* He is now the man it the moon. (Cf. A751, Q221.3.) U.S.: Baughman.

Q236. *Punishment for deceiving (divine) emperor.* Chinese: Graham:

Q237. *Idolatry punished.* Jewish: *Neuman.

Q240. Sexual sins punished.

C100. Sex tabu. T400. Illicit sexual relations.

Q241. *Adultery punished.* (Cf. Q411.0.1, Q413.2, Q414.0.2, Q416.1.1, Q418.1, Q421.0.2, Q421.0.6, Q424.2, Q428.1, Q431.8, Q432.2, Q434.1, Q451.1.5, Q451.2.4, Q451.4.8, Q451.5.1, Q451.6.1, Q451.14, Q455.2, Q456.0.1, Q457.3, Q458.0.1, Q461.3, Q466.1, Q469.1, Q473.0.2, Q473.1.1, Q473.2.1, Q478.1, Q478.2, Q478.3, Q484, Q493.1, Q499.2.1, Q537.1, Q552.3.0.3, Q555.2, Q587.) **Encyc. Rel. Ethics s.v. "adultery"; *Schoepperle 446ff.; *Penzer II 88 n. 1, VI 189 n. 2; Pauli (ed. Bolte) No. 228; Herbert III 134, 472, 574; Boccaccio Decameron V No. 8 (*Lee 166); *Chauvin VIII 120 No. 104; Alphabet Nos. 35—37; Wesselski Bebel I 175 No. 18; Grimm No. 4; Loomis White Magic 99; Foulché-Delbosc and Krappe "La légende du roi Ramire" Revue Hispanique LXXVIII (1930) 489—543. — Irish myth: *Cross; Icelandic: *Boberg; Spanish Exempla: Keller; Italian Novella: *Rotunda; Greek: Fox 197 (cf. K1563); Jewish: *Neuman; India: *Thompson-Balys; Buddhist myth: Malalasekera II 794, 1369; Chinese: Eberhard FFC CXX 127; Easter Island: Métraux Ethnology 114; Marquesas: Handy 113, 118; Hawaii: Beckwith Myth 170; Tonga: Gifford 76, 119; N. A. Indian: *Thompson Tales 344 n. 240; S. A. Indian (Toba): Métraux MAFLS XL 120, 161; Africa (Congo): Grenfell 817.

A2237.1. Animal reveals mistress's adultery: punished by master. B24.1. Satyr reveals woman's infidelity. B131.3. Bird betrays woman's infidelity. B134.1. Dog betrays woman's infidelity. C115. Tabu: adultery.

E263. Adulteress returns from dead as devastating dragon. E411.2. Adulterous person cannot rest in grave. H400. Chastity test. K1500. Deception connected with adultery. M13. Sentence applies to king's own son. Those caught in adultery are to have their eyes put out. When the king's son is found guilty he insists on the punishment. He finally compromises by having one of his own and one of his son's eyes put out. T481. Adultery.

Q241.1. *Desire to commit adultery punished.* Irish myth: Cross.

Q458.0.6. Flogging as punishment for desire to commit adultery.

Q241.2. *Lover refuses to take back unfaithful paramour.* English romance: Malory IX 39.

Q242. *Incest punished.* (Cf. Q414.0.3, Q421.0.6, Q431.8.1, Q451.4.3, Q451.7.3, Q520.3, Q541.3, Q552.19.4.) Spanish Exempla: Keller; Jewish: Neuman; India: Thompson-Balys.

A751.1. Man in the moon is person thrown or sent there as punishment for incest. A1018.2. Flood as punishment for incest. C114. Tabu: incest. E692.6. Youth reincarnated as root in punishment for incest. T410. Incest. T415. Brother-sister incest.

Q242.1. *Cohabitation of godfather and godmother punished.* (Cf. P296.) Andrejev FFC LXIX 240.

Q242.2. *Father-daughter incest punished.* India: *Thompson-Balys.

Q242.3. *Punishment for man who makes advances to sister-in-law.* India: Thompson-Balys.

Q242.4. *Father of incestuous children punished.* Eskimo (Bering Strait): Nelson RBAE XVIII 481, (Cumberland Sound): Boas BAM XV 209.

Q243. *Incontinence punished—miscellaneous.* (Cf. Q414.0.3, Q414.0.3.1, Q431.5.3, Q433.6, Q451.1.4.1, Q458.2.1.) Irish myth: *Cross; Jewish: *Neuman; India: *Thompson-Balys; Chinese: Graham.

A1355.1. Origin of menstruation—Eve and the serpent. It is a punishment because Eve had intercourse with the serpent. C110. Tabu: sexual intercourse.

Q243.0.1. *Punishment by extinction of royal line for sexual incontinence.* Irish myth: Cross.

Q243.0.2. *Suspected incontinence unjustly punished.* India: Thompson-Balys.

Q243.1. *Prostitution punished.*

E411.2.1. Priest's concubine cannot rest in grave. E501.5.1.2. Prostitutes pursued in wild hunt.

Q243.1.1. *Harlot punished by being burned (in hell).* Irish myth: *Cross.

Q243.1.2. *Punishment for forcing a girl to become prostitute.* India: Thompson-Balys.

Q243.2. *Seduction punished.* (Cf. K1360, Q421.0.7, Q431.5, Q458.2.3, Q531.5.) Italian Novella: *Rotunda; S. A. Indian (Tucuna): Nimuendaju BBAE CXLIII (3) 724, (Huamachuco): Métraux RMLP XXXIII 151.

Q243.2.1. *Attempted seduction punished.* (Cf. Q424.3, Q431.5.1, Q469.10.1.) Icelandic: Boberg; Italian Novella: Rotunda.

Q243.3. *Punishment for taking concubine.* (Cf. Q499.2.2.) Irish myth: Cross.

Q243.4. *Punishment for taking heathen wives.* Spanish Exempla: Keller.

Q243.5. *Punishment for consorting with one of lower class.* India: *Thompson-Balys.

Q243.6. *Tiger instead of girl in box tears lecherous teacher to pieces.* India: *Thompson-Balys.

Q244. *Punishment for ravisher.* (Cf. Q411.7, Q421.0.3, Q431.6, Q451.6.0.1, Q467.4, Q552.1.2.) India: *Thompson-Balys.

Q244.0.1. *Ravisher is forced to marry girl and then is executed.* Italian Novella: *Rotunda.

Q244.1. *Punishment for attempted rape.* (Cf. Q411.2.) Italian Novella: Rotunda.

Q244.2. *Knight who ravished nun captured when she miraculously appears before him on his horse and holds reins until he is taken.* Spanish Exempla: Keller.

Q244.3. *Prostitute with venereal disease sent to lecherous king.* India: Thompson-Balys.

Q245. *Punishment for refusal to marry after girl is pregnant.* (Cf. Q263, Q451.2.1.)

K1353. Woman deceived into sacrificing honor. T72. Woman won and then scorned.

Q246. *Mortal's attempt to defile goddess punished.* Greek: Frazer Apollodorus II 34 n. 2 (Iasion and Demeter).

Q246.1. *Goddess killed for infidelity with mortal.* Hawaii: Beckwith Myth 37

Q247. *Punishment for desertion of fairy mistress.* (Cf. F302, F361, Q469.11.) Irish myth: Cross.

Q248. *Punishment for banishing wife at wish of paramour.* (Cf. Q241, Q556.9.) Irish myth: Cross.

Q251. *Punishment for refusal to have children.* (Cf. Q431.4, Q552.9, T572.) *Type 755; Fb "barn" IV 26a; Bolte Zs. f. Vksk. XIV 114; Lithuanian: Balys Legends Nos. 392ff.

Q251.1. *Punishment for abortion.* Buddhist myth: Malalasekera II 918.

Q252. *Punishment for breaking betrothal.* (Cf. Q416.0.1.) Jewish: bin Gorion Born Judas VI 237ff., 316.

Q252.1. *Wife stealing punished with death.* (Cf. K1371.) Marquesas: Handy 103.

Q253. *Sodomy punished.* (Cf. Q414.0.11, T463.) Italian Novella: Rotunda.

Q253.0.1. *Sodomy punished by death.* Italian Novella: Rotunda.

Q253.0.2. *Sodomist rebuked by youth.* Italian Novella: Rotunda.

Q253.1. *Bestiality punished.* (Cf. T465.) India: Thompson-Balys; Marquesas: Handy 121; Samoa: Beckwith Myth 103.

Q253.2. *Homosexuality punished.* Jewish: *Neuman.

Q254. *Girl punished for becoming pregnant.* India: Thompson-Balys.

Q255. *Punishment of woman who prefers mortal lover to gods.* India: Thompson-Balys.

A180. Gods in relation to mortals. T111.1. Marriage of mortal and a god.

Q256. *Punishment for clandestine lover of princess.* India: Thompson-Balys.

Q257. *Refusal of conjugal relations punished.* Jewish: *Neuman.

Q260. Deceptions punished. (Cf. Q551.2, Q558.10.) India: Thompson-Balys.

Q261. *Treachery punished.* (Cf. Q413.8, Q414.0.5, Q414.0.6.1, Q417.2, Q423, Q431.2, Q431.10, Q433.7, Q451.1.3, Q451.4.4, Q451.5.4, Q469.7.1, Q552.1.5, Q581.0.1.) Irish myth: *Cross; Missouri French: Carrière; Spanish: Espinosa II Nos. 113, 119, III No. 264, Espinosa Jr. Nos. 75, 80, 106, 110, 126, 138—42; Greek: Grote I 88f., 109, 171, 203; Jewish: *Neuman; India: *Thompson-Balys; Eskimo (Mackenzie Area): Jenness 87, (West Hudson Bay): Boas BAM XV 551f.; Tuamotu: Stimson MS (z-G. 3/1122, T-G. 3/912); Hawaii: Beckwith Myth 87, 331; Tonga: Gifford 101, 142; S. A. Indian (Chiriguano): Métraux RMLP XXXIII 180.

B131.2. Bird reveals treachery. B133.2. Horse reveals treachery. J1172.3. Ungrateful animal returned to captivity. K800. Fatal deception. K2200. Villains and traitors.

Q261.1. *Intended treachery punished.* (Cf. Q210.1, Q552.2.3.4.) Irish myth: Cross.

Q261.2. *Treacherous wife punished.* (Cf. K2213.)

Q261.2.1. *Treacherous wife abandoned by lover for fear of treachery.* India: Thompson-Balys.

Q262. *Impostor punished.* (Cf. K1900, Q413.3, Q414.0.6, Q414.1.1, Q416.0.3, Q431.7, Q433.4, Q458.0.4, Q552.1.3.) English: Wells 42 (Arthour and Merlin); Breton: Sébillot Incidents s.v. "usurpateur", "imposteur"; Missouri French: Carrière; Spanish: Keller, Espinosa Jr. Nos. 106—110, Espinosa II Nos. 133—135; India: *Thompson-Balys.

Q263. *Lying (perjury) punished.* (Cf. Q431.17, Q451.1.7, Q451.3.2, Q451.5.3, Q451.7.1, Q488.1, Q551.6.1, Q551.8.5, Q551.9.2, Q552.1.7, Q558.2, Q558.15, Q591.) *Fb "sværge" III 692b, "ed" I 234; Wienert FFC LVI 55 (ET 146), 104 (ST 166, 455); Scala Celi 103b No. 556; Alphabet Nos. 380, 417. — Irish myth: *Cross; Icelandic: *Boberg; Finnish-Swedish: Wessman 19 No. 177; Spanish: Keller, Espinosa Jr. Nos. 115, 188, Espinosa II No. 94; Jewish: *Neuman; India: *Thompson-Balys; Buddhist myth: Malalasekera I 113, 150, II 529, 1272; Hawaii: Beckwith 153; Tuamotu: Stimson MS (T-G. 3/711); Philippine (Tinguian): Cole 98; Eskimo (Greenland): Rasmussen III 160; Africa (Fjort): Dennett 89 No. 22, (Ibo, Nigeria): Thomas 124, (Dahome): Einstein 29.

A2239.1. Hare punished for perjury: eyes deep in head. B133.4. Horse refuses to carry one who speaks falsehood. E411.3. Perjurer cannot rest in grave. H914. Tasks assigned because of mother's foolish boasting. The mother foolishly boasts to the king that the daughter can perform an impossible task (often spinning). K1353. Woman deceived into sacrificing honor. M101. Punishment for broken oaths. T72. Woman won and then scorned.

Q263.1. *Death as punishment for perjury.* Irish myth: *Cross.

Q265. *False judging punished.* (Cf. Q551.8.1, Q558.16, Q559.8.) India: Thompson-Balys.

Q265.1. *Bribed false judge punished.* (Cf. J1192.) Alphabet No. 433; Spanish Exempla: Keller; Jewish: *Neuman.

Q265.1.1. *Unjust judges punished in hell.* Irish myth: *Cross.

Q265.2. *Punishment for (undeserved) satire.* (Cf. Q558.8.) Irish myth: *Cross.

Q265.2.1. *Blotches on face of satirist (judge) as punishment for wrongful satire (judgment).* Irish myth: *Cross.

Q265.3. *Judge must yield bench to son because he had made a false judgment.* Spanish Exempla: Keller.

Q265.4. *Punishment for undeserved curse.* Irish myth: Cross.

Q266. *Punishment for breaking promise.* Jewish: *Neuman; India: Thompson-Balys; Chinese: Eberhard FFC CXX 187.

Q266.1. *Man promises more to church than he can possibly provide: punished.* Finnish-Swedish: Wessman 18 No. 176.

Q267. *Hypocrisy punished.*

Q267.1. *Devil comes for hypocrite.* Italian Novella: Rotunda.

G303. Devil. K2000. Hypocrites. R11.2.1. Devil carries off wicked people.

Q268. *Flattery punished.* Jewish: Neuman; Spanish Exempla: Keller (Q393.1.)

Q270. Misdeeds concerning property punished. India: Thompson-Balys.

M368. Prophecy: punishment for misappropriation of property.

Q271. *Debtor punished.* (Cf. Q421.0.1, Q473.0.1, Q491.2, Q499.5.)

P536. Punishment for failure to pay tax.

Q271.1. *Debtor deprived of burial.* (Cf. Q421.0.1, Q491.) See all references to E341 (The grateful dead). **A. Esmein "Débiteurs privés de sepulture" Mélanges d'histoire du droit (Paris, 1886) 244ff.; S. Riccobono "Cristianesimo e diritto privato" Revista di diritto civile III (1911) 43ff.; Antonucci Lares I No. 2 (1930) 3—5.

Q271.2. *Devil condemns rich man who does not repent until ready to die.* Scala Celi 57b No. 322; Spanish Exempla: Keller.

Q271.3. *Woman on visit to world of dead may not return until she pays debt to dead.* India: Thompson-Balys.

Q272. *Avarice punished.* (Cf. Q552.3.5, Q589.1.0.1, W151.) *Hdwb. d. Märchens I 188 nn. 154, 166, 167; Crane Liber de Miraculis 86 No. 10; Icelandic: *Boberg; Irish myth: *Cross; Lithuanian: Balys Index No. 774*; Spanish: Boggs FFC XC 98, 760C*, 836C*, Keller; India: *Thompson-Balys; Chinese: Graham, Eberhard FFC CXX 67, 196; Buddhist myth: Malalasekera II 268, 556, 1264; Tonga: Gifford 207; Tuamotu: Beckwith Myth 504; Maori: ibid. 374; Eskimo (Greenland): Rink 396; Africa (Wakweli): Bender 63, 106, (Fang): Tessman 117, (Jaunde): Heepe 247ff.; West Indies: Flowers 568.

A2011.2. Creation of ant: avaricious man transformed. A2238. Animal characteristics: punishment for greed. D876. Magic treasure animal killed. (Goose that laid the golden egg.)

Q272.1. *Devil carries off rich man.* Pauli (ed. Bolte) No. 281; Crane Vitry 204 No. 170; Scala Celi 60b, 80a Nos. 322, 456.

Q272.1.1. *Devil carries off rich man at death.* Spanish Exempla: Keller.

R11.2.1. Devil carries off wicked people.

Q272.2. *Avaricious man has neck broken when top of his treasure chest falls on him.* Spanish Exempla: Keller.

Q272.3. *Avaricious miser tries to eat his adored money and chokes to death.* Spanish Exempla: Keller.

Q272.4. *Avaricious woman and her gold consumed by hell's fires which burn in her grave.* Spanish Exempla: Keller.

Q273. *Usury punished.* Pauli (ed. Bolte) No. 198; Alphabet Nos. 231, 278, 287, 794; Scala Celi 154b, 168a Nos. 852, 955—959; Spanish Exempla: Keller; Jewish: *Neuman.

B151.1.1.2.1. Ass carries usurer's body to the gallows instead of to the church. He has been denied burial in the church. E411.4. Usurer cannot rest in grave. N277. Oxen bear dead usurer to gallows to be buried. They are allowed to go where they will. P435. Usurer. X510. Jokes concerning usurers.

Q273.1. *Devil comes for usurer.* (Cf. R11.2.1.) Scala Celi 168a Nos. 953, 954; Alphabet No. 758; Italian Novella: Rotunda.

Q273.1.1. *Dead usurer fed molten silver by devil.* Crane Vitry 203 No. 168; Alphabet No. 785; Mensa Philosophica No. 221; Scala Celi 168a No. 953; Spanish Exempla: Keller.

Q273.2. *Usurer refused burial.* Italian Novella: Rotunda.

E411.4. Usurer cannot rest in grave.

Q273.3. *Usurer punished in hell.* *Crane Vitry Nos. 167—170 and passim; Spanish Exempla: Keller.

Q273.4. *Church built by usurer's money made to collapse by devil.* Spanish Exempla: Keller.

Q274. *Swindler punished.* (Cf. Q414.0.6.1, Q456.0.2, Q491.1.1, Q557.3.)

E411.5. Swindler cannot rest in grave.

Q274.1. *Devils carry away stones of church built with ill-gotten money.* Scala Celi 84a No. 481.

Q274.2. *Devil suffocates swindling merchant.* (Cf. Q425.) Italian Novella: Rotunda.

Q274.3. *Use of false weights and measures punished.* Jewish: *Neuman.

Q275. *Remover of landmarks punished.* Kuhn Sagen aus Westfalen I 40f. No. 34, 118 No. 127, 177 No. 187; Hoffman JAFL II 33; Frahm Am Urquell II 202.

C846. Tabu: removing landmarks. E416. Man who removes landmarks cannot rest in grave.

Q276. *Stinginess punished.* (Cf. Q551.2.8, Q589.4.) India: *Thompson-Balys; Buddhist myth: Malalasekera I 342.

J1522. Rebuke to the stingy. J1561. Inhospitality repaid. W152. Stinginess.

Q277. *Covetousness punished.* Jewish: *Neuman, Moreno Esdras (Q332).

Q280. **Unkindness punished.** Irish: Beal XXI 320; Missouri French: Carrière; Jewish: Neuman; India: *Thompson-Balys; Chinese: Eberhard FFC CXX 127; Africa (Duala): Lederbogen JAS IV 67, (Bulu): Krug 109, (Congo): Weeks Congo 216.

A973. Origin of stones: punishment for discourtesy. L432. Impoverished husband begs from wife's new husband. He has formerly refused this man charity. L435. Self-righteousness punished.

Q281. *Ingratitude punished.* (Cf. Q551.6.3, Q597.2.) Irish: Beal XXI 331; Spanish: Keller, Espinosa III No. 264, Espinosa Jr. No. 41; Jewish: *Neuman; India: *Thompson-Balys; Buddhist myth: Malalasekera II 1159; Maori, Samoa, Tonga: *Beckwith Myth 504f.; Africa: Woodson 64, (Wakweli): Bender 50, Sieber 89ff., (Bantu): Einstein 148, (Lokele): Grenfell 820, (Jaunde): Heepe 89, (Fang): Tessman 188; West Indies: Flowers 568; Jamaica: Beckwith MAFLS XVII 267 No. 76.

J1172.3. Ungrateful animal returned to captivity. W154. Ingratitude.

Q281.1. *Ungrateful children punished.* (Cf. Q551.1, Q557.1, Q557.2, Q588.) Irish: Cross, O'Suilleabhain 46, Beal XXI 317; Jewish: *Neuman; India: Thompson-Balys.

D444.2. Transformation: meat to toad. Punishment for ungrateful son. J121.1. Ungrateful son reproved by naive action of his own son: preparing for old age. Man gives his old father half a carpet to keep him warm. Child keeps the other half and tells his father that he is keeping it for him when he grows old. P236. Undutiful children. S20. Cruel children.

Q281.1.1. *Devils carry off girl who abuses her mother.* Scala Celi 99a No. 531; Spanish Exempla: Keller.

R11.2.1. Devil carries off wicked people.

Q281.1.2. *Girl cruel to her mother is slain by God.* Spanish Exempla: Keller.

Q281.2. *Ungrateful ruler is deposed.* Italian Novella: Rotunda.

Q281.3. *Woman eats flesh and leaves cat only bones of fish cat has caught for them.* Cursed by cat. India: Thompson-Balys.

M437.1. Curse: "What I carry may you carry; what you carry may I carry." Cat bears girls, woman kittens.

Q281.4. *Ungrateful king raises old woman's rent; miraculous punishment.* (Cf. W154.2.) India: Thompson-Balys.

Q283. *Irreverent young people punished by outraged old man.* Icelandic: Boberg; Koryak: *Jochelson JE VI 365f.; Eskimo: *Boas BAM XV 361; N. A. Indian (Tsimshian): Boas BBAE XXVII 95.

Q284. *Reproach concerning physical deformity (blemish) punished.* (Cf. Q411.9.) Irish myth: Cross.

Q285. *Cruelty punished.* (Cf. E501.3.1, Q415.3.1.) Spanish: Espinosa Jr. No. 187; Jewish: *Neuman; India: *Thompson-Balys; Africa: Stanley 61, 103.

Q285.1. *Cruelty to animals punished.* India: Thompson-Balys.

Q285.1.1. *Punishment for cutting off bird's tongue.* (Cf. Q451.4, Q552.5.1.) Finnish-Swedish: Wessman 19 No. 182; Japanese: Ikeda.

A2344.2. Why animal has no tongue. S163. Mutilation: cutting out tongue.

Q285.1.1.1. *Man slits tongue of magpie so that it can learn to speak.* His fingernails grow out like bird's claws as punishment. Wales: Baughman.

Q285.1.2. *Punishment for breaking bird's nest.* Finnish-Swedish: Wessman 19 No. 183.

Q285.1.2.1. *Boy reaches into bird's nest for pigeon's eggs.* A stone in the nest holds his hand for three days and nights. He is finally released by prayers. Wales: Baughman.

Q285.2. *Cruelty to sick persons punished.* Finnish-Swedish: Wessman 19 No. 181.

Q285.3. *Cruel mutilation punished.* (Cf. Q411.5.) Irish myth: Cross.

Q285.4. *Slave-driving punished.* (Cf. P270, Q291.2, Q558.7.) Irish myth: Cross; Jewish: *Neuman; Buddhist myth: Malalasekera II 706.

Q286. *Uncharitableness punished.* (Cf. Q494.1.1, Q552.3.0.1, Q571.2, Q572.2, Q574.2, Q585.1, Q595.3.) Irish: O'Suilleabhain 93, 129, 131, Beal XXI 330, 337; Spanish: Espinosa Jr. Nos. 186, 202—04; Swiss: Jegerlehner Oberwallis 300 No. 16; India: *Thompson-Balys; Chinese: Werner 255; Africa (Ila, Rhodesia): Smith and Dale II 415 No. 14.

D444.1. Transformation: money of the hard-hearted to scorpions. L435. Self-righteousness punished. V420. Reward of the uncharitable.

Q286.1. *Uncharitableness to holy person punished.* (Cf. Q1.1, Q553.3.5, Q556.11, Q589.1.) Type 766*; *Pauli (ed. Bolte) No. 329; Irish: *Cross; O'Suilleabhain 22, Beal XXI 307; Spanish: Espinosa Jr. Nos. 183f., 202—04; Hawaii: Beckwith Myth 192.

Q286.2. *Priest will not bury dead unless paid in advance.* Ruler has him buried alive with the corpse. (Cf. Q456.2.) Italian Novella: *Rotunda.

Q287. *Refusal to grant request punished.* (Cf. Q499.4.) Irish myth: Cross.

Q288. *Punishment for mockery.* (Cf. Q556.8, Q583.1.) Irish myth: *Cross; S. A. Indian (Chiriguano): Métraux RMLP XXXIII 181.

Q291. *Hard-heartedness punished.* (Cf. Q415.2.) Irish: O'Suilleabhain 61, 130, Beal XXI 324, 337; Jewish: *Neuman.

Q291.1. *St. Peter's mother dropped from heaven because of hard-heartedness.* She is permitted to go to heaven on a stalk, but is weighted down by people holding to her skirts. She shakes them off. (Cf. Q172.) *Type 804; *BP III 538; Köhler-Bolte I 60.

Q291.2. *Punishment of hard-hearted masters in other world.* (Cf. Q285.4.) Lithuanian: Balys Legends Nos. 467—71; India: Thompson-Balys.

Q292. *Inhospitality punished.* (Cf. P320, Q45, Q551.6.7, Q556.7, W158.) Irish: *Cross, O'Suilleabhain 53; Finnish: Kalevala rune 33; Swiss: Jegerlehner Oberwallis 323 No. 94; Spanish Exempla: Keller; Jewish: *Neuman; India: Thompson-Balys; Buddhist myth: Malalasekera II 824; Hawaii: Beckwith Myth 174; Africa (Wachaga): Gutmann 93, (Loango): Pechuël-Loesche 110.

Q292.1. *Inhospitality to saint (god) punished.* (Cf. Q1.1.) *Loomis White Magic 101; Lithuanian: Balys Index No. 772*; Russian: Andrejev No. 796I*; Swiss: Jegerlehner Oberwallis 295 No. 13; Spanish: Espinosa Jr. No. 181; Greek: Fox 20, 94; India: Thompson-Balys; S. A. Indian (Chincha): Alexander Lat. Am. 231.

Q292.2. *Inhospitality to orphans punished.* Lithuanian: Balys Index No. 3728.

Q292.3. *Abuse of hospitality punished.* Irish myth: *Cross.

Q295. *Monkey destroys nest of bird who has made sport of him.* Japanese: Ikeda; Indonesia: DeVries's list No. 52.

Q296. *Injustice punished.* (Cf. Q265, Q552.1.6.) Irish myth: *Cross; Jewish: Neuman; India: Thompson-Balys.

D1318.1.1. Stone bursts as sign of unjust judgment. U10. Justice and injustice.

Q296.1. *Sack of flour pushed down on peasant who accuses his wife of theft from it.* Icelandic: Boberg.

Q297. *Slander punished.* Jewish: *Neuman.

Q300. Contentiousness punished. (Cf. W188.)

Q301. *Jealousy punished.* (Cf. W181.) Penzer III 177f.; Missouri French: Carrière; Spanish Exempla: Keller; Italian Novella: *Rotunda; Jewish: Neuman; India: Thompson-Balys; Africa (Konnoh): Willans 139.

Q302. *Envy punished.* (Cf. Q551.6.6, W195.) Irish myth: Cross; India: Thompson-Balys.

Q302.1. *Envy punished: the found purse.* Three men find a purse. They are loath to pick it up, since they will have to divide. The king sees this and assigns them their proper punishments. Chauvin II 120 No. 107.

Q304. *Scolding punished.* Africa (Ila, Rhodesia): Smith and Dale II 412 No. 10.

Q305. *War-making punished.* (Cf. Q553.3.1.) Spanish Exempla: Keller.

Q306. *Quarrelsomeness punished.* (Cf. Q551.7.3.) Irish myth: Cross; Africa (Wakweli): Bender 62.

Q312. *Fault-finding punished.* (Cf. Q431.12, Q451.4.6, Q557.8, W128.) Jewish: Neuman; India: Thompson-Balys.

Q312.1. *Punishment for finding fault with God's works in heaven.* *Type 801; BP III 297ff.

F13. Man admitted into heaven but must not find fault. L435.3. Self-righteous tailor in heaven expelled.

Q312.2. *Devil carries off fault-finding people.* (Cf. R11.2.1.) Scala Celi 54b No. 306.

Q312.3. *Punishment for finding fault with God's forgiveness of sin.* *Type 756B.

Q312.4. *Fault-finding with God's handling of weather.* Spanish Exempla: Keller.

Q313. *Bad temper punished.* India: Thompson-Balys.

Q314. *Scandal-mongering punished.* (Cf. Q451.4.2.) Jewish: *Neuman; India: Thompson-Balys.

Q320. Evil personal habits punished.

Q321. *Laziness punished.* (Cf. Q495.1.) Spanish: Espinosa Jr. No. 188; Jewish: Neuman; India: Thompson-Balys; Chinese: Eberhard FFC CXX 127; Africa (Wakweli): Bender 104f.

A2031.1. Creation of fly: punishment for laziness. A2032.1. Creation of flea: punishment for laziness. A2233. Animal characteristics: punishment for laziness. A2233.1. Animals refuse to help dig well (make road) and are punished. G282. Witches punish lazy spinning women. K1636. Maids must rise even earlier. W111. Laziness.

Q321.1. *Women who will not sew are cast from community.* Spanish Exempla: Keller.

Q322. *Dirtiness punished.* (Cf. Q432.1, Q433.3, W115.) Spanish Exempla: Keller; India: Thompson-Balys.

Q323. *Unthriftiness punished.* Alphabet No. 218; Italian Novella: *Rotunda.

Q325. *Disobedience punished.* (Cf. Q431.3, Q451.7.0.2.3, Q456.0.3, Q458.0.2, Q552.1.0.1.1, Q593.) Alphabet No. 441; Spanish: Keller, Espinosa Jr. Nos. 104, 216; Jewish: *Neuman; India: Thompson-Balys; Eskimo (Greenland): Rink 428, (Bering Strait): Nelson RBAE XVIII 473; Tuamotu: Stimson MS (T-G. 3/629); S. A. Indian (Chiriguano): Métraux RMLP XXXIII 177; Africa (Wakweli): Bender 108, (Duala): Lederbogen Märchen 84, (Congo): Weeks Congo 214, (Luba): DeClerq ZsKS IV 193; West Indies: Flowers 569.

A2234. Animal characteristics: punishment for disobedience. V245.1. Angel scourges mortal for disobedience to God. W126. Disobedience.

Q326. *Impudence punished.* (Cf. Q411.10, Q413.5.) Irish myth: Cross; Africa (Bushongo): Torday 241.

Q327. *Discourtesy punished.* (Cf. Q221.1, Q583.2.) Irish myth: Cross.

Q330. Overweening punished. (Cf. Q552.19.1, Q582.5.)

C53.2. Tabu: arrogance toward deity. C450. Tabu: boasting. C770. Tabu: overweening pride.

Q331. *Pride punished.* (Cf. Q552.19.5.) Penzer IV 142f.; Irish myth: Cross; Spanish Exempla: Keller; Jewish: *Neuman; India: *Thompson-Balys; Africa (Bulu): Krug 110.

L400. Pride brought low. Q4. Humble rewarded, haughty punished. Q552.1.1. Lightning strikes monk who despises humility. Q552.5. Monstrous births as punishment for girl's pride. W165. False pride.

Q331.1. *Devil torments old man who has laid aside his humility.* Scala Celi 105a No. 572.

Q331.2. *Vanity punished.*

Q331.2.1. *Woman's vain display punished.* Italian Novella: *Rotunda.

Q331.2.1.1. *Devil impersonates woman's maid at her toilette.* Italian Novella: Rotunda.

G303.3.1.12.1. Devil in form of woman. Lures (punishes) woman.

Q331.2.1.2. *Vain woman has her cheeks miraculously burned.* (Cf. Q550.) Italian Novella: Rotunda.

Q331.2.1.3. *Husband rubs off paint from wife's cheeks.* Threatens to scrape them the next time. Italian Novella: Rotunda.

Q331.2.1.3.1. *Husband puts soot on wife's cheeks to discourage her from using paint.* Italian Novella: Rotunda.

Q331.2.1.4. *Vain woman wears corset so tight that it stifles her to death.* Italian Novella: Rotunda.

E21.2. Resuscitation when strangling corset-lace breaks.

Q331.2.1.5. *Clothes-proud woman trips over long skirt.* Devil laughs. Spanish Exempla: Keller.

Q331.2.2. *Jackal demands to be praised as god:* runs with pack of hounds. India: Thompson-Balys.

Q333. *Boldness punished.*

Q333.1. *"God has no use for me, and the devil will not take me."* On the way home the bold woman is strangled by the devil. (Cf. Q582.5.) Lithuanian: Balys Legends No. 376f.

Q338. *Immoderate request punished.* (Cf. Q501.8, Q559.6, Q572.4, Q582.6, Q585.2.) Type 555; Irish myth: *Cross; Jewish: Neuman; India: Thompson-Balys.

A2232. Animal characteristics: punishment for immoderate request. A2232.3. Beetle makes immoderate request; ant moderate: inverse awards. A2723.1. Discontented pine tree: cause of pine needles. Pine tree given silk leaves, glass leaves, etc. Always discontented. Finally given her needles again. C773.1. Tabu: making unreasonable requests. D1720.1. Man given power of wishing. D1761.0.1. Wishes granted without limit. D1761.0.2. Limited number of wishes granted. D1904. Love-compelling man sickens of bargain. J500. Prudence and discretion. J510. Prudence in ambition. J530. Prudence in demands. L420. Overweening ambition punished .

Q338.1. *Request for immortality punished by transformation into tree.* N. A. Indian: *Thompson Tales 276 n. 18.

A575. Departed deity grants requests to visitors.

Q338.2. *The devil's likeness.* A squire demands somebody to paint a living picture of the devil; when he sees it, he dies. Lithuanian: Balys Index No. 3355, Legends Nos. 681—84.

Q340. Meddling punished. India: Thompson-Balys.

A2237. Animal characteristics: punishment for meddling.

Q341. *Curiosity punished.* Spanish Exempla: Keller; India: Thompson-Balys; Africa (Luba): DeClerq ZsKS IV 189, (Cameroon): Rosenhuber 52.

E501.18.1.3. Wild hunt harmful to the curious. J1546. Overcurious wife learns of the senate's deliberations. K713.1.4. Animal persuaded to be tied through curiosity to learn secret names. K730.1. Animal trapped through curiosity as to what the trap is. K814. Overcurious dupe enters trickster's basket and is killed. T258. The curious wife. W137. Curiosity.

Q342. *Inquisitiveness punished.* (Cf. Q557.5.) Wienert FFC LVI 49 (ET 89), 95 (ST 84); Jewish: Neuman; Africa: Weeks Congo 207.

G520. Ogre deceived into self-injury. J655.1. Birds discuss the trap. One of them is caught in it.

Q380. Deeds punished—miscellaneous.

J1675.2. Clever ways of breaking bad news to a king, who will kill bearer of bad tidings. P422.1. Lawyers punished in hell.

Q381. *Punishment for gambling.* (Cf. N0, Q433.8.) Jewish: Neuman; Indonesia: DeVries's list No. 182.

Q385. *Captured animals avenge themselves.* N. A. Indian: *Thompson Tales 313 n. 126a.

Q386. *Dancing punished.* Scala Celi 61b No. 336; Lithuanian: Balys Legends Nos. 347—352; Spanish Exempla: Keller.

C51.1.5. Tabu: dancing in churchyard. C94.1.1. The cursed dancers. Dancers rude to holy man (Jesus) cursed and must keep dancing till Judgment Day.

Q386.1. *Devil punishes girl who loves to dance.* Scala Celi 62a No. 338; England, U.S.: Baughman; Finnish: Aarne FFC XXXIII 40 No. 24**; Finnish-Swedish: Wessman 10 No. 81, 13 No. 112.

E238.1. Dance with the dead. G303.9.8.2. Devil plays fiddle at weddings.

Q386.2. *Drunken dancers punished.* India: Thompson-Balys.

Q387. *Jesting punished.*

Q387.1. *Devil carries off jester.* (Cf. R11.2.1.) Scala Celi 77b No. 441.

Q388. *Freemasonry punished.*

Q388.1. *Freemasons forced to dance till they sweat blood.* Finnish-Swedish: Wessman 13 No. 114.

Q391. *Punishment for singing worldly songs.* (Cf. Q411.10.1.)

Q391.1. *Prince of devils gives up seat to man who goes to hell for singing worldly songs.* Scala Celi 25b No. 169.

F402.2.1. King of demons (Asmodeus).

Q392. *Punishment of evil magician who has caused plague.* German: H. Büschner Heide-Sagen a. d. Münsterlande 9, Klose Führer d. dt. Sagen u. Märchenwelt d. Grafschaft Glatz 104.

Q393. *Evil speech punished.* Italian Novella: Rotunda; Buddhist myth: Malalasekera I 50.

Q393.1. *Punishment for talking too much.* Monk punished in hell's fires for this fault. Spanish Exempla: Keller.

Q393.2. *Gossiping punished.* Africa: Casati I 319.

Q394. *Uxoriousness punished.* Irish myth: Cross.

Q395. *Disrespect punished.* Hawaii: Beckwith Myth 411, Tahiti: ibid. 244.

Q400—Q599. Kinds of punishment.

Q400. Kinds of punishment—general. *Child V 492 s.v. "punishments"; Irish myth: Cross.

A486. The Furies. Goddesses of vengeance. A751.1. Man in the moon is person thrown or sent there as punishment. A2230. Animal characteristics as punishment A2720. Plant characteristics as punishment. C900. Punishments for breaking tabu. D881.1. Recovery of magic object by use of magic apples. These apples cause horns to grow. E755.2. Souls in hell. K581. Animal "punished" by being placed in favorite environment. R153.2.1. Father hides children from murderous mother. After many years they come forth and she dies of fright.

Q401. *Chain of punishments.* Horse must break leg, since he has broken leg of man who broke leg of dog which bit leg of fox. *Wesselski Hessische Blätter f. Vksk. XXXII 21.

N261. Train of troubles from sparrow's vengeance. N258. Train of troubles from lost horseshoe nail. Z20. Cumulative tales.

Q402. *Punishment of children for parents' offenses.* Jewish: Neuman.

Q403. *Punishment not meted out to persons below twenty years.* Jewish: *Neuman.

Q404. *Punishment comes in seventh generation.* Jewish: *Neuman.

Q410. Capital punishment. Jewish: *Neuman; India: Thompson-Balys.

S110.3. Princess builds tower of skulls of unsuccessful suitors.

Q411. *Death as punishment.* (Cf. Q455, Q456, Q458.2, Q558, Q582.) F. Ström On the Sacral Origin of the Germanic Death Penalties (Stockholm, 1942); *Roberts 211; Irish myth: *Cross; Missouri French: Carrière; Spanish: Espinosa Jr. Nos. 108, 133, 141; Jewish: Neuman; India: *Thompson-Balys; Buddhist myth: Malalasekera II 556; S. A. Indian (Toba): Métraux MAFLS XL 120; Africa (Wakweli): Bender 43.

B275.1. Animal executed for crime. C920. Death for breaking tabu. H331.5.0.1. Loser in bride-race must die. H512. Guessing with life as wager. H541.1. Riddle propounded on pain of death. H542. Death sentence escaped by propounding riddle king (judge) cannot solve. H901. Tasks imposed on pain of death. H1594.0.1. Death as penalty for losing footrace. P12.4. King who intends rape killed. Attackers flee into exile. W155.4. Hardhearted man refuses reprieve for father's murderers.

Q411.0.1. *Husband kills returning adulteress.* (Cf. Q241.) Italian Novella: Rotunda; Maori: Dixon 80.

Q411.0.1.1. *Adulterer killed.* Irish myth: *Cross.

Q411.0.1.2. *Man (fairy) kills wife's lover.* Irish myth: *Cross.

Q411.0.1.3. *Faithless wife (mistress) seized by husband's (lover's) poet, who leaps to death with her in his arms.* Irish myth: Cross.

Q411.0.1.4. *Death for repeated adultery.* Buddhist myth: Malalasekera II 1369.

Q411.0.2. *Husband kills wife and paramour.* Italian Novella: *Rotunda.

K1550. Husband outwits adulteress and paramour.

Q411.1. *Punishment: winning as wife and then killing.* Type 956B; *BP I 373.

T72.1. Maid eloping with pretended lover is forced by him to strip.

Q411.2. *Undesired suitor hiding under girl's bed is killed.* Italian Novella: Rotunda.

Q411.2.1. *Undesired suitor killed asleep in his tent.* Icelandic: *Boberg; Jewish: Judith and Holofernes.

K959.2. Murder in one's sleep. K1371.1. Lovers steals bride from wedding with unwelcome suitor. R111.1.9. Princess rescued from undesired suitor.

Q411.3. *Death of father (son, etc.) as punishment.* Irish myth: *Cross.

Q451.3.3.1. Son stricken dumb as punishment for father's opposition to holy person. Q451.7.2.1. Blinding of father as punishment for ravisher. Q469.11. Baby son hurled into battle as punishment for desertion of fairy mistress. Q558.13.1. Mysterious death of son as punishment for opposition to holy person. Q558.15.1. Mysterious death of son as punishment for lying (perjury). Q559.9. Saints miraculously cause child to fall over cliff as punishment for mother's washing clothes in holy well. S452. Outcast wife commits suicide when confronted with heads of relatives killed in revenge for her wrong-doing.

Q411.4. *Death as punishment for treachery.* Irish myth: *Cross.

Q411.4.1. *Man killed at once for treacherously slaying overlord.* Irish myth: Cross.

Q411.4.2. *Woman who disrobes to attract attention of hostile fighter killed.* Irish myth: *Cross.

Q411.5. *Hero kills mutilators of girl.* Irish myth: Cross.

Q411.6. *Death as punishment for murder.* (Cf. Q211.) Irish myth: *Cross; Icelandic: *Boberg.

Q411.7. *Death as punishment for ravisher.* (Cf. Q244.) Irish myth: Cross; Icelandic: *Boberg.

Q411.8. *A man in every house in the land killed as punishment for abduction by their king.* Irish myth: Cross.

Q411.9. *Death as punishment for reproach concerning physical deformity (blemish).* (Cf. Q284.) Irish myth: *Cross.

Q411.10. *Death as punishment for impudence.* (Cf. Q326.) Irish myth: Cross.

Q411.10.1. *Man killed because of scornful singing.* (Cf. Q391.) Icelandic: *Boberg.

H509.4. Tests of poetic ability. Q91.3. King rewards poem.

Q411.11. *Death as punishment for desecration of holy places (images, etc.).* (Cf. Q222.) Irish myth: *Cross.

Q411.11.1. *Desecrating a sanctuary (saint's house) by murder punished.* Irish myth: *Cross.

Q411.11.2. *Hanging as punishment for stealing from a church.* Irish myth: *Cross.

Q411.12. *Maidens slain in revenge for deaths of young men.* Irish myth: *Cross.

K774. Capture by sight of woman's breasts. K832.3. Female confederate disrobes before hero, who is attacked when he looks away.

Q411.13. *Death as punishment for thievery.* Irish myth: Cross.

Q411.13.1. *Charge of theft avenged by assault.* Icelandic: Boberg.

Q411.14. *Death as punishment for spying on uncanny persons.* Irish myth: Cross.

Q411.15. *Death as punishment for dropping on emperor's coat.* Icelandic: FSS 125, 168—70, Boberg.

Q412. *Punishment: millstone dropped on guilty person.* *Type 720; BP I 412ff., *423; Liebrecht 296; *Fb "møllesten" II 650; Herrmann Saxo II 568 n. 2, Grimm Deutsche Rechtsalterthümer II 277. — Jewish: Neuman.

Q413. *Punishment: hanging.* *DeCock Volkssage 74; *Hdwb. d. Abergl. III 1438ff.; Irish: O'Suilleabhain 107, Beal XXI 334; Icelandic: *Boberg; Jewish: Neuman; India: *Thompson-Balys; Marquesas: Handy 63.

F1044. Man suddenly acquires long gray beard on scaffold at execution. P175. Slave killed. P175.1. Slave hanged. S113.1. Murder by hanging.

Q413.0.1. *Threat of hanging.* Icelandic: *Boberg.

Q413.1. *Hanging as punishment for theft.* (Cf. Q212.) *Fb "hænge" I 731b; Irish myth: *Cross; Icelandic: *Boberg; Italian Novella: *Rotunda.

Q413.2. *Hanging as punishment for adultery.* (Cf. Q241.) Icelandic: *Boberg; German: Grimm No. 4; Italian Novella: Rotunda.

Q413.3. *Hanging as punishment for imposture.* (Cf. Q262.) Italian Novella: Rotunda.

Q413.4. *Hanging as punishment for murder.* (Cf. Q211.) Icelandic: *Boberg; Italian Novella: Rotunda.

Q413.5. *Hanging as punishment for impudence.* (Cf. Q326.) Icelandic: *Boberg.

Q413.5.1. *Impudent suitor or his messenger hanged or threatened with hanging.* Icelandic: *Boberg.

Q413.6. *Hanging as punishment for denying pagan gods.* (Cf. Q225.2.) Der Heiligen Leben und Leiden 101 (Santa Barbara).

Q413.7. *Hanging as punishment for silence about hidden treasure.* Icelandic: Boberg.

Q413.8. *Hanging as punishment for treachery.* (Cf. Q261.) Icelandic: *Boberg.

Q413.8.1. *Hanging by one foot as punishment for treachery.* Italian Novella: Rotunda.

Q414. *Punishment: burning alive.* **W. Foerster Der Feuertod als Strafe in der altfr. erzählenden Dichtung (Halle, 1913); *Fb "brænde" IV 69ab, "teglovn"; Dickson 74; Pauli (ed. Bolte) No. 232; Alphabet No. 353; Grimm No. 3 (Type 710). — Irish myth: *Cross; Icelandic: *Boberg; French Canadian: Barbeau JAFL XXIX 20; Spanish: Keller, Espinosa Jr. Nos. 140, 161; Italian: Basile Pentamerone II No. 2, Rotunda; Jewish: *Neuman; India: *Thompson-Balys; Chinese: Eberhard FFC CXX 35 No. 22; S. A. Indian (Huamachuco): Métraux RMLP XXXIII 151; Africa (Luba): DeClerq ZsKS IV 222.

G275.3. Witch burned. K955. Murder by burning. K1612. Message of death fatal to sender. M341.2.7.1. Prophecy: sinners to be burnt by fire on Doomsday. Q551.9. Miraculous burning as punishment. R175. Rescue at the stake. S112. Burning to death. V252.2. Virgin Mary saves criminal from fire at stake.

Q414.0.1. *Burning as punishment for uxoricide.* (Cf. Q211.3.) Africa (Fjort): Dennett 54 No. 19.

Q414.0.2. *Burning as punishment for adultery.* (Cf. Q241.) Pauli (ed. Bolte) No. 229; Irish myth: *Cross; Spanish: Boggs FFC XC 57 No. 425; Italian Novella: *Rotunda.

Q414.0.3. *Burning as punishment for incest (incontinence).* (Cf. Q242, Q243.) Child II 41—48 passim, 113—25 passim, III 508b, V 292b; Irish myth: *Cross.

D1865.2.1. Girl becomes more beautiful as she is burned, but her brother, who loves her incestuously, turns to charcoal.

Q414.0.3.1. *Burning monastery and monks in it as punishment for incontinence.* Cent Nouvelles Nouvelles No. 32; Heptameron No. 31.

Q414.0.4. *Burning as punishment for ravisher.* (Cf. Q244.) Malone PMLA XLIII 406.

Q414.0.4.1. *Ravisher's grave and body miraculously burnt.* Scala Celi 111a No. 619; Wright Latin Stories 112.

Q414.0.4.2. *Burning as punishment for abductor.* Irish myth: *Cross.

Q414.0.5. *Burning as punishment for traitor.* (Cf. Q261.) Icelandic: *Boberg; Breton: Sébillot Incidents s.v. "bûcher"; Missouri French: Carrière; Italian Novella: Rotunda.

Q414.0.5.1. *Burning for traitor: unwittingly suggested by culprit.* Italian Novella: Rotunda.

Q414.0.6. *Burning as punishment for impostor.* (Cf. Q262.) Missouri French: Carrière; Spanish: Espinosa Jr. No. 106; Italian Novella: *Rotunda; India: Thompson-Balys; Africa (Fjort): Dennett 130.

Q414.0.6.1. *Burning as punishment for counterfeiting.* (Cf. Q261.) Italian Novella: Rotunda.

Q414.0.7. *Innocent queen burned at stake.* *Fb. "brænde" IV 69b.

Q414.0.8. *Demons burn heretics at stake.* (Cf. Q225.1.) Scala Celi 103b Nos. 555, 556.

Q414.0.9. *Burning as punishment for betraying the confessional.* (Cf. Q224.) Italian Novella: Rotunda.

Q414.0.10. *Burning for witchcraft.* Icelandic: *Boberg; Italian Novella: Rotunda.

Q414.0.11. *Burning for sodomy.* (Cf. Q253.) Italian Novella: Rotunda.

Q414.0.12. *Burning as punishment for murder.* (Cf. Q211.) Irish myth: *Cross; Icelandic: *Boberg; Africa (Bankon): Ittman 100.

Q414.0.12.1. *Woman saved from being burned as punishment for killing impudent suitor.* Icelandic: FSS 240, Boberg.

Q414.0.13. *Burning as punishment for fratricide.* (Cf. Q211.9.) Irish myth: Cross.

Q414.1. *Punishment: boiling in oil (lead, tar).* DeCock Volkssage 80; Child II 312 n., 327, IV 480a, V 53, 56, 230; Icelandic: FSS 243; India: *Thompson-Balys.

F872.2. Bath of boiling oil. S112.1. Boiling to death. Often in pitch or oil.

Q414.1.1. *Boiling in tar as punishment for impostor.* (Cf. Q262.) Africa (Angola): Chatelain 49 version B.

Q414.2. *Punishment: imprisonment in white-hot iron house.* Irish myth: Cross (cf. also S112.6); Welsh: MacCulloch Celtic 101.

Q414.3. *Punishment: burning and scattering ashes.* Italian: Basile Pentamerone V No. 9.

E431.9. Ashes of dead thrown on water to prevent return.

Q414.3.1. *Punishment: crushing in rice mill and scattering ashes.* India: Thompson-Balys.

Q414.4. *Punishment: dancing to death in red-hot shoes.* Type 709; *BP I 450ff., *464; *Loomis White Magic 118.

C94.1.1. The cursed dancers. D2061.1.2. Persons magically caused to dance selves to death. Q388.1. Freemasons forced to dance till they sweat blood.

Q414.5. *Punishment: king hung between two fires.* Icelandic: Boberg.

Q414.6. *Woman cast on husband's funeral pyre as punishment.* India: Thompson-Balys.

P16.4.1. Suttee.

Q415. *Punishment: being eaten by animals.* (Cf. Q453, Q557.) *DeCock Volkssage 88; Irish: O'Suilleabhain 46, Beal XXI 317.

Q415.0.1. *Punishment: being eaten by demon.* India: Thompson-Balys.

Q415.1. *Punishment: being eaten by dogs.* Eskimo: Thompson Tales 4, 272 n. 2.

Q415.1.1. *Punishment: transformation to deer which is devoured by dogs.* Greek: Frazer Apollodorus I 323 (Acteon).

C312.1.1. Tabu: man looking at nude goddess. D661. Transformation as punishment.

Q415.1.2. *Punishment: tying man to horses and setting vicious hounds after him.* (Cf. Q416, S117.) Scottish: Campbell-McKay No. 25.

Q415.2. *Mice devour hard-hearted man.* (Hatto and the Mouse Tower.) (Cf. Q291.) *Fb "rotte" III 83a; Veckenstedt (Veckenstedt's) Zs. f. Vksk. I (1888—9) 364ff.; **Beheim-Schwartzbach Die Mäusenturmsage von Popiel und Hatto (Posen, 1888); *Wehrhan Die Sage 51; *Liebrecht 1ff.; Jewish: Neuman.

Q415.3. *Punishment: man eaten by worms (snake).* Finnish-Swedish: Wessman 19 No. 180; Jewish: Neuman; India: Thompson-Balys.

Q415.3.1. *Cobras placed in boxes and given to cruel parents, so that they are bitten.* (Cf. Q285.) India: Thompson-Balys.

Q415.4. *Punishment: being fed to lions (wild beasts).* Italian Novella: *Rotunda; Jewish: Neuman.

Q415.5. *Punishment: being devoured by tiger.* India: *Thompson-Balys.

Q415.6. *Bears devour the wicked.* Jewish: *Neuman.

Q415.7. *Wolves kill person for quenching holy fire.* (Cf. Q222.) Irish myth: *Cross.

Q415.7.1. *Wolves and birds eat bodies of slayers of poet.* Irish myth: Cross.

Q415.8. *Heretic preaching against God's creation worried to death by fly.* (Cf. Q225.) Spanish Exempla: Keller.

Q415.9. *Punishment: being eaten by fish.* Tuamotu: Stimson MS (z-G. 3/1301); Hawaii: Beckwith Myth 504.

Q416. *Punishment: drawing asunder by horses.* (Cf. Q469.12.) Child V 157; BP I 306; Grimm Deutsche Rechtsalterthümer II 272; DeCock Volkssage 91. — Irish myth: Cross; Icelandic: FSS 42, Boberg; Spanish: Espinosa Jr. Nos. 126, 143; Greek: Frazer Apollodorus I 331 n. I (Lycurgus); India: Thompson-Balys.

S117. Death by dragging behind horse. S139.2. Slain person dismembered.

Q416.0.1. *Quartering by horses as punishment for breaking betrothal.* (Cf. Q252.) Estonian: Aarne FFC XXV 136 No. 93.

Q416.0.2. *Quartering by horses as punishment for murder.* (Cf. Q211.3.) Icelandic: *Boberg; Italian Novella: *Rotunda.

Q416.0.2.1. *Quartering by horses as punishment for uxoricide.* (Cf. Q211.3.) Italian Novella: Rotunda.

Q416.0.3. *Quartering by horses as punishment for impostor.* (Cf. Q262.) Icelandic: *Boberg.

Q416.1. *Punishment: trampling (kicking) to death by horses.* East Gothic: De la Saussaye 135; Grimm Deutsche Rechtsalterhümer II 273; Liebrecht Orient und Occident II 270; G. Kurth Histoire poetique des Merovingiens 420ff. — Icelandic: *Boberg; Indonesia: Snouck-Hurgronje De Atjehers II 142.

Q416.1.1. *Adulteress kicked to death by mule as punishment.* (Cf. Q241.) *Fischer-Bolte 217.

Q416.2. *Punishment: dragging to death by a horse.* Cheremis: Sebeok-Nyerges; Lithuanian: Balys Index Nos. 452*f., 481*; India: Thompson-Balys.

Q416.2.1. *Punishment: drawing at the tails of horses.* (Cf. S117.) Irish myth: Cross; Jewish: *Neuman.

Q416.2.2. *Punishment: dragging to death tied to horns of a bull.* Greek: Grote I 241.

Q416.3. *Punishment: trampling by elephants.* India: *Thompson-Balys.

Q416.3.1. *Punishment: being gored to death by elephant.* India: Thompson-Balys.

Q417. *Punishment: dropping and dashing to pieces.* (Cf. Q551.10.) Von Amira Sitzb. bair. Akad. XXXI (3) 136ff.; Irish myth: Cross; Spanish: Boggs FFC XC 49 No. 327F*.

J1184.1. Adulteress hurled from high rock escapes injury: she may not be punished again. K1041. Borrowed feathers. Dupe lets himself be carried aloft by bird and dropped.

Q417.1. *Murderess forced to leap from cliff.* (Cf. Q211.) Irish myth: *Cross.

Q417.2. *Traitor thrown into pit so that he sticks to the waist and is then chased out of the country.* (Cf. Q261.) Icelandic: Boberg.

Q417.3. *Bridge to world of dead cut from under wicked person so that he falls into hell.* (Cf. F152.) India: Thompson-Balys.

Q418. *Punishment by poisoning.* (Cf. S111.) India: Thompson-Balys.

Q418.1. *Murder of faithless wife with poisoned salad.* (Cf. Q241.) Heptameron No. 36.

Q418.2. *Venomous snake put into the mouth as punishment for murder of newborn children.* (Cf. Q211.4.) Icelandic: Boberg.

Q421. *Punishment: beheading.* DeCock Volkssage 75; *Roberts 211; Irish myth: Cross; Icelandic: *Boberg; French Canadian: Sister Marie Ursule; Jewish: *Neuman; India: *Thompson-Balys.

Q421.0.1. *Beheading as punishment for debt.* (Cf. Q271.) *Fb "gjæld" I 448.

Q421.0.2. *Beheading as punishment for adultery.* (Cf. Q241.) Pauli (ed. Bolte) Nos. 229, 230; Italian Novella: Rotunda; India: Thompson-Balys.

Q421.0.3. *Beheading as punishment for rape.* (Cf. Q244.) Italian Novella: *Rotunda.

Q421.0.4. *Beheading as punishment for murder.* (Cf. Q211.) Irish myth: *Cross; Italian Novella: *Rotunda.

Q421.0.5. *Beheading as punishment for mutilation.* Italian Novella: Rotunda.

Q421.0.6. *Beheading as punishment for incest.* (Cf. Q242.) Italian Novella: *Rotunda.

Q421.0.7. *Beheading as punishment for seduction.* (Cf. Q243.2.) Italian Novella: Rotunda.

Q421.0.8. *Beheading for persecution of wife.* (Cf. S410.) Italian Novella: Rotunda.

Q421.1. *Heads on stakes.* Punishment by beheading and placing the heads on stakes. *Taylor Romanic Review IX 21ff.; *BP III 368, IV 113; *B. Lewis Classical Mythology and Arthurian Romance 107ff.; Child V 482 s.v. "heads". — Irish myth: *Cross; Icelandic: *Boberg; India: Thompson-Balys; Japanese: Ikeda; Africa: Frobenius Atlantis III 78; Cape Verde Islands: Parsons MAFLS XV (1) 214 No. 73.

G512.1.2.1. Ogre's head and hands cut off and hung above city gate. H901.1. Heads placed on stakes for failure in performance of task. Unsuccessful youths are beheaded and heads exposed. Hero sees them when he sets out to accomplish his task. S110.3. Princess builds tower of skulls of unsuccessful suitors. S139.2.2.1. Heads of slain enemies impaled upon stakes.

Q421.1.1. *Head cut off and hung on tree outside village.* India: *Thompson-Balys.

Q421.2. *Man beheaded in place where he turned his back on saint.* (Cf. Q227.) Irish myth: Cross.

Q421.3. *Punishment: cutting throat.* India: Thompson-Balys.

Q422. *Punishment: stoning to death.* (Cf. Q220.1.1.) Von Amira Sitzb. bair. Akad. XXXI (3) 155ff.; R. Hirzel Abh. sächs. Ges. der Wiss. Phil.-Hist. Klasse XXVII No. 7. — Icelandic: Corpus Poeticum Boreale I 344, *Boberg; Spanish Exempla: Keller; Italian Novella: *Rotunda; Jewish: *Neuman; India: *Thompson-Balys.

Q422.0.1. *Punishment: beating to death.* India: Thompson-Balys.

Q423. *Punishment: breaking upon a wheel.* Von Amira Sitzb. bair. Akad. XXXI (3) 106ff.; Icelandic: Boberg; Irish myth: Cross; Italian Novella: Rotunda.

S181.1. Being bound to a bladed wheel.

Q424. *Punishment: strangling.* (Cf. Q469.5, S113.) *DeCock Volkssage 77; Marquesas: Handy 113, 129.

Q424.0.1. *Strangling as punishment for murder.* (Cf. Q211.) Irish myth: Cross.

Q424.1. *King strangles falcon when it kills eagle.* (Cf. Q211.6.) Köhler-Bolte I 583; Italian Novella: *Rotunda.

Q424.2. *Strangling as punishment for adultery.* (Cf. Q241.) Italian Novella: Rotunda.

Q424.3. *Man strangles friar for attempting to seduce his wife.* (Cf. Q243.2.1.) Italian Novella: Rotunda.

Q425. *Punishment: suffocating.* (Cf. Q274.2.)

Q426. *Wolf cut open and filled with stones as punishment.* *Type 333; BP I 37, *40; Spanish: Espinosa III No. 212, Espinosa Jr. Nos. 32—34; Cape Verde Islands: *Parsons MAFLS XV (1) 312 n. 1.

S139.5. Murder by cutting up adversary's stomach so that intestines fall out.

Q426.1. *Punishment for murder by fatal enema.* (Cf. Q211.4.2.) Africa (Wakweli): Bender 86.

Q427. *Punishment: opening own veins and bleeding to death.* (Seneca) Alphabet No. 224.

Q428. *Punishment: drowning.* (Cf. Q552.19.) Irish myth: *Cross; Jewish: *Neuman; India: *Thompson-Balys.

C923. Drowning as punishment for breaking tabu. S461. Tale-bearer unjustly drowned for lack of proof of accusation.

Q428.1. *Drowning as punishment for adultery.* (Cf. Q241.) Irish myth: *Cross; Italian Novella: *Rotunda.

Q428.2. *Magic swine cause robbers to be drowned.* (Cf. B183, Q212.) Irish myth: Cross.

Q428.3. *Drowning as punishment for disturbing holy person.* (Cf. Q227.) Irish myth: Cross.

Q429. *Capital punishment—miscellaneous.*

Q429.1. *Punishment: culprit eaten by cannibals.* Buddhist myth: Malalasekera II 824.

Q429.2. *Death at hands of foreign invaders as punishment.* Jewish: Moreno Esdras.

Q429.3. *Cutting into pieces as punishment.* India: *Thompson-Balys.

Q429.4. *Punishment: squeezing to death.* India: Thompson-Balys.

Q430. Abridgment of freedom as punishment.

Q430.1. *Imposition of tabu as punishment.* Irish myth: Cross.

C901. Tabu imposed.

Q431. *Punishment: banishment (exile).* *Boje 63; Dickson 78; Gaster Thespis 304; Irish: *Cross, O'Suilleabhain 88, Beal XXI 328; Icelandic: *Boberg; Greek: Frazer Apollodorus I 350 n. 1 (Oedipus), Grote I 172; Jewish: *Neuman; India: *Thompson-Balys; Chinese: Eberhard FFC CXX 38, 143; Hawaii: Beckwith Myth 205, 214; S. A. Indian (Tupinamba): Métraux RMLP XXXIII 169.

C617. Forbidden country. F252.4. Fairies banished from fairyland. L111.1. Exile returns and succeeds. M373. Expulsion to avoid fulfillment of prophecy. S322. Children abandoned (driven forth, exposed) by hostile relatives. Z174.1. Inverted shoes at doors to indicate banishment.

Q431.0.1. *Saint prefers to die in exile.* Irish myth: Cross.

Q431.1. *Voluntary exile as punishment for murder.* (Cf. Q211, Q431.9.) Greek: Fox 93 (Herakles).

Q431.2. *Banishment for treachery.* (Cf. Q261.) Italian Novella: Rotunda; India: Thompson-Balys.

Q431.2.1. *Elder brothers banished for treachery.* (Cf. K2211, Q261.) Spanish: Boggs FFC XC 49 No. 328A*.

Q431.2.2. *Treachery punished by banishment to desert isle.* (Cf. S145.) Heptameron No. 67.

Q431.2.3. *King's foster brothers banished for lawlessness.* Irish myth: *Cross.

Q431.3. *Banishment because of disobedience.* Maiden wants to become nun and not marry. (Cf. Q325.) Spanish Exempla: Keller; India: Thompson-Balys; Chinese: Werner 260.

Q431.4. *Banishment till rose grows from table for preventing childbirth.* (Cf. F971.2, Q251, T572).) *Type 755.

Q431.5. *Banishment for seduction.* (Cf. Q243.2.) Italian Novella: *Rotunda.

Q431.5.1. *Banishment for attempted seduction.* (Cf. Q243.2.1.) Icelandic: *Boberg; Italian Novella: *Rotunda.

Q431.5.2. *Banishment for abduction of bride (girl).* Icelandic: *Boberg.

Q431.5.3. *Princes banished as punishment for lewd conduct with female subjects* (Cf. Q243.) India: Thompson-Balys.

Q431.6. *Banishment for rape.* (Cf. Q244.) Italian Novella: *Rotunda.

Q431.7. *Banishment for imposture.* (Cf. Q262.) Italian Novella: Rotunda.

Q431.8. *Banishment as punishment for adultery.* (Cf. Q241.) Irish myth: Cross; Italian Novella: Rotunda.

Q431.8.1. *Banishment as punishment for incest.* (Cf. Q242.2.) India: *Thompson-Balys.

Q431.9. *Banishment for murder.* (Cf. Q211.) Icelandic: *Boberg.

Q431.9.1. *Banishment for attempted murder.* Italian Novella: *Rotunda.

Q431.9.2. *Exile as punishment for parricide.* (Cf. Q211.1.) Irish myth: *Cross.

Q431.10. *Banishment for assault on king's tax collectors.* Icelandic: Boberg.

Q431.11. *Banishment as punishment for breach of faith with animals.* (Cf. Q263.) Irish myth: Cross.

Q431.12. *Banishment as punishment for fault-finding.* (Cf. Q312.) Irish myth: Cross.

Q431.13. *Banishment for desecration of holy places.* (Cf. Q222.) Icelandic: *Boberg.

Q431.14. *Berserks banished because of defeat.* Icelandic: Boberg.

Q431.15. *Banishment as punishment for robbery.* (Cf. Q212.) Irish myth: Cross.

Q431.16. *Boy banished for breaking women's water pots.* India: *Thompson-Balys.

Q431.17. *Banishment for lying.* (Cf. Q263.) India: Thompson-Balys.

Q431.18. *Banishment for association with those of another faith.* India: Thompson-Balys.

Q431.19. *Banishment for laziness.* (Cf. Q321.) India: Thompson-Balys.

Q432. *Punishment: ejectment.*

Q432.1. *Buzzard hatched by hawk ejected for fouling nest.* (Cf. Q322.) Herbert III 37ff.; Hervieux IV 276 No. 4; Cent Nouvelles Nouvelles No. 68.

Q432.2. *Adulteress ejected into street clad only in her shirt.* (Cf. Q241, Q243, Q473.) Cent Nouvelles Nouvelles No. 8; Italian Novella: *Rotunda.

Q433. *Punishment: imprisonment.* Icelandic: *Boberg; Missouri French: Carrière; Spanish: Espinosa Jr. Nos. 139, 206f.; Jewish: *Neuman; India: *Thompson-Balys.

R0. Captivity. R40. Places and conditions of captivity. R41. Captivity in tower (castle, prison). R111.2. Princess (duchess) rescued from tower.

Q433.1. *Imprisonment for adultery.* (Cf. Q241.) Heptameron No. 61; Italian Novella: *Rotunda.

Q433.1.1. *Adulteress confined in a cage.* (Cf. Q241.) Malone PMLA XLIII 415f.

Q433.2. *Defeated giants imprisoned in lower world.* Gaster Thespis 160; Greek: Fox 8 (Titans), Grote I 8.

A162.1. Fight of the gods and giants. A531. Culture hero overcomes monsters. A1071. Fettering of underground monster.

Q433.3. *Zeus has embassy of dogs imprisoned for fouling his court.* (Cf. Q322.) *BP III 555; Dh IV 137ff.

A2232.8. Dogs' embassy to Zeus chased forth; dogs seek ambassador: why dogs sniff each other under leg. B220. Animal kingdom (or community).

Q433.4. *Imprisonment for imposture.* (Cf. Q262.) Italian Novella: Rotunda.

Q433.5. *Imprisonment for attempted seduction.* (Cf. Q243.2.1.) Italian Novella: Rotunda.

Q433.6. *Priest imprisoned for incontinence.* (Cf. Q243.) Italian Novella: *Rotunda.

Q433.7. *Imprisonment for treachery.* (Cf. Q261.) Italian Novella: Rotunda.

Q433.8. *Imprisonment for gambling.* (Cf. Q381.) Italian Novella: Rotunda.

Q433.9. *Wicked son confined on island.* Irish myth: Cross.

Q433.10. *Earl hunting in the king's forest imprisoned.* Icelandic: Boberg.

Q433.11. *Undesired suitor's messengers imprisoned.* Icelandic: *Boberg.

Q433.12. *Punishment: abridgment of freedom till extravagant boast is confirmed.* Irish myth: *Cross.

Q433.13. *War prisoners shut up between stones.* Icelandic: Boberg.

Q434. *Punishment: fettering.*

A1071. Fettering of underground monster.

Q434.1. *Adulteress and paramour fettered.* (Cf. Q241.) Malone PMLA XLIII 405, 407, 421.

Q434.2. *War prisoners fettered.* Icelandic: *Boberg.

Q434.3. *Fettering to oak.* Icelandic: *Boberg.

Q435. *Magic imprisonment in cleft tree.* New Guinea: Dixon 137. Cf. Caliban in Shakespeare's Tempest and Fradubio in Spenser's Faerie Queene Book I.

D1413. Magic object holds person fast. K1111. Dupe puts hand (paws) into cleft of tree (wedge, vise).

Q436. *Excommunication from religious association as punishment.* Jewish: *Neuman.

Q437. *Sale into slavery as punishment.* Jewish: *Neuman; Buddhist myth: Malalasekera II 526.

Q437.1. *Criminal's wife and children sold into slavery.* *Chauvin VI 163 No. 327.

P170. Slaves. R61. Person sold into slavery. S210.1. Child sold into slavery.

Q438. *Punishment: abandonment in forest.* (Cf. S143.) India: *Thompson-Balys.

Q450. Cruel punishments.

P253.1. Brother about to drink blood of seemingly guilty sister. R51. Mistreatment of prisoners. S. Unnatural cruelty.

Q450.1. *Torture as punishment.* Irish myth: Cross; Jewish: *Neuman.

Q450.1.1. *Torture as punishment for murder.* (Cf. Q211.) Irish myth: Cross; India: Thompson-Balys.

Q451. *Mutilation as punishment.* (Cf. S160.) Missouri French: Carrière; Marquesas: Handy 78, 121.

Q451.0.1. *Hands and feet cut off as punishment.* Icelandic: Snorra Edda Skaldsk XLI, Herrmann Saxo II 571, *Boberg.

Q451.0.2. *Threat to cut off hand or foot.* Icelandic: *Boberg.

Q451.0.3. *Strong girl breaks impudent suitor's right hand and left foot.* Icelandic: *Boberg.

Q451.0.4. *Hands and feet cut off as punishment for robbery.* (Cf. Q212.) Irish myth: Cross.

Q451.1. *Hands cut off as punishment.* (Cf. S161.) *Type 706; *BP I 295; **Däumling Studie über den Typus des Mädchens ohne Hände (München, 1912); Krappe Zeitschrift für Englische Philologie XLIX 361—69; Missouri French: Carrière; Spanish Exempla: Keller; Latin American: *Knedler Hispanic Review X 314ff.; Italian Novella: Rotunda; India: *Thompson-Balys; Japanese: Ikeda.

Q451.1.1. *Hand cut off as punishment for theft.* (Cf. Q212.) *Penzer V 61 n. 1, 143 n., VI 19; *Chauvin VI 80 No. 249; Icelandic: *Boberg; India: *Thompson-Balys.

Q451.1.2. *Hand cut off for contempt of court.* Italian Novella: Rotunda.

Q451.1.3. *Hand cut off for treachery.* (Cf. Q261.) Italian Novella: Rotunda.

Q451.1.4. *Hand cut off (falls off) as punishment for murder.* (Cf. Q211.) Irish myth: *Cross.

Q451.1.4.1. *Hand cut off as punishment for fornication.* (Cf. Q243.) Irish myth: Cross.

Q451.1.5. *Arms cut off as punishment for adultery.* (Cf. Q241.) Heptameron No. 48.

Q451.1.6. *Right hands cut off enemy's messengers.* Icelandic: *Boberg.

Q451.1.7. *Arms cut off as punishment for slandering.* (Cf. Q263.) Eskimo (Cumberland Sound): Boas BAM XV 207.

Q451.2. *Laming as punishment.* (Cf. S162.) Icelandic: *Boberg; Jewish: Neuman; India: *Thompson-Balys.

Q451.2.0.1. *Limbs cut off (drop off) as punishment.* Irish myth: *Cross.

Q451.2.0.2. *Boring hole through heel as punishment.* Jewish: Neuman.

Q451.2.0.3. *Hamstringing as punishment.* Eskimo (Greenland): Rasmussen I 244.

Q451.2.1. *Youth lamed by man whose daughter he refuses to marry.* (Cf. Q245.) Köhler-Bolte I 120; *Krappe Herrig's Archiv CLVIII 9ff.; *P. Maurus Wielandsage in der Literatur (Münchner Beiträge zur rom u. eng. Philologie XXV (1902)).

Q451.2.2. *Feet cut off as punishment for theft.* (Cf. Q212.) Penzer V 143 n.; India: *Thompson-Balys.

Q451.2.3. *Foot cut off as punishment for murder.* (Cf. Q211.) Irish myth: Cross.

Q451.2.4. *Legs cut off as punishment for adultery.* (Cf. Q241.) Heptameron No. 48.

Q451.3. *Loss of speech as punishment.* *Type 710; *BP I 13ff.; Icelandic: *Boberg; Jewish: *Neuman.

A2344.2. Why animal has no tongue. A2422. How animal lost voice (or power of speech). C401. Tabu: speaking during certain time. C944. Dumbness as punishment for breaking tabu. D758. Disenchantment by maintaining silence. D2020. Magic dumbness. J213. Choice: loss of beauty or speech. Q550. Miraculous punishments. Q583.2. Man stricken dumb for surly speech.

Q451.3.1. *Dumbness as punishment for hiding children.* Fb "stum".

D2021.1. Dumbness as curse.

Q451.3.2. *Dumbness as punishment for lying.* (Cf. Q263.) Irish myth: Cross.

Q451.3.3. *Dumbness as punishment for opposition to holy person.* (*Cf. Q227.) Irish myth: Cross.

Q451.3.3.1. *Son stricken dumb as punishment for father's opposition to holy person.* (Cf. Q411.3.) Irish myth: Cross.

Q451.3.4. *Dumbness as punishment for blasphemy.* Spanish Exempla: Keller.

Q451.4. *Tongue cut off as punishment.* DeCock Volkssage 93; Spanish: Boggs FFC XC 98 No. 836G*, Espinosa II No. 94; India: Thompson-Balys; Chinese: Graham; Japanese: Ikeda; Korean: Zong in-Sob 145 No. 64.

A2344.2. Why animal has no tongue. S163. Mutilation: cutting (tearing) out tongue.

Q451.4.1. *Tongue cut off as punishment for theft.* (Cf. Q212.) *Penzer V 61 n. 1, 143 n.

Q451.4.2. *Tongue cut out as punishment for gossip.* (Cf. Q314.) Wienert FFC LVI 39; Halm Aesop No. 416.

Q451.4.3. *Tongue cut off as punishment for incest.* (Cf. Q242.) Italian Novella: Rotunda.

Q451.4.4. *Tongue cut off as punishment for treachery.* (Cf. Q261.) Italian Novella: Rotunda.

Q451.4.5. *Tongue cut out as punishment for murder.* (Cf. Q211.) Irish myth: Cross.

Q451.4.6. *Tongue cut out as punishment for fault-finding (satire).* (Cf. Q312.) Irish myth: *Cross.

Q451.4.7. *Man pulls out his own tongue in remorse.* India: Thompson-Balys.

Q451.4.8. *Tongue cut off as punishment for alleged adultery.* (Cf. Q241.) Icelandic: Boberg.

Q451.4.8.1. *Tongue cut (bitten) off as punishment for unfaithfulness to wife.* Spanish Exempla: Keller.

Q451.4.9. *Hanging by tongue as punishment.* Cheremis: Sebeok-Nyerges.

Q451.4.10. *Punishment: stretching tongue to enormous length.* Korean: Zong in-Sob 145 No. 64.

Q451.5. *Nose cut off as punishment.* Bødker Exempler 280 No. 24; Irish myth: *Cross; India: *Thompson-Balys; Africa: Frobenius Atlantis IV 196.

P522.1.1. A nose for a nose. P536.1. Nose cut off for failure to pay tax.

Q451.5.1. *Nose cut off as punishment for adultery.* (Cf. Q241.) *Penzer II 88 n. 1, V 82 n. 1, 123, 156, VI 188 n. 1, IX 76; Saxo Grammaticus (ed. Elton) 71; Italian Novella: *Rotunda.

K1512. The cut-off nose. K1911. The false bride.

Q451.5.1.1. *Mistress's nose cut off as punishment for faithlessness.* Icelandic: *Boberg.

Q451.5.2. *Nose cut off as punishment for theft.* (Cf. Q212.) Penzer II 60ff.

Q451.5.3. *Nose of falsely accusing bishop bitten off.* (Cf. Q263.) Dickson 46.

Q451.5.4. *Nose cut off as punishment for treachery.* (Cf. Q261.) Italian Novella: Rotunda.

Q451.6. *Ears cut off as punishment.* Irish myth: Cross; Missouri French: Carrière; India: *Thompson-Balys; Africa: Frobenius Atlantis IV 196.

Q451.6.0.1. *Girl (fairy) bites off ear of ravisher.* (Cf. F304.4.1, Q244.) Irish myth: *Cross.

Q451.6.1. *Ears cut off as punishment for adultery.* (Cf. Q241.) *Penzer V 82 n. 1, 156; Africa (Fang): Einstein 53, Trilles 168.

Q451.6.2. *Ear cut off as punishment for theft.* (Cf. Q212.) Nouvelles Récréations No. 56.

Q451.7. *Blinding as punishment.* *Fb "blind" IV 45b, "øje" III 1165a; Irish myth: *Cross; Icelandic: MacCulloch Eddic 322; Spanish: Espinosa Jr. No. 137; Greek: Frazer Apollodorus I 367 n. 1; Jewish: *Neuman; India: *Thompson-Balys.

C943. Loss of sight for broken tabu. M13. Sentence applied to king's own son. Those caught in adultery are to have their eyes put out. S165. Mutilation: putting out eyes.

Q451.7.0.1. *Loss of one eye as punishment.* Hdwb. d. Märchens I 477a n. 5; Icelandic: *Boberg.

Q451.7.0.2. *Miraculous blindness as punishment.* (Cf. Q559.2.) Irish myth: Cross.

Q451.7.0.2.1. *Miraculous blindness as punishment for opposition to holy person.* (Cf. Q227, Q571.1.) Irish myth: *Cross.

Q451.7.0.2.2. *Miraculous blindness as punishment for theft.* (Cf. Q212.) *Loomis White Magic 98; Irish myth: Cross.

Q451.7.0.2.3. *Miraculous blindness as punishment for disobedience.* (Cf. Q325.) Irish myth: Cross.

Q451.7.0.2.4. *Miraculous blindness as punishment for criminal intent.* (Cf. Q210.1.) Irish myth: Cross.

Q451.7.0.2.5. *Miraculous blindness as punishment for spying (on druids, fairies, witches, etc.).* Irish myth: *Cross.

Q451.7.1. *Blinding as punishment for perjury.* (Cf. Q263.) Pauli (ed. Bolte) No. 493; Spanish Exempla: Keller.

Q451.7.2. *Blinding as punishment for ravisher.* (Cf. Q244.) Herbert III 206; Oesterley No. 50.

Q451.7.2.1. *Blinding (of father) as punishment for ravisher.* (Cf. Q411.3.) Irish myth: *Cross.

Q451.7.2.2. *Blinding as punishment for attempt to violate girl (queen).* Icelandic: *Boberg.

Q451.7.3. *Blinding as punishment for incest.* (Cf. Q242.) Italian Novella: Rotunda.

Q451.7.4. *Blinding as punishment for murder.* (Cf. Q211.) Irish myth: *Cross; Italian Novella: Rotunda; India: Thompson-Balys.

Q451.7.5. *Wicked son blinded.* Irish myth: Cross; Spanish Exempla: Keller.

Q451.8. *Punishment: thong of leather cut from back.* DeCock Studien 9f.; Cosquin Contes indiens 179; Fb "rem" III 39a; Norwegian: R. Berge Eventyr II 49, 66, 71; Russian: Ralston Russian Folk Tales 146.

Q451.9. *Punishment: woman's breasts cut off.* Zupitza Zs. f. Vksk. XI 91; Child Nos. 5, 80, 81; Scotch: Campbell Tales I lxxxix—xc. See also Peele's "King Edward the First".

Q451.9.1. *Punishment: woman suspended by her breasts.* Jewish: Neuman.

Q451.10. *Punishment: genitalia cut off.* Liebrecht 94ff.; DeCock Volkssage 86; Spanish Exempla: Keller; Italian Novella: *Rotunda; Jewish: *Neuman; India: Thompson-Balys.

Q451.10.1. *Punishment: castration.* (Cf. K2111.3.) Herrmann Saxo II 354.

Q451.11. *Piecemeal mutilation as punishment.* Marquesas: Handy 78; Tonga: Gifford 67.

Q451.11.1. *Deception punished by piecemeal mutilation.* Italian Novella: Rotunda.

Q451.12. *Lips sewed together as punishment for slander.* (Cf. Q263.) Icelandic: Boberg.

Q451.13. *Punishment: head split into many pieces.* India: *Thompson-Balys.

Q451.14. *Adulteress's pregnant belly pierced with pounder.* (Cf. Q241.) India: Thompson-Balys.

Q452. *Punishment: snake sucks woman's breasts.* Herbert III 9; *Klapper Erzählungen des Mittelalters 175ff., 372f.; Oesterley 683f.; Herrtage EETS (ES) XXXIII 275ff.

Q453. *Punishment: being bitten by animal.* (Cf. Q415.)

Q453.1. *Punishment: being bitten by ants.* India: Thompson-Balys.

Q453.2. *Punishment: being bitten by scorpion.* India: Thompson-Balys.

Q455. *Walling up as a punishment.* (Cf. S125.) *Type 652; BP II 121ff., *124; Fb "indmure" II 24; Spanish: Espinosa Jr. Nos. 110, 140f.; Italian: Basile Pentamerone I No. 2; Jewish: Neuman; India: *Thompson-Balys.

Q455.1. *Walling up as punishment for murder of children.* (Cf. Q211.4.) *Type 652; BP II 121ff.; Fb "indmure".

Q455.2. *Walling up as punishment for adultery.* (Cf. Q241.)

Q455.2.1. *Adulteress walled up with corpse of paramour.* Italian Novella: Rotunda.

Q455.2.1.1. *Adulteress confined in room containing the corpse of her paramour.* She becomes ill and dies. Italian Novella: *Rotunda.

Q456. *Burial alive as punishment.* (Cf. S123.) *Müllenhoff Deutsche Alterthumskunde (ed. Roediger, Berlin, 1920) IV 244ff.; **Feilberg "Levende Begravet" (Årbog for dansk Kulturhistorie [1892] pp. 1—60); DeCock Volkssage 83. — Irish myth: *Cross; Icelandic: Boberg; Greek: Aeschylus Prometheus Bound 366, 1016; Jewish: Neuman; India: *Thompson-Balys.

Q456.0.1. *Burial alive as punishment for adultery.* (Cf. Q241.) *Schoepperle II 420 n. 1; Irish myth: *Cross.

Q456.0.2. *Burial alive as punishment for swindling.* (Cf. Q274.) Alphabet No. 755.

Q456.0.3. *Burial alive as punishment for disobedience to king.* (Cf. Q325.) Greek: Frazer Apollodorus I 373 n. 2 (Antigone).

V62.1. Funeral rites forbidden.

Q456.1. *Punishment: burial alive up to the breast (neck).* BP I 432; Köhler-Bolte I 571; Cowell Jātaka I 130; India: *Thompson-Balys; Buddhist myth: Malalasekera II 597.

Q456.1.1. *Cast-forth wife buried up to the waist for seven years and despitefully used.* Wesselski Märchen 174 No. 64.

Q456.2. *Burial alive for uncharitableness.* (Cf. Q286.2.) Italian Novella: *Rotunda.

Q457. *Flaying alive as punishment.* Grimm Deutsche Rechtsalterthümer II 291; DeCock Volkssage 85f.; Fb "menneskehud" II 579; Irish: O'Suilleabhain 43, Beal XXI 316; Swiss: Jegerlehner Oberwallis 309 No. 18.

J167. Wisdom from continual reminder of foolishness in the past. Unjust judge skinned and his skin stretched over a footstool kept in the presence of judges, so as to remind them to be just. S114. Murder by flaying.

Q457.1. *Flaying alive as punishment for contesting with a god.* Greek: *Frazer Apollodorus I 30 n. 1 (Apollo and Marsyas).

C50. Tabu: offending the gods.

Q457.2. *Devil flays impious person.* (Cf. G303, Q220.) Finnish: Aarne FFC XXXIII 42 No. 50**; Finnish-Swedish: Wessman 12 No. 108.

Q457.3. *Flaying alive as punishment for adultery.* (Cf. Q241.) Italian Novella: Rotunda.

Q457.4. *Flaying alive as punishment for opposition to holy person.* (Cf. Q227.) Irish myth: Cross.

Q458. *Flogging as punishment.* *Roberts 212; Spanish: Espinosa Jr. Nos. 109, 164f.; Jewish: Neuman; India: *Thompson-Balys.

P237. Daughters flogged by parents Q223.9.2. Musician flogged for eating a kid on Friday (day of fast). T331.6. Saint flogs woman who tempts him. V245.1. Angel scourges mortal for disobedience to God.

Q458.0.1. *Flogging as punishment for adultery.* (Cf. Q241.) Malone PMLA XLIII 410.

Q458.0.2. *Flogging as punishment for disobedience to rulers.* (Cf. Q325.) Alphabet No. 441; Spanish: Espinosa Jr. No. 142.

Q458.0.3. *Flogging as punishment for theft.* (Cf. Q212.) Italian Novella: *Rotunda.

Q458.0.4. *Flogging as punishment for imposture.* (Cf. Q262.) Italian Novella: Rotunda.

Q458.0.5. *Flogging as punishment for reviling church.* (Cf. Q225.) Irish myth: Cross.

Q458.0.6. *Flogging as punishment for desire to commit adultery.* (Cf. Q241.1.) Irish myth: Cross.

Q458.1. *Daily beatings as punishment.* Chauvin V 266 No. 154 and frequently elsewhere in Chauvin.

Q458.2. *Flogging to death as punishment.* (Cf. Q410, S122.) Africa (Fang): Trilles 270.

Q458.2.1. *Brother flogs unchaste sister to death.* (Cf. Q243.) Child II 102.

Q458.2.2. *Flogging to death as punishment for theft.* (Cf. Q212.) Fb "piske" II 834.

Q458.2.3. *Flogging to death as punishment for seduction.* (Cf. Q243.2.) Italian Novella: Rotunda.

Q461. *Impalement as punishment.* Chauvin V 3 No. 2; Taylor Romanic Review IX 21ff.; India: Thompson-Balys; Hindu: Penzer I 111, Meyer Hindu Tales 226.

Q461.1. *Impalement as punishment for faithlessness.* Enemy chief has the faithless widow of his victim impaled. Italian Novella: Rotunda.

T231.3.1. Widow offers city to enemy who has killed her husband, if he will marry her.

Q461.2. *Bodies from which limbs have been cut hung on stakes as punishment.* Irish myth: *Cross.

Q461.3. *Impaling as punishment for adultery.* (Cf. Q241.) India: Thompson-Balys.

Q462. *Crucifixion as punishment.* (Cf. Q522.1.) Irish myth: Cross; Spanish Exempla: Keller; Jewish: *Neuman; Hindu: Tawney I 147, 396.

Q462.1. *Punishment: nailing to pillar.* India: Thompson-Balys.

Q462.2. *Punishment by hanging up by the feet.* Eskimo (Smith Sound): Kroeber JAFL XII 179.

Q463. *Spiked-cask punishment.* Rolling down hill in a cask with spikes on inside. DeCock Volkssage 87; BP I 108; Sébillot France I 302, II 90, 271, IV 293ff.; Fb "spigertønde"; Child II 343, IV 30 n. 32, V 48; *Page JAFL LIX 20ff.; Italian: Basile Pentamerone V No. 8; Icelandic: Boberg.

Q464. *Covering with honey and exposing to flies.* DeCock Studien 11ff.; Boccaccio Decameron II No. 9; *Gaster Beiträge zur vgl. Sagen- und Märchenkunde 21; Grimm Deutsche Rechtsalterthümer (1828) 701; Icelandic: Heinzel Beschreibung der isländischen Saga 162, Boberg; Breton: Sébillot Incidents s.v. "supplice"; Italian Novella: *Rotunda; Jewish: *Neuman.

K1212. Lover left standing in snow while his mistress is with another. He later tricks her into standing a whole day in July in a tower naked exposed to the sun and flies.

Q465. *Throwing into a pit as punishment.* Jewish: Neuman; India: *Thompson-Balys.

Q465.1. *Throwing into pit of snakes as punishment.* *Type 403; BP I 99ff.; Krappe "The Snake Tower" Scandinavian Studies XVI (1940) 22—33. — Icelandic: *Boberg; India: *Thompson-Balys.

R41.3.1. Prison filled with snakes.

Q465.2. *Prisoners put into pit filled with corpses in order to starve.* Icelandic: Boberg.

R51.1. Prisoners starved.

Q465.3. *Punishment: pushing into well.* India: *Thompson-Balys.

Q465.4. *Punishment: throwing into water-filled lime pit.* Jewish: Neuman.

Q466. *Embarkation in leaky vessel as punishment.* *Type 612; BP I 126, *127.

N781. Hero embarks in rudderless boat. .S141. Exposure in boat.

Q466.0.1. *Embarcation in rudderless boat as punishment.* Icelandic: Herrmann Saxo II 650.

Q466.0.2. *Punishment: setting adrift in boat.* Irish myth: Cross.

Q466.1. *Husband substitutes leaky vessel so that his wife and paramour are drowned.* (Cf. Q241.) *Fischer-Bolte 131.

Q466.2. *Punishment: abandonment on cliff that is submerged at high tide.* Icelandic: Boberg; Maurer Bekehrung des norwegischen Stammes I 301 and n. 8.

F945. Person gradually submerged by sea.

Q467. *Punishment by drowning.* (Cf. Q552.19.) India: *Thompson-Balys; Chinese: Graham.

Q467.1. *Casting into water in sack (barrel) as punishment.* (Cf. Q474, S142.) H. Goldsmith Zs. f. vgl. Rechtswissenschaft LXI—LXII; Fb "sæk" III 720b, "tønde" III 934b; Italian: Basile Pentamerone IV No. 6.

Q467.2. *Thief cast into water in a sack containing a cock, a snake, and a monkey.* He had stolen a sacred statue of gold. (Cf. Q212, Q220.) Italian Novella: Rotunda.

Q467.3. *Punishment: drowning in swamp.* (Cf. Q474.) Grimm Rechtsalterthümer II 276ff.; Icelandic: *Boberg.

Q467.3.1. *Punishment: sea-spell chanted by druidess causes rival to drown.* Irish myth: Cross.

Q467.4. *Man thrown into waterfall as punishment for alleged violating of princess.* (Cf. Q244.) Icelandic: FSS 110, Boberg.

Q467.5. *Marooning as punishment.* Hawaii: Beckwith Myth 499f.; Tuamotu: Stimson MS (z-G 13/346).

Q469. *Other cruel punishments.*

Q469.1. *Adulteress caused to fall down stairs from which steps have been removed.* (Cf. Q241.) *Fischer-Bolte 217.

Q469.2. *Punishment: climbing red-hot rod.* (Cf. S112.2.) Jamaica: Beckwith MAFLS XVII 75 No. 68.

Q469.3. *Punishment: grinding up in a mill.* Liebrecht 258f.; Fb "male" II 535a; India: Thompson-Balys.

Q469.4. *Punishment: millstone hung around neck.* Woman has had desire to kill frog. (Cf. Q211.8.) Tobler 28.

Q469.5. *Punishment: choking with smoke.* This given a lawyer who has "sold smoke", i.e., idle words. BP III 495 n.; *Pauli (ed. Bolte) No. 786; Scala Celi 7b No. 48.

Q469.6. *Heart and liver of murderer torn out.* (Cf. Q211.) Icelandic: *Boberg; Chinese: Werner 339.

Q469.6.0.1. *Heart of murderer cut out.* (Cf. Q211.) Irish myth: Cross.

Q469.6.1. *Heart and liver of son to be torn out.* (Cf. S194.) French Canadian: Sister Marie Ursule.

Q469.7. *Punishment: twisting entrails from body.* Fb III 776a; Mannhardt Wald- und Feldkulte I 28; Heinzel Beschreibung der isländischen Saga 162.

Q559.11. Man miraculously made to excrete his entrails for heresy.
S139.1. Murder by twisting out intestines.

Q469.7.1. *Man fettered with the entrails of his own sons as punishment for treachery.* (Cf. Q261.) Icelandic: MacCulloch Eddic 146 (Loki).

Q469.8. *Punishment: sawing in twain.* Italian Novella: Rotunda.

P461.3. Soldier is ordered to fire enemy's armada. Is caught and sawed in two.

Q469.9. *Punishment: boring hot irons through ears.* (Cf. S112.2.) Italian Novella: Rotunda.

Q469.9.1. *Punishment: tearing off flesh with hot pincers.* Italian Novella: Rotunda.

Q469.9.2. *Punishment: piercing with needles.* India: Thompson-Balys.

D2063.1.1. Tormenting by sympathetic magic.

Q469.10. *Scalding as punishment.*

Q469.10.1. *Scalding as punishment for attempted seduction.* (Cf. Q243.2.1.) Italian Novella: Rotunda.

Q469.10.2. *Scalding as punishment for theft.* (Cf. Q212.) Italian Novella: Rotunda.

Q469.10.3. *Scalding as punishment for insult.* Italian Novella: Rotunda.

Q469.11. *Baby son hurled into battle as punishment for desertion of fairy mistress.* (Cf. Q247, Q411.3.) Irish myth: Cross.

Q469.12. *Murderer torn limb from limb.* (Cf. Q211, Q416.) Irish myth: Cross; Icelandic: Boberg; Jewish: Neuman.

Q469.13. *Hands in cleft log as punishment.* (Cf. K1111, Q435.) India: Thompson-Balys.

Q470. Humiliating punishments. Irish myth: *Cross; India: Thompson-Balys.

D2063. Magic discomfort. K1218.1.4. Importunate lover (priest) is forced to hide in chest. K1218.6. Importunate lover beaten and sent on street bearing a humiliating placard. M348. Curse: humiliation. Q523. Humiliating penances. S175. Horses mutilated: tails cut off and manes torn off with the skin in order to humiliate their owner.

Q471. *Spitting in face as punishment.* Spanish: Espinosa Jr. No. 138; Jewish: *Neuman; India: Thompson-Balys.

Q471.1. *Persecuted queen meanly clothed and set where all are commanded to spit on her.* Köhler-Bolte I 571.

Q471.2. *Beggar avenges self on queen who spits at him by disguising as prince and spitting in her face.* India: Thompson-Balys.

Q472. *Branding as punishment.* (Cf. H55.) BP III 114 n. 1; Cosquin Études 428ff.; *Fischer-Bolte 215; Child II 240ff., 513a, III 514, IV 476, V225b; Icelandic: *Boberg; Spanish: Espinosa III No. 192; India: *Thompson-Balys; Hindu: Meyer Hindu Tales 110.

Q473. *Punishment: disgraceful journey through streets.* (Cf. Q432.2.)

Q473.0.1. *Insolvent debtor drawn through streets.* (Cf. Q271.) Breton: Sébillot Incidents s.v. "débiteur".

Q473.0.2. *Corpse of adulteress drawn through streets.* (Cf. Q241.) Icelandic: Boberg.

Q473.1. *Punishment: riding through street on bull.*

Q473.1.1. *Adulteress ridden through street on bull.* (Cf. Q241.) *Wesselski Hodscha Nasreddin II 185 No. 349.

Q473.2. *Punishment: tying to horse's tail.* Fb "hest" IV 212a; Icelandic: Boberg.

Q473.2.1. *Wife's paramour tied to horse's tail and conducted through streets.* (Cf. Q241.) Malone PMLA XLIII 413.

Q473.3. *Seducer, who had disguised as woman, is led naked through streets.* (Cf. Q243.2.) Cent Nouvelles Nouvelles No. 45; Italian Novella: *Rotunda.

K1321.1.2. Seducer successfully disguises as a washerwoman for fifteen years. Finally exposed.

Q473.4. *Importunate lover put asleep in street.* Italian Novella: Rotunda.

D1972. Lover's magic sleep at rendezvous. K1218. Importunate lovers led astray.

Q473.5. *Punishment: sending out of town on donkeys.* India: *Thompson-Balys.

Q473.5.1. *Punishment: shaving head and covering with tar and driving forth on back of donkey to sound of drum.* Stranger thinks he is being honored. India: Thompson-Balys.

J953. Self-deception of the lowly.

Q473.5.2. *Riding backwards on donkey as punishment.* India: Thompson-Balys.

Q473.6. *Punishment: princess to display self on roof.* India: Thompson-Balys.

Q474. *"Cucking-stool" as punishment.* (Cf. Q467.3, Q467.1.) Victim is suspended in a basket over filth and thrown in. *Spargo Virgil the Necromancer (Cambridge, Mass., 1934) 147ff.; *J. Grimm Deutsche Rechtsalterthümer (ed. Hensler u. Hübner, Leipzig, 1899) II 162, 363ff.

Q475. *Tar and feathers as punishment.* (Cf. K31.1, K216.2.) *Fb "tjære" III 811a, "fjer" I 301; Icelandic: *Boberg; Japanese: Ikeda.

Q475.1. *Tar and feathers as punishment for vanity.* Type 833*.

Q475.2. *Shower of pitch as punishment.* Roberts 208.

Q476. *Exposing mistress's person (excepting face) to her husband (paramour's friends).* Italian Novella: *Rotunda.

Q478. *Frightful meal as punishment.* Buddhist myth: Malalasekera II 597.

H1567.1. Frightful meal as test of leadership. Q491.5. Skull used as drinking cup. S183. Frightful meal. S183.1. Person forced to eat hearts (flesh) of relatives (drink blood).

Q478.1. *The Eaten Heart.* Adulteress is caused unwittingly to eat her lover's heart. (Sometimes other parts of his body.) (Cf. Q241.) **Matzke MLN XXVI 1; **K. Nyrop Sangerens Hjærte (København, 1908); *Child V 482 s.v. "heart"; Clouston Tales II 187ff.; *v. d. Hagen I cxvi; DeCock Volkssage 94ff.; *Hibbard 253ff.; Boccaccio Decameron IV Nos. 1, 9 (Lee 116, 143); Schofield PMLA XV 123; Malone PMLA XLIII 413, 430; Nunes "A lenda de coração comido" Revista Lusitana XXVIII 5—15.—Italian Novella: *Rotunda; India: *Thompson-Balys; Marquesas: Handy 104; Hawaii: Beckwith Myth 136; Eskimo (Cumberland Sound): Boas BAM XV 223, (Greenland): Rasmussen III 241; N. A. Indian: *Thompson Tales 344 n. 241; Cape Verde Islands: *Parsons MAFLS XV (1) 140 n. 1.

G60. Human flesh eaten unwittingly. T82. Bath of blood of beloved to cure love-sick empress. B635.1.1. Eaten meat of bear lover causes unborn son to have animal characteristics.

Q478.1.1. *Man sends his daughter the heart of her lover.* She pours poison over it and drinks the potion. Italian Novella: Rotunda.

Q478.1.2. *Adulteress made to drink from paramour's skull.* (Cf. Q241, Q491.5.) Heptameron No. 32.

Q478.1.2.1. *Adulteress forced to eat out of lover's skull.* Irish myth: Cross.

Q478.1.3. *Adulteress punished by having skeleton of her former paramour hang in her room.* Heptameron No. 32.

Q478.1.4. *Adulteress forced to have lover's head before her at meals.* Irish myth: Cross.

Q478.2. *Adulteress compelled to eat with dog.* (Cf. Q241, Q478.) *Chauvin VIII 162 No. 170; Malone PMLA XLIII 430; Gibb History of the Forty Vezirs 331ff.; Irish myth: Cross.

Q478.3. *Adulteress compelled to eat a dog's leavings.* (Cf. Q241, Q523.3.) Malone PMLA XLIII 405—430 passim.

Q478.4. *Punishment: using fat rendered from daughter's mutilated corpse to cook with and to light candles.* India: Thompson-Balys.

Q478.5. *Punishment: eating ashes instead of food.* India: Thompson-Balys.

Q478.5.1. *Punishment: eating ashes (coal) mixed with food.* India: Thompson-Balys.

Q481. *Princess (queen) compelled to keep an inn.* (Cf. Q523.5.) *Type 304; BP II 503; Fb "kro" II 303.

H11.1. Recognition by telling life history.

Q482. *Punishment: noble person must do menial service.* (Cf. A181, H465.) Irish: *Cross, Beal XXI 319f., O'Suilleabhain 53; Missouri French: Carrière; Greek: Grote I 54; Jewish: Neuman; India: *Thompson-Balys; Tuamotu: Stimson MS (z-G. 13/48, z-G. 3/1386).

Q482.1. *Princess serves as menial.* *Type 425; India: Thompson-Balys.

Q482.1.1. *Second wife (slave) must serve as menial.* Irish myth: *Cross.

Q482.2. *Queen placed in kitchen and abused by butcher.* Irish myth: Cross. Welsh: MacCulloch Celtic 101.

Q482.2.1. *Queen forced to do menial service rescued by son.* Irish myth: *Cross.

Q482.2.2. *Queen ordered to go and live in woodcutter's house as servant.* India: Thompson-Balys.

Q482.3. *Nobleman after death must serve as menial.* *Herbert III 283ff.

Q482.4. *Cast-forth wife must sit at horse-block of palace and tell story to each newcomer and offer to carry him inside.* Irish myth: *Cross; Welsh: MacCulloch Celtic 94.

Q482.5. *Queen made to scare crows away in fields.* India: Thompson-Balys.

Q482.6. *Punishment: man must do women's work.* Jewish: Neuman.

Q483. *Princess must sell goods on market as punishment.* *Type 304, 900; BP I 443ff., II 505; India: Thompson-Balys.

Q483.1. *Condemned queen exposed in leather on market place.* India: Thompson-Balys.

Q484. *Husband fondles second wife in presence of first as punishment for adultery.* (Cf. Q241.) Malone PMLA XLIII 423.

Q485. *Noble person must live in hovel.*

Q485.1. *Princess married to lowly hero must live in slave quarters.* Africa (Kordofan): Frobenius Atlantis IV 216ff. No. 19.

L132. Pig-sty abode for unpromising hero (heroine).

Q486. *Criminal's property destroyed as punishment.* Jewish: Neuman.

Q486.1. *Criminal's house burned down.* *Chauvin VI 163 No. 327; Irish myth: *Cross.

Q486.1.1. *Sinful city burnt as punishment.* Jewish: Moreno Esdras (Q488), Neuman.

Q487. *Adulteress forced to wear symbolic dress.* Husband makes her dress in coarse cloth except for her undefiled parts which are covered with gold brocade. (Cf. Q241.) Cent Nouvelles Nouvelles No. 49; Italian Novella: *Rotunda.

Q488. *Cutting hair as punishment.*

Q488.1. *Lying goat punished by being half-shorn.* (Cf. Q263, K1151.) *Type 212; *BP I 346ff.

Q488.2. *Head shaved as punishment.* India: *Thompson-Balys.

Q491. *Indignity to corpse as punishment.* (Cf. Q271.1.) Jewish: *Neuman; India: Thompson-Balys.

Q491.1. *Disgraceful burial as punishment.* Jewish: Neuman.

Q491.1.1. *Swindler buried on dungheap.* (Cf. Q274.) Spanish: Boggs FFC XC 143 No. 1720.

Q491.1.2. *Burial in deserted barn as punishment for desecration of holy places.* (Cf. Q222.) Irish myth: Cross.

Q491.2. *Debtor's corpse flogged.* (Cf. Q271.) *Fb "gjæld" I 448.

Q491.3. *Devil beats wicked man's corpse.* Estonian: Aarne FFC XXV 124 No. 50.

Q491.4. *Toads and snakes devour corpse of rich man in his grave.* Scala Celi 74b No. 426; Herbert III 99 No. 65, 666 No. 261; Irish: Beal XXI 327, O'Suilleabhain 74.

Q491.5. *Skull used as drinking cup.* (Cf. Q478.1.2.) DeCock Volkssage 96ff.; Icelandic: *Boberg; Italian Novella: Rotunda; India: Thompson-Balys.

F866.4. Cup made of skulls. M316. Prophecy: strength to be gained when milk is drunk from hero's skull. S183.1. Person forced to eat hearts (flesh) of relatives (drink blood).

Q491.6. *Corpse of murderer mutilated.* (Cf. Q211.) Italian Novella: *Rotunda; Greek: Grote I 275, 278.

Q491.6.1. *Murderer's corpse cut into pieces.* Irish myth: Cross.

Q491.7. *Punishment: throwing dead body into river.* Africa (Fang): Trilles 270.

Q492. *Woman must relight magic fires as punishment.* Magician in revenge for ill-treatment causes the lights of the city to go out. They can be relighted only from the naked body of the woman in the public square. None can be relighted until all have applied their torches. Spargo Virgil the Necromancer (Cambridge, Mass., 1934) 199ff.; *Oertel Studien zur vgl. Literaturgeschichte VIII 113; Spanish Exempla: Keller; Italian Novella: *Rotunda.

D2158.2. Magic extinguishing of fires. K1211. Vergil in the basket. A lover who is to be pulled up to his mistress's window is left hanging in the basket in the public gaze. K1212. Lover left standing in snow.

Q493. *Punishment: being saddled and ridden as horse.* India: *Thompson-Balys.

Q493.1. *Adulteress transformed to mare and stirruped.* (Cf. Q241.) *Penzer VI 8.

Q494. *Loss of social position as punishment.* Jewish: Neuman.

Q494.1. *Line of kingship taken from king who defies saint.* (Cf. Q227.) Irish myth: *Cross; Jewish: Neuman.

Q494.1.1. *Uncharitable king loses power.* (Cf. Q286.) Irish myth: Cross.

Q494.2. *Removal from priesthood as punishment.* Jewish: *Neuman.

Q495. *Punishment: unseemly exposure of body.* Jewish: Neuman.

Q495.1. *Lazy wife taken naked in bundle of straw to a wedding.* (Cf. Q321.) Type 902*; Lithuanian: Balys Index No. 902*; Estonian: Aarne FFC XXV No. 902*; Russian: Andrejev No. 902*; Japanese: Ikeda.

Q497. *Beard shaved as punishment for murder.* (Cf. Q211, P672.) Italian Novella: Rotunda.

Q497.1. *Moustache pulled out as punishment.* India: Thompson-Balys.

Q499. *Other humiliating punishments.* Irish myth: Cross.

Q499.1. *Humiliating kiss as punishment.*

Q499.1.1. *Humiliation through kissing a leper as punishment.* Irish myth: *Cross.

Q499.2. *Humiliating death as punishment.* (Cf. Q411.) Irish myth: *Cross.

Q499.2.1. *Humiliating death as punishment for adultery.* (Cf. Q241.) Irish myth: Cross.

Q499.2.2. *Humiliating death as punishment for taking concubine.* (Cf. Q243.3.) Irish myth: Cross.

Q499.3. *Sacrament refused as punishment for desecration of holy place.* (Cf. Q222.) Irish myth: Cross.

Q499.4. *Satirizing as punishment for refusal to grant request.* (Cf. Q287.) Irish myth: *Cross.

Q499.4.1. *Satirizing as punishment for breaking treaty.* Irish myth: Cross.

Q499.5. *Debtor clerics forbidden churchly offices.* (Cf. Q271.) Irish myth: Cross.

Q499.6. *Penance for three years and a half for eating horseflesh.* Irish myth: *Cross.

C221.1.1.2. Tabu: eating horsemeat. C756.4. Tabu: entering chariot less than three weeks after having eaten horseflesh.

Q499.7. *Humiliating marriage as punishment.* India: *Thompson-Balys.

L161. Lowly hero marries princess. T62. Princess to marry first man who asks her. T91.6.4. Princess falls in love with lowly boy.

Q499.8. *Humiliating penance: king to rub nose five times on red hot griddle.* India: Thompson-Balys.

Q500. Tedious punishments.

Q501. *Unremitting torture as punishment.*

Q501.1. *Punishment of Sisyphus.* Must keep rolling a great stone up hill. It continually falls down. Reinach Revue Archéologique 1903 (4) Series I 154ff.; Greek: Frazer Apollodorus I 78 n. 3.

C51.4. Tabu: revealing secrets of god. D1649.1. Magic object keeps falling down.

Q501.2. *Punishment of Tantalus.* Stands in a pool that ever recedes from his thirsty lips; branches of fruit spring away from him; stone over his head continually threatens to fall. Reinach Revue Archéologique 1903 (4) series I 154ff.; *Frazer Pausanias V 392; Greek: *Frazer Apollodorus II 154 n. 2; Jewish: *Neuman.

A1074.5. Fettered monster kept just out of reach of water. D1432.1. Water gradually envelops girl filling pitcher. R111.2.3. Princess rescued from giant's cave where she is fettered to a chair by the hair in front of food which she cannot reach.

Q501.2.1. *When hungry man tries to gather fruit it flies out of his reach.* India: Thompson-Balys.

Q501.2.2. *Punishment: delicious food always fills with maggots just as man is about to eat it.* India: Thompson-Balys.

Q501.3. *Punishment of Loki.* A serpent above him continually drops venom in his face. Icelandic: Boberg.

Q501.4. *Punishment of Prometheus.* Chained to a mountain with eagle preying on his vitals, which are restored nightly. (Punishment for theft of fire.) Greek: *W. Schmid Untersuchungen zum gefesselten Prometheus (Stuttgart, 1929), Fox 13, *Frazer Apollodorus I 228 n. 2; Jewish: Neuman.

A1074.4. Fettered monster preyed upon by vulture. A1415. Theft of fire. C948.4. Man's liver snatched away because of broken tabu.

Q501.5. *Punishment of Ixion.* Lashed to a wheel which revolves continually. Greek: Fox 144, *Frazer Apollodorus II 148 n. 1.

Q501.6. *Punishment of Io.* Transformed to cow with gadfly ceaselessly pursuing. Greek: Fox 29.

Q501.7. *Unremittent thirst as punishment.* Irish myth: Cross.

Q501.7.1. *Salt food without drink as punishment for man who accepts Christianity.* (Cf. Q232.) Irish myth: Cross.

Q501.8. *Ceaseless humming (singing) as punishment for immoderate request.* (Cf. Q338.) Irish myth: *Cross.

Q501.9. *Spirit in hell must bathe people endlessly.* (Cf. Q578.) Spanish Exempla: Keller.

Q502. *Wandering as a punishment.*

Q502.1. *The Wandering Jew.* Ceaseless wandering with inability to die as punishment for blasphemy. (Cf. Q221.3.) Type 754**; **L. Neubaur Die Sage vom Ewigen Jude[2] (Leipzig, 1893); **Zirus Ahasverus, der Ewige Jude (Stoff- und Motivgeschichte der deutschen Literatur No. 6 [Berlin, 1930]); Gielen de Wandelende Jood (Amsterdam, 1931); *K. Nyrop Den evige Jøde (København, 1907); **Neubaur Zs. f. Vksk. XXII 33, Zentralblatt für Bibliothekswesen XXVIII 495ff.; *Dübe Zs. F. Vksk. XVII 143; *Bolte ibid. XIX 308; G. Paris. Légendes du moyen âge[2] (1904) 149ff.; *Fb "Jerusalems skomager" II 40, IV 246a; *Wehrhan 50; Taylor MLN XXXIII 394ff.; Anderson Journal of English and Germanic Philology XLVI 367—82; Braddy California Folklore Quarterly IV 82f.; Bagatti Franciscan Studies IX 1—9. — Finnish-Swedish: Wessman 105 No. 933; Lithuanian: Balys Index No. 778*; Estonian: Aarne FFC XXV No. 754*.

E411. Dead cannot rest because of a sin. F571. Extremely old person.

Q502.2. *Punishment: wandering till iron shoes are worn out.* *Types 400, 425; *BP II 272; Missouri French: Carrière; Italian: Basile Pentamerone V No. 4.

H241. Worn-out shoes as proof of long journey. H1125. Task: traveling till iron shoes are worn out. H1583.1. Time measured by worn iron shoes.

Q502.3. *Tribe's long wandering in wilderness as punishment.* Jewish: Neuman.

Q503. *Wandering after death as punishment.*

E411. Dead cannot rest because of a sin. E501.3. Wild huntsmen wander because of sin. E511. The Flying Dutchman. A sea captain because of his wickedness sails his phantom ship eternally without coming to harbor.

Q503.1. *Skull of suicide must roll in dust until it has saved a life.* Man uses the skull to kill an owl that was about to kill a rabbit; thus after 777 years of rolling it has saved a life and is freed. (Cf. Q211.5.) Köhler-Bolte I 406.

Q545. Murderer's penance complete when he kills a greater murderer. R261.1. Pursuit by rolling head.

Q511. *Punishment: carrying corpse of murdered man.* (Cf. Q211.) RTP II 267, VIII 586; FL IX 375ff. No. 3; Zs. f. österreichische Volkskunde VII 197; Irish myth: *Cross.

Q511.1. *Punishment: carrying corpse of murdered man until stone as long as murdered man is found.* This is to be put on the grave. Irish: MacCulloch Celtic 72, Cross.

Q511.2. *Punishment: carrying corpse of murdered man until another can be induced to take it.* Africa (Gold Coast): Barker and Sinclair 66 No. 9.

Q512. *Punishment: performing impossible task.* (Cf. H1010.)

Q512.0.1. *Performing impossible task as punishment for murder.* (Cf. Q211.) Irish myth: Cross.

Q512.1. *Punishment: filling leaky vessels with water from a bottomless jar.* (Cf. H1023.2.) Greek: Fox 31.

Q512.2. *Punishment: binding together sand and string.* (Cf. H1021.1.) Swiss: Jegerlehner Oberwallis 304 No. 24.

Q512.3. *Punishment: ridding country of pests.* Irish myth: *Cross.

Q520. Penances. *Types 756ABC; *BP III 463; **Andrejev FFC LIV, LXIX 126 ff., 234ff.; *Toldo II 87; Irish: Beal XXI 316, *Cross; Jewish: *Neuman.

B253.3. Fox fasts as penance. E451.2. Ghost laid when penance is done. M292. Wife undertakes man's penances for him: also to go to heaven for him? Q172.3. Man admitted to heaven as reward for penance.

Q520.0.1. *Substitutions for penances.* Irish myth: *Cross.

Q520.1. *Murderer does penance.* (Cf. Q171.1.1, Q211.) *Types 756BC; **Andrejev FFC LIV, LXIX 85, 118ff., 238ff.; Italian Novella: Rotunda.

D1549.7. Murdered man's head will cause earth to burn up or sea to boil: must be carried about.

Q520.2. *Robber does penance.* (Cf. Q212.) *Types 756B; **Andrejev FFC LXIX 81, 118ff., 236ff; Spanish Exempla: Keller;. Italian Novella: *Rotunda.

Q520.3. *Life-long penance for brother-sister marriage.* *Bolte Zs. f. Vksk. XXVIII 75.

Q242. Incest punished. T415. Brother-sister incest.

Q520.4. *King who loved to give death sentence accepts penance of always postponing sentence until thirty days period of examination has passed.* Spanish Exempla: Keller.

Q520.5. *Penance in wilderness as punishment for men who left holy orders to marry.* (Cf. Q226.) Spanish Exempla: Keller.

Q520.6. *Warrior retires to a cloister which he later defends against robbers.* Icelandic: Boberg.

Q521. *Tedious penances.* (Cf. H1110, Q500.)

Q521.1. *Doing penance till green leaves grow on a dry branch.* *Types 756ABC; *BP III 463; **Andrejev FFC LIV 34, LXIX 126, 129ff., 241ff.; Irish: O'Suilleabhain 49; Spanish: Espinosa II Nos. 79f., Espinosa Jr. No. 186; Chinese: Eberhard FFC CXX 143.

F971.1. Dry rod blossoms. Z61. Never. Various ways of expressing this idea.

Q521.1.1. *Penance: crawling on knees and watering a dry staff until it blooms. Types* 756BC; **Andrejev FFC LIV 34, LXIX 132; *BP III 471 n. 1; Scala Celi 136a No. 755; Alphabet No. 568.

Q521.1.2. *Penance: carrying water in mouth from a distance and watering dry staff until it blooms.* *Types 756BC; **Andrejev FFC LIV 34, LXIX 133; *BP III 471 n. 1.

Q521.2. *Penance: carrying bag of stones (one for each murder) on the back until it falls off.* (Cf. Q211.) *Type 756C; *Andrejev FFC LIV 35.

Q521.3. *Penance: carrying iron hoop on head until it falls off.* *Types 756C; *Andrejev FFC LIV 35.

Q521.4. *Penance: pasturing black sheep until they become white.* *Types 756C; *Andrejev FFC LIV 35.

Q521.5. *Penance: ferryman setting people over a stream until relieved by another.* *Types 460, 461; *Aarne FFC XXIII 138.

H1292.8. Question (on quest): When will a ferryman be released from his duty? Answer: When he is able to get out of the boat and leave the oar in another's hand.

Q521.6. *Penance: holding midnight mass until someone will make responses.* *Sébillot RTP X 584, XIII 179, XV 621; Ireland: Baughman, O'Suilleabhain 27, Beal XXI 308; Spanish: Espinosa II Nos. 70f.

Q521.7. *Penance to be done until seven spires of Benares are reduced to powder and rebuilt.* India: Thompson-Balys.

Q522. *Self-torture as penance.* *Andrejev FFC LXIX 127, 156.

Q522.1. *Self-crucifixion as penance.* (Cf. Q462.) *Andrejev FFC LXIX 156f.

Q522.2. *Penance: killing oneself with wooden knife.* *Andrejev FFC LXIX 156.

Q522.3. *Penance: creeping naked through thorns.* *Type 756B; *Andrejev FFC LXIX 127; Hdwb. d. Märchens I 202a; Irish: O'Suilleabhain 44, Beal XXI 316; Spanish Exempla: Keller.

Q522.4. *Penance: pilgrimage with hands and loins weighted with iron.* Child II 128.

Q522.5. *Penance: iron band forged round a man's waist.* Child I 172.

Q522.6. *Penance: hanging for a thousand years head downward over a fire of chaff.* Hindu: Keith 168.

Q522.7. *Penance: wearing friar's cord about bare skin.* Heptameron No. 41.

Q522.8. *Penance: man wears huge serpent coiled around him in lieu of clothing.* Spanish Exempla: Keller.

Q523. *Humiliating penances.* (Cf. Q470.)

Q523.1. *Penance: crawling to Rome on knees.* *Andrejev FFC LXIX 127.

Q523.1.1. *Penance: crawling to grave on knees.* Irish: O'Suilleabhain 48.

Q523.2. *Penance: walking on all-fours like beast.* Herbert III 131, 339, 465, 571; *Williams 10; Spanish Exempla: Keller.

Q523.3. *Penance: eating food offered to dogs.* *Dickson 257 n. 80; English: Wells 136 (Sir Gowther); Irish: Beal XXI 330; Spanish: Boggs FFC XC 86 No. 756B.

Q478.3. Adulteress compelled to eat a dog's leavings.

Q523.4. *Penance: living under stairs as mendicant.* *Dickson 255 n. 77; Alphabet No. 600 (Alexius).

K1815.1.1. Pious pilgrim dies unknown in his father's house.

Q523.5. *Penance: planting garden and offering free hospitality to all.* (Cf. Q481.) *Type 756C; *Andrejev FFC LIV.

Q523.6. *Penance: slain cats, dogs, etc. to be hung up and covered with grain by man who has killed them.* Köhler-Bolte I 261.

Q523.7. *Penance: seven years' service for seven days' neglect of religious duty.* (Cf. Q223.) Jewish: bin Gorion Born Judas[2] I 179f., 374.

Q523.8. *Penance: performing all services asked for by anyone.* Klapper Erzählungen des Mittelalters 112 No. 101.

Q523.9. *Penance: king to take off crown and lick spittle from ground.* India: Thompson-Balys.

Q523.10. *Penance: fasting in sackcloth and ashes.* Jewish: *Neuman.

Q524. *Fearful penances.* Irish myth: Cross.

H1400. Tests of fear.

Q524.1. *Penance: spending lonely night in cave.* Irish myth: *Cross.

Q524.2. *Penance: lying the first night with every corpse brought to certain church.* Irish myth: *Cross.

Q525. *Dangerous penances.* Irish myth: Cross.

Q525.1. *Penance: staying on rock in dashing sea.* Irish myth: Cross.

Q526. *Pilgrimage as penance.* Irish myth: *Cross.

Q527. *Penance: inviting one Brahmin for dinner every Wednesday.* India: Thompson-Balys.

Q535. *Negative penances.* Irish myth: Cross.

Q535.1. *Penance: not to speak.* *Krappe Balor 181ff.; *Toldo II 91; *Dickson 255 nn. 76, 77; English: Wells 136 (Sir Gowther); Spanish: Boggs FFC XC 86 No. 756B, Keller.

C401. Tabu: speaking during certain time.

Q535.2. *Penance: lioness foregoes meat.* Her two cubs are killed. The jackal tells her that he has had the same experience. She gives up eating meat and lives on grass. Chauvin II 105 No. 68; Bødker Exempler 302 No. 71; Spanish Exempla: Keller.

B250. Religious animals.

Q535.3. *Refraining from sexual intercourse as penance.* (Cf. C110.) Irish myth: Cross.

Q535.4. *Lone fasting as penance.* Jewish: Neuman.

Q537. *Penance: resisting temptation.* (Cf. T330.)

Q537.1. *Penance: adulteress masks as monk and lives chastely in monastery.* (Cf. Q241.) Toldo Zs. f. Vksk. XIV 52 (St. Theodora).

Q537.2. *Cleric tempts self among beautiful women, lives chastely.* Irish myth: Cross.

Q541. *Sitting (standing) in uncomfortable position as penance.*

Q541.1. *Penance: sitting in water.* *Dickson 91f. nn. 57—69; *Toldo II 94f.; Irish myth: *Cross.

Q541.1.1. *Standing in (Jordan and Tigris) rivers as penance (by Adam and Eve).* (Cf. A1331.) Irish myth: *Cross.

Q541.2. *Penance: standing in water for forty days.* Dh I 228ff.; Irish: O'Suilleabhain 49, Beal XXI 318.

Q541.3. *Penance: Gregory on the stone.* Standing on a stone (pillar) as penance for incest. (Cf. Q242, T415.) *Type 933; Köhler-Bolte Zs. f. Vksk. VI 173 to Gonzenbach No. 85; *Baum PMLA XXXI 562 n. 59; *Toldo II 89.

Q541.4. *Penance: keeping self suspended on two iron hooks placed under armpits.* Irish myth: *Cross.

Q541.5. *Penance: staying for ten months rooted to one spot, with eyes closed, while birds build nests in one's hair.* India: Thompson-Balys.

Q542. *Penance: giving all earnings to poor.* Spanish: Boggs FFC XC 86 No. 756B.

Q544. *Penance: being locked in cellar (well) with key thrown into water.* *Type 756B; *Andrejev FFC LXIX 127, 248.

R41.3. Captivity in dungeon.

Q545. *Murderer's penance complete when he kills a greater murderer and prevents a crime.* (Cf. Q211.) *Type 756C; **Andrejev FFC LIV; Wesselski Archiv Orientální II 39ff.

J210. Choice between evils. Q503.1. Skull of suicide must roll in dust till it has saved a life.

Q550. Miraculous punishments.

A1115.2. Why the sea is salt. Magic salt mill is stolen by sea-captain, who takes it aboard and orders it to grind. It will stop only for its master; ship sinks and mill keeps grinding salt. D444.1. Transformation: money of the hard-hearted to scorpions. D471.1. Transformation: bread to stone. As punishment. D472.1. Transformation: food to muck. As punishment. D475.2.3. Transformation: money to ashes (leaves). F171.6. Mysterious punishments in otherworld. N339.5. Uxorious king is burned to death while taking an alcohol bath. Q331.2.1.2. Vain woman has her cheeks miraculously burned. Q451.3. Loss of speech as punishment. Q451.7.0.1. Loss of eye as punishment.

Q550.1. *Supernatural manifestations at death of wicked person.* Finnish-Swedish: Wessman 1 Nos. 7, 8, 9.

D2141.0.5. Storm at death of wicked person. E410. The unquiet grave. Dead unable to rest in peace. F960.2. Extraordinary nature phenomena at death of holy person.

Q551. *Magic manifestations as punishments.*

Q551.1. *Undutiful son punished by toad clinging to face.* (Cf. Q281.1.) *BP III 167; Köhler-Bolte I 473ff.; *Ward II 664; Herbert III 343; Pauli (ed. Bolte) No. 437; Irish: Beal XXI 317.

A751.3.1. Man in moon a frog which has jumped into person's face and remains there.

Q551.1.1. *Betel-nut grows upon a person's knee as a punishment.* Philippine (Tinguian): Cole 56.

Q551.2. *Punishment: animal skin grows on man's back.* He had masked in the skin in order to cheat. *Type 831; Irish myth: *Cross; India: Thompson-Balys.

D2171.3. Magic adhesion to animal. K1810. Deception by disguise. Q260. Deceptions punished.

Q551.2.1. *Magic adhesion to object as punishment (for opposition to holy person).* (Cf. D2171.1, Q227.) Irish myth: *Cross.

Q551.2.2. *Miraculous adhesion of objects to human hand as punishment for working on holy day.* (Cf. Q223.6.) *Loomis White Magic 55.

Q551.2.3. *Thief rendered unable to remove burden of stolen goods from his back.* (Cf. Q212.) *Loomis White Magic 55, 98.

Q551.2.4. *Corpse of murdered man sticks to murderer's back.* (Cf. Q211.) *Loomis White Magic 55.

Q551.2.5. *Instrument or tool for unlawful work becomes attached to person holding it.* *Loomis White Magic 55.

Q551.2.6. *Sacrilege and blasphemy punished by magic adhesion.* (Cf. Q221.3.) *Loomis White Magic 55f.

Q551.2.7. *Priest's concubine is unable to rise from stone.* She is finally freed by prayers and repentance. (Cf. Q243.1.) England: Baughman.

Q551.2.8. *Punishment for stinginess: bundle of fuel (pitcher of lime) sticks to man's head.* (Cf. Q276.) India: Thompson-Balys.

Q551.2.8.1. *Punishment for cupidity: rich man's foot caught in church door:* extricated only when he sends money to beggar. India: Thompson-Balys.

Q551.3. *Punishment: transformation.* (Cf. D661.) Greek: Grote I 32.

Q551.3.1. *Punishment: transformation of lovers into lion and lioness for desecrating temple.* They have had sexual relations in the temple. It was believed that lions do not mate with each other; hence their sin could not be repeated. Greek: *Frazer Apollodorus I 401 n. 2.

B750. Fanciful habits of animals. C51.1. Tabu: profaning shrine.

Q551.3.2. *Punishment: transformation into animal.* (Cf. Q226.2.) S. A. Indian (Toba): Métraux MAFLS XL 31.

Q551.3.2.1. *Punishment: Loki's son transformed into wolf which tears his brother to pieces.* Icelandic: MacCulloch Eddic 146.

D113.1. Transformation: man to wolf. S73.1. Fratricide.

Q551.3.2.2. *Punishment: woman transformed into bird.* India: Thompson-Balys.

Q551.3.2.3. *Punishment: transformation into frog.* India: Thompson-Balys.

Q551.3.2.4. *Punishment: transformation into monkey.* India: *Thompson-Balys.

Q551.3.2.5. *Punishment: man transformed to a mass of worms.* India: Thompson-Balys.

Q551.3.2.6. *Punishment: transformation to ass.* India: Thompson-Balys.

Q551.3.2.7. *Punishment: transformation to dog.* India: Thompson-Balys.

Q551.3.2.8. *Punishment: transformation to calf.* India: Thompson-Balys.

Q551.3.3. *Punishment: calf's head in murderer's hand turns to corpse's head.* (Cf. Q211.) *BP I 276 n. 2, II 535.

D475.3. Transformation: calf's head to death's head.

Q551.3.3.1. *Punishment: melon in murderer's hand turns to murdered man's head.* Africa (Fulah): Equilbecq II 205ff. No. 43.

Q551.3.4. *Transformation to stone as punishment.* India: Thompson-Balys.

D231. Transformation: man to stone.

Q551.3.4.1. *Scoffers turned to stone by saint.* (Cf. Q225.) Irish myth: Cross.

Q551.3.4.2. *Man curses wind; he is turned to stone, along with sack from which he is sowing.* (Cf. Q221.) England: *Baughman.

Q551.3.4.3. *Nun breaks her vow.* She is turned to stone. (Cf. Q226.) U.S.: Baughman.

Q551.3.5. *Punishment: transformation into other object.* India: Thompson-Balys.

Q551.3.5.1. *Punishment: transformation into falling star.* India: Thompson-Balys.

Q551.3.5.2. *Punishment: transformation into tree.* India: Thompson-Balys.

Q551.4. *Punishment: animals become sick.*

Q551.4.1. *Punishment: horses become sick.* India: *Thompson-Balys.

Q551.5. *Reincarnation as punishment.* (Cf. E600, Q584.3.) India: Thompson-Balys; Buddhist myth: Malalasekera I 222, 342, 424, 479, 597, 740, 1148, II 355, 670, 691, 792, 918, 1028, 1272.

Q551.5.1. *Reincarnation into degraded form as punishment.* India: *Thompson-Balys.

Q551.5.1.1. *Punishment: man reborn as girl.* (Cf. Q292.1.) India: *Thompson-Balys.

D10. Transformation to person of different sex. E605.1. Reincarnation with change of sex.

Q551.5.1.2. *Punishment: king and queen reborn as children of scavenger.* India: Thompson-Balys.

Q551.5.1.3. *Dying priest looks greedily on ripe plum: is reincarnated as insect feeding within plum.* India: Thompson-Balys.

Q551.6. *Magic sickness as punishment.* Irish myth: Cross; Icelandic: Boberg; Jewish: *Neuman; Chinese: Eberhard FFC CXX 187.

D2064. Magic sickness. Q572. Magic sickness as punishment remitted.

Q551.6.0.1. *Punishment: men stricken with leprosy.* India: *Thompson-Balys.

Q551.6.0.2. *Punishment: death from unknown disease before end of three days for having obtained food by force from monastery.* Irish myth: Cross.

Q551.6.1. *Magic sickness as punishment for lying (perjury).* (Cf. Q263, Q583.4.) Irish myth: *Cross.

Q551.6.2. *Magic sickness as punishment for opposition to holy person.* (Cf. Q227, Q572.3.) Irish myth: *Cross.

Q551.6.2.1. *Magic sickness as punishment for tanning shoes with bark from saint's tree.* Irish myth: Cross.

Q551.6.3. *Magic sickness as punishment for ingratitude.* (Cf. Q281.) Irish myth: *Cross.

Q551.6.4. *Magic sickness as punishment for theft.* (Cf. Q212, Q557.4, Q572.1.) *Loomis White Magic 98; Irish myth: Cross.

Q551.6.5. *Magic sickness as punishment for desecration of holy places (images, etc.).* (Cf. Q222.) Irish myth: *Cross.

Q551.6.5.1. *Magic manifestation: blood flows suddenly from mouth of blasphemer.* (Cf. Q221.3.) Spanish Exempla: Keller.

Q551.6.5.2. *Magic manifestation: eyes fall out of head of blasphemer.* (Cf. Q451.7.0.2.) Spanish Exempla: Keller.

Q551.6.6. *Emaciation caused by envy.* (Cf. Q302.) Irish myth: Cross.

Q551.6.7. *Magic sickness (death) as punishment for inhospitality.* (Cf. Q292.) Irish myth: *Cross.

Q551.7. *Magic paralysis as punishment.* Loomis White Magic 98f.; Irish myth: Cross; Spanish Exempla: Keller; Jewish: *Neuman.

D2072. Magic paralysis. Q573. Magic paralysis as punishment remitted.

Q551.7.1. *Magic paralysis as punishment for opposition to holy person.* (Cf. Q227, Q573.1, Q583.3.) Irish myth: *Cross.

Q551.7.1.1. *Heretic suddenly becomes tongue-tied.* India: Thompson-Balys.

Q551.7.2. *Magic paralysis as punishment for theft.* (Cf. Q212.) *Loomis White Magic 98; Irish myth: Cross.

Q551.7.3. *Magic paralysis as punishment for quarrelsomeness.* (Cf. Q306.) Irish myth: *Cross.

Q551.8. *Deformity as punishment.* Irish myth: Cross; Jewish: Neuman.

D1403. Magic object maims. D2062. Maiming by magic. H244. Person magically disfigured when he speaks falsely.

Q551.8.1. *Deformity as punishment for false judging.* (Cf. Q265.) Irish myth: *Cross.

Q551.8.2. *Deformity as punishment for desecration of holy places (images, etc.).* (Cf. Q222.) Irish myth: *Cross.

Q551.8.3. *Deformity (putridity) as punishment for murder.* (Cf. D2061.1.4, Q211.) Irish myth: *Cross.

Q551.8.4. *Man's eye bursts forth when he urges saint to marry.* (Cf. Q227, Q451.7.0.2.) Irish myth: Cross.

Q551.8.5. *Head falls off when man lies to saint.* (Cf. Q263.) Irish myth: *Cross.

Q551.8.6. *Magic punishment: tongue protrudes from mouth of sinner and blindness follows.* Spanish Exempla: Keller.

Q551.8.7. *Punishment: face distorted.* India: Thompson-Balys; Buddhist myth: Malalasekera II 600, 808.

Q551.9. *Miraculous burning as punishment.* (Cf. Q414.) Irish myth: Cross; Jewish: *Neuman; India: Thompson-Balys.

Q551.9.1. *Miraculous burning as punishment for opposition to holy person.* (Cf. Q227.) Irish myth: *Cross; India: Thompson-Balys.

Q551.9.2. *Magic burning to death as punishment for perjury.* (Cf. Q263.) Spanish Exempla: Keller.

Q551.10. *Person miraculously lifted into air and dashed to death as punishment for blasphemy.* (Cf. Q221.3, Q417.) Irish myth: Cross.

Q551.10.1. *Person miraculously lifted into air and dashed to death as punishment for scoffing at church teachings.* (Cf. Q225.) Irish myth: Cross.

Q551.11. *Magic forgetfulness as punishment.* Jewish: *Neuman.

Q551.12. *Premature aging as punishment.* (Cf. D1890.) Jewish: *Neuman.

Q552. *Prodigy as punishment.* Irish myth: *Cross; West Indies: Flowers 569f.

Q552.0.1. *Death from elements as punishment for unjust judgment (by poets).* Irish myth: *Cross.

Q552.1. *Death by thunderbolt as punishment.* *Pauli (ed. Bolte) No. 458; *Blinkenberg The Thunderweapon in Religion and Folklore (Cambridge, Eng., 1911); *P. Saintyves Pierres magiques (Paris, 1936). — Irish: *Cross, Beal XXI 336, O'Suilleabhain 123; Finnish-Swedish: Wessman 18 Nos. 165, 173; Lithuanian: Balys Index No. 3267;

Spanish Exempla: Keller; Greek: Frazer Apollodorus II 34 n. 2 (Iasion), 52 n. 2 (Asopus); Jewish: *Neuman.

A157.1. Thunderweapon. Stone weapons (axes) brought down by thunderbolt (from Thunder God). F968. Extraordinary thunder and lightning. L472. Zeus smites Capaneus while he is climbing a ladder. M447. Curse: one to be stricken by thunder.

Q552.1.0.1. *Destruction of property by thunderbolt as punishment.* (Cf. Q595.) Irish myth: *Cross.

Q552.1.0.1.1. *Thunderbolt demolishes fortress as punishment for disobedience (to saint).* (Cf. Q227, Q325.) Irish myth: Cross.

Q552.1.0.2. *Thunder slays people for disregard of him.* Lithuanian: Balys Tautosakos Darbai VI 135f.

A162.3. Combat between thundergod and devil. L471. The man scorns the storm: killed by it.

Q552.1.1. *Lightning strikes monk who despises humility.* (Cf. Q331.) Scala Celi 102b No. 152; Pauli (ed. Bolte) No. 455; Alphabet No. 116.

Q552.1.2. *Ravisher killed by thunderbolt.* (Cf. Q244.) Italian Novella: Rotunda.

Q552.1.3. *Impostor killed by lightning.* (Cf. Q262.) Chinese: Eberhard FFC CXX 110 No. 65.

Q552.1.4. *Death by thunderbolt as punishment for opposition to holy person.* (Cf. Q227.) Irish myth: *Cross.

Q552.1.5. *Death by thunderbolt as punishment for treachery.* (Cf. Q261.) Irish myth: Cross.

Q552.1.6. *Death by thunderbolt as punishment for injustice.* (Cf. Q296.) Irish myth: Cross.

Q552.1.7. *Woman who accused saint of raping her is struck by lightning.* (Cf. Q263.) Spanish Exempla: Keller.

Q552.1.8. *Infidel defies God to strike him with lightning.* God does. (Cf. Q221.3.) U. S.: Baughman.

Q552.1.8.1. *Cattle thief calls on God to strike him with lightning if he has ever stolen a cow or calf.* Lightning strikes him. U.S.: Baughman.

Q552.2. *Sinking of earth as punishment.* Irish myth: Cross; Finnish-Swedish: Wessman 18f. Nos. 164, 188; India: Thompson-Balys; Tuamotu: Henry Ancient Tahiti (Honolulu, 1928) 511.

Q552.2.0.1. *Quaking of earth as punishment.* (Cf. D2148.) Irish myth: Cross; Jewish: *Neuman.

Q552.2.0.1.1. *Earth quakes when saint is opposed.* (Cf. Q227.) Irish myth: *Cross.

Q552.2.1. *Land sinks and lake appears as punishment.* *Fb "so" III 449b; Loomis White Magic 41, 101; England: Baughman; Lithuanian: Balys Index No. 787*; Chinese: Werner 405.

Q552.2.2. *Grave sinks so that grave-robbers cannot get out.* (Cf. Q212.2.) Estonian: Aarne FFC XXV 116 No. 17.

Q552.2.3. *Earth swallowings as punishment.* (Cf. F940, Q221.4.3.) Irish: *Cross, Beal XXI 327, O'Suilleabhain 79; Lithuanian: Balys Index

Nos. 3610, 3748, Legends Nos. 467f., 470f; Jewish: *Neuman; India: *Thompson-Balys.

L424. Man who has never known unhappiness or want is swallowed up by earth with all his household. M448. Curse: to sink into earth.

Q552.2.3.1. *Girl sinks into earth for dancing in church.* (Cf. C51.1.5, Q386.) Fb "kirkegaard" II 129.

Q552.2.3.1.1. *Earth swallows man who opposes saint (holy man).* (Cf. Q227.) Loomis White Magic 44; Irish myth: *Cross; Buddhist myth: Malalasekera I 798, II 1220.

Q552.2.3.1.2. *Earth swallows man as punishment for sacrilege (blasphemy, heresy, etc.).* (Cf. Q221.3.) *Loomis White Magic 101; Irish myth: *Cross.

Q552.2.3.1.3. *Man who angers saint sinks into earth to his knees.* (Cf. Q227.) Irish myth: Cross.

Q552.2.3.2. *Earth swallows object as punishment.* Irish myth: Cross.

Q552.2.3.2.1. *Earth swallows mill in which saint's grain was refused grinding.* (Cf. Q227.) Irish myth: *Cross.

Q552.2.3.2.2. *Earth swallows heretical city.* (Cf. Q225.1.) Irish myth: *Cross.

Q552.2.3.2.3. *Island sinks for man's offense to saint.* (Cf. Q227.) Irish myth: *Cross.

Q552.2.3.3. *Saint causes parricide to sink into earth to his knees.* (Cf. D1713, Q211.1.) Irish myth: Cross.

Q552.2.3.4. *Earth swallows man intending treachery.* (Cf. Q261.1.) Irish myth: Cross.

Q552.3. *Failure of crops during reign of wicked king.* (Cf. Q552.10.1.) Irish: MacCulloch Celtic 72, *Cross; Icelandic: *Boberg; Greek: Grote I 171, 203; Jewish: Neuman; India: *Thompson-Balys.

A1101.1.1. Reign of peace and justice (under certain king). C563.3. Tabu: king allowing rapine during his reign. C938. Rulers of inferior character after tabu is broken. D2081. Land made magically sterile. F970. Extraordinary behavior of trees and plants.

Q552.3.0.1. *Failure of crops as punishment for uncharitableness.* (Cf. Q286.) Irish myth: Cross.

Q552.3.0.2. *Failure of crops as punishment for murder.* (Cf. Q211.) Irish myth: Cross.

Q552.3.0.3. *Failure of crops and milk as punishment for adultery.* (Cf. Q241.) Irish myth: Cross.

Q552.3.0.4. *Failure of crops for mistreating the dead.* Africa (Cameroon): Mansfield 233.

Q552.3.1. *Famine as punishment.* *Loomis White Magic 95, 102; Irish myth: *Cross; India: Thompson-Balys.

Q552.3.1.1. *Sterility of land as punishment for parricide.* (Cf. Q211.1.) Irish myth: Cross.

Q552.3.2. *Famine as punishment for oppression by victors.* Irish myth: Cross.

Q552.3.3. *Drought as punishment.* Irish myth: Cross; Jewish: Neuman; India: Thompson-Balys.

Q552.3.4. *Food magically disappears.* India: Thompson-Balys; Hawaii: Beckwith Myth 431.

Q552.3.5. *Punishment for greed: streams of sugar, molasses, and milk from anchorite's tomb dry up and petrify because of townspeople's greed.* (Cf. Q272.) India: Thompson-Balys.

Q552.3.6. *Punishment: water famine.* India: *Thompson-Balys.

Q552.3.7. *Murrain upon cattle as punishment.* Jewish: *Neuman.

Q552.4. *Ear of stolen animal protrudes from thief's mouth.* (Cf. Q212.) Irish: Plummer cxliii, *Cross; *Loomis White Magic 98.

Q552.4.1. *Stolen animal cries out from stomach of thief.* *Loomis White Magic 98; Spanish Exempla: Keller.

Q552.5. *Monstrous births as punishment for girl's pride.* (Cf. M437, Q331, T550.) Child I 210; Ireland, U.S.: Baughman.

Q552.5.1. *Man who cuts off tongue of swallow has dumb children.* (Cf. Q285.1.1.) Finnish-Swedish: Wessman 19 No. 182; Japanese: Ikeda.

Q552.6. *Rich lord who robs poor widow of her cow chokes on first mouthful.* (Cf. Q212.) Herbert III 35ff.

Q552.7. *Mary-image descends and chastises clerk who scoffs at its rude carving.* (Cf. Q225.) Ward II 676 No. 61.

Q552.8. *Dead cock rises, crows, and spatters scoffers so that they become leprous.* (Cf. Q225.) Alphabet No. 117.

Q552.9. *Punishment: woman who has prevented birth of children casts no shadow.* (Cf. Q251.) *Type 755; *Fb "skygge" III 347ab; Finnish-Swedish: Wessman 19 No. 186.

F1038. Person without shadow.

Q552.10. *Plague as punishment.* Irish myth: *Cross; Swiss: Jegerlehner Oberwallis 165; German: O. Busch Nordwestthüringer Sagen 145, E. Handreck Müllersagen 194, O. Schöppner Sagenbuch d. bairischen Lande I 72; Spanish Exempla: Keller; Jewish: *Neuman.

C941.4. Plague for breaking tabu. F493. Spirit of plague. Q146. Reward: end of plague. V362. Plague from Jews' poisoning wells.

Q552.10.1. *Recurrent plague during reign of wicked king.* (Cf. Q552.3.) Irish myth: Cross.

Q552.11. *Punishment: meeting frightful apparition.* (Ghost, mysterious animal, devil.) Finnish-Swedish: Wessman 17ff. Nos. 158—161, 167, 169-71, 179.

Q552.12. *Punishment: shipwreck.* Irish myth: *Cross; Finnish-Swedish: Wessman 18 Nos. 174—75.

Q552.13. *Fire from heaven as punishment.* (Cf. F797, F962.2.) Irish myth: *Cross; Jewish: *Neuman.

Q552.13.0.1. *Punishment by arrows of fire from heaven.* Jewish: Neuman.

Q552.13.0.2. *Sword (of fire) from heaven drawn upon sinners.* Jewish: Neuman.

Q552.13.0.3. *Gods pour torrents of hot ashes on kingdom as punishment.* Buddhist myth: Malalasekera II 601.

Q552.13.1. *Death by fire from heaven as punishment.* *Loomis White Magic 35; Irish myth: Cross.

Q552.13.1.1. *Death by fire from heaven as punishment for opposition to holy person.* (Cf. Q227.) Irish myth: *Cross.

Q552.13.1.2. *Death by fire from heaven as punishment for scoffing at church teachings.* (Cf. Q225.) Irish myth: Cross.

Q552.13.2. *Destruction of property by fire from heaven as punishment.* (Cf. Q595.) Irish myth: Cross.

Q552.13.2.1. *City of king who opposed saint miraculously burned.* (Cf. Q227.) Irish myth: Cross.

Q552.13.2.2. *Church which refused to bury saint miraculously burned.* (Cf. Q227.) Irish myth: Cross.

Q552.13.3. *Fire from heaven consumes adulterous wife who has slandered an abbot.* (Cf. Q227, Q414.0.3.) *Loomis White Magic 111.

Q552.14. *Storm as punishment.* (Cf. D905.) Jewish: *Neuman; India: Thompson-Balys.

Q552.14.0.1. *Storm as punishment for affront to disguised supernatural spirit.* (Cf. Q221.) S. A. Indian (Chamacoco): Métraux MAFLS XL 28.

Q552.14.1. *Fortress built on Sunday destroyed by tempest.* (Cf. C631, Q223.6.) Irish myth: Cross.

Q552.14.2. *Punishment: flood of mud after which crops of corn come up with black (smutted) ears.* India: Thompson-Balys.

Q552.14.3. *Mass of sand advances like a tidal wave upon city.* India: Thompson-Balys.

Q552.14.4. *Rain of stones as punishment.* India: Thompson-Balys.
F962. Extraordinary precipitation (rain, snow, etc.).

Q552.14.5. *Hail as punishment.* Jewish: *Neuman.

Q552.15. *Punishment: cloud cuts off view of man promised all he can see for expelling saint.* (Cf. Q227.) Irish myth: Cross.
D901. Magic cloud. K185. Deceptive land purchase.

Q552.16. *Food and drink refused saint miraculously become putrid.* (Cf. D2096, Q227.) Irish myth: Cross.

Q552.16.1. *Food concealed from saint miraculously changed to stones.* (Cf. Q551.3.) Irish myth: Cross.

Q552.16.1.1. *Fishermen cut fish into pieces and claim that they have none.* Saint says, "If you have none, may you have them; if you have, may they be stones." Pieces of fish are changed to stones. (Cf. A977.5.2.) Irish myth: Cross.

Q552.16.1.2. *Women carrying cheeses concealed pretend that they are carrying webs or balls of thread.* Saint changes cheeses to stones. (Cf. A977.5.1.) Irish myth: Cross.

Q552.17. *Punishment: grave fills with sand when digger attempts to bury sinner over holy man.* (Cf. Q222.) Irish myth: Cross.

Q552.18. *Punishment: disappearance of ill-gotten gains.* (Cf. Q585, Q595.) Irish myth: Cross; Jewish: *Neuman.

Q552.18.1. *Gold and silver demanded of saint disappear.* (Cf. Q227.) Irish myth: Cross.

Q552.18.1.1. *Cowl demanded as ransom from saint bursts into flame.* Irish myth: Cross.

Q552.18.2. *Drink refused saint disappears.* (Cf. Q227.) Irish myth: Cross.

Q552.18.3. *Payment for ransom disappears when prisoner is not released.* Irish myth: *Cross.

Q552.19. *Miraculous drowning as punishment.* (Cf Q428, Q467.) Irish myth: Cross; Jewish: *Neuman.

A920.1.3. Lake bursts forth to drown thief. A1018. Flood as punishment. C923. Death by drowning for breaking tabu. F930. Extraordinary occurrences concerning seas or waters.

Q552.19.0.1. *Drowning caused by magic wind as punishment of braggart.* (Cf. D906, Q330.) Irish myth: Cross.

Q552.19.1. *Miraculous drowning as punishment for opposition to saint (holy man).* (Cf. Q227.) Irish myth: *Cross; Buddhist myth: Malalasekera I 1042.

Q552.19.2. *Miraculous drowning as punishment for desire to murder.* (Cf. Q211.8.) Irish myth: Cross.

Q552.19.3. *Miraculous drowning as punishment for theft.* (Cf. Q212.) Irish myth: *Cross.

Q552.19.4. *Miraculous drowning as punishment for man's flight with stepmother.* (Cf. Q242.) Irish myth: Cross.

Q552.19.5. *Miraculous drowning as punishment for haughtiness.* (Cf. Q331.) Irish myth: *Cross.

Q552.19.6. *Flood as punishment for murder (fratricide).* (Cf. Q211.) Irish myth: Cross.

Q552.20. *Eclipse as punishment.* India: Thompson-Balys.

Q552.20.1. *Miraculous darkness as punishment.* Jewish: *Neuman.

Q552.21. *Man vomits heart as punishment and lives without it till his death.* India: Thompson-Balys.

Q552.22. *Punishment: city and inhabitants hurled down precipice.* India: Thompson-Balys.

Q552.23. *Punishment: being suspended between heaven and earth.* India: Thompson-Balys.

Q552.24. *Punishment: lava flow.* Hawaii: Beckwith Myth 500.

Q552.25. *Earthquake as punishment.*

Q552.25.1. *Earthquake at dragon's death.* Icelandic: Boberg.

Q552.25.2. *Earthquake at witch's death.* Icelandic: Boberg.

Q553. *Divine favor withdrawn as punishment.* Jewish: *Neuman.
N134.1.3. Persons lose luck as punishment.

Q553.1. *Virgin Mary withdraws the sacrament from a scoffer.* (Cf. Q225.) Pauli (ed. Bolte) No. 551.

Q553.2. *Punishment: angel ceases to appear to self-righteous hermit.* Type 756A; Köhler-Bolte I 147f., 578; Spanish: Espinosa II No. 81, Espinosa Jr. No. 186.

Q553.3. *Sterility as punishment.* (Cf. T591.) Jewish: *Neuman.

Q553.3.1. *God refuses king a son on account of his many wars.* (Cf. Q305.) Chinese: Werner 256.

Q553.3.0.1. *Sterility of women as punishment.* Jewish: Moreno Esdras (Q578.3); India: Thompson-Balys.

Q553.3.2. *Children of incestuous father die without issue.* (Cf. Q242.) Irish myth: Cross.

Q553.3.3. *Sterility as punishment for breaking saint's covenant.* (Cf. Q227.) Irish myth: Cross; Greek (Herodotus): Classical Philology 39 (1944) 179f.

Q553.3.4. *Sterility as punishment for parricide.* (Cf. Q211.1.). Irish myth: Cross.

Q553.3.5. *Sterility as punishment for uncharitableness to holy person.* (Cf. Q286.1.) Irish myth: Cross.

Q553.3.6. *Painful birth of children as punishment.* Jewish: Neuman.

Q553.3.7. *Punishment: reduced number of children.* Jewish: *Neuman.

Q553.4. *Death of children as punishment.* Jewish: *Neuman.

Q553.4.1. *Child taken from parents because they have ceased to think of God.* (Cf. Q223.1.) Köhler-Bolte I 148.

Q553.5. *Punishment: small catch of fish for child-murderers.* Fisherman and his wife have always caught three fishes. From greed they kill their child in order to have more fish for themselves. But they thereafter catch but two fishes. (Cf. Q211.4.) Type 832.

Q553.6. *Failure in all efforts as punishment.* Loomis White Magic 100; Jewish: Moreno Esdras (Q479.1); India: Thompson-Balys.

Q553.7. *Rains withheld until king remembers to have monks' huts roofed as promised.* (Cf. Q266.) Buddhist myth: Malalasekera II 288.

Q554. *Mysterious visitation as punishment.*

Q554.1. *Punishment: devil carries off thief.* (Cf. Q212.) Pauli (ed. Bolte) No. 378.

Q554.2. *Devil in roof of church into which he thrusts voices of loud singers.* (Cf. Q223.) Alphabet No. 123.
G303.24.1. Devil accuses congregation of sins. R11.2.1. Devil carries off wicked people.

Q554.3. *Mysterious stranger blows ashes into face of scoffer and chokes him to death.* (Cf. Q225.) Pauli (ed. Bolte) No. 666.

Q554.4. *Mysterious wolf enters church and kills blaspheming priest.* (Cf. Q225.) Pauli (ed. Bolte) No. 550.

Q554.5. *Mysterious animal punishes penitent.* Returning from the pope he is met by a mysterious animal who jumps on his back. Then in the man's room, whither he has carried the animal, a three hours' noise is heard as of a fight. Neither man nor beast is found in the room. (Cf. Q557.) Köhler-Bolte I 132; Euphorion IV 332; Irish: Beal XXI 317, O'Suilleabhain 46; Gascon: Bladé Contes pop. de Gascogne II 201 No. 13.

Q554.6. *Cheaters visited by god in animal form.* Frightened into restitution. India: Thompson-Balys.

D101. Transformation: god to animal. K2320. Deception by frightening.

Q554.7. *Creditor in former existence comes to confiscate riches of unkind man in next existence.* (Cf. Q281.) India: Thompson-Balys.

Q555. *Madness as punishment.* (Cf. D2065.) *Loomis White Magic 98; Irish myth: *Cross; Greek: *Frazer Apollodorus I 146 n. 2, 183 n. 3; Jewish: *Neuman; India: *Thompson-Balys.

Q555.1. *Madness as punishment for scoffer.* (Cf. Q225.) Pauli (ed. Bolte) No. 457.

Q555.2. *Madness as punishment for adulterer.* (Cf. Q241.) Alphabet No. 36; Irish myth: Cross; Greek: Aeschylus Eumenides 341.

Q555.3. *Madness as punishment for thieves.* (Cf. Q212.) *Loomis White Magic 98.

Q555.4. *Punishment for incest: father and son maddened; cut off their sexual organs.* India: Thompson-Balys.

Q556. *Curse as punishment.* Roberts 217; Irish: *Cross, O'Suilleabhain 83, Beal XXI 328; Jewish: *Neuman; India: Thompson-Balys.

C987. Curse as punishment for breaking tabu. D1792. Magic results from curse. M205.2. Curse as punishment for broken promise. M400. Curses. Q576. Curse as punishment remitted. Q589.2. Man goes forth naked: cursed with nakedness throughout life.

Q556.0.1. *Curse threatened to enforce demand.* Irish myth: *Cross.

Q556.0.2. *Voice from heaven pronounces curse of destruction on city.* India: Thompson-Balys.

F966. Voices from heaven (or from the air).

Q556.1. *Curse for participation in Crucifixion.* (Cf. Q221.2.) Dh II 216ff., 219ff.; England: Baughman.

Q556.2. *Mark of Cain.* Permanent mark as curse on a murderer. (Cf. Q211.) *Frazer Old Testament I 78ff.; Irish myth: *Cross; Spanish Exempla: Keller.

Q556.3. *Curse for leaving home.* Italian Novella: Rotunda.

Q556.4. *Man has color of the dead as result of saint's curse for disobedience.* (Cf. Q227.) Irish myth: Cross.

Q556.4.1. *Child born with one eye blinded as result of saint's curse.* Irish myth: Cross.

Q556.5. *Saint decrees offenders will not be able to fortify their dwellings.* Fences fall, earth gapes when dug. (Cf. D2192, Q227, Q552.) Irish myth: Cross.

Q556.6. *Curse for plundering church: king loses battles.* (Cf. Q222.) Irish myth: Cross.

Q556.7. *Curse for inhospitality.* (Cf. Q292.) Irish myth: *Cross.

Q556.7.1. *Curse for enforced hospitality.* Irish myth: *Cross.

Q556.8. *Curse for mockery.* (Cf. Q288.) Irish myth: *Cross.

Q556.9. *Curse for banishing wife at wish of paramour.* (Cf. Q248.) Irish myth: Cross.

Q556.10. *Curse for murder.* (Cf. Q211.)

Q556.10.1. *Saint curses murderer with shortness of life here and hell beyond.* Irish myth: Cross.

Q556.11. *Curse for uncharitableness.* (Cf. Q286.1.) Irish myth: *Cross.

Q556.12. *Curse for stealing.* (Cf. Q212.)

Q556.12.1. *Thievish abbot to be eaten by wolves: curse by saint.* Irish myth: Cross.

Q557. *Miraculous punishment through animals.* (Cf. Q415, Q552.4, Q554.5, Q582.6, Q589.1, Q589.1.0.1, Q597.) Jewish: *Neuman.

B200. Animal with human traits. B250. Religious animals. B591. Animal avenges murder. C918. Mare from water world disappears when she is scolded and her halter used for common purposes. F915. Victim speaks from swallower's body. F982.3. Hawk carries hand of man to saint displeased by his handclasp. V134.3. Fish in water from certain well: water refuses to boil till fish are returned to well.

Q557.1. *Poisonous toad sits on food of undutiful children.* (Cf. Q281.1.) Tobler Epiphanie der Seele 25.

Q557.2. *Serpent chokes woman's undutiful son.* (Cf. Q281.1.) Alphabet No. 359.

Q557.3. *Eagle (ape) carries off ill-gotten gain.* Makes away with the receipts of a merchant who had watered his wine. (Cf. Q274.) Italian Novella: *Rotunda.

Q557.4. *Mouse causes hair of thief to fall out.* (Cf. Q551.6.4.) Irish myth: Cross.

Q557.5. *Saint's pet crane pecks out eye of spying person.* (Cf. Q342, Q580.) Irish myth: Cross.

Q557.6. *Snake strikes person for opposing saint.* (Cf. Q227.) Irish myth: Cross.

Q557.7. *Tiger seizes bride and bridegroom at threshold of house because groom has failed to worship deity before ceremony.* (Cf. Q223.) India: Thompson-Balys.

Q557.8. *People given charm to dispel flies grumble: flies return a thousandfold.* (Cf. Q312.) India: *Thompson-Balys.

Q558. *Mysterious death as punishment.* (Cf. Q411, Q574, Q591.1.)

Q558.1. *Scoffing priest mysteriously stricken dead.* (Cf. Q225.) Pauli (ed. Bolte) Nos. 455, 486.

Q558.2. *Perjurer stricken dead.* (Cf. Q263.) Icelandic: Boberg; Finnish-Swedish: Wessman 19 No. 177.

Q558.3. *Usurer flees city to escape plague.* On his return he boasts that God did not get him. He takes the plague and dies. (Cf. Q221.3.) Italian Novella: Rotunda.

Q558.4. *Blasphemer stricken dead.* (Cf. Q221.3.) England: Baughman; Irish myth: *Cross; Spanish Exempla: Keller (Q221.3.3); Italian Novella: Rotunda.

Q558.5. *Man in anger throws stone at the image of the Virgin.* Is stricken dead. (Cf. Q222.) Italian Novella: Rotunda.

Q558.6. *Mysterious death as punishment for theft.* (Cf. Q212.) *Loomis White Magic 98; Irish myth: *Cross.

Q558.7. *Slave-driver mysteriously stricken dead.* (Cf. Q285.4.) Irish myth: Cross.

Q558.8. *Mysterious death as punishment for wrongful satire.* (Cf. Q265.2.) Irish myth: *Cross.

Q558.9. *Mysterious death as punishment for murder.* (Cf. Q211.) Irish myth: *Cross.

Q558.9.1. *Mysterious death of son as punishment for murder.* Irish myth: Cross.

Q558.10. *Mysterious death as punishment for feigning sleep.* (Cf. Q260.) Irish myth: Cross.

Q558.11. *Animals which eat of saint's body stricken dead.* (Cf. B275.3, Q220.) Irish myth: Cross.

Q558.12. *Mysterious death as punishment for worshiping idols on All-Saints-Day.* Irish myth: Cross.

Q558.13. *Mysterious death as punishment for opposition to holy person.* (Cf. Q227, Q574.1.) Irish myth: *Cross.

Q558.13.1. *Mysterious death of son as punishment for opposition to holy person.* (Cf. Q411.3.) Irish myth: *Cross.

Q558.13.2. *Mysterious death as punishment for disbelief in druidism.* Irish myth: Cross.

Q558.14. *Mysterious death as punishment for desecration of holy places (images, etc.).* (Cf. Q222.) Irish myth: *Cross.

Q558.14.1. *Animals stricken dead for desecration of holy places.* (Cf. D2089.3.) *Loomis White Magic 102; Irish myth: *Cross.

Q558.15. *Mysterious death as punishment for lying (perjury).* (Cf. Q263.) Irish myth: Cross.

Q558.15.1. *Mysterious death of son as punishment for lying (perjury).* Irish myth: Cross.

Q411.3. Death of father (son, etc.) as punishment.

Q558.16. *Mysterious death as punishment for false judging.* Irish myth: Cross.

Q558.17. *Death by ulcer for destroying churches.* (Cf. Q222.) Irish myth: *Cross.

Q558.18. *Saints bring about miraculous death because of desecration of sanctuaries.* (Cf. C51.1, Q222, V220.) Irish myth: *Cross.

Q559. *Other miraculous punishments.*

Q559.1. *Devils instead of angels visit woman who has forgotten God in her prosperity.* U.S., England: Baughman; Russian: Andrejev No. 796*.

Q559.2. *Punishment: man stricken blind.* (Cf. Q451.7.0.2.) Irish: Beal XXI 336; Icelandic: *Boberg; Finnish-Swedish: Wessman 18 No. 172; Jewish: *Neuman; India: *Thompson-Balys.

Q559.3. *Body of murdered man cannot be moved nor can water be drawn from a well to wash it.* Leads to exposure of murderer. Italian Novella: Rotunda.

N271. Murder will out.

Q559.4. *Peasants punished for working on feast day.* They cannot leave the field for several days. (Cf. Q223.) Italian Novella: Rotunda.

Q559.5. *Girl punished for jeering at saint.* Is stricken dumb and distaff sticks to her hand. (Cf. Q227.) Italian Novella: Rotunda.

Q559.5.1. *Birth of child prevented until girl confesses slander.* She has accused a bishop of fathering the child. Spanish Exempla: Keller.

Q559.5.2. *Girl's hand withers as punishment for broken oath to God.* Spanish Exempla: Keller.

Q559.6. *Poets lose ability to compose verse as punishment for immoderate request.* (Cf. Q338.) Irish myth: *Cross.

Q559.7. *Punishment: body will not decay after death because man broke saint's covenant.* (Cf. Q227.) Irish myth: Cross.

Q559.8. *Half of house in which false judgment is given slips down hill.* (Cf. Q265.) Irish myth: *Cross.

Q559.9. *Saints miraculously cause child to fall over cliff as punishment for mother's washing clothes in holy well.* (Cf. Q222, Q411.3.) Irish myth: Cross.

Q559.10. *Magic boat keeps thief at sea until he promises to throw ill-gotten gains into sea.* (Cf. D1654.6, Q212.) Irish myth: Cross.

Q559.11. *Man miraculously made to excrete his entrails for heresy.* (Cf. Q225.1, Q469.7.) Spanish Exempla: Keller.

Q560. Punishments in hell. (Cf. Q174.) Fb "helvede" IV 209a; Wienert FFC LVI 41; Krappe "Notes on Dante's Inferno" Archivum Romanicum VI 376—385, XI 592—603; Festskrift til Feilberg 202. — Irish: *Cross, Beal XXI 319—23, O'Suilleabhain 51, 53, 58; Icelandic: *Boberg; Lithuanian: Balys Legends Nos. 391, 467f., 470f., 585; Spanish: Espinosa Jr. Nos. 202, 204, Keller; Greek: Grote I 129; Egyptian: Müller 179f.; Jewish: *Neuman, Moreno Esdras; India: *Thompson-Balys; Buddhist myth: Malalasekera I 598.

A671. Hell. Lower world of torment. E481.1. Land of dead in lower world. E481.6.1. Land of dead in north. E752. Lost souls. E755.2. Souls in hell (Hades). F171.6.1. Man in otherworld loaded down with wood. Then more and more put on him. F171.6.5. Man in otherworld kindles fire. M341.2.7.1. Prophecy: sinners to be burnt by fire on Doomsday. Q291.1. St. Peter's mother dropped from heaven because of hard-heartedness.

Q560.1. *Punishments in land of dead (detailed).* India: Thompson-Balys.

Q560.1.1. *Punishments in other world: people reincarnated as buffaloes and killed.* Chinese: Graham.

Q560.2. *Respite from hell.*

E755.2.0.1. Souls leave hell on Sundays. Q174. Reward: release from hell. Q570. Punishment and remission.

Q560.2.1. *Souls in hell not punished on Sabbath.* Irish myth: Cross; Jewish: Neuman.

Q560.2.1.1. *Three hours of respite on Sunday for tormented in hell.* Irish myth: *Cross.

Q560.2.2. *Certain number of souls released from hell every Saturday through virtue of saint.* Irish myth: *Cross.

Q560.2.3. *Soul (of Judas) tormented on rock in sea on certain days as respite from pains of hell.* Irish myth: *Cross.

Q560.3. *Sinners endure hell tortures for one year.* Jewish: *Neuman.

Q561. *Punishments being prepared in hell.*

Q561.1. *Bed heating in hell for certain person.* *Type 756B; **Andrejev FFC LXIX 106ff.; *Fb "seng" III 187a; Lithuanian: Balys Legends No. 391.

Q561.2. *Kettle heating in hell for certain person.* *Type 756B; *Andrejev FFC LXIX 106ff.

C325. Tabu: looking into pots in hell. E755.2.1. Souls of drowned in heated kettles in hell.

Q561.3. *Seat (room) heating in hell for certain person.* *Type 756B; *Andrejev FFC LXIX 106ff.; Irish: Beal XXI 311, O'Suilleabhain 33.

Q561.4. *Palace in other world of the dead where are rooms full of tongues, hands, etc. of men committing sins in this world.* India: Thompson-Balys.

Q562. *Pain of souls tormented in hell alternately ebbs and flows.* Irish myth: *Cross.

Q562.1. *Girdles of sinners in hell alternately scorch with heat and cold.* Irish myth: *Cross.

A671.3.3. Alternate heat and cold in hell.

Q562.2. *Souls in hell alternately drowned and burned.* Irish myth: *Cross.

C927.3. Burning and drowning as punishment for breaking tabu.

Q562.3. *Souls tormented in hell alternately borne up to firmament and cast down to depths.* Irish myth: *Cross.

Q563. *Punishments in hell fitted to crimes.* (Cf. Q580.) Zs. f. celtische Phil. IX 413ff.; Irish myth: *Cross.

Q563.1. *Punishment in hell fitted to the grade of wickedness.* Jewish: *Neuman.

Q564. *Letter sent to the relatives from man punished in hell.* Lithuanian: Balys Legends Nos. 467f.

Q565. *Man admitted to neither heaven nor hell.* He has tricked the devil. *Type 330; *BP II 149ff., 163ff.; Fb "helvede" I 589a, "himmerige" I 611a; Irish: Beal XXI 329, O'Suilleabhain 90; U.S.: *Baughman; Spanish: Espinosa Jr. Nos. 8, 210, 213; American Negro (Georgia): Harris Remus 156 No. 32.

A1942.1. Snipe from man admitted neither to heaven nor to hell. J1616. St. Peter not guiltless. Soldiers are admitted neither to hell nor to heaven. They remind Peter of his denial of Christ. He admits them.

Q565.1. *Person to be received by neither earth nor heaven.* Irish myth: Cross.

Q566. *Punishments by heat in hell.* (Cf. A671.2.4.) Irish myth: *Cross; Jewish: *Neuman; Buddhist myth: Malalasekera I 885.

Q567. *Punishments by cold in hell.* *Krappe Bulletin Hispanique XXXIX 18; Irish myth: Cross; Jewish: Neuman.
A671.3. Frigidity of hell. E481.7. Icy inferno. E755.2.5. Icy hell.

Q567.1. *Sharp icy hoods (cowls) worn by sinners in hell.* Irish myth: *Cross.

Q569. *Other punishments in hell.* Irish myth: Cross.

Q569.1. *Sinners in hell forced to sit in dark puddles up to their middles* (Cf. A689.1.) Irish myth: *Cross; Jewish: *Neuman.

Q569.2. *Sinners in hell swallowed by dragons.* Irish myth: *Cross.
B11.3.6. Dragons live in hell.

Q569.3. *Sinners in hell fall into mouth of devil.* Irish myth: *Cross.

Q569.4. *Sinners in hell painfully suspended.* Jewish: Neuman.

Q569.5. *Smokers in otherworld are locked in smoky rooms.* Cheremis: Sebeok-Nyerges.

Q570. Punishment and remission. Irish myth: Cross.
D1713. Magic power of hermit (saint).

Q570.1. *Magic foul disease as punishment for persecution of Christians remitted.* Spanish Exempla: Keller.

Q571. *Magic blindness as punishment remitted.* (Cf. Q451.7.0.2.) Spanish Exempla: Keller.

Q571.1. *Magic blindness as punishment for opposition to holy person remitted.* (Cf. Q227.) O'Grady Silva Gadelica II 7; Irish myth: *Cross.

Q571.2. *Magic blindness as punishment for uncharitableness remitted.* (Cf. Q286.) Irish myth: Cross.

Q572. *Magic sickness as punishment remitted.* (Cf. Q551.6.)

Q572.1. *Magic sickness as punishment for theft remitted.* (Cf. Q212.) O'Grady Silva Gadelica II 37; Irish myth: Cross.

Q572.2. *Magic sickness as punishment for uncharitableness remitted.* (Cf. Q286.) Irish myth: Cross.

Q572.3. *Magic sickness as punishment for opposition to holy person remitted.* (Cf. Q227.) Irish myth: Cross.

Q572.4. *Magic sickness as punishment for immoderate request remitted.* (Cf. Q338.) Irish myth: Cross.

Q572.5. *Saint deprives enemy king of speech.* King repents, speech restored. Irish myth: Cross.

Q573. *Magic paralysis as punishment remitted.* (Cf. Q551.7.)

Q573.1. *Magic paralysis as punishment for opposition to holy person remitted.* Cf. O'Grady Silva Gadelica II 28; Irish myth: Cross.

Q573.2. *Magic paralysis as punishment for scorning of bishop remitted.* Icelandic: Boberg.

Q574. *Mysterious death as punishment remitted.* (Cf. Q558.) Irish myth: Cross.

E121.4. Resuscitation by saint.

Q574.1. *Mysterious death as punishment for opposition to holy person remitted.* (Cf. Q558.13.) O'Grady Silva Gadelica II 71; Irish myth: *Cross.

Q574.2. *Mysterious death of animals as punishment for uncharitableness remitted.* (Cf. D2089.3, Q286.) Irish myth: Cross.

Q575. *Magic putrefaction of food as punishment for opposition to holy person remitted.* (Cf. Q227.) O'Grady Silva Gadelica II 26; Irish myth: Cross.

D2096. Magic putrefaction.

Q576. *Curse as punishment remitted.* (Cf. Q556.) Irish myth: Cross.

Q576.1. *Curse of loss of victory for opposition to holy person remitted.* (Cf. Q227.) Irish myth: Cross.

Q577. *Sentence to hang remitted.* Italian Novella: Rotunda.

Q578. *Spirit in hell remitted from humiliating punishment of bathing people.* (Cf. Q501.9.) Spanish Exempla: Keller.

Q580. Punishment fitted to crime. Irish myth: *Cross; Jewish: *Neuman; West Indies: Flowers 570.

Q101. Reward fitting to deed. Q557.5. Saint's pet crane pecks out eye of spying person. Q563. Punishments in hell fitted to crimes. T257.2.1. Wife exposes bald head of second wife to disgrace her. Hair marvellously regrows.

Q581. *Villain nemesis.* Person condemned to punishment he has suggested for others. *Cox 503 and passim (under head "villain nemesis"): *Fb "dom" IV 101b; *Wesselski Theorie 139; Köhler-Bolte Zs. f. Vksk. VI 64 to Gonzenbach No. 13; Pauli (ed. Bolte) No. 116; Wienert FFC LVI 49 (ET 83), 51 (ET 109, 110), 59 (ET 199), 132 (ST 382), 135 (ST 406, 447); Halm Aesop Nos. 18, 326. — Irish myth: *Cross; Italian: Basile Pentamerone I No. 2, III No. 10, V Nos. 8, 9; Jewish: *Neuman; India: Thompson-Balys.

Q581.0.1. *Loss of life as result of one's own treachery.* (Cf. Q261.) Irish myth: *Cross.

Q581.1. *Unusual murder avenged in like manner.* Scottish: Campbell-McKay No. 17; Spanish Exempla: Keller; India: Thompson-Balys.

Q581.2. *Villain in hiding killed by blow aimed at his victim.* India: Thompson-Balys.

Q581.3. *Those planning to drown others drowned.* Jewish: Neuman.

Q581.3.1. *Drowning as punishment for drowning.* Eskimo (Cumberland Sound): Boas BAM XV 165.

Q582. *Fitting death as punishment.* (Cf. Q411, D2060.) Irish: O'Suilleabhain 125, Beal XXI 336; Jewish: *Neuman; India: Thompson-Balys; Buddhist myth: Malalasekera I 374, II 851, 1353; Africa (Duala): Lederbogen JAS IV 61, (Wakweli): Bender 106f.

Q582.1. *Sisters throw unique jewel into lake; killed and thrown after it.* Revue Celtique XVI 76; Irish myth: Cross.

Q582.2. *Man who brings fire to his house at devil's instigation burns to death.* (Cf. Q233.) Irish myth: Cross.

Q582.3. *Murderer killed by his own spear.* (Cf. Q211.) Irish myth: *Cross.

Q582.3.1. *Man killed by piece of stone flying from rock his victim dies upon.* Irish myth: Cross.

Q582.4. *Man dies from drop of blood of pet hound he has killed.* (Cf. Q211.6.) Irish myth: Cross.

Q582.5. *Man boasts he fears saint no more than hornless sheep; killed by hornless sheep.* (Cf. Q333.1.) Irish myth: Cross.

M341.2. Prophecy: death by particular instrument.

Q582.6. *Woman killed by horse got through immoderate request.* (Cf. Q338, Q557.) Irish myth: *Cross.

Q582.7. *Boy who threw stones at clerics killed by thrown stone.* (Cf. Q227.) Irish myth: Cross.

Q582.8. *Person drinks poison he prepared for another.* Irish myth: *Cross.

S111. Murder by poisoning.

Q582.9. *Man falls dead when he sees his sons whom he has reared in sin all killed.* Spanish Exempla: Keller.

Q583. *Fitting bodily injury as punishment.* Irish myth: Cross; Jewish: *Neuman; Buddhist myth: Malalasekera II 16.

Q583.1. *Man who laughs at blind made blind.* (Cf. Q288, Q451.7.0.2.) Irish myth: Cross.

Q583.2. *Man stricken dumb for surly speech.* (Cf. Q327, Q451.3.) Irish myth: Cross.

Q583.3. *Man seeking to flee saint paralyzed.* (Cf. Q551.7.1.) Irish myth: Cross.

Q583.4. *Lying woman's tongue swells.* (Cf. Q551.6.1.) Irish myth: Cross.

Q584. *Transformation as fitting punishment.* (Cf. D661, Q551.3.)

Q584.1. *Transformer transformed.* Irish myth: Cross.

Q584.2. *Transformation of a man to animal as fitting punishment.* (Cf. D661.) Lithuanian: Balys Index No. 773*; S. A. Indian (Tupinamba): Métraux RMLP XXXIII 133, 172.

Q584.3. *Reincarnation in form fitted to crime.* (Cf. Q551.5.) Buddhist myth: Malalasekera I 50, 829, 1020, II 706, 1050, 1357.

Q585. *Fitting destruction (disappearance) of property as punishment.* (Cf. Q552.18, Q595.) India: Thompson-Balys; Buddhist myth: Malalasekera I 885, II 416, 1264.

K236.3. Tribute paid in enchanted snow. After payment snow takes proper form.

Q585.1. *Man refuses to give to charity: his property disappears.* (Cf. Q286, Q595.3.) Irish myth: *Cross; India: Thompson-Balys.

V421. Shipman refuses alms: ship turned to stone.

Q585.2. *Destruction (disappearance) of property got through immoderate request.* (Cf. Q338.) Irish myth: Cross.

Q585.3. *During rainy spring, farmer wishes that Lord would sleep till harvest time.* Farmer himself sleeps until all neighbors have finished harvesting. When he wakes, he finds his crops ruined. (Cf. Q235.) England: *Baughman.

Q585.4. *Food disappears because of wastefulness.* India: *Thompson-Balys.

Q586. *Son on gallows bites his mother's (father's) nose off: punishment for neglect in youth.* *Types 756B, 838; *Andrejev FFC LXIX 88; Wienert FFC LVI 83 (ET 493), 128 (ST 365, 499); Halm Aesop No. 351; *Pauli (ed. Bolte) No. 19; Crane Vitry 259 No. 287; *Chauvin VIII 113 No. 95 n. 1; Alphabet No. 217. — Spanish Exempla: Keller; India: *Thompson-Balys.

Q587. *Jealous husband kills bird which wife falsely says she has been listening to.* She has really been conversing with her lover. (Laüstic.) *Warncke Lais der Marie de France[2] cxxvi.

K1500. Husband outwits adulteress and paramour. Q241. Adultery punished. Q478.1. The Eaten Heart. Adulteress is caused unwittingly to eat her lover's heart. T36. Girl sleeps in garden to meet lover. W181. Jealousy.

Q588. *Ungrateful son punished by having a son equally ungrateful.* (Cf. Q281.1.) BP I 135.

J121.2. Undutiful son rebuked by father. S21. Cruel son.

Q589. *Punishment fitted to crime—miscellaneous.* Irish myth: Cross.

Q589.1. *Horses fail when owner refuses load to saint.* (Cf. Q286.1, Q557.) Irish myth: *Cross.

Q589.1.0.1. *Man cannot drive cow by himself which he refused to share.* (Cf. Q272.) Irish myth: Cross.

Q589.2. *Man goes forth naked: cursed with nakedness throughout life.* (Cf. Q556.) Irish myth: Cross.

Q589.3. *Punishment for stinginess: amends made by being generous and liberal.* (Cf. Q276.) India: Thompson-Balys.

Q590. Miscellaneous punishments.

Q591. *Punishment: lie becomes truth.* (Cf. Q263.) *Loomis White Magic 100; Irish: Beal XXI 327, O'Suilleabhain 74; Japanese: Ikeda.

Q591.1. *Punishment: death pretended becomes real.* Revue Celtique xxvii 297; Irish myth: *Cross.

K1860. Deception by feigned death (sleep).

Q591.1.1. *King tests saint by having man feign death; saint perceives trick and causes man to be dead.* Irish myth: Cross.

Q591.2. *Punishment: man says salt he carries is stones; it immediately becomes so.* Irish myth: *Cross.

A2721.3.1. Man tells Jesus he is sowing stones. D471.5. Transformation: salt to stone.

Q591.2.1. *Punishment: man says sugar he carries is earth; it becomes so.* India: Thompson-Balys.

Q591.3. *Man dies from pretended illness.* Irish myth: Cross.

Q593. *Dead mother appears and makes disobedient child eat fatal serpent.* (Cf. Q325.) Jamaica: *Beckwith MAFLS XVII 263 No. 66.

Q594. *Punishment: taking snakes as foster children.* *Type 751B.

Q595. *Loss or destruction of property as punishment.* (Cf. Q552.1.0.1, Q552.13.2, Q552.14.1, Q585, Q552.18.) Irish myth: Cross; Jewish: *Neuman; Africa (Fang): Tessman 195.

Q595.1. *Fortress ravaged when saint is refused admittance.* (Cf. Q227.) Irish myth: Cross.

Q595.2. *Cattle killed, crops burned as punishment for abduction.* (Cf. Q213.) Irish myth: Cross.

Q595.3. *Uncharitable king loses wealth.* (Cf. Q286, Q585.1.) Irish myth: Cross.

Q595.4. *Loss of money as punishment.* Jewish: Moreno Esdras (Q585.1).

Q595.4.1. *Tribute as punishment for trickery.* Irish myth: Cross (Q261.2).

Q596. *Punishment in effigy.*

Q596.1. *Quartering in effigy for uxoricide.* (Cf. Q211.3.) Italian Novella: Rotunda.

Q597. *Animals avenge injury.* (Cf. Q557.)

Q597.1. *Snake carries into fire man who has banned snakes.* Finnish: Aarne FFC XXXIII 46 No. 79; Estonian: Aarne FFC XXV 132 No. 79.

Q597.2. *Birds take back their feathers from ungrateful wolf to whom they have lent them.* (Cf. Q281.) Cape Verde Islands: *Parsons MAFLS XV (1) 310 n. 1; West Indies: Flowers 570.

Q597.3. *Bees sting honey-thieves.* (Cf. Q212.) Wienert FFC LVI *67 (ET 312), 98 (ST 122); Halm Aesop No. 288.

Q598. *Punishment: fighting all who pass through forest.* Dickson 69 n. 16.

Q599. *Other punishments.*

Q599.1. *Punishment: marrying shrewish wife.* India: Thompson-Balys.
T251. The shrewish wife.

R. CAPTIVES AND FUGITIVES

DETAILED SYNOPSIS

R0 —R99. Captivity
- R0. Captivity
- R10. Abduction
- R40. Places of captivity
- R50. Conditions of captivity
- R70. Behavior of captives

R100—R199. Rescues
- R100. Rescues
- R110. Rescue of captive
- R130. Rescue of abandoned or lost persons
- R150. Rescuers
- R170. Rescue—miscellaneous motifs

R200—R299. Escapes and pursuits
- R200. Escapes and pursuits
- R210. Escapes
- R220. Flights
- R260. Pursuits

R300—R399. Refuges and recapture
- R300. Refuges and recapture
- R310. Refuges
- R350. Recapture of fugitive

R. CAPTIVES AND FUGITIVES

R0—R99. Captivity.

R0. Captivity.

B278. Captured animal ransoms self. D2078. Imprisoning by magic. F165.6.1. Otherworld (fairyland) as place of sorrowful captivity. F302.3.1.4. Fairy abducts whomever she falls in love with. F375. Mortal imprisoned in otherworld (fairyland). F387. Fairy captured. K700. Capture by deception. Q385. Captured animals avenge themselves. Q433. Punishment: imprisonment. V151.1. Captive released because of ability to recite beginning of Genesis.

R1. *Wild man captured and tamed.* *Dickson 116 n. 44, 122; N. A. Indian: *Thompson Tales 319 n. 152.

F567. Wild man.

R2. *God holds the devil captive for three years.* Dh. I 184.

R3. *King imprisons another king's embassy.* Thien Motive 10.

R4. *Surprise capture.* Irish myth: *Cross.

K2350. Military strategy.

R4.1. *Enemy surprised while bathing: taken.* Irish myth: *Cross.

R5. *Capture on field of battle.* Irish myth: Cross; Icelandic: *Boberg; Jewish: Neuman.

R5.1. *Enemy host imprisoned by earthen walls thrown up by hero's chariot wheels.* Irish myth: *Cross.

R5.2. *Hero captured by being pressed between shields from all sides.* Icelandic: *Boberg.

R6. *Messenger of Death imprisoned.* India: Thompson-Balys.

R7. *Men held captive in the Land of Women.* (Cf. F112.) India: Thompson-Balys.

R8. *Gods captured.* India: *Thompson-Balys.

R9. *Captivity—miscellaneous.*

R9.1. *Sun captured.*

R9.1.1. *Sun captured during visit to earth.* India: Thompson-Balys.

R9.1.2. *Sun and Moon captured by creditor, thus causing eclipse.* India: Thompson-Balys.

R9.1.3. *Sun and Moon imprison each other.* India: Thompson-Balys.

R9.2. *Grain and pulse in human form imprisoned by wicked king.* India: Thompson-Balys.

R9.3. *Ogress captured and reformed.* India: Thompson-Balys.

R9.4. *Fire-maiden imprisoned in iron house.* India: Thompson-Balys.

R9.5. *Cow imprisoned until it promises not to eat men.* India: Thompson-Balys.

R9.6. *King imprisons all living creatures.* India: Thompson-Balys.

R10. Abduction. **Feilberg Bjærgtagen (København, 1910), Nissens Historie; **Hdwb. d. Märchens I 541ff.; Irish myth: *Cross; Jewish: *Neuman; N. A. Indian (California): Gayton and Newman 86, (Zuñi): Benedict II 334.

F320. Fairies carry people away to fairyland. F420.5.2.2. Water-spirits abduct person. F460.4.4.1. Mountain-men abduct persons. G303.9.5. The devil as an abductor. G440. Ogre abducts person. H1385. Quest for lost persons. K1300. Seduction. P19.2.1. King abducts woman to be his paramour. Q213. Abduction punished. R110. Rescue of captive. R161.1. Lover rescues his lady from abductor. R225. Elopement. W153.12. Miser is kidnapped and held for ransom.

R10.1. *Princess (maiden) abducted.* (Cf. R11.1, R12.1, R13.1, R16.1, R17.1, R25.1, R31.) *Types 301, 302, 311, 312; *Hdwb. d. Märchens I 553b nn. 296—315; Feilberg Bjærgtagen (København, 1910). — Irish myth: *Cross; Icelandic: *Boberg; Breton: Sébillot Incidents s.v. "princesse"; Spanish: Espinosa II No. 133—135; Italian Novella: Rotunda; Greek: Grote I 156; India: *Thompson-Balys; Chinese: Graham; Indonesia: DeVries's list No. 220.

H1219.3. Quest assigned as punishment by father of abducted girl. K1310. Seduction by disguise or substitution. K1321. Seduction by man disguising as woman. K1321.2. Man disguised as woman abducts princess. K1332. Seduction by taking aboard ship to inspect wares. K1333. Seduction by having maiden placed in floating chest. K1334. Seduction (or wooing) on an aerial journey. K1371. Bride-stealing. K1831.2.2. Lover in disguise as duke's son takes service by king with his followers in order to abduct his sister. K1914. Abductor pretends to have been sent to fetch princess by lover. P15.2. King demands subject's wife for himself. R111. Rescue of captive princess. T151.0.1. Respite ruse. Captive maiden assigns quest, agreeing to marry when it is accomplished.

R10.1.1. *Maiden abducted by soldiers.* Italian Novella: *Rotunda.

R10.1.2. *Lover abducts maiden from cruel father and brother.* Italian Novella: Rotunda.

K2211. Treacherous brother. R225. Elopement. S11. Cruel father.

R10.2. *Pretended abduction.* Adulterous wife plots own abduction by paramour. Irish myth: Cross.

R10.3. *Children abducted.* Icelandic: Boberg.

R10.4. *Hero abducted by witch who loves him.* Icelandic: Boberg.

R10.4.1. *Abduction of bridegroom and killing of his bride planned as giantess's revenge.* Icelandic: Lagerholm 56—58, Boberg.

R11. *Abduction by monster (ogre).* (Cf. G440.) **Feilberg Bjærgtagen (København, 1910); Spanish: Espinosa II Nos. 133—135, III Nos. 141f.; India: *Thompson-Balys; Buddhist myth: Malalasekera II 129, 1060; S. A. Indian (Toba): Métraux MAFLS XL 39.

R11.1. *Princess (maiden) abducted by monster (ogre).* (Cf. R10.1.) *Types 301, 302, 311, 312; *BP I 398, 404, II 301, 317, III 434; Hdwb. d. Märchens I 544b, 547a nn. 60—79, 140—174; *Fb "brud" IV 64b. — Irish myth: *Cross; Icelandic: *Boberg; Missouri French: Carrière; India: *Thompson-Balys; Chinese: Graham; Korean: Zong in-Sob 221 No. 98; Japanese: Dixon 215 n. 17; Eskimo (Smith Sound):

Kroeber JAFL XII 167; N. A. Indian: *Thompson Tales 341f. nn. 228, 228a, 231, 235.

B81.4. Mermaid captures a maiden. B82.1.1. Merman demands princess. F531.5.7.0.3. Giantess daughter of giant and abducted maiden (therefore helps hero). G535. Ogre's captive princess hero's helper. R151.1. Husband rescues stolen wife.

R11.1.1. *Abduction of girl by half bestial man* (hair on body, nails of dog). India: *Thompson-Balys.

R11.2. *Abduction by devil.*

R11.2.1. *Devil carries off wicked people.* Scala Celi 6b, 43a, 54b, 77b Nos. 39, 246, 306, 441; Fb "fanden" I 267a; Irish: O'Suilleabhain 55, Beal XXI 322; Finnish-Swedish: Wessman 13 Nos. 116, 118; Spanish Exempla: Keller; West Indies: Flowers 571.

Q267.1. Devil comes for hypocrite. Q273.1. Devil comes for usurer. Q281.1.1. Devils carry off girl who abuses her mother. Q312.2. Devil carries off fault-finding people. Q387.1. Devil carries off jester. Q554.1. Punishment: devil carries off thief.

R11.2.1.1. *Devil carries off emperor because of his many murders.* Spanish Exempla: Keller.

R11.2.2. *Abduction by demon.* India: *Thompson-Balys; Buddhist myth: Malalasekera II 507, 1053; Tuamotu: Stimson MS (z-G. 3/1386).

R11.2.2.1. *Abduction by Echo.* India: Thompson-Balys.

A497. Echo. D2065.6. Person abducted by Echo crazed and dumb.

R11.3. *Abduction by giant.* (Cf. F531, G100.) English romance: Malory V 5; Icelandic: *Boberg; India: *Thompson-Balys; Korean: Zong in-Sob 166 No. 72; N. A. Indian (Zuñi): Benedict II 334.

R12. *Abduction by pirates.*

R12.1. *Maiden abducted by pirates (robbers).* (Cf. R10.1.) *Reinhard PMLA XXXVIII 465; Irish myth: *Cross; Italian Novella: *Rotunda; India: *Thompson-Balys; Buddhist myth: Malalasekera I 981.

R12.2. *Man abducted by pirates.* French Canadian: Sister Marie Ursule; Italian Novella: *Rotunda.

R12.2.1. *Child abducted by robbers and brought up in their ways.* Later becomes wealthy and law-abiding. Irish myth: Cross.

R12.3. *Lovers abducted by pirates.* Italian Novella: *Rotunda.

R12.4. *Girl enticed into boat and abducted.* India: *Thompson-Balys.

K1332. Seduction by taking aboard ship to inspect wares.

R13. *Abduction by animal.* Chinese: Graham.

B11.6.8. Dragon flies to its nest with human being. C986. Abduction by animal for breaking tabu. N312. Separation of twins through being carried off by beast.

R13.0.1. *Children carried off by animals.* *Hibbard 270 n. 10, 276; Irish myth: *Cross.

B535. Animal nourishes abandoned child.

R13.1. *Abduction by wild beast.*

R13.1.1. *Baboons abduct boy.* Africa (Hottentot): Bleek 42.

R13.1.2. *Lion carries off child.* Italian Novella: *Rotunda.-

R13.1.3. *Rhinoceros carries off man.* India: Thompson-Balys.

R13.1.4. *Abduction by tiger.*

R13.1.4.1. *Tiger abducts man.* India: Thompson-Balys.

R13.1.4.2. *Abduction of woman by tiger.* India: *Thompson-Balys; Chinese: Graham; S. A. Indian (Chiriguano): Métraux RMLP XXXIII 142.

R13.1.4.2.1. *Tigers abduct princess to be wife of their human ward.* India: *Thompson-Balys.

B535. Animal nurse. T50. Wooing.

R13.1.5. *Wolf abducts person.* Irish myth: *Cross.

R13.1.6. *Girl abducted by bear and made his wife.* India: Thompson-Balys.

B635.1. The Bear's Son.

R13.1.7. *Abduction by monkey.*

R13.1.7.1. *Girl carried off by monkeys.* India: Thompson-Balys.

R13.1.8. *Abduction by rabbit.* India: Thompson-Balys.

R13.1.9. *Abduction by leopard.* India: Thompson-Balys.

R13.1.10. *Abduction by elephant.* India: Thompson-Balys.

R13.1.11. *Abduction by fox.* India: Thompson-Balys.

R.13.2. *Abduction by domestic beast.*

R13.2.1. *Girl carried off by ram.* (Cf. R10.1.) Breton: Sébillot Incidents s.v. "bélier".

R13.2.2. *Bull carries off devil after he has tried to deceive God.* (Cf. A60.) Dh I 35.

R13.2.3. *Abduction by cat.* Irish myth: *Cross.

R13.2.3.1. *Abduction by goddess's cat.* India: Thompson-Balys.

R13.3. *Person carried off by bird.* German: Grimm No. 51; India: *Thompson-Balys; Philippine (Tinguian): Cole 183, 201; N. A. Indian (California): Gayton and Newman 79; Africa (Yoruba): Frobenius Atlantis X 222ff. No. 14.

R13.3.1. *Abduction by ravens.* Irish myth: Cross.

R13.3.2. *Eagle carries off youth.* Greek: Fox 240 (Ganymede); Japanese: Ikeda.

R13.4. *Abduction by reptile.*

R13.4.1. *Abduction by snake.* India: *Thompson-Balys.

R14. *Deity (demigod) abducts person.* Greek: Grote I 35, 83, 261; India: *Thompson-Balys; Philippine (Tinguian): Cole 183.

R16. *Abduction by transformed person.*

R16.1. *Maiden abducted by transformed hero.* (Cf. D658, D2121.7, R10.1.) *Type 516; Rösch FFC LXXVII 112; Spanish: Boggs FFC XC 57 No. 425.

R16.2. *Child carried off by werwolf.* (Cf. D113.1.1.) Hibbard 216.

R16.3. *Woman abducted by (transformed) fairy.* Irish myth: *Cross.

R16.4. *Abduction by tiger-man.* India: Thompson-Balys.

R16.5. *Abduction by elephant-man.* India: Thompson-Balys.

R17. *Abduction by whirlwind.* (Cf. D1520.28.) Hartland Science 175; Icelandic: Boberg; Japanese: Ikeda; Africa (Basuto): Jacottet 160 No. 23.

R17.1. *Whirlwind carries princess away.* (Cf. R10.1.) *Fb "hvirvelvind" I 708.

R18. *Abduction by rejected suitor.* Irish myth: *Cross; Icelandic: *Boberg.

T75.2.1. Rejected suitor's revenge. T92.9. Rival in love killed. T104.1. Rejected suitor wages war.

R22. *Abduction by giving soporific.* Irish myth: Cross.

D1964.3. Magic sleep induced by abductor. K776. Capture by intoxication (or narcotic).

R22.1. *Abduction by giving soporific and rolling up in a cloak.* *Chauvin V 23 No. 13 n. 2.

R22.2. *Abduction by means of sleep-giving music.* Irish myth: Cross.

R23. *Abduction with aid of magic mask which renders invisible.* (Cf. D1361.32.) Irish myth: Cross.

R24. *Abductor in disguise.* (Cf. K1310.) India: Thompson-Balys.

R24.1. *Prince disguised as holy man abducts princess.* India: Thompson-Balys.

R24.2. *Princely suitor in minstrel disguise carries princess away.* India: Thompson-Balys.

R25. *Abduction through underground passage.*

R25.1. *Princess abducted through underground passage.* (Cf. R10.1.) *Type 516; Rösch FFC LXXVII 102; BP I 46ff.; Icelandic: Boberg.

R31. *Light extinguished and woman stolen.* (Cf. R10.1.) Icelandic: *Boberg; N. A. Indian: *Thompson Tales 343 n. 237.

R32. *Abduction by stealing clothes of bathers.* Africa (Cameroon): Lederbogen Märchen II 122f. No. 9.

K1335. Seduction (or wooing) by stealing clothes of bathing girl. R4.1. Enemy surprised while bathing; taken.

R33. *Fairy physician abducted to heal wounded mortals.* (Cf. F344.) Irish myth: Cross.

R35. *Abducted princess gives birth to child.* Icelandic: *Boberg.

R39. *Abduction—miscellaneous.*

R39.1. *Abduction by magician.* India: Thompson-Balys.

R39.2. *Abduction by old woman.* India: Thompson-Balys.

R40. Places of captivity. Missouri French: Carrière.

B11.10.1. Dragon keeps maiden tied with golden chain. D2177. Imprisonment by magic. D2177.1. Demon enclosed in bottle. F165.6.1. Otherworld (fairyland) as place of sorrowful captivity. F375. Mortal imprisoned in otherworld (fairyland). J229.12. Prisoners given choice between emasculation and blinding. K700. Capture by deception. Q435. Magic imprisonment in cleft tree. Q455.2.1.1. Adulteress confined in room containing corpse of her paramour. R100. Rescues. R210. Escapes. T50.1. Girl carefully guarded from suitors.

R41. *Captivity in tower (castle, prison).*

K1931.5. Impostors throw hero into prison. Q433. Punishment: imprisonment. R121. Means of rescue from prison. R211. Escape from prison.

R41.1. *Captivity in castle.* *Type 400; English: Wells 66 (Ywain and Gawain); Irish myth: *Cross; India: *Thompson-Balys.

R41.1.1. *Captivity in subterranean palace.* India: Thompson-Balys.

R41.2. *Captivity in tower.* *Type 310; Dickson 198 n. 8; Irish myth: *Cross; Italian: Basile Pentamerone II No. 1, IV No. 6, Rotunda; India: *Thompson-Balys.

F772.2.1. Brazen tower. M372. Confinement in tower to avoid fulfillment of prophecy. T381. Imprisoned virgin to prevent knowledge of men, marriage, impregnation. Usually kept in a tower.

R41.2.1. *Slandered wife is locked in tower for forty days.* If no champion appears, she is to be burned. Former suitor rescues her. Spanish: Childers.

R41.2.2. *Captivity in bower.* Irish myth: *Cross.

R41.3. *Captivity in dungeon.* Irish myth: *Cross; English: Wells 22 (Sir Beues of Hamtoun); Jewish: Neuman.

Q544. Penance: being locked in cellar with key thrown into water.

R41.3.1. *Prison filled with snakes.* (Cf. Q465.1.) *Boje 92; Hdwb. d. Märchens I 436b nn. 183—198; Irish myth: Cross; Jewish: Neuman.

R41.3.2. *Prison with stream of water in it.* Boje 93.

R41.3.3. *Prison floor with spikes in it.* Boje 91ff.

R41.3.4. *Captivity in well.* India: Thompson-Balys.

R41.4. *Groom as prisoner in his and giantess's bridal chamber.* (Cf. R41.5.) Icelandic: *Boberg.

R41.5. *Abducted princess fettered in hall with 100 doors.* Bridal bed for her and giant in the midst. (Cf. R111.2.3.) Icelandic: Boberg.

R41.5.1. *Queen kept in palace of forty doors, each of them watched by a dog.* Africa (Dahome): Einstein 25.

R41.6. *Captivity in a pillar.* Cheremis: Sebeok-Nyerges.

R41.7. *Captivity in cages.* (Cf. Q433.1.) Cheremis: Sebeok-Nyerges; Jewish: Neuman.

R42. *Captivity in sunken valley.* Irish myth: *Cross.

R43. *Captivity on island.* Irish myth: *Cross; India: *Thompson-Balys.

R45. *Captivity in mound (cave, hollow hill).* *Type 870; *BP III 443ff., 450; *Fb "höj" I 740b, 741; **Liungman Traditionsstudie över sagan om prinsessan i jordkulan (Göteborg, 1925). — Irish myth: *Cross; Icelandic: *Boberg; Spanish: Boggs FFC XC 54 No. 405*A; India: *Thompson-Balys; Chinese: Graham.

F721.2. Habitable hill. R112. Magic rescue of prisoner from mound.

R45.1. *Man confined under roots of tree.* N. A. Indian (Seneca): Curtin-Hewitt RBAE XXXII 705 No. 135.

R45.2. *Imprisonment in lion's den.* Italian: Basile Pentamerone III No. 5; Missouri French: Carrière; Spanish Exempla: Keller; Jewish: Neuman.

R45.3. *Captivity in cave.*

R45.3.1. *Bear keeps human wife captive in cave with stone at entrance.* India: *Thompson-Balys.

R46. *Captivity under water.* India: *Thompson-Balys.

F420.5.2.1.1. Water-maiden enamors man and draws him under water.

R47. *Captivity in lower world.* India: Thompson-Balys.

R49. *Other places of captivity.*

R49.1. *Captivity in tree.* India: Thompson-Balys.

R49.2. *Captivity in an oven.* Cheremis: Sebeok-Nyerges.

R49.3. *Ogre seizes girl and puts her in a drum.* Africa (Luba): DeClerq ZsKS IV 225.

R50. Conditions of captivity.

R51. *Mistreatment of prisoners.* Irish myth: Cross.

A185.2.2. God makes man's hand rigid so he can no longer torment captive. Q450. Cruel punishments.

R51.1. *Prisoners starved.* Irish myth: Cross; Jewish: Neuman.

Q465.2. Prisoners put into pit filled with corpses in order to starve. S123.4. Avenger plans to let Atilla starve in mountain chamber.

R51.2. *Prisoners confined in chains.* Irish myth: *Cross; Jewish: Neuman.

R51.3. *Prisoners mutilated.* Irish myth: Cross; Jewish: Neuman.

R51.4. *Prisoner massacred.* Jewish: Neuman.

R53. *Captivity as refuge for the captive.* Type 870.

R53.1. *Woman hidden in underground chamber or mud cabin.* (Cf. R45.) Icelandic: *Boberg.

R53.2. *Woman hidden in sacred place which her lover is not supposed to dare to enter.* Icelandic: *Boberg.

R53.3. *Girl locked up in order to postpone wedding.* Icelandic: Göngu-Hrólfs saga 306.

R53.4. *Faithful servant locks his master and his friend up in a little house built from wood from their wrecked ships;* they falsely think themselves betrayed. Icelandic: Boberg.

H1556. Tests of fidelity. P361. Faithful servant. R169.4. Hero rescued by servant.

R54. *Hero locked up while his father is murdered.* Icelandic: Boberg.

R61. *Person sold into slavery.* *Types 506, 888; Italian Novella: *Rotunda; Jewish: Neuman; Africa (Fang): Einstein 151.

K1812.11. Incognito prince (king) sold into slavery. P173. Captive king's sons made slaves. Q42.4. Man frees slave (incognito prince). Q437.1. Criminal's wife and children sold into slavery. R111.1.6. Princess ransomed from slavery. R152.2. Woman disguised as man sells herself into slavery in order to ransom (free) her husband (lover). S210.1. Child sold into slavery.

R70. Behavior of captives. Irish myth: *Cross.

F848.1. Girl's long hair as ladder into tower. J861.1. Consoled by a drop of honey. Man in pit surrounded by perils thus comforts himself. Q54.2. Captive knight freed for keeping his word.

R71. *Captive prince joins captor out of gratitude for his freedom.* (He had refused to promise that he would not fight again.) (Cf. W27.) Italian Novella: *Rotunda.

R72. *Defiant prisoners refuse to accept grace even from their father unless it is granted them all.* (Cf. M165.) Hdwb. d. Märchens II "Gnade ausbitten"; Icelandic: Boberg.

R74. *Defeated warriors go into the conqueror's service.* Icelandic: *Boberg.

M161.5. Rather die than go in the enemy's service.

R74.1. *Defeated enemy turns conqueror's best friend.* Icelandic: *Boberg.

R74.2. *Defeated enemy's son turns conqueror's man.* Icelandic: *Boberg.

R74.3. *Defeated enemy holds rank and country when he promises to pay tax to conqueror.* Icelandic: *Boberg.

R74.3.1. *Imprisoned king's son released when he promises to be a faithful subject and pay tax.* Icelandic: *Boberg.

R75. *Surrendering.*

K777. Capture of castle by pretending to surrender and entering.

R75.1. *Defeated surrender their city.* Icelandic: *Boberg.

R75.2. *Warriors surrender after chief's death.* Icelandic: Boberg.

R75.2.1. *Warriors flee after chief's death.* Icelandic: Boberg.

R81. *Woman suckles imprisoned relative through prison wall.* **Köhler-Bolte I 373, II 387; *Fb "datter" IV 94b; *DeCock Studien en Essays 23ff.; *Crane Vitry 232f. No. 238; *Oesterley No. 215; Herbert III 220; Alphabet No. 166; Scala Celi 39a No. 220; *Krappe Bulletin Hispanique XXXIX 28. — Spanish: Keller, Espinosa II No. 17; Jewish: Neuman.

H807. Formerly I was daughter, now I am mother; I have a son who was the husband of my mother. (Girl has suckled her imprisoned father through a crack in the prison wall.) T215.2. Wife offers starving husband milk from her breasts.

R81.1. *Woman suckles husband isolated on rock.* Irish myth: Cross.

R82. *Captive sends secret message outside* (in orange or on handkerchief). India: *Thompson-Balys.

R83. *Baker, disguised as old woman, substitutes for princess in cell when he brings bread to her.* India: Thompson-Balys.

R84. *Prisoner's sustenance from outside prison.* (Cf. R81.) Jewish: *Neuman.

R85. *Captive protected by angel from abductor.* Jewish: *Neuman.

R100—R199. Rescues.

R100. Rescues.

B360. Animals grateful for rescue from peril of death. B370. Animal grateful to captor for release. B544. Animal rescues captive. D795. Maiden disenchanted, deserted, and refound. D1390. Magic object rescues person. D1391. Magic object saves person from execution. D1393. Magic object helps fugitive. D1395. Magic object frees person from prison. D1421.5.1. Magic horn summons army for rescue. F913. Victims rescued from swallower's belly. G671. Wild man released from captivity aids hero. P21. Queen intervenes for condemned courtiers. Q42.1.2. Man who divides food with beggar is later released from captivity by him. Q53. Reward for rescue.

R110. Rescue of captive.

R110.1. *Goddess delivers and restores goods of man thrown into jail.* India: Thompson-Balys.

R111. *Rescue of captive maiden.* (Cf. H1385.1, R10.1.) *Sparnaay 45ff.; Hdwb. d. Märchens I 550a nn. 219, 220, 554b; Breton: Sébillot Incidents s.v. "princesse"; French Canadian: Barbeau JAFL XXIX 18; Spanish: Espinosa II Nos. 133—35, III Nos. 140, 143; India: *Thompson-Balys; N. A. Indian: Thompson CColl II 334ff.

R111.0.1. *All man's property offered to rescuer of stolen daughter.* India: Thompson-Balys.

R111.1. *Princess (maiden) rescued from captor.* India: *Thompson-Balys.

T68. Princess offered as prize.

R111.1.1. *Rescue of princess from ogre.* See references to R11.1. Type 590; BP III 1; *Basset RTP III 562; English: Wells 64 (The Avowynge of King Arthur), 66 (Ywain and Gawain), 70 (Libeaus Disconus); Irish myth: *Cross: Spanish: Espinosa III No. 143; Italian: Basile Pentamerone IV No. 3; India: *Thompson-Balys; Japanese: Anesaki 307, 359; N. A. Indian (Zuñi): Benedict II 341.

B82.1.2. Harp music makes merman restore stolen bride. G550. Rescue from ogre.

R111.1.2. *Princess rescued from robbers.* *Types 506B, 970**; *BP III 490ff.; *Liljeblad Tobiasgeschichte; Icelandic: Boberg; Italian: Basile Pentamerone I No. 7; India: *Thompson-Balys.

R111.1.3. *Rescue of princess (maiden) from dragon.* *Types 300, 303; *Hartland Perseus III 1—65 passim; **Ranke FFC CXIV; *BP I 534; *Loomis White Magic 119. See also references to B11.10 and B11.11. — Icelandic: *Boberg; Missouri French: Carrière; Spanish: Espinosa II Nos. 133—135, Espinosa Jr. Nos. 68f.; Greek: *Frazer Apollodorus I 158 n. 3; India: *Thompson-Balys; Japanese: Ikeda.

B11.10. Sacrifice of human being to dragon. B11.11. Fight with dragon.

R111.1.4. *Rescue of princess (maiden) from giant (monster).* (Cf. G100.) *Dickson 132 n. 106; *Brown Iwain 50 n. 1; Irish myth: *Cross; English: Wells 117 (Sir Torrent of Portyngale); Icelandic: *Boberg; India: Thompson-Balys; Japanese: Ikeda.

R111.1.5. *Rescue of woman from snake-husband.* (Cf. B604.1.) Jamaica: *Beckwith MAFLS XVII 272 No. 85.

R111.1.6. *Princess ransomed from slavery.* (Cf. R61.) *Type 506A; India: Thompson-Balys.

R111.1.6.1. *Queen rescued from slavery.* Irish myth: Cross.

R111.1.7. *Rescue of princess (maiden) from magician.* (Cf. D1711.) Irish myth: *Cross; Icelandic: *Boberg.

R111.1.8. *Rescue of maidens from witches.* (Cf. G200.) Icelandic: *Boberg.

R111.1.9. *Princess rescued from undesired suitor.* Icelandic: *Boberg.

H217.2. Decision by single combat or holmgang as to who is going to marry girl. H335.4.4. Suitor task: to kill (defeat) unwelcome suitor. K1371.1. Lover steals bride from wedding with unwelcome suitor.

M149.2. Vow rather to die than marry unwelcome suitor. Q411.2.1. Undesired suitor killed asleep in his tent. T320. Escape from undesired lover.

R111.1.10. *Rescue of princess (queen, maiden) from supernatural being who has won her at game of chance.* Irish myth: *Cross.

R111.1.11. *Maiden rescued from rakshasa.* India: *Thompson-Balys.

R111.1.12. *Princess rescued from captivity of elephant.* India: Thompson-Balys.

R111.1.13. *Rescue of girl from tigers.* Chinese: Graham.

R111.1.13.1. *Rescue of woman from bear's cave.* Cheremis: Sebeok-Nyerges; India: Thompson-Balys.

R111.2. *Princess rescued from place of captivity.* India: Thompson-Balys.

R111.2.1. *Princess(es) rescued from lower world.* *Type 301; *BP II 300; French Canadian: Barbeau JAFL XXIX 25; Missouri French: Carrière; Spanish: Espinosa II 133—135; India: Thompson-Balys; Indonesia: Dixon 215.

F81.1. Orpheus. F101. Return from lower world.

R111.2.1.1. *Stolen woman rescued from lower world.* India: Thompson-Balys.

R111.2.2. *Rescue of princess from mountain.* *Type 530; *BP III 111; Icelandic: De la Saussaye 143, 144 (Siegfried and Brunhilde).

D1330.1. Waberlohe. H331.1.1. Suitor contest: riding up glass mountain.

R111.2.3. *Princess rescued from giant's cave where she is fettered to a chair by the hair.* (Cf. R41.5.) Icelandic: *Boberg.

R111.2.3.1. *Rescue of earl's daughter from giant's cave where she is chained to the wall (a pillar).* Icelandic: *Boberg.

R111.2.4. *Princess rescued from temple where she is imprisoned.* Icelandic: Bósa saga 30ff ch. 8, 114ff ch. 12, Boberg.

R111.2.5. *Girl rescued from tree.* Chinese: Graham.

R111.3. *Means of rescuing princess.*

R111.3.1. *Girl rescued by traveling through air.* Jones PMLA XXIII 563; India: *Thompson-Balys.

D2135. Magic air journey. R215. Escape from execution pyre by means of wings.

R111.4. *Hero returns rescued princess to her betrothed.* Type 506; BP III 490ff.

R111.5. *Nobleman rescues lady from treacherous servant.* Italian Novella: Rotunda.

R111.6. *Girl rescued and then abandoned.* Types 300, 303; *Ranke FFC CXIV.

R111.7. *Joint rescuers quarrel over rescued princess.* Type 653; India: Thompson-Balys; Africa (Konde): Gemuseus und Berger ZsES XXIII 1ff., (Tanga): Nassau JAFL XXVIII 30ff. No. 5, (Vai): Ellis 200f. No. 18.

H621. Skillful companions create woman: to whom does she belong? R166. Brothers having extraordinary skill rescue princess.

R111.8. *Rescued person stolen from rescuer.*

R111.8.1. *Rescued woman stolen from rescuer by demon.* India: Thompson-Balys.

R111.8.2. *Rescued woman stolen from rescuer by other men.* India: Thompson-Balys.

R112. *Magic rescue of prisoner from mound.* (Cf. R45.) *Fb "höj" I 740b; Irish myth: Cross; Spanish: Espinosa III No. 140; India: Thompson-Balys.

R112.1. *Three blasts on horn before sunrise to rescue prisoner from mound.* *Fb "höj" I 740b.

R112.2. *Riding three times around hill to free captive confined within.* Fb "ride" III 52b.

D1791. Magic power by circumambulation.

R112.3. *Rescue of prisoners from fairy stronghold.* Irish myth: *Cross.

R115. *King transformed to parrot frees captured parrots* (Cf. D641.) *Fischer-Bolte 209.

R115.1. *Husband transformed into mouse so he can enter cave-prison of his wife.* India: Thompson-Balys.

R116. *Rescue from robbers' den.* (Cf. R111.1.2.) *Type 851; BP I 188ff.; French Canadian: Sister Marie Ursule; Jewish: Neuman; India: *Thompson-Balys.

R117. *Rescue from being burned.* (Cf. R175.) Icelandic: Lagerholm 117—18, *Boberg; Jewish: *Neuman.

R121. *Means of rescue from prison.*

F848.1. Girl's long hair as ladder into tower. K500. Escape from death or danger by deception. K521.4.5. Adulteress escapes disguised as an old woman. K655. Prisoner kills his watchers who enter to torture him. R152.1. Disguised wife helps husband escape from prison. R211. Escape from prison.

R121.1. *Princess pulled through prison window by hand and freed.* Cape Verde Islands: Parsons MAFLS XV (1) 280 No. 91, 283 No. 92.

R121.2. *Rescuer impersonates captive and deceives blind guardian while captive escapes.* Mangaia (Cook Group): Dixon 75.

D1611. Magic object answers for fugitive.

R121.3. *House burned (torn) down to deliver man imprisoned in it.* *Chauvin VI 74 No. 239.

R121.4. *Ants carry silk threads to prisoner, who makes rope and escapes.* They have thread tied to their feet. Fischer-Bolte 212.

B544. Animal rescues captive. H506.4. Test of resourcefulness: putting thread through coils of snail shell. Thread tied to ant who pulls it through.

R121.5. *Ariadne-thread.* Prisoner given a thread as a clue to find his way out of the labyrinth in which he is being confined. *Herbert III 204; Oesterley No. 63; Greek: Frazer Apollodorus II 135 n. 3.

R135.1. Crumb (grain) trail eaten by birds. Lost persons cannot find way back. R162. Rescue by captor's daughter (wife, mother).

R121.6. *Rescue from prison by saint, who enters and breaks fetters.* (Cf. R165.) Alphabet No. 436; *Loomis White Magic 89, 93; Icelandic: *Boberg.

D1766.1.7. Saint opens prison door by prayer.

R121.6.1. *Saint appears to captor in vision and demands prisoner's release.* (Cf. R165.) Irish myth: Cross.

R121.6.2. *Locks marvelously open for person.* Irish myth: Cross (F1088.4); Jewish: Neuman.

R121.7. *Lovers ransomed from prison.* Italian Novella: *Rotunda.

R121.8. *Fairy mound destroyed to rescue person confined in it.* Irish myth: *Cross.

R121.9. *Stream carries communication between prisoner and rescuer.* Irish myth: Cross.

H35.4. Recognition by unique manner of carving chips. These sent down stream for recognition. H135.2. Milk poured into stream as signal.

R121.10. *With her teeth woman files away chain tying up husband.* India: Thompson-Balys.

R122. *Miraculous rescue.* Irish myth: Cross.

B522.4. Eagle carries off condemned child. D2120. Magic transportation. F1088. Extraordinary escapes.

R122.1. *Prisoner whirled away in blaze of fire.* Irish myth: Cross.

R122.2. *Prisoner carried off in cloud.* (Cf. D2121.7.) Irish myth: Cross.

R123. *Boon granted after prayer and widow's son is released from prison.* India: Thompson-Balys.

R130. Rescue of abandoned or lost persons.

B322.1. Hero feeds flesh to helpful eagle. Eagle is rescuing him by carrying him on his back. B563.4.1. Animal leads lost man home.

R131. *Exposed or abandoned child rescued.* Gaster Oldest Stories 171; Icelandic: *Boberg; Irish myth: *Cross; Missouri French: Carrière; Spanish: Espinosa II No. 19, Espinosa Jr. Nos. 138—41; India: *Thompson-Balys.

B535. Animal nurse. N820. Human helpers. P270. Foster relatives. R150. Rescuers. S140. Cruel abandonments and exposures. S350. Fate of abandoned child.

R131.0.1. *Nurse begs alms from door to door so as to keep child and nurture him.* India: Thompson-Balys.

R131.0.2. *Miraculous rescue of all exposed children.* Jewish: Neuman.

R131.1. *Hunter rescues abandoned child.* *Type 930; *Aarne FFC XXIII 56, 59; Missouri French: Carrière; Italian Novella: Rotunda; Greek: Fox 22 (Telephos), 57 (Atalanta).

R131.2. *Miller rescues abandoned child.* *Types 707, 930; BP II 380ff.; *Aarne FFC XXIII 61; Spanish: Espinosa Jr. No. 116.

R131.2.1. *Miller rescues drowning princess.* French Canadian: Sister Marie Ursule.

R131.3. *Herdsman rescues abandoned child.* (Cf. S351.2.) India: Thompson-Balys.

R131.3.1. *Shepherd rescues abandoned child.* (Cf. N841.) *Type 930; Hartland Perseus III 3 ff.; *Aarne FFC XXIII 56ff.; Dickson 101, 170; *Nutt FLR IV 1ff. — Roman: Fox 307 (Romulus and Remus); Italian Novella: Rotunda; Greek: Longus Daphnis and Chloe, Fox 43 (Zethos and Amphion), 48 (Oedipus), 118 (Paris).

R131.3.2. *Goatherd rescues abandoned child.* Greek: Fox 280.

R131.3.3. *Cowherd rescues abandoned child.* Irish myth: *Cross, MacCulloch Celtic 74; English: Wells 20 (William of Palerne); Greek: *Frazer Apollodorus I 338 n. 1.

R131.3.3.1. *Person pushed into well by wife rescued by cowherd.* India: Thompson-Balys.

R131.3.4. *Swineherd rescues abandoned child.* Irish myth: *Cross; India: *Thompson-Balys.

R131.4. *Fisher rescues abandoned child.* *Types 707, 930; BP II 380ff.; *Boje 65, 126; *Aarne FFC XXIII 62; English: Wells 14 (The Lay of Havelok); Italian Novella: Rotunda.

R131.5. *Servant rescues abandoned child.* Irish myth: *Cross; Icelandic: Gunnlaugs saga Ormstungu ch. 3, Boberg; Italian Novella: Rotunda.

R131.6. *Peasant rescues abandoned child.* Icelandic: Boberg; Spanish: Espinosa Jr. No. 139; Italian Novella: Rotunda; Babylonian: Spence 17, 157; India: *Thompson-Balys.

H92. Identification by necklace. H111. Identification by garment.

R131.7. *Merchant rescues abandoned child.* (Cf. N851.) Dickson 104 n. 13; Jewish: *Neuman.

R131.8. *Other workmen rescue abandoned child.*

R131.8.1. *Horse-keeper rescues abandoned child.* Greek: *Frazer Apollodorus I 82 n. 2.

R131.8.2. *Gardener rescues abandoned child.* India: *Thompson-Balys; Palaung tribe: Scott Indo-Chinese 276.

R131.8.3. *Washerman rescues abandoned child.* Palaung tribe: Scott Indo-Chinese 277.

R131.8.4. *Smith rescues abandoned child.* (Cf. N855.) Krappe Balor 3; Irish myth: Cross; Icelandic: De la Saussaye 143.

R131.8.5. *Forester rescues abandoned child.* *Boje 125ff.; Sparnaay 43; Chinese: Ferguson 41.

R131.8.6. *Potter rescues abandoned child(ren).* India: *Thompson-Balys.

R131.8.7. *Gold-washer rescues abandoned child.* India: *Thompson-Balys.

R131.8.8. *Barber rescues and befriends abandoned boy.* India: Thompson-Balys.

R131.9. *Porter rescues abandoned child.* English: Wells 126 (Lai Le Freine).

R131.10. *Hermit rescues abandoned child.* (Cf. N843, R169.2.) English: Wells 96 (Chevalere Assigne); Italian Novella: Rotunda; India: *Thompson-Balys.

R131.10.1. *Woman disguised as hermit rescues abandoned child.* (Cf. K1837.3.) Italian Novella: Rotunda.

R131.11. *Exalted person rescues abandoned child.* Dickson 170.

R131.11.1. *Princess rescues abandoned child.* Sparnaay 33; Dickson 37, 170; Jewish: *Neuman; China: Eberhard FFC CXX 99ff. No. 58, FFC CXXVIII 76f. No. 34.

R131.11.2. *King rescues abandoned child.* Dickson 170 n. 24; Italian: Basile Pentamerone III No. 2; Jewish: *Neuman; India: *Thompson-Balys.

N836.1. King adopts hero (heroine). S354. Exposed infant reared at strange king's court (Joseph, Oedipus).

R131.11.3. *Prince rescues abandoned child.* Italian: Basile Pentamerone V No. 8.

R131.11.4. *Deity rescues abandoned child.* India: Thompson-Balys.

R131.11.5. *Minister's son recovers prince's lost wife for him.* India: Thompson-Balys.

R131.12. *Fairy rescues abandoned child.* (Cf. F311.) Krappe Balor 3; Irish myth: Cross.

R131.13. *Palmer rescues abandoned child.* (Cf. N846.1.) English: Wells 118 *(Octovian).

R131.14. *Sailors rescue abandoned child.* Italian: Basile Pentamerone III No. 2.

R131.15. *Children abandoned in a boat survive storm and are rescued.* Italian Novella: Rotunda.

R131.16. *Angel rescues abandoned child.* Jewish: Neuman.

R131.17. *Coyote rescues abandoned child(ren).* N. A. Indian (California): Gayton and Newman 89.

R131.18. *Pious woman rescues abandoned child.* Irish myth: Cross.

R131.19. *Bard (poet) rescues abandoned child.* Irish myth: *Cross.

R131.20. *Indians rescue abandoned children.* French Canadian: Sister Marie Ursule.

R133. *Vanished wife rescued.*

R133.1. *Hero finds his vanished wife and disenchants her.* India: Thompson-Balys.

R133.2. *Lost wife restored by conjurer.* Eskimo (Cumberland Sound): Boas BAM XV 246.

R135. *Abandoned children (wife, etc.) find way back by clue (breadcrumb, grain, pebble, etc.).* They have dropped the objects while being led away. *Types 327, 431, 620, 955; *BP I 115ff., 124, 370; Köhler-Bolte I 134; *Penzer III 104 n. 2; Fb "ært" III 1153b, "gryn" IV 187a; *Saintyves Perrault 310. — Irish myth: Cross; Italian: Basile Pentamerone V No. 8; Japanese: Ikeda; Indonesia: *Dixon 227 n. 35, DeVries's list No. 147; Philippine: Fansler MAFLS XII 442; Lkuñgen: Hill-Tout JAI XXXVII 334; S. A. Indian (Warrau): Métraux RMLP XXXIII 145; Africa (Kaffir): Theal 120.

B151.2.0.1. Bird shows way by dropping feathers. K321. Thief learns location of dupe's food supply by strewing ashes. R121.5. Ariadne-thread.

R135.0.1. *Stolen wife makes trail of speaking spittle for husband.* Spittle speaks and directs him. Jamaica: Beckwith MAFLS XVII 263 No. 67.

D1316.3. Speaking spittle reveals truth. D1611.5. Magic spittle impersonates fugitives.

R135.0.2. *Trail of grain (seeds).* (Cf. R267.) India: *Thompson-Balys.

R135.0.2.1. *Trail of rice husks.* India: *Thompson-Balys.

R135.0.3. *Trail of jewels.* India: *Thompson-Balys.

R135.0.4. *Trail of shreds of dress.* India: *Thompson-Balys.

R135.0.5. *Trail of thread.* India: *Thompson-Balys.

R135.0.6. *Trail of ashes.* India: *Thompson-Balys.

R135.0.7. *Trail of flowers.* India: Thompson-Balys.

R135.1. *Crumb (grain) trail eaten by birds.* Lost persons cannot find way back. *Types 327, 431; Missouri French: Carriére; Japanese: Ikeda.

R135.1.1. *Feathers left to mark trail blown away by wind.* S. A. Indian (Warrau): Métraux RMLP XXXIII 145.

R137. *Mermaid rescues heroine who has been thrown overboard.* (Cf. B81.) Italian: Basile Pentamerone IV No. 7; India: Thompson-Balys.

R138. *Rescue from shipwreck.* Icelandic: *Boberg; India: Thompson-Balys.

R138.1. *Mermaid rescues hero (boy) from shipwreck.* Icelandic: Lagerholm 164f., Boberg.

R138.2. *Gam rescues hero as boy from shipwreck.* Icelandic: Lagerholm 163—164.

B31.2. The bird Gam.

R141. *Rescue from well.* India: *Thompson-Balys.

R142. *Exposed children swallowed by earth; vomited up when grown.* (Cf. F900.) Jewish: Neuman.

R143. *Abandoned man befriended by a Centaur.* (Cf. B21.) Greek: Grote I 109.

R150. Rescuers. Missouri French: Carrière.

B53.1. Drowning man rescued by siren. B540. Animal rescuer or retriever. B541.2. Fox rescues man from sea. B541.4. Dog rescues drowning man. F601.4. Extraordinary companions rescue hero (heroine). H1385. Quest for lost persons. N730. Accidental reunion of families. N800. Helpers. R121.6. Rescue from prison by saint, who enters and breaks fetters. R131. Exposed or abandoned child rescued. S251. Virgin Mary rescues child promised to the devil.

R151. *Husband rescues wife.* Irish myth: Cross.

F322.2. Man rescues his wife from fairyland. N658. Husband arrives home just in time to save wife and her father from being burned to death in their home. T210. Faithfulness in marriage.

R151.1. *Husband rescues stolen wife.* (Cf. H1385.3, R11.1.) Krappe Revue Celtique XLVIII (1931) 94—123; Irish myth: *Cross; Spanish: Boggs FFC XC 46 No. 316; India: *Thompson-Balys; Japanese: Ikeda; N. A. Indian: *Thompson Tales 342 n. 235; Africa (Ila, Rhodesia): Smith and Dale II 399 No. 1.

R151.1.1. *Husband frees wife who has sold herself into slavery in order to ransom him.* Italian Novella: Rotunda.

R151.2. *Husband rescues wife from burning at stake.* (Cf. R175.) *Dickson 78.

R151.3. *Husband rescues wife from cannibal.* (Cf. G10.) Chinese: Graham.

R152. *Wife rescues husband.* Type 316; Missouri French: Carrière; Greek: Grote I 462f.; Jewish: Neuman; India: *Thompson-Balys.

K1353. Woman deceived into sacrificing honor. Ruler promises to release her brother (husband) but afterward refuses to do so. T210. Faithfulness in marriage.

R152.1. *Disguised wife helps husband escape from prison.* (Cf. R121.) *Types 880, 888, 890; Spanish Exempla: Keller; Italian Novella: Rotunda; West Indies: Flowers 521.

R152.2. *Woman disguised as man sells herself into slavery in order to ransom (free) her husband (lover).* (Cf. K1837.) Italian Novella: *Rotunda.

R152.3. *Wives change clothes with their imprisoned husbands when allowed to visit them.* Husbands escape. Greek: Grote I 463.

R152.4. *Wife gets back her husband from land of serpents by charming him with her beautiful dance.* India: Thompson-Balys.

B225.1. Kingdom of serpents. F81.1. Orpheus.

R152.5. *Transformed wife takes husband out of captivity.* India: Thompson-Balys.

D641. Transformation to reach difficult place.

R153. *Parents rescues child.* (Cf. S351.)

R153.1. *Parents rescue son.*

R153.1.1. *Parents rescue son from lower world on rope.* Africa (Basuto): Jacottet 86 No. 13.

R153.2. *Father rescues children.*

R153.2.1. *Father hides children from murderous mother.* After many years they come forth and she dies of fright. *Type 765.

Q211.8. Punishment for desire to murder. S12. Cruel mother.

R153.3. *Father rescues son(s).* Icelandic: Lagerholm 170ff., *Boberg.

R153.3.1. *Father rescues son captured by enemy.* Type 899*; Spanish Exempla: Keller.

R153.3.2. *Father rescues son stolen by animals.* Africa (Bushmen, South of Zambesi): Theal 56.

R153.3.3. *Old robber frees his three sons: relates frightful adventures.* In order to free them he must relate three adventures, each more frightful than the last. *Type 953; *BP III 369; Wesselski Märchen 217 No. 29.

H924. Tasks assigned prisoner so that he may escape punishment. J1185. Execution escaped by story-telling.

R153.3.4. *Father rescues son from prison.* Italian Novella: Rotunda.

R153.3.5. *Fathers thrust sons above water even as they themselves drown.* Spanish Exempla: Keller.

R153.3.6. *Father hides son from Satan.* Jewish: Neuman.

R153.4. *Mother rescues son.*

R153.4.1. *Mother rescues fettered son.* Icelandic: Boberg.

R153.4.2. *Mother hides twin (triplet) sons to keep them from death.* (Cf. S314.) Africa (Fang): Tessman 90, Einstein 56.

R153.5. *Father rescues daughter.* Irish myth: *Cross; Icelandic: Lagerholm 134ff., *Boberg; Eskimo (Greenland): Rasmussen III 85, (Central Eskimo): Boas RBAE VI 584, (Cumberland Sound): Boas BAM XV 164.

N732.1. Father unwittingly buys daughter who has been sold into slavery.

R154. *Children rescue parents.* India: Thompson-Balys.

R154.0.1. *Children rescue mother from lion's den.* Dickson 57 n. 75.

R154.1. *Son rescues mother.* Irish myth: *Cross; India: *Thompson-Balys; Buddhist myth: Malalasekera I 207.

R154.1.1. *Son rescues mother from burning at stake.* (Cf. R175.) *Dickson 128ff. nn. 98, 99.

R154.2. *Son rescues father.* Type 301C*; Irish myth: *Cross; Icelandic: Boberg; India: *Thompson-Balys.

H1385.7. Quest for lost father. J151.1. Wisdom of hidden old man saves kingdom.

R154.2.1. *Son frees father by bringing riddle the king cannot solve.* (Cf. H542.) Spanish: Boggs FFC XC 112 No. 927*B.

R154.2.2. *Son recovers father's bones.* Hawaii: Beckwith myth 259, 263, 346f.; Tahiti: ibid. 266; Maori: ibid. *249.

R154.2.3. *Sons rescue father.* India: Thompson-Balys.

R154.3. *Daughter rescues father.* Rumania: Schullerus FFC LXXVIII No. 879*; Italian Novella: Rotunda; India: Thompson-Balys.

R155. *Brothers rescue brothers.* Icelandic: *Boberg; Missouri French: Carrière; India: Thompson-Balys.

G551.4. One brother rescues another from ogre. H1385.8. Quest for lost brother.

R155.1. *Youngest brother rescues his elder brothers.* (Cf. L31.) *Types 303, 303*, 327**, 471, 551; MacCulloch Childhood 353; *BP I 503ff., 528ff. — Icelandic: *Boberg; Missouri French: Carrière; Arabian: Burton Nights S V 249; Jewish: *Neuman; India: *Thompson-Balys; Indonesia: DeVries's list No. 182; N. A. Indian (Arapaho): Dorsey and Kroeber FM V 23ff. Nos. 10, 11, (Dakota): Wissler JAFL XX 199, (Chinook): Boas BBAE XXV 9ff. Nos. 1, 2, (Quinault): Farrand JE II 114 No. 10, (Caddo): Dorsey CI XLI 58ff. Nos. 32, 33, (Klikitat): Jacobs UWash II 7; Africa (Thonga): Junod 229, (Fjort): Dennett 64 No. 12.

R155.2. *Elder brother rescues younger.* India: Thompson-Balys.

R156. *Brother rescues sister(s).* (Cf. G551.1.) Irish myth: Cross; Icelandic: *Boberg; Spanish: Espinosa II No. 18; Greek: Grote I 156; India: *Thompson-Balys; Chinese: Graham.

R157. *Sisters rescue sisters.* (Cf. G551.2.)

R157.1. *Youngest sister rescues elder.* (Cf. L50.) *Type 311; *BP I 398ff.; *Roberts 219.

R158. *Sister rescues brother(s).* *Type 707; Icelandic: *Boberg; Rumanian: Schullerus FFC LXXVII No. 879*; India: *Thompson-Balys.

R161. *Lover rescues his lady.* Irish myth: *Cross; Icelandic: Boberg; West Indies: Flowers 571.

R161.0.1. *Hero rescued by his lady.* Irish myth: *Cross; India: Thompson-Balys.

R161.1. *Lover rescues his lady from abductor.* Irish myth: *Cross; English: Wells 80 (Sir Tristrem); India: Thompson-Balys.

R161.2. *Princess rescued by blind man restores his sight and marries him.* India: Thompson-Balys.

R161.3. *Lover rescues his lady from drowning.* Icelandic: *Boberg.

R161.4. *Lover rescues his lady from the gallows.* England, U.S.: *Baughman, Child No. 95.

R162. *Rescue by captor's daughter (wife, mother).* Types 516, 975**; *Rösch FFC LXXVII 102; *Loomis White Magic 117; Basset RTP XVI 614; Irish myth: Cross; English: Wells 85 (The Sowdone of Babylone); Icelandic: *Boberg; Greek: *Frazer Apollodorus II 135 n. 3 (Ariadne); India: *Thompson-Balys.

G530. Ogre's relative aids hero. K640. Escape by help of confederate. K646. Fugitive's confederate misdirects pursuer. K781. Castle captured with assistance of owner's daughter. She loves the attacker. N831. Girl as helper. R121.5. Ariadne-thread. Prisoner given a thread as a clue to find his way out of the labyrinth in which he is being confined. T32.1. Lovers' meeting: hero in heroine's father's prison from which she helps him escape. T91.6.4.1. Sultan's daughter in love with captured knight.

R163. *Rescue by grateful dead man.* (Cf. E341.) *Types 505—508; **Liljeblad passim; India: Thompson-Balys.

R164. *Rescue by giant.* (Cf. G100.) India: Thompson-Balys.

R164.1. *Giant rescues maiden.* Dickson 154.

R164.2. *Giant rescues woman from burning at stake.* (Cf. R175.) *Dickson 130 n. 102.

R165. *Rescue by saint (holy man).* (Cf. R121.6.) Alphabet No. 560; *Loomis White Magic 93; Irish: Plummer cxlix, *Cross.

D2074.2.5.1. Imprisoned cleric comes to answer saint's prayers in ritual. N848. Saint as helper. R121.6.1. Saint appears to captor in vision and demands prisoner's release. R176. Executioner miraculously blinded; condemned man saved.

R165.1. *Rescue of poor girl by St. Nicholas.* Saint keeps her from being sold into slavery. Spanish Exempla: Keller.

R165.2. *Innocently hanged person saved by saint.* Icelandic: Boberg.

R165.3. *Abducted wife brought back by fakir.* India: Thompson-Balys.

R166. *Brothers having extraordinary skill rescue princess.* *Type 653; BP III 45ff.; *Köhler-Bolte I 198, 439; Italian: Basile Pentamerone V No. 7; Japanese: Ikeda.

F660. Remarkable skill. R111.7. Joint rescuers quarrel over rescued princess.

R167. *Master rescues disciple.* India: Thompson-Balys.

R168. *Angels as rescuers.* Irish myth: Cross (R169.12); Jewish: *Neuman.

R169. *Other rescuers.*

R169.1. *Hero in disguise of foolish knight, then of black knight, rescues lady.* (Cf. R222.) English: Wells 147 (Ipomadon).

R169.2. *Boys rescued from beasts by hermit.* (Cf. N843, R131.10.) Dickson 105.

R169.3. *Boy saved by werwolf.* (Cf. D113.1.1.) English: Wells 19 (William of Palerne).

R169.4. *Hero rescued by servant.* (Cf. P361, R53.4.) *Type 519, 851; India: Thompson-Balys.

R169.4.1. *Rescue of bride from mysterious perils by hidden faithful servant.* Type 516; *Rösch FFC LXXVII 128; India: *Thompson-Balys.

N342.1. Faithful servant guarding master's wife from danger falsely condemned for betraying his master. T175. Magic perils threaten bridal couple.

R169.4.2. *Rescue of king's children by faithful servant.* Icelandic: Boberg.

R169.5. *Hero rescued by friend.* Icelandic: *Boberg.

R169.5.1. *Hero's wife rescued by his faithful friend.* India: Thompson-Balys.

R169.6. *Youth saved from death sentence by father's friend.* Italian Novella: Rotunda.

H1558.1. Test of friendship: the half friend.

R169.7. *Royal minister rescues abandoned queen(s).* (Cf. P110.) India: Thompson-Balys.

R169.8. *Predestined rescuer.* South Africa: Bourhill and Drake 237ff. No. 20.

R169.9. *Boy rescued by childless woman.* Africa (Fang): Tessman 91.

R169.10. *Unpromising hero as rescuer.* (Cf. L100.) India: Thompson-Balys.

R169.10.1. *Fool rescues girl and wins her for his wife.* India: Thompson-Balys.

R169.11. *Unknown helper(s) emerge(s) in the last moment and turn(s) out later to be well known.* (Cf. R222.) Icelandic: *Boberg.

R169.12. *Hero rescued by sailors.* French Canadian: Sister Marie Ursule.

R169.13. *Child rescued by nurse.* Irish myth: *Cross.

R169.14. *Wounded hero restored in peasant's house.* Icelandic: Boberg.

R169.15. *Rescue by stranger.* India: Thompson-Balys.

R169.16. *Death as rescuer.* (Cf. R185.) Africa (Dahomé): Einstein 27.

R170. Rescue—miscellaneous motifs.

R175. *Rescue at the stake.* (Cf. R151.2, R154.1.1, R164.2, R215.) *Dickson 78 n. 40; *Boje 116ff.; English: Wells 97 (Chevalere Assigne); Icelandic: *Boberg; Jewish: *Neuman; India: Thompson-Balys; West Indies: Flowers 572.

D643.1. Transformation to falcon in order to rescue condemned man at the gallows. D1391. Magic object saves person from execution. D2141.0.7. Storm raised by incantation. Extinguishes execution fire. J1181. Execution escaped by use of special permissions granted the condemned. K551. Respite from death granted until particular act is performed. N686. Hero's (heroine's) identity established as he is on the point of being executed. P512. Condemned woman may be freed by marrying a rogue. V252.2. Virgin Mary saves criminal from fire at stake.

R175.1. *Escape from sacrificial altar on ram with golden fleece.* Greek: Grote I 117.

R176. *Executioner miraculously blinded: condemned man saved.* Jewish: *bin Gorion Born Judas[2] I 39, 361, Neuman.

R181. *Demon enclosed in bottle released.* *Type 331; *BP II 414ff., IV 321; Jewish: Neuman, **Levi Revue des Etudes Juives LXXXV 137; India: *Thompson-Balys; Japanese: Ikeda.

D2177.1. Demon enclosed in bottle. F403.2.2.4. Spirit in bottle (bag) as helper.

R181.1 *Demon imprisoned in tree released.* India: Thompson-Balys.

R182. *True rescuer hidden by girl when he arrives to claim her.* India: Thompson-Balys.

R185. *Mortal fights with "Death".* (Cf. R169.16.) *BP III 293; Greek: *Frazer Apollodorus I 92 n. 3, Fox 38, 107 (Alcestis, Sisyphus); India: Thompson-Balys.

T211.1. Wife dies so that husband's death may be postponed. Z111. Death personified.

R185.1. *Mortal deceives Angel of Death.* (Cf. V233.) Jewish: Neuman.

R187. *Horn of Roncevalles.* Hero calls aid of waiting soldiers on horn. *Thien Motive 32; Old French: Chanson de Roland.

R187.1. *Dord fían.* A call used by members of a fían (warrior band) for summoning aid. Irish myth: Cross.

R188. *Rescued person horrifies rescuers: e.g., they swoon on seeing him.* Scottish: Campbell-McKay No. 2 and note.

R191. *King (prince) returns home (from exile) and rescues his native country.* Icelandic: *Boberg.

L111.1. Exile returns and succeeds.

R200—R299. Escapes and pursuits.

R200. Escapes and pursuits.

R210. Escapes. Irish myth: Cross; India: Thompson-Balys.

A1070. Fettered monster's escape at end of world. D642. Transformation to escape difficult situation. D671. Transformation flight. D672. Obstacle flight. D2165. Escapes by magic. G561. Ogre tricked into carrying his prisoners home in bag. K500. Escape from death or danger by deception. K608. Escape by laughing and crying at same time. K622. Captive plays further and further from watchman and escapes. N255. Escape from one misfortune into worse.

R211. *Escape from prison.* Icelandic: *Boberg; Missouri French: Carrière.

D2074.2.5.1. Imprisoned cleric comes to answer saint's prayers in ritual. R41. Captivity in tower (castle, prison). R121. Means of rescue from prison. R311.2. King escapes pursuers through hollow tree in his hall.

R211.1. *Giant breaks from tower prison.* Dickson 130 n. 102; Japanese: Ikeda.

R211.2. *Captive bores way out of prison.* Icelandic: *Boberg; Swiss: Jegerlehner Oberwallis 313 No. 98; Korean: Zong in-Sob 174 No. 75.

R211.3. *Escape through underground passage.* Italian: Basile Pentamerone II No. 7.

R211.4. *Escape from slavery (pirates).* (Cf. R61.) Italian Novella: *Rotunda.

R211.5. *Captive hews through iron prison with sword.* Irish myth: Cross.

F625. Strong man: breaker of iron.

R211.6. *Captive knocks prison roof off.* (Cf. F627.) Irish myth: *Cross.

R211.7. *Escape from pit of snakes by means of rope.* (Cf. Q465, R41.3.1.) Icelandic: *Boberg.

R211.8. *Rescue from prison by beheading giant keeper.* French Canadian: Sister Marie Ursule.

R211.9. *Escape from prison because of bribed guards.* Buddhist myth: Malalasekera II 355.

R212. *Escape from grave.*

R212.1. *Man buried alive with king escapes from the tomb.* Follows noise made by sea animal and finds way out to sea. Chauvin VII 19 No. 373D n. 3.

P16.4. Person buried with dead king.

R212.1.1. *Man buried alive escapes from tomb when thief tries to rob it.* Italian Novella: Rotunda.

R212.1.2. *Captive buried alive to his neck fastens his teeth on jackal that comes to eat him and companions.* Rest flee when they hear him howl. In struggles to get free jackal loosens earth around captive, who manages to free himself. Buddhist myth: Malalasekera II 570.

R212.2. *Man buried alive with beloved escapes, as thieves break open the tomb.* Icelandic: Boberg.

R213. *Escape from home.*

R213.1. *Prince escapes from home in order to see world.* India: *Thompson-Balys.

R214. *Animal eludes bird watchman and escapes from his hole.* Indonesia: DeVries's list No. 112.

R215. *Escape from execution.*

R215.1. *Escape from execution pyre by means of wings.* *Type 575.

F1021.1. Flight on artificial wings. R111.3.1. Girl rescued by traveling through air. R175. Rescue at the stake.

R215.1.2. *Escape from execution pyre through underground passage.* Hdwb. d. Märchens I 600b. nn. 17—18.

R215.2. *Escape from death by boiling oil.* Irish myth: Cross.

R215.3. *Escape from execution on flying wooden horse.* (Cf. D1626.1.) India: *Thompson-Balys; Buddhist myth: Malalasekera II 839.

R216. *Escape from ship while captors quarrel.* Italian Novella: Rotunda.

R216.1. *Escape from ship by jumping into the sea.* Icelandic: *Boberg.

R217. *Inscription accidentally seen tells hero how to escape captivity.* Africa (Swahili): Steere 331ff.

R218. *Escape from fairyland.* (Cf. F210.) Irish myth: *Cross.

R219. *Escapes—miscellaneous.*

R219.1. *Man carried off on bed escapes by grasping tree limbs as he passes under tree.* India: *Thompson-Balys.

R219.2. *Man and wife escape from land of dead upon a vine.* (Cf. E481.) Philippine (Tinguian): Cole 185.

R220. Flights. India: Thompson-Balys.

A2221.5. Animal blessed for helping holy fugitive. A2231.7.1. Animal cursed for betraying holy fugitive. A2711.3. Plant blessed for helping holy fugitive. A2721.4. Plant cursed for betraying holy fugitive. B184.1.6. Flight on magic horse. D670. Magic flight. D1436. Magic hair stretches after fugitive. D1551. Waters magically divide and close. D1552.4. Mountain opens and lets ship on wheels, permitting magician's escape. D1611. Magic object answers for fugitive. D1612.1. Magic objects betray fugitive. D1813.4. Fugitives' way revealed by magic. K630. Escape by disarming (making pursuit difficult). Q46. Reward for protecting holy fugitive. T311.1. Flight of maiden to escape marriage.

R221. *Heroine's three-fold flight from ball.* Cinderella (Cap o' Rushes) after meeting the prince at a ball (church) flees before identification is possible. Repeated three times. *Type 510; **Cox 1—121, 437—446 passim; Missouri French: Carrière; Spanish: Espinosa Jr. Nos. 123f.; Italian: Basile Pentamerone I No. 6; India: Thompson-Balys.

C761.3. Tabu: staying too long at ball. H36.1. Slipper test. Identification by fitting of slipper. H151.6. Heroine in menial disguise discovered in her beautiful clothes: recognition follows. K1816.0.2. Girl in menial disguise at lover's court. L102. Unpromising heroine. N711.6. Prince sees heroine at ball and is enamoured.

R222. *Unknown knight.* (Three days' tournament.) For three days in succession an unknown knight in different armor wins a tournament and escapes without recognition. Finally identified by tokens. **Weston The Three Days Tournament; *Types 314, 502; *BP III 111; *Child V 44ff.; *Webster Kittredge Memorial Volume 227; Bruce MLN XXIV 257; *Hibbard 226 n. 2; *Fb "hest" I 598a; Zs. f. Vksk. IV 98; RTP VIII 82. — English: Wells 48 (Lancelot of the Laik), 147 (Ipomadon); Icelandic: *Boberg; Missouri French: Carrière; French Canadian: Barbeau JAFL XXIX 18; India: Thompson-Balys; N. A. Indian: *Thompson CColl II 349ff., 407, (Wichita): Dorsey JAFL XVI 160, (Skidi Pawnee): Dorsey MAFLS VIII Nos. 40, 41.

H331.2. Suitor contest: tournament. H1561.1. Test of valor: tournament. L225. Hero refuses reward. Rides away without it. P561. Tournaments. R169.1. Hero in disguise of foolish knight, then of black knight, rescues lady. R169.11. Unknown helper(s) emerge(s) in the last moment and turn(s) out later to be well known. T236. Woman enamored of an unknown knight in a tournament loses interest.

R224. *Girl flees to escape incestuous brother.* India: *Thompson-Balys.

T311.1. Flight of maiden (bridegroom) to escape marriage. T415.1. Lecherous brother.

R225. *Elopement.* *Type 516; Rösch FFC LXXVII 106; *Thien Motive 27; *Boje 110ff.; *Krappe Revue Hispanique LXXVIII (1930) 489—543. — Irish myth: *Cross; Icelandic: *Boberg; Missouri French: Carrière; Italian Novella: Rotunda; Greek: *Frazer Apollodorus II 174

n. 1 (Helen); India: *Thompson-Balys; Buddhist myth: Malalasekera II 860.

D2143.1.10. Wizard sells charm to raise rainstorm to enable eloping couple to escape pursuers. K1371.1. Lover steals bride from wedding with unwelcome suitor. N318.2. Princess accidentally elopes with wrong man. R312.1. Forest as refuge of eloping lovers. R315.1. Cave as eloping lovers' refuge. R355. Eloping girl recaptured by parents. T92.4. Girl mistakenly elopes with wrong man. T100. Marriage.

R225.1. *Elopement on winged horse.* Type 516; Rösch FFC LXXVII 110.

B542.2. Escape on flying horse.

R225.2. *Lovers elope to prevent girl's marriage to undesired fiancé.* Cent Nouvelles Nouvelles No. 98.

R227. *Wife flees from husband.* (Cf. P210, T200.) India: Thompson-Balys.

R227.1. *Wife flees from animal husband.* India: Thompson-Balys.

R227.2. *Flight from hated husband.* Irish myth: *Cross.

R227.3. *Supernatural wife finds garment stolen from her by husband and leaves him.* India: Thompson-Balys.

C31. Tabu: offending supernatural wife. D361.1. Swan Maiden. F302.4.2. Fairy comes into man's power when he steals her wings. K1335. Seduction (or wooing) by stealing clothes of bathing girl.

R228. *Children leave home because their parents refuse them food.* Irish myth: Cross.

R231. *Obstacle flight—Atalanta type.* Objects are thrown back which the pursuer stops to pick up while the fugitive escapes. *Pauli (ed. Bolte) No. 526; Köhler-Bolte I 430; Irish myth: Cross; Icelandic: *Boberg; Spanish: Espinosa II Nos. 122—25; Greek: Roscher Lexikon s.v. "Absyrtos"; India: Thompson-Balys; Buddhist myth: Malalasekera II 860; Japanese: Anesaki 224; N. A. Indian: *Thompson Tales 342 n. 232; S. A. Indian (Toba): Métraux MAFLS XL 74; Africa (Gold Coast): Barker and Sinclair 99 No. 18, 125 No. 22, (Zulu): Callaway 145, (Angola): Chatelain 101 No. 6, (Kaffir): Theal 46 No. 2, (Yoruba): Ellis 269 No. 4.

D672. Obstacle flight. D672.1. Magic objects as decoy for pursuer. F381.2.1. Escape from pursuing fairies by strewing path with bananas. H331.5.1.1. Apple thrown in race with bride. Distracts girl's attention, and as she stops to pick it up, suitor passes her. (Atalanta.) J351. Bodily member sacrificed to save life. K622.2. Escape from captor by throwing objects to great distance which captor tries to procure. K671. Captive throws his hat to lions who fight over it while he escapes. K672. Captive throws his shoe at serpent who chokes while he escapes.

R231.1. *Ogre tries to retain fugitive by tempting him with gold ring;* but he takes ring by cutting off the hand. Icelandic: Boberg.

R231.2. *Fugitive cuts tail of camel caught by pursuer and it turns into grass.* India: Thompson-Balys.

R231.2.1. *Helpful animal's tail cut off so pursuers who hang onto tail are shaken off into river.* India: Thompson-Balys.

R265. Pursuer (witch, giant) pulls out tail of fugitive's horse.

R233. *Fugitive kills pursuer and takes his extraordinary horse to continue flight.* Boje 96ff.

R235. *Fugitives cut support of bridge so that pursuer falls.* Indonesia: Dixon 229.

R236. *Pursuers aided by magic weather phenomenon.* Jewish: *Neuman.

R236.1. *Fugitive aided by magic mist.* Irish myth: *Cross; Jewish: Neuman.

D1361.1. Magic mist of invisibility. K532.1. Escape in mist of invisibility.

R236.2. *Sun sets at high noon to hide fugitive.* (Cf. F965.) Jewish: *Neuman.

R236.3. *Earthquake saves fugitive.* Jewish: Neuman.

R236.4. *Fugitive has magic wind against him, pursuer with him (caused by goddess).* Icelandic: Boberg.

R241. *Flight on skis; two on one pair.* Icelandic: *Boberg.

R242. *Flight carrying friend (girl) on back.* Icelandic: *Boberg.

R243. *Fugitives aided by helpful animal.* (Cf. B520.)

R243.1. *Pursuer misdirected by animal to help fugitive.* India: Thompson-Balys.

D1393.4. Tree points way to fugitive but misdirects enemy.

R244. *Ships burned to prevent flight.* Icelandic: Boberg.

R245. *Whale-boat.* A man is carried across the water on a whale (fish). (He usually deceives the whale as to the nearness of the land or as to hearing thunder. As a consequence the whale runs into the shore or is killed by lightning.) *Loomis White Magic 91; cf. Aarne FFC XXIII 137; Maori: Dixon 8; N. A. Indian: *Thompson Tales 327 n. 179; Jamaica: Beckwith MAFLS XVII 256f. Nos. 38, 39, 275 No. 86; Cape Verde Islands: Parsons MAFLS XV (1) 310 n. 1.

B175.1. Magic salmon carries hero over water. B472. Helpful whale. B541.1. Escape from sea on fish's back. B551.1. Fish carries man across water. B552.1. Alexander carried by two birds with meat held in front of them. J1172.4. Turtle released by man to carry him across stream. J1761.1. Whale thought to be island. K952.1. Ungrateful river passenger kills carrier from within. K1042. Water bird takes dupe to sea; shakes him off into water. K1177. Dupe deceived concerning the thunder; finally killed by it. M205.1.1.1. Fish (whale) carrying man through water shakes him off when man strikes him with coconut. S131.1. River carrier (whale, crocodile) throws passenger off and drowns him.

R245.1. *Crocodile-boat.* Trickster props his jaws apart and leaves him. India: Thompson-Balys.

K952.1. Ungrateful river passenger kills carrier from within.

R245.2. *Snake king takes fleeing captives across river.* Buddhist myth: Malalasekera I 785.

R246. *Crane-bridge.* Fugitives are helped across a stream by a crane who lets them cross on his leg. The pursuer is either refused assistance or drowned by the crane. N. A. Indian: *Thompson Tales 340 n. 227.

B463.3. Helpful crane. B523. Animals save man from pursuer. B555. Animals serve as bridge across stream. Q2. Kind and unkind.

R246.1. *Stone bridge appears for fugitives.* Disappears and drowns pursuers. Loomis White Magic 130.

R251. *Flight on a tree, which ogre tries to cut down.* **Parsons Zs. f. Ethnologie LIV 1-29; Bolte Zs. f. Vksk. XXXIII—XXXIV 38; Japanese: Ikeda; Korean: Zong in-Sob 9 No. 3; Africa (Togo): Einstein 12f.; Cape Verde Islands: Parsons MAFLS XV (1) 121 n. 3, 125, 131f.;

American Negro (Georgia): Harris Friends 91 No. 12. Cf. Thompson Tales 341 n. 230. Most African references in B421.

B524.1.2. Dogs rescue fleeing master from tree refuge. R311. Tree refuge.

R252. *Flight by vaulting on stick.* N. A. Indian (California): Gayton and Newman 92.

R253. *Escape from nest of giant bird by seizing two young birds and jumping.* Philippine (Tinguian): Cole 201.

R255. *Formula for girl fleeing: behind me night, etc.* "Behind me night and before me day that no one shall see where I go." *Type 510B; *BP II 46; Ainu: Ikeda (Type 175).

R257. *Fugitives sustain selves on apples.* Hdwb. d. Märchens I 90b no. 3.

R260. Pursuits. Missouri French: Carrière; India: Thompson-Balys.

D1432. Waters magically pursue man. D1813.2. Pursuit revealed by magic. F932.1. River pursues fugitive. K897.2.1. Giant impales self on javelin fugitive holds behind himself. Z49.2. Cumulative pursuit.

R261. *Pursuit by rolling object.*

C91.1. The offended rolling stone. D1430. Magic object pursues.

R261.1. *Pursuit by rolling head.* *Kittredge Gawain and the Green Knight 189 n. 1; Japanese: Ikeda; N. A. Indian: *Thompson Tales 343 nn. 238, 238a, *Alexander N. A. Myth. 290 n. 37; cf. JAFL II 69; (California): Gayton and Newman 79; S. A. Indian (Cashinawa): Métraux BBAE CXLIII (3) 684, (Chaco, Warrau, Shipaya): Lowie ibid. 54f., (Tenetehara): Wagley-Galvão ibid. 148; Africa (Congo): Weeks 207 n. 4.

D1641.7.1. Self-rolling head. E261.1. Wandering skull pursues man. F493.0.3.1. Pestilence in form of a head. F531.1.2.0.1. Gigantic head. G361.2. Great head as ogre. Q503.1. Skull of suicide must roll in dust until it has saved a life.

R262. *Magic eel pursues man over land.* Irish myth: Cross.

R265. *Pursuer (witch, giant) pulls out tail of fugitive's horse.* Fb "hale" IV 197b; cf. Burns "Tam O' Shanter"; India: Thompson-Balys.

G100. Giant ogre. G200. Witch. G273.4. Witch powerless to cross stream. R231.2.1. Helpful animal's tail cut off so pursuers who hang onto tail are shaken off into river.

R267. *Fugitives trailed by mustard seeds (ashes) dropped from bag.* (Cf. R135.) India: *Thompson-Balys; Africa (Kaffir): Theal 127ff.

K321. Thief learns location of dupe's food supply by strewing ashes.

R268. *Dew in footprints reveals man's way.* Icelandic: *Boberg.

R271. *Pursuit by fire.* N. A. Indian (California): Gayton and Newman 82.

R272. *Pursuer follows successive night campfires (each brighter than last).* Chinese: Graham.

R300—R399. Refuges and recapture.

R300. Refuges and recapture.

R310. Refuges. *Encyc. Rel. & Ethics s.v. "Asylum".

D1380.1. Waberlohe. Magic fire surrounds and protects. F942.1. Ground opens and swallows up person. K515. Escape by hiding. P322. Guest given refuge. S445. Abandoned wife hidden under a tub.

R311. *Tree refuge.* Type 162*; *Fb "træ" III 865a; *Hdwb. d. Märchens I 199a; BP I 429, II 195f. — Breton: Sébillot Incidents s.v. "arbres"; Missouri French: Carrière; India: *Thompson-Balys; Chinese: Graham; Japanese: Ikeda; N. A. Indian: *Thompson Tales 341 n. 230; S. A. Indian (Toba): Métraux MAFLS XL 62; Africa (Zulu): Callaway 145, 346.

A1023. Escape from deluge on tree. F811.10.1. Hollow tree as residence for hero. F1045. Night spent in tree. H135.1. Recognition by trimmed leaf thrown from tree hiding place. N711.1. King (prince) finds maiden in woods (tree) and marries her. N776. Light seen from tree lodging place at night leads to adventures. R251. Flight on a tree, which ogre tries to cut down. R351. Fugitive discovered by reflection in water.

R311.1. *Trees magically hide a fugitive.* Dh II 40ff.; N. A. Indian: Kroeber JAFL XXI 225.

R311.1.1. *Thorn-brake as refuge.* Irish myth: Cross.

R311.2. *King escapes pursuers through hollow tree in his hall.* Icelandic: Boberg.

R311.3. *Stolen child found in hollow tree.* India: Thompson-Balys.

R311.4. *Stretching tree refuge for fugitive.* (Cf. D482.1.) India: *Thompson-Balys.

R312. *Forest as refuge.*

R312.1. *Forest as refuge of eloping lovers.* (Cf. R225.) Schoepperle 391ff.; Irish myth: *Cross.

R313. *Princess hides in straw.* *Fb "halmstrå" I 540.

R314. *Negro takes refuge under princess's throne.* Malone PMLA XLIII 407.

R315. *Cave as refuge.* Irish myth: *Cross; Jewish: *Neuman; India: Thompson-Balys; Eskimo (Greenland): Rasmussen I 150.

B523.1. Spider web over hole saves fugitive.

R315.1. *Cave as eloping lovers' refuge.* (Cf. R225, T35.) Schoepperle 391ff.; Irish myth: Cross.

R315.2. *Christians crushed in cave where they take refuge from heathen.* Icelandic: Boberg.

R316. *Refuge on rock in sea.* Finnish: Kalevala rune 4.

R316.1. *Refuge on island.* Icelandic: Boberg.

R317. *Well (spring) as refuge.* Fb "kilde" II 118b; Irish myth: Cross; Africa (Benga): Nassau 225 No. 33, (Kaffir): Theal 129, (Basuto): Jacottet 160 No. 23.

R318. *Girl hidden in skin of her dead mother.* Köhler-Bolte I 346.

R318.1. *Boy hidden under skin in order not to be seen and prophesied about.* Icelandic: Örvar-Odds saga 12—13.

R321. *Escape to the stars.* Fugitives rise in the air and become stars. (Cf. R324.) Greek: Fox 250; Hindu: Keith 76; Japanese: Ikeda; Korean: Zong in-Sob 218 No. 98; Eskimo (West Hudson Bay): Boas BAM XV 360; N. A. Indian: Thompson Tales 291f. nn. 71, 71a; S. A. Indian (Chiriguano): Métraux RMLP XXXIII 158, 164, (Jivaro): ibid. 149.

R321.1. *Sister escapes to the stars to avoid marrying brother.* He is the thunder and her face is lightning. India: Thompson-Balys.

A736.1. Sun sister and moon brother. A1141. Origin of lightning. A1142. Origin of thunder. T415. Brother-sister incest.

R321.2. *Escape to moon.* Pursued hero escapes to moon. India: Thompson-Balys.

R322. *Eagle's nest as refuge.* Scottish: Campbell-McKay 1 n., 25; N. A. Indian (California): Gayton and Newman 95.

R323. *Refuge in upper world.*

R323.1. *Murderer escapes to sky on sky rope.* (Cf. F51.) India: Thompson-Balys.

R323.2. *Murderer escapes to sky in magic chariot.* Greek: Euripides' Medea.

R324. *Refuge in air.* Fugitive supernaturally rises in air to escape. (Cf. R321.) India: Thompson-Balys.

R324.1. *Escape from battle by flying in air.* Irish myth: *Cross; Eskimo (Mackenzie Area): Jenness 81, 86, (West Hudson Bay): Boas BAM XV 315, 541f., (Labrador): Hawkes GSCan XIV 151, (Greenland): Rasmussen III 99f., Rink 320, 455, 460.

R325. *Church (altar) as refuge.* Fb "kirke" II 125b; Irish myth: *Cross; Greek: Frazer Apollodorus I 276 n. 4; Jewish: *Neuman; Gaster Thespis 303f.; Japanese: Ikeda.

C51.1. Tabu: profaning shrine.

R325.1. *Devil chases ghost of wicked man until he puts his head into chapel window.* (Cf. E754.) England: *Baughman.

R325.2. *Idol cracks open to grant refuge to fugitive in answer to prayer; then closes again.* India: Thompson-Balys.

R325.3. *Saint offers murderer refuge.* Irish myth: Cross.

R326. *Escape to fairyland.* (Cf. F210.) Irish myth: *Cross.

R327. *Earth opens to rescue fugitive.* India: *Thompson-Balys.

F940. Extraordinary underground (underwater) disappearance.

R331. *Hero takes refuge at king's court.* *Dickson 143 nn. 140—42; Deutschbein 34; *Boje 74ff.

N836.1. King adopts hero (heroine).

R335. *Roof as refuge for pursued animals.* West Indies: *Flowers 573—75, Parsons MAFLS XVIII (3) 26 No. 6.

R336. *Refuge under kettle.* Icelandic: Boberg.

R341. *Escape by intervention of Providence.* (Cf. F942.1.)

R341.1. *Lightning strikes branch on which man is being hanged.* Delay gives him chance to prove his innocence. (Cf. R175.) U.S.: *Baughman.

R345. *Cities of refuge.* Jewish: *Neuman.

R350. Recapture of fugitive.

J1146.1. Detection by pitch-trap.

R351. *Fugitive discovered by reflection in water.* *Type 408; *Cox 503; *Cosquin Contes indiens 85ff.; *Köhler-Bolte I 281; Köhler-Bolte Zs. f. Vksk. VI 64 to Gonzenbach No. 14; Malone PMLA XLIII 399. — India: *Thompson-Balys; Chinese: Graham; Japanese: Ikeda; Indonesia: DeVries's list No. 212, Dixon 140 n. 21, 226 n. 33; New Hebrides, Torres Straits, New Guinea: ibid. 140 n. 21; Melanesia: ibid. 226 n. 33; N. A. Indian: *Thompson Tales 352 n. 270.

J1791. Reflection in water thought to be the original of the thing reflected. R311. Tree refuge. T11.5. Falling in love with reflection in water.

R351.1. *Milk drops from woman's breast on tiger's leg and reveals her hiding place in tree.* S. A. Indian (Chiriguano): Métraux RMLP XXXIII 156, 161.

N696. Fugitive in tree urinates from fright; pursuers think it rain and leave

R352. *Lovers fleeing from slavery are recaptured.* (Cf. R211.4.) Italian Novella: *Rotunda.

R355. *Eloping girl recaptured by parents.* (Cf. R225.) Type 516; Rösch FFC LXXVII 111.

S. UNNATURAL CRUELTY

DETAILED SYNOPSIS

S0—S99. Cruel relatives
- S 0. Cruel relatives
- S10. Cruel parents
- S20. Cruel children and grandchildren
- S30. Cruel step- and foster relatives
- S40. Cruel grandparents
- S50. Cruel relatives-in-law
- S60. Cruel spouse
- S70. Other cruel relatives

S100—S199. Revolting murders or mutilations
- S100. Revolting murders or mutilations
- S110. Murders
- S140. Cruel abandonments and exposures
- S160. Mutilations
- S180. Wounding or torturing

S200—S299. Cruel sacrifices
- S200. Cruel sacrifices
- S210. Children sold or promised
- S220. Reasons for promise (sale) of child
- S240. Children unwittingly promised (sold)
- S250. Saving the promised child
- S260. Sacrifices

S300—S399. Abandoned or murdered children
- S300. Abandoned or murdered children
- S310. Reasons for abandonment of children
- S330. Circumstances of murder or exposure of children
- S350. Fate of abandoned child

S400—S499. Cruel persecutions
- S400. Cruel persecutions
- S410. Persecuted wife
- S430. Disposal of cast-off wife
- S450. Fate of outcast wife
- S460. Other cruel persecutions

S. UNNATURAL CRUELTY

S. Unnatural cruelty.

D1357. Magic object makes person cruel. J1675.2. Clever ways of breaking bad news to a king who will kill bearer of bad tidings. M2. Inhuman decisions of king.

S0—S99. Cruel relatives.

S0. Cruel relative.

K2210. Treacherous relatives. K2211. Treacherous brother. Usually elder brother. K2212. Treacherous sister. Usually elder sister. P200. The family.

S10. Cruel parents. *Types 327AB, 517, 832; Irish myth: Cross; India: Thompson-Balys. See also S300—S399, Abandoned or murdered children, and many of the motifs in S200—S299, Cruel sacrifices.

G72. Unnatural parents eat children. L52. Abused youngest daughter. M411.1 Curse by parent.

S11. *Cruel father.* *Types 451, 516, 671, 706, 725, 870; *Rösch FFC LXXVII 120; *Schlauch Constance and other accused Queens 40; Irish myth: *Cross; Jewish: *Neuman; India: *Thompson-Balys; N. A. Indian: *Thompson Tales 326 n. 177.

H1210.1. Quest assigned by father. K1614. Father delivering daughter to be eaten by cannibal is himself eaten.

S11.1. *Father mutilates children.* (Cf. S160.) *Type 706; Greek: Fox 74 (Phineus).

S11.2. *Jealous father sends son to upper world on stretching tree.* N. A. Indian: *Thompson Tales 332 n. 199; Africa (Benga): Nassau 176 No. 23.

D482.1. Transformation: stretching tree. A tree magically shoots upward. F54.1. Tree stretches to sky. K1113. Abandonment on stretching tree.

S11.3. *Father kills child.*

S11.3.1. *Man who doubts his children's paternity kills them.* Murders wife and paramour. Italian Novella: Rotunda.

S11.3.2. *Father kills deformed children.* (Cf. S325.0.1.) Irish myth: Cross.

S11.3.3. *Father kills son.* India: Thompson-Balys.

S11.3.3.1. *Father kills son (for stealing).* Irish myth: *Cross.

Q212. Theft punished.

S11.3.3.2. *Father murders his two sons for whining.* Tonga: Gifford 24.

S11.3.4. *Cruel father, learning that he is to be killed by his son, puts to death all children born to him.* (Cf. M375.) Irish myth: Cross.

S11.3.5. *Cruel king slays brother and brother's son.* Irish myth: *Cross.

S11.3.6. *Father throws boy into river (sea).* Africa (Congo): Weeks Jungle 407, (Cameroon): Rosenhuber 20 No. 3, (Fang): Tessman 91.

S11.3.7. *Father orders son assassinated.* (Cf. K512.) Buddhist myth: Malalasekera II 529; Africa (Fang): Tessman 92.

S11.3.8. *Father eats own children.* (Cf. G10.) Buddhist myth: Malalasekera I 920; Africa (Pangwe): Tessman 108, 365.

S11.4. *Father plans child's death.* India: Thompson-Balys.

S11.4.1. *Jealous father vows to kill daughter's suitors.* Irish myth: *Cross.

E765.4.3. Father will die when daughter bears son. H913.2.1. Task assigned at suggestion of father (of prospective bride). M311.1. Prophecy: king's grandson will dethrone him. M343.2. Prophecy: murder by grandson. P234. Father and daughter. T50.1.2. Girl carefully guarded by father. T91.1. Giant's daughter loves hero. T97. Father opposed to daughter's marriage. T314. Father kills daughter lest she become prostitute.

S11.4.2. *Father kisses son while planning to kill him.* Icelandic: Boberg.

S11.4.3. *Cruel fathers threaten to kill their children if they are of undesirable sex.* India: Thompson-Balys.

S11.4.4. *Cruel father seeks to kill infant son.* Irish myth: *Cross.

S11.5. *Father banishes son at request of fairy wife.* (Cf. F302, S322.4.3.) Irish myth: Cross.

S11.6. *Father flogs child.* India: Thompson-Balys.

S12. *Cruel mother.* *Types 511, 590, 706, 765, 781; *BP I 551, III 2; *Boje 62f.; *Child V 475 s.v. "Cruel". — Breton: Sébillot Incidents s.v. "mère"; French Canadian: Barbeau JAFL XXIX 14; Missouri French: Carrière; Spanish: Keller, Espinosa Jr. Nos. 115, 148f., Espinosa II Nos. 115f.; Italian Novella: *Rotunda; Eskimo: Rink 389, Kroeber JAFL XII 181; Africa (Basuto): Jacottet 76 No. 12, 168 No. 24, 190 No. 28, (Angola): Chatelain 30 No. 1.

E225. Ghost of murdered child. H491.1. In large family father unwilling but mother willing to sell children. H914. Tasks assigned because of mother's foolish boasting. R153.2.1. Father hides children from murderous mother. S322.2. Jealous mother casts daughter forth.

S12.1. *Treacherous mother marries ogre and plots against son.* *Type 590; *BP III 1; N. A. Indian: Thompson CColl. II 392.

S12.1.1. *Treacherous mother and paramour plan son's death.* India: Thompson-Balys.

S12.2. *Cruel mother kills child.* Spanish: Espinosa Jr. Nos. 139, 151, 157; India: *Thompson-Balys.

B524.4. Supernatural bird prevents mother from killing babe.

S12.2.1. *Mother feeds newly-born illegitimate child to dog.* (Cf. S312.) Italian Novella: Rotunda.

S12.2.2. *Mother throws children into fire.* Jewish: *Neuman.

S12.2.3. *Mother forces child to break eating tabu: child dies.* Africa (Fang): Tessman 162.

S12.3. *Mother orders son's death.* Icelandic: Völsunga saga ch. 6—8, 40 (38), 43 (41); Italian Novella: Rotunda; India: Thompson-Balys.

K948. King lured to send sons on dangerous quests, where they are killed. P23.4. Queen suffers son to be killed in order to spurn to fight and revenge her first husband. P230.2. Mother dislikes her children in forced marriage. P230.3. Queen dislikes son who is unlike her and loves a poor girl; therefore she promises her daughter to the warrior who kills them. P231. Mother and son. P232.1. Wicked mother and her sons do everything to prevent daughter's marriage with beloved.

S12.4. *Cruel mother blinds son.* Spanish Exempla: Keller; Eskimo (Greenland): Rink 99, Rasmussen I 312, III 201, Holm 31.

S12.5. *Cruel mother expels (drives away) child.* India: Thompson-Balys.

S12.5.1. *Girl impregnated by god driven from home by mother.* S. A. Indian (Chiriguano): Métraux RMLP XXXIII 164.

S12.6. *Cruel mother refuses children food.* Eskimo (Central): Boas RBAE VI 625, (Cumberland Sound): Boas BAM XV 168; Cook Islands: Clark 77.

S12.7. *Mother tells healthy sons to wipe soiled hands on lame son.* Africa (Wakweli): Bender 79.

S20. Cruel children and grandchildren.

K2214.1. Treacherous daughter. K2214.1.1. Daughter has aged father cremated with dead husband to honor the latter. P236. Undutiful children. Q281.1. Ungrateful children punished.

S20.1. *Children sell mother.* N. A. Indian (Zuñi): Benedict 340.

S20.2. *Child hides food from starving parents.* Marquesas: Handy 114.

S21. *Cruel son.* Irish myth: Cross; Spanish: Espinosa III Nos. 139, 151, 157; Buddhist myth: Malalasekera II 287, 547, 632; Africa (Fang): Einstein 161.

J121. Ungrateful son reproved by naive action of his own son: preparing for old age. N332.4.1. Youth accidentally takes the poison he intended for his father. Q588. Ungrateful son punished by having a son equally ungrateful.

S21.1. *Son buries aged mother alive.* Swiss: Jegerlehner Oberwallis 326 No. 4.

S21.2. *Son blinds father.* (Cf. Q451.7, S165.) Irish myth: Cross; Italian Novella: Rotunda.

S21.3. *Son gives mother as hostage.* Irish myth: Cross.

S21.4. *King banishes mother to stables.* India: Thompson-Balys.

S21.5. *Cruel son tries to sterilize father.* Jewish: *Neuman.

S22. *Parricide.* (Cf. Q211.1.) Irish myth: *Cross; Icelandic: *Boberg; Jewish: Neuman; Buddhist myth: Malalasekera I 35, 1148, II 651, 1101, 1169; Tonga: Gifford 189.

S22.1. *Parricide to obtain kingship.* Irish myth: Cross.

K2214. Treacherous children. P16. End of king's reign.

S22.1.1. *Adopted son plots death of parents. Usurps the throne.* Italian Novella: Rotunda.

S22.2. *Prince plans to kill wicked father for cruelty.* India: Thompson-Balys.

S22.3. *Father learns that his son is planning to kill him.* Gives his son a weapon to do so. Son repents. Italian Novella: Rotunda.

S25. *Cruel grandson.*

S25.1. *Boy kills his grandfather.* Jewish: Neuman; India: Thompson-Balys.

S30. Cruel step- and foster relatives.

K2212.1. Treacherous stepsisters.

S31. *Cruel stepmother.* *Types 403, 425, 432, 450, 451, 480, 502, 510, 511, 516, 590, 592, 706, 708, 709, 720; BP I 42ff., 70ff., 79ff., 165ff., 207ff., 227ff., 412ff., *421, 427ff., 450ff., II 45ff., 229ff., 490ff., III 60ff., 137, 338f.; **W. Lincke Das tiefmuttermotiv im Märchen der germanischen Völker (Berlin, 1933); *MacCulloch Childhood 150; *Cox Cinderella passim; Böklen Sneewittchenstudien passim; *Arfert Unterschobene Braut passim; Rösch FFC LXXVII 120; Ranke FFC CXIV 154ff.; *Child V 497 s.v. "stepmother"; *Fb "stifmoder"; Dh III 414ff. — Irish myth: *Cross; Icelandic: *Boberg; Breton: Sébillot Incidents s.v. "marâtre"; French Canadian: Barbeau JAFL XXIX 14; Spanish: Boggs FFC XC 63 No. 453; Italian: Basile Pentamerone I No. 6, III No. 10, V No. 8, Rotunda; Greek: Grote I 103, 116; Jewish: *Neuman, *bin Gorion Born Judas[2] I 375; India: *Thompson-Balys; Hindu: Penzer I 185; Chinese: Ferguson 162, Eberhard FFC CXX 52f., 109, 125; Japanese: Ikeda, Anesaki 324; Korean: Zong in-Sob 201f. No. 97; Indonesia: DeVries's list No. 209, Dixon 238f.; Hawaii, Micronesia, Melanesia: ibid 89 nn. 97—102; N. A. Indian: *Thompson CColl II 382ff.; S. A. Indian (Karib): Métraux RMLP XXXIII 147; Africa (Cameroon): Mansfield 228; Jamaica: Beckwith MAFLS XVII 269 No. 81.

E221.2.1. Dead wife returns to reprove husband's second wife for abusing her stepchildren. G205. Witch stepmother. H363. Deceased wife marriage test. J134.1. Cock's second mate lets her stepchildren starve: woman warns husband accordingly. K1911. The false bride (substitute bride). K2056. Hypocritical stepmother weeps as she tells departing husband she will take good care of stepchildren though they beat her (she beats them instead). K2111.1. Woman makes vain overtures to stepson and accuses him of murder. K2211.2. Treacherous foster brother. L55. Stepdaughter heroine. L55.1. Abused stepdaughter. M411.1.1. Curse by stepmother. S322.3. Jealous co-wife kills woman's children. T154. Cruel stepmother enchants stepdaughter on eve of wedding.

S31.1. *Adulteress and paramour plot against her stepson.* They fear that he may betray them. Fischer-Bolte 214.

S31.2. *Children enchanted by stepmother.* (Cf. D683.) Irish myth: *Cross; Icelandic: *Boberg.

S31.3. *Cruel bird stepmother feeds young ones with thorns.* India: *Thompson-Balys.

S31.4. *Cruel stepmother feeds children with fish spines (thorns) to kill them.* India: Thompson-Balys.

S31.5. *Girl persuades her father to marry a widow who has treated her kindly.* *Roberts 136.

S32. *Cruel stepfather.* Type 970**; Icelandic: Boberg; India: *Thompson-Balys.

S33. *Cruel stepbrother.* (Cf. K2211.3.) Irish myth: Cross.

S34. *Cruel stepsister(s).* Icelandic: Boberg; India: Thompson-Balys; Chinese: Graham.

S36. *Cruel foster father.* Hawaii: Beckwith Myth 480.

S37. *Cruel foster son.* (Cf. S22.1.1.) S. A. Indian (Warrau): Métraux RMLP XXXIII 146, (Jivaro): ibid. 148, (Amuesha): ibid. 150.

S40. Cruel grandparents.

S41. *Cruel grandmother.* Breton: Sébillot Incidents s.v. "grand'mère"; India: Thompson-Balys; Africa (Basuto): Jacottet 254 No. 37.

S42. *Cruel grandfather.* Kills his grandchildren. Italian Novella: Rotunda.

S50. Cruel relatives-in-law. Chinese: Graham.

K2211.1. Treacherous brother-in-law. K2212.2. Treacherous sister-in-law. K2218. Treacherous relatives-in-law.

S51. *Cruel mother-in-law.* See references to K2110.1 and K2215, many of which have the present motif. *Type 706; *BP I 295ff.; *Dickson 25 n. 26, 29 n. 3, 30 n. 4, 31 n. 9, 41 n. 40; Saintyves Perrault 67; **Däumling Studie über den Typus des Mädchens ohne Hände (München, 1912); *Andree (1878) 159; Hibbard 26; Schlauch Constance and Accused Queens 40. — English: Wells 96 (Chevalere Assigne), 118 (Octovian), 130 (Emare); Rumanian: Schullerus FFC LXXVIII No. 1480*; Italian: Basile Pentamerone V No. 5, *Rotunda; India: *Thompson-Balys; Hindu: Penzer III 44f.; Buddhist myth: Malalasekera I 342, 736; Chinese: Eberhard FFC CXX 125, 189; New Guinea: Dixon 136; S. A. Indian (Chiriguano): Métraux RMLP XXXIII 177; Cape Verde Islands: Parsons MAFLS XV (1) 180 n. 1.

S322.6. Cruel mother-in-law casts woman's children forth.

S51.1. *Cruel mother-in-law plans death of daughter-in-law.* India: *Thompson-Balys.

S52. *Cruel father-in-law.* *Type 516; *Rösch FFC LXXVII 120; *BP I 46ff.; Breton: Sébillot Incidents s.v. "gendre"; Spanish: Espinosa II Nos. 99—103, 105; India: Thompson-Balys; Eskimo (Greenland): Rasmussen III 85, (Smith Sound): Kroeber JAFL XII 168.

S54. *Cruel daughter-in-law.* India: Thompson-Balys; Chinese: Eberhard FFC CXX 256f.; Marquesas: Handy 111.

S54.1. *Burned and underbaked bread.* Wishing to rid herself of her father-in-law, the daughter-in-law starts to feed him burned bread; but the old man begins to thrive on it. When she tries underbaked bread, he dies very soon. Lithuanian: Balys Index No. 2427*.

S55. *Cruel sister-in-law.* Chinese: Graham.

S56. *Cruel son-in-law.* India: Thompson-Balys; Marquesas: Handy 126; S. A. Indian (Chiriguano): Métraux RMLP XXXIII 177.

S56.1. *Lover asks girl to kill her father.* India: Thompson-Balys.

S60. Cruel spouse.

H492.1. Husband refuses to murder wife for high honors; wife agrees to murder husband. K2213. Treacherous wife.

S62. *Cruel husband.* *Type 760, 887. See references to H461. Icelandic: *Boberg; French Canadian: Barbeau JAFL XXIX 14; India: *Thompson-Balys; Chinese: Graham; Hawaii: Beckwith Myth 152; Eskimo: Boas BAM XV 188, 310, 331.

F301.5. Elf-knight entices maiden away and kills her. H461. Test of wife's patience. J122. Naive remark of child: "You forgot to strike mother." K1916. Robber bridegroom. Robber marries girl under pretence of being a fine gentleman. S400. Cruel persecutions. T88. Husband forsakes wife when she is stricken by plague.

S62.1. *Bluebeard.* Girl marries murderous husband. *Type 312; cf. Type

955; *BP I 404ff.; Child I 47; Swiss: Jegerlehner Oberwallis 312f. Nos. 73, 77; Spanish: Espinosa Jr. Nos. 91—93.

S62.2. *Man has bride drowned so that he may marry another.* Italian Novella: Rotunda.

S62.3. *Barren wife exposed by husband.* Jewish: Neuman.

S62.4. *Husband leaves wife to die of thirst.* Marquesas: Handy 99.

S63. *Spouse murder pact.* Princess kills her husband. Prince kills his wife. Murderers marry and usurp the throne. Italian Novella: Rotunda; India: Thompson-Balys.

S70. Other cruel relatives. Missouri French: Carrière.

S71. *Cruel uncle.* Irish myth: *Cross; English: Wells 19 (William of Palerne); Breton: Sébillot Incidents s.v. "oncle"; Italian Novella: *Rotunda; Greek: Aeschylus Agamemnon 1220 (Atreus); India: Thompson-Balys; Buddhist myth: Malalasekera II 447, 1303; Hindu: Keith 177; Chinese: Graham; Hawaii: Beckwith Myth 422; Samoa: ibid. 473; Mono: Wheeler No. 29; N. A. Indian: *Thompson Tales 313 n. 127.

S71.1. *Cruel uncle poisons nephew (king).* Irish myth: *Cross.

P16. End of king's reign. S111. Murder by poisoning.

S72. *Cruel aunt.* Italian: Basile Pentamerone IV No. 7; India: *Thompson-Balys; Chinese: Graham.

K2211. Treacherous brother. K2212. Treacherous sister.

S73.1. *Fratricide.* Krappe Revue des Études Anciennes XXXV (1933) 146ff.; Irish myth: *Cross; Icelandic: *Boberg; Greek: Grote I 219; Jewish: Neuman; Buddhist myth: Malalasekera II 13; Tonga: Gifford 83; Maori: Clark 157, Beckwith 157.

F960.6. Extraordinary nature phenomena on night of fratricide. Q211.9. Fratricide punished.

S73.1.0.1. *Murder of stepbrother (foster brother).* Irish myth: *Cross.

S73.1.1. *Fratricide in order to gain control of kingship.* Irish myth: *Cross; Buddhist myth: Malalasekera II 492.

S73.1.2. *Brother kills and eats brother.* (Cf. G10.) Tonga: Gifford 27, Mono: Wheeler No. 22.

S73.1.3. *Elder brother threatens to kill younger as soon as he is born.* Hawaii: Beckwith Myth 436.

S73.1.4. *Fratricide motivated by love-jealousy.* (Cf. T257.) Irish myth: Cross.

S73.2. *Person banishes brother (sister).* Irish myth: Cross.

S73.3. *Man blinds brother.* (Cf. S165.) Irish myth: *Cross.

S74. *Cruel nephew.* Irish myth: Cross; Spanish Exempla: Keller.

S74.1. *Nephew (niece) kills uncle.* Irish myth: *Cross.

S100—S199. Revolting murders or mutilations.

S100. Revolting murders or mutilations.

S110. Murders. Irish myth: *Cross; Jewish: *Neuman; India: Thompson-Balys.

D711. Disenchantment by decapitation. D1361.8. Heart of unborn child renders person invisible. D2135.1. Power of flying from eating children's hearts. E12. Resuscitation by decapitation. F615. Strong man evades death. Vain attempts to kill him. G10. Cannibalism. G321. Cliff-ogre. Kicks victims over cliff. G327. Swinging ogre. Girls who swing their lovers over pit, cut rope, and later devour them. G331. Pot-tilter. Ogre who tilts a pot so that victims are drawn into it. G332. Sucking monster. Giant (sometimes a giant hall or cave) sucks in its victims. G341. Sharp-elbowed women. Kill with their elbows. H931. Tasks assigned in order to get rid of hero. K950. Various kinds of treacherous murder. Q211. Murder punished.

S110.1. *Old people killed in famine.* *Wesselski Märchen 237 No. 48; Fb "gammel" IV 174a; Icelandic: *Boberg.

F969.7. Famine. F1041.1.11.1. Suicide from fear of starving. J151.1. Wisdom of hidden old man saves kingdom. K231.1.1. Mutual agreement to sacrifice family members in famine. K1603. Man falls into sacrificial grave prepared for others.

S110.1.1. *Child condemned to be killed in famine.* Irish myth: Cross.

S110.2. *Man kills all guests, hoping some day to kill rival.* Dickson 83 n. 47.

S110.3. *Princess builds tower of skulls of unsuccessful suitors.* Malone PMLA XLIII 414; India: Thompson-Balys.

H310. Suitor tests. A suitor is put to severe tests by his prospective bride or father-in-law. H331.5.0.1. Loser in bride-race must die. H901.1. Heads placed on stakes for failure in performance of task. Q410. Capital punishment. Q421.1. Heads on stakes. Punishment by beheading and placing the heads on stakes. T70. The scorned lover.

S110.3.1. *Princess makes necklace of heads of unsuccessful suitors.* India: Thompson-Balys.

S110.4. *Prince resolves to drive relatives from his domain.* Kills many. Italian Novella: Rotunda.

S110.5. *Murderer kills all who come to certain spot.* India: Thompson-Balys.

S111. *Murder by poisoning.* *Type 709; *Böklen 100ff.; *Child V 491 s.v. "Poisoning"; Irish myth: *Cross; Icelandic: *Boberg; Spanish: Espinosa II Nos. 115f., Espinosa Jr. Nos. 143, 145; Missouri French: Carrière; Italian Novella: Rotunda; Jewish: *Neuman; India: *Thompson-Balys; Buddhist myth: Malalasekera II 80, 491, 510, 816.

B776. Venomous animals. N332. Accidental poisoning. Q418. Punishment by poisoning. Q582.8. Person drinks poison he prepared for another. S71.1. Cruel uncle poisons nephew king.

S111.1. *Murder with poisoned bread.* *Type 709; *Böklen 102; India: *Thompson-Balys; Africa (Basuto): Jacottet 80 No. 12.

S111.2. *Murder with poisoned lace.* *Type 709; *BP I 450ff.; *Böklen 104.

S111.3. *Murder with poisoned comb.* *Type 709; *BP I 450ff.; *Böklen 109.

S111.4. *Murder with poisoned apple.* *Type 709; *BP I 450ff.; *Böklen 100; Italian Novella: Rotunda.

S111.5. *Murder with poisoned book.* King wets finger to turn leaves and falls dead. *Chauvin V 276 No. 156 n. 3.

S111.6. *Murder with poisoned robe.* Consumes wearer. Greek: Fox 115, *Frazer Apollodorus I 123; India: Thompson-Balys.

S111.7. *Murder with poisoned slippers.* Africa (Thonga): Junod 266ff., (Swahili): Baker FL XXXVIII 299ff. No. 16.

E21.4. Resuscitation by removal of poisoned slippers.

S111.8. *Murder by feeding poisonous snake.* English ballad: Child No. 12 (Lord Randal); Icelandic: *Boberg; India: Thompson-Balys.

S111.9. *Murder by placing a poisoned fingernail on step.* India: *Thompson-Balys.

S112. *Burning to death.* (See notes to K955 and Q414.) Irish myth: *Cross; English: Wells 97 (Chevalere Assigne); Spanish Exempla: Keller; India: *Thompson-Balys; Africa (Basuto): Jacottet 192 No. 28.

A1861.2. Creation of monkeys: old woman thrown into fire. E15. Resuscitation by burning. E446.2. Ghost laid by burning body. G512.3.1. Ogre killed by throwing hot stones (metal) into his throat. G512.3.2. Ogre burned in his own oven. H1511. Heat test. Attempt to kill hero by burning him in fire. K851. Deceptive game: burning each other. Dupe burned (boiled) to death. K951.1. Murder by throwing hot stones in the mouth. K955. Murder by burning. K1612. Message of death fatal to sender. K2135. The complaint about bad breath. K2214.1.1. Daughter has aged father cremated with dead husband to honor the latter. N482.1. Secret learned by burning hand. P16.3.1.1. Attempt to kill old king by suffocating in bathroom. Q414. Punishment: burning alive. S326.1. Disobedient child burned.

S112.0.1. *City burned with all inhabitants.* Irish myth: *Cross.

S112.0.2. *House (hostel) burned with all inside.* Irish myth: *Cross; Marquesas: Handy 132; Easter Island: Métraux Ethnology 386; Hawaii: Beckwith Myth 514.

S112.1. *Boiling to death.* Often in pitch or oil. *Cosquin Études 360ff.; Spanish: Boggs FFC XC 83 No. 711A*; Greek: *Frazer Apollodorus I 321 n. 1; India: Thompson-Balys; Japanese: Ikeda.

D1865.2. Beautification by boiling and resuscitation. D1885. Rejuvenation by boiling. E15.1. Resuscitation by boiling. Q414.1. Punishment: boiling in oil (lead, tar).

S112.2. *Murder with hot iron.* Bored through eye or nose. *Krappe Balor 4ff.; Icelandic: Herrmann Saxo II 592, Boberg; India: Thompson-Balys.; Africa (Fjort): Dennett 52 No. 8.

K1011. Eye-remedy. Under pretence of curing eyesight the trickster blinds the dupe. (Often with a glowing mass thrust into the eye.) Q469.2. Punishment: climbing red-hot rod. Q469.9. Punishment: boring hot iron through ear.

S112.2.1. *Murder by hot iron through heart.* Icelandic: Herrmann Saxo II 592, Boberg.

S112.2.2. *Murder by driving red-hot iron spits through soles of feet and into shins.* Irish myth: *Cross.

S112.3. *Murder by hot lead poured into ear.* (Cf. S115.1.) *Fb "øre" III 1180b, 1181a.

S112.4. *Attempted murder by live coals in garments.* India: Thompson-Balys.

S112.5. *Murder by feeding on over-hot food.* Person forced to eat. India: *Thompson-Balys.

H1511.2. Burning food test. K1043. Dupe induced to eat sharp (stinging, bitter) fruit.

S112.6. *Murder by roasting alive in oven furnace).* Jewish: *Neuman; Tonga: Gifford 190.

S112.7. *Son takes mother to woods and tries to burn her up while she sleeps.* India: Thompson-Balys.

S113. *Murder by strangling.* See references to Q424. Irish myth: Cross; Chinese: Werner 267.

Q424. Punishment: strangling.

S113.1. *Murder by hanging.* Dickson 186 n. 60; Icelandic: *Boberg; Missouri French: Carrière.

H1533. Hanging test. Unavailing attempt to kill hero by hanging. K852. Deceptive game: hanging each other. Dupe really hanged. Q413. Punishment: hanging.

S113.1.1. *Slaves killed by hanging.* Icelandic: *Boberg.

S113.1.2. *Prisoners taken in war (enemy's messengers) hanged.* Icelandic: *Boberg.

S113.2. *Murder by suffocation.* Irish myth: Cross; Spanish Exempla: Keller; West Indies: Flowers 575.

Q274.2. Devil suffocates swindling merchant. Q469.5. Punishment: choking with smoke.

S113.2.1. *Devil cuts off hand of woman and suffocates her.* Pauli (ed. Bolte) No. 289; Scala Celi 57b No. 321.

S161. Mutilation: cutting off hands.

S113.2.2. *Suffocating in bathroom.* Icelandic: Boberg; Danish: Grundtvig No. 121; Lithuanian: M. Boehm u. F. Sprecht Lettische-Litauische Volksmärchen (Jena, 1924) 193 No. 11.

S113.2.3. *Murder by luring to feast and suffocating.* All holes are stopped and house set afire. India: Thompson-Balys.

K811.1. Enemies invited to banquet and killed. K2013. Enemy invited for marriage with relative attacked.

S114. *Murder by flaying.* *Fb "hud" I 661; Icelandic: *Boberg; Jewish: Neuman.

J167. Wisdom from continual reminder of foolishness in the past. Unjust judge skinned and his skin stretched over a footstool kept in the presence of judges, so as to remind them to be just. Q457. Flaying alive as punishment.

S114.1. *Skin of murdered person found in enemy's house.* Koryak: *Jochelson JE VI 377.

S115. *Murder by stabbing.* Heptameron No. 40; Icelandic: Herrmann Saxo II 592; Japanese: Ikeda.

K916. Dancer stabs spectator.

S115.1. *Murder by stabbing in ear.* (Cf. S112.3.) Koryak: Jochelson JE VI 236, 265; N. A. Indian: *Thompson Tales 350 n. 264.

S115.2. *Murder by sticking needle through head.* Italian: Basile Pentamerone V No. 9; Eskimo (Greenland): Holm 52, Rasmussen III 65, (Cumberland Sound): Boas BAM XV 185.

S115.2.1. *Murder by driving nail through head.* West Africa: Nassau Fetischism in West Africa (London, 1904) 337ff. No. 2.

S115.3. *Murder by piercing with pins and needles.* India: *Thompson-Balys.

S116. *Murder by crushing.* (Cf. S167.) Irish myth: Cross; Icelandic: Herrmann Saxo II 592, Boberg; Africa (Basuto): Jacottet 168 No. 24.

S116.1. *Murder by grinding in mill.* Irish myth: *Cross; India: *Thompson-Balys.

S116.2. *Pregnant woman crushed beneath chariot.* (Cf. S185.) Irish myth: Cross.

S116.3. *Murder by breaking back.* Icelandic: *Boberg.

S116.4. *Murder by crushing head.* Icelandic: *Boberg.

S116.5. *Murder by crushing beneath falling tree.* India: Thompson-Balys; Tonga: Gifford 184.

S116.6. *Murder by trampling of horses (elephants).* English romance: Malory IX 25; Buddhist myth: Malalasekera I 647.

S117. *Death by dragging behind horse.* *Fb "hest" I 599b; India: *Thompson-Balys.

J2132. Numskull dragged. Q415.1.2. Punishment: tying man to horses and setting vicious hounds after him. Q416. Punishment: drawing asunder by horses. Q416.2. Punishment: dragging to death by horse.

S118. *Murder by cutting.*

S118.1. *Murder by cutting adversary in two.* Icelandic: *Boberg.

S118.2. *Murder by cutting throat.* Africa (Cameroon): Mansfield 228.

S121. *Murder by slamming down chest-lid.* Done while victim is looking into the chest. *Type 720; *BP I 412ff., 422; *Cox 479; *Hdwb. d. Märchens I 91b n. 36; Italian: Basile Pentamerone I No. 6; Icelandic: *Boberg.

K434.3. Girl tells thief that money is in chest.

S122. *Flogging to death.* (Cf. Q458.2.) Fb "piske" II 834; Icelandic: Boberg; Hawaii: Beckwith Myth 152.

S123. *Burial alive.* **Feilberg "Levende begravet" (Årbog for dansk Kulturhistorie, 1892); *Liebrecht 284; *Fb "høj" I 741b, "levende" II 403a—404a, "jord" II 45b. — Irish: *Cross, O'Suilleabhain 74, Beal XXI 327; Swiss: Jegerlehner Oberwallis 326 No. 4; Breton: Sébillot Incidents s.v. "enterrement"; Spanish: Espinosa Jr. Nos. 203f.; Greek: Sophocles' Antigone; India: *Thompson-Balys; Society Islands: Henry Ancient Tahiti (Honolulu, 1928) 557; Eskimo (Greenland): Rink 221, 232, Rasmussen II 94, III 53, (Cumberland Sound): Boas BAM XV 171, (Central Eskimo): Boas RBAE VI 639, (Mackenzie Area): Jenness 34, (Labrador): Hawkes GSCan XIV 161, (Ungava): Turner RBAE VI 262.

P16.4. Persons buried with dead king. Q456. Burial alive as punishment. S21.1. Son buries aged mother alive. S261. Foundation sacrifice. S266. Burial of live girl to banish plague.

S123.0.1. *Hostages buried alive.* Irish myth: *Cross.

S123.1. *Burial alive of drugged person.* *Chauvin VI 15 No. 188 n. 1.

S123.2. *Burial of living husband or wife with dead spouse.* Type 612; *BP I 126ff., 128; *Chauvin VII 20 No. 373D; Missouri French: Carrière.

P16.4.1. Suttee. Burning of wife with dead king. T211.2.1. Wife throws herself on husband's funeral pyre.

S123.2.1. *Burial of living man with dead blood brother.* Icelandic: *Boberg.

S123.3. *Living children buried with dead mother.* Child I 180, 185, IV 450a (No. 15).

S123.4. *Avenger plans to let king starve in mountain chamber.* Icelandic: Boberg.

R51.1. Prisoners starved.

S123.5. *Burial alive of maiden to keep her safe from rival.* Icelandic: Boberg.

S123.6. *Enemies buried alive up to their necks and exposed to jackals.* (Cf. Q456.1.) Buddhist myth: Malalasekera II 570.

S125. *Immolation.* Greek: Grote I 278f.; Jewish: Neuman; S. A. Indian (Inca): Rowe BBAE CXLIII (2) 317.

Q455. Walling up as punishment. S261. Foundation sacrifice.

S125.1. *Self-immolation.* Hindu: Tawney I 163, 398, 522, II 255, 490, 546, 558, 560, Panchatantra III 8 (tr. Ryder 334).

S127. *Murder by throwing from height.* Greek: Grote I 278.

S131. *Murder by drowning.* Hdwb. d. Märchens I 346b nn. 130—46; English: Wells 96 (Chevalere Assigne); Irish myth: *Cross; Icelandic: *Boberg; Missouri French: Carrière; Jewish: Neuman; Buddhist myth: Malalasekera II 651; Marquesas: Handy 53; Maori: Beckwith Myth 318; Eskimo (Greenland): Holm 56, Rasmussen I 363, III 200, (Labrador): Hawkes GSCan XIV 152, (Central Eskimo): Boas RBAE VI 637; Africa (Fang): Einstein 153.

S131.1. *River carrier (whale, crocodile) throws passenger off and drowns him.* India: Thompson-Balys; Africa (Madagascar): Renel II 207f. No. 119.

K1042. Water bird takes dupe to sea: shakes him off into water. R245. Whale-boat.

S132. *Murder by starvation.* (Cf. R51.1, S123.4.) Jewish: *Neuman; India: Thompson-Balys; Buddhist myth: Malalasekera II 287.

S133. *Murder by beheading.* (Cf. Q421.) India: Thompson-Balys.

S135. *Murder by springing bent tree.* Man bound to it is torn to pieces. (Cf. H1522.1.) Fb "træ" III 865b; India: Thompson-Balys; Icelandic: *Boberg.

S139. *Miscellaneous cruel murders.*

S139.1. *Murder by twisting out intestines.* (Cf. K1444, Q469.7.) *Fb "tarm" III 776a; Icelandic: *Boberg; Easter Island: Métraux Ethnology 66, 384.

S139.2. *Slain person dismembered.* Irish myth: *Cross; Spanish Exempla: Keller; Greek: Frazer Apollodorus II 72 n. 1; India: Thompson-Balys.

D1884. Rejuvenation by dismemberment. E14. Resuscitation by dismemberment. Q416. Punishment: drawing asunder by horses.

S139.2.1. *Head of murdered man displayed before his own house.* *Siberian and North Pacific Coast of America: Jochelson JE VI 381.

H901.1. Heads placed on stakes for failure in performance of tasks.

S139.2.1.1. *Head of murdered man taken along as trophy.* Icelandic: *Boberg; Jewish: Neuman; Philippine (Tinguian): Cole 43, 77.

S452. Outcast wife commits suicide when confronted with heads of relatives killed in revenge for her wrong-doing.

S139.2.2. *Other indignities to corpse.* Irish myth: Cross.

P555.2. Corpses of dead foes dismembered. Q491. Indignity to corpse as punishment.

S139.2.2.1. *Heads of slain enemies impaled upon stakes.* (Cf. Q421.1.) Irish myth: *Cross; Icelandic: *Boberg.

S139.2.2.1.1. *Heads (tongues) of slain enemies as trophies.* Irish myth: *Cross.

S139.2.2.1.2. *Impaled head used as target.* Irish myth: Cross.

S139.2.2.1.3. *Custom: sitting upon head of slain enemy.* Irish myth: *Cross.

S139.2.2.1.4. *Heads of defeated enemies hung on conqueror's saddle.* India: Thompson-Balys.

S139.2.2.1.5. *Hand of slain enemy nailed to castle.* Irish myth: Cross.

S139.2.2.1.6. *Heads brandished to intimidate foe.* Irish myth: *Cross.

S139.2.2.2. *Dead man gutted and filled with stones.* India: Thompson-Balys.

S139.2.2.3. *Dead dog buried with enemy.* Irish myth: Cross.

S139.2.2.3.1. *Corpse buried face down as indignity.* Irish myth: *Cross.

S139.2.2.4. *Parts of corpses used in sport.* Irish myth: Cross.
P203. Game with ancestors' bones.

S139.2.2.4.1. *Head used as ball.* Irish myth: *Cross.

S139.2.2.4.2. *Brains of enemies fashioned into balls (as trophies for play).* Irish myth: *Cross.

S139.2.2.4.3. *Chess board and men made from bones of slain enemies.* Irish myth: Cross.

S139.2.2.5. *Corpses burned as fuel for cooking.* Irish myth: Cross.

S139.2.2.6. *Corpse drawn asunder.* Irish myth: Cross.

S139.2.2.7. *Ash (hazel) stakes thrust through bodies of slain warriors.* India: Thompson-Balys.
D712.10. Disenchantment by driving stake through body. D950.6. Magic ash tree (quicken, rowan). E434. Magic protection against revenants. E442. Ghost laid by piercing grave with stake.

S139.2.2.8. *Ashes of murdered person passed through sieve and remains put to manure heap.* India: Thompson-Balys.

S139.3. *Captured women hanged and crucified.* Irish myth: Cross.

S139.4. *Murder by mangling with axe.* Irish myth: Cross.

S139.5. *Murder by cutting off uvula.* Icelandic: Boberg.

S139.6. *Murder by tearing out heart.* India: Thompson-Balys; Icelandic: *Boberg.

S139.7. *Murder by slicing person into small pieces.* Hawaii: Beckwith Myth 154; Tuamotu: Stimson MS (TpG. 3/912).

S139.8. *Murder by biting the throat.* Icelandic: *Boberg.

S140. Cruel abandonments and exposures. India: Thompson-Balys.
K1113. Abandonment on stretching tree. L111.1. Exile returns and succeeds. L111.2. Foundling hero (heroine). N732.3. Parents accidentally

meet daughter who has survived their attempt to drown her. R131. Exposed or abandoned child rescued. S300. Abandoned or murdered children. S312.1. Child of incest exposed. S433. Cast-off wife abandoned on island.

S140.1. *Abandonment of aged.* Type 981*; *Encyc. Religion Ethics s.v. "Abandonment and exposure"; *F. Brouga-Brey Revista de dialectologia y tradiciones populares (Madrid) I 496—573; India: Thompson-Balys; Buddhist myth: Malalasekera II 547; Chinese: Eberhard FFC CXX 116; Japanese: Ikeda; Korean: Zong in-Sob 186 No. 82.

K231.1.1. Mutual agreement to sacrifice family members in famine. P16.3. King killed when old. S110.1. Old people killed in famine.

S141. *Exposure in boat.* A person (usually woman or child) set adrift in a boat (chest, basket, cask). *Types 590, 675, 708, 930; BP I 489, II 236f., III 2; **Cosquin Études 199ff., 215ff.; Chauvin VII 95ff.; *Hertel Zs. f. Vksk. XIX 83; *Aarne FFC XXIII 60; *Penzer II 4, VII 81 n. 1; Dickson 35 n. 16, 41f. nn. 40, 42, 169f. n. 23; *Krappe Balor 3ff., 17ff. nn. 57—60; *Sparnaay 31ff., 50; *Frazer Old Testament II 437ff.; *Fb "å" III 1187b, "båd" IV 87a; *Schoepperle II 374 n. 4; Hibbard 276; *Basset 1001 Contes II 371. — Irish myth: *Cross; Breton: Sébillot Incidents s.v. "enfant"; French Canadian: Barbeau JAFL XXIX 14; Spanish: Espinosa Jr. No. 116; Italian: Basile Pentamerone III No. 2, *Rotunda; Greek: Frazer Apollodorus I 155, Grote I 86, *103, Fox 22, 33, 307; Egyptian: Müller 116; Babylonian: Spence 16; Jewish: *Neuman, bin Gorion Born Judas[2] I 165, 372; India: *Thompson-Balys; Buddhist myth: Malalasekera II 103, 633; Japanese: *Ikeda; Chinese: Ferguson 192; Palaung tribe: Scott Indo-Chinese 276; Indonesian: DeVries's list No. 219; Tonga: Gifford 154; Tuamotu: Stimson MS (T-G. 3/45); Marquesas: *Beckwith Myth 502 n. 4; Eskimo (Cumberland Sound): Boas BAM XV 167, (Labrador): Hawkes GSCan XIV 152, (Ungava): Turner RBAE XI 261; N. A. Indian: *Thompson Tales 313 n. 131.

H157. King finds note with children in casket floated down river identifying them as his. H263.1. Exposure in boat as test of sin. K1333. Seduction by having maiden placed in floating chest. K1931.1.1. Impostor tries to push foster brother into the water and then cuts rope. L111.2.1. Future hero found in boat (basket, bushes). N781. Hero embarks in rudderless boat. Q466. Embarkation in leaky vessel as punishment. S331. Exposure of child in boat (floating chest). S431. Cast-off wife exposed in boat.

S141.1. *Man springs ashore and pushes companion in boat out to sea.* Icelandic: *Boberg.

S141.2. *Father saves himself in storm and forgets his two children.* They are abandoned in a boat. Italian Novella: Rotunda.

S141.3. *Exposure astride a log of wood floated down river.* India: *Thompson-Balys.

S142. *Person thrown into the water and abandoned.* *Types 450, 506, 612, 667*, 707; *BP I 79ff., 126ff., II 380ff., III 490ff.; *Krappe Balor 12 n. 43; *Fb "spinde" III 492b; Dickson 86. — Irish: MacCulloch Celtic 167, *Cross; Icelandic: Boberg; Italian: Basile Pentamerone IV No. 7; India: *Thompson-Balys; Buddhist myth: Malalasekera II 526; Tahiti: Handy 408; Tonga: Gifford 122; Tuamotu: Stimson MS (T-G. 3/45, 403, z-G. 3/1117).

K1931.1. Impostors throw hero overboard into sea. Q467.1. Casting into water in sack (barrel) as punishment. S432. Cast-off wife thrown into water.

S143. *Abandonment in forest.* *Types 327, 450, 708, 872*; BP I 79ff., 115ff.; *Dickson 35 n. 16; *Sparnaay 41ff.; Roberts 128. — English: Wells 118 (Octovian); Icelandic: Boberg; Breton: Sébillot Incidents s.v. "abandon"; French Canadian: Barbeau JAFL XXIX 14; Missouri French: Carrière; Spanish: Espinosa II 99-105, Espinosa Jr. Nos. 142—45; Greek: Grote I 109; India: *Thompson-Balys.

M371.0.1. Abandonment in forest to avoid fulfillment of prophecy. N316. Separation in jungle (forest). Q438. Punishment: abandonment in forest. S345. Parents trick children into going on hunt, then abandon them in forest. S441. Cast-off wife and child abandoned in forest. S465. Abandoned person in woods comforted by prophet and birds.

S143.1. *Child abandoned in hollow tree.* English: Wells 126 (Lai Le Freine); Irish myth: *Cross.

S143.2. *Abandonment in tall tree.* India: *Thompson-Balys; S. A. Indian (Mundurucú): Horton BBAE CXLIII (3) 294, (Sherente): Lowie ibid. (1) 515.

H151.14.1. Recognition by tear falling from tree where girl has been abandoned. K1113. Abandonment on stretching tree.

S143.2.1. *Tortoise placed in tall tree and left.* India: Thompson-Balys; Africa: Weeks Congo 209ff. No. 6.

S143.3. *Mutilated man on horseback chased into the forest.* Icelandic: Boberg.

S143.4. *Husband abandons wife in childbirth in jungle.* (Cf. S430.) India: *Thompson-Balys.

S144. *Abandonment in desert.* *Type 310; BP I 97ff.; India: Thompson-Balys.

S144.1. *Abandonment alone on foreign coast.* English: Wells 80 (Sir Tristrem).

S145. *Abandonment on an island.* (Marooning.) *Type 506, 890; BP III 490ff.; Icelandic: *Boberg; Breton: Sébillot Incidents s.v. "abandon"; French Canadian: Morin JAFL XXX 147; Italian Novella: *Rotunda; Greek: Frazer Apollodorus II 53 n. 5; Papua: Ker 7, 112; Hawaii: Beckwith Myth 358; Eskimo (Greenland): Holm 56, Rasmussen III 200, (Labrador): Hawkes GSCan XIV 152, (Central): Boas RBAE VI 637, (Cumberland Sound): Boas BAM XV 163, 166; N. A. Indian: *Thompson CColl II 405ff.

K1616. Marooned man reaches home and outwits marooner. S433. Cast-off wife abandoned on island.

S146. *Abandonment in pit.* Chauvin VII 108 No. 379bis; Irish myth: *Cross; Icelandic: Lagerholm 161—63, Boberg; Missouri French: Carrière; Hebrew: Genesis ch. 37, *Neuman; India: *Thompson-Balys; Hawaii: Beckwith Myth 41.

H1535.1. Pit test. K1931.4. Impostors throw hero into pit. S435. Cast-off wife abandoned in pit. T581.2. Child born of woman abandoned in pit.

S146.1. *Abandonment in well.* India: *Thompson-Balys.

S146.2. *Abandonment in cave.* Tuamotu: Beckwith Myth 471.

S147. *Abandonment on mountain.* *Type 675; Irish myth: Cross.

S147.1. *Abandonment on cliff.* French Canadian: Sister Marie Ursule; Greek: Aeschylus Prometheus Bound; India: Thompson-Balys.

S147.1.1. *Abandonment on cliff near nest of a bird.* S. A. Indian (Mundurucú): Horton BBAE CXLIII (3) 294.

S148. *Abandonment in bonds that cannot be loosed.* Irish myth: Cross.

S152. *Children abandoned in box in potter's kiln.* India: Thompson-Balys.

S153. *Abandonment in stable.* India: *Thompson-Balys.

S160. Mutilations. Nouvelles de Sens No. 24; Irish myth: Cross; India: Thompson-Balys.

A128. Mutilated god. C948. Mutilation as punishment for breaking tabu. G313. Procrustes. Monster makes men fit his bed. Tall men sawed off, short men stretched. H56.2. Mutilation of children's bodies for identification. K1111. Dupe puts hand (paws) into cleft of tree (wedge, vise). M201.4. Covenant between saints confirmed by cutting off their thumbs. M375.3. Child mutilated to avoid fulfillment of prophecy. Q211.6.1. Punishment for flaying live calf. Q451. Mutilation as punishment. R51.3. Prisoners mutilated. S11.1. Father mutilates children.

S160.1. *Self-mutilation.* (Cf. T327.1, T327.2, T333.) Irish myth: *Cross; Icelandic: *Boberg; India: Thompson-Balys; Hindu: Penzer III 21 n.; Chinese: Werner 314.

J2411.4. Imitation of magician unsuccessful. Person does self injury.

S160.2. *Jealous women mutilate her who is most attractive to men.* Irish myth: Cross.

S160.3. *Fairies mutilate mortals.* (Cf. F362.) Irish myth: Cross.

S160.4. *Mutilation of envoys.* (Cf. R51.3.) Buddhist myth: Malalasekera II 701.

S160.5. *Moon mutilates his earth mistress.* Eskimo (Smith Sound): Kroeber JAFL XII 180.

S161. *Mutilation: cutting off hands (arms).* Heptameron No. 48; Irish myth: *Cross; Icelandic: *Boberg; Missouri French: Carrière; Spanish: Keller, Espinosa II Nos. 99—103, Espinosa Jr. No. 137; Jewish: *Neuman; India: *Thompson-Balys; Buddhist myth: Malalasekera I 710, 885; Eskimo (Labrador): Hawkes GSCan XIV 151.

A128.4. God with one hand. Hand cut or bitten off. F515.0.1. Person without hands. H333.2 Suitor test: tribute of his severed hands. Q451.1. Hands cut off as punishment. S113.2.1. Devil cuts off hand of woman.

S161.0.1. *Masons who build mausoleum of princess lose their right hands so they may never again construct so fine a building.* (Cf. S165.7, W181.2.) India: Thompson-Balys.

S161.1. *Mutilation: cutting off fingers.* *Fb "guld ring" I 514a; *Dickson 41 n. 41; Icelandic: *Boberg; Buddhist myth: Malalasekera I 22; Eskimo (Greenland): Rink 17, Rasmussen III 58, (Smith Sound): Kroeber JAFL XII 168, (Ungava): Turner RBAE XI 262, (Labrador): Hawkes GSCan XIV 152, (Cumberland Sound): Boas BAM XV 165, (Central): Boas RBAE VI 584, 586, 637.

S161.1.1. *Child's finger-ends cut off to give long life.* Irish myth: Cross.

S162. *Mutilation: cutting off legs (feet).* *Type 519; *Krappe Archiv f. d. Studium d. neueren Sprachen CLX 161ff.; Irish myth: *Cross; Icelandic: *Boberg; India: *Thompson-Balys; Buddhist myth: Malalasekera I 710, 885; Hawaii: Beckwith Myth 242.

A128.3.1. God with one leg (foot). J2413.4.1. Fowl makes another animal believe that he has had his leg cut off. Q451.2. Laming as punishment.

S162.1. *Fighting on stumps of legs after they have been cut off at knee.* Child V 497 s.v. "stumps"; Icelandic: Boberg.

S162.2. *Hamstringing.* E. H. Meyer Germanen 161f.; *P. Maurus Wielandsage in der Literatur (Müncher Beiträge zur rom. und eng. Philologie XXV [1902]); Icelandic: *Boberg.

S162.3. *Mutilation: cutting off toes.* Icelandic: *Boberg.

S162.4. *Mutilation: cutting off heelbone.* Icelandic: *Boberg.

S162.5. *Mutilation: crushing feet and turning them backward.* Icelandic: *Boberg.

S163. *Mutilation: cutting (tearing) out tongue.* Often to prevent revelation of secret. Irish myth: *Cross; Spanish: Boggs FFC XC 67 No. 510, Keller; Greek: Fox 70 (Philomela), Grote I 181; India: Thompson-Balys; Japanese: Ikeda; Tuamotu: Stimson MS (T-G. 3/600); Koryak, American Indian: *Jochelson JE VI 372.

A2344.2. Why animal has no tongue. K825. Victim persuaded to hold out his tongue: cut off. Q451.4. Tongue cut off as punishment.

S164. *Mutilation: knocking out teeth.* Icelandic: *Boberg.

S165. *Mutilation: putting out eyes.* *Types 310, 533, 590, 613; *BP I 97ff., II 273ff., 468ff., III 1ff.; **Christiansen FFC XXIV 46ff.; *Cox 501; Gaster Thespis 332f. — Irish myth: *Cross; Icelandic: *Boberg; Missouri French: Carrière; Breton: Sébillot Incidents s.v. "yeux"; Spanish: Boggs FFC XC 63, 67 Nos. 455, 510, Espinosa II 99—103, 111—112, Espinosa Jr. No. 137; Greek: *Grote I 183, Fox 74 (Phineus); Jewish: Neuman; India: *Thompson-Balys; Buddhist myth: Malalasekera I 111, 1163; Chinese: Eberhard FFC CXX 250 No. 193; Tahiti: Beckwith Myth 251; Hawaii: ibid. 248; Eskimo (Cumberland Sound): Boas BAM XV 165, (Central Eskimo): Boas RBAE VI 585; N. A. Indian: *Thompson CColl II 391ff.

E781.2. Eyes bought back and replaced. G511. Ogre blinded. J2423. The eye-juggler. K1011. Eye-remedy. Under pretence of curing eyesight the trickster blinds the dupe. K1465. The blinded slave's revenge. M225. Eyes exchanged for food. A starving man lets himself be blinded in return for food. Q451.7. Blinding as punishment. R176. Executioner miraculously blinded: condemned man saved. S21.2. Son blinds father. S73.3. Man blinds brother.

S165.1. *Eyes of beheaded person gouged out.* Greek: Frazer Apollodorus I 278 n. 1.

S165.2. *Crane pecks out tiger's eyes.* India: Thompson-Balys.

S165.3. *Blinding by thrusting needles into eyes.* Irish myth: Cross.

S165.4. *Eyes torn out and filled with sand.* India: *Thompson-Balys.

S165.5. *Necklace made of torn out human eyes.* India: Thompson-Balys.

S165.6. *Human eyes used as fishbait.* Hawaii: Beckwith Myth 245.

S165.7. *Artisan who has built palace blinded so he cannot build another like it.* (Cf. S161.0.1, W181.2.) Buddhist myth: Malalasekera I 489, 672.

S166. *Mutilation: skin cut from back.* Hdwb. d. Märchens II 102a n. 140; Icelandic: Herrmann Saxo II 447, Boberg; Missouri French: Carrière; Spanish: Espinosa III Nos. 163—7; India: Thompson-Balys.

Q457. Flaying alive as punishment. S114. Murder by flaying.

S166.1. *Mutilation: beard torn off with the skin (and cheeks).* (Cf. S187.1.) Icelandic: *Boberg.

S166.2. *Mutilation: cheek and chin cut off, but held together by biting the beard.* Icelandic: *Boberg.

S166.3. *Mutilation: shoulder-skin torn off in wrestling.* Icelandic: Göngu-Hrólfs saga 264.

S166.4. *Mutilation: cheeks cut off.* (Cf. S166.2.) Icelandic: *Boberg.

S166.5. *Mutilation: chin and lips cut off.* Icelandic: *Boberg.

S166.6. *Blood-eagle cut on man's back by flaying and salting.* Icelandic: Herrmann Saxo II 656, *Boberg.

S167. *Mutilation by crushing.* (Cf. S116.) Irish myth: *Cross.

S167.1. *Mutilation: crushing victim's limbs.* India: Thompson-Balys.

S168. *Mutilation: tearing off ears.* Icelandic: *Boberg.

S172. *Mutilation: nose cut off or crushed.* Icelandic: *Boberg.

S172.1. *Angry paramour bites off his mistress's nose.* India: Thompson-Balys; Buddhist myth: Malalasekera I 318, 328.

S173. *Mutilation: breaking (two, three) ribs.* Icelandic: *Boberg.

F624.3.1. Strong man throws carriage with horses and driver on top of haystack and breaks the driver's ribs.

S175. *Horses mutilated: tails cut off and manes torn off with the skin in order to humiliate their owner.* (Cf. J1169.5.) Icelandic: Boberg.

Q470. Humiliating punishments.

S176. *Mutilation: sex organs cut off.* (Cf. Q241, Q451.10.) Icelandic: *Boberg; Spanish Exempla: Keller.

S176.1. *Mutilation: emasculation.* Irish myth: *Cross; Eskimo (Greenland): Rasmussen I 270, III 293.

S180. Wounding or torturing.

E10. Resuscitation by rough treatment. K1016. Beetles and barley introduced into wounds on pretence of healing them. K1111. Dupe puts hand (paws) into cleft of tree (wedge, vise). K1111.1. Ogre's (dwarf's) beard caught fast. K1212. Lover left standing in snow while his mistress is with another. He later tricks her into standing a whole day in July in a tower naked exposed to the sun and flies. Q464. Covering with honey and exposing to flies. Q501. Unremitting torture as punishment.

S181. *Wounding by trapping with sharp knives (glass).* *Type 432; *BP II 261ff.; Italian: Basile Pentamerone II Nos. 2, 5; India: *Thompson-Balys.

K1565. Blades (broken glass) to wound and detect wife's lover.

S181.1. *Victim bound to a bladed wheel.* (Cf. Q423.) *Loomis White Magic 118.

S182. *Girl fastened by hair to rafter.* *Fb "hår" I 771b.

R111.2.3. Princess rescued from giant's cave where she is fettered to a chair by the hair.

S182.1. *Man hanged by hair to tree.* Cheremis: Sebeok-Nyerges.

S182.2. *Girl pulled about by her hair.* Buddhist myth: Malalasekera II 706.

S183. *Frightful meal.* (Cf. Q478.) Irish myth: Cross.

S183.0.1. *Person forced to eat red-hot meal.* Irish myth: Cross.

S183.1. *Person forced to eat hearts (flesh) of relatives (draw blood).* Irish myth: *Cross.

S183.2. *Person forced to eat loathsome animal.* Irish myth: *Cross.

S185. *Cruelty to pregnant woman.* Irish myth: Cross; India: Thompson-Balys.

S116.2. Pregnant woman crushed beneath chariot. S324. Pregnant woman ordered by husband to kill child to be born.

S185.1. *Co-wife forces pregnant woman to perform lowly tasks.* (Cf. T257.2.) Irish myth: *Cross.

T257.2. Jealousy of rival wives.

S185.2. *King demands intercourse with woman in childbed.* Irish myth: *Cross.

S186. *Torturing by beating.* Der Heiligen Leben und Leiden 100ff. (Santa Barbara); Buddhist myth: Malalasekera I 587.

S187. *Torturing by scratching.*

S187.1. *Torture by tearing out the sides (of a person).* (Cf. S166.1.) Der Heiligen Leben und Leiden 100f. (Santa Barbara); Jewish: Neuman.

S187.2. *Hair combed with iron combs.* India: Thompson-Balys.

S191. *Driving insane by keeping awake.* Nouvelles Récréations No. 68.

S200—S299. Cruel sacrifices.

S200. Cruel sacrifices.

S21.3. Sons give mother as hostage.

S210. Children sold or promised. *Type 930; Aarne FFC XXIII 54; BP I 98; Grimm Nos. 12, 31, 55, 92, 181; India: *Thompson-Balys; Japanese: Ikeda.

B11.10. Sacrifice of human being to dragon. S10. Cruel parents. V115.2. Girl sold for new church bell.

S210.1. *Child sold into slavery.* English: Wells 22 (Sir Beues of Hamtoun); Greek: Grote I 163; India: *Thompson-Balys; Buddhist myth: Malalasekera II 946. See also story of Joseph.

Q437.1. Criminal's wife and children sold into slavery. R61. Person sold into slavery.

S210.2. *Child sold to be killed.* Jewish: *Neuman.

S211. *Child sold (promised) to devil (ogre).* See also references to S220—S259, practically all of which apply here. *Types 314, 400, 502, 756B, 810; BP II 329, III 463, 531; *Cosquin Études 365, 542ff.; *Wesselski Märchen 242 No. 52; *Andrejev FFC LXIX 46; Sebillot France III 446, IV 127; Gaster Exempla 248 No. 352. — Lappish: Qvigstad FFC LX 42 No. 29AB; Swiss: Jegerlehner Oberwallis 293 No. 1, 300 No. 2; Breton: Sébillot Incidents s.v. "enfant", "diable"; French Canadian: Barbeau JAFL XXIX 17; Missouri French: Carrière; Spanish: Espinosa II Nos. 99—103, Espinosa Jr. No. 66; India: *Thompson-Balys; Indonesia: DeVries's list No. 147; Philippine: Fansler MAFLS XII 210, 212; Africa: Werner African 214.

C12.4.1. Mother wishes lazy daughter may marry devil. Devil appears and marries her. C25.1. Child threatened with ogre. Latter takes child off. G461. Youth promised to ogre visits his home. H1273.1. Quest to devil in hell for return of contract. K218.2. Devil cheated of his victim by boy having bible under his arm. M211. Man sells soul to devil.

S211.1. *Child of woman and devil taken to his father.* Type 756B; *Andrejev FFC LXIX 49.

S212. *Child sold to magician.* *Type 325; *Cosquin Études 523; BP II 60; Jones PMLA XXIII 567; India: *Thompson-Balys.

S213. *Child promised to wood-spirit.* (Cf. F441.) Type 667*.

S214. *Child promised to mermaid.* (Cf. B81.) Köhler-Bolte I 178; Irish myth: Cross.

S215. *Child promised to animal.* (Cf. B620.1.) India: *Thompson-Balys; Africa: Werner African 223.

H188. Princess appears before crane (who had demanded her in marriage) and is recognized by him despite loathly disguise. S221.1. Bankrupt father sells his daughters in marriage to animals. (Sometimes to pay gambling debt.) S232. Daughter promised to tiger in marriage for help in carrying load. S247. Daughter unwittingly promised to dog rescuer.

S215.1. *Girl promises herself to animal suitor.* *Type 440; BP I 1ff.; India: Thompson-Balys.

S216. *Mothers exchange children.* India: Thompson-Balys.

S220. Reasons for promise (sale) of child.

S10. Cruel parents.

S221. *Child sold (promised) for money.* *Type 756B; *Andrejev FFC LXIX 50ff., 56ff., *223, 227 n., *230 n.; Fb "sælge" III 722a; *Ward II 661 No. 4 (wife sold); Spanish: Boggs FFC XC 65 No. 471B*, Espinosa II No 117.

S221.1. *Bankrupt father sells his daughters in marriage to animals.* (Sometimes to pay gambling debt.) (Cf. S215.) *Types 425C, 552A; *BP II 234ff., III 424ff.; Spanish: Espinosa Jr. No. 65; India: *Thompson-Balys; Buddhist myth: Malalasekera I 149, II 1013.

F451.5.18.1. Dwarf promises money and property to mortal father for hand of daughter. N1. Gamblers. T68. Princess offered as prize.

S221.2. *Youth sells himself to an ogre in settlement of a gambling debt.* (Cf. M211, S215.) *Type 313; BP I 442.

S222. *Man promises (sells) child in order to save himself from danger or death.* *Types 310, 425C, 756B, 500; BP I 490ff.; MacCulloch Childhood 421; *Andrejev FFC LXIX 51, 58, 229 n.; India: *Thompson-Balys.

T52.7. Princess asked for in return for sparing palace. T69.3. Man gives daughter in return for his release.

S222.1. *Woman promises her unborn child to appease offended witch.* Italian: Basile Pentamerone II No. 1.

S222.2. *Woman promises unborn daughter to snake as wife for ferrying her across stream.* India: Thompson-Balys.

B551.4. Water snake carries man across water.

S222.3. *Woman promises unborn child to tiger if he will spare her.* India: Thompson-Balys.

S222.4. *Sultan's daughter demanded by giant ogre as price for letting his subjects alone.* India: Thompson-Balys.

S223. *Childless couple promise child to the devil if they may only have one.* *Type 756B; *BP III 107; *Wesselski Märchen 242 No. 52;

*Andrejev FFC LXIX 49, 52, *223ff.; Icelandic: *Boberg; India: *Thompson-Balys; Africa (Swahili): Steere 379.

C758.1. Monster born because of hasty wish of parents. M219.1. Bargain with the devil for an heir. S271. Sacrifice of child to remove barrenness. T548.1. Child born in answer to prayer.

S223.0.1. *Robert the Devil.* Childless couple wish for a child even if he comes from the devil. He is diabolical. *Wells 784; *Hibbard 49ff. (Sir Gowther); *Krappe Mod. Lang. Rev. XXIV (1929) 200ff.; Irish myth: Cross.

T548.1. Child born in answer to prayer. T556. Woman gives birth to a demon. T614. Diabolical child kills his wet-nurses.

S223.0.2. *Maid pledged to devil dresses conspicuously.* Finnish-Swedish: Wessman 14 No. 124.

S223.1. *Girl promises unborn child to devil if he will suffer the birth pangs.* Finnish: Aarne FFC XXXIII 40 No. 31**; Lithuanian: Balys Index No. 3254, Legends Nos. 370ff.

S223.2. *Mother curses her unborn child.* (Cf. M411.1.) *Type 756B; *Andrejev FFC LXIX 49.

S223.3. *An old maid promises the devil her first born.* She wishes to get a husband. Lithuanian: Balys Legends No. 391.

S223.4. *Childless couple promise one of two children to devil if they may only have them.* India: *Thompson-Balys.

S224. *Child promised to devil for acting as godfather.* (Cf. N411.) *Types 314, 502, 756B; *BP II 319ff., 329; Andrejev FFC LXIX 50; Breton: Sébillot Incidents s.v. "filleul".

S225. *Child promised to devil for help on road with broken wagon.* Andrejev FFC LXIX 50, 56, 228 n.

S226. *Child promised to devil for directions out of woods when father is lost.* *Andrejev FFC LXIX 51, 58, 229 n.; BP II 483f.

S227. *Child promised to devil in exchange for a good catch of fish.* *Andrejev FFC LXIX 51, 60, 230 n.; Irish: O'Suilleabhain 38, Beal XXI 314.

S228. *Daughter promised to monster as bride to secure flower (bird) she has asked for.* *Type 425C; *Tegethoff 12, 18; *BP II 229ff., *232 n. 2; India: *Thompson-Balys.

L221. Modest request: present from the journey. T118. Girl married to (enamored of) a monster.

S232. *Daughter promised to tiger in marriage for help in carrying load.* (Cf. B620.1.) India: *Thompson-Balys.

S233. *Children given in return for being taught magic.* India: *Thompson-Balys.

S234. *Children sold in exchange for food.* Africa (Wakweli): Bender 60.

S235. *Angry man gives away his daughter to a beggar.* Chinese: Eberhard FFC CXX 248 No. 193.

S240. Children unwittingly promised (sold). (Cf. S211.) *Types 314, 400, 710, 756B; *BP II 329; *Fb "frugtsommelig" I 376, "ufødt" III 926a; *Andrejev FFC LXIX 50ff., 56ff., 223; *MacCulloch Childhood 418; Irish: Baughman; Italian: Basile Pentamerone I No. 8.

S240.1. *Girl promised unwittingly by her parents to ogre.* India: Thompson-Balys.

S241. *Child unwittingly promised: "first thing you meet."* (Jephthah's vow.) *Types 425, 810; *BP II 329, 483; *Fb "først" I 404, "møde" II 647a; Wünsche 34f.; *Tegethoff 18; *Cox Cinderella 511; *Andrejev FFC LXIX 50, 62, 228 n.; Johnston MLN XXII 233. — French Canadian: Barbeau JAFL XXIX 17; Spanish: Espinosa Jr. No. 66; N. A. Indian (Zuñi): Boas JAFL XXXV 66 No. 2.

S241.1. *Unwitting bargain with devil evaded by driving dog over bridge first.* The child has been unwittingly promised (the first thing that goes over the bridge). Kittredge Witchcraft 206, *518 n. 19; Hazlitt Shakespeare Jest Books I 86f. No. 67; Mensa Philosophica No. 11.

D526. Transformation through greeting. First creature to be greeted will be transformed. J1169.4. The ass beheaded. King vows to sacrifice first thing he meets. It is a miller driving an ass. Miller pleads that the ass preceded him. They behead the ass. K210. Devil cheated of his promised soul. K527. Escape by substituting another person in place of the intended victim.

S241.2. *Devil is to have last one who leaves "black school".* Fb. "fanden" I 267b; Scotland, England: Baughman.

G303.19. Devil takes the hindmost.

S241.3. *Princess promised unwittingly to madman: "what you ask for."* India: Thompson-Balys.

S242. *Child unwittingly promised: "what you have at home."* The man thinks it is a cat (dog). *Types 316, 710; *BP I 21; Köhler-Bolte I 312; *Andrejev FFC LXIX 50, 62, 228 n.; Finnish-Swedish: Wessman 54 No. 455; Spanish: Espinosa II Nos. 99—103.

S242.1. *Child unwittingly promised: "What you wife has under her belt."* BP I 98f.; Danish: Grundtvig No. 33.

S243. *Child unwittingly promised: Nix-Naught-Nothing.* The child born while the father is away is named Nix-Naught-Nothing. Köhler-Bolte I 279; English: Jacobs English Fairy Tales 33.

K193. Deceptive bargain based on an unusual name.

S245. *Child unwittingly promised: what is born on your farm.* Two women agree that what is born on the farm of each belongs exclusively to the owner. The child of one is born on the farm of the other. Africa (Fjort): Dennett 58 No. 11.

S247. *Daughter unwittingly promised to dog rescuer.* (Cf. B620.1.) Without knowing that a dog has rescued her, the father offers her in marriage to her rescuer. India: *Thompson-Balys; Chinese: Werner 421; Japanese: Ikeda:

S250. Saving the promised child.. Missouri French: Carrière.

H1273.1. Quest to devil in hell for return of contract. K210. Devil cheated of his promised soul.

S251. *Virgin Mary rescues child promised to the devil.* *Meyer Romania XXXIII 163ff.; Ward II 632 No. 29, Herbert III 504; Spanish: Espinosa II Nos. 99—103.

M211. Man sells soul to devil. R150. Rescuers. V250. The Virgin Mary.

S252. *Vain attempt to save promised child.*

S252.1. *Vain attempt to save promised child by use of substitute.* *Type 425.

K527. Escape by substituting another person. K1840. Deception by substitution. K1920. Substituted children.

S252.2. *Vain attempt to save promised child by evasions.* India: Thompson-Balys.

S255. *Deity saves person about to be sacrificed.* (Cf. S263.2.1.) India: *Thompson-Balys.

S255.1. *Deity promises deliverance of promised child to mother in dream.* India: *Thompson-Balys.

S255.2. *Child sacrificed to deity returned to mother alive and whole after the ablution and ceremonial rites in honor of her.* India: Thompson-Balys.

S260. Sacrifices. (Cf. S255.) Irish myth: *Cross.

A1545. Origin of sacrifices. B11.10.0.1. Sacrifice of animals to dragon. B82.2. Merman demands cattle as offering. D1766.2. Magic results produced by sacrifices. K1614. Father delivering daughter to be eaten by cannibal is himself eaten. T301. Sacrifice of virginity. V10. Religious sacrifices.

S260.1. *Human sacrifice.* *Penzer IV 65 n.; *Encyc. Religion Ethics s.v. "Human sacrifice"; *V. Manzini La superstizione omicida e i sacrifici umani, con particolare riguardo alle accuse contro gli Ebrei (2d. ed., Padua, 1930); Krappe Hessische Blätter für Volkskunde XXVI (1927) 18—25. — Irish myth: *Cross; Icelandic: *Boberg; Spanish: Keller, Espinosa Jr. Nos. 61, 68f.; Greek: Fox 183; Jewish: *Neuman; India: *Thompson-Balys; Buddhist myth: Malalasekera I 189, II 54, 851; Marquesas: Beckwith 269, Handy 73; N. A. Indian (Sia): Alexander N. Am. 203, (Hopi): ibid. 205, (Zuñi): ibid. 201, *Benedict 342; Africa (Bushongo): Torday 250.

B11.10. Sacrifice of human being to dragon. P16.4.1. Suttee. Burning of wife with dead king. P361.3. Faithful servant sacrifices sons to save life of king. Sons resuscitated and servant enriched. V361. Christian child killed to furnish blood for Jewish rite.

S260.1.1. *Child sacrifice as religious rite.* Irish: *Cross, Beal XXI 329, O'Suilleabhain 90; Jewish: *Neuman; N. A. Indian (Aztec): Alexander Lat. Am. 72.

S260.1.2. *Sacrifice of sister on advice of yogi.* India: Thompson-Balys.

S260.1.3. *Prisoners sacrificed to goddess.* Irish myth: Cross.

S260.1.4. *Sacrifice of child to save life of another.* (Cf. S268.) Korean: Zong in-Sob 44 No. 26.

S261. *Foundation sacrifice.* A human being buried alive at base of the foundation of a building or bridge. *Krappe Balor 165 n. 1; *Gaidoz Mélusine IV (1888) No. 2; Krappe Revue Celtique XLIII (1926) 124ff. — Irish myth: *Cross; English: Wells 39 (Arthour and Merlin), 42 (Nennius' Historia Britonum); Welsh: MacCulloch Celtic 200; Finnish: Aarne FFC XXXIII 46 No. 81; Finnish-Swedish: Wessman 73 No. 620; Lithuanian: Balys Index No. 3519; Estonian: Aarne FFC XXV 133 No. 81; Spanish: Espinosa III Nos. 139, 151, 157; India: *Thompson-Balys; Japanese: Ikeda.

C931. Building falls because of breaking of tabu. D2192. Work of day magically overthrown at night. S125. Immolation.

S261.0.1. *Human blood mixed with rice to make leaky tanks hold water.* India: Thompson-Balys.

S261.1. *Child as foundation sacrifice smiles and wins freedom.* The king asks him why he smiles. "One first expects mercy from the parents; if they have none, then from the king. Now only God will have mercy." *Krappe Balor 171ff.; Penzer VII 87 n. 1, 88—96, 250ff.; *DeVries "De Sage van het ingemetselde Kind" Nederlandsche Tijdschrift voor Volkskunde XXXII (1917); India: *Thompson-Balys.

H637.1. What is hardest? — Parent's heart (said by child being sacrificed). J120. Wisdom learned from children. N456. Enigmatical smile (laugh) reveals secret knowledge.

S262. *Periodic sacrifices to a monster.* *Schoepperle II 326ff.; *Panzer Beowulf 276ff.; *Frazer Pausanias V 143; Brown Iwain 17 and passim; *Freytag Am Urquell I (1890) 179ff., 197ff.; *Fb "glarbjærg" I 459, "jomfru" II 43; Chauvin VI 110 No. 274. — Irish myth: *Cross; Missouri French: Carrière; Spanish: Espinosa III Nos. 139, 151, 157; Greek: *Frazer Apollodorus I 207 n. 2, II 119 n. 2, 134 n. 1; India: *Thompson-Balys; Buddhist myth: Malalasekera I 189, II 573, 1188; Japanese: Ikeda; Africa (Basuto): Jacottet 154 No. 22, (Fang): Trilles 166.

B11.10. Sacrifice of human being to dragon. B16.2.1. Devastating fox. Monthly human sacrifice.

S262.0.1. *One man disappears each night.* English: Beowulf; Icelandic: *Boberg.

S262.1. *Woman given to devastating monster as wife to appease it.* Irish myth: *Cross; Japanese: Ikeda; N. A. Indian (Creek): Alexander N. Am. 71.

S262.2. *Tribute of youths regularly sent to foreign king.* English: Wells 80 (Sir Tristrem).

S262.2.1. *Youths and maidens as yearly tribute to monsters (Fomorians).* Irish myth: *Cross.

S262.3. *Sacrificial victim chosen by lot.* (Cf. N126.) Icelandic: *Boberg; Buddhist myth: Malalasekera II 793; West Africa: Tauxier La Noir du Yatenga (Paris, 1917) 496f. No. 1, (Hausa): Basset Mélusine III 226f. No. 2, (Senegambia): Bérenger-Feraud II 185ff. No. 2.

S262.4. *Girl offers to sacrifice herself to dragon in place of her parents.* India: Thompson-Balys.

S263. *Sacrifice to appease spirits (gods).* (Cf. K1603, T211.1.1.) Irish myth: Cross; Japanese: Ikeda.

S263.1. *Highest ranking man in land to be sacrificed for good crops.* Icelandic: *Boberg.

S263.2. *Child sacrificed to gain favor of gods.* Penzer II 214ff.; Irish myth: Cross; Greek: Frazer Apollodorus II 111, Fox 52, 126; India: Thompson-Balys.

S263.2.1. *Gods furnish substitute for child sacrifice.* (Cf. S255.) Irish myth: *Cross; Greek: Frazer Apollodorus II 192 n. 1; Jewish: *Neuman.

S263.2.2. *Daughters sacrificed to avert famine.* *Frazer Pausanias II 78.

S263.2.3. *Man shows himself willing to sacrifice his child to prove his desire to follow God.* He is prevented by abbot. Spanish Exempla: Keller.

S263.3. *Person sacrificed to water spirit to secure water supply.* India:

*Thompson-Balys; Africa (Lamba): Doke MAFLS XX 14 No. 11, (Hausa): Basset Mélusine III 226f. No. 2, (Fulah): Frobenius Atlantis VI 182ff. No. 4.

A1111. Impounded water.

S263.3.1. *Human sacrifice to water serpent to secure tribal prosperity.* Africa Tauxier La Noir du Yatenga (Paris, 1917) 496f. No. 1, (Senegambia): Béranger-Feraud II 185ff. No. 2.

S263.3.2. *Serpent in stream demands pair of human eyes for drink of water.* (Cf. M225.) India: Thompson-Balys.

S263.3.3. *Raja sacrifices his entire family so as to purify lake water.* India: Thompson-Balys.

S263.4. *Sacrifice to river-god who has stopped boat in mid-stream.* India: *Thompson-Balys; Africa (Basuto): Jacottet 152ff. No. 22.

S263.4.1. *Sacrifice to offended gods, who hold ship back.* Icelandic: Herrmann Saxo II 586; Greek: Frazer Apollodorus II 111.

D2072.0.3. Ship held back by magic.

S263.5. *Sacrificial suicide.* (Cf. S264.1.2.) Irish myth: Cross.

S263.5.1. *Saints (monks) sacrifice themselves (to avert plague).* Irish myth: *Cross.

S263.5.2. *Monks sacrifice themselves (to save king and princes from pestilence).* Irish myth: Cross.

S263.5.3. *Man leaps from vessel into jaws of sea-beast, so as to save remaining passengers.* Irish myth: Cross.

S263.6. *Man sacrifices his wife to procure wealth in jars.* India: Thompson-Balys.

S264. *Sacrifice to rivers and seas.* *Fb "sø" III 731a, "å" III 1187b.

D1311.11.1. River says, "The time has come but not the man."

S264.1. *Man thrown overboard to placate storm.* (Cf. S263.5.3.) Type 973*; Child V 496 s.v. "Ships"; Chauvin VII 30 No. 212 n. 2; Irish myth: *Cross; Icelandic: *Boberg; Jewish: bin Gorion Born Judas[2] I 227; Buddhist myth: Malalasekera I 1024; Korean: Zong in-Sob 107 No. 57.

C41.3. Tabu: crossing water when spirits are offended.

S264.1.1. *Man carried on top of mast ready to be sacrificed to storm spirit.* India: *Thompson-Balys.

S264.1.2. *Woman drowns herself as sacrifice to water-gods to save husband's boat from capsizing.* (Cf. S263.5.) Japanese: Ikeda.

S264.2. *Sacrifice to tank.* India: Thompson-Balys.

S265. *Sacrifice of strangers.* Greek: *Frazer Apollodorus I 224 n. 1, II 273 n. 2; Japanese: Ikeda.

S265.1. *Hostages sacrificed.* Irish myth: *Cross.

S266. *Burial of live girl to banish plague.* German: Knoop Sagen u. Erzählungen aus Posen 123.

S267. *Flood stopped by sacrifice of boy and girl.* N. A. Indian (Zuñi): Benedict 337.

S268. *Child sacrificed to provide blood for cure of friend.* (Cf. S260.1.4.) *Type 516; **Rösch FFC LXXVII 138ff., 161ff.; BP I 56; *Chauvin VIII 195 No. 235; *Wells 787 (Amis and Amiloun); Hibbard 70ff.; Scala Celi 10a No. 64; Alphabet No. 55. — Italian: Basile Pentamerone IV No. 9, Rotunda; India: *Thompson-Balys; Japanese: Ikeda.

E113. Resuscitation by blood. H1558. Tests of friendship. P310. Friendship. P361.3. Faithful servant sacrifices sons to save life of king.

S268.1. *Sacrifice of child demanded as cure for feigned sickness.* India: *Thompson-Balys.

B335.2. Life of helpful animal demanded as cure for feigned sickness. D866.2. Magic object destroyed to cure feigned sickness. H1212. Quest assigned because of feigned illness.

S268.1.1. *Prince's life can only be prolonged if servant sacrifices his only son to goddess.* India: *Thompson-Balys.

S268.2. *Son sold for transfusion of blood to sick king.* India: Thompson-Balys.

S271. *Sacrifice of child to remove barrenness.* Penzer I 154; Chauvin V 176 No. 100; India: Thompson-Balys.

J2067.1. Sacrifice of one son to get another. S223. Childless couple promise child to the devil if they may only have one. T510. Miraculous conception.

S272. *Sacrifice of brothers promised if girl is born.* *Type 451; BP I 71ff.

S272.1. *Flight of brothers from home to avoid being sacrificed.* *Type 451; BP I 70.

S273. *Child bought to serve as sacrifice to demon.* Penzer VII 87 n. 1; India: Thompson-Balys.

S274. *Sacrifice as an agricultural rite.* Irish myth: *Cross.

S276. *Sacrifice as protection against disease.* Irish myth: *Cross.

S300—S399. Abandoned or murdered children.

S300. Abandoned or murdered children.

E225. Ghost of murdered child. G261. Witch steals children. P230. Parents and children. S10. Cruel parents. T600. Care of children.

S301. *Children abandoned (exposed).* *Types 327, 450, 590, 675, 920, 930; *De Vries FFC LXXIII 40ff.; *Penzer VII 81 n. 1, 82 n. 250; *Boje 65; *Cosquin Études 199ff.; *Prato RTP IV 178; **Nutt FLR IV 1ff.; **Hartland FLJ IV 308; *Aarne FFC XXIII 60; Cowell Jātaka V 230; Dickson 152. — Irish myth: *Cross; Icelandic: *Boberg; Breton: Sébillot Incidents s.v. "enfant"; Spanish: Espinosa II Nos. 99—103, 119; Italian: Basile Pentamerone V No. 8, *Rotunda; Jewish: *Neuman; India: *Thompson-Balys; Chinese: Eberhard FFC CXX 94f.; Tuamotu: Beckwith Myth 471; Tonga: Gifford 122; Hawaii: Beckwith Myth 523; Easter Island: Métraux Ethnology 369, 385; N. A. Indian: *Thompson Tales 349 n. 255, (California): Gayton and Newman 89, (Zuñi): Benedict II 335; West Indies: Flowers 576.

M312.7. Prophecy of luck for outcast child.

S302. *Children murdered.* Irish myth: *Cross; Jewish: *Neuman.

S302.1. *All new-born male children slaughtered.* Jewish: *Neuman.

S303. *Son killed at instigation of lover.* India: Thompson-Balys.

S303.1. *Woman asks suitor to kill the child of his first wife.* Africa (Cameroon): Mansfield 228.

S310. Reasons for abandonment of children. (Cf. K2015, M371, M373, M375.)

S311. *Undesirable children exposed, desirable preserved.* *Frazer Old Testament II 437ff.; Icelandic: Boberg.

S311.1. *Parents successively bury alive their sons who mention something about smith's, potter's, washerman's, and tom-tom beater's trade,* but keep fifth child who says something about being future king. India: Thompson-Balys.

S312. *Illegitimate child exposed.* (Cf. S12.2.1, T640.) *Encyc. Religion Ethics s.v. "Abandonment and exposure"; *Nutt FLR IV 1ff.; Frazer Apollodorus I 252 n. 2; Aarne FFC XXIII 63; *Hertel Zs. f. Vksk. XIX 83ff., 91. — Irish myth: *Cross; Icelandic: *Boberg; Italian Novella: Rotunda; India: *Thompson-Balys.

S312.1. *Child of incest exposed.* (Cf. T410.) *Type 933; Köhler-Bolte Zs. f. Vksk. VI 173 (to Gonzenbach No. 85); *Baum PMLA XXXI 562 n. 59; Krappe Neuphilologische Mitteilungen XXXIV (1933) 11—22; Irish myth: *Cross; Icelandic: Boberg.

S312.2. *Violated woman's child exposed.* Icelandic: *Boberg.

S312.3. *Posthumous child to be exposed.* Icelandic: Boberg.

T645.1. Sword left posthumous son to kill father's murderer. T682. Hero a posthumous son.

S312.4. *Woman abandons baby boy (of which she was artificially impregnated) in forest.* India: Thompson-Balys.

S313. *Child of supernatural birth exposed.* (Cf. T520.) *Nutt FLR IV 1ff.; Gaster Thespis 255; Greek: Grote I 103; Jewish: Neuman; India: Thompson-Balys.

S314. *Twins (triplets) exposed.* (Cf. T587.) *Krappe Balor 17 n. 55; Dickson 103 n. 10; Gaster Thespis 255; Italian Novella: Rotunda; Greek: Grote I 103.

S321. *Destitute parents abandon children.* *Encyc. Religion Ethics s.v. "Abandonment and exposure"; *Type 327; *BP I 123; Missouri French: Carrière; Greek: Grote I 103; India: *Thompson-Balys; Chinese: Eberhard FFC CXX 256 No. 200a; Korean: Zong in-Sob 43 No. 25.

S321.1. *Children abandoned in famine.* Eskimo (Greenland): Rasmussen I 374, (Mackenzie Area): Jenness 34a; N. A. Indian (Zuñi): Benedict II 335; Africa (Wachaga): Gutmann 142.

S322. *Children abandoned (driven forth, exposed) by hostile relative.* *Roberts 128; Irish myth: *Cross; Spanish: Espinosa II No. 114, Espinosa Jr. No. 140.

S322.0.1. *Orphaned boy deprived of his inheritance by relatives.* India: *Thompson-Balys.

S322.1. *Father casts daughter forth.* Spanish: Espinosa II Nos. 107f., 154, Espinosa Jr. Nos. 120—123.

M21. King Lear judgment.

S322.1.1. *Father who wanted son exposes (murders) daughter.* Irish myth: *Cross; Greek: Fox 56 (Atalanta); India: *Thompson-Balys; Indonesia: DeVries's list No. 203.

S322.1.2. *Father casts daughter forth when she will not marry him.* (Cf. T411.1.) *Type 510B; BP II 45; Cox passim; Krappe Zeitschrift für englische Philologie XLIX 361—69; Spanish: Espinosa II Nos. 99—103.

S322.1.2.1. *Exposure in jungle for refusing to marry according to father's wishes.* India: Thompson-Balys.

S322.1.3. *Father condemns daughter to death because he believes her unchaste.* Type 883A; India: Thompson-Balys; Africa (Somali): Kirk FL XV 319ff. No. 3, Reinisch Die Saho-Sprache (Wien, 1889) I 76ff. No. 3.

S322.1.4. *Princess humiliated by father after she has married loathly bridegroom.* India: Thompson-Balys.

S322.1.5. *Boy turned out of doors by father.* India: Thompson-Balys.

S322.1.5.1. *King, jealous of son, banishes him and his wife.* Buddhist myth: Malalasekera I 210.

S322.2. *Jealous mother casts daughter forth.* (Cf. S12.) *Type 709; Africa (Angola): Chatelain 30 No. 1.

S322.2.1. *Mother exposes child (for fear of jealous co-wife).* Irish myth: *Cross.

S322.3. *Jealous co-wife kills woman's children.* (Cf. K2222.) India: *Thompson-Balys; Africa (Basuto): Jacottet 246 No. 36, (Zulu): Callaway 237.

S322.3.1. *Jealous co-wife demands murder of woman's children.* India: *Thompson-Balys.

S322.3.2. *Jealous concubine plots against real wife's daughter.* Chinese: Graham.

S322.4. *Evil stepmother casts boy forth.* *Types 592; India: *Thompson-Balys.

S322.4.1. *Banishment (death) of stepchildren demanded as cure for feigned illness.* India: Thompson-Balys.

B335.2. Life of helpful animal demanded as cure for feigned sickness. H1212. Quests assigned because of feigned illness. Q431. Punishment: banishment (exile).

S322.4.2. *Evil stepmother orders stepdaughter to be killed.* Irish myth: *Cross.

S322.4.3. *Stepmother irritates two stepsons so that one kills the other.* India: Thompson-Balys.

S322.5. *Repulsed lover kills woman's child.* Dickson 73 n. 26.

S322.6. *Jealous mother-in-law and sisters cast woman's children forth.* Roberts 132; Italian Novella: Rotunda; India: *Thompson-Balys.

K2110.1. Calumniated wife. K2212. Treacherous sister. S51. Cruel mother-in-law.

S322.7. *Evil stepmother works stepdaughter to death in absence of merchant husband.* India: Thompson-Balys.

S324. *Pregnant woman ordered by husband to kill child to be born.* Irish myth: Cross.

S325. *Diseased child exposed.* Africa (Kaffir): Kidd 224 No. 1.

S325.0.1. *Monstrous (deformed) child exposed.* (Cf. S11.3.2, T550.) Irish myth: Cross; Greek: Grote I 55; Chinese: Graham; Marquesas: Handy 114; Tonga: Gifford 31, 60.

S325.0.1.1. *Child born with caul exposed.* Irish myth: Cross.

S326. *Disobedient children cast forth.* India: Thompson-Balys; Indonesia: DeVries's list No. 205.

S326.1. *Disobedient child burned.* Irish myth: Cross.

S327. *Child cast out because of his stupidity.* Type 563; Grimm No. 36; India: Thompson-Balys.

S327.1. *Father wants to kill son because of foolish boasting.* India: Thompson-Balys.

S327.2. *Baby ordered killed because it pulls beard of father (raja).* India: Thompson-Balys.

P672. Pulling a man's beard as an insult.

S327.3. *Half-wit abandoned because of his tricks.* Eskimo (Kodiak): Golder JAFL XXII 23.

S328. *Mother sells her child to heathen sailors.* Boje 63, *67.

S329. *Reasons for abandonment of children—miscellaneous.*

S329.1. *Child exposed so as to avoid death decree.* India: Thompson-Balys.

S330. Circumstances of murder or exposure of children.

K1921.1. Son of the king and of the smith exchanged. S142. Person thrown into the water and abandoned. S143. Abandonment in forest. S143.1. Child abandoned in hollow tree. S146. Abandonment in pit.

S331. *Exposure of child in boat (floating chest).* See references for S141, nearly all of which refer to this motif. Type 930; W. R. Halliday Indo-European Folk Tales and Greek Legend (London, 1933) 55; Irish myth: Cross; Missouri French: Carrière; Greek: Grote I 103; Jewish: *Neuman; India: *Thompson-Balys; Buddhist myth: Malalasekera I 558, 931; Japanese: Ikeda; Philippine (Tinguian): Cole 152.

S141. Exposure in boat. S431. Cast-off wife exposed in boat.

S332. *Queen hides her child and accuses wolf of eating it.* Malone PMLA XLIII 437.

S333. *Child's ankles pierced before exposing him.* Greek: *Frazer Apollodorus I 344 n. 1 (Oedipus).

S334. *Tokens of royalty (nobility) left with exposed child.* (Cf. H80.) *Penzer VII 81 n. 1; Irish myth: Cross; English: Wells 134 (Sir Degare), 126 (Lai Le Freine); Greek: Fox 71.

S334.1. *Child exposed with twelve years' supply of food and attendants.* India: Thompson-Balys.

S335. *Child exposed at palace gate.* Penzer VII 81 n. 1, 82 n., 250.

S336. *Abandoned child wrapped in straw.* DeVries FFC LXXIII 326f.

S337. *Children enticed into grain pot and imprisoned.* India: Thompson-Balys.

S338. *Father abandons his daughter in forest and leaves axes tied so that they move in wind.* Daughter thinks he is cutting wood. *Roberts 137.

S341. *Exposure prevented.*

S341.1. *Exposure given up on account of newborn son's protesting stanza.* Icelandic: Boberg.

F611.3.2. Hero's precocious strength. T585. Precocious infant.

S342. *Mother induced by rival to kill her children.* India: *Thompson-Balys.

S345. *Parents trick children into going on hunt, and then abandon them in forest.* (Cf. S143.) India: Thompson-Balys.

S350. Fate of abandoned child. India: Thompson-Balys; Chinese: Eberhard FFC CXX 54 No. 33; Japanese: Ikeda.

D1821.6. Magic sight given to abandoned child. F615. Strong man evades death. Vain attempts to kill him. G25. Abandoned infant lives by eating corpse of murdered father. H80. Identification by tokens. H90. Identification by ornaments. H110. Identification by cloth or clothing. K512. Compassionate executioner. A servant charged with killing the hero (heroine) arranges the escape of the latter. L111.1. Exile returns and succeeds. L111.2. Foundling hero. N731.3. Father unexpectedly meets abandoned son and reinstates him. P361.5. Abandoned maiden helped by her faithful nurse. R131. Exposed or abandoned child rescued. S371. Abandoned daughter's son becomes hero.

S350.1. *Infant condemned to death saved by a smile.* Irish myth: Cross.

S350.2. *Child driven out (exposed) brought up in secret.* Irish myth: *Cross.

A516. Expulsion and return of culture hero.

S351. *Abandoned child cared for by mother secretly.* (Cf. R153.) Africa (Zulu): Callaway 236, (Basuto): Jacottet 128ff. No. 18.

S351.0.1. *Abandoned child made over to its own mother (sister) acting as wet nurse.* Jewish: *Neuman.

S351.1. *Abandoned child cared for by grandmother (aunt, foster mother).* Irish: *Cross, MacCulloch Celtic 167; N. A. Indian (California): Gayton and Newman 91.

S351.2. *Abandoned child reared by herdsman.* (Cf. R131.3.) Irish myth: Cross; Greek: Grote I 241, 263; Buddhist myth: Malalasekera I 458.

S351.2.1. *Abandoned princess, brought up by herdsmen, becomes wife of king.* Irish myth: *Cross; Buddhist myth: Malalasekera I 378.

S352. *Animal aids abandoned child(ren).* (Cf. B535.) Missouri French: Carrière; India: *Thompson-Balys; S. A. Indian (Sherenti): Lowe BBAE CXLIII (1) 515; West Indies: Flowers 576.

S352.1. *Animal preserves fire for abandoned children in a clam shell.* N. A. Indian: *Thompson Tales 347, 349 nn. 247, 255.

S353. *Abandoned child reared by supernatural beings.* India: *Thompson-Balys; Maori: Dixon 42.

S353.1. *Deity nurtures and rears abandoned child.* India: *Thompson-Balys; Buddhist myth: Malalasekera II 1366.

S353.2. *Exposed children miraculously fed by angels.* Jewish: Neuman.

S354. *Exposed infant reared at strange king's court (Joseph, Oedipūs).*

*Type 931; Irish myth: *Cross; Jewish: Neuman, bin Gorion Born Judas[2] I 165, 372; India: Thompson-Balys.

L111.1. Exile returns and succeeds. N836.1. King adopts hero (heroine). R131.11.2. King rescues abandoned child.

S354.1. *Abandoned child adopted and found by queen.* India: *Thompson-Balys.

S354.2. *Travelers find exposed baby girl and take her to emperor's court.* India: Thompson-Balys.

S354.3. *Prince (princess) adopts exposed child.* Jewish: Neuman; Africa (Wachaga): Gutmann 142.

S355. *Exposed child carried off by wild beast.* (Cf. R13.) Dickson 169ff.

S356. *Children left at home seek exposed brothers and sisters.* Indonesia: DeVries's list No. 207.

S357. *Abandoned sister rescued by brothers.* When she is refused entrance to house, she makes complaint in a song and brothers bring her clothes. Lithuanian: Balys Index No. 883C*.

S361. *Bird carries food from deserted child to starving parents.* N. A. Indian: *Thompson Tales 348 n. 250.

S362. *Starving parents come to abandoned child for food.* Jewish: *Neuman (Joseph); Sulka of New Britain: Dixon 132 n. 2; N. A. Indian: *Thompson Tales 349 n. 255.

S365. *Maltreated children transformed.* (Cf. D642.)

S365.1. *Maltreated children transformed to doves.* India: Thompson-Balys.

S366. *Abandoned children return and kill parents.* N. A. Indian (California): Gayton and Newman 89.

S371. *Abandoned daughter's son becomes hero.* *Dixon 130, 132 n. 2, 136 nn. 10, 11; Greek: Grote I 854; India: *Thompson-Balys.

S375. *Old woman's maledictions inform abandoned hero of his parentage and future.* He has knocked her over (broken pots). *Cosquin Contes indiens 398.

M301.2.1. Enraged old woman prophesies for youth. M411.5. Old woman's curse. N825.3. Old woman helper.

S376. *Tree feeds abandoned children with its sap.* India: Thompson-Balys.

S378. *Deserted children become Thunder.* N. A. Indian (California): Gayton and Newman 91.

A1142. Origin of thunder R321. Escape to the stars.

S400—S499. Cruel persecutions.

S400. Cruel persecutions.

S401. *Unsuccessful attempts to kill person in successive reincarnations (transformations).* Egyptian: Petrie Egyptian Tales (London, 1895) I 36ff., Von Sydow "Den fornegyptiska Sagan om de två Bröderna"

Yearbook of the New Society of Letters of Lund, 1930, 53ff.; India: *Thompson-Balys.

D610. Repeated transformations. E670. Repeated reincarnation. H1510. Tests of power to survive. K1911.2.1. True bride transformed by false.

S410. Persecuted wife. *Types 450, 705, 706, 707, 708, 712, 872*; *BP II 236, 284; *Schlauch Constance and Accused Queens (New York, 1927); *Hibbard 29, 35ff.; *Wehrhan 51; *Krappe Anglia XLIX 361ff. — Missouri French: Carrière; Spanish: Keller, Espinosa II No. 105; India: *Thompson-Balys; Eskimo (Greenland): Rasmussen I 365, III 104, Rink 441, (Cumberland Sound): Boas BAM XV 198.

A773.2. Pleiades six repudiated wives. C867.1. Tabu: abusing women or children. D688. Transformed mother suckles child. E323.1.1. Dead mother returns to suckle child. H465. Test of wife's endurance. Haughty princess married to beggar and must endure poverty and menial work. K1911. The false bride (substitute bride). K2110.1. Calumniated wife. K2155.1. Blood smeared on innocent person brings accusation of murder. P210. Husband and wife. Q414.0.7. Innocent queen burned at stake. Q421.0.8. Beheading for persecution of wife. Q456.1.1. Cast-forth wife buried up to waist. Q471.1. Persecuted queen meanly clothed and set where all are commanded to spit on her. Q481. Princess (queen) compelled to keep an inn. Q482.1. Princess serves as menial. S62. Cruel husband. T292. Wife sold unwillingly by husband.

S411. *Wife banished.* India: *Thompson-Balys; Buddhist myth: Malalasekera II 526.

S411.1. *Misunderstood wife banished by husband.* She has decorated the house for his homecoming, but he thinks that she is expecting a paramour. *Type 890 (Christiansen Norske Eventyr 113); Japanese: Ikeda.

S411.2. *Wife banished for some small fault.* India: *Thompson-Balys.

S411.2.1. *Queen banished for saying that man's condition depends on what kind of wife he has.* India: Thompson-Balys.

S411.3. *Barren wife sent away.* India: *Thompson-Balys.

S411.4. *Wife banished because she eats by stealth.* India: Thompson-Balys.

K1984.2. The girl who ate so little.

S412. *Heroine taunted with her unknown past.* (Cf. F302.) Dickson 74.

S412.1. *Husband expels wife because her industry indicates her peasant origin.* Chinese: Graham.

S413. *Unfaithful husband and his mistress persecute his wife.* Italian Novella: Rotunda.

S413.1. *Ogress-wife orders raja to turn out his six wives.* India: *Thompson-Balys.

S413.2. *Second wife orders husband to persecute first.* India: *Thompson-Balys.

S414. *Woman abandoned when with child.* Buddhist myth: Malalasekera II 1038.

S416. *Queen banished when she defeats king in argument.* India: *Thompson-Balys.

S430. Disposal of cast-off wife.

S431. *Cast-off wife exposed in boat.* *Hertel Zs. f. Vksk. XIX 83ff.

S141. Exposure in boat. S331. Exposure of child in boat (floating chest).

S431.1. *Cast-off wife and child exposed in boat.* Hibbard 26ff.; English: Wells 115 (Sir Eglamour of Artois), 117 (Sir Torrent of Portyngale), 129 (Emare), Chaucer's Man of Law's Tale; Italian: Basile Pentamerone I No. 3; Greek: *Frazer Apollodorus I 155 n. 3; India: Thompson-Balys; Japanese: Ikeda.

S432. *Cast-off wife thrown into water.* (Cf. S142.) *Types 403, 450, 707; India: *Thompson-Balys; N. A. Indian: *Thompson CColl II 382ff., (Teton): Dorsey JAFL II 137.

S433. *Cast-off wife abandoned on island.* (Cf. S145.) Type 890 (Christiansen Norske Eventyr 113); Spanish: Espinosa II Nos. 105, 119.

S435. *Cast-off wife abandoned in pit.* (Cf. T581.2.) India: *Thompson-Balys; Indonesia: DeVries's list No. 202.

S436. *Cast-off wife's head shaven.* India: Thompson-Balys.

S437. *Cast-off wife sent to herd cows.* India: Thompson-Balys.

S438. *Abandoned queen blinded.* India: *Thompson-Balys.

S441. *Cast-off wife and child abandoned in forest.* (Cf. S143.) India: *Thompson-Balys.

S442. *Outcast wife and her son live in poverty.* India: *Thompson-Balys.

S445. *Abandoned wife hidden under a tub.* Cox 501; Grimm No. 9.

S446. *Rejected wife asks to take away only what she brought.* Type 887; Chinese: Graham.

S450. Fate of outcast wife.

S451. *Outcast wife at last united with husband and children.* *Types 706, 712, 938; *Loomis White Magic 118; *Chauvin VI 167ff. No. 327. Chauvin discusses the following stories having this motif: St. Clement, St. Eustace, Crescentia, Hildegarde, Florence, Octavianus, Sebile, Genevieve of Brabant, Euriant, the Maiden without Hands, Helena of Constantinople, the Count of Toulouse. — Missouri French: Carrière; Spanish: Espinosa II Nos. 105, 119, Espinosa Jr. Nos. 138—41; India: *Thompson-Balys; Indonesia: DeVries's list Nos. 201, 202.

H152.3. Abandoned wife recognized among workers. N251. Man pursued by misfortune .... He finally recovers all.

S452. *Outcast wife commits suicide when confronted with heads of relatives killed in revenge for her wrong-doing.* Irish myth: Cross.

S453. *Exposed woman helped by magician.* India: Thompson-Balys.

S460. Other cruel persecutions.

S461. *Tale-bearer unjustly drowned for lack of proof of accusation.* Irish myth: Cross.

N340. Hasty killing or condemnation (mistake). Q428. Punishment: drowning.

S463. *Jealous wife has merchant turn out queen and son, whom he had befriended and taken into his home.* India: Thompson-Balys.

S464. *Deity appears before persecuted youngest brother and gives him a flock of sheep.* India: Thompson-Balys.

S465. *Abandoned person in woods comforted by prophet and birds.* (Cf. S143.) *Grünwald Hessische Blätter für Vksk. XXX—XXXI 315.

S466. *Practice of one's religion forbidden.* Jewish: *Neuman.

S471. *Persecuted sons of co-wife.* (Cf. K2222.) India: Thompson-Balys.

S481. *Cruelty to animals.* India: Thompson-Balys; Chinese: Eberhard FFC CXX 181 No. 123.

T. SEX

DETAILED SYNOPSIS

T600—T699. Care of children

T600. Care of children
T610. Nurture and growth of children
T640. Illegitimate children
T670. Adoption of children
T680. Care of children—miscellaneous motifs

T. SEX

T. Sex.

A1313. Origin of sex-organs. A1355.1. Origin of menstruation—Eve and the serpent. B754.1.1. Hyena changes sex yearly. D10. Transformation to person of different sex. D1982.1. Magic door invisible to women. F302.3.4. Fairies entice men and then harm them. F565.1. Amazons. Women warriors M130. Vows concerning sex. M369.2. Prophecies concerning love and marriage. N131.1. Luck changed after cohabitation. Q451.10. Punishment: genitalia cut off. S176.1. Mutilation: emasculation. X700. Humor concerning sex.

T0—T99. Love.

T0. Love. Irish myth: *Cross.

A475. God of love. A475.1. Goddess of love. C453. Tabu: boasting of love-conquest. D658. Transformation to seduce. D856. Magic object obtained by gaining love of owner. D1355. Love-producing magic object. D1900. Love induced by magic. F420.5.1.3. Water-spirits help lovers. F585.1. Fatal enticements of phantom women. F771.13. Castle warmed by love. No fire is required because love makes perpetual summer. G262.0.1.1. Lamia devours her lover. G264. La Belle Dame Sans Merci. Witch entices men with offers of love and then deserts or destroys them. J491. Old sweetheart chosen in preference to new. J1737. Foolish lover ignorant of mistress's flaws. J1791.6. Diving for reflection of beautiful woman. K1210. Humiliated or baffled lovers. K1300. Seduction. K1500. Deceptions connected with adultery. M369.2. Prophesies concerning love and marriage.

T1. *Zeus gives man modesty, but it leaves when love enters.* Wienert FFC LVI 36; Halm Aesop No. 148.

T2. *The relative pleasures of love.* Do men or women have the greater pleasure in sexual intercourse? Man who has been transformed to woman answers that women have the greater pleasure. The goddess blinds him as punishment. Krappe Science of Folklore 6f.; Penzer VII 227; Greek: Frazer Apollodorus I 367 n. 1; India: Thompson-Balys.

J99.1. Relative pleasure of sexes in love taught by parable. Q451.7. Blinding as punishment.

T3. *Omens in love affairs.*

T3.1. *Blue fortunate in love matters.* English: Child II 182, 512a.

D1812.5. Future learned through omens. Z140. Color symbolism.

T4. *Person wants to learn art of love.*

T4.1. *Herdsman to learn art of love so he can become a holy man.* India: Thompson-Balys.

T6. *Love as inducement to idolatry.* Jewish: *Neuman.

T8. *Sexual desire as original sin.* Jewish; Neuman.

T10. Falling in love. India: Thompson-Balys.

D1314.1.3. Magic arrow shot to determine where to seek bride. D1900. Love induced by magic. H1381.3.1.2. Quest for bride for oneself.

T10.1. *Sluggish prince reformed by falling in love.* *bin Gorion Born Judas[2] IV 38, 276.

T10.1.1. *Gambler reformed by falling in love.* Italian Novella: Rotunda.

T10.1.2. *Love transforms crude individual into a polished courtier.* Italian Novella: Rotunda.

T10.2. *Angel of love compels man to fall in love.* Jewish: Neuman.

T10.3. *Girl continually falling in love.* India: *Thompson-Balys.

T11. *Falling in love with person never seen.*

H1381.3.1. Quest for bride.

T11.1. *Love from mere mention or description.* *Type 516; *Rösch FFC LXXVII 100; *Chauvin V 132 No. 112; *Penzer X 214 s.v. "Love by mere mention"; Malone PMLA XLIII 399; *Dickson 188 n. 63; Hibbard 208 n. 18, 226 n. 1; *Cross MPh XII 612 n. 3; Moore PMLA XXIX (1914) 527f.; Fb "hår" IV 241b. — Irish myth: *Cross; Icelandic: *Boberg; Italian: Basile Pentamerone IV No. 7, *Rotunda; India: *Thompson-Balys.

T11.1.1. *Beauty of woman reported to king causes quest for her as his bride.* India: *Thompson-Balys; Chinese: Graham.

H1381.3.1.1. Quest for bride for king. P15.2. King demands subject's wife for himself.

T11.2. *Love through sight of picture.* *Types 403, 516, 900; *BP I 45ff., 443ff.; *Rösch FFC LXXVII 98; Philippson FFC L 11f.; *Penzer X 214 s.v. "love with a painting", 263 s.v. "picture, falling in love"; Fb "portræt" II 863; *Köhler-Bolte I 127, 520ff., 527; Wesselski Archiv Orientální II 430; Herbert III 204; Oesterley No. 62. — English: Wells 81 (Sir Tristrem); Icelandic: *Boberg; Breton: Sébillot Incidents s.v. "portrait"; Missouri French: Carrière; Arabian: Burton Nights S II 194ff.; India: *Thompson-Balys; Chinese: Graham, Eberhard FFC CXX 61f., 252; Japanese: Ikeda; Indonesia: DeVries's list No. 218.

H21. Recognition through picture. H1381.3.1.1.1. Quest for bride for king like picture he has seen. H1381.3.1.2.1. Quest for unknown woman whose picture has aroused man's love. M151.2.1. Vow not to reign and to starve to death unless picture's original is found.

T11.2.0.1. *Ugly picture of suitor makes girl refuse him.* Icelandic: Boberg.

T11.2.1. *Love through sight of statue.* *Type 516; *Rösch FFC LXXVII 99; Köhler-Bolte I 520 ff., 527; Icelandic: Boberg; India: Thompson-Balys.

T11.2.1.1. *Youth makes statue of girl and seeks a girl like the statue.* Icelandic: Boberg; India: Thompson-Balys; Buddhist myth: Malalasekera I 63, 76, II 476, 1090; Chinese: Chavannes 500 Contes I 374 No. 107.

D435.1.1. Statue comes to life. Galateia.

T11.3. *Love through dream.* Falling in love with a person seen in a dream. *Type 516; *BP I 45; *Rösch FFC LXXVII 100; *Chauvin V 132 No. 112; *Penzer III 82 n. 2, IX 36 n. 1; *Moore PMLA XXIX 527f.; Rohde Griechische Roman 45ff.; Dunlop-Wilson II 258; Bédier Fabliaux (1895) 113ff.; *Krappe Revue Hispanique LXXXI 5ff. — Irish: MacCulloch Celtic 78, *Cross; Icelandic: M. Moe in Edda 1914 p. 245, *Boberg; Arabian: Basset 1001 Contes I 136, II 68; India: *Thompson-Balys; Korean: Zong in-Sob 73 No. 40, 136 No. 63; Indonesia: J. Brandes Tijdschrift voor Indische Taal-, Land-, en Volkenkunde XLI 295f., 469, Jeynboll Supplement Catalogus Jav. — Madoereesche Handschriften I 53ff.; Hawaii: Beckwith Myth 231; N. A. Indian (Yana): Curtin Creation Myths 425ff.; Africa: Frobenius Atlantis III 247; Cape Verde Islands: Parsons MAFLS XV (1) 211f. No. 73, 220 No. 74.

D1812.3.3.9. Future husband (wife) revealed in dream. D1976.2. Future spouse met during magic sleep. H24. Recognition through dream.

T11.3.1. *Lovers meet in their dreams.* Irish myth: Cross; Persian: Carnoy 341; India: Thompson-Balys; Hindu: Penzer III 82.

T11.3.2. *Dream about a marriage with another's wife.* India: Thompson-Balys.

T11.4. *Love through sight of something belonging to unknown princess.* Hdwb. d. Märchens II 103b. nn. 169—76; India: Thompson-Balys.

T11.4.1. *Love through sight of hair of unknown princess.* **Golther Die Jungfrau mit den goldenen Haaren (Leipzig, 1893); *Cosquin Contes indiens 50 n. 2, 351ff.; Köhler-Bolte II 328ff.; Chavannes III 258 No. 470; Icelandic: Boberg; India: *Thompson-Balys; Japanese: Ikeda; Philippines: Dixon 169.

D1355.5. Magic hair produces love. H75. Identification by a hair. H1213.1.1. Quest for princess caused by sight of one of her hairs dropped by a bird (or floating on river).

T11.4.1.1. *Love through sight of hair of unknown hero.* India: *Thompson-Balys; N. A. Indian (Shasta): Thompson Tales 196.

T11.4.2. *Love through sight of slipper of unknown princess.* *Cosquin Études 8; Saintyves Perrault 115; India: *Thompson-Balys.

T11.4.3. *Love through finding lady's wreath.* Cowell Jātaka IV 144; Buddhist myth: Malalasekera I 586.

T11.4.3.1. *Love through seeing bouquet.* India: Thompson-Balys.

T11.4.4. *Love through seeing marks of lady's teeth in fruit which she has bitten.* Indonesia: DeVries Volksverhalen II 89ff. No. 110.

T11.4.5. *Love through finding lady's handkerchief.* India: Thompson-Balys.

H113. Identification by handkerchief. H35.3. Recognition by unique needlework.

T11.4.6. *Love through finding lady's ornament (ring, comb, etc.).* India: Thompson-Balys.

T11.4.7. *Falling in love at receipt of girl's amulet.* Jewish: Neuman.

T11.5. *Falling in love with reflection in water.* Princess thus first sees prince. Malone PMLA XLIII 400; India: Thompson-Balys; Japanese: Ikeda.

R351. Fugitive discovered by reflection in water.

T11.5.1. *Falling in love with one's own reflection in water.* (Narcissus.) Italian Novella: Rotunda; Ovid Metamorphoses Bk. 3.

T11.6. *Wish for wife red as blood, white as snow, black as raven.* Italian: Basile Pentamerone IV No. 9, V No. 9.

Z65.1. Red as blood, white as snow.

T11.7. *Love through sight in magic mirror.* (Cf. D1163.) Icelandic: *Boberg.

T11.8. *Falling in love with beautiful voice.* India: *Thompson-Balys; Buddhist myth: Malalasekera II 1185.

T12. *Love through prophecy that prince shall marry the fairest.* *Type 516; *Rösch FFC LXXII 100.

H1301.1. Quest for the most beautiful bride.

T13. *Woman falls in love as result of husband's praise of her suitor.* Italian Novella: *Rotunda.

K1544. Husband unwittingly instrumental in wife's adultery.

T15. *Love at first sight.* Irish myth: *Cross; Icelandic: *Boberg; Italian Novella: Rotunda; Jewish: *Neuman; India: *Thompson-Balys; Buddhist myth: Malalasekera I 614, II 355, 1369.

T15.1. *Princess so lovely that everyone falls in love with her.* India: Thompson-Balys.

T16. *Man falls in love with woman he sees bathing.* Jewish: *Neuman; India: *Thompson-Balys.

D361.1. Swan Maiden. K1335. Seduction (or wooing) by stealing clothes of bathing girl. N716. Lover sees beloved first while she is bathing.

T16.0.1. *Woman falls in love with man she sees bathing.* India: *Thompson-Balys.

T16.0.2. *Bathing woman sees hero and falls in love with him.* India: Thompson-Balys.

T16.1. *Man falls in love by the sight of woman's white arms.* Icelandic: MacCulloch Eddic 110f.

T16.2. *Man falls in love on seeing dead body of beautiful girl.* (Cf. T466.) India: Thompson-Balys.

T21. *Mutual love through accidental drinking of love philtre.* Schoepperle II 587a s.v. "potion"; English: Wells 80 (Sir Tristrem).

D1355. Love-producing magic object. D1425. Magic object draws lover (husband) to woman. D1426. Magic object draws woman to man. D1900. Love induced by magic.

T22. *Predestined lovers.* Future wife or husband assigned by destiny. (Cf. T54.) India: *Thompson-Balys.

D1825.1.2. Magic view of future lover.

T22.1. *Lovers mated before birth.* Fate compels their union as soon as they meet. Chinese: Chavannes 500 Contes I 377 No. 108.

T22.2. *Predestined wife.* (Cf. M312.1.) Basset 1001 Contes II 208 n. 1; Finnish-Swedish: Hackman FFC VI No. 930*; Lithuanian: Balys Index No. 934A*; Chinese: Eberhard FFC CXX 202 No. 149, FFC CXXVIII 179 No. 95; Japanese: Ikeda.

T22.3. *Predestined husband.* Icelandic: Hdwb. d. Märchens I 450a n. 534; Italian: Basile Pentamerone, Introduction; Japanese: Ikeda.

T22.4. *Lovers fated to marry each other born at same time;* identical prophecies for both. (Cf. T61.5.) Jewish: Neuman; India: Thompson-Balys.

T24. *The symptoms of love.* *Penzer VII 139 n. 2; *Rohde Der griechische Roman 157ff.; Irish myth: Cross; India: *Thompson-Balys.

T24.1. *Love-sickness.* *Penzer II 9 n. 2, 10 n., III 68 n. 1; Irish myth: *Cross; Icelandic: *Boberg; Breton: Sébillot Incidents s.v.

"amoureux"; Italian Novella: *Rotunda; Jewish: *Neuman; Japanese: Ikeda.

D1355.0.1. Spear produces love-sickness. D2064.0.1. Magic love-sickness. T82. Bath of blood of beloved to cure love-sick empress.

T24.1.1. *Night emissions from lusting after certain woman bring man near death.* India: Thompson-Balys.

T24.2. *Swooning for love.* *Type 516; *Rösch FFC LXXVII 98; India: *Thompson-Balys; Hindu: Penzer II 10 n.; Chinese: Graham.

T24.2.1. *Fainting away for love (or sexual desire).* (Cf. F1041.1.6.1.) India: Thompson-Balys.

T24.2.2. *Swooning for fright that lover shall be killed.* Icelandic: Boberg.

T24.2.3. *Fainting away from seeing an extraordinary beauty.* India: *Thompson-Balys.

T24.3. *Madness from love.* *Chauvin VI 51 No. 217 n. 2; Irish myth: *Cross; Icelandic: Göngu-Hrólfs saga 300; Italian Novella: *Rotunda; India: *Thompson-Balys.

T24.4. *Woman takes on lover's deformity (while conversing with him).* Irish myth: *Cross.

T24.5. *Boy turns red and white from love.* Icelandic: *Boberg.

T24.6. *Lover refuses food and drink.* India: *Thompson-Balys.

T24.7. *Waiting for twenty-two years to see a beauty.* India: *Thompson-Balys.

T24.8. *Man promises to sacrifice self in order to marry beloved.* India: Thompson-Balys.

T25. *Miraculous healing from a passionate love.* *Loomis White Magic 124; Irish myth: *Cross. (T24.3.1).

T26. *Attention distracted by sight of beloved.*

N8. Gambler's attention distracted by women.

T26.1. *Finger cut because of absorption in the charms of beloved.* The person cutting food cannot take his eyes off the man (woman) opposite him. *Köhler-Bolte I 579, II 79ff., 83ff.; Jewish: *Neuman.

H331.6.1.1. Princess wins wrestling match with suitor by revealing her breast. He looks and is beaten. K92.3. Girl distracts opponent's attention so that gambling lover wins. K774. Capture by sight of women's breasts. Women with uncovered breasts meet hero. He averts his face and is captured.

T27. *Unusual success in love.* *Loomis White Magic 82.

F112.1. Man on Island of Fair Women overcome by loving women.

T27.1. *Thirty young girls fall in love with a young man.* *Loomis White Magic 82.

T27.2. *Seventy princesses in love with hero.* He loves only the youngest one. India: Thompson-Balys.

T27.3. *Hundred rajas fall in love with one woman.* India: Thompson-Balys.

T28. *Princess falls in love with a man disguised as a woman.* India: Thompson-Balys.

K1321. Seduction by man disguising as woman.

T29. *Falling in love—miscellaneous.*

T29.1. *Boy and girl fall in love when curtain is pulled aside.* India: Thompson-Balys.

T30. Lovers' meeting. Italian Novella: Rotunda.

D1965. Guardian magically made to sleep while girl goes to lover. K1826.1.1. Lover disguised as monk or friar meets sweetheart. N455.4. King overhears girl's boast as to what she should do as queen. Marries her. N710. Accidental meeting of hero and heroine. N831. Girl as helper.

T31. *Lovers' meeting: hero in service of heroine.* As page, or the like. Dickson 143. Cf. Folie Tristan.

T31.1. *Lovers' meeting: hero in service of lady's father.* *Type 314; Malone PMLA XLIII 421; Boccaccio Decameron II No. 6; Missouri French: Carrière; Italian Novella: Rotunda.

T32. *Lovers' meeting: heroine heals hero's wounds.* (Cf. T67.2.) *Dickson 148 n. 158; Icelandic: *Boberg.

T32.1. *Lovers' meeting: hero in heroine's father's prison from which she helps him to escape.* Icelandic: *Boberg.

R162. Rescue by captor's daughter (wife, mother). T91.6.4.1. Sultan's daughter in love with captured knight.

T33. *Man transformed to animal kept as pet by heroine.* (Cf. D658.) Malone PMLA XLIII 401f.

T34. *Lovers meet at social gathering.*

T34.1. *Sudden love as woman pours drink for man at festival.* Icelandic: *Boberg.

T34.2. *Falling in love while playing game.*

T34.2.1. *Falling in love while playing draughts.* Danish: Grundtvig No. 238; Icelandic: Boberg.

T35. *Lovers' rendezvous.* (Cf. R315.1.) Irish myth: *Cross; Missouri French: Carrière.

T35.0.1. *Lover late at rendezvous; detained by incessant talker.* Chauvin V 155 No. 78 n. 1.

D1964.2. Magic sleep induced by disappointed suitor. D1972. Lover's magic sleep at rendezvous. A lover (husband) is to meet his mistress but magically oversleeps. N391. Lover who is detained away beyond stipulated time returns to find sweetheart married.

T35.0.2. *Magic sleep causes lover to miss appointment with mistress.* Irish myth: Cross.

T35.1. *Fountain (well) as lovers' rendezvous.* Malone PMLA XLIII 402; Nouvelles de Sens No. 3; Irish myth: Cross; Missouri French: Carrière; Jewish: Neuman.

T35.2. *Pavilion as lovers' rendezvous.* *Dickson 61 n. 4.

T35.3. *Girl intoxicates nurse to keep rendezvous with lover.* Italian Novella: Rotunda.

T35.4. *Hesitation in making up mind spoils lovers' rendezvous.* (Cf. J2166.) Cent Nouvelles Nouvelles No. 81; Italian Novella: *Rotunda.

T35.5. *Lover goes to see his beloved in her husband's (or her father's) house, defiant of the danger.* Icelandic: *Boberg.

T36. *Girl sleeps in garden to meet lover.* Discovered next morning and married. Boccaccio Decameron V No. 4; von der Hagen II *xi, 71 No. 25; Italian Novella: *Rotunda.

T37. *Lover finds lady in tomb apparently dead.* She revives and marries him. Boccaccio Decameron X No. 4 (Lee 313ff.); Italian Novella: *Rotunda.

K522.0.1. Death feigned to avoid unwelcome marriage. K1538. Death feigned to meet paramour. K1862. Death feigned to meet lover. N694. Apparently dead woman revives as she is being prepared for burial.

T37.0.1. *"Poisoned" woman revives.* Husband tries to poison wife. Student substitutes sleeping potion for poison, takes her from the tomb. When she revives he claims her as his own. Italian Novella: *Rotunda.

K512. Compassionate executioner. K1856. Sleeping potion substituted for poison.

T37.1. *Despairing lover at lady's tomb takes poison.* She revives to learn of his fatal error and shares his fate. (Romeo and Juliet.) Italian Novella: *Rotunda.

N343. Lover kills self believing his mistress dead.

T41. *Communication of lovers.*

K1549.5. Unfaithful wife communicates with lover by pouring milk into stream.

T41.1. *Communication of lovers through hole in wall.* Italian Novella: *Rotunda; Greek: Fox 201 (Pyramus and Thisbe); Japanese: Ikeda; N. A. Indian (Malecite): Mechling GSCan VI No. 21, (Fox): Jones PAES I 145 (the last two tell of sexual relations through hole in a tent).

K1561. The husband meets the paramour in the wife's place. Beats him (or cuts off privates).

T41.2. *Communication of lovers through hole in floor.* India: Thompson-Balys.

T41.3. *Lovers' signal.* Informs lover when he must come. Irish myth: Cross; India: Thompson-Balys.

T42. *Conversation of lovers.*

T42.1. *Unacquainted lovers converse in sign language.* Penzer VI 247f.

T42.2. *Lovers converse in figures of speech not understood by others.* Irish myth: *Cross.

T45. *Lover buys admission to woman's room.* *Type 900; BP I 446; *Philippson FFC L 26f.; *Fb "guldrok" I 514b, "guldhaspe" I 513b.

K1330. Girl tricked into man's room (or power). K1340. Entrance into girl's (man's) room (bed) by trick. K1361. Beggar buys right to sleep before the girl's door, at foot of bed, in the bed. K1361.2. Progressive purchase of favors: the anatomical progression. K1581.8. Lover's gift regained: refusal to leave bed. Woman fearing exposure, returns his money.

T46. *Suitor outwits watchman to meet lady.*

T46.1. *To reach beauty young man climbs eight fences watched by one hundred guards.* Tonga: Gifford 187.

T47. *Heroine hidden by stepmother when suitor comes.* *Roberts 222.

T50. Wooing. India: Thompson-Balys.

A753.1. Moon as wooer. A1550. Origin of customs of courtship and marriage. D642.3.1. Pursued sweetheart becomes tree. D1310.4.2. Magic plant bears fruit to indicate that heroine is ready to marry. D1314.1.3. Magic arrow shot to determine where to seek bride. H310. Suitor tests. H316. Apple thrown indicates princess's choice. H360. Bride test. H511.1. Three caskets. Princess offered to man who chooses correctly from three caskets. J642.1. Lion suitor allows his teeth to be pulled and his claws to be cut. He is then killed. K1300. Seduction. K1372. Woman engaged by trick. M217. Devil bargains to help man win woman. R13.1.4.2.1. Tigers abduct princess to be wife of their human ward. R225. Elopement. X760. Jokes on courtship.

T50.1. *Girl carefully guarded from suitors.* Hdwb. d. Märchens I 551a nn. 228—36; Irish myth: *Cross; Icelandic: *Boberg; Jewish: Neuman; India: *Thompson-Balys; West Indies: Flowers 577.

T381. Imprisoned virgin to prevent knowledge of men.

T50.1.1. *Girl carefully guarded by mother.* (Cf. K1349.4.) Irish myth: Cross; S. A. Indian (Chiriguano): Métraux RMLP XXXIII 151, 165.

T50.1.2. *Girl carefully guarded by father.* Irish myth: *Cross; Africa (Togo): Einstein 12f.

T50.1.3. *Girl carefully guarded from suitors by hag.* Irish myth: *Cross.

T50.1.4. *Cat and dog as guards of imprisoned beauty.* (Cf. B576.1.) India: Thompson-Balys.

T50.2. *King likes his daughter so much that he does not wish to marry her to anyone.* Icelandic: *Boberg.

T50.2.1. *King unwilling to marry his daughter to a man not her equal.* Icelandic: *Boberg.

T50.3. *Mythical being asks for girl in marriage.* (Cf. T111.) S. A. Indian (Chiriguano): Métraux RMLP XXXIII 158f.

T51. *Wooing by emissary.* *Schoepperle I 188 n. 3, 202; Icelandic: Hálf saga ok Hálfsrekka 69, *Boberg; Missouri French: Carrière; India: Thompson-Balys.

H1381.3.1.1. Quest for bride for king. T133.2. Royal bride conducted by embassy to husband's kingdom.

T51.1. *Wooing emissary wins lady's love for himself.* *Köhler-Bolte II 328ff.; Schoepperle passim; English: Wells 43 (Arthour and Merlin); Icelandic: *Boberg; Missouri French: Carrière; India: *Thompson-Balys; S. A. Indian (Chiriguano): Métraux RMLP XXXIII 159; Africa (Zulu): Callaway 210.

H492.2. Husband has friend woo his wife for him (as test). She is seduced. K1094. Treacherous counselor persuades king's son to woo his father's young bride. K1371.1. Lover steals bride from wedding with unwelcome suitor. K1952.5. Wooing emissary poses as king and suitor but is refused.

T51.1.1. *Wooing emissary admitted to woman's room.* Elopes with her. (Cf. K1349.1.5.) Icelandic: Boberg.

T51.2. *King wooes through his daughter and the princess's maiden.* Icelandic: Boberg.

T51.3. *Match arranged by means of pictures of both parties.* India: Thompson-Balys.

T51.3.1. *Messengers seek wife for hero to resemble image they carry with them.* Buddhist myth: Malalasekera II 354.

T52. *Bride purchased.* *Type 890 (Christiansen Norske Eventyr 113); *Fb "brud" IV 64a; Irish: MacCulloch Celtic 130, *Cross; Icelandic: *Boberg; Jewish: *Neuman; Greek: *Grote I 157, 163; India: *Thompson-Balys; Chinese: Graham; Philippine (Tinguian): Cole 57; Africa (Fang): Tessman 175f.

A1555.2. Origin of custom of purchasing wives. F343.8. Fairy leaves goats as purchase price for girl he has carried off. H317. Long term of service imposed on suitor. H318. Suitor preferred who will pay enormous sum for bride.

T52.1. *Prince buys twig (flower) (enchanted girl) from her mother.* (Cf. D212, D215.) Type 652; BP II 125; Italian: Basile Pentamerone I No. 2.

T52.2. *Purchase money instead of bride given to suitor to settle dispute.* Africa (Fjort): Dennett 74ff. No. 16.

T52.3. *Bride purchased for her weight in gold.* East Africa: Rochemonteix Quelques Contes Nubiens (Cairo, 1888) 48ff. No. 4.

T52.4. *Dowry given at marriage of daughter.* Icelandic: Boberg; Jewish: *Neuman; India: Thompson-Balys.

T52.4.1. *Amount of dowry fixed by custom in bride's family.* India: Thompson-Balys.

T52.5. *Attempt to purchase wife.* Chinese: Graham.

T52.6. *Rich girl gives poor suitor necklace with which to pay her bride-price.* India: Thompson-Balys.

T52.7. *Princess asked for in return for sparing palace.* (Cf. S222.) India: Thompson-Balys.

T52.8. *Absent man's wife demanded in law court in payment of debt by creditor.* India: Thompson-Balys.

T52.9. *Village given to bride-to-be as part of her dowry.* Buddhist myth: Malalasekera I 698.

T53. *Matchmakers.* India: Thompson-Balys.

T53.0.1. *Matchmakers arrange weddings.* India: *Thompson-Balys.

T53.1. *Incognito prophet as matchmaker.* Jewish: bin Gorion Born Judas[2] I 177f., 374.

K1811. Gods (saints) in disguise visit mortals. N810. Supernatural helpers.

T53.2. *Christ as matchmaker.* *Type 822. See references for T125.

T125. Lazy boy and industrious girl matched. Jesus (incognito) as matchmaker.

T53.3. *Saint as matchmaker.* Irish myth: *Cross.

T53.4. *God occupied with matchmaking.* Jewish: *Neuman.

T53.5. *Barber as matchmaker.* India: Thompson-Balys.

T54. *Choosing bride by horoscope.* (Cf. B152.2, M302.4, T22.) Chinese: Chavannes 500 Contes I 376 No. 108.

T55. *Girl as wooer.* Forthputting woman. *Cross MPh XII 612 n. 3; Hibbard 208 n. 18; Irish myth: *Cross; Icelandic: *Boberg; Italian Novella: Rotunda; Jewish: Neuman; India: Thompson-Balys.

C192. Tabu: refusing to elope with woman who desires it. C901.1.3.1. Tabu imposed by forthputting woman. C929.1. "Shame and disgrace" threatened for refusing love of forthputting woman. F302.3. Fairy woos mortal man. H316. Suitor test: apple thrown indicates princess's choice. H607.3. Princess declares her love through sign language.

K778.2. Amazonian woman disguised as leper seduces and binds enemies. K1386. Man won over by woman's obscene trick. K1393. Woman seduces boy by feigning illness. T146. Polyandry.

T55.1. *Princess declares her love for lowly hero.* *Type 314; *Dickson 144 n. 146; Missouri French: Carrière; Jewish: *Neuman; Africa (Ibo, Nigeria): Thomas 120.

L162. Lowly heroine marries prince (king). Q87.2. Reward for resisting princess's advances. T121. Unequal marriage.

T55.1.1. *Princess declares love for courtier.* Italian Novella: *Rotunda.

T55.2. *Servant-girl helps prince if he will make her chief wife.* Malone PMLA XLIII 400.

T55.3. *Lady in love with ruler enlists friend's aid.* Rendezvous arranged. Italian Novella: Rotunda.

T55.4. *Little girl will give prince marvelous objects if he promises to marry her later.* India: Thompson-Balys.

T55.4.1. *Gift made by bride to husband.* Irish myth: *Cross.

T55.5. *Princess feigns sickness to woo hero.* Only marriage to him will cure her. India: Thompson-Balys.

H1212. Quest assigned because of feigned illness. K1818. Disguise as sick man.

T55.6. *Person (man, woman) exhibits figure.* Irish myth: *Cross; Jewish: Neuman.

C312.1. Tabu: man looking at nude woman. F397. Fairy woman exhibits her figure to warriors. H1596. Beauty contest. K774.2. Sight of unclothed women calms rage of youthful hero. Q411.4.2. Woman who disrobes to attract attention of hostile fighter killed.

T55.6.1. *Maidens (women) request hero to exhibit figure.* Irish myth: *Cross.

T55.7. *Princess elects herself husband from the young men present.* (Cf. H311, H362, T131.0.1.) Type 530.

T55.8. *Princess declares love by presenting cup of drink at feast.* Krappe Revue Hispanique LXXXI (1933); Irish myth: Cross.

T55.9. *Harper as love messenger sent by girl.* Irish myth: *Cross.

T55.10. *Princess offers reward for securing prince as husband for her.* India: Thompson-Bays.

T55.11. *Princess transforms self to woo.* (Cf. D658.) India: Thompson-Balys.

T56. *Means of attracting sweetheart.*

D1426.1. Magic flute compels woman to come to man. K1335. Seduction (or wooing) by stealing clothes of bathing girl.

T56.1. *Bride attracted by music.* India: *Thompson-Balys.

T56.1.1. *Bride attracted by flute.* India: Thompson-Balys; Chinese: Eberhard FFC CXX 209 No. 157; Japanese: Ikeda; N. A. Indian: Kroeber JAFL XXI 224; West Indies: Flowers 577.

T56.2. *Image of God of Love sent to fetch bride.* (Cf. A475.) *Penzer I 77 n. 1.

T56.3. *Forgotten fiancée sends lover false diamond inscribed with Christ's last words:* "Oh Lord why hast Thou forsaken me?" Lover returns. (Cf. D2003.) Italian Novella: *Rotunda.

T56.4. *Beautiful woman enticed by wonderful flower.* India: Thompson-Balys.

T57. *Declaration of love.*

T57.1. *Lover declares himself by showing her own reflection to his beloved.* (Cf. T91.6.1.1.) Heptameron No. 24.

T58. *Wooing the strong and beautiful bride.* *Type 519; Icelandic: *Boberg.

G519.1.3. Ogress lured into bridal bed and killed. H345. Suitor test: overcoming princess in strength.

T61. *Betrothal.* Irish myth: Cross; Icelandic: Boberg; Jewish: *Neuman.

M146. Vow only to marry a certain woman. T69.2. Parents affiance children without their knowledge. T135. Wedding ceremony. Z151. Ring broken as token of broken engagement.

T61.1. *Betrothal by lovers' drinking each other's blood.* *Fb "blod" IV 46b.

C165. Tabu: marriage with person whose blood one has drunk. E714.1. Soul (life) in the blood. P312. Blood-brotherhood. Friends take oath of brotherhood by means of mixing their blood.

T61.2. *Parting lovers pledge not to marry for seven years.* Child V 488 s.v. "Marriage".

T61.3. *At betrothal maid makes shirt for her lover.* Child V 496 s.v. "Shirt"; Icelandic: *Boberg.

T61.4. *Betrothal ceremony.*

T61.4.1. *Liquor brewed for betrothal.* India: Thompson-Balys.

T61.4.2. *At betrothal ceremony both parties drink out of the loving-cup.* India: Thompson-Balys.

T61.4.3. *Engagement ritual: intermediary sprinkles girl with flour.* India: Thompson-Balys.

T61.4.4. *Token of betrothal sent to parents of a proposed bridegroom;* acceptance means agreement to proposed match. India: Thompson-Balys.

T61.4.5. *Betrothal by gold ring.* Icelandic: *Boberg.

T61.4.5.1. *Dying lover sends his sweetheart his ring.* (Cf. T81.) Icelandic: Boberg.

T61.5. *Children born on same night betrothed.* (Cf. B311, T22.4.) Irish myth: Cross.

T61.5.1. *Betrothal of hero to princess while both are still in cradle.* Scottish: Campbell-McKay No. 23; India: Thompson-Balys.

T61.5.2. *Children ten and twelve years old betroth themselves.* Icelandic: Boberg.

T61.5.3. *Unborn children promised in marriage to each other.* Jewish: Neuman; India: Thompson-Balys; Buddhist myth: Malalasekera II 1097; Madagascar: Renel I 168ff. No. 30.

T62. *Princess to marry first man who asks for her.* *Type 900; BP I 443ff.; *Philippson FFC L 21f.; *Chauvin V 234 No. 134 n. 1; India: *Thompson-Balys.

C664. Injunction: to marry first woman met. D1812.5.0.7. Divination from first person (thing) met. M138.1. Vow to marry off two daughters to first two men father looks on the following morning. N125.4. Districts named from first person met in each. N710. Accidental meeting of hero and heroine. Q499.7. Humiliating marriage as punishment. T456. Bed-partner to receive payment from first man she meets in the morning. It so happens: she marries the man and he makes her wealthy.

T62.1. *Man to marry first woman who gives him alms.* India: Thompson-Balys.

T62.2. *Minister's daughter to marry first bachelor who arrives.* Korean: Zong in-Sob 112 No. 58.

T63. *Princess's husband selected by elephant bowing to him.* (Cf. H171.1.) India: Thompson-Balys.

T64. *King seeks bride only because counsellors insist.* *Thien Motive 4; Chaucer's Clerk's Tale; Irish myth: *Cross; Icelandic: *Boberg.

H1381.3.1.1. Quest for bride for king.

T65. *Betrothal restrictions.*

T65.1. *Maiden will not give her troth to two brothers successively.* English: Child V 487 s.v. "Maid".

T65.1.1. *Girl formally betrothed can never marry another should anything happen to prevent her from marrying the first.* India: Thompson-Balys.

T65.2. *Mercenary soldier (exile) unsuitable as husband.* Irish myth: *Cross.

T66. *Help in wooing.* (Cf. B582.)

T66.1. *Grateful dead man helps hero win princess.* *Type 506; India: Thompson-Balys. See references for E341 (the grateful dead).

T66.2. *Grateful little boys help hero win girl.* Chinese: Graham.

T67. *Prince offered as prize.*

T67.1. *Marriage to prince as reward for disenchanting him.* (Cf. L162.) Italian: Basile Pentamerone Int.

T67.2. *Marriage to prince as reward for curing him.* Italian: Basile Pentamerone II Nos. 2, 5; India: Thompson-Balys.

Q94. Reward for cure. T32. Lovers' meeting: heroine heals hero's wounds.

T67.3. *Prince will marry girl who will rescue him from embarrassing position.* Italian: Basile Pentamerone V No. 1.

T67.3.1. *King marries girl who frees him from the clutches of magic doll.* (Cf. D1268.) Italian Novella: *Rotunda.

T68. *Princess offered as prize.* Irish myth: Cross; Icelandic: *Boberg;

Missouri French: Carrière; Spanish: Espinosa Jr. Nos. 130f.; Jewish: *Neuman; India: *Thompson-Balys.

B620.1. Daughter promised to animal suitor. H331. Suitor contests: bride offered as prize. H335. Tasks assigned suitors. Bride as prize for accomplishment. H346. Princess given to man who can heal her. H507.1. Princess offered to man who can defeat her in repartee. H508.2. Bride offered to man who can find answer to question. H511. Princess offered to correct guesser. H551. Princess offered to man who can out-riddle her. N2.6.2. Daughter as wager. Q53. Reward for rescue. Q91.1. Princess given in marriage to clever thief. Q112. Half of kingdom as reward. S221.1. Bankrupt father sells his daughters in marriage to animals.

T68.1. *Princess offered as prize to rescuer.* *Types 300, 301, 302, 303, 304, 506, 653; *Hartland Perseus III 1—65; *MacCulloch Childhood 17f.; Irish myth: Cross; Italian: Basile Pentamerone I No. 7; India: *Thompson-Balys; Chinese: Werner 420; Africa (Angola): Chatelain 89 No. 5.

B11.11. Dragon fight. H335. Tasks assigned suitors. Q53.3. Maiden queen offers her hand as reward for rescuing her town. R111.1. Princess rescued from captor.

T68.2. *Earl's daughter as reward to knight who helped to kill fierce buffalo.* Icelandic: Boberg.

T68.3. *Princess as prize to man who saves his country.* Chinese: Graham.

T68.4. *Vanquished king gives hero his daughter and control over his kingdom.* India: Thompson-Balys.

T68.5. *Girl marries hunter when he promises to return to monkey brothers their human form* (Cf. D118.) India: Thompson-Balys.

T69. *Wooing—miscellaneous motifs.*

T69.1. *100 brothers seek 100 sisters as wives.* (Seven—seven, fifty—fifty, etc.) Type 303*; Rumanian: Schullerus FFC LXXVIII No. 303*; Greek: Aeschylus Prometheus Bound 853.

T69.1.1. *Three brothers married to three sisters.* Icelandic: *Boberg.

T69.1.2. *Seven princesses sought by seven princes.* India: *Thompson-Balys.

T69.2. *Parents affiance children without their knowledge.* Type 516; Rösch FFC LXXVII 101; Jewish: *Neuman; India: Thompson-Balys.

T69.2.1. *Parents wooing one of seven daughters for their son.* Chinese: Graham.

T69.2.2. *Parents decide princess can marry no one who weighs more than she.* India: Thompson-Balys.

T69.3. *Man gives daughter in return for his release.* (Cf. S222.) Irish myth: Cross.

T69.3.1. *Raja betroths his daughter to visitor's son as a compensation for murder.* India: Thompson-Balys.

T69.4. *Bashful suitor directs his wooing to an oak.* Icelandic: Boberg.

H13.2. Recognition by overheard conversation with objects.

T69.5. *Father punishes daughter by giving her to poor man in marriage.* Chinese: Graham.

T70. The scorned lover. Chinese: Graham.

K401.3. Stolen goods left in suitor's room. Impoverished lover falsely accused in order to be rid of him. K1210. Humiliated or baffled lovers. S110.3. Princess builds tower of skulls of unsuccessful suitors.

T71. *Women scorned in love.* *Dickson 87ff. nn. 50, 55; Penzer II 109, 120ff., III 109f., IV 91, 104ff., V 259 n. 1; Irish myth: *Cross; Icelandic: *Boberg; Jewish: Neuman; India: Thompson-Balys.

C31. Tabu: offending supernatural wife. F302.3.3.1. Fairy avenges herself on inconstant lover (husband). F361. Fairy's revenge. K2111. Potiphar's wife. T331. Man unsuccessfully tempted by woman. W34.1. Man constrained to elope with leader's fiancée resists her blandishments.

T71.1. *Accidental death fate of woman scorned in love.* Irish myth: *Cross.

T71.2. *Woman avenges scorned love.* Icelandic: *Boberg; Babylonian: Gilgamesch-Epos VI 6ff.

T71.2.1. *Woman scorned in love complains of man's coldness.* Irish myth: *Cross.

T72. *Woman won and then scorned.* Irish myth: *Cross; Italian Novella: *Rotunda; India: Thompson-Balys.

K1353. Woman deceived into sacrificing honor. Q245. Punishment for refusal to marry after girl is pregnant. R111.6. Girl rescued and then abandoned.

T72.1. *Maid eloping with pretended lover is forced by him to strip.* Child V 487 s.v. "Maid".

K1645. Woman ordered to strip has lover turn his back: pushes him into water. Q411.1. Punishment: winning as wife and then killing.

T72.2. *Nobleman marries poor girl and then abandons her.* Italian Novella: Rotunda.

T72.2.1. *Prince marries scornful girl and punishes her.* India: *Thompson-Balys.

T72.3. *Woman sets out to kill man who has won and then scorned her.* Ruler brings about their reconciliation. Italian Novella: *Rotunda.

T72.4. *Woman entertains two lovers on alternate nights.* They expose the deception and scorn her in public. Cent Nouvelles Nouvelles No. 33; Italian Novella: *Rotunda.

T75. *Man scorned by his beloved.* Icelandic: *Boberg; Italian Novella: Rotunda; India: *Thompson-Balys; Africa (Ekoi): Talbot 357.

T311. Woman averse to marriage.

T75.0.1. *Suitors ill-treated.* Icelandic: *Boberg.

T75.0.2. *Mortal woman rejects deity for human lover.* India: Thompson-Balys.

T75.1. *Scorn of unloved suitor punished.* Types 402*, 906*; Icelandic: Boberg.

T75.2. *Scorned lover kills successful one.* Italian Novella: *Rotunda.

T75.2.1. *Rejected suitors' revenge.* Icelandic: *Boberg.

R18. Abduction by rejected suitor. T104.1. Rejected suitor wages war.

T75.3. *Unrequited love expressed in song (poem).* English romance: Malory X 86; Spanish: Childers.

T75.4. *Lady humiliates lover after he leaves wife for her.* Chinese: Graham.

T75.5. *Scorned lover becomes an anchorite.* (Cf. T330.)

T75.6. *Divine hand catches scorned lover as he plunges from minaret top to die.* India: Thompson-Balys.

T76. *Princess calls her suitors ugly names.* *Type 900; *BP I 443ff.; *Philippson FFC L 14; Italian: Basile Pentamerone IV No. 10.

T77. *Maid vexes suitor by pretense.* Noble maid who is to marry knight pretends to be beggar's daughter. Child V 487 s.v. "Maid".

T80. Tragic love. Italian Novella: Rotunda; Jewish: Neuman; India: Thompson-Balys.

A968.2. Cliff from lovers' leap. E419.6. Lovers buried apart found in one grave each morning. F1841.1.1.4. Hearts break when lovers are told beloved is dead. K1087.1. Message falsified to bring about death of lovers. N339.4. Groom killed by bolt of lightning on wedding night. N343. Lover kills self believing his mistress dead. N345. The falcon of Sir Federigo. P214. Wife drinks blood of slain husband.

T81. *Death from love.* *Penzer II 8, 9 n. 2, 10, V 39, VII 69 n. 1, 103, 258, VIII 98; Irish myth: *Cross; Jewish: *Neuman; India: *Thompson-Balys; Chinese: Eberhard FFC CXX 69, 209 No. 157.

A773.3. Pleiades girls who died of grief. F1041.1.1. Death from broken heart. T24.1. Love sickness. T211. Faithfulness in marriage to death.

T81.1. *Man dies at bedside of dying sweetheart.* Italian Novella: Rotunda.

T81.2. *Death from unrequited love.* Virgil Aeneid IV 505ff. (Dido); Italian Novella: *Rotunda.

T81.2.1. *Scorned lover kills self.* India: *Thompson-Balys.

T81.2.1.1. *Scorned lover (woman) threatens to kill self.* India: *Thompson-Balys.

T81.3. *Girl falls dead on lover's body.* Italian Novella: *Rotunda.

T81.4. *Man dies when the bride who had been denied him kisses him.* Italian Novella: Rotunda.

T81.5. *Sick lover dies from exertion of embracing beloved.* Heptameron No. 50.

F1041.1.5. Death from excessive joy. J2572. Heart may not be able to stand winning mistress.

T81.6. *Girl kills herself after lover's death.* Herrmann Saxo II 94; Icelandic: *Boberg; India: *Thompson-Balys.

T81.7. *Woman dies on hearing of lover's or husband's death.* (Cf. T211.9.1.) Icelandic: *Boberg.

T81.8. *Wife swallows hot coal and dies because her husband is unfaithful.* Spanish Exempla: Keller.

T82. *Bath of blood of beloved to cure love-sick empress.* Herbert III 212; Oesterley No. 281; Wesselski Mönchslatein 60 No. 50.

D1500.1.7.3. Magic healing blood. Q478.1. The Eaten Heart. Adulteress is caused unwittingly to eat her lover's heart. T24.1. Love-sickness.

T83. *Hero and Leander.* Lover drowned as he swims to see his mistress. *Von der Hagen I cxxviii; *Fb "svömme" III 695b; Italian Novella: Rotunda; Greek: Fox 202.

T83.1. *Girl drowns as she swims to see her lover.* Her brothers deceive her with false signal light. Italian Novella: *Rotunda.

T84. *Lovers treacherously separated.* Irish myth: Cross.

T85. *Woman mourns dead lover.*

T85.1. *Woman thinking lover dead erects cenotaph and mourns before it.* Chauvin V 153 No. 75 n. 1.

T85.2. *Princess hangs up weapons of dead lover as continual reminder.* *Wesselski Mönchslatein 80 No. 69.

T85.3. *The Pot of Basil.* Mistress keeps murdered lover's skull in flower-pot. *Belden PMLA XXXIII 327ff.; Boccaccio Decameron IV No. 5 (Lee 136); Italian Novella: Rotunda.

T85.4. *Lover's body kept embalmed for years by grieving mistress.* (Cf. T211.4.) *Hibbard 266.

T85.4.1. *Ring of Fastrada.* (Tove's magic ring.) Lover keeps body of dead mistress (wife) intact by means of magic ring. When ring is removed from her finger, the body immediately decays and he is cured of his love. **A. Pauls Der Ring der Fastrada (Aachen, 1896); **K. Nyrop Fortids Sagn og Sange 1: Tove's Tryllering (København, 1907); *Chauvin II 202 No. 48; *Moth Danske Studier (1915) 97ff.; *BP I 463f.; *G. Paris Journal des Savants Nov. 1896; Euphorion VI 186.

D1076. Magic ring. D1585. Magic object saves corpse from corruption. T211.4.1. Wife's corpse kept after death. T334. Monk cures himself of desire for dead sweetheart. He digs up her remains.

T86. *Lovers buried in same grave.* *Chauvin V 107 No. 37; Heptameron Nos. 50, 70; Boccaccio Decameron IV No. 8 (Lee 140); Irish myth: Cross; Icelandic: *Boberg; Italian Novella: *Rotunda; India: *Thompson-Balys.

E631.0.1. Twining branches grow from graves of lovers.

T86.1. *Rival suitors kill each other over woman's love.* Woman dies of broken heart and all three are buried in the same grave. Italian Novella: Rotunda.

T86.2. *Lovers die at the same time.* Icelandic: FSS 267, Boberg.

T86.3. *Mistress springs into dead lover's grave.* Irish myth: *Cross.

T86.4. *Girl and boy promised to each other by parents both die when they see each other after girl's marriage to another.* India: Thompson-Balys.

T87. *Lovers forbidden to marry starve themselves to death.* Italian Novella: Rotunda.

T88. *Woman stricken by plague and forsaken by her husband is sought out by unsuccessful lover and dies in his arms.* Italian Novella: Rotunda.

T88.1. *Love kept up even after one of the parties is married to another.* Icelandic: Boberg.

T89. *Tragic love—miscellaneous motifs.*

T89.1. *Woman falls in love with dying warrior.* Irish myth: Cross.

T89.1.1. *Princess married to mortally wounded prince and both left in jungle.* India: Thompson-Balys.

T89.2. *Woman sacrifices herself in order to save beloved.* India: Thompson-Balys.

T90. Love—miscellaneous motifs.

T91. *Unequals in love.* Irish myth: Cross; India: Thompson-Balys.

B610. Animal paramour. B620. Animal suitor. J414. Marriage with equal or with unequal. T110. Unusual marriage. T121. Unequal marriage.

T91.1. *Giant's daughter loves hero.* See references to G530.2. Icelandic: De la Saussaye 337, *Boberg; Irish myth: *Cross; India: *Thompson-Balys.

G530.2. Help from ogre's daughter. N812.4. Giantess helps the man she loves.

T91.1.1. *Giant's daughter has child by hero.* Icelandic: *Boberg.

T91.2. *Love of mortal and devil.*

T91.2.1. *Devil would be maid's paramour.* (Cf. G303.9.4.7.) Child V 283; Lithuanian: Balys Index No. 368*f., 3265.

T91.3. *Love of mortal and supernatural person.* India: *Thompson-Balys; S. A. Indian (Cashinawa): Métraux BBAE CXLIII (3) 684, (Toba): Métraux MAFLS XL 23.

T91.3.1. *Supernatural lover performs girl's work.* Jamaica: Beckwith MAFLS XVII 267 No. 78.

T91.3.2. *Love of goddess for mortal.* (Cf. T111.1.) Penzer V 33; Greek: Fox 245.

T91.3.3. *God enamored of mortal.* (Cf. A188.) Greek: Grote I 85f., 139, 164; India: *Thompson-Balys.

T91.3.3.1. *God falls in love with a woman of low caste.* India: Thompson-Balys.

T91.4. *Age and youth in love.*

J21.3. "Do not go where an old man has a young wife": counsel proved wise by experience. J445.2. Foolish marriage of old man and young girl.

T91.4.1. *Mature married woman in love with callow youth.* Malone PMLA XLIII 418.

J445.1. Foolish youth in love with ugly old mistress.

T91.4.1.1. *Old teacher wishes to marry his young girl pupil.* India: Thompson-Balys; Buddhist myth: Malalasekera II 860.

T91.5. *Rich and poor in love.*

T91.5.1. *Rich girl in love with poor boy.* Spanish: Boggs FFC XC 54 No. 405A*; India: *Thompson-Balys; Chinese: Eberhard FFC CXX 247 No. 192.

M312.1. Prophecy: wealthy marriage for poor boy.

T91.5.1.1. *Daughter of merchant develops intimacy with slave.* Buddhist myth: Malalasekera I 897.

T91.6. *Noble and lowly in love.*

T91.6.1. *Lowly person falls in love with king (queen).* Italian Novella: Rotunda.

T91.6.1.1. *Courtier in love with queen.* Queen asks him whom he loves. He holds up a mirror to her as answer. (Cf. T57.1.) Italian Novella: *Rotunda.

T91.6.2. *King (prince) in love with a lowly girl.* (Cf. L162, T121.8.) Icelandic: *Boberg; Jewish: *Neuman; India: *Thompson-Balys; Buddhist myth: Malalasekera II 1185.

T91.6.2.0.1. *King covets subject's wife.* India: *Thompson-Balys.

T91.6.3. *Prince falls in love with minister's daughter.* India: Thompson-Balys.

T91.6.3.1. *Prince falls in love with merchant's daughter exposed in jungle.* India: Thompson-Balys.

T91.6.4. *Princess falls in love with lowly boy.* (Cf. L161.) *Type 314; *Boje 74ff.; Penzer V 250, VIII 115ff.; Krappe "The Legends of Amicus and Amelius and of King Horn" Leuvensche Bijdragen XVI (1924) 14—17; Breton: Sébillot Incidents s.v. "jardinier"; Italian Novella: Rotunda; India: *Thompson-Balys; N. A. Indian: Thompson CColl II 348ff.

T91.6.4.1. *Sultan's daughter in love with captured knight.* Dickson 133 n. 109; English: Wells 85 (The Sowdone of Babylone).

K781. Castle captured with assistance of owner's daughter. She loves the attacker. R162. Rescue by captor's daughter (wife, mother). T32.1. Lovers' meeting: hero in heroine's father's prison from which she helps him to escape.

T91.6.4.1.1. *Princess falls in love with knight.* Marries him after her husband's death. Italian Novella: Rotunda.

T91.6.4.1.2. *Hostile amazon's daughter loves hero.* Irish myth: *Cross.

T91.6.4.2. *Princess falls in love with a king who becomes a slave.* India: Thompson-Balys.

T91.6.4.3. *Princess runs away with hunchback.* Buddhist myth: Malalasekera II 910.

T91.7. *Unequals in love—miscellaneous.*

T91.7.1. *Brahmin in love with washerwoman.* India: Thompson-Balys.

T91.7.2. *Falling in love with someone of a different caste.* India: Thompson-Balys.

T92. *Rivals in love.* Irish myth: *Cross; Missouri French: Carrière; India: Thompson-Balys.

A773.1. Pleiades a princess and six suitors from whom she could not choose. J414.1. Wife chosen instead of fairy mistress. They let man choose between them. J414.2. Prince prefers first love to princess he later marries. J496. Choice of friend over mistress. P319.6. Successful rival gives his lady to unsuccessful friend. T86.1. Rival suitors kill each other over woman's love. T75.2.2. Refused suitor attacks successful one but is killed.

T92.0.1. *Girl promised to three different suitors;* because she is unable to settle the dispute she eats poison and dies. India: Thompson-Balys.

T92.1. *The triangle plot and its solutions.* Two men in love with the same woman; two women with the same man. *Dickson 243 n. 48; Irish myth: *Cross; India: Thompson-Balys.

T92.1.1. *Young wife of old man (king) loves (is loved by) younger man.* Irish myth: *Cross.

T92.1.2. *Would-be unfaithful wife.* Irish myth: *Cross.

T92.2. *Three victims of love.* Girl loves boy; boy loves singing girl; singing girl loves the girl. All die of despair. *Chauvin V 110 No. 44.

T92.3. *Girl leaves rescuer for younger lover.* Dickson 119 nn. 55, 56.

T92.3.1. *Girl leaves rescuer and elopes with his friend.* India: Thompson-Balys.

T92.4. *Girl mistakenly elopes with the wrong lover.* The preferred suitor overtakes them, finds them asleep and waits for them to awaken. He himself falls asleep and when he wakes they have gone. Italian: L. de Francia Novellino (Torino, 1930) Gaulteruzzi MS No. 99, Rotunda.

D1972. Lover's magic sleep at rendezvous. R225. Elopement.

T92.4.1. *Hero falls asleep while sweetheart is being married to another.* India: Thompson-Balys.

T92.4.2. *Letter falsified and elopement with false lover arranged.* India: Thompson-Balys.

T92.4.3. *In darkness of night trickster instead of her chosen lover elopes with girl.* Tonga: Beckwith Myth 536.

T92.5. *Lover kills his rival brother.* Irish myth: Cross; India: *Thompson-Balys.

T92.6. *Mother and daughter as rivals in love.* Irish myth: *Cross.

T92.7. *Rival lovers do battle for girl.* (Cf. T86.1.) Irish myth: Cross.

T92.8. *Sisters in love with same man.* Irish myth: Cross; Icelandic: Boberg; India: Thompson-Balys.

P252.7. Eighteen sisters kill one another.

T92.9. *Father and son as rivals in love.* India: *Thompson-Balys.

T92.9.1. *Parricide because of father-son rivalry for girl's love.* India: Thompson-Balys.

T92.10. *Rival in love killed.* Icelandic: *Boberg; India: Thompson-Balys.

H335.4.3. Suitor task: to kill all earlier suitors. M149.3. Vow to kill more successful rival. R18. Abduction by rejected suitor. T75.2.1. Rejected suitors' revenge.

T92.11. *Rivals contesting for the same girl.* Cheremis: Sebeok-Nyerges; India: Thompson-Balys.

T92.11.1. *Rival suitors discomfit each other.* Lithuanian: Balys Index No. 1692*, 1693.

T92.12. *Two smiths as rivals for love of girl.* Irish myth: Cross.

T92.12.1. *The tailor and the smith as rivals.* The tailor declares that the smith is blind and the smith declares that the tailor is a fool. At the wedding in church, the smith drops a hot piece of iron into the tailor's boot. Lithuanian: Balys Index No. 1693A*; Estonian: Aarne FFC XXV No. 1631*.

T92.13. *Older warrior preferred as suitor.* Icelandic: *Boberg.

T92.14. *Three lovers mourn for dead girl:* one throws himself into her funeral pyre; another gathers together the ashes and vows to spend his life sitting upon them; third resolves to turn fakir. India: Thompson-Balys.

T211.2.1. Wife throws herself on husband's funeral pyre.

T93. *Fate of disappointed lover.*

P319.6. Successful rival gives his mistress to unsuccessful friend.

T93.1. *Disappointed lover becomes a wild man in the woods.* (Cf. F567.) *Dickson 116 n. 44; Irish myth: *Cross; Italian Novella: *Rotunda.

T93.2. *Disappointed lover turns hermit.* (Cf. V472.) Heptameron No. 64, 19; Italian Novella: Rotunda.

T93.2.1. *Lover becomes friar and sweetheart nun when unable to marry.* Heptameron No. 19.

T93.3. *Disappointed lover kills self.* Italian Novella: Rotunda.

T93.4. *Disappointed lover buys poison for girl.* Druggist substitutes sleeping potion. Girl revives and is reconciled. Italian Novella: Rotunda.

T93.5. *Tragic love between a Pari and a mortal man;* they never meet again, but continually roam the earth seeking each other. India: Thompson-Balys.

T95. *Lover opposed to sweetheart's relatives.* Irish myth: *Cross; Italian Novella: *Rotunda.

T95.0.1. *Princess falls in love with father's enemy.* India: Thompson-Balys.

T95.1. *Lover kills his lady's relatives in fight.* Irish myth: *Cross; English: Child V 496 s.v. "Slaughter"; Italian Novella: *Rotunda; India: Thompson-Balys.

T96. *Lovers reunited after many adventures.* Boccaccio Decameron Book V (Lee 157ff.); Irish myth: Cross; Icelandic: Boberg; Missouri French: Carrière; Italian Novella: *Rotunda; India: *Thompson-Balys.

N730. Accidental reunion of families. T102. Hero returns and marries first love. T298. Reconciliation of separated couple.

T97. *Father opposed to daughter's marriage.* Irish myth: *Cross.

E765.4.3. Father will die when daughter bears son. H913.2.1. Task assigned at suggestion of jealous father (of prospective bride). M311.1. Prophecy: king's grandson will dethrone him. M343.2. Prophecy: murder by grandson. P234. Father and daughter. S11.4.1. Jealous father vows to kill daughter's suitors. T131.1.2. Father's consent to daughter's marriage necessary.

T99. *Love—additional motifs.* Irish myth: Cross.

T99.1. *Death from excess of women.* (Cf. F112.1.) Irish myth: *Cross.

T99.2. *Girl wants to marry lover even if he is mutilated.* Icelandic: Áns saga Bogsveigis 350, Boberg.

T100—T199. Marriage.

T100. Marriage. *E. Westermarck The History of Human Marriage (2 vols. London, 1925); Hdwb. d. Abergl. I 1522; Irish myth: Cross; Jewish: *Neuman.

A1555. Origin of marriage. C160. Tabu connected with marriage. H300. Tests connected with marriage. J482. King advised to marry maid rather than widow. J482.1. Woman refuses second marriage. J482.2. Better to marry ugly than fair wife. K522.0.1. Death feigned to escape unwelcome marriage. K523.0.1. Illness (madness, dumbness, etc.) feigned to escape unwelcome marriage. K1210. Humiliated or baffled lovers. K1218. Importunate lovers led astray. K1223.1. Bride escapes from foolish husband and leaves goat as substitute in bed. K1300. Seduction or deceptive marriage. P210. Husband and wife. R225. Elopement. R355. Eloping girl recaptured by parents. T415.5. Brother-sister marriage.

T102. *Hero returns and marries first love.* Types 611, 884, 885**, 886; Icelandic: Boberg.

J414.2. Prince prefers first love to princess he later marries. J491. Old sweetheart chosen in preference to new. T96. Lovers reunited after many adventures. T298. Reconciliation of separated couple.

T104. *Foreign king wages war to enforce demand for princess in marriage.* *Boje 74ff., 78; Icelandic: *Boberg.

T104.1. *Rejected suitor wages war.* (Cf. T75.2.1.) Icelandic: *Boberg.

T104.2. *Victor demands defeated king's daughter (widow) in marriage.* Icelandic: *Boberg.

T110. Unusual marriage. India: Thompson-Balys.

A762.1. Star husband. Star takes mortal maiden as wife. B82.1. Merman marries maiden. B81.2. Mermaid marries man. B600. Marriage of person to animal. D732. Loathly Lady. Man disenchants loathsome woman by embracing her. D733. Loathly Bridegroom. Woman disenchants loathsome man by embracing him. E474 Cohabitation of living person and ghost. G81. Unwitting marriage to cannibal. J21.3. "Do not go where an old man has a young wife." J21.4. "Do not marry a girl from abroad." J414.1. Wife chosen instead of fairy mistress. J445.1. Foolish youth in love with ugly old mistress. P512. Condemned woman may be freed by marrying a rogue. T91. Unequals in love.

T111. *Marriage of mortal and supernatural being.* *Type 425; *Tegethoff 16; Krappe MLR XXIV (1929) 200ff.; India: *Thompson-Balys; Chinese: Graham.

A188. Gods and goddesses in love with men. B640.1. Marriage to beast by day and man by night. C31. Tabu: offending supernatural wife. C32. Tabu: offending supernatural husband. F300. Marriage with fairy F402.2.3. Child of demon king marries mortal. F420.6.1. Marriage of mortals and water-spirits. F441.2.3.1.1. Man marries spirit of willow tree. F460.4.1. Mountain-girl marries mortal man.

T111.0.1. *Marriage to supernatural wives who disappear.* *Holmström Svanjungfrumotivet 11ff.; Lithuanian: Balys Index Nos. 404*, 423*; India: Thompson-Balys; Mono-Alu: Wheeler Nos. 17, 35.

T111.0.2. *Supernatural wife summoned by bell.* Italian: Basile Pentamerone I No. 2.

T111.1. *Marriage of a mortal and a god.* Irish: MacCulloch Celtic 13, *Cross; Greek: cf. the various love affairs of Zeus with mortal maidens; India: *Thompson-Balys; Hindu: Tawney I 256, 302, 335, 351, 560f.; Maori: Dixon 57.

A188. Gods and goddesses in love with men. B641.3. Marriage to god in bull form. Q255. Punishment of woman who prefers mortal lover to gods. T91.3.2. Love of goddess for mortal.

T111.1.1. *Maiden chooses disguised god as husband.* Buddhist myth: Malalasekera I 648.

T111.1.2. *Man marries the daughter of a god.* Korean: Zong in-Sob 137 No. 63; S. A. Indian (Chiriguano): Métraux RMLP XXXIII 161f.

T111.2. *Woman from sky-world marries mortal man.* India: *Thompson-Balys; Japanese: Ikeda; Philippine (Tinguian): Cole 110; Africa (Fjort): Dennett 60 No. 12, (Congo): Weeks 206 No. 3, (Angola): Chatelain 131 No. 13.

A762.1. Mortal marries star-girl. C15.1. Wish for star-husband realized. F420.6.1. Marriage (or liaison of mortals and water-spirits.

T111.2.1. *Hero marries star in form of girl.* Chinese: Graham.

T111.2.1.1. *Star-wife gives birth to a human baby.* Chinese: Graham.

T111.2.2. *Marriage of mortal and moon.* (Cf. A753.1.) Eskimo (Kodiak): Golder JAFL XVI 29, (West Hudson Bay): Boas BAM XV 307, (Cumberland Sound): ibid. 198, (Greenland): Holm 47, Rasmussen III 307; S. A. Indian (Viracocha): Steward-Métraux BBAE CXLIII (3) 550.

T111.2.3. *Sun has a woman for his wife.* S. A. Indian (Warrau): Métraux RMLP XXXIII 145.

T111.3. *Marriage of man with woman who has come from an egg.* India: *Thompson-Balys.

C963. Person returns to original form when tabu is broken. E155.3. Nightly resuscitation of man with external soul. E474. Cohabitation of living person with ghost. T542. Birth of human being from an egg.

T111.4. *God as lover of giantess (18 giantesses).* Icelandic: *Boberg.

T111.5. *Marriage of mortal and dwarf.* Eskimo (Greenland): Rink 183, 209, (Labrador): Hawkes GSCan XIV 151, (Cumberland Sound): Boas BAM XV 170—3; Koryak: Jochelson JE VI 154, 201, 227.

F451.5.18. Dwarf loves mortal girl.

T111.6. *Marriage of mortal and angel.* Jewish: *Neuman.

T113. *Marriage to man alive by night but dead by day.* India: *Thompson-Balys.

B640.1. Marriage to beast by day and man by night. E155.3. Nightly resuscitation of man with external soul. E474. Cohabitation of living person and ghost.

T113.1. *Sorceress marries a man every morning and transforms him to some kind of animal in the evening.* (Cf. D621.) India: Thompson-Balys.

T115. *Man marries ogre's daughter.* India: Thompson-Balys.

G530.2. Ogre's daughter as helper.

T117. *Marriage of person and object.* India: Thompson-Balys.

T461. Person enamored of an object.

T117.1. *Marriage of girl to a dagger.* Penzer I 242, 244.

T117.2. *Marriage of girl to a sword.* Penzer I 257; India: Thompson-Balys.

T135.3.1. Sword and shield as proxy at wedding ceremony.

T117.3. *Marriage of girl to a drum.* Penzer I 257.

T117.4. *Marriage of girl to an idol.* Penzer I 244.

T117.5. *Marriage with a tree.* Frazer Golden Bough I 195f.; India: Thompson-Balys; N. A. Indian: Thompson Tales 304 n. 109o.

T117.5.1. *Marriage to tree by day, man by night.* (Cf. D621.2, T113.) India: Thompson-Balys.

T117.6. *Marriage to a flower.* India: Thompson-Balys.

T117.7. *Marriage to a gourd.* India: Thompson-Balys.

T117.8. *Marriage to doll.* India: *Thompson-Balys.

T117.9. *Marriage to river.* Mono: Wheeler No. 34.

T117.10. *Plant wife (in form of a woman).* Mono-Alu: Wheeler Nos. 17, 35.

T117.11. *Marriage to a statue.* Saintyves Saints Successeurs 255—57.

T118. *Girl (man) married to (enamored of) a monster.* *Types 306, 506; *Liljeblad passim; *BP III 83; *Kittredge Harvard Studies and Notes in Philology VIII 250; Irish myth: *Cross; India: *Thompson-Balys; Japanese: Ikeda.

G81. Unwitting marriage to cannibal. F531.5.7. Giants marry human beings. S228. Daughter promised to monster as bride to secure flower (bird) she has asked for. S262.1. Woman given to devastating monster as wife to appease it. T232. Woman deserts husband for unworthy lover.

T118.1. *Monster husband invisible.* Africa (Basuto): Jacottet 152ff. No. 22.

D1980. Magic invisibility. E482. Land of shades. F412. Visibility of spirits.

T118.2. *Marriage of dragon girl to orphan boy.* Chinese: Graham.

T121. *Unequal marriage.* Child V 500 s.v. "Unequal"; Irish myth: Cross; India: Thompson-Balys.

J414. Marriage with equal or with unequal. J445.2. Foolish marriage of old man and young girl. K1816.10.1. Noble man disguises as cobbler to woo wood-cutter's daughter. L161. Lowly hero marries princess. L161.1. Marriage of poor boy and rich girl. L162. Lowly heroine marries prince (king). M312.1. Prophecy: wealthy marriage for poor boy. M312.1.1. Prophecy: wealtny marriage for poor girl. N227. Man who is impoverished is given high post by princess in disguise. Marries her. P41. Princess cannot be married to someone of low caste, though he passes suitor test. T31.1. Lovers' meeting: hero in service of lady's father. T55.1. Princess declares her love for lowly hero. T72.2. Nobleman marries poor girl and then abandons her. T91. Unequals in love.

T121.1. *Knight weds peasant girl.* English: Wells 60 (Syre Gowene and the Carle of Carelyle).

T121.2. *Noblewoman weds shepherd.* Cent Nouvelles Nouvelles No. 57; Italian Novella: Rotunda.

T121.3. *Princess marries courtier.* Italian Novella: *Rotunda; India: *Thompson-Balys.

T121.3.1. *Princess marries lowly man* (Cf. L161.1.) Jewish: Neuman; India: *Thompson-Balys.

T121.4. *Ruler marries fugitive noblewoman.* Italian Novella: Rotunda.

T121.5. *Wealthy girl marries deformed and penniless philosopher.* Italian Novella: Rotunda.

T121.5.1. *Princess marries saint.* India: Thompson-Balys.

T121.5.2. *Rich girl marries fakir.* India: Thompson-Balys.

T121.6. *Man weds his bondmaid.* Irish myth: Cross; Jewish: Neuman.

T121.7. *Rich girl marries servant.* Chinese: Eberhard FFC CXX 249.

T121.8. *King (rich man) weds common girl.* (Cf. L162, T91.6.2.) Icelandic: *Boberg; India: *Thompson-Balys; Buddhist myth: Malalasekera I 938, II 1091.

T121.8.1. *Infertile raja marries beggar woman in hope of having a son.* India: Thompson-Balys.

T122. *Marriage by royal order.* Widow hesitates to marry. Queen sends her a letter ordering her to marry the bearer (a suitor). Italian Novella: Rotunda; India: Thompson-Balys.

T125. *Lazy boy and industrious girl matched.* Jesus (incognito) as matchmaker. *Type 822.

T125.1. *Fool given intelligent wife; lame man hardworking wife.* India: Thompson-Balys.

T125.2. *Blind girl marries lame man.* (Cf. H886.) India: Thompson-Balys.

T126. *Fantastic marriage.*

T126.1. *Marriage of Mother Earth and ogre.* India: Thompson-Balys.

T126.2. *Marriage of mountain and cockle-shell.* India: Thompson-Balys.

T126.3. *Marriage of earth and sky.* India: Thompson-Balys.

T130. Marriage customs. Jewish: *Neuman.

A1550. Origin of customs of courtship and marriage. D1812.5.1.8. Bad omen for two bridal processions to meet.

T131. *Marriage restrictions.*

A1556. Origin of sexual restrictions. C160. Tabu connected with marriage. C567.1. Tabu: eloping with king's daughter. H360. Bride test. M130. Vows concerning sex. Q240. Sexual sins punished. T65. Betrothal restrictions.

T131.0.1. *Princess has unrestricted choice of husband.* (Cf. T55.7.) India: *Thompson-Balys.

T131.0.1.1. *Father promises that girl may wed only man of her choice.* Irish myth: Cross; Icelandic: *Boberg.

T131.1. *Relative's consent to marriage necessary.*

T131.1.1. *Brother's consent for sister's marriage needed.* Child I 142ff.; Heptameron No. 40; Icelandic: *Boberg; Japanese: Ikeda.

Z31.1. Pif Paf Poltrie. The suitor sent from one relation to the other for consent to the wedding.

T131.1.2. *Father's consent to son's (daughter's) marriage necessary.* Irish myth: Cross; Icelandic: Boberg.

T131.1.2.1. *Girl must marry father's choice.* Irish myth: Cross (T131.8.1); Icelandic: *Boberg.

T131.1.2.2. *King chooses bridegroom for daughter from boys' pictures.* India: Thompson-Balys.

T131.1.2.3. *Father demands that son break all relations with his beloved.* India: *Thompson-Balys.

T131.1.2.4. *Son refuses to marry father's choice.* India: Thompson-Balys.

T131.1.3. *Marriage against will of parents.* India: *Thompson-Balys.

T131.2. *Younger child may not marry before elder.* Hdwb. d. Abergl. II 566; Irish myth: *Cross; Icelandic: Rittershaus No. 2; Indonesia: Pleyte Bataksche Vertellingen 184f., Wilken Bijdragen tot de Taal-, Land-, en Volkenkunde van Nederlandsch-Indië I 142; Africa (Zulu): Callaway 323.

C169.2. Tabu: giving younger daughter in marriage before elder.

T131.3. *Eldest daughter will marry man only if he will marry all her sisters too.* Africa (Angola): Chatelain 119 No. 10.

T145.1. Marriage to five women, each with separate duties.

T131.4. *Widow may not remarry.* *Frazer Pausanias III 198.

J482.1. Woman refuses second marriage. If husband is good she will fear to lose him; if bad she will repent. T291. Why widows do not remarry. (1) Only her property is wanted; (2) her husband is still in her heart; (3) if new husband is bad it will not be well, if he is good there will be the fear that he will die.

T131.5. *Exogamy. Marriage only outside the group.* India: *Thompson-Balys.

T131.5.1. *Marriage within clans sanctioned because of incest-origin of tribe.* India: Thompson-Balys.

T131.6. *Girl will marry on condition she is to be only wife.* Irish myth: Cross.

T131.7. *King may not marry girl who has been wife of another.* Irish myth: *Cross; Jewish: Neuman.

C563. Tabus of kings. P13. Customs connected with kings. P18. Marriage of kings. T381.0.1. Girl intended for marriage with king cloistered.

T131.8. *Different religion as obstacle for marriage.* India: Thompson-Balys.

T131.9. *Brahmin may marry from all four castes.* India: Thompson-Balys.

T132. *Preparation for wedding.*

T132.1. *Girl fattened before wedding.* Africa (Zulu): Callaway 202, (Kaffir): Theal 67, (Ekoi): Talbot 7, 357.

T132.2. *Parents become servants to secure funds for wedding.* India: Thompson-Balys.

T133. *Travel to wedding.*

T133.1. *Faithful servant accompanies bride to new home.* Icelandic: *Boberg; Spanish: Espinosa Jr. No. 93.

T133.2. *Royal bride conducted by embassy to husband's kingdom.* (Cf. T51.) Dickson 31.

T133.3. *Drummer beats drums before bride on way to wedding.* Nouvelles Récréations No. 49.

T133.4. *Bridegroom and his men come for the bride.* Icelandic: *Boberg.

T133.5. *Mounting upon horse to fetch bride.* India: Thompson-Balys.

T133.6. *Groom's mother visits bride-to-be and puts the betrothal ring on her finger.* India: Thompson-Balys.

T134. *Conduct of bridal couple before ceremony.*

T134.1. *Bridal couple must never see each other before wedding.* Chinese: Werner 375.

T134.2. *Betrothed parties do not see each other until night of the wedding.* India: Thompson-Balys.

T134.3. *Man who has once been married helps groom to dress for wedding.* India: Thompson-Balys.

T135. *Wedding ceremony.*

T61. Betrothal.

T135.1. *Marriage formula: "You are mine and I am yours".* *BP II 58.

T135.2. *Touching of privates considered a marriage pact.* Koryak: *Jochelson JE VI 381.

T135.3. *Wedding by proxy.* India: *Thompson-Balys.

T135.3.1. *Sword and shield as proxy at wedding ceremony.* India: *Thompson-Balys.

T117.2. Marriage of girl to a sword.

T135.4. *Groom's sword makes vermillion mark on bride's forehead as wedding ceremony.* India: *Thompson-Balys.

T135.5. *Marriage by exchange of garlands.* India: *Thompson-Balys.

T135.6. *Marriage by drinking festival.* (Cf. T136.1.) Icelandic: Boberg.

T135.7. *The bride must have someone to give her away, usually her father or brother.* Icelandic: Boberg.

T135.8. *Two or more weddings at one time as the end of a tale.* Icelandic: *Boberg; India: Thompson-Balys.

T135.9. *Wedding ceremony in church.* Icelandic: *Boberg.

T135.10. *Marriage custom: going round and round fire (pillar, etc.).* India: *Thompson-Balys.

T135.11. *Bride and groom drink from same cup as part of ceremony.* India: *Thompson-Balys.

T135.12. *Bodies of would-be bride and groom besmeared with turmeric and mustard-oil.* India: Thompson-Balys.

T135.13. *Bride and groom look into a big mirror while old member of family knocks both their heads together.* India: Thompson-Balys.

T135.14. *Wedding-canopy over bride and groom.* Jewish: *Neuman.

T135.15. *Breaking a glass during wedding ceremony.* Jewish: *Neuman.

T136. *Accompaniments of wedding.*

T136.1. *Wedding feast.* Icelandic: *Boberg; India: Thompson-Balys; Africa (Zulu): Callaway 66.

H151.2. Attention drawn by helpful animal's theft of food from wedding table: recognition follows.

T136.2. *Rice thrown at weddings.* *Crane Vitry 249 No. 265; Herbert III 22; *Hdwb. d. Abergl. I 1649, III 385f., IV 168f.; Frazer Golden Bough I 254; Mannhardt Wald und Feldkulte I 222.

T136.3. *Amusements at wedding.* Icelandic: *Boberg.

T136.3.1. *Dancing at wedding.* Jewish: Neuman.

T136.3.2. *Marriage odes sung at wedding feast.* Jewish: *Neuman.

T136.4. *Gifts at wedding.* Jewish: *Neuman; India: *Thompson-Balys.

T136.4.1. *Gifts for bridal couple by a special ceremony with the bride on a bridebench.* Icelandic: *Boberg.

T136.4.2. *Parting gifts after wedding.* Icelandic: *Boberg.

T136.4.3. *Bride scatters presents among groom's relations.* India: Thompson-Balys.

T137. *Customs following wedding.*

M352. Prophecy of particular perils to prince on wedding journey.

T137.1. *Advice to a parting bride.* Dickson 165 n. 10.

T137.2. *Bride and bridegroom conducted to bridal bed.* Icelandic: *Boberg.

T137.2.1. *Bride and groom simultaneously touch hearthstones and put one foot down inside threshold as they enter groom's house.* India: Thompson-Balys.

T137.3. *Groom invited after marriage ceremony into female apartments to eat wedding breakfast with the bride.* India: Thompson-Balys.

T137.4. *Groom becomes a member of bride's family.* India: Thompson-Balys.

T137.5. *Bride (and party) fetched by groom and party after wedding.* India: Thompson-Balys.

T137.6. *Journey to husband's home accompanied by attendants.* India: Thompson-Balys.

T141. *Assignment of bride to another.* Icelandic: Boberg.

K1371.1. Lover steals bride from wedding with unwelcome suitor.

T141.1. *Dying man assigns bride to his brother.* Child I 376, 378 n.

T141.2. *Wives exchanged.* Irish myth: *Cross; India: Thompson-Balys; Eskimo (Cumberland Sound): Boas BAM XV 223, (Greenland): Holm 75.

T141.3. *Hero assigns the bride he has won to another.* Icelandic: *Boberg.

T143. *Infant marriages.* India: *Thompson-Balys.

T145. *Polygamous marriages.* Irish myth: *Cross; Icelandic: *Boberg; Jewish: *Neuman; India: *Thompson-Balys; Africa (Duala): Lederbogen Märchen 82, (Fang): Trilles Legends 263f.

A164.3. Polygamy among the gods.

T145.0.1. *Polygyny.* Irish myth: Cross.

T145.1. *Marriage to five women, each with separate duties.* India: Thompson-Balys; Africa (Benga): Nassau 169 No. 22.

T131.3. Eldest daughter will marry man only if he will marry all her sisters too.

T145.1.1. *Man requires seven women.* Irish myth: Cross.

T145.1.2. *Seven wives each to have the husband one day a week.* India: Thompson-Balys.

T145.1.3. *Man married to several sisters.* India: *Thompson-Balys.

T145.2. *Second wife taken because first is barren.* India: *Thompson-Balys.

T145.3. *Competition in ale-brewing between king's two wives.* Icelandic: *Boberg.

H460. Wife test.

T145.4. *Man's two wives each claim part of his body: they torment him.* India: *Thompson-Balys.

T145.5. *Man pulled down stairs by his two wives.* India: Thompson-Balys.

T145.6. *Polygamist must love all his wives.* India: Thompson-Balys.

T145.7. *Man's senior wife ugly but diligent; his second, beautiful but lazy.* Africa (Fang): Trilles 264.

T145.8. *Polygamy so that head wife may be quickly replaced for wrongdoing.* Africa (Konnoh): Willans 139.

T146. *Polyandry.* Woman with two husbands. Irish myth: *Cross; Icelandic: Boberg; India: *Thompson-Balys.

A164.5. Polyandry among the gods.

T146.1. *Several men marry one woman.* Grimm No. 4; Jewish: Neuman.

T563.1. Child of three fathers born with three stripes. T586.3. Multiple birth as result of relations with several men.

T146.2. *Woman requires thirty men.* Irish myth: Cross.

T147. *Marriages made at annual festival.* Irish myth: *Cross; India: Thompson-Balys.

T148. *Matriarchy.* Irish myth: *Cross; Jewish: Neuman.

A164.4. Matriarchy among the gods. T55. Girl as wooer.

T148.1. *Son named for mother.* Irish myth: *Cross.

T150. Happenings at weddings. *Hdwb. d. Abergl. IV 148ff.; India: Thompson-Balys.

A185.5. Deity assists at mortal's wedding. D2006.1.5. Forgotten fiancée attracts attention by magically stopping wedding carriage of new bride. F322.1. Changeling bride. Fairies steal bride and leave a substitute. F417.1. Spirits borrow from mortals at weddings; return goods later. J1171.2. Solomonic judgment: the divided bride. J2462. Foolish bridegroom follows instructions literally. K1371. Bride stealing. N318.2. Princess accidentally elopes with wrong man. N681. Husband (lover) arrives home just as wife (mistress) is to marry another. R31. Light extinguished and woman stolen. R225. Elopement.

T151. *Year's respite from unwelcome marriage.* *Type 300, 301; *Loomis White Magic 120; Irish myth: *Cross; Welsh: MacCulloch Celtic 94; English: Wells 135 (Sir Degare); Icelandic: *Boberg; India: *Thompson-Balys.

K522.0.1. Death feigned to escape unwelcome marriage. N681. Husband (lover) arrives home just as wife (mistress) is to marry another.

T151.0.1. *Respite ruse.* Captive maiden assigns quest, agreeing to marry when it is accomplished. Irish myth: *Cross.

R10.1. Princess (maiden) abducted. H1210. Quest assigned. K550. Escape by false plea.

T151.0.2. *Father giving away daugnter makes condition: son-in-law not to see daughter as his wife during one year.* Africa (Dahome): Einstein 25.

T151.1. *Six months' respite from unwelcome marriage.* India: *Thompson-Balys.

T151.2. *Thirty days' respite from unwelcome marriage.* India: *Thompson-Balys.

T151.3. *Other respites from unwelcome marriage* (three months, two years, etc.). India: *Thompson-Balys.

T152. *Bride wounded accidentally on way home.* Fatal wound from bridegroom's sword. Child I 142b.

T153. *Bridegroom slain on way to bride.* Child I 142, 386, IV 179ff.

T154. *Cruel stepmother enchants stepdaughter on eve of wedding.* (Cf. D5, S31.) Icelandic: Boberg.

T155. *Old beggar transforms wedding party into wolves.* (Cf. D113.1.) Dh III 454; Finnish: Aarne FFC VIII 14 No. 75, XXXIII 53 No. 75; Estonian: Aarne FFC XXV 130 No. 73, 145 No. 38; Lithuanian: Balys Index No. 3674; Livonian: Loorits FFC LXVI 63 No. 160.

T156. *Marriage for a night to evade law.* In order to have girl escape unwelcome marriage, the hero agrees to marry her and give her up the next day. He puts up a large bond as pledge to give her up. But he gets hold of the money by trickery and keeps her. *Chauvin V 45 No. 18 n. 1.

K231. Debtor refuses to pay his debt. K1915.1. Monk becomes husband to girl at night, so that his friend may have dowry.

T156.1. *Marriage for a night to insure heir of warrior destined to be slain (next day) in battle.* Irish myth: *Cross.

T157. *Affianced wife of chieftain falls in love with another man at betrothal feast, drugs the company with sleeping potion, and forces man of her choice to elope with her.* Irish myth: *Cross.

T160. Consummation of marriage. India: Thompson-Balys.

C117. Nuptial tabu. Husband and wife forbidden intercourse for definite time. D2006.1.4. Forgotten fiancée buys place in husband's bed and reawakens his memory. H38.2.3. Recognition of maidservant substitute bride by her habitual conversation. J1306. How marriage was consummated. K1843. Wife deceives husband with substituted bedmate. K1844. Husband deceives wife with substituted bedmate. K1911. The false bride (substituted bride). K2052. The oversensitive bride. T92.4. Girl mistakenly elopes with the wrong lover. T288. Wife refuses to sleep with unbeloved husband.

T161. *Jus primae noctis.* Overlord claims right of sleeping the first night with subject's wife. Liebrecht Orient und Occident II 541f., Liebrecht 94, 416; Herrmann Saxo II 324; *Hertz Abhandlungen 207ff.; *Hdwb. d. Abergl. III 746; *Wesselski Archiv Orientální I 82f. — Irish: MacCulloch Celtic 140, *Cross; Swiss: Jegerlehner Oberwallis 319 No. 21; French: Sébillot France IV 285; Jewish: *bin Gorion Born Judas[2] I 363, *Neuman; India: Thompson-Balys.

A1556.4. Origin of jus primae noctis. P19.2. King may have any woman to be his paramour if he makes her a settlement. S185.2. King demands intercourse with woman in childbed. T281. Sex hospitality.

T161.0.1. *King deflowers all twelve year old girls.* India: Thompson-Balys.

T161.1. *Lover allowed to sleep with woman first few nights after her marriage to another.* India: Thompson-Balys.

T162. *Feast of "bedding and handspreading" before consummation of marriage.* Irish myth: Cross.

T165. *Girl may remain virgin for three days after marriage.* (Cf. C117.) *Fb "brud" IV 64b; *DeVries Zs. f. deutsche Philologie LIII 276f.; Hdwb: d. Abergl. III 739; Icelandic: *Boberg; Italian Novella: Rotunda.

T165.1. *Consummation of marriage postponed until revelation by dream* of future of family has been secured. DeVries Zs. f. deutsche Philologie LIII 277.

T165.2. *One year to elapse between ceremony and consummation of marriage.* Italian Novella: Rotunda.

T165.3. *Twenty-four hours to elapse before consummation of marriage.* Italian Novella: Rotunda.

T165.4. *Bride and groom separated on wedding night.* Italian Novella: Rotunda.

T165.5. *Three years asked before consummation of marriage as trick.* Icelandic: *Boberg.

T165.6. *Consummation of marriage postponed till couple return home.* India: Thompson-Balys.

T165.7. *For first six months bride of prince is only to sit an hour or two in his house.* India: Thompson-Balys.

T166. *Bride afraid of intercourse refuses consummation until judge orders it in court.* Cent Nouvelles Nouvelles No. 86.

T166.1. *Bride refuses to sleep with ugly groom.* India: Thompson-Balys.

T166.2. *Bridegroom must be taught sexual intercourse.* Chinese: Graham.

J1744. Ignorance of marriage relations. J2462. Foolish bridegroom follows instructions literally.

T171. *Bridegroom driven from bridal chamber by magic.* Usually by hornets or wasps. *Type 559; *BP II 454; Italian: Basile Pentamerone III No. 5; Japanese: Ikeda; N. A. Indian: Thompson CColl II 411ff.

T172. *Dangers to husband in bridal chamber.* India: *Thompson-Balys.

K1210. Humiliated or baffled lovers.

T172.0.1. *All husbands have perished on bridal night.* See references to F547.1.1, F582, F582.1. *Types 506—08; India: *Thompson-Balys.

F547.1.1. Vagina dentata. Woman kills her husbands with her toothed vagina. F582. Poison damsel. Woman nourished on poison is fatal to her husbands. Sometimes the poisoning is from fatal look, or breath, sometimes from intercourse. F582.1. Serpent damsel. Woman has serpent inside which comes out and kills her bridegrooms.

T172.1. *Bridal chamber filled with coiled snakes.* Greek: Frazer Apollodorus I 93.

T172.2. *Bridal chamber invaded by magic dragon (serpent).* (Cf. B176.1.) *Types 507AB, 516; Liljeblad passim; Italian: Basile Pentamerone IV No. 9; India: *Thompson-Balys.

T172.2.1. *Grateful dead man kills princess's monster husband.* (Or otherwise renders her innocuous to the bridegroom.) *Type 506—08.

E341. The grateful dead. T118. Girl married to a monster.

T172.3. *Bride's monster-father tries to kill husband, but is defeated.* Icelandic: Boberg.

T173. *Murderous bride.* India: *Thompson-Balys.

T173.1. *Strong bride tries to stifle husband in bed.* *Type 519.

K1844.1. Husband has his strong servant substitute in bed with strong wife. The supernaturally strong wife is about to kill her husband.

T173.2. *Hostile brides kill husbands in the bridal bed.* *Encyc. Britannica 13 s.v. "Danaus"; Frazer Apollodorus I 143 n. 1; Lithuanian: Balys Index No. 306A*; India: *Thompson-Balys.

K872. Judith and Holofernes: girl from enemy camp chosen to sleep with intoxicated general kills him in bed.

T175. *Magic perils threaten bridal couple.* The perils are various—magic horse, poison, enchanted clothes, etc. *Type 516; **Rösch FFC LXXVII 123ff.; Italian: Basile Pentamerone IV No. 9; India: *Thompson-Balys; Korean: Zong in-Sob 155 No. 68.

M352. Prophecy of particular perils to prince on wedding journey. N342.1. Faithful servant guarding master's wife from danger falsely condemned for betraying his master. R169.4.1. Rescue of bride from mysterious perils by hidden faithful servant.

T175.1. *Falling furniture threatens bridal couple.* Furniture etc. arranged by jealous rival so that it will fall. India: *Thompson-Balys.

T177. *Bridegroom magically impelled to leave his bride.* Irish myth: *Cross; Italian: Basile Pentamerone I Nos. 7, 9. See also all references to Forgotten Fiancée (D2003).

T294. Husband (wife) of supernatural being longs for old home and visits relatives. T376.1. Man leaves earthly bride for service of Virgin.

T181. *Dangerous husband.* (Cf. T172.) India: Thompson-Balys.

T182. *Death from intercourse.* India: Thompson-Balys.

F1041. Extraordinary physical reactions of persons.

T190. Marriage—miscellaneous motifs.

T192. *Marriage by force.* India: Thompson-Balys.

T200—T299. Married life.

T200. Married life.

C31. Tabu: offending supernatural wife. C32. Tabu: offending supernatural husband. C713. Forsaken merman. D732. Loathly lady. D733. Loathly bridegroom. D735.1. Beauty and the beast. D1978.4. Hero wakened from magic sleep by wife who has purchased place in his bed from false wife. D2003. Forgotten fiancée. D2006.1.4. Forgotten fiancée buys place in husband's bed and reawakens his memory. E221.1. Dead wife haunts husband on second marriage. H1187. Task left by departing husband for wife to accomplish. H1385.3. Quest for vanished wife (mistress). H1385.4. Quest for vanished husband. J229.1. Choice: staying at home with loving wife or going to tavern and having unfaithful wife. Man chooses latter. J461.2. Common wives of man debate as to which has helped him most. J482. King advised to marry maid rather than widow. J1151.1.2. Husband discredited by absurd truth. J1540. Retorts between husband and wife. J1545. Wife outwits her husband. J1701. Stupid wife. J1713. Foolish married couples. J2301. Gullible husbands. J2353. The wife multiplies the secret. J2511. The silence wager. A man and his wife make a wager as to who shall speak first. J2516.3.1. Wife follows written instructions. J2523. The obedient husband. K1911. The false bride (substitute bride). N2.6. Wife as wager. N681. Husband (lover) arrives home just as wife (mistress) is to marry another. P210. Husband and wife. Q115.1. Reward: any boon that may be asked—king's wife demanded. R227.2. Flight from hated husband.

T201. *Marriage destroys friendship.* Lover and mistress live together and are happy; become unhappy as soon as they marry. *Pauli (ed. Bolte) Nos. 215, 217.

T202. *The happy couple: wife blind, husband deaf.* Italian Novella: Rotunda.

T203. *Peace in marriage more important than truth.* Jewish: Neuman.

T210. Faithfulness in marriage. India: Thompson-Balys.

E321. Dead husband's friendly return. E322. Dead wife's friendly return. E756.5. Saved soul of woman assists her husband's soul in battle against demons. H400. Chastity test. H430. Chastity index. H492. Test of faithfulness of husband and wife. J482.1.1. Woman refuses a second marriage. J1545.4. The exiled wife's dearest possession. J1545.6. Wife by cleverness wins back fortune overbearing husband has foolishly lost and humbles him. M254. Promise to be buried with wife if she dies first. N455.6. Husband learns of wife's fidelity through conversation overheard. Q83. Reward for marital fidelity. Q394. Uxoriousness punished. R151. Husband rescues wife. R152. Wife rescues husband.

T210.1. *Faithful wife.* Korean: Zong in-Sob 106ff. No. 57.

D733.2. Swine bridegroom. Bride disenchants him by her love.

T210.2. *Faithful husband.* Jewish: *Neuman; Chinese: Eberhard FFC CXX 252.

T211. *Faithfulness to marriage in death.* Herrmann Saxo II 94; Icelandic: *Boberg; Korean: Zong in-Sob 30 No. 13.

F1041.1.1.3. Heart breaks from sorrow. K1353. Woman deceived into sacrificing honor. Ruler promises to release her brother (husband) but afterwards refuses to do so. M135. Vow never to remarry. T455.2. Woman sacrifices her honor to free her husband (brother) from prison.

T211.1. *Wife dies so that husband's death may be postponed.* Greek: Euripides' Alcestis. *Grote I 108.

D1855.2. Death postponed if substitute can be found. E165. Resuscitation of wife by husband giving up half his remaining life. (Sometimes vice versa.) R185. Hercules fights with "Death" and rescues Alcestis.

T211.1.1. *Woman drowns herself as sacrifice to water-gods to save husband's boat from capsizing.* Japanese: Anesaki 304.

C41.3. Tabu: crossing water when spirits are offended. S263. Sacrifice to appease spirits (gods).

T211.1.2. *Husband learning from augurs that his wife will die if he saves self from serpent, lets self be bitten to death.* Spanish Exempla: Keller.

T211.1.3. *Wife offers to sacrifice her right arm for husband's safe return.* India: Thompson-Balys.

T211.1.4. *Female deer offers herself instead of her mate, who has been captured.* Hunter, struck by her sacrifice, lets both go. India: Thompson-Balys.

T211.2. *Wife's suicide at husband's death.* (Cf. T81.7.) Icelandic: *Boberg; India: *Thompson-Balys.

T211.2.1. *Wife throws herself on husband's funeral pyre.* Icelandic: *Boberg; Greek: Frazer Apollodorus I 375 n. 3 (Evadne); Spanish Exempla: Keller; India: *Thompson-Balys.

P16.4.1. Suttee. Wife burned with dead king. S123.2. Burial of living husband or wife with dead spouse. V61.2. Dead burned on pyre.

T211.2.1.1. *Wife prefers to be burned together with husband even though she was forced to marry him* and she has helped to prepare the revenge. Icelandic: Boberg.

T211.2.2. *Wife promises to die with husband.* India: Thompson-Balys.

T211.3. *Husband and wife kill themselves so as not to be separated.* Chinese: Werner 400.

A968.2. Cliff from lovers' leap. Lovers in despair throw themselves from a high place. This becomes a cliff.

T211.3.1. *Husband falls on sword when his wife dies.* Spanish Exempla: Keller.

T211.3.2. *Wife hangs self because her husband has been killed.* Spanish Exempla: Keller.

T211.4. *Spouse's corpse kept after death.*

T211.4.1. *Wife's corpse kept after death.* Type 612; Wesselski Märchen 188, 191; BP I 463f.; Moth Danske Studier (1915) 97ff.; Pauls Der Ring der Fastrada (Aachen, 1896); Chauvin II 201ff.; Cowell Jātaka II 108.

T85.4. Lover's body kept embalmed for years by grieving mistress. T85.4.1. Ring of Fastrada. Lover keeps body of dead mistress intact by means of magic ring.

T211.4.2. *Husband's corpse kept after death.*

T211.4.2.1. *Wife will not give up dead body of husband to God of Death.* India: Thompson-Balys.

T211.5. *Man becomes a hermit after his wife's death.* *Dickson 264 n. 85.

T211.6. *Widowed she-fox rejects suitors who do not resemble her deceased husband.* *Type 65; BP I 362; *Taylor JAFL XLVI 78; Fb "ræv" III 113b.

T211.7. *Girl forced to marry before sweetheart's return is faithful to her husband.* When she refuses to give her former fiancé a kiss, he falls dead. She goes to his funeral and falls dead over his body. Italian Novella: *Rotunda.

F1041.1.1. Death from broken heart. T81.3. Girl falls dead on lover's body. T86. Lovers buried in same grave.

T211.8. *Wife unwilling to deceive her husband for the man she loves.* Icelandic: Boberg.

T211.9. *Excessive grief at husband's or wife's death.* Icelandic: *Boberg.

T211.9.1. *Wife dies of grief for death of husband.* (Cf. T81.7.) Irish myth: Cross.

T211.9.1.1. *Wife swoons realizing her husband is dead.* India: Thompson-Balys.

T211.9.2. *Man kills self in grief for wife.* Irish myth: Cross.

T211.9.2.1. *Grieving man goes to die where his wife's corpse lies.* India: Thompson-Balys.

T212. *Loving couple die of separation.* Penzer II 9.

T212.1. *Constancy of wife brings husband back to life.* India: Thompson-Balys.

T213. *Husband (wife) sickens as result of separation from spouse.* Irish myth: Cross.

T215. *Faithfulness of married couple in misfortune.* India: Thompson-Balys.

T215.1. *Wife carries mutilated husband on her back so that he may beg.* Paris Zs. f. Vksk. XIII 4.

T215.2. *Wife offers starving husband (father) milk from her breasts.* Irish: MacCulloch Celtic 179, *Cross.

R81. Woman suckles imprisoned relative through prison wall.

T215.3. *Husband nourishes starving wife with his own flesh and blood.* Paris Zs. f. Vksk. XIII 5.

T215.4. *Wife puts out one of her eyes to show sympathy with her husband.* He has lost an eye in a tournament and is ashamed to return to her. She shows that it makes no difference in her love. Von der Hagen I cxxiv; Spanish Exempla: Keller.

T215.5. *Fugitive returns to his family so that they may collect reward from his capture.* Italian Novella: Rotunda.

T215.6. *Woman swims nightly to husband's prison and arranges his escape.* Spurns the attentions of treacherous suitor. (Cf. R152.) Italian Novella: Rotunda.

T215.7. *Wife travels for years with sick husband in order to have him cured.* Icelandic: Lagerholm 107—15, Boberg.

T215.7.1. *Wife alone does not desert leprous husband.* Jewish: Neuman; Buddhist myth: Malalasekera II 1060.

T215.8. *Woman sells her hair to feed starving husband.* Jewish: Neuman.

T216. *Loathly bridegroom carried on back in basket by wife.* Indonesia: Dixon 211.

D733. Loathly bridegroom. Woman disenchants loathsome man by embracing him. L54.1. Youngest daughter agrees to marry a monster.

T217. *Wife refuses to become unfaithful although she knows her husband to be so.* Italian Novella: Rotunda.

T221. *Woman's naivité proves her fidelity.* Man is rebuked for having bad breath. He reproves his wife for never having told him. "I thought that men liked it as I did." He realizes that his wife has not known any other man. Spanish Exempla: Keller; Italian Novella: Rotunda.

T222. *Wife hides husband's unfaithfulness from emperor and even shelters his mistress.* Spanish Exempla: Keller.

T224. *Husband tempted by own wife disguised in fine clothes: says he will touch no woman save his wife.* She puts on her old clothes. India: Thompson-Balys.

K1814.1. Prince marries dancing girl not knowing that she is his former wife. T235. Husband transforms himself to test his wife's faithfulness.

T230. Faithlessness in marriage. Irish myth: *Cross; India: Thompson-Balys.

A2237.1. Animal reveals mistress's adultery: punished by master. B131.3. Bird betrays woman's infidelity. B134.1. Dog betrays woman's infidelity. C12.4. Man commends wife to devil. Devil guards wife's chastity. D662. Transformation to cure inconstant husband. H400. Chastity test. H492. Test of faithfulness of husband and wife. J229.1. Choice: staying at home with loving wife or going to tavern and having unfaithful wife.

Man chooses latter. J221.1. King overlooks wife's unfaithfulness rather than to cause troubles of state. J882.1. Man with unfaithful wife comforted when he sees the queen's unfaithfulness. J1182.1. To be beaten by deceiver of husband. J1184.1. Adulteress hurled from high rock escapes injury: she may not be punished again. J1532. Adulteress's absurdity rebuked. J2301. Gullible husbands. K713.1.7. Faithless wife ties husband's hair to bed, allowing lover to kill him. K1500. Deceptions connected with adultery. K1813.1. Disguised husband wins his faithless wife's love. K1814. Woman in disguise wooed by her faithless husband. K1843. Wife deceives husband with substituted bedmate. K2213. Treacherous wife. R227.2. Flight from hated husband. T383. Futile attempts to keep wife chaste. T481. Adultery.

T230.1. *Wife and husband believe each unfaithful at the slightest provocation.* India: Thompson-Balys.

T230.2. *Faithless wife causes her husband to go insane.* India: Thompson-Balys.

T231. *The faithless widow.* Irish myth: *Cross.

K2052.4. The oversensitive or hypocritical widow. K2213.1. Matron of Ephesus. P22. Queen marries murderer of her fiancé. P214. Wife drinks blood of slain husband.

T231.1. *Faithless widow betrothed anew at husband's funeral.* Pauli (ed. Bolte) No. 751.

T231.2. *Faithless widow fans husband's grave.* She does not want to remarry until the body is cold (or the earth on the grave is dry). *Wesselski Mönchslatein 85 No. 72; Chinese: Werner 149.

T231.3. *Faithless widow ready to marry messenger who brings news of husband's death.* The husband, however, has only feigned death to test her. (Cf. T235.) *Type 1350.

T231.3.1. *Faithless widow offers city to killer of her husband if he will marry her.* Italian Novella: Rotunda; India: Thompson-Balys.

T231.4. *Faithless widow's heartlessness repels the new suitor.* She obeys him when he tells her to knock out the teeth of her dead husband. Fearing like treatment, he leaves. Type 1352*.

T231.5. *Faithless widow marries slayer of husband.* Irish myth: *Cross.

T232. *Woman deserts husband for unworthy lover.* (Deformed, mutilated, monstrous, or of different race.) *Penzer V 153 n. 1; Malone PMLA XLIII 418ff.; Strauch Enikels Weltchronik, lines 25177ff. — Irish myth: Cross; Italian Novella: *Rotunda; Palestine: Schmidt-Kahle Volkserzählungen aus Palästina I 139ff.; India: *Thompson-Balys; Buddhist myth: Malalasekera II 109; Indonesia: Coster-Wijsman 148.

T118. Girl married to (enamoured of) a monster.

T232.1. *Woman consorts with leper.* Italian Novella: Rotunda.

T232.2. *Adulteress chooses loathly paramour.* Heptameron No. 20; Italian Novella: Rotunda.

T232.3. *Adulteress poisons husband in order to be with swineherd.* Italian Novella: Rotunda.

T232.4. *Woman enamored of repulsive and abusive lover.* India: Thompson-Balys.

T118. Girl married to (enamored of) a monster. T481.1. Adulteress roughly treated by her lover.

T232.5. *Faithless wife pays her paramour for enjoying herself with him.* India: *Thompson-Balys.

T233. *Wronged wife goes to wronged husband.* Italian Novella: *Rotunda.

T235. *Husband transforms himself to test his wife's faithfulness.* (Cf. T231.3.) Greek: Fox 72.

K1531. Husband transformed to goat must witness wife's adultery. K1568. Husband in disguise begs food of his wife's suitors. K1810. Deception by disguise. N15. Chastity wager. A man makes a wager on his wife's chastity.

T236. *Woman enamored of an unknown knight in a tournament loses interest when she finds that it is her husband.* (Cf. R222.) Pauli (ed. Bolte) No. 750.

T237. *Old man married to young, unfaithful wife.* Irish myth: Cross; Italian Novella: Rotunda.

T238. *Adulteress on her death-bed reveals the illegitimacy of her children.* Did not want her husband to be burdened with their bringing up. Cent Nouvelles Nouvelles No. 51; Italian Novella: *Rotunda.

T241. *Series of husbands try in vain to control adulteress.* India: Thompson-Balys.

T243. *Fight between husband and lover for kingdom and wife.* Irish myth: Cross; India: *Thompson-Balys.

T244. *Woman reveals whereabouts of husband to enemy in revenge for desertion.* Irish myth: Cross.

T244.1. *Woman reveals whereabouts of husband to hungry bear in revenge for desertion.* India: Thompson-Balys.

T245. *Man unfaithful even on wedding night.* India: Thompson-Balys.

H1552.1. Which was most generous—husband, robber, or lover?

T247. *Object stolen (left) as token that infidelity has been discovered.* Irish myth: *Cross.

T247.1. *Substituted sword.* Husband leaves wooden sword in scabbard of wife's paramour upon discovering their infidelity. Irish myth: Cross.

T249. *Faithlessness in marriage—miscellaneous.*

T249.1. *Adulterous wife convicted commits suicide.* Irish myth: *Cross.

T249.2. *Husband and wife (king and queen) each unfaithful to other.* Irish myth: *Cross.

T250. Characteristics of wives and husbands.

H461. Test of wife's patience. Griselda. J1151.1.1. Talkative wife discredited. J1546. Overcurious wife learns of the senate's deliberations. W111.3. The lazy wife. W111.4. Lazy husband. Z153. Princess crushes lotus flower to show that she will be submissive.

T251. *The shrewish wife.* *Penzer II 159f.; Hanna Lindberg "The Shrew", argbiggans typ i den Engelska Literaturen intill Shakespeare (Tavastehus, 1900); India: *Thompson-Balys.

J2412.5. Healing with the cherry tree. K583. Wolf punished by being married. Q599.2. Punishment: marrying shrewish wife. S51. Cruel mother-in-law.

T251.0.1. *Man ejected from heaven for folly of marrying twice.* Spanish: Boggs FFC XC 126 No. 1410.

T251.0.2. *Christ, not having married, knew nothing about suffering.* So thinks the man after hearing all about Christ's torments. Spanish: Boggs FFC XC 129 No. 1516A.

T251.0.3. *Man reprimanded by judge for marrying several times.* The man replies that he was always looking for a good wife. Spanish: Childers.

T251.1. *Avoiding the shrewish wife.*

T251.1.1. *Belfagor.* The devil frightened by the shrewish wife. A man persuades his shrewish wife to let herself be lowered into a well. When he comes to pull her out he raises a genie (devil) who is glad to escape from the woman. Later he frightens the devil by telling him that his wife has escaped. *Type 1164; **Axon The Story of Belfagor in Literature and Folklore (1902); *BP I 382, 388, IV 176 n. 1; *Prato RTP IV 174; *Bolte Zs. f. Vksk. XV 104; Child V 107f., 305a; *Chauvin VIII 152 No. 154. — Rumanian: Schullerus FFC LXXVIII No. 1164I*; Spanish: Boggs FFC XC 50 No. 332; Italian Novella: *Rotunda; India: *Thompson-Balys.

K212. Devil cheated by being frightened. K2325. Devil frightened by threatening to bring mother-in-law.

T251.1.1.1. *Devil flees shrewish wife and enters body of a duke.* Exorcised by telling him that they are sending for his wife. Italian Novella: *Rotunda.

T251.1.2. *Late husband chooses to remain in Purgatory rather than to return to his shrewish wife.* Spanish: Boggs FFC XC 129 No. 1516.

T251.1.2.1. *Husband chooses to go to hell rather than join shrewish wife in heaven.* Pauli (ed. Bolte) No. 757.

T251.1.2.2. *Man in hell declares that life there is much better than on earth with his wife.* Bargain with the devil: should the latter not be able to endure life with his wife for three years, the man would be released from hell. The devil is the loser. Lithuanian: Balys Index No. 1164B*.

T251.1.3. *Man had rather remain transformed to mule than to live with his shrewish wife.* Spanish: Boggs FFC XC 86 No. 754C*.

T251.1.4. *Man forces devil to take back the shrewish wife.* Spanish: Boggs FFC XC 41 No. 301.

T251.1.5. *Minstrel throws wife into sea: her tongue the heaviest thing on board.* Ordered to throw all heavy articles overboard. *Pauli (ed. Bolte) No. 138; Mensa Philosophica No. 61; Italian Novella: *Rotunda.

T251.1.6. *Thief overhears and oversees quarrel of two jealous wives.* Arraigned before judge, he asks any punishment be given him rather than that of having two wives. India: Thompson-Balys.

T251.2. *Taming the shrew.* By outdoing his wife in shrewishness the husband renders her obedient. *Types 900, 901; *BP I 443; **Philippson FFC L; *Wesselski Arlotto II 229 No. 95; *Gigas "Et eventyrs vandring" Litteratur og Historie (3e samling) (København, 1902); *Krappe Études ital. II 141ff.; *Wesselski Märchen 216 No. 24; Köhler-Bolte I 137; Chauvin II 155 No. 27. — Spanish Exempla: Keller; Italian Novella: Rotunda; India: *Thompson-Balys.

H386. Bride test: obedience. N12. Wager on the most obedient wife. The husband tames his shrewish wife so that he wins the wager. W31. Obedience.

T251.2.1. *Shrew tamed by setting another shrew against her.* Crane Vitry 218 No. 200; Herbert III 16.

T251.2.2. *Husband dons armor and forces the household to shout: "Long live the Master!"* Takes off his breeches and dares his wife to put them on. Establishes his mastery in the home. Italian Novella: *Rotunda.

T251.2.3. *Wife becomes obedient on seeing husband slay a recalcitrant horse.* Italian Novella: *Rotunda.

T251.2.3.1. *Husband tries to reform wife by killing a recalcitrant horse in her presence.* She thinks he has lost his mind and continues in her ways. Italian Novella: Rotunda.

T251.2.4. *The wicked queen reformed.* While asleep she is made to exchange places with the cobbler's wife. She thinks she is in hell. The cobbler teaches her to obey and fear her husband. Lithuanian: Balys Index No. 904*; Russian: Andrejev No. 901I*; Prussian: Plenzat 49.

K1840. Deception by substitution. Q325. Disobedience punished.

T251.2.5. *Shrewish wife driven from home but when in danger, runs to husband and receives protection.* She is a good wife thereafter. Africa (Congo): Grenfell 819.

T251.3. *St. Peter's wife meets him with a broom handle.* She is waiting for him at the rear door of the house. Type 754**.

T251.4. *Socrates and Zanthippe: "After thunder rain".* He thus remarks as she empties slops on his head. *Wesselski Arlotto II 258 No. 183; *Pauli (ed. Bolte) No. 471; England: Baughman.

J1250. Clever verbal retorts.

T251.5. *Strength in words, in herbs, and in stones.* When first two do not cure shrewish wife, the last does. (Cf. J1563.6, J1581.2, J2412.5.) Pauli (ed. Bolte) No. 134; Mensa Philosophica No. 58.

T251.6. *The browbeaten husband from under the table: "The man always has a man's heart."* Type 1366*; Spanish: Boggs FFC XC 141 No. 1705.

T251.7. *Husband will not search for shrewish wife who has run away from him.* Wesselski Bebel II 145 No. 142.

T251.8. *Shrewish wife gives husband heating every morning.* India: *Thompson-Balys.

T251.9. *Husband consoled by seeing woman even more shrewish than his wife.* (Cf. J882.) India: Thompson-Balys.

T251.10. *Wife beats her husband and eats up everything he earns.* India: Thompson-Balys.

T251.11. *Fakir thankful for shrewish wife: she is a thorn in his flesh and warns him from neglecting the ways of righteousness.* India: Thompson-Balys.

T252. *The overbearing wife.*

T252.1. *Unsuccessful search for man who can rule his wife.* Type 1375*.

T252.2. *Cock shows browbeaten husband how to rule his wife.* (Cf. J21.16, J130.) *Type 670; **Aarne FFC XV 49ff.; Fb "kok" IV 272b; Italian Novella: Rotunda; India: Thompson-Balys.

T252.2.1. *King sees how male stork kills his unfaithful wife.* Follows its example. Scala Celi 7a No. 40; Oesterley No. 82; Spanish Exempla: Keller.

T252.2.2. *Monkey (jackal, etc.) shows husband how to rule his wife.* India: *Thompson-Balys.

T252.2.2.1. *King tells jackal his statistics are wrong since there are more men than women.* Jackal: husbands ruled by their wives counted as women. India: Thompson-Balys.

T252.3. *Wife threatens husband with death if he will not tell secrets.* *Type 670; **Aarne FFC XV 48ff.; India: *Thompson-Balys.

C420.1. Man (woman) persuaded to reveal fatal secret. C425. Tabu: revealing knowledge of animal languages. K975. Secret of strength treacherously discovered. K2213. Treacherous wife. N440. Valuable secrets learned. N456. Enigmatical smile (laugh) reveals secret knowledge.

T252.4. *Prize for husband who rules his wife.* (Ham, egg.) *Köhler-Bolte III 609; Fb "æg" III 1142a.

T252.4.1. *Man claims prize (boots) as ruler of his house, but is afraid to carry the boots lest he soil his clean shirt and anger his wife.* Pauli (ed. Bolte) No. 753; Italian Novella: Rotunda.

T252.5. *Men rulers in their house asked to sing.* No man in congregation does so. Priest alone sings. Next year he cannot, for then he has a maid. Wesselski Bebel II 148 No. 157; Pauli (ed. Bolte) No. 811.

T252.6. *Wife threatens suicide if she does not have her own way.* India: Thompson-Balys.

T252.7. *Vexed woman brings pot down on husband's head in presence of guest.* India: Thompson-Balys.

T253. *The nagging wife.* India: *Thompson-Balys.

T253.1. *Nagging wife drives husband to prepare for suicide.* *Type 670; **Aarne FFC XV 48ff.

T253.2. *Woman advised that nagging will never make a husband virtuous.* Pauli (ed. Bolte) No. 135.

T253.3. *Saint composes hymn to free himself from the mala vita in which he lives with his wife.* Irish myth: Cross.

T254. *The disobedient wife.*

H473. Test of wife's obedience. H1557. Tests of obedience. N12. Wager on most obedient wife. W126. Disobedience.

T254.1. *The husband shows his wife poison to avoid: she takes it and dies.* Chauvin II 155 No. 27; Krappe Bulletin Hispanique XXXIX 38; Spanish Exempla: Keller; Italian Novella: *Rotunda.

T254.2. *Husband forbids wife to ride on the dog: she immediately does* so and is bitten. Pauli (ed. Bolte) No. 705.

T254.3. *Man with obedient wife looks young; with disobedient, old.* India: Thompson-Balys.

T254.4. *Man forbids wife to open chest.* Loaded crossbow placed in it. She opens it and is killed. Italian Novella: Rotunda.

T254.5. *Husband warns wife not to enter empty furnace.* She does so and it falls in upon her. Spanish Exempla: Keller.

T254.6. *Disobedient wife punished.*

T254.6.1. *Wife refuses to bring husband warm water: is beaten.* India: Thompson-Balys.

T255. *The obstinate wife or husband.* (Cf. J2511.) *Type 1365; India: *Thompson-Balys; Japanese: Ikeda.

T255.1. *The obstinate wife: cutting with knife or scissors.* At the end of the argument the man throws his wife into the water. As she sinks she makes with her finger the motion of shearing with the scissors. *Type 1365B; *Köhler-Bolte I 136; *Taylor Washington Univ. Studies IV 181 n. 28; *Crane Vitry 223 No. 222; Bédier Fabliaux (1895) 46ff.; *Pauli (ed. Bolte) No. 595; Moe Samlede Skrifter I 209ff.; Spanish Exempla: Keller.

T255.2. *The obstinate wife sought for up-stream.* When she falls into the stream, the husband concludes that she would be too obstinate to go with the current. *Type 1365A; *Crane Vitry 225f. No. 227; Köhler-Bolte I 506 n. 1; *Wesselski Hodscha Nasreddin I 270 No. 276; *Moe Samlede Skrifter I 212; *Pauli (ed. Bolte) No. 142; Italian Novella: *Rotunda; India: Thompson-Balys.

T255.3. *The obstinate wife: sign of the louse.* She calls her husband a lousy head. He throws her into the stream. As she sinks she makes a sign of cracking a louse. *Type 1365C; *Crane Vitry 222f. No. 221; *Bédier Fabliaux 46; *Pauli (ed. Bolte) No. 872; Herbert III 17; Italian Novella: *Rotunda.

T255.4. *The obstinate wife: the third egg.* The husband and the wife dispute as to who shall eat the third egg. She pretends to die. At the grave she asks him, "Do I eat two of the three eggs?" and he gives his consent. She jumps up and cries out "I eat two!" and everyone flees except a lame man who exclaims, "Poor me and the other one!" Spanish: Boggs FFC XC 123 No. 1365D*.

T255.4.1. *The obstinate wife: insists on eating three of the five eggs.* Italian Novella: *Rotunda.

T255.5. *The dish which the husband detests and the wife keeps serving him.* He affects to like it and thus gets rid of it. Type 1390*; India: Thompson-Balys.

T255.6. *Obstinate wife refuses to take cover off boiling kettle.* Is beaten by husband. Italian Novella: Rotunda.

T255.7. *Man warns his wife that he has dreamed that she is attacked by a wolf.* She pays no heed to him and the dream comes true. Italian Novella: *Rotunda.

T256. *The quarrelsome wife or husband.* Penzer II 159f., 180; India: Thompson-Balys.

T256.0.1. *Quarrel between husband and wife explained by their having been previously a tiger and a dog.* India: Thompson-Balys.

T256.1. *Quarrelsome wife conquered by silent husband.* *Pauli (ed. Bolte) No. 470.

T256.2. *Medicine against quarrelling: the wife must take one dose and keep it in her mouth for ten minutes as soon as her husband is angry.* Spanish: Childers; India: *Thompson-Balys.

T256.3. *Quarrelsome wife reproved by a good whipping.* India: Thompson-Balys.

T257. *Jealous wife or husband.* Irish myth: *Cross; Italian Novella: Rotunda; Jewish: Neuman; India: *Thompson-Balys.

F1041.1.9. Death from jealousy. M137. Vow never to be jealous of one's wife. Q301. Jealousy punished. S11.3.1. Man who doubts his children's paternity kills them. S73.1.4. Fratricide motivated by love-jealousy. W181. Jealousy.

T257.0.1. *Heavenly maidens are not jealous.* India: Thompson-Balys.

T257.1. *Woman jealous of a fair maid in her house.* Fears her attraction for her husband. Alphabet No. 796; India: *Thompson-Balys.

T257.1.1. *King's wives jealous of his attention to pet animal.* India: Thompson-Balys.

T257.2. *Jealousy of rival wives.* Penzer III 99; Irish myth: *Cross; India: *Thompson-Balys.

D665.1. Transformation of rival in love (marriage) to be rid of him. K2222. Treacherous co-wife. P217. Co-wife. S185.1. Co-wife forces pregnant woman to perform lowly tasks. S322.2.1. Mother exposes child for fear of jealous co-wife. T92. Rivals in love.

T257.2.1. *Wife exposes bald head of second wife to disgrace her.* Hair marvelously regrows. Irish myth: Cross.

T257.2.2. *Jealous wife (mistress) transforms rival to hound.* (Cf. B182.1.0.2.) Irish myth: *Cross.

T257.3. *Decision not to punish a jealous husband: he already suffers enough.* Wesselski Bebel I 127 No. 23.

T257.4. *Husband jealous of wife who goes to confession is punished by the priest.* When the husband sees the priest take her behind the altar to punish her he volunteers to take the punishment. The wife says, "Pound him well. I am a terrible sinner." Mensa Philosophica No. 72; *Wesselski Mönchslatein No. 74. Cf. Italian Novella: Rotunda.

T257.5. *Jealous husband kills nightingale which his wife gets up to hear.* Herbert III 201; Oesterley No. 121.

T257.5.1. *Woman's scented hair attracts deer: husband jealous.* India: *Thompson-Balys.

T257.6. *Jealous king causes massacre of handsome young captives.* Jewish: Neuman.

T257.7. *Husband's unjust jealousy forces wife to commit adultery.* Italian Novella: *Rotunda; Heptameron No. 47.

K1544. Husband unwittingly instrumental in wife's adultery.

T257.7.1. *Wife repays husband's supposed adultery by doing likewise.* India: Thompson-Balys.

T257.8. *Jealous husband objects to wife's enjoyment of intercourse: thinks she has had previous experience.* Nouvelles Récréations No. 39.

T257.9. *Jealous husband spends all his earnings as skillful smith bribing courtiers not to talk to his wife,* and at last locks her up in hut in the forest. Icelandic: FSS 14—18, XCVIII, Boberg.

T257.10. *Trickster sends jealous wife after husband: steals food.* (Cf. K343.) India: Thompson-Balys.

T257.11. *Jealous wife ties husband to her so that he cannot get away to meet another woman.* India: Thompson-Balys.

T258. *The curious wife.* India: *Thompson-Balys.

C324. Tabu: looking into jug. H1554.1. Test of curiosity: mouse in jug. J1546. Overcurious wife learns of the senate's deliberations. J2370. Inquisitive fool. Q341. Curiosity punished. W137. Curiosity.

T258.1. *The curious wife: wait and see.* A man and his wife overhear thieves planning to rob the house, put the man out of the way, and have their will of the wife. The man wants to raise an alarm. She says, "Wait and see." *Wesselski Hodscha Nasreddin II 242 No. 538.

T258.1.1. *Husband insists on knowing wife's secret.* India: Thompson-Balys.

T258.2. *Wife insists upon knowing husband's secret.* Type 670; India: Thompson-Balys.

T261. *The ungrateful wife.* (Cf. W154.) India: Thompson-Balys.

T261.1. *Husband takes wife's place and receives punishment for her adultery.* She is ungrateful. Pauli (ed. Bolte) No. 31.

T263. *The hypocritical wife.* Shows what she has done for her husband, but not what she has done for herself. Pauli (ed. Bolte) No. 569.

T265. *Jewels of Cornelia.* She shows her children as her jewels. Pauli (ed. Bolte) No. 141.

T268. *Beautiful woman married to hideous man:* he is thankful, she patient. She says that they have thus both gained paradise. *Chauvin V 174 No. 98.

T271. *The neglected wife.* Italian Novella: Rotunda; Icelandic: *Boberg.

T315.2. The continent husband.

T271.1. *Woman gets rid of impotent husband and remarries.* Italian Novella: Rotunda.

T311.2. Woman prefers to remain chaste rather than keep an impotent husband.

T271.1.1. *Mistress of impotent husband sends her maid to find a man for her.* India: Thompson-Balys.

T272. *The silent wife.*

T272.1. *Silent wife brought to speech by dangers to her husband.* (Cf. F954.) India: Thompson-Balys.

T274. *Wife cannot keep secret.* India: *Thompson-Balys.

H472. Test of wife's ability to keep secret. J1151.1.1. Talkative wife discredited. J2353. The wife multiplies the secret (husband has spit up white feather, etc.).

T275. *The spendthrift wife.* India: Thompson-Balys.

T280. Other aspects of married life.

T281. *Sex hospitality.* Host gives his wife (daughter) to his guest as bed companion. *Encyc. Religion Ethics s.v. "Adultery"; Irish: MacCulloch Celtic 149, *Cross; Welsh: MacCulloch Celtic 488; English: Wells 60 (Syre Gowene and the Carle of Carelyle); Icelandic: *Boberg.

A591. Semi-divine hero granted free access to men's wives. F302.1.1. Mortals given fairy mistresses during visit to fairyland. P14.13. King gives his own wife as reward. P325. Host surrenders his wife to his guest. T161. Jus primae noctis. T331.2. Knight unsuccessfully tempted by host's wife. T484. Maidservant given to lover's companion as bed-partner.

T281.1. *Sex hospitality given to druid.* Irish myth: Cross.

T281.2. *Sex hospitality given to king (prince).* Irish myth: *Cross; Icelandic: *Boberg.

T282. *Handmaid given as wife unto husband by barren wife.* Jewish: Neuman.

T282.1. *First (barren) wife insists her husband should take second wife.* Jewish: *Neuman.

T283. *Wife withholds intercourse from husband to enforce demand.* Cf. Aristophanes' Lysistrata. India: Thompson-Balys.

T284. *Frightened wife shows marks of affection for husband.* This is so rare that he pardons the robber who has caused the fright. Chauvin II 97 No. 52; Panchatantra III 9 (tr. Ryder 341); Bødker Exempler 295 No. 57; Spanish Exempla: Keller; India: Thompson-Balys.

T285. *Mistress has always said her "Aves": Virgin Mary refuses to help wife against her rival.* The wife tells this to the mistress, who repents. *Ward II 621 No. 30; Herbert III 18; *Crane Vitry 223 No. 223; Wesselski Mönchslatein 190 No. 149; Scala Celi 115a No. 639.

F302.5.1. Fairy mistress surrenders man to his mortal wife. J414.1. Wife chosen instead of fairy mistress. V254.1. Saying of "Aves" obliterates sin.

T286. *Sight of mistress's ring causes husband to withhold himself from his wife.* English: Wells 80 (Sir Tristrem).

T287. *Why separation of a good woman from a bad man is a benefit.* N. A. Indian (Kaska): Teit JAFL XXX 457.

T288. *Wife refuses to sleep with detested husband.*

T160. Consummation of marriage.

T288.1. *Wife curses unbeloved husband who attempts to force her.* India: Thompson-Balys.

T291. *Why widow does not remarry.* (1) Only her property is wanted; (2) her husband is still in her heart; (3) if new husband is bad it will not be well, if he is good there will be the fear that he will die. Pauli (ed. Bolte) No. 222.

J482.1.1. Woman refuses second marriage. If husband is good she will fear to lose him; if bad she will repent. J482.1.2. Widow refuses second marriage so her brother can't kill a second husband. T131.4. Widow may not remarry. T210. Faithfulness in marriage.

T291.1. *Wife keeps vow never to wed after her husband's death.* Spanish Exempla: Keller.

T292. *Wife sold unwillingly by husband.* *Hibbard 8; Irish myth: *Cross.

T292.1. *Wives traded.* Chinese: Graham.

T294. *Husband (wife) of supernatural being longs for old home and visits relatives.* India: *Thompson-Balys; Japanese: Ikeda; Siberian and N. A. Indian: Jochelson JE VI 366.

C713. Forsaken merman. C713.2. Tabu: wife of supernatural husband seeing old home. F374. Longing in fairyland to visit home. T177. Bridegroom magically impelled to leave his bride.

T295. *Husband's indiscreet boast about wife brings about his death.* King regards his wife as so beautiful that he has a friend view her naked through a crack in the wall. Wife learns of his act, goes over to the man who has viewed her, and with the latter brings about the king's death. Italian Novella: *Rotunda.

T296. *Wife buys (sells) privilege of sleeping one night with husband.* (Cf. D2006.1.4.) Jewish: Neuman.

T298. *Reconciliation of separated couple.* India: *Thompson-Balys.

K1814. Woman in disguise wooed by her faithless husband. K1843.2. Wife takes mistress's place in husband's bed. N730. Accidental reunion of families. T96. Lovers reunited after many adventures. T102. Hero returns and marries first love.

T299. *Other aspects of married life—miscellaneous.*

T299.1. *Sleeping with head laid in wife's lap as sign of tenderness.* India: Thompson-Balys.

T299.2. *Wife gives wise warning to husband.*

T299.2.1. *Man warned by wife against stepping on red cloth.* Chinese: Graham.

T299.2.2. *Wife warns departing hero against seductions of women.* Chinese: Graham.

T300—T399. Chastity and celibacy.

T300. Chastity and celibacy. *Penzer III 172 n. 2; *Encyc. Religion Ethics III 474 s.v. "Chastity"; **J. Main Religious Chastity (New York, 1913); *E. Fehrle Die kultische Keuschheit im Altertum (Giessen, 1910). — Irish myth: Cross; Missouri French: Carrière; Jewish: *Neuman.

A476. Goddess of chastity.. C111. Tabu: loss of chastity. D1714.1. Magic power of chaste woman. D1825.4.2. Magic power to see whether girl is a virgin. D1964.1. Savage elephant lulled to sleep by virgin. D2061.2.5. Hunter reduced to ashes by power of heroine's chastity. H400. Chastity test. H412.1. Chastity ordeal: passing under magic rod. H413.4. Special power of chaste woman. M131. Vow of chastity. M133. Vow: man will love only a virgin. Q87. Reward for preservation of chastity. V461.3. Chastity as clerical virtue.

T301. *Sacrifice of virginity.* Penzer I 275f.; *Hartland Tylor Anthropological Volume 189.

T302. *Methods of ascetics.* India: Thompson-Balys.

T310. Celibacy and continence. *Encyc. Religion Ethics III 271ff. s.v. "Celibacy"; Eskimo (Cumberland Sound): Boas BAM XV 163, 166, 261, (Greenland): Rink 410, Rasmussen I 137, 363, III 85, 154, 200, (Central): Boas RBAE VI 583, 637, (Mackenzie Area): Jenness 49.

A1556.2. Origin of celibacy. F112. Journey to Land of Women. F566. Celibate people. J1264. Repartee concerning clerical incontinence.

T310.1. *Ceremonial continence.* *Frazer Fasti IV 206ff.; **E. Fehrle Die kultische Keuschheit im Altertum (Giessen, 1910).

T310.1.1. *"Night of Sabbath" (Friday night) only devoted to conjugal pleasures.* Jewish: *Neuman.

T311. *Woman averse to marriage.* (Cf. T321.1, T327.3.) India: Thompson-Balys.

T311.0.1. *Woman's aversion to marriage motivated through a dream.* Chauvin V 125 No. 59, 130 No. 112.

C168.1. Woman marries in spite of warning dream. Bears blind child who soon dies. D1812.3.3. Future revealed in dream.

T311.1. *Flight of maiden (bridegroom) to escape marriage.* Type 888*; cf. Type 510B; *Toldo II 306; Alphabet No. 310; Irish myth: *Cross; Icelandic: *Boberg; Italian Novella: Rotunda; Greek: Aeschylus Suppliants line 5; India: Thompson-Balys.

R220. Flights. R224. Girl flees to escape incestuous brother. T411.1. Unnatural father wants to marry his daughter.

T311.2. *Woman prefers to remain chaste rather than keep an impotent husband.* (Cf. T271.1.) Italian Novella: Rotunda.

T311.2.1. *Girl commits suicide rather than marry man she does not love.* Chinese: Eberhard FFC CXX 262.

T311.3. *Girl remains a virgin after both her suitors are killed in battle.* Italian Novella: Rotunda.

T311.4. *Maiden queen prefers to fight instead of marrying,* but is at last conquered and married. Icelandic: Herrmann Saxo II 292, *Boberg.

T312. *Saint's daughter dies when wooed.* Alphabet No. 390.

T312.1. *Woman dies when spoiled of her sanctity.* Irish myth: Cross.

T313. *Ravished girl's virginity restored by Virgin Mary.* Ward II 703 No. 33; *Hibbard 12ff.

D1387. Magic object preserves chastity.

T313.1. *Ravished girl's virginity restored by saint.* *Loomis White Magic 85; Irish myth: *Cross.

T313.1.1. *Pregnant nun's virginity restored through power of saint.* Irish myth: *Cross.

T314. *Father kills daughter lest she become prostitute.* Alphabet No. 774.

T314.1. *Father kills daughter lest she become the property of a tyrant.* Italian Novella: Rotunda.

T471.3. Husband sends wife poison to avoid having her ravished by the enemy.

T315. *Continence in marriage.*

T315.1. *Marital continence by mutual agreement.* Pauli (ed. Bolte) No. 689; Chaucer Second Nun's Tale (St. Cecelia); *Toldo II 304ff.; Jewish: *Neuman, Gaster Exempla 200 No. 73.

T315.2. *The continent husband.* (Cf. T271.)

T315.2.1. *The audacious water and the continent husband.* A woman with a continent husband (lover) splashes water on her thighs as she crosses a stream and then reproves it for being bolder than her husband. She thus calls attention to her situation. *Schoepperle 413ff.; *Köhler-Bolte II 346f.; Irish myth: *Cross.

H13. Recognition by overheard conversation with animals or objects. Person not daring to reveal self directly thus attracts attention and recognition. J1675.3. King's capriciousness censured: the ass in the stream.

T315.2.2. *Wife reproves continent husband by showing conduct of cock and hens.* Nouvelles Récréations No. 32.

T315.2.2.1. *Wife reforms continent husband by having walls of bedroom painted with erotic scenes.* India: Thompson-Balys.

T315.3. *Woman continent in two marriages to become a nun.* Irish myth: Cross.

T317. *The repression of lust.* (Cf. D1356.) Spanish Exempla: Keller.

T317.1. *Repression of lust through sitting in water.* Dickson 92f. nn. 70, 71; Alphabet No. 750.

T317.2. *Repression of lust through prayer.* Alphabet No. 14; Spanish Exempla: Keller.

T317.3. *Repression of lust through preaching.* Alphabet No. 638.

T317.4. *Repression of lust through fasting.* Cent Nouvelles Nouvelles No. 99; Spanish Exempla: Keller; Italian Novella: *Rotunda.

T317.5. *Man and woman in chaste love for twenty-five years.* Italian Novella: Rotunda.

T317.6. *Monk finds that only abuse and cruel treatment from his fellow monks can conquer his lust.* Spanish Exempla: Keller.

T318. *Wife proves her faithfulness.* Had substituted for husband's mistress. Proves legitimacy of her child by producing tokens and by child's missing toe (like her husband's four-toed foot). Italian Novella: *Rotunda.

D659.7. Transformation: wife to mistress. K1843.2. Wife takes mistress's place in husband's bed.

T320. Escape from undesired lover. Heptameron No. 26; Irish myth: Cross; Icelandic: Schlauch Romance in Iceland (New York, 1934) 105f., *Boberg.

D642.3. Transformation to escape lover. D1385.3. Marriage ring protects from devil. D1386. Magic object protects from unwelcome lover. D1386.1. Magic sword protects woman from fairy lover in husband's absence. K522.0.1. Death feigned to escape unwelcome marriage. K675. Sleeping potion given to man who is to pass the night with a girl. K1210. Humiliated or baffled lovers. Q87. Reward for preservation of chastity. R111.1.9. Princess rescued from undesired suitor.

T320.1. *Oft-proved fidelity.* Repeated attempts to seduce innocent woman. She escapes them all. *Types 881, 882, 883AB, 888, 892; *Loomis White Magic 95; Irish myth: *Cross; Italian Novella: *Rotunda; India: Thompson-Balys.

K443.2. Clever wife gets money from those who attempt to seduce her. K2112. Woman slandered as adulteress.

T320.1.1. *Virginity saved in spite of torture.* Undesired suitors give up task. Italian Novella: Rotunda.

T320.2. *Girl kills man who threatens her virtue.* Irish myth: *Cross; Italian Novella: Rotunda; India: Thompson-Balys.

T320.2.1. *Woman escaping from slavery kills man who would ravish her.* Italian Novella: Rotunda.

T320.3. *Bride puts to flight man who attempts to ravish her.* Italian Novella: Rotunda.

T320.3.1. *Widow dons late husband's armor to put would-be ravisher to flight.* Italian Novella: Rotunda.

T320.4. *Wife escapes lust of king by shaming him.* Spanish Exempla: Keller; India: Thompson-Balys.

J81. The dishes of the same flavor. T481.5. King covets his subject's wife.

T320.4.1. *Woman escapes king's lust by inducing bad breath.* India: Thompson-Balys.

T320.5. *Girl gives up wealth and flees to escape lecherous emperor.* Spanish Exempla: Keller.

T320.6. *Wife sets fire to house to escape undesired lover.* India: Thompson-Balys.

T321. *Escape from undesired lover by miracle.* Icelandic: Boberg.

T321.1. *Maid pledged to celibacy is given, at her prayer, a beard.* BP III 242.

T321.2. *Girl named Mary has virginity spared by knight who has bought her.* The Virgin appears to her. *Ward II 628 No. 16, 697 No. 9; Scala Celi 115a No. 641; Von der Hagen III 451.

T321.3. *Girl's virginity spared by knight when he sees her surrounded by the Virgin and her train.* In her straits the girl has prayed for help. *Herbert III 356; Irish: Beal XXI 327.

T321.4. *Girl prays to Virgin to spare her virginity.* Two soldiers quarrel over possessing her. Captain slays her, thus "saving" her. Italian Novella: Rotunda.

T321.5. *Magic sickness (discomfort) prevents lover from raping woman.* Icelandic: *Boberg.

T321.6. *In answer to maiden's prayer saint changes boat's course and guides it to another place.* India: Thompson-Balys.

T322. *Girl strikes man who tries to kiss her.* Pauli (ed. Bolte) Nos. 618, 619.

T322.1. *Woman kicks lecherous monk down the stairs.* Heptameron No. 46A.

T322.2. *Princess threatens to kill amorous king.* French Canadian: Sister Marie Ursule.

T322.3. *Undesired lover drugged and carried out.* India: Thompson-Balys.

T322.4. *Girl pleads vow of chastity to repel lover.* India: Thompson-Balys.

G303.16.19.5. Demon has to serve girl whom he cannot persuade to break vow of chastity. M131. Vow of chastity.

T323. *Escape from undesired lover by strategy.*

K1223. Mistress deceives lover with a substitute.

T323.1. *Princess escapes from undesired lover by fleeing disguised as a bishop.* Italian Novella: Rotunda.

K1812.8. Incognito queen (princess). K1826. Disguise as churchman. K1837. Disguise of woman in man's clothes.

T323.2. *Princess evades unwelcome lover by putting on foul-smelling skin-coat.* India: Thompson-Balys.

T324. *Girl's virginity saved by the kindness of an emissary.* Makes the lord believe she is a relative. Italian Novella: Rotunda.

T325. *Chaste woman resists advances of a conqueror.* Italian Novella: Rotunda.

T325.1. *Chaste woman promises conqueror drug of invulnerability.* Has him try it on her. Cuts her head off. *Bonner Byzantion XIV 142ff.

T326. *Suicide to save virginity.* Spanish Exempla: Keller.

M149.2. Vow rather to die than marry unwelcome suitor.

T326.1. *Girls drown selves to save their virginity.* Alphabet No. 773; Italian Novella: Rotunda.

T326.2. *Man is killed defending sweetheart's honor.* She kills herself. Italian Novella: Rotunda.

T326.3. *Martyrdom to preserve virginity.* Der Heiligen Leben und Leiden 100ff. (Santa Barbara).

T327. *Mutilation to repel lover.* (Cf. S160, T333.) Heptameron No. 10; Irish myth: Cross; India: Thompson-Balys.

T327.1. *Maiden sends to her lecherous lover (brother) her eyes (hands, breasts) which he has admired.* Type 706; **Williamson Philological Quarterly XI 149; *BP I 303; *Crane Vitry 158 No. 57; Herbert III 72, 611; Hervieux IV No. 120; *Penzer III 20f.; Alphabet No. 136; *bin Gorion Born Judas[2] IV 175, 283; Pauli (ed. Bolte) Nos. 11, 12; Krappe Bulletin Hispanique XXXIX 40; Nouvelles de Sens No. 12. — Spanish Exempla: Keller; Italian: Basile Pentamerone III No. 2; N. A. Indian: *Thompson Tales 273 n. 6; Africa (Bangola): Weeks 122.

T327.2. *Woman successfully prays for disease to repel lover.* India: Thompson-Balys.

T327.3. *Saint plucks out her eye when urged to marry.* Irish myth: *Cross.

T327.4. *Maidens befoul selves with blood to escape rape.* Spanish Exempla: Keller.

T327.5. *Woman raises sores on her body to preserve chastity.* India: Thompson-Balys.

T327.6. *Princess takes on loathsome disguise to avoid unwelcome demon-lover.* India: Thompson-Balys.

T327.7. *Girl escapes from undesired lover by cutting off her plaits of hair.* Lithuanian: Balys Index No. 871*; Russian: Andrejev No. 871*.

T328. *Girl lives in sepulchre to preserve chastity.* Scala Celi 33a No. 184.

T330. Anchorites under temptation. *Toldo II 304ff.; *Loomis White Magic 187 n. 140; Italian Novella: Rotunda.

D733.1. Hairy anchorite. Beast-like man seduced by beautiful woman becomes human and handsome. Q537.2. Cleric tempts self among beautiful women; lives chastely. T75.5. Scorned lover becomes an anchorite. V131.1. Sight of holy fringe on garment restrains a man from fornication and reforms the harlot.

T331. *Man unsuccessfully tempted by woman.* (St. Anthony.) Alphabet Nos. 128, 795; Wesselski Mönchslatein 103 No. 87; Krappe Bulletin Hispanique XXXIX 30; Irish myth: *Cross; Spanish Exempla: Keller; Jewish: *Neuman, Gaster Exempla 192 Nos. 34, 34A; India: *Thompson-Balys; Buddhist myth: Malalasekera I 168, 887, 1034, II 37, 226, 594, 616, 707, 716, 892, 996, 1052, 1214, 1322.

C686. Injunction: to forsake woman who arouses love. T55. Girl as wooer. T71. Woman scorned in love. T317. The repression of lust. V461.3. Chastity as a clerical virtue. W34.1. Man constrained to flee with leader's fiancée resists her blandishments.

T331.1. *Monk unsuccessfully tempted in nunnery.* Alphabet No. 127.

T331.2. *Knight unsuccessfully tempted by host's wife.* **Kittredge Gawain and the Green Knight.

T281. Sex hospitality. Host gives his wife (daughter) to his guest as bed companion.

T331.3. *Woman masks as man to deceive anchorite.* Toldo I 347.

T331.4. *No place secret enough for fornication.* Monk thus repels temptress. Herbert III 21; *Crane Vitry 243f. Nos. 256, 257.

U232. No place secret enough for sin. V465.1.2.2. Nun tempted into sinning with man who tells her God can't see things that happen in the dark.

T331.5. *Anchorite saved by a miracle.* When he is about to give in to temptation a dove flies out of his mouth. On repenting the dove re-enters his mouth. Italian Novella: *Rotunda.

T331.6. *Saint flogs woman who tempts him.* Irish myth: Cross.

Q227. Punishment for opposition to holy person. Q458. Flogging as punishment.

T331.7. *Saint sleeps with maidens without sinning.* Another saint, who doubts fact, undergoes same test and perceives its effacy. Irish myth: Cross.

T331.8. *Monk unsuccessfully tempted by woman he formerly loved.* Heptameron No. 64.

T331.9. *Monk yells "thief" to repel temptress.* When she seeks him in his bed he screams. He says she steals his most valuable possession, virtue. Spanish Exempla: Keller.

T332. *Man tempted by fiend in woman's shape.* (Or woman by fiend in man's shape.) *Kittredge Witchcraft 211, 525 n. 49; *Herbert III 357ff.; Chauvin II 226 No. 3; Gaster Exempla 213 No. 136; *Toldo II 307ff., 310ff.; Pauli (ed. Bolte) No. 887; Wesselski Mönchslatein 72 No. 63; Alphabet No. 257. — Lithuanian: Balys Index No. 816*; Finnish-Swedish: Wessman 11 No. 86; Spanish Exempla: Keller; Italian Novella: *Rotunda.

D12. Transformation: man to woman. F471.2. Incubus. A demon who comes in sleep and has sexual intercourse with one. G303.9.4.6. Devil tempts saints. G303.9.4.7. Devil tempts girl.

T332.1. *Woman sent by deity to tempt self-righteous anchorite.* India: Thompson-Balys.

T333. *Man mutilates himself to remove temptation.* *Mensa Philosophica No. 104; Italian Novella: Rotunda.

S160. Mutilations. T327. Mutilation to repel lover. V256.3 Saint cuts off hand to repress lust.

T333.1. *Tempted man bites out his tongue and spits it in temptress's face.* *Herbert III 343; Alphabet No. 138; Scala Celi 15b No. 186.

T333.2. *Tempted man burns off his fingers.* Frightens his temptress. Wesselski Mönchslatein 23 No. 18; *Crane Vitry 236 No. 246; Herbert III 20; Scala Celi 13b No. 80; *Krappe Bulletin Hispanique XXXIX 34. — Spanish Exempla: Keller; Italian Novella: Rotunda.

T333.3. *Man disfigures his face to remove temptation.* Alphabet No. 659; Spanish Exempla: Keller.

T333.3.1. *Tempted rabbi tears out his eyes to escape temptation.* Jewish: Neuman.

T333.4. *Tempted holy man mutilates genitals.* Irish myth: Cross; Jewish: Neuman.

T333.5. *Hero cuts off head and wraps it in napkin so he will not be tempted by sight of virgins.* India: Thompson-Balys.

T334. *Monk cures himself of desire for dead sweetheart.* He digs up her remains. *Crane Vitry 236 No. 245; Herbert III 20.

T85.4.1. Ring of Fastrada.

T334.1. *Monk goes into desert to avoid temptation of women, the prime source of sin.* Spanish Exempla: Keller.

T335. *Saint exposes self to temptation but preserves chastity.* Thus insures self greater reward in Heaven. Irish myth: *Cross:

T336. *Sight or touch of woman as source of sin.* Alphabet Nos. 16, 527, 732, 776; Scala Celi 121b, 156b Nos. 666, 874; Mensa Philosophica No. 104; Herbert III 343, 434; Spanish Exempla: *Keller.

T336.1. *Woman's girdle as source of sin.* Pauli (ed. Bolte) No. 378.

T336.2. *Woman's voice as source of sin.* Jewish: Neuman.

T337. *Woman wagers that she can seduce anchorite.* Alphabet No. 528; Italian Novella: *Rotunda.

N15. Chastity wager. V229.20. Downfall of an ascetic (saint).

T337.1. *Saint's enemy, wishing to cause saint to violate his oath never to "commit folly and utter lie," induces his daughter to tempt saint.* Saint perceives trick and avoids sin. Irish myth: Cross.

T338. *Virtuous man seduced by woman.* Nouvelles de Sens No. 15; India: Thompson-Balys.

T338.1. *Ascetic successfully tempted: kills son born in consequence.* India: Thompson-Balys.

T350. Chaste sleeping together. Irish myth: *Cross.

C117. Nuptial tabu. Husband and wife forbidden intercourse for definite time. H1472. Test: sleeping by princess three nights without looking at her or disturbing her. H1556.4.1. Lover's fidelity tested by going to bed with mistress and only kissing.

T351. *Sword of chastity.* A two-edged sword is laid between the couple sleeping together. *Type 303; *BP I 554, IV 202; *Cox Cinderella 488 n. 21; *Huet Romania XXXVI 50; *Chauvin V 62 No. 19 n. 2, VIII 194 No. 235 n. 1; *Fb "sværd" III 690a; Hdwb. d. Märchens I 104a; Gaster Exempla 242 No. 330; *Hibbard 69 n. 8; Tardel Untersuchungen zur mittelhochdeutschen Spielmannspoesie (Schwerin, 1894) 22 n. 2; Thien 24; Günter Die christliche Legende des Abendlandes 21; *Schoepperle II 430ff.; Köhler-Bolte Zs. f. Vksk. VI 76 (to Gonzenbach No. 40); Child V 497 s.v. "sword". — Irish myth: Cross; Icelandic: *Boberg; Italian: Basile Pentamerone I No. 9, *Rotunda; Jewish: *Neuman; India: Thompson-Balys.

K1311.1. Husband's twin brother mistaken by woman for her husband.

T351.1. *Bed-cover of chastity.* Similar to sword of chastity. Italian: Basile Pentamerone I No. 7.

T352. *Boy sleeps between couple to safeguard their virtue.* Irish myth: *Cross.

T353. *Object set between beds of couple sleeping in same room.* Irish myth: *Cross.

T354. *Chaste sleeping together to torment woman.* Man remains utterly impassive. India: Thompson-Balys.

T355. *Chaste sleeping together with six sisters-in-law one by one.* India: Thompson-Balys.

T356. *Young man sleeps on girl's mat without touching her to signify his desire.* S. A. Indian (Brazil): Oberg Mato Grosso 110.

T360. Chastity and celibacy—miscellaneous.

P12.9. Kings overcomes passion for beautiful captives and sends them back untouched to their people.

T362. *Nun refuses to look at man.*

T362.1. *Nun so opposed to seeing men that she refuses to see St. Martin.* Spanish Exempla: Keller.

F647.4. Marvelous sensitiveness: woman blushes in presence of male statue.

T371. *The boy who had never seen a woman: the Satans.* When he sees a girl and asks his father what it is, the father tells him it is Satan. Asked what he most likes he says, "The Satans." *Type 1678; *Chauvin III 105 No. 16; Herbert III 5; *Crane Vitry 169f. No. 82; Alphabet No. 170; Scala Celi 15b No. 89; Boccaccio Decameron IV (proem) (*Lee 110); Nouvelles de Sens No. 2. — U.S.: Baughman; Spanish Exempla: Keller; Italian Novella: *Rotunda; Jewish: bin Gorion Born Judas IV 169, 282.

J147. Child confined to keep him in ignorance of life. Useless. L122. Unsophisticated hero. T617. Boy reared in ignorance of the world.

T371.1. *Boy is denied sight of all women except his mother and his nurse until he is eighteen.* He falls in love with the first woman who is more attractive than his mother. Italian Novella: Rotunda.

T372. *Adulterous love changed into a chaste one.* Italian Novella: Rotunda.

T373. *Heavy chastity belt imposed on wife.* Italian Novella: Rotunda.

T376. *Young man betrothed to statue.* Man puts marriage ring on finger of statue of Venus (Virgin Mary). She afterwards forbids him the embraces of an earthly bride. **Baum PMLA XXXIV 523ff.; Alphabet Nos. 48, 465, 656; Ward II 609 No. 22, 621 No. 31, 626 No. 7; Scala Celi 111b No. 620.

T376.1. *Man leaves earthly bride for service of Virgin.* *Crane Miraculis 89 No. 16, 98 No. 35; Wesselski Mönchslatein 60 No. 51; Wells 170; Spanish Exempla: Keller.

T177. Bridegroom magically impelled to leave his bride.

T381. *Imprisoned virgin to prevent knowledge of men (marriage, impregnation).* Usually kept in a tower. (Danaë.) *Types 310, 516; *Krappe Balor 2ff., 11 nn. 38, 39; *Hertel Zs. f. Vksk. XIX 83ff. (chest on water); *Rösch FFC LXXVII 103, 107f.; *Krappe Le Moyen Age 96ff.; *Loomis White Magic 119. — Irish myth: *Cross; Italian Novella: Rotunda; Greek: *Frazer Apollodorus I 153 n. 3, 154 n. 1, *Hartland Perseus chap. 1; Babylonian: Spence 157; Jewish: *Neuman; India: *Thompson-Balys; Korean: Zong in-Sob 5 No. 2; N. A. Indian: *Thompson Tales 277 n. 21b; West Indies: Flowers 578.

C756.2. Tabu: letting sun shine on girl before she is thirty years old. D1965.1. Guardian magically made to sleep while lover visits maiden. K1349.4. Lover visits guarded maiden while harper puts mother to sleep. M372. Confinement in tower to avoid fulfillment of prophecy. R41. Captivity in tower (castle, prison). S322.1.3. Father condemns daughter to death because he believes her unchaste. T50.1. Girl carefully guarded from suitors. T521. Conception from sunlight.

T381.0.1. *Girl intended for marriage with king cloistered.* Irish myth: *Cross.

T381.0.2. *Wife imprisoned in tower (house) to preserve chastity.* Italian Novella: *Rotunda.

T381.1. *Guarded maiden first seen by hero in church.* *Type 516; Rösch FFC LXXVII 103; Icelandic: Boberg.

N711.4. Prince sees maiden at church and is enamored.

T381.1.1. *Guarded maiden first seen by hero in otherworld.* Irish myth: Cross.

T382. *Attempt to keep wife chaste by carrying her in box.* In spite of all precautions she meets men. *Hertel Zs. f. Vksk. XIX 83ff.; Wesselski Märchen 185; Jewish: *Neuman; India: *Thompson-Balys; Buddhist myth: Malalasekera II 1053; Japanese: Ikeda.

F1034.2. Magician carries mistress with him in his body. She in turn has paramour in hers. K1510. Adulteress outwits husband.

T383. *Other futile attempts to keep wife chaste.* Italian Novella: *Rotunda.

T386. *Message of chastity: uncooked meat left behind.* Man conducting a woman leaves uncooked meat behind each night of the journey as a sign to the husband following that she has not been touched. *Schoepperle II 414, 419; Irish myth: *Cross.

T400—T499. Illicit sexual relations.

T400. Illicit sexual relations.

C110. Sex tabu. K1300. Seduction or deceptive marriage. K1500. Deception connected with adultery. Q240. Sexual sins punished.

T401. *Virgin Mary as protectress of illicit lovers.* Ward II 604 No. 8, 606 No. 14, 612 No. 29, 618 No. 39, 621 No. 30, 626 No. 6, 638 No. 6, 650 No. 1, *663 No. 12, 668 No. 15; Herbert III 24; *Crane Vitry 257 No. 282, Miraculis 308 No. 2; *Pauli (ed. Bolte) No. 887; Wells 166f. (Vernon Miracles Nos. 3, 7); Wesselski Mönchslatein 47 No. 40, 72 No. 63.

K1841.1. The nun who saw the world (Sister Beatrice). The Virgin takes the place of the nun in the nunnery while the latter is living a life of shame. V250. The Virgin Mary. V465.1.2. Incontinent nun.

T401.1. *Pregnant abbess secretly delivered of her child by Virgin Mary.* *Wesselski Mönchslatein 51 No. 44; *Crane Miraculis 99 No. 36; Alphabet No. 13; Spanish Exempla: Keller; Italian Novella: Rotunda.

T410. Incest. **O. Rank Das Inzest-Motiv in Dichtung und Sage (Leipzig u. Wien, 1912); *Child V 484 s.v. "Incestuous"; Irish myth: *Cross; Arabian: Burton Nights I 110 n., II 172 n.; India: Thompson-Balys; Indo-Chinese: Dixon 165 *n. 47; Indonesia: Dixon 172.

A112.1. God from incestuous union. A751.1. Man in the moon is person thrown or sent there as punishment for incest. A1006.2. New race from incest after world calamity. A1018.2. Flood as punishment for incest. A1273.1. Incestuous first parents. C114. Tabu: incest. D1741.6. Loss of magic power through incest. N365. Incest unwittingly committed. N681.3. Incest accidentally averted. Q242. Incest punished. S312.1. Child of incest exposed.

T410.1. *Master discovers that slave girl he wants to marry is a near relative.* Type 938*; U.S.: Baughman.

T411. *Father-daughter incest.* *Köhler-Bolte II 190ff.; *Krappe Review of Religion (1941) 3—17; Heptameron No. 30. — Irish myth: *Cross, MacCulloch Celtic 74f.; English: Wells 176 (The Tale of an Incestuous Daughter); Danish: De la Saussaye 166 (Helgi); Italian Novella: Rotunda; Greek: Grote I 149; India: *Thompson-Balys; Hindu: Keith 75 (Prajāpati); Maori: Dixon 164 n. 46; Eskimo (Greenland): Rasmussen III 198.

M344.1. Father-daughter incest prophecy. N365.2. Unwitting father-daughter incest. V132.1. Holy water prevents a man from committing incest with his daughter.

T411.1. *Lecherous father.* Unnatural father wants to marry his daughter. (Manekine.) *Types 510B, 706; BP I 295ff., *301 n. 5, II 45ff.; *Hibbard 25ff.; *Cox Nos. 131—208; Saintyves Perrault 187ff.; Köhler-Bolte I 420, II 184ff.; Wienert FFC LVI *83 (ET 497), 115 (ST 256); Cosquin Études 3ff.; Rohde Der griechische Roman 37ff., 448; Dickson 199. — Irish myth: Cross; English: Wells 129 (Emare); Swiss: Jegerlehner Oberwallis 325 No. 6; Breton: Sébillot Incidents s.v. "père"; Italian: Basile Pentamerone II No. 6, III No. 2, *Rotunda; Greek: *Frazer Apollodorus I 46 n. 1; India: Thompson-Balys; N. A. Indian: *Thompson Tales 304 n. 109p; Africa (Ibo, Nigeria): Thomas 139.

S322.1.2. Father casts daughter forth when she will not marry him. T311.1. Flight of maiden to escape marriage.

T411.1.1. *Father by trickery secures priest's advice to marry his own daughter.* If a man raise a lamb, shall he eat it himself or let another eat it? *Cosquin Études 9.

K1350. Woman persuaded (or wooed) by trick.

T411.1.2. *Father feigning death returns in disguise and seduces daughter.* N. A. Indian: **Schmerler JAFL XLIV 196ff.

K1315. Seduction by impostor. K1325. Seduction by feigned death.

T411.2. *Girl got with child by intoxicated father.* Irish myth: *Cross.

T411.2.1. *Daughters seduce drunken father.* Jewish: *Neuman.

T412. *Mother-son incest.* *Types 931, 933; *Sparnaay 50ff.; Köhler-Bolte II 173ff., 182ff. — Irish: MacCulloch Celtic 90, *Cross; English: Wells 116 (Sir Eglamour of Artois); Danish: Grundtvig No. 294; Jewish: *Neuman; India: *Thompson-Balys; Buddhist myth: Malalasekera II 603; Oceanic: Dixon 164 nn. 33—44; Indonesia: Hambruch Malaiische Märchen 299, Bezemer Volksdichtung aus Indonesien 81; S. A. Indian (Chiriguano): Métraux RMLP XXXIII 162.

A164.1.1. Mother-son marriage of the gods. G303.11.1.1. The devil's son is with his mother at night in his father's place. H94.8. Recognition by medallion. Prevents incest. M344. Mother-incest prophecy. In spite of all precautions the youth marries his mother. N365.1. Boy unwittingly commits incest with his mother. N383.3. Mother dies of fright when she learns that she was about to commit incest with her son. N681.3.1. Man about to consummate marriage with own mother when he is identified by a plaque. P231. Mother and son.

T412.1. *Mother guilty of incest with son forgiven by Pope (Virgin Mary).* Wesselski Mönchslatein 21 No. 16; Alphabet Nos. 206, 320; Spanish Exempla: Keller.

T412.2. *Incognito son tempts mother to see whether all women are wicked.* Scala Celi 87a No. 509; Icelandic: Gerling Islandzk Æventyri 7 No. 1.

T412.3. *Mother guilty of incest with son whose honor she is testing.* Heptameron No. 30.

T412.4. *Boy courts his mother, is driven off by father.* Africa (Konnoh): Willans 136.

T415. *Brother-sister incest.* *Type 933; *Bolte Zs. f. Vksk. XXVIII 75; *Sparnaay 30; Köhler-Bolte II 173ff., 182ff.; Baum PMLA XXXI 562 n. 59; Schröder Germanisch-Romanische Monatschrift XIX 13; Chauvin V 197 No. 115; *Krappe Archiv für das Studium der neueren Sprachen 167 (1935) 161—176; Heptameron Nos. 30, 33. — Irish: MacCulloch Celtic 25, 90, *Cross; Welsh: MacCulloch Celtic 98; Icelandic: De la Saussaye 251, Boberg; Spanish Exempla: Keller; Italian Novella: Rotunda; Persian: Carnoy 310; Egyptian: Müller 119; Jewish: Neuman; India: *Thompson-Balys; Philippine: Dixon 164 n. 45; N. A. Indian: *Thompson Tales 274 n. 8; Africa (Fang): Einstein 189.

A511.1.3.2. Demigod son of king's unmarried sister by her brother. A736.1.1. Sun sister and moon brother. A1331.2. Paradise lost because of brother-sister incest. A1552.1. Why brother and sisters do not marry. F1075. Blood of brother and sister (and smoke from their funeral pyres) refuses to mingle. N365.3. Unwitting brother-sister incest. P253. Sister and brother. Q541.3. Penance: Gregory on the stone. Standing on a stone (pillar) as penance for incest. R321.1. Sister escapes to the stars to avoid marrying brother. T550.3. Misshapen child from brother-sister incest.

T415.1. *Lecherous brother.* Wants to seduce (marry) his sister. Lithuanian: Balys Index No. 314A*; Spanish Exempla: Keller; India: *Thompson-Balys; Chinese: Werner 408; N. A. Indian: *Thompson Tales 305 n. 109.

T415.2. *Brother repels incestuous sister.* *Bolte Zs. f. Vksk. XXVIII 75; N. A. Indian: *Demetrocoupoulou JAFL XLVI 101—125.

T415.3. *Lovers reared as brother and sister learn to their joy that they are not related.* *Bolte Zs. f. Vksk. XXVIII 75; Italian Novella: *Rotunda.

T415.4. *Two lovers give each other up when they learn that they are brother and sister.* *Bolte Zs. f. Vksk. XXVIII 75; India: Thompson-Balys.

T415.5. *Brother-sister marriage.* Icelandic: Boberg; Greek: Fox 164 (Zeus and Hera), *Frazer Pausanias II 84; India: Thompson-Balys; N. A. Indian (Klikitat): Jacobs UWash II 31; Africa (Fang): Tessman 185.

A164.1. Brother-sister marriage of the gods. A1552.3. Brother-sister marriage of children of first parents.

T415.6. *Suicide to prevent brother-sister marriage.* India: Thompson-Balys.

T415.7. *When boy cannot have his sister for a wife he asks for one of her eyes and ears instead.* India: Thompson-Balys.

T417. *Son-in-law seduces mother-in-law.* Italian Novella: Rotunda; N. A. Indian: *Thompson Tales 305 n. 109s.

T417.1. *Mother-in-law seduces son-in-law.* Italian Novella: *Rotunda; S. A. Indian (Guaporé): Lévi-Strauss BBAE CXLIII (3) 379.

K1315.7.1. Seduction by pretending to instruct (or to need instruction) for marital duties.

T418. *Lustful stepmother.* Irish myth: *Cross; Icelandic: *Boberg; Italian Novella: *Rotunda; Greek: Euripides Hippolytus; S. A. Indian (Viracocha): Steward-Métraux BBAE CXLIII (3) 551.

K2111. Potiphar's wife.

T418.1. *Lustful stepfather.* Italian Novella: *Rotunda.

T421. *Man marries his aunt (mother's sister).* Irish myth: *Cross; Greek: Frazer Apollodorus II 98 n. 1.

T423. *Youth attempts to seduce his grandmother.* Cent Nouvelles Nouvelles No. 50; Italian Novella: *Rotunda.

T425. *Brother-in-law seduces (seeks to seduce) sister-in-law.* Irish myth: *Cross; India: *Thompson-Balys.

T450. Prostitution and concubinage. *Encyc. Religion Ethics III 809 s.v. "concubinage"; *Penzer X 272 s.v. "prostitution", X 288 s.v. "sacred prostitution"; Pauli (ed. Bolte) No. 218; Irish myth: *Cross; Italian Novella: Rotunda; India: *Thompson-Balys.

E411.2.1. Priest's concubine cannot rest in grave. E501.2.4. Courtisans in wild hunt. E501.5.1.2. Prostitutes pursued in wild hunt. J229.4. Better send an ugly woman to the devil than a pretty one. Man chooses ugly mistress. J1115.8. Clever prostitute. J1351. Women call each other prostitutes. J1551.1. Imagined intercourse, imagined payment. K425. King's daughter put into brothel to catch thief. Q243.1.1. Harlot punished by being burned in hell fire.

T450.1. *Wife born to be prostitute.* Husband unable to change her ways, submits to them. Cent Nouvelles Nouvelles No. 91.

T450.2. *Woman disappointed in love threatens to become prostitute.* India: *Thompson-Balys.

T450.3. *Prostitution to avoid starvation.* India: *Thompson-Balys.

T450.4. *Prostitute has favorite lover.* India: Thompson-Balys.

T451. *Devil causes girl to become prostitute.* Destroys the girl's family and begets on her a boy. English: Wells 42 (Arthour and Merlin).

T452. *Bawds.* Professional go-betweens. *Chauvin VI 17 No. 189 n. 1; Bødker Exempler 280 No. 23; Spanish Exempla: Keller.

T452.1. *Mother acts as procuress of bedmate for her son.* India: Thompson-Balys.

T453. *Getting advice from a woman in bed.* Icelandic: *Boberg.

C195. Tabu: taking the advice of a woman. J155. Wisdom (knowledge) from women. J155.8. Wisdom from a harlot to a king. N131.1. Luck changed after cohabitation.

T453.1. *Hero learns feats of arms through gratifying woman's lust.* Irish myth: *Cross.

T453.2. *Prostitute gets advice from customer.* India: Thompson-Balys.

T455. *Woman sells favors for particular purpose.* Irish myth: *Cross.

H551.2. Woman gives self to solver of riddles. K1353.1. Trickster offers food for woman's favors which will completely satisfy him. K1357. Youth tricks lady with promise of shoes. K1358. Girl shows herself naked in return for youth's dancing hogs. K1361. Beggar buys right to sleep before the girl's door, at foot of bed, in the bed. K1361.2. Progressive purchase of favors: the anatomical progression. K2231. Treacherous mistress. M200. Bargains and promises.

T455.1. *Woman sells favors to obtain a jewel.* Icelandic: MacCulloch Eddic 123 (Freja), 176 (Frigg); Spanish: Boggs FFC XC 108 No. 900A*.

T455.1.1. *Woman sells favors to obtain many jewels.* India: *Thompson-Balys.

T455.2. *Woman sacrifices her honor to free her husband (brother) from prison.* *Bolte Zs. f. Vksk. XII 65.

K1353. Woman deceived into sacrificing honor. Ruler promises to release her brother (husband) but afterwards refuses to do so. T211. Faithfulness to marriage in death.

T455.2.1. *Woman commits adultery to obtain aid for husband in battle.* Irish myth: *Cross.

T455.3. *Woman sells favors for beautiful clothes.* Italian: Basile Pentamerone IV No. 10.

T455.3.1. *Women sells favors for new shoes.* (Cf. K1357.) Type 1731; Italian Novella: Rotunda.

T455.4. *Parents urge girl to trade her favors for truce with hostile warrior.* Irish myth: *Cross.

T455.5. *Woman gives favors to pay for help across river.* India: Thompson-Balys.

T455.6. *Woman sells favors for large sum of money (property).* India: *Thompson-Balys.

T455.7. *Princess gives herself to Turks of her own accord in order to save her people.* India: Thompson-Balys.

T456. *Bed-partner to receive payment from first man she meets in the morning.* It so happens: she marries the man and he makes her wealthy. Greek: Roscher Lexikon s.v. "Acca".

N125.4. Districts named for first person met in each. N700. Accidental encounters. T62. Princess to marry first man who asks for her.

T456.1. *Girl dares not receive gift from a man as it may be supposed to be payment for her favors.* Icelandic: Lagerholm 21.

T457. *Sacred prostitution.* *Penzer Poison Damsels 131ff.

T458. *Woman enjoys the ravishings of the enemy.* Italian Novella: Rotunda.

T460. Sexual perversions.

T461. *Person enamored of an object.*

T117. Marriage of person and object.

T461.1. *Woman enamored of a river.* Greek: *Frazer Apollodorus I 82 n. 1.

T461.2. *Women cohabit with magic house pillars.* Eskimo (Greenland): Rink 442, Rasmussen I 223.

T461.3. *Tree as wife.* Koryak: Jochelson JE VI 367, 255, 275; Eskimo (Greenland): Rasmussen III 101; N. A. Indian: *Thompson Tales 304 n. 1090.

T462. *Lesbian love.* Jewish: Neuman; India: Thompson-Balys.

T462.1. *Lesbian love: women give birth to monsters as result.* India: Thompson-Balys; N. A. Indian (Navaho): Matthews MAFLS V 81, (Fox): Jones PAES I 151ff.

C101. Sex tabu broken: child born without bones. F112. Journey to Land of Women.

T463. *Homosexual love (male).* Icelandic: Corpus Poeticum Boreale I 137; Spanish Exempla: Keller; Italian Novella: Rotunda; Jewish: *Neuman; India: Thompson-Balys.

C113. Tabu: sodomy. K1843.2.4. Wife substitutes for sodomist husband. Q253. Sodomy punished.

T465. *Bestiality.* Intercourse of a human being and an animal. Irish myth: *Cross; Jewish: *Neuman, Leviticus 18: 23; Babylonian: Gilgamesch-Epos VII; India: Thompson-Balys; West Indies: Flowers 578.

B23.1. Minotaur. B600. Marriage of person to animal. Q253.1. Bestiality punished.

T465.1. *Sheep born with human head as a result of bestiality.* Wienert FFC LVI 38f.

T465.2. *Foal born of Loki after dealing with mythical stallion.* Icelandic: MacCulloch Eddic 90.

T465.3. *Homocentaurus born as a result of bestiality.* Icelandic: *Boberg; Greek: Fox 61.

T465.4. *Children are spotted like leopards as result of bestiality.* U.S.: Baughman.

T465.5. *Pig born with head like that of man as a result of bestiality.* U.S.: Baughman.

T466. *Necrophilism: sexual intercourse with dead human body.* Spanish Exempla: Keller; Jewish: *Neuman; India: Thompson-Balys.

E474. Cohabitation of living person and ghost. T16.2. Man falls in love on seeing dead body of a beautiful girl.

T467. *The amorous bite.* Penzer II 305.

T470. Illicit sexual relations—miscellaneous motifs.

T471. *Rape.* Irish myth: *Cross; Icelandic: *Boberg; Italian Novella: *Rotunda; India: Thompson-Balys.

C118. Tabu: violating woman. F304.4. Mortal violates fairy woman. J1174. Clever decisions concerning kissing and rape. M13.1. Ruler has son beheaded for rape. Q244. Punishment for ravisher.

T471.0.1. *Fines imposed for rape.* Irish myth: Cross.

T471.1. *Man unwittingly ravishes his own sister.* (Cf. N365.3.) Finnish: Kalevala rune 35.

T471.2. *Wild man as ravisher of women.* (Cf. F567.) Dickson 120 nn. 58—60.

T471.3. *Husband sends wife poison to avoid having her ravished by the enemy.* Italian Novella: Rotunda.

T314.1. Father kills daughter lest she become the property of a tyrant.

T475. *Unknown (clandestine) paramour.* Irish myth: Cross.

H58. Tell-tale hand-mark. Clandestine lover is identified by paint marks left on his skin by his mistress. H81. Clandestine lover recognized by tokens. H480. Father tests. Tests as to who is unknown father of child. Q256. Death sentence for a clandestine lover of a princess. T645. Paramour leaves token with girl to give their son.

T475.1. *Unknown paramour discovered by string clue.* Japanese: Anesaki 341, Ikeda.

T475.2. *Hero lies by princess in magic sleep and begets child.* Italian: Basile Pentamerone V No. 5; India: Thompson-Balys; Icelandic: Boberg.

D1960. Magic sleep. H81.1. Hero lies by sleeping girl and leaves identification token with her.

T475.2.1. *Intercourse with sleeping girl.* India: Thompson-Balys.

T476. *Incognito mistress.* King's mistress secretly becomes hero's without revealing identity. *Chauvin V 219 No. 129 n. 2.

T481. *Adultery.* *Encyc. Religion Ethics s.v. "adultery"; Irish myth: *Cross; Icelandic: *Boberg; Jewish: *Neuman; India: Thompson-Balys; Eskimo (West Hudson Bay): Boas BAM XV 223, (Mackenzie Area): Jenness 87.

A112.8. God from adulterous union. A164.2. Adultery among the gods. A1556.3. Origin of adultery. B134.1. Dog betrays woman's infidelity. E263. Adulteress returns from dead as devastating dragon. E411.2. Adulterous person cannot rest in grave. F254.5. Fairies commit adultery. F345.2. Supernatural person reveals marital infidelity. J1146. Detection by strewing ashes. Trespasser (lover, mistress, ghost, fairy, etc.) leaves footprints in the ashes. K1500. Deceptions connected with adultery. N386. Lover's wound breaks while he is in bed with mistress. He bleeds to death (or is discovered because of the blood). Q241. Adultery punished. T230. Faithlessness in marriage. T247. Object stolen (left) as token that infidelity has been discovered. N339.11. Woman commits suicide and suffocates baby unintentionally when she discovers her adultery.

T481.1. *Adulteress roughly treated by her lover.* *Fischer-Bolte 217; India: Thompson-Balys.

T481.2. *Queen's illicit passion for diseased man.* Penzer V 181, 183.

T481.2.1. *Queen commits adultery with low-born man.* Africa (Fang): Einstein 162.

T481.3. *Adulteress sells self to devil for money.* Scala Celi 112a No. 625.

T450. Prostitution.

T481.4. *Wife seduces husband's servant (pupil).* Irish myth: *Cross.

T481.5. *King takes subject's wife while her husband is sent away.* Icelandic: *Boberg; Danish: Grundtvig No. 145.

T320.4. Wife escapes lust of king by shaming him.

T481.6. *Queen begets son with duke while the king is in war.* Icelandic: *Boberg.

T481.7. *Woman advises husband to kill guest, else she will make him chase husband and marry her instead.* Icelandic: Boberg.

T482. *Day husband: night husband.* Woman has two husbands: juggler at home only at night, robber only in day. They do not know about each other. (Similarly, day wife: night wife.) Chauvin V 254 No. 151 n. 1.

T484. *Maidservant given to lover's companion as bed-partner.* (Cf. T281.) *Schoepperle I 254ff.; Irish myth: *Cross.

T485. *Fruit-picking time used for sexual promiscuity.* India: Thompson-Balys.

T491. *Man has a son not his wife's; wife has a daughter not her husband's.* Children become lovers. Irish myth: Cross.

T492. *Queen makes all men who come to serve her copulate with her.* India: Thompson-Balys.

T494. *Black nipples of girl's breasts reveal her loss of virginity.* S. A. Indian (Chiriguano): Métraux RMLP XXXIII 154, 159.

T500—T599. Conception and birth.

T500. **Conception and birth.** *Rank Mythus von der Geburt des Helden; **Fellinger Schwangerschaft und Geburt in der altfranzösischen Literatur (Göttingen, 1907); **Hartland Primitive Paternity; *Hdwb. d. Abergl. II 806; McDaniel Conception, Birth and Infancy (Miami, Florida, 1948). — Irish myth: Cross.

A431. God (goddess) of fertility. A477. Goddess of childbirth. A511. Birth and rearing of culture hero. A1221. Mankind from unusual primeval mating. A1234.1. Earth as virgin mother of Adam. A1351. Origin of childbirth. A1560. Origin of customs connected with birth. B144.1. King of fishes prophesies hero's birth. B311. Congenital helpful animal. Born at same time as master and (usually) by same magic means. D1352. Magic object has prenatal influence. D1812.5.0.17. Divination by choice of roads: which son to be born first. F172. No time, no birth, no death in otherworld. F315. Fairy predicts birth of child. H493. Virility test for husband. J1270. Repartee concerning the parentage of children. J2063. Distress over imagined troubles of unborn child. M311. Prophecy: future greatness of unborn child.

T510. **Miraculous conception.** *Type 516; *BP I 544; *Hartland Perseus I 71ff.; *Chauvin V 43 No. 18 n. 1; **Hartland Paternity; Hdwb. d. Abergl. II 808; *Frobenius Zeitalter des Sonnengottes I 223—263; *Rösch FFC LXXVII 96; Hdwb. d. Märchens I "Abstammung, wunderbare"; Loomis White Magic 16. — English: Wells 31 (Geoffrey's life of Arthour), 39 (Nennius' Historia Britonum), 42 (Arthour and Merlin), 101 (King Alisaunder); Breton: Sébillot Incidents s.v. "conceptions", RTP XV 471, 552, 597; Greek: *Frazer Apollodorus I 21 n. 5; Jewish: *Neuman; India: *Thompson-Balys; N. A. Indian: *Thompson Tales 323 n. 166e; S. A. Indian (Tupinamba): Métraux RMLP XXXIII 172.

D1925. Fecundity magically induced. S223. Childless couple promise child to the devil if they may only have one. S271. Sacrifice of child to remove barrenness. V312. Belief in Immaculate Conception.

T511. *Conception from eating.* *BP I 544; *Hartland Perseus I 71ff.; Hdwb. d. Abergl. II 1032; Frobenius Zeitalter des Sonnengottes I 236ff., 250ff.; *Toldo I 337. — Irish myth: *Cross; Jewish: Neuman, Gaster Oldest Stories 84; Egyptian: Müller 115; Indonesia: Dixon 236; Koryak: Jochelson JE VI 324, 380; Eskimo (Greenland): Rink 437, 444, (Bering Strait): Nelson RBAE XVIII 461, (Aleut): Golder JAFL XVIII 85, (Cumberland Sound): Boas BAM XV 248; N. A. Indian: *Thompson Tales 323 n. 166h; S. A. Indian (Central Brazil): Ehrenreich Int. Cong. Americanists XIV 661.

A1411.2. Theft of light by being swallowed and reborn. B635.1.1. Eaten meat of bear lover causes unborn son to have animal characteristics. D1793. Magic results from eating or drinking. D1925.1. Barrenness removed by eating or drinking. J1532.1. The Snow-Child. A sailor's wife bears a son in his absence and says that it came from eating snow. Later the husband makes away with the boy who, he says, melted in the sun.

T511.0.1. *Queen and maidservant conceive from eating same food.* Their sons are like brothers. (Cf. P311.4.) Köhler-Bolte I 512; BP I 545.

T511.1. *Conception from eating a fruit.* (Cf. F611.1.8.) *Type 301; *BP I 544; Chauvin V 43ff.; Gypsy: Aichele Zigeunermärchen 316; Turkish: Manzel Türkische Märchen II No. 7; India: *Thompson-Balys; Chinese: Eberhard FFC CXX 91; Indonesia: Verbeck Malaiische Erzählungen 139; S. A. Indian (Yunca): Alexander Lat. Am. 228, (Huarochiri): Métraux RMLP XXXIII 169.

T511.1.1. *Conception from eating apple.* *Type 708; BP II 236; *Hdwb. d. Märchens I 91a n. 14; Chauvin VI 84 No. 252; *Fb "æble" III 1135b; Irish myth: *Cross; Icelandic: Boberg; India: Thompson-Balys.

D981.1. Magic apple. D1347.1. Magic apple produces fecundity.

T511.1.2. *Conception from eating berry.* Finnish: Kalevala rune 50.

T511.1.3. *Conception from eating mango.* India: *Thompson-Balys.

T511.1.4. *Conception from eating orange.* India: Thompson-Balys.

T511.1.5. *Conception from eating lemon.* Africa (Kordofan): Frobenius IV 216ff. No. 19.

T511.1.6. *Conception from eating a peach.* Chinese: Eberhard FFC CXX 103.

T511.2. *Conception from eating plant.* French: Sébillot France III 528; Jewish: Neuman; India: Thompson-Balys.

T511.2.0.1. *Conception from eating root.* India: *Thompson-Balys.

T511.2.0.2. *Conception from eating leaves.* India: Thompson-Balys.

T511.2.1. *Conception from eating mandrake.* (Cf. D965.1.) **Frazer Old Testament II 372ff.; Loomis White Magic 20.

T511.2.2. *Conception from eating watercress.* Irish myth: Cross.

T511.3. *Conception from eating vegetable.* India: Thompson-Balys.

T511.3.1. *Conception from eating peppercorn.* Rumanian: *Schullerus FFC LXXVIII No. 315A, 327D*.

T511.3.2. *Conception from eating spinach.* India: Thompson-Balys.

T511.4. *Conception from eating flower.* Chinese: Eberhard FFC CXX 92, 108; Indonesia: v. Ronkel Catalogus Malaiische Handschriften te Batavia 153.

T511.4.1. *Conception from eating rose.* Red rose brings boy, white rose a girl. Fb "rose" III 80a; Italian: Basile Pentamerone II No. 8.

T511.5. *Conception from eating animal.*

T511.5.1. *Conception from eating fish.* *Types 301, 705; *BP I 544; Irish myth: *Cross; Indonesia: Jeynboll Supplement Catalogus Sundaneesche Handschriften 26; S. A. Indian (Tupinamba): Métraux MAFLS XL 158.

T511.5.2. *Conception from swallowing worm (in drink of water).* *Schoepperle II 275, 277; MacCulloch Celtic 140; Irish myth: *Cross.

A1411.2. Theft of light by being swallowed and reborn. E607.2. Person transforms self, is swallowed and reborn in new form.

T511.5.3. *Conception from eating louse.* N. A. Indian: Kroeber JAFL XXI 224.

T511.5.4. *Conception from eating bird.* India: Thompson-Balys.

T511.6. *Conception from eating parts of human being.*

T511.6.1. *Conception from eating woman's heart.* *DeVries FFC CX 217ff.; Icelandic: De la Saussaye 263.

T511.6.2. *Conception from eating finger-bones.* S. A. Indian (Bakairi): Alexander Lat. Am. 312, Lévi-Strauss BBAE CXLIII (3) 347.

T511.7. *Conception from eating food.*

T511.7.1. *Conception after eating honey given by lover.* S. A. Indian (Toba): Métraux MAFLS XL 157.

T511.7.2. *Pregnancy from eating an egg.* Chinese: Eberhard FFC CXX 91, 103.

T511.7.3. *Conception from eating meat.* India: Thompson-Balys.

T511.8. *Conception from eating—miscellaneous.*

T511.8.1. *Conception from swallowing a stone.* Chinese: Eberhard FFC CXX 92.

T511.8.2. *Conception from eating medicines.* India: *Thompson-Balys.

T511.8.3. *Conception from eating mess of fairy pottage.* Irish myth: Cross.

T511.8.4. *Conception from eating grain (seed).* India: *Thompson-Balys; Chinese: Eberhard FFC CXX 93.

T511.8.5. *Woman impregnated after accidentally partaking of crane's dung.* India: Thompson-Balys.

T511.8.6. *Conception from swallowing a pearl.* Chinese: Eberhard FFC CXX 92.

T512. *Conception from drinking.* *BP I 544; *Hartland Perseus I 71ff.; *Penzer I 95 n. 2; *Schoepperle II 276; Irish myth: Cross; Hindu: Keith 166; Indonesia: Dixon 238 n. 52; Central Caroline Islands: ibid. 251; Eskimo (Bering Strait): Nelson RBAE XVIII 461.

T512.1. *Conception from drinking elixir from goat's horns.* Penzer III 218.

T512.2. *Conception from drinking urine.* Hdwb. d. Märchens I 85; Frobenius Zeitalter des Sonnengottes I 226ff.; India: *Thompson-Balys; Chinese: Chavannes 500 Contes I 80 No. 23, II 283 No. 342, III 233 No. 453; Indonesia: De Vries Volksverhalen II 362 No. 110; Africa: Frobenius Atlantis II 57.

T512.2.1. *Child develops from man's urine.* S. A. Indian (Mataco): Métraux MAFLS XL 132.

T512.3. *Conception from drinking water.* Icelandic: Herrmann Saxo II 585, Boberg; India: *Thompson-Balys; Chinese: Eberhard FFC CXX 93 No. 51.

T512.3.1. *Conception from drinking holy water.* (Cf. D1242.1.2.) Irish myth: *Cross.

T512.4. *Conception from drinking saint's tears.* Irish myth: Cross.

T512.5. *Impregnation from licking spittle.* India: *Thompson-Balys.

T512.6. *Conception from drinking sperm.* (Cf. T531.1.) Buddhist myth: Malalasekera II 37; S. A. Indian (Chiriguano): Métraux MAFLS XL 159, (Huarochiri): Métraux RMLP XXXIII 169.

T512.7. *Conception from drinking dew.* Chinese: Eberhard FFC CXX 93.

T513. *Conception from wish.* (Cf. T548.1.) *Types 675, 708; *Hartland Primitive Paternity I 27f.; *Fb "frugtsommelig" I 376b, "ønske" III 1178b, 1179a; Missouri French: Carrière; Italian: Basile Pentamerone I No. 3.

T513.1. *Conception through another's wish.* Italian Novella: Rotunda.

T513.1.1. *Impregnation by magician's power.* Eskimo (Greenland): Rink 148, Rasmussen II 217; S. A. Indian (Tupinamba): Métraux RMLP XXXIII 168.

T514. *Conception after reciprocal desire for each other.* India: Thompson-Balys.

T514.1. *Conception after anchorite blesses woman in love with him.* India: Thompson-Balys.

T515. *Impregnation through glance.* England: Baughman; Rumanian: Schullerus FFC LXXVIII No. 315; Cape Verde Islands: Parsons MAFLS XV (1) 289 No. 94.

T515.1. *Impregnation through lustful glance.* N. A. Indian (Yana): Curtin Creation Myths 348. Cf. the "greenclad woman" in Ibsen's Peer Gynt.

T516. *Conception through dream.* *Type 650; Christiansen Norske Eventyr 92; Egyptian: Legrain Louqsor sans les Pharaons 119; Chinese: Ferguson 37, 60, Werner 132, Eberhard FFC CXX 93; Korean: Zong in-Sob 127, 201 Nos. 61, 97.

T517. *Conception from extraordinary intercourse.*

T517.1. *Conception from hand or foot.* *Hartland Primitive Paternity I 19; Icelandic: MacCulloch Eddic 275.

T517.2. *Conception through mother's side.* (Cf. T584.1.) *Hartland Primitive Paternity I 21.

T517.3. *Conception through ear.* *Hartland Primitive Paternity I 19.

T518. *Conception from divine impregnation.* Penzer VIII 114 n. 1; Spanish Exempla: Keller; India: Thompson-Balys; Philippine (Tinguian): Cole 180; S. A. Indian (Chiriguano): Métraux RMLP XXXIII 159.

T521. *Conception from sunlight.* *BP III 89 n. 2; Frazer Golden Bough X 74ff.; Baumann Mensch en Maatschappij VI 263; *Hartland Primitive Paternity I 25ff., 90ff.; Gaster Oldest Stories 169. — India: Thompson-Balys; Chinese: Werner 130, Eberhard FFC CXX 91; Japanese: Ikeda; Korean: Zong in-Sob 5 No. 2; Siberian: Holmberg Siberian 398; Samoa, Fiji: Dixon 165 nn. 49f.; N. A. Indian: *Thompson Tales 277 n. 21a; Aztec: Krickeberg Märchen der Azteken 230, 247; S. A. Indian (Tunja): Alexander Lat. Am. 201, (Karib): Métraux RMLP XXXIII 146, (Warrau): ibid. 145.

C842. Tabu: exposure to sunlight. C756.2. Tabu: letting sun shine on girl before she is thirty years old. D567. Transformation by sunlight. T381. Imprisoned virgin to prevent knowledge of men (marriage, impregnation).

T521.1. *Conception from moonlight.* *Hartland Primitive Paternity I 98: Chinese: Eberhard FFC CXX 91; N. A. Indian: Thompson Tales 277 n. 21a.

T521.2. *Conception from rainbow.* Chinese: Eberhard FFC CXX 92.

T521.3. *Conception from rays of a dragon.* Chinese: Eberhard FFC CXX 91.

T522. *Conception from falling rain.* *Hartland Primitive Paternity I 24; Baumann Mensch en Maatschappij VI 266; N. A. Indian: *Thompson Tales 323 n. 166g.

T523. *Conception from bathing.* (Cf. D1788.) *Hartland Primitive Paternity I 23; Jewish: Neuman; India: Thompson-Balys; Africa (Zulu): Callaway 335.

T524. *Conception from wind.* (Cf. A715.2, F611.1.9.) *Hartland Primitive Paternity I 22; BP II 300; Hdwb. d. Abergl. II 810; Baumann Mensch en Maatschappij VI 264; Finnish: Kalevala rune 1; Chinese: Eberhard FFC CXX 92; Japanese: Ikeda; Minahassa (Celebes): Dixon 158; N. A. Indian: *Thompson Tales 277 n. 21.

T525. *Conception from falling star.* Irish myth: Cross.

T525.1. *Impregnation by star.* Chinese: Eberhard FFC CXX 92.

T525.2. *Impregnation by a comet.* Chinese: Eberhard FFC CXX 92.

T526. *Conception because of prayer.* Korean: Zong in-Sob 4 No. 1.

T527. *Magic impregnation by use of charm (amulet).* India: Thompson-Balys.

T528. *Impregnation by thunder (lightning).* Chinese: Eberhard FFC CXX 91.

T531. *Conception from casual contact with man.* *Hartland Primitive Paternity I 18, 26; Jewish: Neuman; India: Thompson-Balys; Hawaii: Beckwith Myth 229; Philippine (Tinguian): Cole 144; N. A. Indian: *Thompson Tales 323 n. 166f.

B631.3. Fish bears man-children. Has swallowed rinsings of man's mouth.

T531.1. *Conception from having licked semen-stained loincloth.* (Cf. T512.6.) India: Thompson-Balys.

T532. *Conception from other contacts.* Chinese: Eberhard FFC CXX 92, 103; Eskimo (Greenland): Rink 437, Rasmussen III 305; Marquesas: Handy 85; S. A. Indian (Tapirapé): Wagley-Baldão BBAE CXLIII (3) 253.

T532.1. *Conception from contact with magic object.* *Hartland Primitive Paternity I 17f.

T532.1.1. *Conception from plucking flower.* (Cf. C515.) Greek: Fox 190.

T532.1.1.1. *Conception from smelling flower.* Rumanian: Schullerus FFC LXXVIII No. 315; India: Thompson-Balys.

T532.1.2. *Conception from embracing magic tree.* Hindu: Keith 159.

T532.1.2.1. *Conception from embracing holy image.* French: Sébillot France IV 159.

T532.1.3. *Impregnation by leaf of lettuce.* Greek: Fox 166.

T532.1.4. *Conception by smell of cooked dragon heart.* Italian: Basile Pentamerone I No. 9; India: Thompson-Balys.

T532.1.4.1. *Conception after smelling ground bonedust.* India: Thompson-Balys.

T532.2. *Conception from stepping on an animal.* French: Sébillot France III 15.

T532.3. *Conception from fruit thrown against breast.* Indonesia: Bezemer Volksdichtung aus Indonesien 409ff.

T532.3.1. *Conception from flowers hidden in breast.* S. A. Indian (Amuesa): Métraux RMLP XXXIII 129, 149.

T532.4. *Cow touched by arrow becomes pregnant.* N. A. Indian (Blackfoot): Uhlenbeck Blackfoot Texts (Verhandelingen der Akademie van Wetenschappen te Amsterdam, 1912) 18f.

T532.5. *Conception from putting on another's girdle.* Hawaii: Frobenius Zeitalter des Sonnengottes I 225.

T532.5.1. *Conception from touching another's garment.* Buddhist myth: Malalasekera I 376.

T532.6. *Conception from putting ball into bosom.* Mexican: Frobenius Zeitalter des Sonnengottes I 234ff.

T532.7. *Woman becomes pregnant after eagle sits on her head.* India: Thompson-Balys.

T532.8. *Impregnation by shadow of Bhimsen.* India: Thompson-Balys.

T532.8.1. *Conception after shadow of man has fallen on bathing birl.* India: Thompson-Balys.

T532.9. *Miraculous conception from God's bow.* India: Thompson-Balys.

T532.10. *Conception from hiss of cobra.* India: Thompson-Balys.

T533. *Conception from spittle.* (Cf. T541.8.2.) Fb "spytte" III 515b; Philippine (Tinguian): Cole 16, 105; S. A. Indian (Quiché): Alexander Lat. Am. 171, (Maya): Métraux RMLP XXXIII 169, (Mocoví): Métraux MAFLS XL 98.

T534. *Conception from blood.* (Cf. T541.1, T563.2.) *Fb "blod" IV 47a.

T535. *Conception from fire.* (Cf. F611.1.10.) Irish myth: Cross.

T535.1. *Conception from heat of fire.* *Hartland Primitive Paternity I 98ff.

T536. *Conception from feathers falling on woman.* N. A. Indian (Aztec): Alexander Lat. Am. 60.

T537. *Conception from scarification.* Pigeons scarify woman on loins. Africa (Zulu): Callaway 55.

T538. *Unusual conception in old age.* Loomis White Magic 20; Jewish: Neuman; S. A. Indian (Inca): Rowe BBAE CXLIII (2) 318.

T539. *Miraculous conception—miscellaneous.*

T539.1. *Hero enters womb of sleeping woman and is reborn.* India: Thompson-Balys; Hindu: Keith 194, 222.

E607.2. Person transforms self, is swallowed and reborn in new form.

T539.2. *Conception by a cry.* Max Müller Sacred Books of the East V 69, 71 (Persian); cf. Carnoy 289.

T539.3. *Conception from intercourse with demon.* Irish myth: *Cross; Jewish: *Neuman.

C112. Tabu: sexual intercourse with unearthly beings. F301. Fairy lover. F471.2. Incubus (demon lover). F471.2.0.1. Demon lover.

T539.4. *Heifers covered by supernatural bull conceive miraculously.* Irish myth: Cross.

T539.5. *Magic impregnation from faraway husband.* Chinese: Eberhard FFC CXX 102 No. 59.

T540. Miraculous birth. *BP I 544; *Hartland Perseus ch. 4, 5, 6, Primitive Paternity passim; *Fb "barn" IV 27a; *Penzer II 136 n. 1; Jewish: *Neuman; India: Thompson-Balys; Chinese: Eberhard FFC CXX 94 No. 53; Indonesia: DeVries's list Nos. 157, 159; N. A. Indian: *Thompson Tales 323 n. 166.

A511.1. Birth of culture hero. B630. Offspring of marriage to animal. B754.7. Unusual parturition of animal. C33.1. Tabu: mentioning origin of supernatural child. S313. Child of supernatural birth exposed. T578. Pregnant man.

T540.1. *Supernatural birth of saints.* *Toldo I 320 n. 2; Loomis White Magic 20; India: Thompson-Balys; Japanese: Ikeda.

T584.0.3. Birth of holy person painless. V220. Saints.

T541. *Birth from unusual part of person's body.* Irish myth: Cross; Japanese: Ikeda.

T541.1. *Birth from blood.* Greek: *Frazer Apollodorus I 5 n. 4, Fox 6, 262; Philippine (Tinguian): Cole *15, 63, 71, 124.

T541.1.1. *Birth from blood-clot.* Hatt Asiatic Influences 80ff.; Oceanic: *Dixon 109, 251 n. 25; Mono-Alu: Wheeler No. 01; New Hebrides: Codrington 406; N. A. Indian: *Thompson Tales 322 n. 165, (California): Gayton and Newman 68; Africa (Zulu): Callaway 72, 105, (Kaffir): Theal 149.

A1263.1.1. Man created from blood-clot.

T541.1.1.1. *Boy created by saint from blood-clot.* Irish myth: Cross.

T541.2. *Birth from wound or abscess.* *Type 705; Fb "orm" II 759b; Oceanic: Dixon 113, 234 n. 44, 251 nn. 18—22; Haiti: Alexander Lat. Am. 29; Africa: *Werner 156f., 222.

T541.2.1. *Birth from wound or abscess on body of father.* Cosquin Études 257, Contes indiens 196ff.; Moe Samlede Skrifter I 43ff.; Greek: Grote I 10; India: *Thompson-Balys; Philippine (Tinguian): Cole 18 n. 2, 30 n. 3, 38, 81, 87, 144, 151; N. A. Indian: *Thompson Tales 341 nn. 228, 229; Africa (Mkulwe): Einstein 18f.

T541.2.1.1. *Child born of splinter in hand (foot).* India: Thompson-Balys; N. A. Indian: *Thompson Tales 341 n. 228.

T541.3. *Birth from tears.* India: Thompson-Balys; Hindu: Keith 141; N. A. Indian: *Thompson Tales 323 n. 166a.

T541.4. *Birth from person's head.* *Fb "barn" IV 27a; Greek: *Frazer Apollodorus I 25 n. 2; India: Thompson-Balys; Hindu: Keith 121.

T541.4.1. *Birth from mouth.* Jewish: Neuman.

T541.5. *Birth from man's thigh.* *Fb "barn" IV 27a; Gaster Oldest Stories 127.

T541.5.1. *Birth from woman's thigh.* Japanese: Ikeda.

T541.6. *Birth from an arm.* Micronesia: Dixon 251 nn. 18—22; S. A. Indian (Toba): Métraux MAFLS XL 98.

T541.7. *Birth from an eye.* Micronesia: Dixon 251 nn. 18—22.

T541.8. *Birth from secretions of the body.* N. A. Indian: *Thompson Tales 323 n. 166b.

A1263.3. Man created from rubbings of skin.

T541.8.1. *Birth from excrement.* Jewish: *Neuman.

T541.8.2. *Birth from spittle.* (Cf. T533.) S. A. Indian (Yana): Curtin Creation Myths 348.

T541.8.3. *Birth from mucus from the nose.* Hindu: Keith 141; N. A. Indian: *Thompson Tales 352 n. 269.

T541.8.3.1. *Child born through nose.* India: Thompson-Balys; Africa (Upoto): Einstein 122.

T541.9. *Birth from contact of severed male genitals with ground.* Greek: Frazer Apollodorus I 5 n. 4.

T541.10. *Birth from semen thrown on ground.* Irish myth: Cross; Greek: Frazer Apollodorus II 90 n. 1.

T541.11. *Birth from lotus issuing from a god's navel.* Hindu: Keith 120.

T541.12. *Birth from nine mothers.* (Cf. A112.5.) Icelandic: MacCulloch Eddic 153 (Heimdall).

T541.13. *Birth from man's shoulder.* India: Thompson-Balys.

T541.14. *Birth through the ear.* Africa (Upoto): Einstein 122.

T541.15. *Birth through the back.* Africa (Upoto): Einstein 122.

T541.16. *Birth from knee.* S. A. Indian (Tucuna): Nimuendajú BBAE CXLIII (3) 724.

T542. *Birth of human being from an egg.* (Cf. F611.1.11.) *Type 650; Christiansen Norske Eventyr 92; *Fb "æg" III 1142b; Greek: Frazer Apollodorus II 23 n. 7, 25 n. 1, Fox 24f., 203; India: *Thompson-Balys; Hindu: Keith 139; Indo-Chinese: Scott Indo-Chinese 276, 292; Chinese: Graham; Buddhist myth: Malalasekera I 757, 787; Korean: Zong in-Sob 5 No. 2; S. A. Indian (Chincha): Alexander Lat. Am. 230; Africa (Basuto): Jacottet 110.

T542.1. *Shepherdess born of red and blue egg.* India: Thompson-Balys.

T543. *Birth from plant.* Japanese: Ikeda; Africa (Gold Coast): Barker and Sinclair 77 No. 12, (Ekoi): Talbot 133ff., (Ibo, Nigeria): Thomas 76.

T543.0.1. *Twig, born of a woman, is planted and becomes a girl.* (Cf. T555.) BP II 125.

T543.1. *Birth from a tree.* Greek: Fox 198; Chinese: Eberhard FFC CXX 84; Indonesia: DeVries's list No. 159.

T543.2. *Birth from flower.* Irish myth: Cross; Armenian: Ananikian 45; Hindu: Penzer VI 15 n. 3.

T543.2.1. *Birth from lotus.* Buddhist myth: Malalasekera I 299, II 135, 247, 527, 1150.

T543.3. *Birth from fruit.* *Penzer VI 15. n. 3; Armenian: Ananikian 45; India: *Thompson-Balys; Japanese: Anesaki 313, Ikeda; Africa (Ekoi): Talbot 134.

T555.1. Woman gives birth to a fruit.

T543.3.1. *Birth from orange.* India: Thompson-Balys.

T543.4. *Birth from fungus.* Africa (Ekoi): Talbot 135.

T543.5. *Birth from gourd.* India: *Thompson-Balys.

T543.6. *Birth from grass (grain).*

T543.6.1. *Birth from wheat.* India: Thompson-Balys.

T543.7. *Birth from vegetable.* India: Thompson-Balys.

T544. *Birth from mineral.*

T544.1. *Birth from rock.* Ploss Das Kind I 33; Gaster Oldest Stories 125; Caucasian: von Löwis of Menar Archiv f. Religionwiss. XIII 509ff., XV 305; Greek: Fox 213; Chinese: Eberhard FFC CXX 94 No. 52; Melanesia: Dixon 119, Codrington 156.

T544.2. *Boy forged from iron* (Cf. F611.1.12.) *Type 540; Christiansen Norske Eventyr 92; *Fb "jærn" II 60b.

T545. *Birth from ground.* Greek: Grote I 52; Hindu: Keith 127; N. A. Indian: *Thompson Tales 314 n. 139.

F516.2.1. Six-armed earth-born men.

T546. *Birth from water.*

T546.1. *Birth from sea-foam.* N. A. Indian (Zuñi): Stevenson RBAE XXIII 24.

A114.1. Deity born from sea-foam. A114.1.1. Goddess born from sweat of rock washed by sea. A1261.1. Man created from sea-foam.

T546.2. *Birth from hailstone.* India: Thompson-Balys.

T547. *Birth from virgin.* Saintyves Saints Successeurs 220ff., 271—77; Greek: Grote I 10, 55; S. A. Indian (Chiriguano): Métraux RMLP XXXIII 154.

V312. Belief in Immaculate Conception.

T548. *Birth obtained through magic or prayer.* Buddhist myth: Malalasekera II 1163, 1258; S. A. Indian (Inca): Rowe BBAE CXLIII (2) 318.

D1347. Magic object produces fecundity. D1925. Fecundity magically induced.

T548.1. *Child born in answer to prayer.* *Prato RTP IV 177; Toldo I 321 n. 1; Spanish: Boggs FFC XC 77, 113 Nos. 650, 936; Italian: Basile Pentamerone I No. 2; Jewish: Neuman, Gaster Thespis 270f.; India: *Thompson-Balys; Chinese: Eberhard FFC CXX 76f.; Japanese: Ikeda; Korean: Zong in-Sob 1 No. 4, 171 f. No. 74; West Indies: Flowers 578.

C758.1. Monster born because of hasty wish of parents. D1766.1. Magic results produced by prayer. J2067.1. Sacrifice of one son to get another. Q140. Miraculous or magic rewards. S223. Childless couple promise child to the devil if they may only have one. T513. Conception from wish. T553. Thumbling born as result of hasty wish of parents.

T548.1.1. *Hateful or lovely child to be born first?* Childless parents' prayer answered: they are to have two children, one hateful, one lovely. Choice as to which is to come first. Köhler-Bolte I 520ff.

T548.2. *Magic rites for obtaining a child.* *Type 711; Christiansen Norske Eventyr 98; Penzer VI 14; Hawaii: Beckwith Myth 284.

T548.3. *Magic elixir to procure a child.* Penzer III 218f.

T548.4. *Charity rewarded by birth of child.* India: Thompson-Balys.

T549. *Miraculous birth—miscellaneous.*

T549.1. *Vegetable comes to life at woman's prayer.* Africa (Gold Coast): Barker and Sinclair 77 No. 12.

T549.2. *Thrown cane becomes child.* N. A. Indian (California): Gayton and Newman 75.

T549.3. *Boy born from fish's belly.* India: Thompson-Balys.

T549.3.1. *Fish when slit open gives up baby boy.* India: Thompson-Balys.

T549.4. *Child born from miscarried fetus.* Philippine (Tinguian): Cole 68, 83, 89.

T549.4.1. *Child born from placenta.* Philippine (Tinguian): Cole 79.

T550. Monstrous births. *Types 425, 708; *Hibbard 48 n. 6; Tegethoff 24; BP II 236; Irish: MacCulloch Celtic 155, *Cross; U.S.: Baughman; Breton: Sébillot Incidents s.v. "accouchement"; Eskimo (Greenland): Rasmussen III 145.

B20. Beast-men. Combinations of bestial and human forms. B96. Beast with human head and shape of smith's bellows. B634. Monstrous offspring from animal marriage. C101. Sex tabu broken: child born without bones. C993. Unborn child affected by mother's broken tabu. E474.1. Offspring of living and dead person. F510. Monstrous persons. L112.1. Monster as hero. M437. Curse: monstrous birth. Q552.5. Monstrous births as punishment for girl's pride. S325.0.1. Monstrous (deformed) child exposed.

T550.1. *Monster child helps mother.* *Type 708; BP II 236; Japanese: Ikeda.

T550.2. *Abnormally born child has unusual powers.* *Fb "ufødt" III 961b; Japanese: Ikeda; West Indies: Flowers 578.

T550.3. *Misshapen child from brother-sister incest.* (Cf. T415.) Halliday Indo-European Folk-Tales (London, 1933) 134; Greek: Fox 33: Chinese: Werner 408.

T550.4. *Monstrous birth because mother sees horrible sight.* England: Baughman; Ploss Das Kind 21ff.

T550.5. *Blemished children born of monstrous parent.* Irish myth: Cross.

T550.6. *Only half a son is born by queen who ate merely half of mango.* (Cf. F525, T589.2.) India: Thompson-Balys.

T550.7. *Poor woman gives birth to child who has no body (merely head or skull).* India: Thompson-Balys.

T551. *Child with extraordinary members (limbs).*

T551.1. *Child born without limbs.* English: Wells 122 (The King of Tars); Africa (Kaffir): Theal 72.

F516.1. Armless people.

T551.1.1. *Child born as formless lump of flesh.* Icelandic: Ragnars saga Lodbrokar (ed. Olsen, Copenhagen, 1906—08) 129; *Schlauch Chaucer's Constance and Accused Queens (New York, 1927) 126; *Hornstein Philological Quarterly XX 1; Buddhist myth: Malalasekera II 782, 1268f.

T551.2. *Child born with two heads.* (Cf. F551.0.2.1.) Africa (Angola): Chatelain 117 No. 9.

T551.3. *Child born with animal head.* Type 711; Christiansen Norske Eventyr 99.

T551.3.1. *Child with dog's head.* India: Thompson-Balys.

T551.3.2. *Child with hawk's head.* India: Thompson-Balys.

T551.3.3. *Monstrous birth: child with donkey's head.* India: Thompson-Balys.

T551.3.4. *Child with cow's head.*

T551.3.4.1. *Person born with cow's ears.* (Cf. F511.2.2.) Chinese: Graham.

T551.3.4.2. *Child born with horns.* Greek: Grote I 18.

T551.4. *Boy born with one side flesh and one iron.* Africa (Kaffir): Theal 129.

D2031.4.1. Druid makes self appear ugly on one side, beautiful on other. F525.1.1. Man with one side of stone (iron).

T551.4.1. *Child born beautiful on one side, hairy on other.* Hibbard 45ff. (King of Tars); Irish myth: Cross.

T551.5. *Child born half man, half fish.* Italian Novella: Rotunda.

T551.6. *Child born without mouth.* Irish myth: *Cross.

T551.7. *Child born with one ear.* Irish myth: Cross.

T551.8. *Child born with caul (containing serpent).* Irish myth: *Cross.

T551.9. *Child born with claws as result of curse by dying peddler murdered by its parents.* U.S. (New York State): *Baughman (M411.3.1.1).

T551.10. *Monstrous birth — nine faces, nine arms, nine feet.* Chinese: Graham.

T551.11. *Birth of one-eyed child.* (Cf. F512.1.) India: Thompson-Balys.

T551.12. *Child born with one leg.* Eskimo (Greenland): Rasmussen I 179.

T551.13. *Child born hairy.* Jewish: Neuman.

T551.13.1. *Child born with long hair.* Jewish: *Neuman.

T551.13.2. *Child born with long beard.* Jewish: Neuman.

T551.14. *Child with all of its organs out of place.* Buddhist myth: Malalasekera I 270.

T551.15. *Child born blood-red.* Jewish: *Neuman.

T552. *Child born bearing an object.*

H71.7. Child born with chain around neck. Sign of royalty.

T552.1. *Girl born with red string around neck.* Fb. "rød".

T552.2. *Child born with snake around neck.* Fb. "slange"; Italian Novella: Rotunda.

T552.2.1. *Child born bearing lizard in each hand.* Irish myth: Cross.

T552.2.2. *Child born holding worm (in each hand).* Irish myth: *Cross.

T552.3. *Child born carrying knife and calabash.* Africa (Ekoi): Talbot 32.

T552.4. *Child born carrying handful of hair.* Africa (Fjort): Dennett 56 No. 10.

T552.5. *Child born with complete armor.* Hartland Perseus III 198; Hungarian: Ipolyi Zs. f. deutsche Mythologie und Sittenkunde II 168; Malay: Overbeck Malaiische Erzählungen 12; Africa: Frobenius Atlantis IV 300, XII 125.

T552.5.1. *Child born wearing helmet.* Irish myth: Cross.

T552.5.2. *Child born with magic iron bow.* India: Thompson-Balys.

T552.5.3. *Child born with knife and shield.* Africa (Upoto): Einstein 120.

T552.6. *Child born carrying a stone.* Irish myth: Cross.

T552.7. *Child born wearing jewel.* India: Thompson-Balys.

T552.8. *Daughter born with a feathered parka.* Eskimo (Kodiak): Golder JAFL XXII 21.

T553. *Thumbling born as result of hasty wish of parents.* They wish for a child, no matter how small he may be. *Type 700; *BP I 389ff.; India: Thompson-Balys; Japanese: Anesaki 286, Ikeda.

C758.1. Monster born because of hasty wish of parents. F535.1. Thumbling. Person the size of a thumb. S223. Childless couple promise child to the devil if they may only have one. T548.1. Child born in answer to prayer.

T554. *Woman gives birth to animal.* Type 441; BP II 236ff., 482ff.; *Fb "hund" I 678b; Irish myth: *Cross; Icelandic: MacCulloch Eddic 279; Italian Novella: Rotunda; Greek: Fox 108, 211; India: Thompson-Balys; Africa (Zulu): Callaway 105, 268, (Kaffir): Theal 148.

B632. Animal offspring from marriage to animal. K2115. Animal-birth slander. A woman is accused of having given birth to animals. M437.1. Curse: "What I carry may you carry; what you carry may I carry." T465. Bestiality.

T554.0.1. *Woman transformed to animal bears animal.* (Cf. T578.2.) Irish: MacCulloch Celtic 169, *Cross.

T554.1. *Tiger, spirit, and man sons of one mother.* India: Thompson-Balys.

T554.2. *Woman bears dog.* India: Thompson-Balys.

T554.3. *Woman bears crane.* India: Thompson-Balys.

T554.4. *Woman bears monkey.* India: *Thompson-Balys.

T554.5. *Woman bears tortoise (turtle).* India: *Thompson-Balys.

T554.6. *Woman bears goat.* India: Thompson-Balys.

T554.7. *Woman gives birth to a snake.* India: Thompson-Balys; S. A. Indian (Brazil): Oberg 108; Africa (Upoto): Einstein 120.

T554.8. *Woman bears frog.* India: Thompson-Balys.

T554.8.1. *Woman gives birth to toad.* Chinese: Graham.

T554.9. *Woman bears three pigs.* Philippine (Tinguian): *Cole 116.

T554.10. *Woman gives birth to a bird.* Mono-Alu: Wheeler No. 20.

T554.11. *Supernaturally impregnated woman gives birth to dragon.* Chinese: Eberhard FFC CXX 102 No. 60.

T555. *Woman gives birth to a plant.* (Cf. T543.0.1.) BP II 125; Italian: Basile Pentamerone I No. 2; Persian: Carnoy 295.

T555.1. *Woman gives birth to a fruit.* Can transform itself to girl. India: Thompson-Balys.

D630. Transformation and disenchantment at will. T543.3. Birth from fruit.

T555.1.1. *Woman gives birth to pumpkin.* Chinese: Eberhard FFC CXX 77.

T555.2. *Queen gives birth to a gourd.* India: Thompson-Balys.

T556. *Woman gives birth to a demon.* Type 433B; Hindu: Meyer Hindu Tales 62, 117, 165.

S223.1. Girl promises unborn child to devil if he will suffer the birth pangs. T554.1. Tiger, spirit, and man sons of one mother.

T557. *Child born with viper in heart (body).* Irish myth: *Cross.

T561. *Child born in a jug (jar).* Penzer IX 89 n. 3; N. A. Indian: Thompson Tales 323 n. 166c; Africa (Kaffir): Theal 149.

T561.1. *Child born in conch shell.* India: *Thompson-Balys.

T561.2. *Child born in a furnace.* India: Thompson-Balys.

T561.3. *Child born in a bag.* India: Thompson-Balys.

T561.4. *Child born in pot.* India: Thompson-Balys; S. A. Indian (Toba): Métraux MAFLS XL 40, 97ff., 129-33, BBAE CXLIII (1) 368.

T562. *White woman bears black child.* Fb "prins og prinsesse" II 876.

T563. *Birthmarks.* Irish myth: Cross; Icelandic: Boberg.

H71.1. Star on forehead as sign of royalty.

T563.1. *Child of three fathers born with three stripes.* Irish myth: *Cross.

T563.2. *Child formed of clot of gore has red birthmark.* (Cf. T541.1.1.) Irish myth: *Cross.

T563.3. *Child born with figure of serpent on his body.* Jewish: *Neuman.

T563.4. *Tattoo on newly born baby's back telling who was his former incarnation.* Korean: Zong in-Sob 76 No. 41.

E600. Reincarnation.

T565. *Woman lays an egg.* (Cf. T542.) Fb "æg" III 1142b; Chinese: Eberhard FFC CXX 77; Korean: Zong in-Sob 5 No. 2; S. A. Indian (Huamachuco): Métraux RMLP XXXIII 151.

T566. *Human son of animal parents.* India: Thompson-Balys.

T569. *Monstrous births—miscellaneous.*

T569.1. *Queen delivered of a piece of flesh;* abandoned and saved, it gradually separates into forms of boy and girl. India: Thompson-Balys.

T569.2. *Woman gives birth to grinding-stone.* Chinese: Eberhard FFC CXX 68.

T570. Pregnancy. India: Thompson-Balys.

C152. Tabus during pregnancy. D1352.1. Magic net has prenatal influence.

T571. *Unreasonable demands of pregnant women.* *Penzer I 97 n. 1, 221ff., II 31, III 60, V 127 n. 2, VII 201, IX 144; Cowell Jātaka Index s.v. "pregnancy"; *M. Bloomfield in Penzer VII vii, JAOS XL 1; Child II 408f., 414; Loomis White Magic 20. — Irish: Mac Culloch Celtic 176, *Cross; India: *Thompson-Balys; Japanese: Ikeda; Philippine (Tinguian): Cole 95, 98; Maori: Dixon 60; Indonesian,

Polynesian: ibid 233 n. 42; Sumatran: ibid. 161; Batak: Voorhoeve 141; Eskimo (Greenland): Rasmussen III 51; Africa (Ekoi): Talbot 374, (Angola): Chatelain 83 No. 4, (Ila, Rhodesia): Smith and Dale II 414 No. 13; West Indies: Flowers 578.

C152.2. Tabu: refusing unreasonable demand of pregnant woman. H936. Tasks assigned because of longings of pregnant woman. H1212.2. Quest assigned by wife through appeal to husband's love for her. N335.2. Pregnant woman demands a bath of blood.

T572. *Prevention of childbirth.*

Q251. Punishment for refusal to have children. Q431.4. Banishment till rose grows from table for preventing childbirth.

T572.1. *Magic prevention of childbirth.* *Type 755; *Hauffen Zs. f. Vksk. X 436ff.; *Kittredge Witchcraft 113f., 442f. nn. 79—84; *Fb "sten" III 554a; Irish myth: *Cross.

T589.8. Woman strives to delay birth until auspicious day.

T572.1.1. *Mother sits on stone to prevent premature birth.* Irish myth: *Cross.

T572.2. *Abortion.* *Encyc. Rel. Ethics VI 54ff.; *Penzer II 229; Irish myth: *Cross; Jewish: Neuman; India: Thompson-Balys.

T572.2.1. *Abortion by vomiting up embryo.* Irish: MacCulloch Celtic 84, *Cross.

T572.2.2. *Abortion by eating.* Child I 341, 343f., 352, 354, III 387, 393, IV 456; Gaster Oldest Stories 121.

T572.2.3. *Hero an abortion thrown into the bushes.* Maori: Dixon 42.

L111. Hero (heroine) of unpromising origin. Z210.1. Lodge-Boy and Thrown-Away as joint adventurers. Of brothers (sometimes twins taken from body of slain mother) one is abandoned and becomes wild. Later he joins his brother.

T572.2.4. *Abortion by fasting.* Irish myth: Cross.

T572.2.5. *Abortion caused by fear.* Irish myth: Cross.

T572.2.6. *Abortion by long bathing.* India: Thompson-Balys.

T573. *Short pregnancy.* Jewish: *Neuman; Koryak: Jochelson JE VI 375; N. A. Indian: *Thompson Tales 309 n. 116; S. A. Indian (Chiriguano): Métraux RMLP XXXIII 142, (Uru-Chipaya): ibid 169, (Inca): Rowe BBAE CXLIII (2) 318.

T573.0.1. *Short pregnancy in animals.* Irish myth: *Cross.

T573.1. *Woman conceives and bears same day.* Irish myth: Cross; India: Thompson-Balys.

T574. *Long pregnancy.* Delayed by an enemy who bewitches the mother. *Toldo I 337, II 313; *Frazer Pausanias V 45f.; *Fb "føde" I 398; Tegethoff 41; Köhler-Bolte Zs. f. Vksk. VI 63 (to Gonzenbach No. 12); Child I 82ff., 489, III 497, V 285b. — Irish: Thurneyson I 274, *Cross; Icelandic: Boberg; Finnish: Kalevala rune 1; Greek: *Frazer Apollodorus I 166 n. 2; Persian: Carnoy 331; Chinese: Wilhelm Chinesische Märchen Nos. 15, 18, 29; Batak: Frazer Golden Bough I 143; Philippine (Tinguian): Cole 180; Madagascar: Dandoyau Contes populaires des Sakalava No. 57.

Q559.5.1. Girl punished for slander against bishop. She is prevented from giving birth to her child until she admits slander is lie. T582.3. Knots to be untied at childbirth.

T574.1. *Long pregnancy: twelve months.* India: *Thompson-Balys.

T574.2. *Long pregnancy: seven years.* Jewish: *Neuman; India: *Thompson-Balys; Buddhist myth: Malalasekera I 208, II 1222.

T575. *Child speaks before birth.* (Cf. A511.1.2.)

T575.1. *Child speaks in mother's womb.* *Chauvin VII 112 No. 379bis n. 1, VIII 63 No. 27; *Fb "ufødt" III 962a; **Colson "L'enfant qui parle avant d'être né" Mélusine V No. 2; Gaidoz Mélusine IV No. 10; *Toldo I 338f.; DeVries FFC LXXIII 322, 325f.; Hdwb. d. Märchens I 102, 520; Child III 367 nn., IV 507a, V 298a; Krappe Zeitschrift für deutsches Altertum LXXII (1935) 161—71; Saintyves Saints Successeurs 253. — Irish: MacCulloch Celtic 207, *Cross; Jewish: *Neuman; Persian: Carnoy 335; India: *Thompson-Balys; S. A. Indian (Aztec): Alexander Lat. Am. 60, (Tupinamba): Métraux RMLP XXXIII 133, (Warrau): ibid. 145; Africa (Angola): Chatelain 85 No. 5, (Kaffir): Theal 89, (Zulu): Callaway 6.

T575.1.1. *Child in mother's womb reveals crime.* BP II 535; Spanish Exempla: Keller.

D1318. Magic object reveals guilt. D1817. Magic detection of crime. N271. Murder will out.

T575.1.1.1. *Child in mother's womb reveals murder.* BP II 535.

T575.1.1.2. *Child in mother's womb reveals adultery.* DeVries FFC LXXIII 322, 325f.

T575.1.1.3. *Child in mother's womb reveals unjust judgment.* DeVries FFC LXXIII 322, 325f.; Loomis White Magic 23f.

T575.1.2. *Future suicide weeps in mother's womb.* Fb "selvmord".

T575.1.3. *Twins quarrel before birth in mother's womb.* *Krappe Balor 31 n. 109; Greek: *Frazer Apollodorus I 145 n. 4; Jewish: *Neuman; N. A. Indian: *Thompson Tales 279 n. 33.

A511.1.2.1. Twin culture heroes quarrel before birth.

T575.1.4. *Future poet chants spell in mother's womb.* Irish myth: Cross.

T575.1.5. *Children in mothers' wombs praise God at birth of Christ.* Irish myth: Cross.

T575.1.5.1. *Embryos in womb join melody and sing.* Jewish: Neuman.

T575.1.6. *Child in mother's belly guides her.* S. A. Indian (Warrau): Métraux RMLP XXXIII 145, (Karib): ibid. 146.

T575.1.6.1. *Unborn child directs his mother on journey.* S. A. Indian (Karib): Métraux RMLP XXXIII 146, (Chiriguano): ibid 154, 160, 165, (Tupinamba): Métraux BBAE CXLIII (3) 132.

T575.2. *Woman talks to her child before it is conceived.* N. A. Indian (Blackfoot): Wissler and Duvall PaAM II 126.

T575.3. *Child speaks from dead mother's womb.* (Cf. T584.2.) India: Thompson-Balys.

T575.4. *Child in mother's womb visible from outside.* Buddhist myth: Malalasekera II 325, 609.

T576. *Prenatal influences.* India: Thompson-Balys.

C152. Tabus during pregnancy.

T577. *Fetus exchanged from one woman to another.* India: Thompson-Balys; Hindu: Keith 171, 223.

T577.1. *Male embryo transformed in womb to female.* Jewish: Neuman.

T578. *Pregnant man.* *Type 705; *Fb "frugtsommelig" I 376b; DeVries FFC LXXIII 268; von der Hagen II 53ff. No. 24; Christensen DF XLVII 227 No. 93, L 72. — Irish myth: Cross; Icelandic: MacCulloch Eddic 145 (Loki); Koryak: Jochelson JE VI 324; Eskimo (Greenland): Rink 444, (West Hudson Bay): Boas BAM XV 326; N. A. Indian: *Thompson Tales 323 n. 166d; Africa (Basuto): Jacottet 196 No. 29.

H791. Riddle: a fish was my father; a man was my mother. Man eats magic fish and becomes pregnant; a girl is taken from his knee. J2321. Man made to believe that he is pregnant (has borne child).

T578.1. *Child incubated in man's thigh.* Greek: *Frazer Apollodorus I 319 n. 3 (Zeus and Dionysus).

T578.2. *Man transformed to female (human or animal) bears offspring.* (Cf. T554.0.1.) Irish myth: *Cross.

T579. *Pregnancy—miscellaneous motifs.*

T579.1. *Sheath and knife as analogy for mother and unborn child.* Child V 486 s.v. "knife"; Eskimo: Rink No. 2.

T579.2. *Girl's blood examined to see if she is pregnant.* Fb "blod" IV 48a.

T579.3. *Seven-year-old girl has child.* Gaster Exempla 230 No. 247.

T579.3.1. *Seven-year-old boy begets child.* Irish myth: Cross.

T579.4. *Mother of saint has healing spittle during pregnancy.* Irish myth: Cross.

T579.5. *Saint performs miracles while yet unborn.* (Cf. D1713.) Irish myth: Cross.

T579.6. *Worm swallowed at conception eats hand of babe before birth.* (Cf. T511.5.2.) Irish myth: Cross.

T579.7. *King demands that his pregnant queen be chained to him.* India: Thompson-Balys.

T579.8. *Signs of pregnancy.*

T579.8.1. *Transparent body of pregnant woman.* Jewish: Neuman.

T579.8.2. *Girl paints face because pregnant.* S. A. Indian (Chiriguano): Métraux RMLP XXXIII 154.

T579.8.3. *Girl betrays pregnancy by dropping milk on brother.* Philippine (Tinguian): Cole 87.

T580. Childbirth. Irish myth: Cross.

A112. Birth of gods. C151. Tabu: man's presence at childbirth. D1361.8. Heart of unborn child renders person invisible. K1923.6. Queen passes off girl-child as boy by having pandits say raja must not see his son for twelve years. Q192. Child given as reward for prayer.

T580.1. *Jewess must entreat Virgin before she can bear her child.* Irish myth: Cross.

T581. *Place and conditions of childbirth.*

T581.1. *Birth of child in forest.* Dickson 168 n. 19; Irish myth: *Cross; Icelandic: *Boberg.

T581.2. *Child born of woman abandoned in pit.* Indonesian, Polynesian: Dixon 234 n. 43.

G72.2. Starving woman abandoned in cave eats newborn babe. S435. Cast-off wife abandoned in pit.

T581.2.1. *Child born to an apparently dead mother in her grave.* *Bolte "Die Sage von der erweckten Scheintoten" Zs. f. Vksk. XX (1910) 353—81; H. Hauvette "La morte vivante" (Paris, 1933); Krappe "L'enfant de la morte" Lettres Romanes I (1947) 297—310.

T581.2.2. *Blind wives fall into a pool where they give birth to children.* India: Thompson-Balys.

T581.2.3. *Children born in dungeon.* India: Thompson-Balys.

T581.3. *Child born in tree.* English: Child II 109; Indonesian, Polynesian: Dixon 234 n. 43.

T581.4. *Child born in stable.* English: Child II 85—99 passim, V 221.

T581.5. *Child born during snowstorm.* Irish myth: Cross.

T581.6. *Noise of battle precipitates birth.* Irish myth: Cross.

T581.7. *Child born on flagstone.* Loomis White Magic 20f.; Irish myth: *Cross.

T581.8. *Woman bears twins at end of footrace* (with king's horses). Irish myth: *Cross.

T581.9. *Child born on beach.* Irish myth: Cross; Icelandic: Örvar-Odds saga 2—5, Boberg.

T581.10. *Twins born in tent; mother abducted.* Icelandic: FSS 246—48, Boberg.

T581.11. *Boy is born in a wrapping of fine cloth.* Buddhist myth: Malalasekera II 1097.

T582. *Precautions at childbirth.* *Penzer II 166ff.; *McDaniel Conception, Birth and Infancy (Miami, 1948); *H. A. Winkler Salomo und die Karina: eine orientalische Legende von der Bezwingung einer Kindbettdämonin (Stuttgart, 1931); Irish myth: Cross.

T582.1. *Avoidance of evil spirits at childbirth.* Armenian: Ananikian 88f.

D2071.1.2. Evil Eye averted by swinging cat over child's cradle.

T582.2. *All locks in house to be shot during childbirth.* English: Child II 498.

T582.3. *Knots to be untied at childbirth.* Particularly knots in the woman's clothes. Aly Hdwb. d. Abergl. V. 19; cf. Frazer Pausanias V 45f.; English: Child I 85.

T582.4. *Knife (other sharp instrument) as childbirth precaution.* Jewish: Neuman.

T583. *Accompaniments of childbirth.*

C150. Tabu connected with childbirth. F312. Fairy presides at child's birth. Sometimes the Norns, the Fates, etc. F316. Fairy lays curse on child. F317. Fairy predicts future greatness of (new-born) child. F960.1. Extraordinary nature phenomena at birth of holy person. M311.0.1 Heroic career prophesied for new-born child. M356.3. Prophecy: (new-born) child will bring evil upon land.

T583.1. *Couvade.* Father goes into confinement at time of childbirth. *Encyc. Religion Ethics II 635b; *Ploss Das Kind I 125; Bouwman Revue Anthropologique XXV 49ff., Lévy-Bruhl L'âme primitive 225ff.; Hdwb. d. Abergl. V 1573; Grimm Deutsche Rechtsalterthümer I 106. — Irish myth: *Cross; Latin American: Alexander Lat. Am. 37f.; Melanesia: Codrington 228ff.

T583.1.0.1. *Husband goes into seclusion at wife's pregnancy.* India: Thompson-Balys.

T583.1.0.2. *Couvade imposed on man during wife's menstruation.* India: Thompson-Balys.

T583.1.1. *Pains of woman in childbirth repeated in person of the man.* English: Child II 109, V 292; U.S.: Baughman.

T583.2. *Calamities at birth of hero.* India: Thompson-Balys.

F960.1.2.1. Extraordinary precipitation at birth of hero.

T583.3. *King leaves bell with his wife for her to ring so he will know when her child is born.* India: *Thompson-Balys.

T584. *Parturition.* Spanish Exempla: Keller.

A477. Goddess of childbirth. B81.6. Mermaid has human midwife. F372.1. Fairies take human midwife to attend fairy woman. F451.5.5. Dwarfs have human woman as midwife. V211.1.4. Virgin suffers no birth pangs at Christ's Nativity.

T584.0.1. *Childbirth assisted by magic.* (Cf. D1501.2.) *Kittredge Witchcraft 114, 443f. nn. 85—102; Irish myth: Cross; Icelandic: *Boberg.

T584.0.2. *Husband acts as midwife when no woman is available.* Boje 125ff.

T584.0.3. *Birth of holy person painless.* Loomis White Magic 16, 20; Irish myth: Cross; Jewish: Neuman.

T584.0.4. *Childbirth assisted by angel.* Irish myth: Cross.

T584.0.5. *While saint's mother was giving birth to the child, she grasps a stout rod which roots and becomes a sturdy tree.* Loomis White Magic 22f.

T584.0.6. *Childbirth assisted by sacred stone.* Irish myth: *Cross.

T584.1. *Birth through the mother's side.* *Hartland Primitive Paternity I 21; Toldo I 340; English: Child I 83, II 309ff., 373ff.; V 227ff.; Irish myth: Cross; Egyptian: Müller 390 n. 34; Persian: Carnoy 290, 331; Hindu: Keith 33; Malagasy: Sibree FLJ II 50; Haiti: Alexander Lat. Am. 29; Bakairi: ibid. 312.

A511.1.1. Culture hero snatched from mother's side. T517.2. Conception through mother's side. T541. Birth from unusual part of person's body.

T584.2. *Child removed from body of dead mother.* *Schoepperle 280 n. 2; Loomis White Magic 21; Irish myth: *Cross; Icelandic: Boberg; Greek: Fox 286; India: Thompson-Balys; Japanese: Ikeda; Oceanic: *Dixon 132 n. 4; N. A. Indian: *Thompson Tales 324 n. 166i; S. A. Indian (Yuracare): Alexander Lat. Am. 314, Métraux RMLP XXXIII 144, (Karib): ibid. 147, (Tupinamba): Métraux BBAE CXLIII (3) 132.

T612. Child born of slain mother cares for itself during infancy. Z210.1. Lodge-Boy and Thrown-Away as joint adventurers. Of brothers (sometimes twins taken from body of slain mother) one is abandoned and becomes wild.

T584.2.1. *Child born of dead mother in grave.* Irish myth: Cross.

T584.2.1.1. *Twins freed from dead mother's body as body rots.* New Hebrides: Codrington 398.

T584.3. *Cesarean operation upon a woman at childbirth as a custom.* Hatt Asiatic Influences 83f.

T584.4. *Piglings cut from bodies of sows and reared.* Irish myth: *Cross.

T584.5. *Extraordinarily long labor at childbirth.*

T584.5.1. *Prolonged labor: woman has childbirth pains for 100 days but is not delivered.* India: Thompson-Balys.

T584.6. *After-birth (placenta) becomes a demon.* India: Thompson-Balys.

T584.7. *Hero is born by splitting mother's womb.* Chinese: Eberhard FFC CXX 93f.

T584.8. *Child helps mother in severing his navel string.* Jewish: *Neuman.

T585. *Precocious infant.* *Toldo I 329; Loomis White Magic 23; Gaster Oldest Stories 69; Irish myth: *Cross; Icelandic: *Boberg; Greek: Fox 79 (Hercules), 92 (Hermes); India: *Thompson-Balys.

A527.1. Culture hero precocious. F305.3. Offspring of fairy and mortal has long hair and beard at birth. F611.3.2. Hero's precocious strength. T615. Supernatural growth. Z251. Boy hero.

T585.1. *Child born full (nearly) grown.* *Ranke FFC CXIV 156; Persian: Carnoy 287; Jewish: Neuman; India: *Thompson-Balys; Korean: Zong in-Sob 5 No. 2; Hawaii: Beckwith Myth 230; S. A. Indian (Aztec): Alexander Lat. Am. 60, (Inca): Rowe BBAE CXLIII (2) 318, (Chiriguano): Métraux RMLP XXXIII 161, 166, (Karib): ibid. 147; Africa (Ekoi): Talbot 126, (Fjort): Dennett 60 No. 12, (Zulu): *Callaway 9; Cape Verde Islands: Parsons MAFLS XV (1) 352.

F611.3.2. Hero's precocious strength. T614. Diabolical child kills his wet-nurses.

T585.1.1. *Child stronger than mother on day of birth.* Irish myth: Cross.

T585.2. *Child speaks at birth.* (Cf. T575.1.) *Penzer II 39 n. 2; *Liebrecht 210ff.; Günter 242 s.v. "redend"; Cowell Jātaka VI 157, 250; Chavannes 500 Contes I 30, 243, 427. — Irish myth: *Cross; Jewish: *Neuman; India: *Thompson-Balys; Buddhist myth: Malalasekera I 151, II 944, 1247; S. A. Indian (Toba): Métraux MAFLS XL 97; Africa: Frobenius Atlantis II 57, IV 278, VII 148, 208, XII 125, (Benga): Nassau 184 No. 24 version 2, (Bahonga): Einstein 247, (Fang): ibid. 57, (Mkulwe): ibid. 18f.

T585.2.1. *Child two months old speaks.* Irish myth: Cross.

T585.2.2. *Child speaks prematurely on first birthday.* Moreno Esdras.

T585.3. *Infant born blind immediately drowns self.* Irish myth: *Cross.

T585.4. *Infant saint rebukes mother's impiety.* Loomis White Magic 23; Irish myth: Cross.

T585.5. *Child born with all his teeth.* Irish myth: Cross.

T585.5.1. *Child born with hairy mane.* Irish myth: Cross.

T585.6. *Newborn child kisses dying mother.* Icelandic: Boberg.

T585.7. *Precocious hero leaves cradle to go to war.* Irish myth: Cross; Icelandic: Boberg.

T585.8. *Child stands (walks) at birth.* Jewish: Neuman; Buddhist myth: Malalasekera I 789, II 299.

T585.9. *Child born circumcised.* Jewish: *Neuman.

T586. *Multiple births.* Irish myth: *Cross; India: Thompson-Balys; Eskimo (Greenland): Rasmussen III 85, 251.

T586.1. *Many children at a birth.* BP I 432; Köhler-Bolte I 467; Jewish: *Neuman; India: Thompson-Balys; Buddhist myth: Malalasekera I 420; Chinese: Eberhard FFC CXX 200f.; N. A. Indian: *Thompson Tales 310 n. 116a; S. A. Indian (Chibcha): Alexander Lat. Am. 199.
L435.2.1. Woman with 365 children.

T586.1.1. *Four children at a birth.* Haiti: Alexander Lat. Am. 30

T586.1.1.1. *Six children at a birth.* Irish myth: Cross.

T586.1.2. *Seven children at a birth.* *Fb "gifte" I 432; *BP I 432; Wesselski Märchen 174 No. 64; *Loomis White Magic 87; India: Thompson-Balys.

T586.1.2.1. *King and queen have seven sons, all named Maine.* Irish myth: *Cross.

T586.1.2.2. *King has six (seven) sons, all named Lugaid.* Irish myth: *Cross.

T586.1.3. *Nine children at a birth.* Ward II 657 No. 9.

T586.1.4. *Five children at a birth for four successive years.* All alive. Italian Novella: Rotunda.

T586.1.5. *Forty sons born in one day.* India: Thompson-Balys.

T586.2. *Extraordinary number of children in family.*

T586.2.1. *King with fifty sons (daughters).* Greek: Fox 20, 30.

T586.2.2. *King with 60,000 sons.* Hindu: Keith 115.

T586.3. *Multiple birth as result of relations with several men.* (Cf. T587.1.) Irish myth: Cross; S. A. Indian (Tenetehara): Wagley-Galvão BBAE CXLIII (3) 148, (Kaigua, Tembé, Apapocuvá-guarani): Métraux RMLP XXXIII 136.

T586.3.1. *Woman ravished by three brothers bears triplets.* Irish myth: *Cross.

T586.3.2. *Triplets killed by tribe at birth.* Africa (Fang): Einstein 56, Trilles 182.

T586.4. *Extraordinary number of animals at birth.*

T586.4.1. *Four calves to one cow at a birth.* Irish myth: *Cross.

T586.5. *Extraordinarily frequent childbirth.*

T586.5.1. *Woman bears child every month.* India: *Thompson-Balys.

T586.5.2. *Child born each day for seven days.* India: Thompson-Balys.

T587. *Birth of twins.* (Cf. T685.) Irish myth: Cross; India: *Thompson-Balys.

F523. Two persons with bodies joined. Siamese twins. S314. Twins exposed.

T587.1. *Birth of twins an indication of unfaithfulness in wife.* (Cf. T586.3.) *Harris Cult of the Heavenly Twins 10ff.; Krappe "Tyndare" Studi e Materiali di Storia delle Religioni XV (1939) 23—29; English: Child II 67 n., 511a, Wells 96 (Chevalere Assigne), 126 (Lai Le Freine), *Hibbard 295; Greek: Fox 79; India: Thompson-Balys.

A515.1.1.1. Twin culture heroes sired by two fathers.

T587.2. *Twins born one with ear of other in mouth.* Irish myth: Cross.

F523. Two persons with bodies joined. Siamese twins.

T587.2.1. *Immediately after birth of twins one puts the other in his mouth:* this twin's body becomes made of iron. India: Thompson-Balys.

T587.3. *Last born twin conceived first.* Jewish: Neuman.

T588. *Motifs associated with the placenta.* India: Thompson-Balys.

T588.1. *Spirits make child from placenta.* Philippine (Tinguian): Cole 185.

T589. *Childbirth—miscellaneous motifs.*

T589.1. *Co-operative birth.* Each of two wives bears a half-boy. They are placed together and form a real boy. Hindu: Keith 156.

T589.2. *Boy cut in two: each half becomes a boy.* N. A. Indian (Shoshonean): Alexander N. Am. 133, (California): Gayton and Newman 92.

F525. Person with half a body.

T589.3. *Birth trees.* Spring forth as hero is born; act as life tokens, etc. (Cf. T589.7.1.) Type 303; Köhler-Bolte I 179; Fb "træ" III 865b; *Kittredge Arthur 171 n. 1; Irish myth: Cross.

B311. Congenital helpful animal. Born at same time as master and (usually) by same magic means. D857. Magic object born with hero.

T589.4. *Birth with veil brings luck.* (Cf. T552.5.1.) Fb. "sejrsskjorte".

T589.5. *New-born child reincarnation of recently deceased person.* Fb "sjæl" III 214a; N. A. Indian: *Alexander N. Am. 281 n. 20.

E741.1.1.1. New star for each birth. A star in the sky for each person.

T589.6. *Where children come from.* Explanations given to children. Hdwb. d. Abergl. IV 1342ff.; v. Wlislocki Germania N. R. XXII 134ff.

T589.6.1. *Children brought by the stork.* *Fb "barn" I 50b.

T589.6.1.1. *Newborn boy placed in the lap of bathing queen by vulture.* India: Thompson-Balys.

T589.6.2. *Children brought by midwife.* *Fb "barn" I 50b.

T589.6.3. *Children said to come from underworld.* Kalevala-seuran Vuosikirjaa IV 243.

T589.6.4. *Children said to come from a well.* Wuttke Deutsche Aberglaube Register s.v. "Kinderbrunnen".

T589.6.5. *Children said to come from cauliflower.* Hdwb. d. Abergl. IV 1348.

T589.6.6. *Children said to come from stones.* Schmidt DF XXXIX 92ff.

T589.7. *Simultaneous births.* Irish myth: Cross.

T589.7.1. *Simultaneous birth of (domestic) animal and child.* Type 303; Irish myth: *Cross.

E765.2. Life bound up with that of animal. Person to live as long as animal lives. B311. Congenital helpful animal. Born at same time as master and (usually) by same magic means. T589.3. Birth trees. Spring forth as hero is born; act as life tokens, etc.

T589.7.2. *Hero born in hour of Christ's Nativity.* Irish myth: *Cross.

T589.8. *Woman strives to delay birth until auspicious day.* Loomis White Magic 20f.; Irish myth: *Cross.

M311.0.1. Hectic career prophesied for (new-born) child. M311.0.2. Prophecy: birth of hero at certain time (in certain place). N127. The auspicious day.

T589.9. *Child with several mothers.* (Heimdal.) Icelandic: MacCulloch Eddic 153.

T590. Conception and birth—miscellaneous motifs.

T591. *Barrenness or impotence induced by magic.* *Kittredge Witchcraft 113, 441 n. 78; *Boje 107; Irish myth: *Cross; Icelandic: Boberg; India: *Thompson-Balys.

Q553.3.3. Sterility as punishment for breaking saint's covenant.

T591.1. *Magic remedies for barrenness or impotence.* Cf. D1347, D1925, D2161.3.11.) Irish myth: Cross; Jewish: *Neuman; India: *Thompson-Balys.

T591.1.1. *Magic potion as remedy for impotence.* Greek: Frazer Apollodorus I 87 n. 3.

T591.1.2. *Milk of hornless, single-colored cow drunk by man to make wife fruitful.* Irish myth: Cross.

T591.2. *Unlucky for a woman to look on the face of a childless person.* India: Thompson-Balys.

T592. *Milk suddenly appears in woman's dry breast.* *Cosquin Études 199ff., 238ff.; India: Thompson-Balys.

F1041. Extraordinary physical reactions of persons. H175.1. Recognition of son by gushing up of milk in mother's breasts. H495. Mother test. J1142.1. Test of mother by weighing milk.

T592.1. *Milk medicine fills woman's breasts with milk.* India: Thompson-Balys.

T595. *Sign hung out informing brothers whether mother has borne boy or girl.* *Type 451; BP I 70ff.; Italian: Basile Pentamerone IV No. 8.

N344.1. Wrong sign put out leads to boys' leaving home. They are to be informed by a sign of a sister is born. Z140.1. Color of flag (sails) on ship to indicate good or bad news.

T596. *Naming of children.*

T596.1. *Angel names child.* Irish myth: Cross.

T596.2. *Children named by numbers (1, 2, 3, etc.).* Hdwb. d. Märchens I 521a; Irish myth: Cross.

L10.1.1. "Thirteen" is name of victorious youngest son. (Youngest of thirteen brothers.)

T597. *Ambitions of father transferred to child at moment of conception.* Irish myth: Cross.

T600—T699. Care of children.

T600. Care of children. **Ploss Das Kind; Fellinger Das Kind in der altfranzösischen Literatur (Göttingen, 1908); *McDaniel Conception, Birth and Infancy (Miami, 1948); Irish myth: *Cross.

B535. Animal nurse. C867.1. Tabu: abusing women and children. J1149.1. Feigned madness unmasked by threatening man's child. J1171.1. Solomon's judgment: the divided child. L111.2. Foundling hero. L111.2.1. Future hero found in boat (basket, bushes). P230. Parents and children. P270. Foster relative. P296. Godparents. R131. Exposed or abandoned child rescued. S123.3. Living children buried with dead mother. S161.1.1. Child's finger-ends cut off to give long life. S300. Abandoned or murdered children.

T601. *Infant bathed in milk.* Irish myth: Cross.

T602. *Weapons and horses procured for boy at his birth.* Icelandic: Hervarar saga 85, Boberg.

T605. *Divine nurse.* Greek: Grote I 52.

T610. Nurture and growth of children.

B251.2.10.1. Brilliantly white cow comes to be milked for infant saint. C875. Tabu: carrying child on one's back into house. G77. Girl child fed on infant boys' flesh to make her grow faster. J2175. Short-sightedness in dealing with children. K515. Children hidden to avoid their execution (death). N811. Supernatural godfather. Q586. Son on gallows bites his mother's (father's) nose off: punishment for neglect in youth. R13.0.1. Children carried off by animals. S300. Abandoned or murdered children.

T611. *Suckling of children.*

B53.2. Man suckled by siren. B535. Animal nurse. E323.1.1. Dead mother returns to suckle child F611.2. Strong hero's suckling.

T611.1. *Child nourished by sucking its own fingers.* *Cosquin Études 208, 256; Toldo I 341; Babylonian: Spence 54.

F552.1.5. Milk from fingers. G332.1. Ogre sucks victim's finger and drinks all his blood.

T611.1.1. *Child nourished by sucking thumb of a god.* Egyptian: Müller 115; India: Thompson-Balys; Hindu: Keith 166.

T611.2. *Child miraculously suckled by his father.* *BP II 296; Icelandic: Boberg.

T611.3. *Witch (fairy) suckles child.* Hoffman-Krayer Zs. f. Vksk. XXV 121 n. 4; Lithuanian: Balys Index No. 3297, Legends No. 528.

T611.4. *Children magically prevented from suckling.* Fb "patte" I 791a.

T611.5. *Child miraculously suckled by saint.* (Cf. V211.1.8.1.) Irish myth: *Cross.

T611.5.1. *Saint has two paps — a pap with milk and a pap with honey:* with these he suckles two infants. Irish myth: Cross.

T611.5.2. *Saint feeds children by cutting off cow's teats and pouring milk into them.* Irish myth: *Cross.

T611.5.3. *Children miraculously suckled by angel.* Jewish: Neuman.

T611.6. *Milk magically appears in woman's breast so as to nourish orphan.* (Cf. T592.) Loomis White Magic 22; India: Thompson-Balys.

T611.7. *Abandoned child saved by seagulls; milk furnished by doe; angel brings bell as drinking utensil.* Loomis White Magic 22.

T611.8. *One woman suckles many babies.* Jewish: *Neuman.

T611.9. *Dead mother's breasts furnish sufficient nourishment for her baby during two years.* *Loomis White Magic 108.

T611.10. *Man suckled by dog (wolf): called Mac Con (Son of Dog).* Irish myth: *Cross.

A511.2.2.1. Culture hero suckled by wolf.

T611.10.1. *Girl suckled by wolf has nail "like a wolf's nail."* Irish myth: Cross.

T611.10.2. *Saint suckled by wolf.* Irish myth: *Cross.

T611.11. *Child nourished by sucking the eyeballs of snake-mother (frog-mother) who left it.* Japanese: Ikeda.

T612. *Child born of slain mother cares for itself during infancy.* Oceanic: Dixon 132, 137; N. A. Indian: *Thompson Tales 319 n. 152.

A511.2.1.1. Abandoned culture hero captured by use of net. T584.2. Child removed from body of dead mother. Z210.1. Lodge-Boy and Thrown-Away as jont adventurers.

T614. *Diabolical child kills his wet-nurses.* (Gowther, Robert the Devil.) *Hibbard 49ff.; *Wells 784.

T615. *Supernatural growth.* (Cf. T585.) *Köhler-Bolte I 405, 544; *Child V 482 s.v. "growth"; Fb "pattebarn" II 792; Gaster Oldest Stories 130. — Irish: MacCulloch Celtic 26, *Cross; Welsh: MacCulloch Celtic 95; Icelandic: MacCulloch Eddic 21, 74; Breton: Sébillot Incidents s.v. "croissance"; Greek: *Frazer Apollodorus I 175 n. 2, Fox 175; Persian: Carnoy 332; Babylonian: Spence 54; Jewish: *Neuman; India: *Thompson-Balys; Chinese: Ferguson 30, Werner 306, *Coyajee JPASB XXIV 179; Japanese: Mitford 189ff., Ikeda; Philippine: Dixon 234, (Tinguian): Cole 30 n. 3, 53, 102; Eskimo (Greenland): Holm 47, Rasmussen I 234, 238, III 153; N. A. Indian: *Thompson Tales 307 n. 112, (California): Gayton and Newman 69; S. A. Indian (Carajá): Métraux MAFLS XL 49, (Toba): ibid. 89, 98, 157, (Tupinamba): Métraux BBAE CXLIII (3) 132, (Cashinawa): ibid. 684, (Yurakare): Métraux RMLP XXXIII 144, (Karib): ibid. 147, (Uru-Chipaya): ibid. 109; Africa: Werner African 221, (Benga): Nassau 185 No. 24, (Basuto): Jacottet 118 No. 17, 70 No. 11, (Ekoi): Talbot 33, 127, 312, (Zulu): Callaway 8ff., 73, 110, (Gold Coast): Barker and Sinclair 147 No. 29, (Boloki): Einstein 112, (Baluba): ibid. 183, (Fang): ibid. 57.

A153.2.1. God's food gives supernatural growth. A511.4.1. Miraculous growth of culture hero. A527.1 Culture hero precocious. F983. Extraordinary growth of animal. F611.3.2. Hero's precocious strength.

T615.1. *Precocious speech.* (Cf. T585.) DeVries "De Sage van het ingemetselde Kind" Nederlandsche Tijdschrift voor Volkskunde XXXII (1917) 1; Irish myth: *Cross; Finnish: Kalevala runes 31, 50; Africa (Kaffir): Theal 72f.

T615.2. *Women old from their birth.* Greek: *Frazer Apollodorus I 155 n. 4.

T615.3. *Precocious wisdom.* Jewish: *Neuman; India: *Thompson-Balys; Chinese: Graham.

T615.4. *Precocious boy supports his widowed mother and himself by use of his wits.* India: Thompson-Balys.

T615.5. *Precocious young child demands weapons.* (Cf. T617.1.) India: Thompson-Balys.

F611.3.3. Strong hero tests weapons.

T617. *Boy reared in ignorance of the world.* English: Wells 72 (Sir Percyvelle of Galles); Irish myth: *Cross; Missouri French: Carrière; Spanish Exempla: Keller; Jewish: Neuman.

J147. Child confined to keep him in ignorance of life. Useless. L122. Unsophisticated hero. M372. Confinement in tower to avoid fulfillment of prophecy. T371. The boy who had never seen a woman: the Satans.

T617.1. *Future hero as child isolated from world kills increasingly larger game with superior weapons.* N. A. Indian (California): Gayton and Newman 69.

T617.2. *Hero learns his name at time of first adventure.* Irish myth: Cross.

T621. *Orphan inquires about parents.* (Cf. L111.4.1.) N. A. Indian (California): Gayton and Newman 69.

T640. Illegitimate children. Irish myth: *Cross; India: Thompson-Balys.

A112.8. God from adulterous union. A511.1.3.1. Demigod son of king's unmarried sister (daughter) by god. H480. Father tests. J1515.1. The father of an illegitimate child must walk in front of the cross. J1661.1.2. Deduction: the king is a bastard. After dinner the king begins to dance. He is therefore called illegitimate. His mother acknowledges an intrigue with a dancer. L111.5. Bastard hero. N126.2. Lots cast to determine father of illegitimate child. S312. Illegitimate child exposed. T156.1. Marriage for a night to insure heir of warrior destined to be slain (next day) in battle. T411.2. Girl got with child by intoxicated father. T481. Adultery. T586.3. Multiple birth as result of relations with several men.

T640.1. *Illegitimate child of nun* (Cf. V465.1.2.) Irish myth: *Cross.

T640.2. *Mother of illegitimate child given as pledge for his crime.* Irish myth: Cross.

T642. *Test of legitimacy of children: exposure to asps.* Asps will bite only foreigners. (Cf. H222.1.) Herbert III 168 No. 16.

T644. *Child betrays his own illegitimacy.* India: Thompson-Balys.

T645. *Paramour leaves token with girl to give their son.* *Type 873; *Potter Sohrab and Rustem 6ff.; Irish myth: Cross; Icelandic: *Boberg; India: Thompson-Balys; Japanese: Ikeda; Hawaii: Beckwith Myth 86, 330, 478f.

H81. Clandestine lover recognized by tokens. H82.6. Token sent with youngster to relatives, that they may take care of him. H480. Father tests. Tests as to who is unknown father of child. H1216. Mother sends son to find unknown father. H1381.2.1. Woman seeks unknown father of her child. H1381.2.2.1. Son seeks unknown father. P233.7. Son must threaten father before he will recognize him as son. T475. Unknown (clandestine) paramour.

T645.1. *Sword left for posthumous son to kill father's murderer.* Krappe Balor 35; Marie de France "Yonec".

S312.3. Posthumous child to be exposed. T682. Hero a posthumous son.

T645.2. *"Keep it if it is a girl; send it to me if it is a boy."* Hero leaving girl says this of the prospective child. Icelandic: *Boberg.

T645.2.1. *"Kill it if it is a girl."* Indonesia: De Vries's list No. 203.

T645.3. *Father orders the mother to send the expected illegitimate boy to him when he can perform certain feats.* Irish myth: Cross; Greek: Fox 97 (Theseus).

T645.4. *Hero leaves bedmate keys to treasure chamber for the son she is supposed to bear.* Icelandic: Boberg.

T646. *Illegitimate child taunted by playmates.* *Type 873; DeVries Edda (1923) 155ff., DeVries Studiën over Faerösche balladen 44ff.; Chauvin V 72; Irish: MacCulloch Celtic 52, *Cross; Welsh: MacCulloch Celtic 200; Missouri French: Carrière; India and China: Cowell Jātaka VI 21, Chavannes 500 Contes III 331; Chinese: Graham; Japanese: Ikeda; Korean: Zong in-Sob 78 No. 44; Oceanic: Dixon 67f., 82, 113; Africa: Frobenius Atlantis IV 273; Jamaica: Beckwith MAFLS XVII 277 No. 89; West Indies: Flowers 579.

C33.1. Tabu: mentioning origin of supernatural child. P36. Dispossessed prince taunted by usurper's son.

T646.1. *Child cries because his father is unknown.* S. A. Indian (Uru-Chipaya): Métraux RMLP XXXIII 169.

T647. *Illegal to care for illegitimate child.* Irish myth: Cross.

T670. Adoption of children. *Encyc. Religion Ethics s.v. "adoption"; Icelandic: Boberg; Missouri French: Carrière; India: Thompson-Balys.

B535. Animal nurse. F311. Fairies adopt human child. K1921. Parents exchange children. N836.1. King adopts hero (heroine). P270. Foster relatives. P312. Blood-brotherhood.

T671. *Adoption by suckling.* Ogress who suckles hero claims him as her son. *Cosquin Études 199ff.; *Roberts 177.

P313. Milk-brotherhood. Friends bound in brotherhood through partaking of milk from the same woman.

T672. *Adopted child reproaches his foster mother and is returned to his real mother.* India: Thompson-Balys.

T673. *Rich but stingy couple adopt young man as their son: everybody is happy.* India: Thompson-Balys.

T674. *Adopted child deserted when own child is born to couple.* India: Thompson-Balys.

T675. *Real mother preferred to foster mothers.* Kid abandoned by his mother suckles the whole flock but is not satisfied. Chauvin III 56 No. 15.

J391. Kind foster parents chosen rather than cruel parents.

T675.1. *Children prefer foster mother.* Gaster Thespis 252.

T676. *Childless couple adopt animal as substitute for child.* India: *Thompson-Balys; Japanese: Ikeda.

T676.1. *Childless woman adopts a serpent (transformed man).* (Cf. D191.) Italian: Basile Pentamerone II No. 5.

T677. *Substitute for a child.* Aged, childless couple carve themselves a child from wood, or make one from snow, clay, and the like. Lithuanian: Balys Index No. 701*; Russian: Andrejev No. 703.

T678. *Adopted child identical with real child reared with him.* *Ranke FFC CXIV 152—4.

T680. Care of children—miscellaneous motifs.

T681. *Each likes his own children best.* Snipe asks sportsman to spare its small ones, easily recognized as being the prettiest in the forest. To be on the safe side he shoots only the ugliest he can find. They are the young snipes. (Often told of the ape.) *Type 247; Dh II 242ff.; Fb "ugle" III 964a; Wienert FFC LVI 77 (ET 426), 146 (ST 509); Herbert III 39ff.; India: Thompson-Balys.

T681.1. *Animals ridicule foolish pride of owl in the beauty of his son's really hideous feet.* Spanish Exempla: Keller.

T682. *Hero a posthumous son.* *Von Sydow Fåvne 40; Icelandic: *Boberg.

S312.3. Posthumous child to be exposed. T645.1. Sword left for posthumous son to kill father's murderer. Z200. Heroes.

T684. *Devil substitutes himself for new-born child.* Köhler-Bolte I 148.

F321. Fairy steals child from cradle.

T685. *Twins.* (Cf. T587.) Saintyves "Les Jumeaux, dans l'ethnographie et la mythologie" Revue anthropologique XXV (1925) 54—9; Icelandic: *Boberg.

A116. Twin gods. H255. Test: which of twins is elder.

T685.1. *Twin adventurers.* *Harris Cult of the Heavenly Twins passim; Dickson 98ff.; Italian: Basile Pentamerone I No. 7; India: *Thompson-Balys; New Hebrides: Dixon 132; N. A. Indian: Thompson Tales 320 n. 155, (Quiché): Alexander Lat. Am. 169ff.

P251. Brothers. Z210. Brothers as heroes.

T685.2. *Hostile twins.* *Dickson 98ff.; *Krappe Balor 30, 143 n. 33, FL XXXIV 189ff.; Gaster Oldest Stories 168.

A511.1.2.1. Twin culture heroes quarrel before birth. T575.1.3. Twins quarrel before birth in mother's womb.

T685.3. *Twins who look exactly alike.* India: Thompson-Balys.

T685.4. *Twins: as twins are reared one born earlier becomes continually weaker, the other stronger.* India: Thompson-Balys.

T686. *Quadruplet heroes.* Haiti: Alexander Lat. Am. 30.

T687. *Triplets (as heroes).* Icelandic: *Boberg.

T688. *Children sleep in village dormitory.* India: Thompson-Balys.

U. THE NATURE OF LIFE

DETAILED SYNOPSIS

U0—U99. Life's inequalities
- U0. Life's inequalities
- U10. Justice and injustice
- U30. Rights of the strong
- U60. Wealth and poverty

U100—U299. Nature of life—miscellaneous motifs
- U110. Appearances deceive
- U120. Nature will show itself
- U130. The power of habit
- U140. One man's food is another man's poison
- U150. Indifference of the miserable
- U160. Misfortune with oneself to blame the hardest
- U170. Behavior of the blind
- U180. In vino veritas
- U210. Bad ruler, bad subject
- U220. Forced peace valueless
- U230. The nature of sin
- U240. Power of mind over body
- U250. Shortness of life
- U260. Passage of time
- U270. Security breeds indifference

U. THE NATURE OF LIFE

U. The nature of life.

N135.3. The luck-bringing shirt. The king is to become lucky when he puts on the shirt of a lucky man. The only man who says that he is lucky has no shirt.

U0—U99. Life's inequalities.

U0. Life's inequalities.

A1599.8. Inequalities of fortune among men. A1618. Origin of inequalities among men.

U10. Justice and injustice.

D1318.1.1. Stone bursts as sign of unjust judgment. D1318.2.1. Laughing fish reveals unjust judgment. J230. Real and apparent values. J1170. Clever judicial decisions. T575.1.1.3. Child in mother's womb reveals unjust judgment. U119.1.2. At a hanging the witnesses are bigger thieves than the culprit. W35. Justice.

U11. *Small trespasses punished; large crimes condoned.*

U11.1. *Ass punished for stealing mouthful of grass; lion and wolf forgiven for eating sheep.* Wesselski Mönchslatein 71 No. 61.

U11.1.1. *Animals confess sins to one another: fox and wolf forgive each other; punish ass.* (Cf. V20.) *Pauli (ed. Bolte) No. 350.

U11.1.1.1. *Animals confess sins to lion holding court.* All the powerful animals forgiven. Ass and lamb are punished. Italian Novella: Rotunda.

U11.1.1.2. *Penitent in confession worries about little sins and belittles the big ones.* *Wesselski Arlotto I 191 No. 17; Italian Novella: Rotunda.

U11.2. *He who steals much called king; he who steals little called robber.* *Pauli (ed. Bolte) No. 351; Scala Celi 20a No. 120; Alphabet No. 334; Spanish Exempla: Keller.

U11.2.1. *Wolf punished for theft; kings honored.* Wesselski Bebel II 126 No. 82.

U12. *Largest burdens laid on smallest asses: best offices to most ignorant men.* *Wesselski Bebel II 121 No. 64.

U14. *Unworthy rewarded instead of the worthy.* Italian Novella: *Rotunda.

U15. *Fool laughs at the absurdities he sees about him.* (1) Sees a man who is to die that day buy shoes. (2) Sees sheriff leading a man to the gallows: a big thief leading a little one. (3) Sees farmer weeping at funeral of his child, while priest (the real father) sings. Wesselski Mönchslatein 193 No. 153.

N456. Enigmatical smile (laugh) reveals secret knowledge.

U15.0.1. *Dwarf king (fairy) laughs at the absurdities he sees about him.* (1) Sees man who is to die that day complain that his shoes are too thin. (Cf. J2174.) (2) Sees women adorn their heads when they are immoral below. (Cf. J2050.) (3) Sees man remove from his wife's garment dust gathered while she lay with another man. (Cf. J2301.3.) (4) Sees persons making plans while forgetting to say, "If God wills." Irish myth: *Cross.

U15.1. *Philosopher laughs at the vanities and sins of the world.* His companion weeps. Spanish: Childers.

U18. *The fathers have eaten sour grapes and the children's teeth are set on edge.* Jewish: Neuman.

U21. *Justice depends on the point of view.*

U21.1. *Hen complains that man eats her, but she eats ant.* Indonesia: DeVries's list No. 101.

U21.2. *A gift of property silences criticism.* A priest who has preached against lucrative places given the clergy is silent when he receives one. Pauli (ed. Bolte) No. 546.

U21.3. *Man complains of injustice of gods' wrecking ship because of one man's sin.* He then kills whole swarm of ants because one has stung him. Wienert FFC LVI 77 (ET 429), 103 (ST 161); Halm No. 118; Irish: O'Suilleabhain 11, Beal XXI 305.

U21.4. *Wolf objects to lion stealing sheep from him although he has himself stolen it.* Wienert FFC LVI 55 (ET 148), 129 (ST 366); Halm No. 279.

U21.5. *Judge reduces penalty when accused is his own son.* India: Thompson-Balys.

U25. *Theft to avoid starvation forgiven.* *Chauvin II 126 No. 128.

U27. *Swallow killed in court house by snake laments injustice in house of justice.* Wienert FFC LVI 50 (ET 100), 140 (ST 464); Halm No. 418.

U30. Rights of the strong. Wienert FFC LVI 147.

J810. Policy in dealing with the great. J910. Humility of the great. J950. Presumption of the lowly. J1909.1. Fisherman fails to make fish dance to his flute. Later in his net they jump about without the aid of the flute.

U31. *Wolf unjustly accuses lamb and eats him.* When all the lamb's defenses are good the wolf asserts the right of the strong over the weak. (Usually accused of stirring up water from lower in stream.) (Cf. U141.) Wienert FFC LVI 50 (ET 97), 148 (ST 526); Halm Aesop No. 274; *Crane Vitry 191 No. 135; Herbert III 12; Alphabet No. 631; Jacobs Aesop 199 No. 2; Italian Novella: Rotunda; Indonesia: DeVries's list No. 83 (monkey and goat).

U31.1. *Cat unjustly accuses cock and eats him.* Although all the cock's defenses are good the cat tells him that she can no longer go hungry and eats him. Italian Novella: Rotunda.

U31.2. *Crow exercises rights of strong over dove who cannot defend self.* Dove at crow's request sings to save her brood which crow kills after song. Spanish Exempla: Keller.

U32. *Smallness of offense no excuse when hunter prepares to kill lark.* She has stolen but a single grain of wheat. Wienert FFC LVI 64 (ET 273), 146 (ST 513); Halm Aesop No. 209.

U33. *Cock killed by his captors in spite of his plea of usefulness to man.* Wienert FFC LVI 49, 64 (ET 88, 280, 281), 146, 148 (ST 514, 527, 528); Halm Aesop Nos. 14, 195, 341.

U34. *Nobleman murders one of the people.* Goes unpunished. Italian Novella: Rotunda.

U34.1. *Nobleman who kills one of the people is brought to justice only after long delay.* Italian Novella: Rotunda.

U35. *Rich man (king) seizes poor widow's (nun's) cow.* Herbert III 40ff. No. 39; Hervieux IV No. 40; Irish myth: *Cross.

U35.1. *King seizes old woman's cow.* Irish myth: *Cross.

U35.1.1. *King seizes poor man's lamb.* Jewish: Neuman.

U35.2. *Nobles ruin peasant's (widow's) crops with impunity.* India: *Thompson-Balys.

U36. *Lion cub killed by bull gives lioness no right to complain.* Wienert FFC LVI 50 (ET 92), 129 (ST 367); Halm Aesop No. 395.

U37. *Wolf as commander orders all booty divided, but keeps his own.* Wienert FFC LVI 47 (ET 58), 103 (ST 157); Halm Aesop No. 281.
J811.1. The lion's share.

U38. *Ruler exiles subject for trivial remark.* Italian Novella: Rotunda.

U41. *Ruler forces bishop to ordain ignorant priest.* Italian Novella: Rotunda.

U42. *Praise what your master likes and scorn what he dislikes.* India: Thompson-Balys.

U60. Wealth and poverty.

U61. *Dividing after God's fashion: little to poor, much to rich.* *Wesselski Hodscha Nasreddin II 233 No. 509, Bebel I 232 No. 149, Mensa Philosophica No. 63.

U63. *Priest has no friends until he becomes bishop: then they flock to him.* Pauli (ed. Bolte) No. 421.

U65. *Wealth is relative: beggar with horse, wife, or dog considered rich by poorer beggar.* Pauli (ed. Bolte) No. 612.

U65.1. *Grass serves as pleasant couch for poor.* Jewish: Neuman.

U66. *Every man has his price.*

U66.1. *Every woman has her price.*

U66.1.1. *Bid raised for queen's favors until she hesitates.* Jester replies, "If a man have goods enough, he might have a sovereign lady." England, U.S.: *Baughman.

U67. *Jester takes cow and tells king people have plenty of milk, for "he who is warm thinks everyone else is."* India: Thompson-Balys.

U68. *Optimist becomes pessimist when his money is stolen.* India: Thompson-Balys.

U71. *Man so constantly enriched by God that he cannot give all his goods to the poor.* Herbert III 7; Crane Vitry 175 No. 97.

U81. *Great possessions bring great risks.* Jewish: Neuman.

U81.1. *Dove's pride in her large brood linked with fear for their loss.* Wienert FFC LVI 44 (ET 21), 141 (ST 470); Halm Aesop No. 358.

U83. *King in exile neglected, but courted when he regains throne.* India: Thompson-Balys.

U84. *Price of object depends on where it is on sale.* India: Thompson-Balys.

U100—U299. The nature of life—miscellaneous motifs.

U110. Appearances deceive. Wienert FFC LVI 123.
K1800. Deception by disguise or illusion.

U111. *Many books do not make a scholar.* Pauli (ed. Bolte) No. 608.

U111.1. *Many books do not make a scholar: youth tricks mother by carrying many books.* Pierre Fai-feu No. 3.

U112. *Beard on she-goats do not make a male.* Wienert FFC LVI 77 (ET 431), 124 (ST 332).

U113. *Big voice: little creature.* (Frogs, crickets.) Wienert FFC LVI 61, *66 (ET 232, 304), 123 (ST 321, 322); Halm Aesop Nos. 172, 248.

U114. *Mountain in labor brings forth a mouse.* Wienert FFC LVI *44 (ET 24), *101 (ST 141); Jacobs Aesop 203 No. 14; Spanish Exempla: Keller.

U115. *The skeleton in the closet.* An apparently happy man lets another see the actual misery of his existence. Pauli (ed. Bolte) No. 223.

U115.1. *Apparently happy woman discloses the skeleton of her slain paramour.* Italian Novella: *Rotunda.
H1195. Task: having woman free from worries make a shirt.

U116. *Hypocrite is acclaimed as saint after his death.* Italian Novella: *Rotunda.

U117. *Man rejects bride because she seems immature.* Her father reassures him that she has had several children already. Italian Novella: Rotunda.
J2427. Numskull praises his daughter as being pregnant.

U119. *Other ways in which appearances deceive.* Italian Novella: Rotunda.

U119.1. *Revelations of a satyr.* Italian Novella: Rotunda.
B24.1. Satyr reveals woman's infidelity.

U119.1.1. *At a funeral of a child a satyr reveals that the real father (officiating priest) sings while the cuckold weeps.* (Cf. U15.) Italian Novella: Rotunda.

U119.1.2. *At a hanging the witnesses are bigger thieves than the culprit.* (Cf. U10.) Italian Novella: Rotunda.

U119.2. *Peasant wishes to exchange places with monks.* Thinks they lead a very easy life. One night's experience in the monastery makes him change his mind. Italian Novella: Rotunda.

U119.3. *Handsome exterior does not indicate beautiful soul.* Angel holds nose when handsome sinner passes. Spanish Exempla: Keller.

U119.4. *An ugly face does not mean an ugly soul.* A noble and holy man who is very ugly is proved to be a saintly soul. Spanish Exempla: Keller.

U119.5. *Stories to show that one's name does not alter his condition.* India: Thompson-Balys.

U120. Nature will show itself.

J512. Animal should not try to change his nature. J1908. Absurd attempt to change animal nature.

U121. *Like parent, like child.*

U121.1. *Crab walks backward: learned from his parents.* *Crane Vitry 152 No. 44; Wienert FFC LVI *63 (ET 258), *103 (ST 159); Halm Aesop No. 187.

U121.2. *Hind, like his mother, flees before the hounds.* Useless for her to urge him to stand up against them. Wienert FFC LVI *63 (ET 256), 103 (ST 158, 501); Halm Aesop No. 130.

U121.3. *Farmer's son and noble's reared in country.* The former takes to toil on farm, the latter to riding and hunting. Spanish Exempla: Keller.

U121.4. *Alleged son of king proved to be bastard when he displays habits of his true father.* Spanish Exempla: Keller.

U121.5. *Father, like son, acts foolishly at king's court.* India: Thompson-Balys.

U121.6. *Butcher's son becomes cruel and atrocious ruler.* India: Thompson-Balys.

U122. *Dungbeetle prefers his dunghill to all other smells.* Wienert FFC LVI 60 (ET 217), 119 (ST 292); Halm Aesop No. 185; Herbert III 35ff.; India: Thompson-Balys.

U122.1. *Beetles treated with as much honor as oxen will not learn to act as oxen.* Spanish Exempla: Keller.

U123. *Hog goes to bath but wallows in the mud.* Chauvin III 39 No. 2.

U124. *Scorpion, in spite of himself, stings the turtle carrying him across the stream.* Is drowned. *Chauvin II 117 No. 95.

K952.1. Ungrateful river-passenger kills carrier from within.

U125. *Wolf loses interest in the sermon when he sees a flock of sheep.* A dervish preaches to him. Chauvin II 125 No. 123; Scala Celi 50b No. 285; Spanish Exempla: Keller.

U125.1. *Heron (crane) loses interest in heaven if there are no snails.* India: *Thompson-Balys.

U126. *Dog allowed to warm self in house begins to bark.* Is chased off. Chauvin III 39 No. 1.

A2232.8. Dogs' embassy to Zeus chased off. J581.1. Wolf as dog's guest sings. J2137.6. Camel and ass together captured because of ass's singing. J2351. Animal betrays himself to his enemies by talking. Q433.3. Zeus has embassy of dogs imprisoned for fouling his court.

U127. *Fawn, in spite of his fine horns, runs from the dog.* Wienert FFC LVI 63 (ET 257), 89 (ST 12): Halm Aesop No. 303.

U128. *Tiger son of human mother scratches her and licks her blood.* India: Thompson-Balys.

U128.1. *Tiger father of human child licks its blood.* India: Thompson-Balys.

U129. *Nature will show itself—miscellaneous.*

U129.1. *Thieving nature of the fox will show itself.* Nouvelles Récréations No. 29.

U129.2. *Prostitute will deceive new lover as always.* India: Thompson-Balys.

U129.3. *Washerman as minister thinks of washing and fails the king.* India: Thompson-Balys.

U130. The power of habit. Wienert FFC LVI 111.

J2527. Thief out of habit robs from his own purse.

U130.1. *Newly rich cannot resist call for distribution of food to beggars.* India: Thompson-Balys.

U131. *Familiarity takes away fear.*

U131.1. *Fox finally converses with lion whom he had feared at first.* Wienert FFC LVI 60 (ET 224), 111 (ST 224); Halm Aesop No. 39; Jacobs Aesop 208 No. 34.

U131.2. *Men at first frightened at camel take him into their service.* Wienert FFC LVI 66 (ET 306), 111 (ST 224); Halm Aesop No. 180.

U133. *Man soon learns to stand the smells of the tannery.* Wienert FFC LVI 81 (ET 474), 111 (ST 226); Halm Aesop No. 368; India: Thompson-Balys.

U133.1. *Farmer prefers stable smells to flowers.* Latter make him ill. Wesselski Mönchslatein 13 No. 8; Spanish Exempla: Keller.

U134. *Knight doesn't want to go to heaven if there are no hunting dogs there.* Spanish Exempla: Keller.

U135. *Longing for accustomed food and living.*

U135.1. *At feast cat chooses rat meat; other animals cannot eat it.* Spanish Exempla: Keller.

U135.2. *Shepherd in king's palace sickens for country air.* India: Thompson-Balys.

U135.3. *Former slave sickens for accustomed food.* Spanish Exempla: Keller; India: Thompson-Balys.

U135.3.1. *Peasant girl married to king longs for peasant ways of eating.* India: Thompson-Balys.

U135.3.2. *Peasants fed white bread demand the rye bread to which they are accustomed.* Pauli (ed. Bolte). No. 570.

U136. *Fisher and hunter exchange catches for variety: soon return to original food.* Wienert FFC LVI 81 (ET 475), 111 (ST 227); Japanese: Ikeda.

U136.1. *Dissatisfied workmen exchange work: still more dissatisfied.* Bødker Exempler 276 No. 14; India: Thompson-Balys.

J512.7. Mouse, bird, and sausage keep house together. When they exchange duties all goes wrong. J2431. A man undertakes to do his wife's work. All goes wrong.

U136.2. *Beasts and fishes exchange places: fatal to both.* India: Thompson-Balys.

U137. *Mill horse when taken to war keeps going in a circle, as he has learned in the mill.* *Liebrecht 110f.

U138. *Habit of dishonesty (thievery) cannot be broken.*

U138.1. *Dishonest silversmith restless until silver ornament is mixed with alloy.* India: Thompson-Balys.

U138.2. *Thieves cannot quit plundering.* India: Thompson-Balys.

U139. *Power of habit—miscellaneous.*

U139.1. *Habitual food and drink continued even when it is harmful.* Bødker Exempler.

U139.2. *Conservatism defies reason.*

U139.2.1. *Conservative but absurd way of slaughtering hog stubbornly kept.* India: Thompson-Balys.

U140. One man's food is another man's poison. Wienert FFC LVI 121.

U141. *Enmity between fisherman and dweller on the river.* Fishing stirs up the water and makes it unfit for drinking. (Cf. U31.) Wienert FFC LVI 84 (ET 512), 121 (ST 303); Halm Aesop No. 25.

U142. *Ox likes loving strokes of man; flea fears them.* Wienert FFC LVI 60 (ET 223), 121 (ST 307); Halm Aesop No. 426.

U143. *Collier and fuller cannot live together: one makes things clean, the other soils them.* Wienert FFC LVI 85 (ET 513), 121 (ST 305); Halm Aesop No. 59.

U144. *Nightingale cannot lodge with birds whose nest is made of manure.* Spanish Exempla: Keller.

U146. *Royalty unable to endure coarse entertainment.*

H41.1. Princess on the pea.

U146.1. *Coarse food, etc., sends adulterous king back to his wife.* India: Thompson-Balys.

U147. *Animals try unsuccessfully to exchange food.* India: *Thompson-Balys.

B392.1. Animals grateful for appropriate food. J512. Animal should not try to change his nature. J1565.1. Fox and crane invite each other. J1903. Absurd ignorance concerning animal's eating and drinking.

U148. *Good weather for one is foul for another.* Cf. Heywood's Play of the Weather.

U148.1. *Bird wants sunshine, worm clouds.* India: Thompson-Balys.

U149. *What is one man's food is another man's poison—miscellaneous.*

U149.1. *Lions despise what asses admire (braying).* India: Thompson-Balys.

U150. Indifference of the miserable.

U151. *Ass indifferent to enemy's approach: he could be no more miserable than now.* Wienert FFC LVI 71 (ET 352), 144 (ST 498).

U160. Misfortune with oneself to blame the hardest. Wienert FFC LVI 117.

U161. *Eagle killed with arrow made with his own feather.* Wienert FFC LVI *64 (ET 277), 117 (ST 273); Halm Aesop No. 4; Spanish Exempla: Keller.

U162. *Tree cut down with axe for which it has furnished a handle.* Wienert FFC LXI *74 (ET 388), 117 (ST 274); Halm Aesop No. 123; Jewish: *Neuman; India: Thompson-Balys.

U170. Behavior of the blind.

N388. Blind men accidentally hurt each other.

U171. *Blind man crosses a narrow bridge which his guide is afraid to attempt.* Alphabet No. 140.

U172. *Two blind men succeed in fooling each other about their blindness.* India: Thompson-Balys.

U173. *Futile attempt to explain to a blind man meaning of "white".* India: Thompson-Balys.

U180. In vino veritas.. Jewish: *Neuman.

U181. *Man unable to persuade wife to confess misdeed to priest succeeds when he makes her drunk.* (Cf. J1141.) Pauli (ed. Bolte) No. 242.

U210. Bad ruler, bad subject.

U211. *No great knights now because no great kings.* Pauli (ed. Bolte) No. 531.

U212. *To have good servants a lord must be good.* Pauli (ed. Bolte) No. 532.

U220. Forced peace valueless.

U221. *Monk under pressure from abbot forgives the crucifix which has fallen and hurt him.* He says that nevertheless there will always be hatred between them. *Wesselski Arlotto II 222 No. 90; *Pauli (ed. Bolte) No. 336.

U230. The nature of sin.

U230.0.1. *Monk leaves monastery when he sees a devil there tempting brethren.* Returns when in the world he sees scores of devils tempting the people. Spanish Exempla: Keller.

U231. *Hermit having rebuked youth falls himself when exposed to the same sin.* Herbert III 5; *Crane Vitry 169 No. 81.

U231.1. *Monk rebukes brethern who succumb to temptation.* When he is exposed to it he understands what temptation is. Spanish Exempla: Keller.

U232. *No place secret enough for sin.* Alphabet No. 3; Wienert FFC LVI 80 (ET 458), 138 (ST 441); Halm No. 354.

T331.4. No. place secret enough for fornication. Monk thus repels temptress.

U235. *Lying is incurable.* A father asks about his son. When he hears that he lies, he gives the son up as hopeless. Other sins may be outgrown. Pauli (ed. Bolte) No. 393; Spanish Exempla: Keller.

U235.1. *Liar cannot be healed even when taking bath in the Ganges.* India: Thompson-Balys.

U236. *False repentance of the sick.* Wolf having eaten too much meat promises God to eat no more meat. When he becomes well he eats as before. Pauli (ed. Bolte) No. 307.

U236.1. *False repentance of the sick, rich man.* After his death it was discovered that he had intended to retrieve his money from church if he recovered. Spanish Exempla: Keller.

K231.3. Refusal to make sacrifice after need is past. M266. Man promises to build church if he is saved at sea.

U240. Power of mind over body.

J2317. Well man made to believe that he is sick. K1889.2. Deceptive cure by illusion.

U241. *King grows lean from fear of death.* *Chauvin VIII 181 No. 213.

U242. *Hares fearing death outrun pursuing dogs.* Wienert FFC LVI 51 (ET 103), 142 (ST 476); Japanese: Ikeda.

U242.1. *The hare's last will.* Surrounded by hunters and hounds, the hare considers to whom each of his members will be allotted. Succeeds in escaping. Lithuanian: Balys Index No. 160*; Prussian: Plenzat 8.

U243. *Courage conquers all and impossible is made possible.* India: Thompson-Balys.

U250. Shortness of life. Jewish: *Neuman.

U251. *The bad custom in the world: the young die as well as the old.* Hence youth enters monastery. *Crane Vitry 184 No. 116; Alphabet No. 212; *Mensa Philosophica No. 181.

U260. Passage of time.

U261. *Time seems short to those who play, long for those who wait.* So says servant girl whose mistress upbraids her for late hours. Wesselski Bebel I 185 No. 39.

U262. *Suffering healed by time.* Jewish: *Neuman.

U270. Security breeds indifference.

U271. *Cat ceases catching rats as soon as he is given a home in a monastery.* Thus with lazy priests. Pauli (ed. Bolte) No. 573.

V. RELIGION

DETAILED SYNOPSIS

V. RELIGION

V. Religion.

A1541. Origin of religious feasts. A2221. Animal characteristic: reward for pious act. A2231. Animal characteristics: punishment for impiety. B250. Religious animals. J564. Intemperance in worship. J1261. Repartee based on levity toward sacred persons and things. Q170. Religious rewards.

V0—V99. Religious services.

V0. Religious services. Irish myth: Cross; Icelandic: *Boberg; Norwegian: Solheim 22; Jewish: *Neuman.

D1766. Magic results produced by religious ceremony. E501.3.8. Wild huntsman wanders for disturbing church service. F382. Exorcising fairies. Fairies disappear when some name or ceremony of the Christian Church is used. G224.1. Witch's charm opposite of Christian. Must be "Without God and Holy Mary" instead of "With God, etc." G243. Witch's sabbath. G285. Witches avoid religious ceremonies. G304.2.4.1. Trolls cannot endure church bells. M183. Religious vows and promises. Q20. Piety rewarded.

V1. *Objects of worship.* *Encyc. Rel. Ethics Index 649b; Irish myth: *Cross; Icelandic: MacCulloch Eddic 214, *Boberg.

V1.1. *Worship of particular gods and goddesses.*

V1.1.1. *Worship of one god.* Jewish: Neuman.

V1.2. *Worship of spirits.*

V1.2.1. *Worship of fairies.* Irish myth: Cross (V1.16, V1.16.1); Icelandic: *Boberg.

V1.2.2. *Worship of devil.* Irish myth: Cross (V1.15, V1.15.1).

V1.2.3. *Worship of "disar".* Icelandic: *Boberg.

V1.2.4. *Worship of angels.* Jewish: *Neuman.

V1.3. *Worship of ancestors.* Encyc. Rel. Ethics I 425—67; Irish myth: Cross; Icelandic: Boberg; India: Thompson-Balys; Chinese: Eberhard FFC CXX 411 s.v. "Ahnenfiguren"; Hawaii: Beckwith Myth 160; Society Islands: Henry Ancient Tahiti (Honolulu, 1928) 561; Tuamotu: Stimson MS (T-G. 3/619); Africa (Cameroon): Mansfield 233, (Fang): Trilles 140.

V1.4. *Worship of heavenly bodies.* Jewish: Neuman.

V1.4.1. *Worship of the sky.* (Cf. A210.)

V1.4.2. *Worship of the sun.* (Cf. A220.) Irish myth: *Cross; Icelandic: Boberg; Jewish: Neuman; India: *Thompson-Balys; Hawaii: Beckwith Myth 12.

V1.4.3. *Worship of moon.* (Cf. A240.) Jewish: Neuman.

V1.4.4. *Worship of stars.* (Cf. A250.) Jewish: Neuman; India: Thompson-Balys.

V1.5. *Worship of manifestations in nature.*

V1.5.1. *Worship of clouds.* (Cf. A283.)

V1.5.2. *Worship of thunder.* (Cf. A284.)

V1.5.3. *Worship of wind.* (Cf. A282.)

V1.5.4. *Worship of storm.* (Cf. A281.)

V1.5.5. *Worship of dawn.* (Cf. A270.)

V1.5.6. *Worship of light.* (Cf. A260.)

V1.5.6.1. *Worship of rainbow.* (Cf. A288.)

V1.5.7. *Worship of frost.* (Cf. A289.1.)

V1.6. *Worship of elements of nature.*

V1.6.1. *Worship of earth.* (Cf. A400.) India: Thompson-Balys.

V1.6.1.1. *Worship of mountains and hills.* (Cf. A495.) Danish: Kristensen Danske Sagn III (1895) 65ff., (1931) 47ff.

V1.6.2. *Worship of water.* (Cf. A420.)

V1.6.2.0.1. *Worship of water-goddess.* India: Thompson-Balys.

V1.6.2.1. *Sacred rivers and lakes.* (Cf. A425.)

V1.6.2.2. *Worship of sea.* (Cf. A421.) Irish myth: Cross.

V1.6.3. *Worship of fire.* (Cf. A493.) Encyc. Rel. Ethics Index 202c; Penzer III 160; Irish myth: *Cross; Jewish: *Neuman.

V1.6.3.1. *Sacred fire.* *Encyc. Rel. Ethics Index 202b; Penzer I 260, II 247—55; Irish myth: *Cross.

V1.6.3.1.1. *(Sacrificial) fire from which all others must be lighted.* Irish myth: *Cross.

V1.6.4. *Worship of minerals and metals.* (Cf. A492.)

V1.6.4.1. *Sacred stones.* Irish myth: *Cross; Icelandic: Corpus Poeticum Boreale I 322, Boberg, Schmidt DF XXXIX 86ff.; Hawaii: Beckwith Myth 88ff.; Tahiti: Henry Ancient Tahiti (Honolulu, 1928) 382.

V1.6.4.2. *Sacred shells.* Tonga: Gifford 52; Tahiti: Henry 391.

V1.7. *Worship of trees and plants.* (Cf. A430, C51.2.2.) *Encyc. Rel. Ethics Index 611b; *Penzer II 96 n. 1, VII 162 n. 1; Schmidt Brandtræer og Ulykkestræer Danske Studier (1928) 54ff.; Irish myth: *Cross; Icelandic: MacCulloch Eddic 214; S. A. Indian (Antilles): Alexander Lat. Am. 25f.

V1.7.1. *Sacred tree.* *Encyc. Rel. Ethics Index 611a; *Fb "træ" III 866a; Wimberly 156; Irish myth: *Cross; Jewish: Neuman.

V1.7.1.1. *Sacred oak.* Irish myth: *Cross; Jewish: Neuman.

V1.7.1.2. *Sacred ash.* Irish myth: *Cross.

V1.7.1.3. *Sacred yew.* Irish myth: *Cross.

V1.7.1.4. *Sacred bo-tree.* India: Thompson-Balys.

V1.8. *Worship of animals.* *Encyc. Rel. Ethics Index 28a; Jewish: *Neuman.

B811. Sacred animals. Q228. Punishment for trying to harm sacred animal.

V1.8.1. *Cow worship.* Encyc. Rel. Ethics Index 142bc; **Burnell FL LVIII 377ff.; *Penzer II 240; Icelandic: Boberg.

V1.8.1.1. *Bull worship.* Irish myth: Cross; Jewish: *Neuman.

V1.8.2. *Horse worship.* Penzer II 57; Icelandic: MacCulloch Eddic 216, *Boberg.

V1.8.3. *Dog worship.* Encyc. Rel. Ethics Index 167b; Jewish: Neuman; Chinese: Werner 422.

V1.8.4. *Swine worship.* Irish myth: Cross; Icelandic: MacCulloch Eddic 109, *Boberg.

M114.3. Vows taken on holy swine.

V1.8.5. *Wolf worship.* Icelandic: Boberg.

V1.8.6. *Serpent worship.* *Encyc. Rel. Ethics Index 539a; *Penzer III 142; Jewish: *Neuman.

V1.8.7. *Bird worship.* (Cf. A132.6.1.) Irish myth: Cross; Jewish: Neuman; Easter Island: Métraux Ethnology 313f.

V1.8.8. *Dragon worship.* Jewish: Neuman; Chinese: Eberhard FFC CXX 103f.

V1.8.9. *Lion worship.* Jewish: Neuman.

V1.8.10. *Ass worship.* Jewish: Neuman.

V1.8.11. *Fish worship.* Marquesas: Handy 104; Hawaii: Beckwith Myth 129.

V1.9. *Worship of tools and implements.*

V1.9.1. *Plow worship.* (Cf. A432.) Irish myth: *Cross.

V1.9.2. *Worship of weapons.* Irish myth: *Cross.

V1.9.3. *Worship of hammer (axe).* Tahiti: Henry Ancient Tahiti (Honolulu, 1928) 147.

V1.10. *Worship of fetish.* (Cf. D1274.) *Encyc. Rel. Ethics Index 200a; Irish myth: *Cross; Jewish: *Neuman; Africa (Fjort): Dennett 96.

V1.10.1. *Man worships a cake which from time to time he eats.* *Chauvin V 24 No. 13 n. 1.

V1.10.2. *Cult of heads.* Irish myth: Cross.

V1.10.3. *Sacred feather.* Tuamotu: Beckwith Myth 289.

V1.11. *Worship of idols.* (Cf. Q558.12, V11.10.) Irish myth: *Cross; Jewish: *Neuman.

V1.11.1. *Worship of golden calf.* Jewish: Neuman.

V1.11.2. *Worship of stone idols.* Jewish: Neuman.

V1.11.3. *Worship of wooden idol.* Icelandic: *Boberg; Hawaii: Beckwith Myth 16.

V4. *Value of religious exercises.*

V4.1. *Religious exercises weighed in balance.* A son doubts whether the words spoken by the priests to whom his father has willed a sum of money is worth so much. The words are put on paper and are found to outweigh the money. Pauli (ed. Bolte) No. 465; Irish: O'Suilleabhain 65, 113, Beal XXI 325, 335.

V5. *Negligence in religious exercise.* (Cf. Q223.)

V5.1. *Virgin Mary reproves a monk who sleeps at altar.* Alphabet No. 284.

V5.2. *Negligent priests buried under bags filled with words omitted from service.* *Crane Vitry 141 No. 19.

V5.3. *Devils cause monk to perspire and stay away from church service.* Pauli (ed. Bolte). No. 260.

V10. Religious sacrifices. *Encyc. Rel. Ethics Index 511b; *Hdwb. d. Abergl. IX Nachträge 19—54, 496—547; Irish: *Cross, Beal XXI 329; Jewish: *Neuman.

A751.1.3. Man in moon as punishment for disdainful sacrifice (Cain). A1545. Origin of sacrifices. B811. Sacred animals. C92.1.0.1. Tabu: killing animals for sacrifice. D1654.17. Throne of goddess's idol is lifted only after goat has been sacrificed. D1766.2. Magic results produced by sacrifices. D2107.1. Horse and weapons needed by hero are provided after incense is offered to Nandia, the bull. E382. Ghost summoned by pouring blod of sacrifices into trench. E433. Ghosts placated by sacrifices. K231.3. Refusal to make sacrifice after need is past. P427.1. Druid performs sacrifice. Q21. Reward for religious sacrifice. Q223.3. Neglect to sacrifice punished. S260. Sacrifices.

V10.1. *Goddess prevents suicide of man despairing of ability to make sacrifice.* India: Thompson-Balys.

V10.2. *God dislikes offerings beyond one's ability.* India: Thompson-Balys.

V11. *Power to which sacrifice is made.*

V11.1. *Sacrifice to tree.* (Cf. V1.1.) *Encyc. Rel. Ethics Index 611a; Fb "træ" III 866a.

V11.2. *Sacrifice to sea.* *Penzer II 72 n. 1, VII 146 n. 1; Irish myth: *Cross; Icelandic: Boberg; India: Thompson-Balys.

V11.2.1. *Sacrifice to river.* India: Thompson-Balys.

V11.3. *Sacrifice to stone.* *Encyc. Rel. Ethics Index 570; *Fb "sten" III 553a; Irish myth: *Cross; Icelandic: MacCulloch Eddic 225, *Boberg; Danish: Schmidt DF XXXIX 90ff.

V11.4. *Sacrifices to Confucius.* Encyc. Rel. Ethics IV 13f.; Chinese: Werner 102.

V11.5. *Sacrifice to wind.* Encyc. Rel. Ethics Index 645b; Icelandic: *Boberg; Swiss: Jegerlehner Oberwallis 307 No. 29; Greek: Euripides Iphigenia at Aulis.

V11.6. *Sacrifice to the dead.* (Cf. A108.1.) *Encyc. Rel. Ethics Index 512b; Irish myth: *Cross.

V11.6.1. *Human sacrifice in connection with funeral.* (Cf. S260.1.) Irish myth: *Cross.

V11.6.2. *Animal sacrifice in connection with funeral.* Irish myth: *Cross.

V11.7. *Sacrifice to animal.* Jewish: Neuman.

V11.7.1. *Sacrifice to serpent.* India: Thompson-Balys.

V11.8. *Sacrifice to saint.* Irish: O'Suilleabhain 89.

V11.9. *Sacrifice to deity.* Jewish: Neuman.

V11.9.1. *Sacrifice to unknown god.* Hawaii: Beckwith Myth 70.

V11.10. *Sacrifice to idols.* (Cf. V1.11.) Jewish: *Neuman.

V12. *Nature of sacrifice.*

V12.1. *Blood as sacrifice.* Irish: O'Suilleabhain 90.

V12.2. *Jewels as sacrifice to sea.* (Cf. V11.2.) *Penzer II 72 n. 1.

V12.3. *Skulls as sacrifice to a god.* India: Thompson-Balys.

V12.4. *Animals as sacrifice.* Irish myth: *Cross; Jewish: *Neuman; India: Thompson-Balys.

B2. Animal totems. B11.10.0.1. Sacrifice of animals to dragon. V16.1. Sacrifices of animals at Passover.

V12.4.0.1. *Sacrifice of animals at the edification of a temple.* Jewish: Moreno Esdras (V17.8).

V12.4.1. *Dog as sacrifice.* Irish myth: Cross; Chinese: Eberhard FFC CXX 218 No. 167.

V12.4.2. *Cat as sacrifice.* Irish myth: *Cross.

V12.4.3. *Pig as sacrifice.* Irish myth: *Cross; Jewish: Neuman; Chinese: Eberhard FFC CXX 218 No. 167.

V12.4.3.1. *Hog as sacrifice.* Icelandic: Boberg; Greek: Homer Odyssey XIV 435; Hawaii: Beckwith Myth 123.

V12.4.4. *Ox (bull) as sacrifice.* Irish myth: Cross; Icelandic: *Boberg: Greek: Homer passim; Jewish: Neuman.

V12.4.4.1. *Cow as sacrifice.* Cheremis: Sebeok-Nyerges.

V12.4.4.1.1. *Heifer as sacrifice.* Greek: Homer passim.

V12.4.4.2. *Calf as sacrifice.* Jewish: *Neuman.

V12.4.5. *Goat as sacrifice.* Icelandic: *Boberg; Jewish: Neuman.

V12.4.6. *Sheep (ram) as sacrifice.* Cheremis: Sebeok-Nyerges; Jewish: Neuman.

V12.4.7. *Hare as sacrifice.* Cheremis: Sebeok-Nyerges.

V12.4.8. *Ass as sacrifice.* *Krappe Classical Philology XLII (1947) 223—34; Jewish: *Neuman.

V12.4.9. *Horse as sacrifice.* *Encyc. Rel. Ethics Index 262b; *Howey 185ff.; Icelandic: *Boberg.

V12.4.10. *Fish as sacrifice.* Hawaii: Beckwith Myth 19, 420; Tahiti: Henry Ancient Tahiti (Honolulu, 1928) 241.

V12.4.11. *Bird as sacrifice.* Jewish: *Neuman.

V12.5. *Gold as sacrifice to false wooden god.* Icelandic: *Boberg.

V12.6. *Thrall as sacrifice.* Icelandic: *Boberg.
S260.1. Human sacrifice.

V12.7. *Eyes (human or animal) as sacrifice.* Marquesas: Handy 134; Hawaii: Beckwith Myth 130, 497.

V12.8. *Flowers as sacrifice.* Hawaii: Beckwith Myth 16.

V12.9. *Libations.* Drink poured out to the gods. Greek: Homer passim; Chinese: Graham.

V12.10. *Incense as sacrifice.* Jewish: *Neuman.

V13. *Sacrifice made when treasure is found.* Fb "skat" III 235b.

V14. *Sacrifice must be without blemish.* Greek: Homer passim; Jewish: Neuman.

V15. *Sacrifice: olive branch laid on altar of Mercy.* Greek: Frazer Apollodorus I 375 n. 2.

V16. *Sacrifice at religious festivals.* Jewish: Neuman.

V16.1. *Sacrifices at Passover.* Jewish: Moreno Esdras, *Neuman.

V17. *Purpose of sacrifice.*

V17.0.1. *Sacrifice to deity in order to obtain favors.* India: Thompson-Balys.

V17.1. *Sacrifice for a good year, crops.* Icelandic: *Boberg.

V17.2. *Sacrifice after committing a sin.* Jewish: Neuman.

V17.3. *Sacrifice to get help in danger.* Icelandic: *Boberg.

V17.4. *Sacrifice for good weather.* (Cf. V17.1.) Icelandic: Örvar-Odds saga 38f.

V17.4.1. *Sacrifice to get snow and good conditions for skiing.* Icelandic: Flateyjarbók I 21f., Boberg.

V17.5. *Sacrifice to get knowledge.*

V17.5.1. *Sacrifice to find out where abducted daughter is.* Icelandic: Flateyjarbók I 219, Boberg.

V17.6. *Sacrifice in order that king may live 300 years.* (Cf. F571.7.) Icelandic: Boberg.

V17.7. *Sacrifice to deity for return of abducted persons.* India: Thompson-Balys.

V17.8. *Sacrifice at edification of temple.* (Cf. V12.4.0.1.) Jewish: Neuman.

V17.9. *Sacrifice by women at childbirth.* Jewish: Neuman.

V18. *Ceremony of sacrifice.* Jewish: *Neuman.

V19. *Religious sacrifices—miscellaneous.*

V19.1. *Rising smoke as sign of acceptance of sacrifice.* Jewish: *Neuman.

V20. Confession of sins. *Encyc. Rel. Ethics Index 133b; *De Vooys

Middelnederlandse Legenden en Exempelen (Den Haag, 1926) 241ff.; *R. Pettazzoni La confessione dei peccati (Bologna, 1929); Jewish: *Neuman; Tahiti: Henry Ancient Tahiti (Honolulu, 1928) 143.

E411.0.2. Unquiet dead sinner taken to priest for absolution. E501.3.4. Wild huntsman wanders because of unshriven death. F1051.1. Barrel filled miraculously with penitent's tears. J1545.2. Husband disguises as a priest to hear his wife's confession. K443.8. Priest induced to betray secrets of confessional: money then exacted from him for silence. K1528. Wife confesses to disguised husband. M292. Wife undertakes man's penances for him: also to go to heaven for him? Q224. Punishment for betraying confessional. T257.4. Husband jealous of wife who goes to confession is punished by priest. U11.1.1.2. Penitent in confessional worries about little sins and belittles the big ones. V468. Priest bribed into betraying a confessional.

V20.1. *Protection of sinners by confession.* *Crane Vitry 245 No. 261, 246f. No. 263; Spanish Exempla: Keller.

V20.1.1. *A man without a confessor is a body without a head.* Irish myth: *Cross.

V20.1.2. *Confessor as "soul-friend".* Irish myth: *Cross.

V21. *Confession brings forgiveness of sin.* Nouvelles de Sens No. 15; Spanish: Keller, Espinosa Jr. No. 182.

V21.1. *Sincere confession miraculously obliterated as sign of forgiveness.* *Crane Vitry 266f. Nos. 301, 302; Alphabet Nos. 205, 209; Scala Celi 44b, 46a, 55a, 56b, 85b, 104a Nos. 251, 258, 308, 316, 493, 561; Ward II 663 No. 12; Herbert III 259, 380, 432, 469.

V21.2. *Woman confesses murder: unharmed by execution fire.* Alphabet No. 466; Scala Celi 47a No. 265; Wright Latin Stories 66.

R175. Rescue at the stake.

V21.3. *Confession of monk who intended to rob monastery brings forgiveness. Eventually elected prior.* Italian Novella: Rotunda.

V21.4. *Prior pardons sinning friar who has confessed.* Italian Novella: Rotunda.

V21.5. *Sinner confesses before sinning and thus is pardoned.* Spanish Exempla: Keller.

V21.6. *Sinner's tearmarks on written confession cause bishop to pardon his sins.* Spanish Exempla: Keller.

V22. *Condemnation because of death without confession.* (Cf. Q223.4.) Alphabet Nos. 231, 455; Spanish: Boggs FFC XC 89 No. 760A*, Keller.

V23. *Miracle to permit confession.*

V23.1. *Unshriven man restored to life in order to confess.* (Cf. V251.) Herbert III 14; *Crane Vitry 267 No. 303; *Crane Miraculis 93 No. 27; English: Wells 167 (Vernon Miracles).

V23.2. *Dumb man recovers speech in order to confess.* *Fb "stum".

F954. Dumb person brought to speak.

V24. *Miraculous manifestation at confession.*

V24.1. *Confession of sins of a pilgrim calms a great storm at sea.* Alphabet No. 174.

V25. *Easy confession not effective.*

V25.1. *Man returns from dead to protest against priest who has been too easy with him at confession.* Pauli (ed. Bolte) No. 303.

V25.2. *Confession without giving up sin punished.* Scala Celi 55a No. 309.

V27. *Penance magically concluded by confession.* Type 756B; *Andrejev FFC LXIX 136ff.

V29. *Confession—miscellaneous motifs.*

V29.1. *Search for confessor.* Great sinner sent from one confessor to another. All say that his sins are too great for forgiveness. Finally he succeeds. *Type 756C; **Andrejev FFC LIV 28ff.; Irish: O'Suilleabhain 46, 48, Beal XXI 317.

V29.2. *Monks shrive selves clean under threat of complete exposure of their sins by brother possessed of fiend.* Alphabet No. 171.

V29.3. *Miracle attests fact that man does not need to confess.* He hangs his sack on a sunbeam. Spanish: Boggs FFC XC 146 No. 1805A.

F1011.1. Clothes hung on sunbeam. V43. Holy man has his own mass. When upbraided for not coming to mass, he hangs his coat on a sunbeam.

V29.4. *Sodomist makes sport of confession.* Italian Novella: Rotunda.

V29.5. *Unnecessary for husband to confess as his wife has already done it for him.* Italian Novella: Rotunda.

V29.6. *Penitent brings manuscript of sins to confession.* Italian Novella: Rotunda.

T257.4.1. Jealous husband writes down wife's sins and hands list to confessor.

V29.6.1. *List of sins: schedule is returned miraculously cleansed of all his sins.* *Loomis White Magic 131.

V29.7. *Confessor and penitent exchange confidences.* Balance sins and cancel wrongs. Italian Novella: Rotunda.

V29.8. *The devil goes to confession.* Performs very severe penance, but cannot bear to humble himself and to stoop before the altar. (Cf. G303.16.9.) Lithuanian: Balys Index No. 818*.

V29.9. *Extortionate confessor demands golden statue.* India: Thompson-Balys.

V30. Sacrament. *Encyc. Rel. Ethics Index 510; DeVooys Middelnederlandse Legenden en Exempelen (Den Haag, 1926) 230ff.; Irish myth: *Cross.

B259.4. Bees build church of wax to contain consecrated host. D1031.1.1. Consecrated bread as magic object. G281. Consecrated wafer kept in mouth in order to be a witch. J1261.2. Disrespect for the sacrament. J1824. Fatal bread. Numskull refuses communion because his sister died shortly after eating the bread.

V30.1. *The eaten god.* *Encyc. Rel. Ethics V 136—39.

G13.1. Ritual cannibalism: corpse of hero (demigod) eaten to acquire his strength.

V30.1.1. *Flesh of Artemis eaten as quail or bear.* Greek: Fox 183.

V31. *Unconsecrated host.*

V31.1. *Host taken away from sinful priest.* Alphabet Nos 689, 691;

Scala Celi 40b, 41a Nos. 229—36; Herbert III 398, 399, 465, 480, 483, 609, 709; Lithuanian: Balys Legends No. 409; Italian Novella: Rotunda.

V31.2. *Unconsecrated host ineffective.* Alphabet No. 162.

V31.3. *Unconsecrated host refused.* Alphabet Nos. 161, 310.

V31.4. *Altar casts away host with louse baked in it.* Alphabet No. 690.

V31.5. *Devil eats unblessed bread.* Scala Celi 64b No. 353.

V32. *Host miraculously given when it is refused a man by the priest.* Pauli (ed. Bolte) No. 129; Alphabet Nos. 160, 420; Spanish Exempla: Keller; Icelandic: Boberg.

V33. *Incredulity as to sacredness of host punished.* Pauli (ed. Bolte) No. 687; Alphabet No. 309.

V33.1. *Incredulity as to sacredness of host confounded by miraculous appearance.* Scala Celi 42a, 65b, 66a Nos. 239, 357—60, 364; Herbert III 539.

V33.1.1. *Incredulity of true transformation of host banished by actual appearance of Jesus's body and blood.* Spanish Exempla: Keller.

V34. *Miraculous working of the host.*

D1031.1.1. Consecrated bread as magic object. N533.4. Consecrated wine used to discover treasure.

V34.1. *Host cures disease.* Alphabet No. 164.

V34.2. *Princess sick because toad has swallowed her consecrated wafer.* *Type 613; **Christiansen FFC XXIV 83f.; *BP I 322ff.

C55. Tabu: losing consecrated wafer. C940.1. Princess's secret sickness from breaking tabu D2064.1. Magic sickness because girl has thrown away her consecrated wafer.

V34.3. *Man who has received sacrament overcomes enemy, a blasphemer.* Alphabet No. 163; Pauli (ed. Bolte) No. 535.

V34.4. *Clothes of knight who kneels in mud before host as it passes miraculously kept clean.* Alphabet No. 492; Spanish Exempla: Keller.

V35. *The stolen sacrament.*

C55.3. Bee-master puts consecrated host into beehive. Has success with his bees. When he dies his spirit haunts the place.

V35.1. *Jews bribe woman to steal host for them: miraculous manifestations.* Scala Celi 64a No. 350.

V35.1.1. *Horse kneels before stolen sacrament.* Pauli (ed. Bolte) No. 556; Mensa Philosophica No. 59; Scala Celi 64a Nos. 349f.

B250. Religious animals.

V35.1.2. *Sacred image miraculously appears on stolen sacrament.* (Cf. V39.5.) Pauli (ed. Bolte) No. 557.

V35.2. *Stolen sacred hosts put into coffin.* Before death, a woman asks to put a bag into coffin. It is filled with hosts. (Cf. C55, D1031.1.1.) Lithuanian: Balys Legends Nos. 628ff.

V39. *Sacrament—miscellaneous motifs.*

V39.1. *Man considering self unworthy to receive host given it by God himself.* Pauli (ed. Bolte) No. 687.

V39.2. *Wicked woman unable to endure presence of host at mass.* English: Wells 151 (Richard Coer de Lyon).

V39.3. *Sacrament effective even from unworthy priest.* Man who has refused such a sacrament shown a vision of a leper giving men good water without harm. Alphabet No. 687; Irish: O'Suilleabhain 126, Beal XXI 334, 337.

V39.4. *Vision of sacrament in form of young child.* Alphabet No. 694; Scala Celi 66a Nos. 360—64; Toldo IV 49ff.; Irish: O'Suilleabhain 109.

V39.5. *Sacred image appears on host.* Woman who has vowed not to use make-up or ornaments thus rewarded. (Cf. V35.1.2.) Italian Novella: Rotunda.

V39.6. *Host given as pledge to keep one's word.* Italian Novella: Rotunda.

V39.7. *Voice from grave asks that it be opened.* Corpse spits out host because he has missed confession. Italian Novella: Rotunda.

G285.1. At communion witches spit out wine over shoulder.

V39.8. *Sick men die and go to hell because they hesitate to take sacrament.* Spanish Exempla: Keller.

V39.9. *Woman who eats before communion cannot swallow the wafer.* Irish myth: *Cross.

V40. Mass. *Encyc. Rel. Ethics Index 368a; Irish myth: *Cross.

K1961.1.2.1. Parody sermon (mass). Q521.6. Penance: holding midnight mass until someone will make responses. V255.2. Virgin gives private mass to devout lady unable to attend. Z140.3. Symbolism of colors in mass vestments. Z176. Symbolism of the mass.

V41. *Masses work miracles.* *Herbert III 273ff. passim; Scala Celi 130b, 131a Nos. 712—16.

D1766.5. Magic produced by saying mass.

V41.1. *Imprisoned miner kept alive by masses performed by his wife.* Ward II 675; Herbert III *85, 284, 324, 365; Alphabet No. 499.

V41.2. *Hearing masses causes triumph in tournament.* Angel takes absent knight's place. He is delayed by going to mass. *Liebrecht 29; Alphabet No. 462; Scala Celi 130b No. 714; *Ward II 662; Spanish Exempla: Keller.

V42. *Masses release souls from hell (purgatory).* Herbert III 284 Nos. 54ff. passim, 473; Alphabet Nos. 613, 652; Scala Celi 111b No. 620; Pauli (ed. Bolte) No. 228; Irish: O'Suilleabhain 99, Beal XXI 332; English: Wells 172 (Trentalle Sancti Gregorii); Swiss: Jegerlehner Oberwallis 298 No. 11; Spanish: Espinosa Jr. Nos. 192—97.

V43. *Holy man has his own mass.* (Cf. F1011.1, V29.3.) When upbraided for not coming to mass, he hangs his coat on a sunbeam. Swiss: Jegerlehner Oberwallis 309 No. 10; Spanish: Boggs FFC XC 147 No. 1805B.

V44. *Faithful attendance at mass outweighs evil deeds.* *Crane Vitry Nos. 223ff. passim; Irish: O'Suilleabhain 98, Beal XXI 331.

V45. *Mass said for dead; they arise and say "Amen".* Scala Celi 133a No. 732.

V46. *Pebble put in box each time mass is heard.* Irish: O'Suilleabhain 127.

V48. *The canonical hours.* Irish myth: *Cross.

B252.2. Birds (in otherworld) call at canonical hours.

V49. *Mass—miscellaneous motifs.*

V49.1. *Werwolves hold mass.* (Cf. D113.1.1, E492, G243.) Köhler-Bolte I 134; Gascon: Bladé Contes pop. de Gascogne II 360 No. 4.

V49.2. *Angel holds mass in church on the day that the king absents himself for sake of hunting trip.* Spanish Exempla: Keller.

V50. Prayer. *Encyc. Rel. Ethics Index 470a; Irish myth: *Cross; Missouri French: Carrière; Jewish: *Neuman.

C713.1. Tabu: merman's wife not to stay till church benediction. D781. Disenchantment by prayer (mass) of pope. D2163.5. Saint's prayer wins battle. D2176.3. Evil spirit exorcised. E341.3. Dead grateful for prayers. E443.2. Ghost laid by prayer. E754.1.1. Condemned soul saved by prayer. J1269.7. Man while praying refuses to salute superior. Q223.1. Neglect to pray punished.

V51. *Learning to pray.* Jewish: Neuman.

V51.1. *Man who does not know how to pray so holy that he walks on water.* *Pauli (ed. Bolte) No. 332; **Andrejev "Tri Starca" Novoje Delo (Kazan, 1922) (see Anderson Zs. f. Vksk. XXX-XXXII 171); Lithuanian: Balys Index No. 827*; Russian: Andrejev No. 827*.

V51.2. *Worldly-minded learn to pray by thinking of their usual business.* Pauli (ed. Bolte) Nos. 334, 338; Scala Celi 37b No. 209.

V51.3. *Woman shows that the Lord's Prayer is the best.* Pauli (ed. Bolte) No. 333.

V51.4. *Woman taught that it is better to pray before Christ's image than before a saint's.* Wesselski Arlotto I 201 No. 26.

V51.5. *"Beatus" best prayer for saving condemned souls.* (Cf. E754.1.1.) Irish myth: *Cross.

V52. *Miraculous power of prayer.* Irish: *Cross, Beal XXI 334, O'Suilleabhain 112; Spanish Exempla: Keller; West Indies: Flowers 579. Cf. Nouvelles de Sens No. 26.

D1273.0.2. Magic spells mixed with Christian prayers. D1766.1. Magic results produced by prayer. D2105.1. Provisions provided in answer to prayer. D2143.1.3. Rain produced by prayer. E63. Resuscitation by prayer. V243. Angel answers mortal's prayer.

V52.1. *Man saved from lechery through prayer.* Alphabet No. 65; Spanish Exempla: Keller.

V52.2. *Continuous prayer sustains man through frightful vigil.* *Type 307; *BP III 534; *Köhler-Bolte II 213ff.; Irish: Beal XXI 313, 319, O'Suilleabhain 37, 53; Japanese: Ikeda.

E251.1.1. Vampire's power overcome by endurance and prayer. H1450. Vigilance test.

V52.3. *Prayer before battle brings victory.* Scala Celi 151b No. 833; Irish myth: *Cross; Spanish Exempla: Keller; Jewish: *Neuman.

V52.4. *Objects supplied through prayer.* Irish myth: Cross.

V52.5. *Prayer restores shattered vessel.* Irish myth: Cross.

D1565.4. Saint's breath restores shattered vessel.

V52.6. *Mariners saved from maelstrom through prayer.* Irish myth: Cross.

V52.7. *Prayer at saint's flagstone averts trouble.* Irish myth: Cross.

V52.8. *Prayer brings death to enemy.* Irish myth: *Cross; Spanish Exempla: Keller; Hawaii: Beckwith Myth 105, 345.

V52.9. *Prayer for protection on journey to land of dead.* Irish myth: Cross.

V52.10. *Prayers of devout woman free husband from death and imprisonment.* Spanish Exempla: Keller.

V52.11. *Prayer of sinner changes his color from black into white.* Spanish Exempla: Keller.

V52.12. *The clever brothers work, the foolish brother only prays;* finally he acquires all the property. Lithuanian: Balys Index No. 1666*.

V52.13. *Saint's Paternoster outweighs ox.* Irish myth: Cross.

V52.14. *Reciting martyrology will prevent decomposition of body of one who recites it.* Irish myth: Cross.

V52.15. *Prayer said by saint into his right hand restores displaced eye of opponent.* Irish myth: *Cross

D996. Magic hand. D1331. Magic object affects eyesight. D1791.1. Dextrorsum circuit. E781. Eyes successfully replaced.

V53. *Prayers of family comfort prisoner.* Alphabet No. 298.

V53.1. *Prayer unfastens boy's fetters.* (Cf. R211.) Hawaii: Beckwith Myth 345.

V55. *Man worships devil's image in order to secure advancement.* Scala Celi 8b No. 56; Alphabet No. 50.

V57. *Purpose of prayer.*

V57.1. *Prayer for good harvest.* India: Thompson-Balys; Maori: Clark 32.

V57.2. *Prayer for shower of gold.* India: Thompson-Balys.

V57.3. *Prayer on special occasions.* Jewish: *Neuman.

V58. *Prayer as ceremony.*

V58.1. *Prayers at sunrise and sunset.* Tahiti: Henry Ancient Tahiti (Honolulu, 1928) 143.

V58.2. *Prayer with face toward east.* Irish myth: Cross.

V58.3. *Repeated circumambulations with prayer.* India: Thompson-Balys.

V58.4. *Handwashing before prayer.* Greek: Homer passim; Jewish: *Neuman.

V58.5. *Prayer shawl.* Jewish: Neuman.

V59. *Prayers answered—miscellaneous.* India: *Thompson-Balys.

V59.1. *Skill in theft granted as answer to prayer.* Africa (Duala): Lederbogen JAS IV 64.

V60. Funeral rites. *Encyc. Rel. Ethics Index 212a; Irish myth: *Cross; India: Thompson-Balys.

A1547. Origin of funeral customs. A1591. Origin of burial. E412.3. Dead without proper funeral rites cannot rest in grave. E431. Precautions at funeral against revenant. F268. Burial among underworld folk. V11.6. Sacrifice to the dead. V255. Virgin Mary has dissolute monk buried in consecrated ground: his only mass is that of the Virgin.

V60.1. *Stones sold at funeral wakes.* India: Thompson-Balys.

V60.2. *Funeral rites by druids.* Irish myth: Cross.

V61. *Various ways of disposing of dead.*

V61.1. *Dead placed on boat.* Encyc. Rel. Ethics Index 79c, 545b; Fb "skib" III 243b; Icelandic: *Boberg. Cf. Beowulf.

V61.2. *Dead burned on pyre.* (Cremation.) *Encyc. Rel. Ethics Index 143c; Icelandic: *Boberg; India: Thompson-Balys.

E431.13. Corpse burned to prevent return. E446.2. Ghost laid by burning body. P16.4.1. Suttee. T211.2. Wife throws herself on husband's funeral pyre.

V61.3. *Coffin buried upright.* Breton: Sébillot Incidents s.v. "cercueil".

V61.3.0.1. *Hero buried in armor, standing with face toward land of enemies.* (Cf. V67.) Irish myth: *Cross.

V61.3.0.2. *Person buried in standing position with friends about him.* Irish myth: Cross.

V61.3.0.3. *Man buried upright beneath kitchen stairway in order that he may watch his family.* Icelandic: *Boberg.

V61.4. *Head buried one place, body another.* Irish myth: Cross; Icelandic: Boberg.

V61.4.1. *Corpse buried face down.* (Cf. S139.2.2.3.1.) Irish myth: Cross.

V61.4.2. *Dismemberment before burial.* Gaster Thespis 242.

V61.5. *King buried in his war car.* Icelandic: *Boberg.

V61.6. *Christian buried in stone coffin.* Icelandic: *Boberg.

V61.7. *Christian buried in wooden coffin.* Icelandic: *Boberg.

V61.8. *Burial in grave-mound.* Icelandic: *Boberg.

V61.8.1. *Chiefs buried in hidden caves.* Tahiti: Henry Ancient Tahiti (Honolulu, 1928) 224.

V61.9. *Lion buried in stone cave with gold letters.* Icelandic: Boberg.

V61.10. *Corpses exposed in tree.* Greek: Argonautica III 205.

V61.11. *Aversion to burial in "strange city".* Irish myth: Cross.

V62. *Restrictions on burial.*

V62.1. *Funeral rites forbidden.* Irish myth: *Cross; Greek: Fox 53, Sophocles' "Antigone".

E341.1. Dead grateful for having corpse ransomed. Q456.0.3. Burial alive as punishment for disobedience to king.

V62.2. *Only usurers to carry body of usurer to grave.* Alphabet No. 793.

V63. *Bones of dismembered person assembled and buried.* (Cf. E30.) Type 720; BP I 412ff., *422.

V64. *Money tied on corpse thrown overboard from ship in order to secure burial.* Child III 342, IV 506.

V64.1. *Shipwrecked each get a piece of the chief's gold ring in order to have gold with them in death.* Icelandic: *Boberg.

E431.11. Coin placed in mouth of dead to prevent return.

V65. *Commemoration of death.* Irish myth: Cross.

V65.1. *Calves kept separate from cows in commemoration of hero's death.* Irish myth: Cross.

V65.2. *Drinking festival in memory of the dead.* Icelandic: *Boberg.

V65.3. *Wedding and funeral festival on same time.* Icelandic: *Boberg.

V65.4. *Professional mourning.* Virgil Aeneid XI 37; Greek: Aeschylus Libation-Pourers 423; India: Thompson-Balys.

V65.4.1. *Funeral song sung over dead.* *Hdwb. d. Abergl. VIII 1071ff.; *E. Reiner Die rituelle Totenklage der Griechen (Stuttgart, 1938); Irish myth: *Cross; Icelandic: Boberg.

A1543.1. Origin of the death chant.

V65.5. *Funeral games.* Virgil Aeneid V 66; Irish myth: *Cross.

V66. *Funeral sermon.*

V66.1. *Witty funeral sermon.* Priest having nothing good to say about man damns him with faint praise or gives anecdotes with unfavorable implications. (Cf. K1961.1.2.1.) *Wesselski Arlotto I 216ff. No. 64.

V67. *Accompaniments of burial.* (Cf. V61.3.0.1.) Irish myth: Cross.

V67.1. *Ornaments (arms, chariots) buried with hero.* Irish myth: *Cross; Icelandic: *Boberg.

V67.2. *Shoes buried with the dead.* Icelandic: MacCulloch Eddic 305.

V67.3. *Treasure buried with the dead.* Icelandic: *Boberg.

V67.3.1. *King buried with immense treasure in the ground of an artificially dried river;* later the normal course of the river is restored. *Krappe "Les funérailles d'Alaric" Annuaire de l'institut de philologie et d'histoire orientales et slaves VII 229—40.

V67.4. *Men buried with dead chief.* Icelandic: *Boberg.

P16.4. Persons buried with dead king.

V67.4.1. *Captain buried with his crew.* Icelandic: *Boberg.

V67.5. *Animals buried with the dead.* Icelandic: *Boberg.

V68. *Preparations for burial.* Irish myth: Cross; Icelandic: Lagerholm 33, *Boberg.

V68.1. *Dead washed (in river).* Irish myth: *Cross.

V68.2. *Dead washed and hair combed.* Icelandic: Boberg.

V68.3. *Dying hero wants to be buried in the clothes of his brother who killed him.* Icelandic: Boberg.

V68.4. *Dead is undressed.* Icelandic: Göngu-Hrólfs saga 245.

V68.4.1. *Dead not to be buried naked.* Jewish: Neuman.

V68.5. *Dead rubbed with red paint.* Africa (Fang): Trilles 140.

V69. *Funeral rites-miscellaneous.*

V69.1. *All dead are buried after battle.* Icelandic: *Boberg.

V69.2. *Hero buried as unknown merchant in foreign country.* Icelandic: Boberg.

V70. Religious feasts and fasts. *Encyc. Rel. Ethics Index 198; Irish myth: *Cross; Jewish: *Neuman.

A1535. Origin of secular feasts. A1541. Origin of religious feasts and fasts. D1505.5.2.1. Dew falling on St. John's Night restores sight. E501.3.5. Wild huntsman wanders for failure to keep fast day. E501.11.1.3. Wild hunt appears on St. John's Night. E501.11.2.2. Wild hunt appears between Christmas and Twelfth Night. E501.11.2.3. Wild hunt appears on feast-days.

V70.1. *The first day of summer.* Icelandic: *Boberg.

V70.1.1. *Festival of Beltane (=May Day).* Irish myth: *Cross.

V70.2. *Whitsuntide.* Icelandic: *Boberg.

V70.3. *Midsummer.* (Cf. A1535.3.) Irish myth: *Cross; Icelandic: Boberg.

V70.3.1. *Feast of Saint John the Baptist.* Irish myth: *Cross.

V463.2. First martyr: John the Baptist.

V70.4. *Harvest-festival.* Icelandic: *Boberg.

V70.5. *Festival of Samhain* (Hallowe'en, Tara [Temair]). Irish myth: *Cross.

A1535.4. Origin of feast of Tara. A1541.3. Origin of Hallowe'en.

V70.6. *Festival of Imbolg (Brigit, Candlemas).* Irish myth: *Cross.

V70.7. *Feast of the new moon.* Jewish: Moreno Esdras (V74).

V70.8. *Festival of Cenn (Crom) Cruaich.* Irish myth: *Cross.

S260.1. Human sacrifice. V1.6.4.1. Sacred stones. V11.3. Sacrifice to stone (Cenn or Crom Cruaich).

V71. *Sabbath.* *Encyc. Rel. Ethics Index 509c; Irish myth: *Cross; Jewish: Moreno Esdras (V71.2.), *Neuman.

C58. Tabu: profaning sacred day. C631.1. Tabu: journeying on Sunday. D1676. Mill refuses to work on Sunday. E501.3.6. Wild huntsman wanders for hunting on Sunday.

V71.1. *Jewish automaton will not work on Saturday.* *Dickson 212 n. 140.

V71.1.1. *Manna does not descend on Sabbath.* Jewish: *Neuman.

V71.2. *Misfortune ascribed to breaking Sabbath.* Irish myth: *Cross.

V71.3. *Various events, from creation to Resurrection, that occurred on Sabbath.* Irish myth: Cross; Jewish: Neuman.

V72. *Christmas.* *Encyc. Rel. Ethics Index 121b; *Hdwb. d. Abergl. IX 979ff., IX Nachträge 864—968; Irish myth: Cross; Icelandic: *Boberg.

B251.1.2. Animals speak to one another at Christmas. F971.5.2. Apples at Christmas.

V72.1. *Little Christmas.* Irish myth: Cross.

V73. *Fasts.* Irish myth: Cross; Jewish: *Neuman.

V73.0.1. *Christ in the desert overcomes devil by fasting.* Irish myth: Cross.

V73.1. *Fast to prevent pestilence.* Irish myth: *Cross.

V73.2. *Fast improves health.* Irish myth: Cross.

V73.3. *Saint causes two youths to be fed with the best food,* says one is doomed to go to hell, the other will practice austerity in his old age. Irish myth: *Cross.

V73.4. *Fasting to secure a prosperous journey.* Jewish: Moreno Esdras (V74.1).

V73.5. *Fasting on "Golden Fridays" as charm against certain misfortunes.* Irish myth: *Cross.

V73.6. *Lent.* Irish myth: Cross.

V73.6.1. *Christ's forty-days' fast called "His Lent".* Irish myth: Cross.

V73.6.2. *Saint remains silent during Lent by holding stone in mouth.* Irish myth: *Cross.

V73.6.3. *Holy man eats pork and beef in Lent because pig is raised on milk, ox on grass;* but refuses to eat cake because it contains weevils (live meat). Irish myth: Cross.

V75. *Easter.* Irish myth: *Cross.

B256.12. Whale raises back so that voyaging clerics can land to celebrate Easter.

V75.1. *Passover.* Jewish: Moreno Esdras, *Neuman.

V80. Religious services—miscellaneous.

V81. *Baptism.* *Encyc. Rel. Ethics Index 61c; Irish: *Cross, Beal XXI 337, O'Suilleabhain 128; Icelandic: *Boberg; Jewish: *Neuman.

D587. Transformation by baptism. D741.2. Disenchantment of monster child when baptized. D1242.1.1. Baptismal water as magic object. D1766.3. Magic powers from baptizing an animal. E176. Resuscitation in order to baptize. E412.2. Unbaptized person cannot rest in grave. V241.4. Angel baptizes saint. V322. Heretical baptism.

V81.1. *Girl having been stolen by mountain-folk must be baptized anew.* *Fb "døbe" I 227.

V81.2. *Tails fall off mountain spirits when they are baptized.* Fb "hale" IV 197b.

V81.3. *Metamorphosis brought about by baptism.* Monster born of union of heathen ruler and Christian maiden becomes a handsome boy on being baptized. Italian Novella: Rotunda.

V81.4. *Baptism of infants.* Maori: Clark 185.

V81.5. *Sea bath as purificatory rite.* Tahiti: Henry Ancient Tahiti (Honolulu, 1928) 144; Hawaii: Beckwith Myth 152, 176.

V82. *Circumcision.* (Cf. F81.3.) *Encyc. Rel. Ethics Index 126c; Spanish Exempla: Keller; Jewish: *Neuman.

V83. *Hymns.* Irish myth: *Cross.

D1275.3. Magic hymn. G303.16.2.4. Devils driven away by hymn.

V84. *Excommunication.* *Encyc. Rel. Ethics Index 193b; Spanish Exempla: Keller; Jewish: *Neuman.

C95. Tabu: giving security for one excommunicated. E412.1. Excommunicated person cannot rest in grave.

V84.1. *Lightning strikes excommunicated person who enters church.* Scala Celi 85b No. 492.

V84.2. *Priest shows power of excommunication over host.* It turns black. Scala Celi 85b No. 495; Herbert III 446 No. 17.

V84.3. *Pirate excommunicated, goes on pilgrimage as penance.* Italian Novella: Rotunda.

V85. *Religious pilgrimages.* (Cf. V84.3.) Chinese: Eberhard FFC CXX 186f.

V86. *Sign of the Cross.* Encyc. Rel. Ethics VI 539b; Fb "kors" II 274; Scala Celi 67b—71b Nos. 373—404 passim.

D1766.6. Magic results from sign of the cross. E443.4. Ghost laid by raising a cross. G303.16.3.4. Devil made to disappear by making sign of the cross. P441.2. Tailoring only trade devil cannot learn. He fails to knot thread because it would make sign of the cross.

V86.1. *Sign of cross protects from injury.*

V86.1.1. *Sign of cross prevents child from being stolen from cradle.* Fb "kors" II 285f.

F321. Fairy steals child from cradle.

V86.1.2. *Sign of cross prevents garment from burning.* Alphabet No. 232.

V86.1.3. *Man dies because he has killed a man with the sign of the cross on his forehead.* Köhler-Bolte I 382.

V86.2. *Martyr with sign of cross on his heart.* (Cf. V254.3.) Herbert III 77, 416, 467, 487, 530; Scala Celi 69b No. 388; Alphabet No. 563.

V86.3. *Punishment for profane use of the cross.* Drunkard kisses cross, thinking it is a bottle of wine. Pauli (ed. Bolte) No. 271.

V86.4. *Miraculous manifestations to scoffers of the cross.* Alphabet. No. 230; English: Wells 97 (Chevalere Assigne), 89 (The Sege of Melayne).

V86.5. *Praying with arms extended so as to form a cross.* Irish myth: *Cross.

V86.6. *Loaf bursts in oven because sign of cross has not been made over it.* Irish myth: *Cross.

V86.7. *The seven significances of the sign of the cross.* Irish myth: Cross.

V87. *Christening.*

N811. Supernatural godfather. P296. Godparents.

V88. *Ceremony of the proclamation of a Buddha.* Chinese: Werner 271.

V91. *Accidental calling on god's name held to outweigh a life of wickedness.* Hindu: Keith 180.

D1766.7.1. Magic results produced in name of deity.

V92. *"Our Lady's Tumbler."* A tumbler, turned monk, dances while others chant psalms. He is praising God in the only way he knows. *Herbert III 417; *Wicksteed Romania II 315; Romanische Forschungen XI 223.

V93. *Religious dancing.* (Cf. A1542.) India: Thompson-Balys.

V96. *Ritual bathing.* Jewish: *Neuman.

V96.1. *Taking bath in a sacred river (Ganges).* India: Thompson-Balys.

V97. *Study of Tora as religious service.* Jewish: *Neuman.

V100—V199. Religious edifices and objects.

V100. Religious edifices and objects. Irish myth: Cross.

V110. Religious buildings. Irish myth: *Cross.

C51.1. Tabu: profaning shrine. C93. Tabu: trespassing sacred precinct.

V111. *Churches.* *Encyc. Rel. Ethics Index 123c; Irish: *Cross, Beal XXI 335, O'Suilleabhain 112.

B259.4. Bees build church of wax to contain consecrated host. C51.1.6. Tabu: discontinuing use of a church. D1314.1.4. Magic arrow indicates place to build church. D1314.10. Fiery pillar guides person to church D1389.1. Magic stone protects church from oppression. F531.3.2.1. Church built where giants throw stones. F531.3.3. Giant astride a church-roof. F531.3.6. Giants carry a church across a stream. F941.2. Church sinks underground. V246.1. Angel tells saint where to build his church.

V111.1. *Visit to certain church protects from drowning on pilgrimage.* (Cf. D1384, D1388.) Irish myth: Cross.

V111.2. *Stones for building church (chapel) miraculously supplied.* (Cf. D931.0.1.) Irish myth: Cross; Icelandic: Boberg.

V111.3. *Place where a church must be built miraculously indicated.* *Loomis White Magic 127f.

V111.3.1. *Birds indicate the site where a church is to be built by making a model of the structure on the spot.* *Loomis White Magic 68.

B155.1. Building site determined by halting of an animal.

V111.3.2. *Divine person points out site for church.* United States: Baughman.

V112. *Temples.* *Encyc. Rel. Ethics Index 591b; Jewish: *Neuman.

V112.0.1. *Ark of the temple.* Jewish: *Neuman.

V112.1. *Spirit huts.* Philippine (Tinguian): Cole 69; Hawaii: Beckwith Myth 112.

V112.2. *Mosques.*

D2136.2.1. Mosque turns round in order to face in the true direction of Mecca after prayers of two saints.

V112.3. *Synagogues.* Jewish: *Neuman.

V113. *Shrines.* (Cf. C51.1.) *Encyc. Rel. Ethics Index 546a; Irish myth: *Cross; Missouri French: Carrière; Jewish: Neuman.

V113.0.1. *Miracles at shrine.* India: Thompson-Balys.

V113.0.2. *Vow to visit shrine.* India: Thompson-Balys.

V113.1. *Cripples at shrine frightened and run away without crutches.* *Herbert III 21; *Crane Vitry 241f. No. 254.

V113.2. *Robbers promise to make offerings to the shrine of a hermit if successful.* India: Thompson-Balys.

V114. *Sacred groves.* *Frazer Golden Bough XII 293 s.v. "Grove(s), sacred"; Irish myth: *Cross.

A435. God of trees and forests. C51.2.2. Tabu: cutting sacred trees or groves. Z111.4. Death excluded from sacred groves.

V114.1. *Sacred groves of druids.* Irish myth: *Cross.

V115. *Church bells.* Encyc. Rel. Ethics Index 69a; Hdwb. d. Abergl. III 868ff.; E. Lippert Glockenläuten als Rechtsbrauch (Freiburg im Breisgau, 1939); *P. Sartori Das Buch von deutschen Glocken (Berlin, 1932). — Irish myth: *Cross; Norwegian: Solheim Register 21.

A1466. Origin of church bell. D1213. Magic bell. D1610.15.1. Church bell speaks. D2141.1.1. Church bell rung as protection against storm. E434.1. Hiding from ghosts under church bell. F451.5.9.3. Dwarfs dislike church bells. G303.16.12. Ringing of church bell causes devil to lose his power. G304.2.4.1. Trolls cannot endure church bells.

V115.1. *Church bell sunk in river (sea).* (Cf. F993.) *Fb. "kirkeklokke" IV 260b; Wales, England: *Baughman; Finnish: Aarne FFC XXXIII 47 No. 88; Finnish-Swedish: Wessman 72 Nos. 608—11; Estonian: Aarne FFC XXV 135 No. 88.

V115.1.1. *Sunken bell travels on sea bottom.* Finnish-Swedish: Wessman 72 No. 609.

V115.1.2. *Raising sunken church bell.* Finnish-Swedish: Wessman 73 No. 620.

V115.1.3. *Sunken church bell cannot be raised.* Finnish-Swedish: Wessman 73 Nos. 612—22.

V115.1.3.1. *Church bell cannot be raised because silence is broken.* (Cf. C401.4.) Finnish-Swedish: Wessman 72f. Nos. 612, 613, 619.

V115.1.3.2. *Church bell cannot be raised because person blasphemes.* England: *Baughman.

V115.2. *Girl sold for new church bell.* (Cf. S210.) England: Child I 91ff.

V115.3. *Devil buys church bell and demoralizes congregation.* They have always come early before since they had no bell to announce the time. Now they wait for the bell. Pauli (ed. Bolte) No. 92.

V115.4. *What church bells say.* Fb "kirkeklokke" IV 260A.

V116. *Altars.* (Cf. V135.) *Encyc. Rel. Ethics Index 18a; Irish myth: *Cross; Jewish: *Neuman.

F1083.1. Altar floats in air. M101.1. False swearer not allowed to approach altar. R325. Church (altar) as refuge.

V117. *Pulpits.*

E434.2. Hiding from ghosts in pulpit.

V118. *Monasteries.* Irish myth: *Cross.

V118.0.1. *Hell as a monastery—the devil, abbot; sinners, monks.* Irish myth: Cross.

V118.1. *Monastery on otherworld island.* Irish myth: Cross.

V118.2. *Subaqueous monastery.* Irish myth: *Cross.

V118.2.1. *Submarine oratory.* Irish myth: *Cross.

V120. Images. *Encyc. Rel. Ethics Index 271b; Irish myth: *Cross; Jewish: *Neuman.

D1268. Magic statue. D1311.7. Oracular image. D1658.1. Objects repay kindness. J1823.1. Misunderstanding concerning images of Christ. Q172.1. Child taken to heaven: offers food to crucifix. V256.2. Miracles of healing performed before image of Virgin Mary.

V120.1. *Images and druids.* Irish myth: Cross.

V121. *Miraculous image of Christ impressed on napkin.* Veronica. Ward II 641 No. 20.

V122. *Image bars way of nun trying to escape convent to join lover.* Wesselski Mönchslatein 74 No. 65.

V122.1. *Image of Jesus descends from cross and wounds nun leaving convent.* Spanish Exempla: Keller.

V123. *Image blamed by suppliant for misfortunes.* Type 1479**, *Wesselski Arlotto I 196 No. 23; Spanish Exempla: Keller; India: Thompson-Balys.

J1853.1.1. Money from the broken statue. Fool sells goods to a statue and when it will not pay him knocks it to pieces. V381. Heathen beats his god because of misfortune.

V123.1. *God under compulsion: suppliant threatens to mutilate (crush) holy image if his wish is not fulfilled.* India: Thompson-Balys.

V124. *Preacher criticizes the likeness of Christ exhibited in his church.* Says that it is unworthy of the original. Italian Novella: Rotunda.

V124.1. *Saint hangs cowl in thornbrake as symbol of Christ on the Cross.* Irish myth: Cross.

V125. *Casting of image of Buddha delayed until a maniac's mite is thrown into the furnace.* Chinese: Werner 401.

V126. *Image of saint speaks.* *Loomis White Magic 124.

V127. *Image of deity in wood (stone).* (Cf. V1.11.) Hawaii: Beckwith Myth 111; Cook Islands: ibid. 131; Marquesas: Handy 122; Tahiti: Henry Ancient Tahiti (Honolulu, 1928) 344.

V128. *Motions of various kinds attributed to images.*

D1622. Image indicates favor to suppliant. D1622.1. Crucifix bows as sign of favor. D1622.2. Image of Virgin bows to indicate favor. D1623.1. Image of Virgin veils and unveils itself. D1624.1. Image of Christ bleeds from thrown stone.

V128.1. *An apple is offered to a statue of the Virgin and her child.* The infant reaches out and takes the fruit. *Loomis White Magic 124.

V128.2. *Portraits exude oil.* *Loomis White Magic 124.

V130. Other sacred objects connected with worship.

V131. *Religious robes (vestments).* *Encyc. Rel. Ethics Index 629c; Gaster Thespis 270f.; Jewish: *Neuman.

V131.1. *Sight of holy fringe on garment restrains a man from fornication and reforms the harlot.* Gaster Exempla 192f. No. 35; Jewish: *Neuman.

T330. Anchorites under temptation.

V131.2. *White robes of druids.* Irish myth: *Cross.

V132. *Holy water.* *Encyc. Rel. Ethics IV 61f.; Irish myth: *Cross; Icelandic: *Boberg.

D1242.1.2. Holy water as magic object. H222.2. Ordeal by holy water.

V132.1. *Holy water prevents a man from committing incest with his daughter.* (Cf. T411.) Alphabet No. 523.

V132.2. *Holy water disperses demons.* (Cf. D1385.) Irish myth: Cross.

V132.2.1. *Holy water removes mark placed on man's face by the devil.* Spanish Exempla: Keller.

V132.3. *Drinking holy water facilitates cursing.* Irish myth: Cross.

V133. *Holy candles.* *Encyc. Rel. Ethics III 188ff.

A2012.1. Creation of bee to provide wax for candles in church.

V134. *Sacred wells.* *Encyc. Rel. Ethics Index 640c; Fb "kilde" II 119; Namn och Bygd XXXIII (1945) 1ff. — Danish: Schmidt Danmarks Helligkilder (DF XXXIII); Irish myth: *Cross; England, Wales, Ireland, U.S.: Baughman; Icelandic: *Boberg.

A427.1. Goddess of springs and wells. C261. Tabu: drinking from certain fountain. D926. Magic well. D1300.3. Magic well of wisdom. D1470.1.35. Magic wishing well.

V134.0.1. *Tree beside holy well.* Irish myth: *Cross.

V134.1. *Oracles and auguries from holy well.* Irish myth: *Cross.

V134.2. *Offerings to holy wells.* Irish myth: *Cross.

V134.3. *Fish in water from certain well: water refuses to boil till fish are returned to well.* Irish myth: *Cross.

V134.4. *Ducks in pool in church: water in which they are placed refuses to boil till ducks are restored to pool.* Irish myth: *Cross.

V135. *Altar cloths.* (Cf. F962.12.2.) Irish myth: Cross.

V135.1. *Poverty-stricken couple wrap newly-born child in altar-coverings.* Italian Novella: Rotunda.

V136. *Bible.* Irish myth: Cross.

V136.1. *Copy of gospels buried with saint.* Irish myth: Cross.

V137. *House of woman who launders clothes for church spared in great fire.* Alphabet No. 76.

V140. Sacred relics. **Saintyves Les réliques et les images légendaires (Paris, 1912); Encyc. Rel. Ethics Index 493a.

D1296. Sacred relic as magic object. F979.7. Hollow in tree grows over, giving sanctuary to relics within. K1976. False miraculous relic. M114.4. Swearing on sacred relics.

V140.1. *Angel reveals (buried) relics to saint.* Irish myth: *Cross.

D1810.5. Magic knowledge from angel. V232.7.1. Angel brings cross as gift to saint.

V140.2. *Saint's relics miraculously recovered.* *Loomis White Magic 127f.

V140.3. *A cow licks the stone under which the secreted body of saint is buried.* *Loomis White Magic 62.

V140.4. *Testing the authenticity of relics: bones are cast into fire; with great noise they jump away from the flames.* *Loomis White Magic 92.

V141. *Possession of relic brings prosperity, its loss sickness.* Wesselski Mönchslatein 113 No. 96.

V142. *Devout possessor of false relics miraculously receives authentic ones.* Alphabet Nos. 89, 402; Spanish Exempla: Keller.

V142.1. *Sham relics perform miracles if faith is great.* India: *Thompson-Balys.

V143. *Saint's bones for lack of worship remove themselves from church.* (Cf. D1641.) Alphabet No. 679.

V143.1. *Saint's bones miraculously removed from reliquary broken in pillage.* Irish myth: Cross.

V143.2. *Relics (images) carried away return to their original church.* *Loomis White Magic 48.

V144. *Belief in miraculous powers of sacred relics.* Irish myth: Cross.

V144.1. *Sacred relics carried in battle to aid victory.* Irish myth: Cross.

V144.2. *The relics of saint protect horses from the attack of wild beasts.* *Loomis White Magic 106.

V150. Sacred objects—miscellaneous.

D1171.6. Magic cup. D1446.3. Shepherd's consecrated staff keeps cow from straying. D1500.1.2. Sacred healing stone. D1500.1.15.1. Consecrated healing ring. D1.10.3. Money from offertory as cure. E64.5.1. Resuscitation by Holy Grail. E163. Man kept alive by consecrated sword. E443.1. Ghost laid by blessing grave.

V151. *Sacred writings.* *Encyc. Rel. Ethics Index 530a; Irish myth: *Cross.

D1266.1. Magic writings (gramerye, runes). D1381.24.1. Reading letter written by Christ protects against attack. D1641.11. Sacred scroll returns to heaven. F962.13.4. Written scroll received from heaven.

V151.1. *Captive released because of ability to recite beginning of Genesis.* (Cf. J1185.) Gaster Exempla 193 No. 38.

V200—V299. Sacred persons.

V200. Sacred persons.

A0. Creator. A100—A499. Gods. A2620. Plants originate from experience of holy person. D1648.1.2. Tree bows down to holy person. D2157.2. Magic quick growth of crops. Reward for helping holy fugitive. K1811. Gods (saints) in disguise reward hospitality and punish inhospitality. Q42.3. Generosity to saint (god) in disguise rewarded. Q46.1. Reward for protecting holy fugitive.

V200.1. *Flame illuminates cradle of sacred person.* (Cf. H41.4.) Saintyves Saints Successeurs 247—48.

V201. *God.* *Encyc. Relic Ethics Index 223b.

A100. Gods. A2612.3. God's tears .ecome peas. J2215. Absurd reasoning about God.

V202. *Sacred spirits.* Hawaii: *Beckwith Myth 104, 107, 108, 180, 382, 447, 512.

F400. Spirits and demons.

V205. *Royal family as sacred.*

P0. Royalty and nobility. P16.6. Kings worshipped after their death.

V205.1. *Third son of king possesses sacred power.* Easter Island: Métraux Ethnology 130.

V210. Religious founders. Jewish: *Neuman.

V211. *Christ.* *DeVooys Middelnederlandse Legenden en Exempelen (Den Haag, 1926) 129ff.; Spanish Exempla: Keller; Jewish: *Neuman.

A2221.3. Markings on animals as recollections of Christ's life and suffering. A2287. Jesus causes animal characteristics. D1381.4.1. Christ's coat of mercy protects Pilate from punishment. D1851.4. Immortality bestowed by Christ. E121.2. Resuscitation by Christ. F621.2.1. Antichrist a giant. F955. Miraculous cure for leprosy. Rage at hearing for first time of Christ's passion causes cure. H1573.3. Power of Christianity tested. M363.1. Coming of Christ (Christianity) prophesied. Q25. Reward for carrying Christ across a stream. V234.2. Angels sing on night of Christ's Nativity. V235.1. Angel announces birth of Christ to shepherds. Z177. Lamb as symbol of Christ.

V211.0.1. *Christ born from crown of Virgin's head.* Irish myth: Cross.

V211.0.2. *Christ conceived on same day He was crucified.* Irish myth: Cross.

V211.0.3. *Seventeen marvels at the birth of Christ.* Irish myth: *Cross.

V211.0.4. *Christ as prophet.* Irish myth: Cross.

V211.0.5. *Christ called "druid".* Irish myth: *Cross.

V211.1. *The Nativity of Christ.* Irish myth: Cross.

A941.5.0.2. Wells break forth at birth of Christ. A2221.1. Animals blessed for honoring infant Jesus. B251.1. Animals rejoice at Christ's birth. B251.10. Animals lick Christ child. F960.1. Extraordinary nature phenomena at birth of holy person. G303.16.19.10. Devil exorcised at time of Christ's Nativity.

V211.1.1. *Air fragrant at Nativity.* (Cf. V222.4.) Irish myth: Cross.

V211.1.2. *Star shines through day of Nativity.* (Cf. F961.2.) Irish myth: Cross.

V211.1.2.1. *Hairy star appears before Nativity.* Irish myth: Cross.

V211.1.3. *Shining cloud marks place of Nativity.* Irish myth: Cross.

V211.1.3.1. *Vast intolerable light on night of Christ's Nativity.* Irish myth: Cross.

V211.1.4. *Virgin suffers no birth pangs at Christ's Nativity.* Irish myth: Cross.

V211.1.5. *Elements silent and motionless at Nativity.* Irish myth: Cross.

V211.1.6. *A "crown of thorns" among gifts given by the shepherds to Joseph, husband of Virgin Mary.* Irish myth: Cross.

V211.1.7. *Three (seven) druids come to adore infant Jesus.* Irish myth: *Cross.

V211.1.8. *The Infant Jesus.* Irish myth: Cross.

V211.1.8.1. *Christ in form of an infant nursed by saint.* Irish myth: Cross.

V211.1.8.2. *Christ in form of an infant fondled by nuns.* Irish myth: Cross.

V211.1.8.3. *Christ as infant in mother's arms causes bare hillside to become field of wheat as protection.* Irish myth: Cross.

V211.2. *Christ on earth.* Irish myth: Cross.

A972.1.1. Indentations on rocks from footprints of Christ. K1811. Gods (saints) in disguise visit mortals. V227. Saints have divine visitors.

V211.2.1. *Fiery pillar as sign of Christ's visit.* (Cf. F964.0.1.) Irish myth: Cross.

V211.2.1.1. *Christ disguised as leper.* Irish myth: *Cross.

V211.2.1.2. *Christ disguised as beggar.* Irish myth: *Cross.

V211.2.1.2.1. *Jesus had "dark hair and a long red beard".* Irish myth: Cross.

V211.2.2. *Christ leaves bachall after visit.* (Cf. D1277.) Irish myth: *Cross.

V211.2.3. *The Crucifixion.* Irish myth: *Cross.

A2221.2. Animals blessed for good services at crucifixion. F960.2. Extraordinary nature phenomena at death of hero.

V211.2.3.0.1. *Angel warns of Christ's danger.* Irish myth: Cross.

V238. Guardian angel.

V211.2.3.0.2. *Smith's wife made nails for the Cross because her husband believed Christ to be a true prophet.* *Loomis White Magic 51f.

V211.2.3.1. *Earth trembles at Crucifixion.* Irish myth: Cross.

V211.2.3.2. *Moon bloody at Crucifixion.* (Cf. F961.3.) Irish myth: Cross.

V211.2.3.3. *Sun darkened at Crucifixion.* (Cf. F965.2.) Irish myth: Cross.

V211.3. *Finding of the Cross.* Irish myth: Cross.

V211.4. *Construction of the Cross.*

V211.4.1. *Cross of Christ made of four kinds of wood.* Irish myth: *Cross.

V211.5. *The five wounds of Christ.* Irish myth: Cross.

V211.5.1. *Blood and wine issue from wound in side of crucified Savior.* Irish myth: *Cross.

V211.6. *Dialogue between Christ and the Virgin Mary.* Irish myth: Cross.

V211.7. *Christ's descent to hell.* Irish myth: Cross.

V211.7.1. *The harrowing of hell.* Irish myth: *Cross.

V211.7.2. *Dialogue (debate) between Christ and Satan (at the harrowing of hell).* Irish myth: *Cross.

V211.7.3. *The three bolts left on hell by Christ.* Irish myth: Cross.

V211.8. *Christ's resurrection (on March 27).* Irish myth: Cross.

V211.9. *Christ's ascent to Heaven (on May 5).* Irish myth: Cross.

V211.10. *Letter (message) of Christ.* Irish myth: *Cross. Cf. North Carolina: Brown Collection I 642.

V211.10.1. *Christ sends message to voyaging clerics.* Irish myth: Cross.

V212. *Buddha.*

V212.1. *Sacred books received from Buddha in person.* Chinese: Werner 340.

V212.2. *Precepts heard from Buddha in person.* India: Thompson-Balys.

V220. Saints. **Toldo Studien zur vgl. Litgsch. I—IX passim; **Saintyves Saints Successeurs 23—26; *Encyc. Rel. Ethics Index 514a. — Norwegian: Solheim Register 22; Jewish: Neuman; Chinese: Eberhard FFC CXX 140—42, 162, 210, 411. For references in addition to those given below, see volume VI s.v. "Saints".

A581.3. Culture hero returns to prove power of saint. A661.0.1.2. Saint Peter as porter of heaven. A725.1. Sun does not set for a year through power of saint. A934.5. Rivers originate through saint's prayer during drought. A941.5. Spring breaks forth through power of saint. A972.1. Indentions on rocks from imprints of gods and saints. A974.1. Certain stones are druids transformed by power of saint. A2002. Origin of insects from various experiences of saints. A2217.3.1. Marks on certain fish from St. Peter's fingerprints. A2231.1. Animal characteristics: punishment for discourteous answer to God (saint). B155.3. Animal determines burial place of saint. B251.2. Animals honor saint. B256. Animal as servant of saint. B524.2.1.1. Saint sends swarm of bees or wasps against the enemy. B771.2. Animal tamed by holiness of saint. C51.2. Tabu: stealing from god or saint. C901.1.6. Tabu imposed by saint. D480.0.1. Things miraculously stretched or shortened if needed by saint. D683.4. Transformation by saint. D812.1. Magic object received from saint. D1093.1. The boomerang effect of hurled missiles caused by saint. D1277. Magic bachall. D1311,16.0.1. Saint's blessing makes stone oracular. D1313.11. Magic fountain indicates road for saint by removing itself. D1331.4.1. Saint's gospel-book causes sight-shifting. D1337.1.6. Beautification by use of saint's spittle. D1344.6. Saint's tunic renders invulnerable. D1344.7. Saint's girdle renders invulnerable. D1344.8. Saint's cowl renders invulnerable. D1355.2.1. Water blessed by saint as love-philtre. D1356.1. Saint's girdle represses lust. D1361.12.1. Saint's tunic renders invisible. D1361.16. Saint's cowl renders invisible. D1364.5. Saint's breath causes magic sleep. D1364.7.1. Liquor blessed by saint causes magic sleep. D1381.2. Saint's spittle protects fugitive from attack. D1381.12. Saint's bachall keeps off enemies. D1385.1. Earth from saint's grave expels demons. D1385.8. Saint's bachall keeps off monsters and ghosts. D1385.12.1. Saint's bell rung against black birds (demons). D1385.19.1. Saint's hose protects woman from devil. D1388.1.1. Saint's bachall protects from shipwreck. D1389.6. Saint's bell carried around tribe averts all danger. D1391.2. Saint's bachall saves prisoner from execution. D1395.4. Saint's bachall enables captive to escape. D1400.1.9. Saint's bell conquers enemies. D1400.1.12. Saint's bachall defeats enemies. D1442.3. Saint's bachall subdues wild animals. D1444.1.1. Saint's bachall catches fish. D1446.1. Saint's bell keeps cattle from straying. D1446.2. Saint's gospel-book keeps cattle from straying. D1524.1.2. Saint's bachall permits him to walk on sea. D1549.2. Saint's girdle causes tree to fall in right direction. D1549.3.1. Saint's bachall drives back flooding river. D1549.3.2. Saint's bachall leads stream through mountain (or up hill). D1549.4. Saint's bachall brings down mountain on heads of enemies. D1549.6. Saint's veil quells volcano. D1551.5. Saint's bachall causes sea to divide. D1563.1.4. Saint's bell starts crops growing. D1564.2. Saint's spittle splits rocks. D1564.3. Saint's bachall splits rock, cuts stone, and cleaves ground. D1565.4. Saint's breath restores shattered vessel. D1566.1.4. Saint's breath kindles lamp. D1566.2.1. Saint's bachall quenches fire. D1567.1. Saint's blood produces fountain. D1567.2. Saint's tears produce fountains. D1567.3. Water poured from saint's bell produces fountain. D1567.4. Saint's bachall produces fountain. D1567.5. Saint's crozier produces fountain. D1572. Magic smoke carries power of saint. D1574. Line drawn by saint's bachall separates calves from their mothers. D1602.2.1. Fallen trees upraised at saint's request. D1602.8. Saint's bell when stolen miraculously returns. D1602.9. Saint's bachall when lost returns. D1610.15.2. Saint's bell speaks. D1622.3. Saint's image lets golden shoe (ring) fall as sign of favor to suppliant. D1652.16. Lime (for building church) miraculously renewed by power of saint. D1654.0.1. Magic immovability of saints (or their possessions). D1674. Iron blessed by saint incapable of wounding. D1677. Mill refuses to work when saint is ill-treated. D1684. Dye blessed by saint colors animals, trees. D1685. Interred body of saint performs signs and miracles. D1713. Magic power of hermit (saint, yogi). D1719.1.1. Contest in magic between druid and saint. D1722. Magic power from saint. D1741.7. Saint causes loss of magic power. D1766.7.3. Magic results produced in name of saint. D1820.1. Magic sight of saints. D1840.1. Magic invulnerability of saints. D1841.3.2.3.1. Saint carries fire in hand to warm guests. D1882.1. Rejuvenation by saint. D1925.4. Barrenness removed by saint's blessing. D1926. Craftsmanship magically bestowed by saint. D1981.2. Magic invisibility of saints. D2031.0.1. Saints causes illusions. D2072.3. Magic paralysis caused by saint. D2084.3. Saint causes dyes to work incorrectly. D2089.4. Saint causes mill to turn backwards. D2102.3. Saint magically produces treasure. D2106.1. Magic multiplication of objects by saints. D2125.1.1.1. Saint rides blessed wave. D2135.3. Stones fly through the air at saint's bidding. D2136.4.1. Saint drives lake into sea. D2140.1. Control of weather by saint's prayers. D2141.0.9. Storm raised by saint. D2143.1.12. Arrival of saint brings rain to rainless land. D2146.2.5. Saint banishes night for a year. D2148.2. Saint is able to produce earthquakes at will. D2148.3. Stopping the eruption of a volcano by a saint. D2149.2. Saint magically causes mountain to melt away. D2149.3. Saint causes sun to come down and cook for him. D2151.0.1. Saint regulates temperature of waters. D2151.1.2.2. Tide held back by saint. D2152.5. Mountain moved by saint. D2156.3. Saint forces beast to bring back stolen child. D2156.4. Wild boar reprimanded by saint. D2156.5. Vicious snakes controlled by saint. D2156.6. Saint destroys disastrous insects. D2157.2.1. Magic quick growth of saint's crops. D2157.3. Withered and dead trees suddenly blossom at saint's command. D2158.1.3. Fire obeys the saints. D2161.5.1. Cure by holy man. D2176.0.1. Saint sanctifies locality against death. D2176.3.3. Evil spirit exorcised by saint. D2182. Flow of cow's milk increased by licking saint's garment. E1.1. Saint cut into pieces or decapitated comes back to life. E64.3.1. Resuscitation by saint's bell. E64.4.1. Resuscitation by saint's bachall. E121.4. Resuscitation by saint. E501.1.6. Saint as leader of wild hunt. E545.7. Holy man converses with entombed dead. F552.1.2. Fingers of saint (angel) give light or fire. F555.3.2. Holy man's hair of enormous length, so long has he remained praying at one spot. F624.0.1. Saint as mighty lifter. F660.2. Unskilled man made skillful by saint's blessing. F866.7.2. Saint able to carry fluid (water, wine or oil) in a broken container, bottomless jar, etc. F930.1. Book dropped in water by saint not wet. F932.2. River arches over saint's body like a vault. F932.3. Stream becomes hot in which saint performs his ascetic devotions. F933.1. Miraculous spring bursts forth for holy person. F971.5.1. Fruit produced out of season at saint's request. F971.6. Flowers spring up when saint strikes ground. F979.1. Sour fruits made sweet by saint. F979.2. Leaves of tree open and close to give saint passage. F979.3. Leaves of tree make melody for saints. F1041.16.4. Heat of saint's anger sets cowl afire. F1051. Prodigious weeping. Usually by saint. F1086. Saint preaches for three days and three nights. G303.6.2.9.1. Saint is able to see devils. G303.9.6.2. Satan attacks saints. G303.16.11.4. Saint expels devil to hell. H984. Tasks performed with help of saint. H1573.2.1. Magic manifestation required as proof in test of saintliness. K405.3. Thief successfully claims that stolen image has been given him by the saint himself. K1811. Gods (saints) in disguise visit mortals. K1827. Disguise as holy man. K1842. Living person acts as image of saint. M364.11. Everyone buried in saint's soil shall go to heaven. M411.8. Saint's (prophet's) curse. M414.3. Saint cursed. N848. Saint (pious man) as helper. Q1.1. Gods (saints) in disguise reward hospitality and punish inhospitality. Q42.3. Generosity to saint (god) in disguise rewarded. Q292.1. Inhospitality to saint (god) punished. Q552.2.3.1.1. Earth swallows man who opposes saint. Q552.2.3.3. Saint causes parricide to sink into earth to his knees. Q558.18. Saints bring about miraculous death because of desecration of sanctuaries. R121.6. Rescue from prison by saint who enters and breaks fetters. R165. Rescue by saint (holy man). R165.2. Innocently hanged person saved by saint. T312. Saint's daughter dies when wooed. T540.1. Supernatural birth of saints. T579.4. Mother of saint has healing spittle during pregnancy. X452.1. No need to give sermon about saint again.

V221. *Miraculous healing by saints.* Encyc. Rel. Ethics Index 246a; Irish myth: *Cross; India: Thompson-Balys; Icelandic: *Boberg.

D1500.1.1.1. Magic healing well dug by saint. D1500.1.1.2. The water of spring which saint caused to flow has curative powers. D1500.1.7.1.1. Magic head (of saint) heals diseases. D1500.1.7.2.1. Healing power of saint's saliva. D1500.1.10.2.1. Wine blessed by saint or received from the saint's hand cures various ills. D1500.1.13.1. Saint's girdle as magic cure. D1500.1.18.1. Dew from saint's grave as cure. D1500.1.33.1.1. Cures by the milk of the mothers of saints. D1500.3.2. Disease transferred to saint's bell. D1500.1.1. Saint causes pain of sick man to be transferred to himself. D1500.4.2.1. Saint's breath makes men drunk. D1505.10. Saint's breath restores sight. D1507.2. Saint's gospel-book restores speech. D1507.3. Saint's bell restores speech. D1507.4. Saint's breath restores speech. D1508.1. Saint's bell restores reason. T579.4. Mother of saint has healing spittle during pregnancy.

V221.0.1. *Relics of saint cure disease.* Alphabet Nos. 398, 432; *Loomis White Magic 104.

D1500. Magic object controls disease. V140. Sacred relics.

V221.0.1.1. *Oil flowing from relics has curative powers.* *Loomis White Magic 104.

V221.0.1.2. *The wine (water) occasionally used to bathe relics assumes healing powers.* *Loomis White Magic 104.

V221.0.1.3. *Shrine of saint carried around to supress pestilence.* *Loomis White Magic 105.

V221.0.2. *Saint miraculously healed.* Irish myth: Cross.

V221.0.2.1. *Crippled saint miraculously receives horse and chariot.* Irish myth: Cross.

V221.0.3. *Miraculous healing power of saint as child.* *Loomis White Magic 25.

V221.1. *Saint cures palsy.* Alphabet No. 731; Irish myth: *Cross.

V221.2. *Saint restores dumb man's speech.* (Cf. D1507.) Alphabet No. 401; Icelandic: *Boberg.

V221.3. *Saint cures leprosy.* Irish myth: *Cross.

D1502.4. Magic object cures leprosy.

V221.3.1. *Leper cured by the kiss of a saint.* *Loomis White Magic 103.

V221.4. *Saint subdues madman.* (Cf. D1508.1.) Irish myth: *Cross.

V221.4.0.1. *Saint cures frenzied animal.* Irish myth: *Cross.

B255. Miracle wrought for animal.

V221.4.0.1.1. *Saint's blessing sufficient to control a mad dog.* *Loomis White Magic 106.

V221.5. *Saint purifies monk with sign of the cross.* (Cf. D1766.6.) Irish myth: Cross.

V221.6. *Saint sustains man on gallows.* Spanish Exempla: Keller.

V221.7. *Woman relieved of incurable malady by kissing letter from saint.* (Cf. D1266.1.) *Loomis White Magic 105.

V221.8. *Wounds cured by saint leave no scars.* *Loomis White Magic 106.

V221.9. *Cut off parts of body attached again by saint.* *Loomis White Magic 84.

V221.10. *Men with enormous and unnatural appetite cured by saint.* Irish myth: Cross.

V221.11. *Saint cures dumb person.* Irish myth: *Cross.

V221.12. *Saint cures blindness.* Irish myth: *Cross.

V222. *Miraculous manifestation acclaims saint.* Alphabet Nos. 345, 354, 602, 637, 762; Irish: Beal XXI 305, 326, 335, O'Suilleabhain 70f., 115; Spanish: Keller, Espinosa Jr. Nos. 45, 182; India: Thompson-Balys.

D1313.11. Magic fountain indicates road for saint by removing itself. D1361.39. Fact that woman bears future saint in womb renders her invisible. D1648.1.2. Tree bows down to holy person. F960.1. Extraordinary nature phenomena at birth of holy person. F961.2.1. Bright star indicates birth of holy person. F960.2.6. Winter's day changes to summer's day at saint's funeral. F979.2. Leaves of tree open and close to give saint passage. H1573.2.1. Magic manifestation required as proof in test of saintliness.

V222.0.1. *Birth of saint predicted by visions of miracles.* Irish myth: *Cross.

M364.7. Coming (birth) of saint prophesied. V510. Religious visions.

V222.0.1.1. *Pillar of fire rises over woman pregnant with future saint.* Irish myth: Cross.

F964.0.1. Pillar of fire in sky.

V222.0.1.2. *Saint identified by pillar of fire above her head.* Irish myth: *Cross.

V222.0.1.3. *Dazzling heavenly light by day and night marks place of saint's birth.* Irish myth: *Cross.

V222.0.2. *Angels appear above place where saint is born.* Irish myth: Cross.

V222.1. *Marvelous light accompanying saint.* Alphabet No. 473; Plummer cxxxviii, clxxviii; Loomis White Magic 27f.; Irish myth: *Cross; Icelandic: *Boberg.

F960.1.3. Exhibition of lights at saint's birth. F969.3.2. Hero's light: appears around head of hero aroused to extraordinary feats of valor. F969.3.1. Marvelous light reveals man hiding from saint.

V222.1.0.1. *Supernaturally bright light marks sleeping infant saint.* Irish myth: Cross.

V222.1.0.2. *"Fair Drop" from Heaven falls upon infant saint.* Irish myth: Cross.

V222.1.1. *Radiance fills church when saint dies.* Irish myth: *Cross.

V222.1.2. *Hand of saint made bright by Lord's touch.* Too splendid for man's sight thereafter. Irish myth: *Cross.

F552.1.2. Fingers of saint give light or fire. F574. Luminous person. V227. Saints have divine visitors.

V222.1.3. *Column of light descends from heaven upon chosen man.* Loomis White Magic 28.

V222.1.4. *Lights shov where the body of saint is buried.* Loomis White Magic 28.

V222.2. *Brake in which saint loses tooth bursts into flame.* Irish myth: Cross.

V222.3. *Choral singing accompanies saint.* Irish myth: Cross.

F966. Voices from heaven (or from the air).

V222.4. *House of saint filled with fragrance.* Irish myth: *Cross.

V211.1.1. Air fragrant at Nativity.

V222.4.1. *Aromatic smell of a saint's body.* *Loomis White Magic 54f.

V222.5. *Oil bursts from ground as saint is made bishop.* Irish myth: Cross.

V222.6. *Bell sounds at approach of saint.* Irish myth: Cross; England: Baughman; India: Thompson-Balys.

D1601.18.1. Self-ringing bell. F960.1.4. Bells ring without human hands when a saint is born.

V222.6.1. *Church bells ring without aid of human hands at death of holy person.* *Loomis White Magic 52.

V222.7. *Dead holy man stretches hand from tomb to honor saint.* Irish myth: *Cross.

E542. Dead man touches living.

V222.8. *Holy man passes through fire for his faith.* Only his clothing burns. Spanish Exempla: Keller.

D1841.3.2. Fire does not injure saint.

V222.9. *Earthquake accompanies entrance of holy man into palace of heathen emperor.* Irish myth: Cross.

V222.10. *Saint falling into an abyss found perched in the branches of a tree which projected from the cliff.* As soon as the man is drawn up, the tree vanishes. *Loomis White Magic 127.

V222.11. *Flowers fall from saint's mouth while he speaks.* (Cf. D1454.2.1.) *Loomis White Magic 95.

V222.12. *Holy man restores a garden to bloom.* India: *Thompson-Balys.

V222.13. *Sun sends shaft of heat to cook meat given persecuted saint.* India: Thompson-Balys.

V222.14. *Roses lose thorns when saint walks on them.* England: Baughman.

V222.15. *Saint changes maggots in the sores of a nun into precious stones.* Spanish Exempla: Keller.

V222.16. *Robbers who enter saint's garden to steal are caused to spade it up for him.* This proves him to be saint. Spanish Exempla: Keller.

V223. *Saints have miraculous knowledge.* Alphabet No. 482; *Loomis White Magic 72f.; Irish myth: *Cross; Swiss: Jegerlehner Oberwallis 307 No. 25.

D1810.0.3. Magic knowledge of saints. D1812.0.2. Saints have foreknowledge of coming of guests. D1817.2. Saints magically detect crime. M301.5. Saints (holy men) as prophets. V511.1.1. Saints have visions of heaven.

V223.1. *Saint gives advice.* Chinese: Eberhard FFC CXX 119f.

V223.2. *Saint warns against poisoned well.* Chinese: Eberhard FFC CXX 114 No. 99.

V223.3. *Saint can perceive the thoughts of another man and reveal hidden sins.* Irish myth: *Cross.

V223.4. *Saint helps with learning.*

V223.4.1. *Truant boy learns long lesson while asleep with head in saint's lap.* Irish myth: *Cross.

V223.5. *Saints blessed with ability to discourse in the native idioms of the people whom they visit.* *Loomis White Magic 72.

V223.5.1. *Saint understands language of wren, fly, cat.* Irish myth: Cross.

B216. Knowledge of animal languages.

V223.6. *Saint as prognosticator.* India: Thompson-Balys.

V223.6.1. *Saint can foretell the weather.* Irish myth: Cross.

V224. *Miraculous replacement of objects (animals) for saint.* Irish myth: Cross.

D1602. Self-returning magic object. D2178. Objects produced by magic. V411.5. Treasure given away by saint miraculously restored. V411.6. Food given away by saint miraculously restored.

V224.1. *Objects used as firewood for saint miraculously replaced.* Irish myth: *Cross.

V224.2. *Food (animals) eaten by saint miraculously replaced.* Loomis White Magic 70; Irish myth: *Cross; India: Thompson-Balys.

D2105. Provisions magically furnished. E32. Resuscitated eaten animal.

V224.3. *Animals stolen from saint miraculously replaced.* Irish myth: *Cross.

C51.2. Tabu: stealing from god or saint. K423.0.1. Stolen animal returns to owner.

V224.4. *Performing fox accidentally killed miraculously replaced for saint.* Irish myth: Cross.

V224.5. *Supply of lime for building church miraculously renewed for saint.* Irish myth: Cross.

V225. *Saints in several places at once.* *Toldo V 343; *Loomis White Magic 131.

V226. *Saints as hermits.* *Toldo II 99; Irish myth: Cross; Icelandic: Boberg.

V227. *Saints have divine visitors.* *Toldo IV 49ff.; Irish myth: *Cross; India: Thompson-Balys.

K1811. Gods (saints) in disguise visit mortals. V235. Mortal visited by angel.

V227.1. *God gives staff of Jesus to saint.* Irish myth: *Cross.

D811. Magic object received from God (a god).

V228. *Immunities of saints* (holy men). (Cf. D1840.)

V228.1. *Saint immune to poisoning.* India: Thompson-Balys.

V228.1.1. *Saint drinks poison without being injured.* Irish myth: *Cross.

V228.2. *Anchorite immune to magician's powers.* India: Thompson-Balys.

V229. *Saints—miscellaneous.* Irish myth: Cross.

V229.1. *Saint commands return from dead with supernatural information.* Irish myth: Cross.

V229.2. *Sanctity of saints.* Irish myth: Cross.

T585.4. Infant saint rebukes mother's impiety. V238. Guardian angel.

V229.2.1. *Saintly babe repeatedly found with arms extended in form of cross.* Irish myth: Cross.

V229.2.2. *Saintly babe disgorges unclean food.* Irish myth: *Cross.

V229.2.3. *Saint will drink only milk of cow milked by faithful woman.* Irish myth: Cross.

V229.2.3.1. *Saint as baby refuses to take mother's breast on Wednesdays and Fridays.* *Loomis White Magic 114.

V229.2.4. *Baptism of a wonder child is accompanied by a variety of phenomena.* *Loomis White Magic 23.

V229.2.5. *Place of saint's martyrdom perpetually green.* *Loomis White Magic 95.

V229.2.6. *Martyrs emit milk instead of blood from their wounds.* *Loomis White Magic 79.

V229.2.6.1. *Saint sheds tears of blood.* Irish myth: Cross.

V229.2.7. *Flowers grow on graves from the mouths or hearts of holy persons.* (Cf. E631.1.) *Loomis White Magic 95.

V229.2.8. *Saint's body remains unspoiled in the earth for a long time.* *Loomis White Magic 43f.

V229.2.9. *Tombs of saints distill oil.* *Loomis White Magic 43.

V229.2.10. *Stones answer "Amen" after saint's preaching.* *Loomis White Magic 126.

V229.2.11. *Miracle saves saint from unjust censure.* Irish myth: Cross.

V229.2.11.1. *Saint causes gluttonous reptile to leap from saint's body into bishop's throat* and then return as proof of bishop's injustice. Irish myth: Cross.

V229.2.12. *Extraordinary longevity of saints.* Irish myth: *Cross.

A191.1. Great age of the gods. D1345. Magic objects gives longevity. D1857. Magic longevity. F571. Extremely old person. Q145. Miraculously long life as reward.

V229.2.12.1. *Seven Irish saints who never died.* Irish myth: *Cross.

V229.2.12.2. *Saint lives for 300 (100?) years without eating food or uttering evil.* Irish myth: *Cross.

V229.2.13. *Saint promises to return from heaven.* Irish myth: Cross.

V229.3. *Saint banishes snakes.* Irish myth: *Cross.

A531.2. Culture hero banishes snakes. A2434.2.3. Why there are no snakes in Ireland.

V229.4. *Saint overcomes (destroys) monsters (dragons).* Irish myth: *Cross.

V229.5. *Saint banishes demons.* Irish myth. *Cross.

A531.1.1. Culture hero banishes demons. D1385.12.1. Saint's bell rung against black birds (demons). D2176.3.3. Evil spirit exorcised by saint. E754.1. Condemned soul recovered. E756. Contest over souls. G303.16. How the devil's power may be escaped or avoided. G303.16.11.4. Saint expels devil to hell.

V229.5.1. *Saint confines monster (dragon) in lake.* Irish myth: *Cross.

V229.6. *Saint in conflict with druid.* Irish myth: *Cross.

A974.1. Certain stones are druids transformed by power of saint. D1719.1.1. Contest in magic between druid and saint. P427. Druid. Q552.2.3.1.1. Earth swallows druid who opposes saint.

V229.6.1. *Saint limits powers of satirist (druid).* Irish myth: Cross.

V229.6.2. *Ale poisoned by druid miraculously purified by saint.* Irish myth: Cross.

V229.6.3. *Druid raised in air, cast down, and brains scattered on stone by power of saint.* Irish myth: Cross.

V229.6.4. *Druid by spells seeks to drive saint from island.* Irish myth: Cross.

V229.7. *Invaders miraculously defeated by saints.* Irish myth: Cross.

V229.7.1. *Saint drives away an army by bringing upon it a dense and smoky cloud.* (Cf. D2163.4.) *Loomis White Magic 123; Irish myth: Cross; India: Thompson-Balys.

V229.8. *Saints create magic concealing mist.* (Cf. D1361.1.) Irish myth: *Cross.

V229.9. *Unusual fuel used by saints: burning stone, snow and icicles, marble pillar, and green timber.* *Loomis White Magic 34f.

V229.10. *Broken objects restored to their original forms by saint.* *Loomis White Magic 82f., 85.

V229.10.1. *Burned clothes restored to their previous form.* *Loomis White Magic 128.

V229.10.2. *Holy man restores cut-off hands and feet.* India: Thompson-Balys.

V229.10.3. *Saint causes grey hair to grow in black.* India: Thompson-Balys.

V229.11. *Saint with tongue of fire (literally).* *Loomis White Magic 34.

V229.12. *Sinful beauty is converted and spends the end of her life doing penance* (Mary Magdalene, Mary of Egypt, and Thais). *Loomis White Magic 109f.

V229.13. *Ground elevates itself to give protection or comfort to saint.* *Loomis White Magic 45.

V229.14. *Saint in anger shows strength: wall broken by his kick.* (Cf. F610.) *Loomis White Magic 131.

V229.15. *Saint disguised as poor man saves almsgiving king from punishment in hell.* Irish myth: Cross.

V229.16. *Lake of milk made through merit of saint.* Irish myth: Cross.

V229.17. *Saint's blessing causes a river to be best place for fishing.* Irish myth: Cross.

V229.18. *Dispute between two saints settled by angel.* Irish myth: Cross.

V229.19. *Objects mourn death of saint (holy man).* India: Thompson-Balys.

V229.20. *Downfall of ascetic (saint).* Chinese: Eberhard FFC CXX 185 No. 126.

T337. Woman wagers that she can seduce anchorite.

V229.20.1. *After birth of son holy person loses miraculous power.* India: Thompson-Balys.

V229.21. *House and family appear overnight to afford hospitality to benighted priests.* (Cf. Q45.1.) U.S.: Baughman.

V229.22. *Severed head of saint speaks so that searchers can find it.* (Cf. D1610.5.) England: Baughman.

V229.23. *Stone turns red when saint's picture is removed.* England: Baughman.

V229.24. *Saint turns snakes to stones.* (Cf. D420.) England: Baughman.

V229.25. *Conversation of animals reveals to man how to become saint.* Chinese: Eberhard FFC CXX 42.

V230. Angels. *Encyc. Rel. Ethics Index 26b; Irish: *Cross, O'Suilleabhain 107, Beal XXI 334; German: Grimm No. 3. For an extensive analysis of angels in Jewish tradition see *Neuman.

A42. Angels as God's advisers. A106.2. Revolt of evil angels against God. A972.2. Indentions on rocks from footprints of fairies (angels). B41.2.1. Angel horse. C13.1. Prince invites angel to wedding. C51.4.2. Tabu: spying on secret help of angels. D683.8. Transformation by angel (God). D1725. Magic power obtained from angels. D1810.5. Magic knowledge from angel. E754.2.2. Souls carried to heaven by angels. E756.1. Devils and angels contest for man's soul. F251.6. Fairies as fallen angels. F403.2.2.2. Angels as familiar spirits. F531.6.1.1. Sons of God and daughters of men. Before the flood angels have relations with human women: origin of giants. G303.1.1.3. God changes an angel into the devil, because he tried to imitate God in creating the world. G303.3.2.2. Devil (Satan) appears as an angel. G303.16.10. Angels save persons from the devil. H634.1. What is the sweetest song? Angel song. H663. Riddle: What is whiter than a swan? An angel. J225.0.1. Angel and hermit. J225.3. Angel takes cup from old man. J225.5. Angel kills man because he loves his child too much. J2212.2. Burial in old grave to deceive angel. K18.1.1. Throwing contest: trickster addresses Angel Gabriel. K311.2. Thief disguised as angel. K1315.1.1. Seduction by posing as Angel Gabriel. K2371.1.6. Heaven entered by trick: angel tricked by drink into telling woman how to enter. L411. Proud king displaced by angel. M301.10. Angels as prophets. N536. Treasure pointed out by angels. N814.1. Man carried through air by angel. Q45.1. Angels entertained unawares. Q553.2. Punishment: angel ceases to appear to self-righteous hermit. Q559.1. Devils instead of angels visit woman who has forgotten God in her prosperity.

V230.1. *Man beholds angels.* Irish myth: *Cross.

V230.2. *Angels powerfuld.* Irish myth: Cross.

V230.3. *Angel and mortal struggle.* Spanish Exempla: Keller.

V231. *Appearance of angel.* Spanish Exempla: Keller; Icelandic: Boberg; Jewish: *Neuman.

V231.1. *Angel in bird shape.* *Fb "fugl" I 380b; Irish myth: *Cross.

V231.2. *Shooting star as angel.* BP III 234.

V231.3. *Angel with four wings.* Irish myth: Cross.

V231.4. *Angel is form of cleric.* Irish myth: Cross.

V231.5. *Angel appears to woman to warn her not to force girl into marriage.* Spanish Exempla: Keller.

V231.6. *Angel in the form of an old man.* Cheremis: Sebeok-Nyerges.

V232. *Angel as helper.* Spanish: Keller, Espinosa Jr. No. 188; Jewish: *Neuman.

D812.10. Magic object received from angel. D1725. Magic power obtained from angels. D1810.5. Magic knowledge from angel. D2161.5.5. Cure by angel. D2162.3. Locality sanctified against pestilence by angel as result of prayer and fasting. F403.2.2.2. Angels as familiar spirits. H1573.0.1. Angel helpers in religious test. N211.3. Angel helps to find lost pin. N536. Treasure pointed out by angels. N814. Helpful angel.

V232.1. *Angel as helper in battle.* English: Wells 76 (Joseph of Aramathie); Italian Novella: Rotunda.

V232.1.1. *Angels appear and help boy prince slay treacherous uncle.* Spanish Exempla: Keller.

V232.2. *Angel carries mortal.* Irish myth: *Cross.

V232.2.0.1. *Angel carries boat to water.* Irish myth: Cross.

V232.2.0.2. *Angel transports saint's staff.* Irish myth: Cross.

V232.3. *Angels supply food to mortal.* Irish myth: *Cross; Jewish: Neuman.

V232.3.1. *Angel shows saint where to dig for water.* Irish myth: *Cross.

V232.4. *Angel looses man's fetters.* (Cf. R121.) Irish myth: Cross.

V232.5. *Angel as guide.* Irish myth: *Cross; Jewish: *Neuman.

V232.5.1. *Angel guides chariot.* Irish myth: *Cross.

V232.6. *Angel reveals location of lost (buried) object.* Irish myth: *Cross.

V232.7. *Gifts from angels.* Irish myth: *Cross; Jewish: *Neuman.

V232.7.1. *Angel brings cross as gift to saint.* Irish myth: Cross.

V232.8. *Angel helps Peter to escape from prison.* Spanish Exempla: Keller.

V232.9. *Angel cleans hearth.* Irish myth: Cross.

V232.10. *Angels build church.* Irish myth: *Cross.

V233. *Angel of death.* *Chauvin VI 184 No. 349; *Fb "engel" I 250; Jewish: *Neuman, bin Gorion Born Judas I 313f., 149f., 371ff., 380.

V233.1. *Angel of death spares mother who is suckling children.* As punishment angel must serve as sexton. Type 795*; Lithuanian: Balys Index No. 795*; Russian: Andrejev No. 795A*; Estonian: Aarne FFC XXV No. 795*.

V234. *Songs of the angels.* *Chauvin VI 106 No. 270; *Loomis White Magic 53; Irish myth: *Cross.

V234.1. *Angels sing in honor of saint.* Irish myth: *Cross.

V234.1.1. *Angels sing to welcome saint.* Irish myth: Cross.

V234.1.2. *Angels sing over saint's body.* Irish myth: *Cross.

V234.1.3. *Angel choir responds when saint receives orders.* Irish myth: *Cross.

V234.2. *Angels sing on night of Christ's Nativity.* Irish myth: *Cross.

V235. *Mortal visited by angel.* Irish: Plummer clxxxii, *Cross; Icelandic: *Boberg; Swiss: Jegerlehner Oberwallis 301 No. 16; Spanish: Keller, Espinosa Jr. No. 186; Jewish: *Neuman.

A182.3. God (angel) speaks to mortal. J225.0.1. Angel and hermit. K1811. Gods (saints) in disguise visit mortals. Q45.1. Angels entertained unawares. U119.3. Angel holds nose when handsome sinner passes. V227. Saints have divine visitors.

V235.0.1. *Mortals visited by angel in vision.* (Cf. V510.) Irish myth: *Cross.

V235.0.2. *Angel invoked by fasting.* Irish myth: *Cross.

V235.1. *Angel announces birth of Christ to shepherds.* Irish myth: Cross.

V235.2. *Angel comforts repentant sinner.* Irish myth: Cross.

V235.3. *Angel bars abbot from his cell because abbot has cast out a sinning monk.* Spanish Exempla: Keller.

V236. *Fallen angels.* Jewish: Neuman.

V236.1. *Fallen angels become fairies (dwarfs, trolls).* *Fb "engel" I 250; Irish: O'Suilleabhain 59, 61, Beal XXI 323f.

A106.2. Revolt of Evil Angels against God.

V237. *Angel bars the way to Baalam's ass.* Numbers 22: 27; Italian Novella: Rotunda.

V238. *Guardian angel.* (Cf. F403.2.2.2, V232, 246.) Irish myth: *Cross; Jewish: Neuman.

V238.1. *Angels hover over mortal (saint).* Irish myth: *Cross.

V238.2. *Angels melt snow around saintly babe.* Irish myth: Cross.

V238.3. *Service of angels marks saint's destination.* Irish myth: Cross.

V238.4. *Air above grave of converted druid full of angels.* Irish myth: *Cross.

V241. *Angels honor mortal.* (Cf. V234.1.) Irish myth: *Cross; Jewish: *Neuman.

V241.1. *Angels attend saint's funeral.* Irish myth: Cross.

V241.1.1. *Angel directs saint's burial.* Irish myth: *Cross.

V241.2. *Angels hold service over (saint's) tomb.* (Cf. V242.) Irish myth: *Cross.

V241.2.1. *Angels shed light upon saint's tomb.* Irish myth: Cross.

V241.3. *Angels run races before saint.* Irish myth: Cross.

V241.4. *Angel baptizes saint.* Irish myth: Cross.

V241.4.1. *Angel names child.* Irish myth: *Cross.

V241.5. *Angels set heavenly veil upon head of pious woman.* Irish myth: Cross.

V242. *Holy place (object) glorified by angel's presence.* (Cf. V421.2.)

V242.1. *Train of angels rises from graveyard.* Irish myth: Cross.

V242.2. *Angel abides in church.* Irish myth: Cross.

V242.2.1. *Angels attend church service.* Irish myth: *Cross.

V242.3. *Angel passes daily over blessed stone.* Irish myth: Cross.

V243. *Angel answers mortal's prayer.* Irish myth: *Cross; Jewish: Neuman.

V243.1. *Angels appear above grave of fallen girl through virtue of prayers said by her lover (young monk).* Irish myth: Cross.

V244. *Angel beseeches at unholy grave of redeemed sinner until body is moved to sanctified ground.* Irish myth. Cross.

V245. *Angel punishes mortal.* Irish myth: Cross; Jewish: *Neuman.

V245.1. *Angel scourges mortal for disobedience to God.* (Cf. Q220, Q325, Q458.) Irish myth: Cross.

V246. *Angel counsels mortal.* (Cf. V232, V238.) Irish myth: *Cross; Jewish: *Neuman.

V246.0.1. *Angel leaves letter (book) with instructions for saint.* Irish myth: *Cross.

V246.0.2. *Angel dictates (gives) book.* Irish myth: *Cross.

V246.1. *Angel tells saint where to build his church.* Irish myth: *Cross.
V111. Churches.

V246.2. *Angel as saint's teacher.* Irish myth: *Cross.

V246.3. *Angel informs saint of coming of guests.* Irish myth: Cross.
D1812.0.2. Saints have foreknowledge of coming of guests.

V247. *Daily life of angels.* Jewish: *Neuman.

V248. *Angels and God.* Jewish: *Neuman.

V249. *Angels—miscellaneous motifs.* Irish myth: Cross.

V249.1. *Angel makes proclamation.* Irish myth: Cross.

V249.2. *Language of angels.*

V249.2.1. *Hebrew the language of the angels.* Irish myth: Cross.

V250. The Virgin Mary. **Crane Liber de Miraculis; *DeVooys Middelnederlandse Legenden en Exempelen 57; Genthe Die Jungfrau Maria: ihre Evangelien und ihre Wunder (Halle, 1852); *Encyc. Rel. Ethics Index 366c. — Irish: *Cross, O'Suilleabhain 59, 78, Beal XXI 307, 314, 323, 327; Spanish: Keller, Espinosa Jr. Nos. 202—04. For references in addition to those given below, see volume VI s.v. "Virgin Mary".

A1355.2. Origin of menstruation: Virgin Mary's garment. A2231.5. Spider vies with Virgin Mary in spinning. A2615.1. Mary hides in ground nail to be used for cross: origin of thistles. B131.6. Bird betrays hiding place of Virgin. D1331.2.3. Virgin Mary's shift as banner causes blindness to opposing army. D1610.21.1. Image of Virgin speaks. D1620.1.4. Statue of Virgin sews for suppliant. D1622.2. Image of Virgin bows to indicate favor. D1623.1. Image of Virgin veils and unveils itself. D1639.2. Image of Virgin saves painter. D1648.1.2.1. Tree bows to help Virgin Mary in childbirth. D2151.1.2.1. Tide held back by Virgin Mary. D2161.5.2. Cure by Virgin Mary. D2163.3. Virgin Mary intercepts an arrow in battle. G303.9.4.8. Devil tempts youth to deny Virgin. G303.16.1. By help of Virgin devil may be escaped. G303.16.2.2. Person saved from devil by prayer to Virgin. K1841. The Virgin Mary substitutes for a mortal. K1971.3.1. Maid behind statue of Virgin advises mistress. M91. Virgin Mary reverses judgments of church. Q32. Reward for offering food to crucifix (Madonna). Q653.1.

Virgin Mary withdraws sacrament from scoffer. Q558.5. Man in anger throws stone at image of Virgin: is stricken dead. S251. Virgin Mary rescues child promised to the devil. T313. Ravished girl's virginity restored by Virgin Mary. T321.2. Girl named Mary has virginity spared by knight who has bought her. The Virgin appears to her. T376. Young man betrothed to statue. Man puts marriage ring on finger of statue of Venus (Virgin Mary). She afterwards forbids him the embraces of an earthly bride. T401. Virgin Mary as protectress of illicit lovers. T401.1. Pregnant abbess secretly delivered of her child by Virgin Mary. T412.1. Mother guilty of incest with son forgiven by pope (Virgin Mary).

V250.1. *Irish saint as "Mary of the Gael"*. Irish myth: *Cross.

V250.2. *Virgin Mary has golden hair*. Irish myth: Cross

V251. *Virgin Mary prevents (retards) death so as to save sinner's soul.* Permits time for repentance and absolution. (Sometimes resuscitation.) Alphabet No. 464; Ward II 606 No. 14, 633 No. 31, 650 No. 1; *Crane Miraculis Nos. 6, 7, 10, 31, 39; Wells 169 (De Miraculo Beate Marie); Scala Celi 123a, 125b Nos. 674, 681. — Spanish Exempla: Keller.

E121.3. Resuscitation by Virgin Mary. E754.1.2. Condemned soul saved by Virgin Mary. V23.1. Unshriven man restored to life in order to confess.

V251.1. *Virgin Mary brings man back to life after he has seen hell's torments*. Spanish Exempla: Keller.

V252. *Virgin Mary defends innocent accused.* Alphabet No. 381; Wesselski Mönchslatein 78 No. 68; *Crane Miraculis No. 34; Icelandic: Boberg.

V252.1. *Virgin Mary returns borrowed money and reveals cheat.* A man borrows money from a Jew with the Virgin as security. Unable to return the money in time, he commits the money to the sea with a prayer to the Virgin. The Jew receives it but claims that the money is not paid. The Virgin reveals the cheat. Ward II 638 No. 10; *Crane Miraculis No. 33; Wells 167 (Vernon Miracles).

V252.2. *Virgin Mary saves criminal from fire at stake.* *Ward II 663 No. 12; Spanish Exempla: Keller.

Q414. Punishment: burning alive. R175. Rescue at the stake.

V253. *Faithfulness to Virgin Mary, even if not to Christ, rewarded.* Alphabet No. 555; Wesselski Mönchslatein 128 No. 113.

V254. *Efficacy of saying "Aves"*. Irish: Beal XXI 335, O'Suilleabhain 114, 117.

V254.1. *Saying of "Aves" obliterates sin.* *Crane Miraculis No. 12; Ward II 605ff. Nos. 10, 18, 20; Herbert III 26; *Crane Vitry 263 No. 296.

Q171. Immunity from punishment for sin as reward. T285. Mistress has always said her "Aves": Virgin Mary refuses to help wife against her rival. The wife tells this to the mistress, who repents.

V254.1.1. *Virgin Mary supports robber on gallows because he once said "Ave Maria"*. Spanish Exempla: Keller.

V254.2. *Ship in storm saved because of sailors' "Ave Maria"*. (Cf. D2141.1.) *Crane Miraculis No. 28; Ward II 626 No. 9, 640 Nos. 12, 14, 15, *677 No. 12.

V254.3. *"Ave" on the tongue.* Because of faithfulness in saying "Aves" the words are found imprinted on the dead man's tongue. (Cf. V86.2.) Ward II 612 No. 29, 677 No. 1, cf. 632 No. 30.

V254.3.1. *Blasphemer paralyzed in all members except tongue which had once said "Ave Maria"*. Spanish Exempla: Keller.

V254.4. *Devil exorcised by "Ave".* Ward II 686 Nos. 74, 75, 77.

V254.5. *Nun forgets to hail Mary and goes into the world to sin.* Alphabet No. 470.

V254.6. *Joseph and Mary threaten to leave heaven when the man who has always prayed to them is refused admittance.* *Type 805*.

V254.7. *Murdered boy still sings "Ave" after his death.* (Chaucer's Prioress's Tale.) **Brown PMLA XXI 486ff.; Ward II 656, 697 and passim; Herbert III 528; Wells Catalogue of Romances 166 (Vernon Miracles).

V254.7.1. *Criminal who said "Ave" beheaded.* His head calls repeatedly, "Ave Maria". Spanish Exempla: Keller.

V254.8. *Virgin Mary will not let devil (authorities) take robber noble who daily says "Ave".* Spanish Exempla: Keller.

V254.9. *Virgin forbids devil to take robber as long as he continues to say two "Aves" daily.* Italian Novella: Rotunda.

V255. *Virgin Mary has dissolute monk buried in consecrated ground: his only mass is that of the Virgin.* *Crane Miraculis Nos. 3, 9; Ward II 607 No. 15, 660 No. 29; Scala Celi 116a, 116b Nos. 644, 645; Spanish Exempla: Keller.

V255.1. *Devotee of Virgin not buried in consecrated ground has lily issue from mouth so that his grave is made known.* Spanish Exempla: Keller; Italian Novella: Rotunda.

V255.2. *Virgin gives private mass to devout lady unable to attend.* Spanish Exempla: Keller

V256. *Miraculous healing by Virgin Mary.* (Cf. D2161.) Irish myth: Cross.

V256.1. *Healing spittle of Virgin Mary.* (Cf. D1500.1.7.2.) Irish myth: Cross.

V256.2. *Miracles of healing performed before image of Virgin Mary.* Irish myth: Cross.

V256.3. *Virgin Mary restores severed hand to Saint John Damascene.* He had cut it off to repress lust. Spanish Exempla: Keller.

T327. Mutilation to repel lover. T333. Man mutilates self to remove temptation.

V256.4. *Virgin Mary saves life of man who at devil's instigation has castrated himself.* She will not, however, restore his severed members. Spanish Exempla: Keller.

V256.5. *Virgin Mary restores life to drowned man who always had saluted her.* Spanish Exempla: Keller.

V261. *Virgin Mary designates favorite for election for office.* *Crane Miraculis No. 13; Ward II 608 No. 19.

V261.1. *Virgin restores office to an ignorant man because of his faith.* Spanish Exempla: Keller.

V261.2. *Virgin pardons man who repented for cheating in election.* Spanish Exempla: Keller.

V262. *Virgin Mary supplies mead for unprepared hostess of the king.* Ward II 614 No. 35.

V263. *Portrait of the Virgin appears to devotee.* *Ward II 611 Nos. 26, 27; *Crane Miraculis Nos. 21, 44.

V264. *Virgin Mary rescues man attacked by the devil.* *Crane Miraculis No. 23; Ward II 612 No. 30; Spanish Exempla: Keller; West Indies: Flowers 580.

V264.1. *Virgin Mary brings man a pact he signed with the devil and frees the man from devil's power.* Spanish Exempla: Keller.

M211. Man sells soul to devil. S251. Virgin Mary rescues child promised to the devil.

V265. *Virgin miraculously prevents nun (monk) from deserting cloister.* Ward II 634 No. 34, 636 Nos. 7, 41, 667 No. 13, 721 No. 17; Spanish Exempla: Keller.

K1841.1. The nun who saw the world (Sister Beatrice). The Virgin takes the place of the nun in the nunnery while the latter is living a life of shame. V475. Renunciation of clerical vows.

V265.1. *Image of Virgin tries in vain to keep nun from leaving convent.* Crane Vitry 160 No. 60; Spanish Exempla: Keller.

V266. *Virgin Mary converts a Jew.* (Cf. V330.) Italian Novella: Rotunda.

V267. *Devotee of Virgin is comforted in the hour of death.* Italian Novella: Rotunda.

V268. *Miracles performed under protection of Virgin Mary.* Italian Novella: Rotunda.

V268.1. *Boy under protection of Virgin Mary pulled from well alive after a week.* Irish myth: Cross.

V268.2. *Virgin Mary saves devotee from death in waves.* Spanish Exempla: Keller.

V268.3. *Virgin Mary destroys Moorish army besieging Constantinople.* Spanish Exempla: Keller.

V268.4. *Virgin Mary saves devotee's son from shipwreck.* Spanish Exempla: Keller.

V268.5. *Image of Virgin Mary works miracles.* Irish myth: Cross.

V271. *Virgin Mary as foster mother.* Type 710; *BP I 13ff.

V275. *Virgin Mary comforts repentant criminals.* Ward II 603 No. 6, 606 No. 12, 610 No. 25, 618 No. 39, 648 No. 44; Spanish Exempla: Keller.

V276. *Virgin Mary appears to erring man.*

V276.1. *Virgin Mary appears to erring monk and exalts him to prayer.* His prayers weave her a garment. Spanish Exempla: Keller.

V276.2. *Virgin Mary appears and pardons monk who has been too overworked to pray to her.* Spanish Exempla: Keller.

V276.3. *Virgin Mary aids repentant slayer of priest.* Priest is resurrected in order to forgive murderer and then is returned to tomb. Italian Novella: Rotunda.

V277. *Virgin Mary appears to devotee.*

V277.1. *Virgin Mary appears to devout nun with infant Jesus.* The nun devoutly prayed to see Him. Spanish Exempla: Keller.

V281. *Devotee of Virgin Mary given present by her.* Ward II 660 No. 28.

V282. *Stella Maris: Virgin Mary as protectress of sailors.* Canney Revue de l'Histoire des Religions CXV (1937) 90ff.; Krappe Review of Religion (1948) 376ff.

V283. *Testament of Virgin Mary.* Irish myth: *Cross.

V284. *During a flood the Virgin descends into the streets to save her image from the flood waters.* U.S.: Baughman.

V290. Other sacred persons. Irish myth: Cross.

D2161.5.4. Cure by Moses.

V291. *Master poets (ollamhs) as sacred persons.* Irish myth: *Cross.

V292. *The Apostles of Christ.*

V292.1. *Appearance of the Apostles.* Irish myth: Cross.

V292.2. *The Twelve Apostles of Ireland.* Irish myth: *Cross.

V293. *Lepers as sacred persons.* Irish myth: Cross.

V294. *The Pope.* Irish myth: Cross.

V300—V399. Religious beliefs.

V300. Religious beliefs.

J1262. Repartee based on doctrinal discussions. Q225. Punishment for scoffing at church teachings.

V310. Particular dogmas.

V311. *Belief in the life to come.* *Encyc. Rel. Ethics Index 272b; Irish myth: *Cross.

V311.0.1. *Doctrine of immortality taught by druids.* Irish myth: *Cross.

V311.1. *Man converted to belief in future life on deathbed.* Feels sure nevertheless that nothing will come of it. Wesselski Bebel I 182 No. 32.

V311.2. *Dying man refuses to believe in life to come.* Italian Novella: Rotunda.

V311.3. *Given choice between life and heaven, person chooses latter.* Irish myth: *Cross.

V312. *Belief in Immaculate Conception.* (Cf. T510.) *Encyc. Rel. Ethics Index 272a; Spanish Exempla: Keller.

V312.1. *Proclamation of dogma of Immaculate Conception stops plague.* Pauli (ed. Bolte) Nos. 552, 553.

V312.2. *Man miraculously dies for opposing dogma of Immaculate Conception.* Attempt to disprove the dogma by false miracle. Sham dead man is to rise if the dogma is not true. He is found to be actually dead. Pauli (ed. Bolte) No. 554.

V313. *Last judgment.* Jewish: Moreno Esdras, *Neuman.

A1002. Doomsday. E750. Perils of the soul. V520. Salvation.

V315. *Belief in the Atonement.* *Encyc. Rel. Ethics Index 48c; Jewish: *Neuman.

V315.1. *Power of repentance.* Jewish: *Neuman.

V316. *Efficacy of prayer.* Jewish: *Neuman.

V316.1. *"He that asks shall receive."* Hermit wants to prove truth of these words of the Gospel and asks for the hand of the princess. Performs the difficult task imposed upon him. Lithuanian: Balys Index No. 779*; Russian: Andrejev No. 841I*

V317. *The chosen people.* Jewish: *Neuman.

V317.1. *Holy land.* Jewish: *Neuman.

V320. Heretics. *Encyc. Rel. Ethics Index 251b; Irish myth: Cross.

Q552.2.3.2.2. Earth swallows heretical city. V351.1. Wise heretic is vanquished in debate with a Christian.

V321. *Insane man burns heretic in his bed: restored to his senses as reward.* Pauli (ed. Bolte) No. 47.

V322. *Heretical baptism.* Heathen baptized into devil's possession. Irish myth: *Cross.

V323. *Atheists.*

V323.1. *Epicureans regarded as atheists.* Jewish: Neuman.

V325. *Baptismal water vanishes before Aryan bishop.* Alphabet No. 95.

V326. *Hero renounces heaven because dead companions (heathen) are not there.* Irish myth: *Cross.

V327. *Author of book against heretic honored by Virgin Mary and angels.* Scala Celi 117b No. 652.

V328. *Man sets fire to his house and perishes in it rather than accept Christianity.* Irish myth: *Cross.

V330. Conversion from one religion to another. *Encyc. Rel. Ethics X 400—403.

M351. Prophecy that youth shall abandon his religion and become Christian. (Baarlam and Josaphat.)

V331. *Conversion to Christianity.* (Cf. M177.1.) Pauli (ed. Bolte) No. 555; Dickson 199 n. 89; Malone PMLA XLIII 413. — Irish: *Cross, O'Suilleabhain 65, Beal XXI 325; Icelandic: *Boberg; English: Wells 88 (Roland and Vernagu); Spanish Exempla: Keller; Jewish: *Neuman; Tahiti: Henry Ancient Tahiti (Honolulu, 1928) 178.

V331.0.1. *Druid converted to Christianity.* Irish myth: *Cross.

V331.0.2. *Three (two) Irishmen who believed in Christianity before the coming of St. Patrick.* (Cf. A1546.3.1.) Irish myth: *Cross.

V331.1. *Conversion to Christianity through miracle.* Dickson 193—98 passim; Alphabet No. 558; Icelandic: *Boberg; Irish: *Cross, O'Suilleabhain 71, 74, Beal XXI 326; English: Wells 91 (Otuel), 119 (Octovian), *Hibbard 45ff.; Italian Novella: *Rotunda.

V331.1.1. *Conversion to Christianity by miracle of seeing blood flow from Jesus' image.* Spanish Exempla: Keller.

V331.1.2. *Conversion to Christianity through appearance of the cross and angels.* Spanish Exempla: Keller.

V331.1.3. *Conversion to Christianity because the heathen gods prove to be less powerful.* *Loomis White Magic 75.

V331.1.4. *Conversion because saint's staff miraculously goes through neophytes' foot.* Irish myth: *Cross.

V331.2. *Conversion to Christianity on pain of death.* *Dickson 188 n. 64, 224; Icelandic: *Boberg.

V331.3. *Miraculous beautification upon conversion to Christianity.* (Cf. D1860.) English: Wells 122 (The King of Tars).

V331.4. *Conversion to Christianity through repentance.* Italian Novella: Rotunda.

V331.5. *Conversion to Christianity through love.* Italian Novella: *Rotunda.

V331.6. *Conversion to Christianity out of gratitude.* Ruler has captive baptize his sister and then marry her. Grateful for past kindnesses. Italian Novella: Rotunda.

V331.7. *Saladin asks to be made a Christian knight.* Italian Novella: Rotunda.

V331.8. *Fairies converted to Christianity.* Irish myth: *Cross.

V331.9. *Swans (transformed children) do not suffer in harsh weather after conversion to Christianity.* Irish myth: *Cross.

B250. Religious animals. D161.1. Transformation man to swan.

V331.10. *Conversion to Christianity because of admiration for Christian virtue.*

V331.10.1. *Conversion to Christianity through show of forgiveness and gentleness.* Spanish Exempla: Keller.

V332. *Baptism of heathen.* *Thien Motive 40f.; Spanish Exempla: Keller.

V336. *Conversion to Judaism.* Jewish: *Neuman.

V340. Miracle manifested to non-believers. Irish myth: *Cross; Icelandic: *Boberg; Jewish: Neuman; India: Thompson-Balys.

F964.2. Fire spares saint's tunic, though wearer is burned. H1573.3. Power of Christianity tested. V353. Saint's bachall pointed at idol defaces it.

V341. *Pagan sybil draws picture of Madonna and Child in sand.* Result of vision. Pauli (ed. Bolte) No. 560.

V342. *Sign of cross intimidates Jews.* Type 1709*.

V343. *Jews protesting against marriage of Jewess and Christian are struck dumb.* Wesselski Mönchslatein 52 No. 62.

V344. *Temple about to be taken over by pagans saved by appearance of a Sign of the Cross (image of the Virgin).* Alphabet No. 708; *Crane Miraculis No. 20.

V345. *Dove flies out of man's mouth.* Impious anchorite has agreed to forsake his religion in return for the possession of a maid. When he repents the dove reenters his mouth. Italian Novella: Rotunda; Spanish Exempla: Keller.

E732.1. Soul in form of dove. M217. Devil (Saracen priest) bargains to help man win woman.

V346. *Skeptic kicked by sacrificial animal.* India: Thompson-Balys.

V347. *Idols found on their faces after saint's arrival.* *Loomis White Magic 89; Irish myth: Cross.

D2176.3.3.1. Demons in stone images driven out by holy man (saint).

V350. Conflicts between religions. Irish myth: *Cross; Jewish: *Neuman.

D1402.13. Druid's spells kill Christian king. D1719.1. Contest in magic. F302.8. Fairy mistress demands mortal lover deny Christian teachings. F399.3. Fairies hate clerics. F402.1.11.1. Spirit sent by druids cause death of Christian king. F460.4.4.4. Mountain-men make sausage of Christians. H1573.1. Belief in Christianity tested. J1825. Turkish ambassador misunderstands Christian ceremonies. Makes ridiculous reports to his king. P426.0.1. In fear of clerics pagans flee into fairy mounds. Q222. Punishment for desecration of holy places. Q227. Punishment for opposition to holy person. Q552.3.3. Drought as punishment for heathen.

V351. *Duel (debate) to prove which religion is better.* Dickson 187 nn. 61, 62; English: Wells 88 (Roland and Vernagu), 91 (Otuel); Spanish Exempla: Keller.

H607.1. Discussion between priest and Jew carried on by symbols.

V351.1. *Wise heretic is vanquished in debate with a Christian.* Italian Novella: Rotunda.

V351.1.1. *Brahmin wins a discussion on religion.* India: Thompson-Balys.

V351.2. *Unbeliever loses argument with hermit.* Italian Novella: Rotunda.

V351.3. *Magician overpowered in contest with a saint.* *Loomis White Magic 75f.

V351.3.1. *Contest of St. Peter with Simon Magus, a magician.* *Loomis White Magic 120.

V351.4. *Prayer-contest to prove which religion is better.* Irish myth: *Cross.

V351.5. *Contest of miraculous powers between a Yogi and a Musselman.* India: Thompson-Balys.

V352. *Pagan disputant with Christian stricken dumb.* English: Wells 76 (Joseph of Aramathie); Spanish Exempla: Keller.

V352.1. *Pagan disputant with Christian bested by the words put in his mouth by God.* Spanish Exempla: Keller.

V354. *Life of heroic age preferable to Christian living.* Irish myth: *Cross.

V355. *Buddhists become slaves of Taoists because they cannot produce rain.* Chinese: Werner 353.

V356. *Christian hero (saint) overthrows heathen idols.* *Boje 82; *Toldo V 339; Irish myth: *Cross; Icelandic: *Boberg.

V356.1. *Saint dispels pagan devils from ancient shrines.* *Loomis White Magic 115.

V356.2. *Pagan shrines and idols, or magic books destroyed by fire from heaven.* *Loomis White Magic 35.

V356.2.1. *Heathen idols sink into earth up to their necks through power of saint.* Irish myth: Cross.

V356.3. *Saint's bachall pointed at idol defaces it.* (Cf. V347.) Irish myth: Cross.

V360. Christian and Jewish traditions about each other. *DeVooys Middelnederlandse Legenden en Exempelen (Den Haag, 1926) 199ff.

A1681.2. Why Jews do not eat pork. D1624.2. Wounds of crucifix bleed. J1613. The rescuers' Sabbath. A Jew, fallen into a pit, refuses to be rescued on Saturday, his Sabbath. The next day he calls for help but the Christians refuse to rescue him on Sunday, their Sabbath. J2336. Jewess makes parents believe that she is to give birth to the Messiah. She bears a girl. J2383. Pity for the poor Jews. On Good Friday an old woman who has heard the Passion Story exclaims, "How hard it was for the Jews who had to watch all night with Christ." P715.1. Jews. W154.19. Ungrateful Jew steals horse of Christian who has lent it to him. X610. Jokes concerning Jews.

V361. *Christian child killed to furnish blood for Jewish rite.* (Hugh of Lincoln.) (Cf. V254.7.) **V. Manzini La superstizione omicida e i sacrifici umani, con particolare riguardo alle accuse contro gli Ebrei (2d ed., Padua, 1930); **Berger Mélusine VIII 169ff.; *Ward II 656 No. 3; *Brown PMLA XXI 486ff. — English: Child III 240ff., IV 497a.

V362. *Plague from Jews' poisoning wells.* German: H. Rauchfuss Alte Geschichte u. neue Sagen aus Thuringen 60.

V363. *Jewish child thrown into oven by father for taking eucharist.* Preserved by Virgin Mary. *Ward II 601; Irish myth: Cross (V35.1.0.1); Spanish Exempla: Keller.

V363.1. *Jewish child resurrected (saved by power of Virgin Mary) after being burned to ashes for eating consecrated bread in Christian church.* Irish myth: *Cross.

V364. *A Christianized Jew becomes a priest.* During Mass, he stabs the consecrated host, blood flows (cf. C55, J1261.2, V30). He kills the other priest who saw him commit the sacrilege, and before killing, forces him to renounce his faith. A miracle exposes the murderer. Lithuanian: Balys Index No. 3270, Legends Nos. 416ff.

V365. *Jewish traditions concerning non-Jews.* Jewish: *Neuman.

V380. Religious beliefs—miscellaneous.

V381. *Heathen beats his god because of misfortune.* (Cf. V123.) *Boje 101; Chinese: Eberhard FFC CXX 238 No. 185.

V382. *Doctor ridicules belief in Devil, Heaven, and Hell.* Italian Novella: Rotunda.

V383. *Religious fanaticism.* Irish myth: Cross.

V383.1. *Prolonged prostration in worship causes death.* Irish myth: Cross.

V383.2. *Hindu drinks water by mistake from Mohammedan's vessel: his fortune turns to evil.* India: Thompson-Balys.

C270. Tabu: drinking certain things.

V385. *Romans won't include Jesus in their pantheon because of his poverty which they hate.* Spanish Exempla: Keller.

V400—V449. Religious virtues.

V400. Charity. *Encyc. Rel. Ethics Index 111c; Spanish Exempla: Keller; Jewish: *Neuman.

D1500.1.10.3. Money from offertory as cure. F1095. Arm grows longer from giving alms.

V410. Charity rewarded. Irish: O'Suilleabhain 22, Beal XXI 307, 337; Spanish: Espinosa Jr. No. 137, 200—204; Jewish: *Neuman.

Q42. Generosity rewarded.

V410.1. *Charity rewarded above prayer or hearing of masses.* Irish: O'Suilleabhain 131; Spanish: Boggs FFC XC 87 No. 756E*.

V410.2. *Prince's motto: charity conquers.* India: *Thompson-Balys.

V411. *Miraculous reward for charities.* India: Thompson-Balys.

V411.1. *Queen gives away a sleeve of her dress: miraculously restored.* Pauli (ed. Bolte) No. 322.

V411.2. *Saint exchanges coat with beggar: gold sleeves miraculously appear.* Herbert III 6; Crane Vitry 173 No. 92.

V411.3. *Man who has given all in charity has foot amputated: restored miraculously.* Alphabet No. 81; Spanish Exempla: Keller.

V411.4. *Stones turn to gold for charitable money-lender.* Hence money borrowed for wedding is never refused by lenders. India: Thompson-Balys.

A1550. Origin of customs of courtship and marriage. D475.1. Transformation objects to gold.

V411.5. *Treasure given away by saint miraculously restored.* Irish myth: *Cross.

V224. Miraculous replacement of objects (animals) for saint.

V411.5.1. *Man earns as much as he gave away for charity in his former life.* India: Thompson-Balys.

V411.6. *Food given away by saint miraculously restored.* Irish myth: *Cross.

V411.7. *Charitable king blows nose after having given to beggar.* Huge ruby appears in his kerchief. Spanish Exempla: Keller.

V411.8. *Jesus appears to St. Martin when he gives his cloak to beggar.* Spanish Exempla: Keller.

V411.9. *Charity miraculously repaid: flame settles on forehead.* India: Thompson-Balys.

V412. *Miraculous manifestations during act of charity.* *Ward III 7; *Crane Vitry Nos. 92, 94, 95.

V412.1. *Bread stolen by St. Nicholas for purpose of feeding poor is miraculously restored.* Spanish Exempla: Keller.

V412.2. *The more bread (flour) the monks give to the poor the more God places in their bins.* (Cf. D1652.1.1.) Spanish Exempla: Keller.

V413. *Son's acts of charity save his father's soul.* English: Wells 175 (The Child of Bristowe).

V414. *Saint shares punishment of sinful man whose cloak he shared in life.* Irish myth: Cross.

V415. *Children envious of money given by deceased father to bishop.* In vision they take their father's body up and find a quittance saying that he has received more than a hundredfold reward. Alphabet No. 302; Spanish Exempla: Keller.

V416. *Act of charity obliterates sin.*

V416.1. *Man convicted of cheating at his bookkeeping is excused when it is learned that he has given the money to the poor.* Spanish Exempla: Keller.

V420. Reward of the uncharitable.

Q286. Uncharitableness punished.

V421. *Shipman refuses alms: ship turned to stone.* Alphabet No. 608.

D471.3. Transformation: ship to stone. Q585.1. Destruction of property uncharitably refused.

V422. *Uncharitable knight drives bargain even in giving alms: devoured by serpents.* His alms of corn turn to serpents. *Herbert III 334 No. 7, 340.

V425. *Uncharitable pope wanders after death.* Alphabet No. 294.

V430. Charity—miscellaneous motifs.

V431. *Charity of usurers ineffective.* Alphabet Nos. 260, 754, 786, 789, 792; Irish: Beal XXI 337; Spanish: Espinosa Jr. No. 213.

E411.4. Usurer cannot rest in grave.

V432. *Man beggars self by charity.* India: *Thompson-Balys.

L432. Impoverished husband begs from wife's new husband.

V433. *Charity of saints.* Irish myth: *Cross.

V434. *Conqueror restores kingship to king for charity.* Irish myth: Cross.

V435. *Pious man charitable to man who has formerly refused him charity.* India: Thompson-Balys.

L432. Impoverished husband begs from wife's new husband.

V436. *Mendicant refuses to accept alms from barren woman.* India: Thompson-Balys.

V437. *Saint repeatedly bestows father's goods upon the poor.* Irish myth: Cross.

V438. *Merit for charity lost by asking work in return.* India: Thompson-Balys.

V440. Other religious virtues. Irish myth: Cross.

V441. *Forgiveness.* Irish myth: Cross.

V441.1. *Saint heals enemy.* Irish myth: *Cross.

V450—V499. Religious orders.

V450. Religious orders. *Encyc. Rel. Ethics Index 384a, 389b; Irish myth: Cross.

J1260. Repartee based on church or clergy. J1265. Repartee based on church government. P120. Church dignitaries. P426. Clergy. P426.3. Monks. P427.1.2. Druids as priests. T93.2. Disappointed lover becomes monk. X410. Jokes on parsons.

V451. *First-born son and one of every ten born thereafter given to Church.* Irish myth: Cross.

V453. *Levites as religious order.* Jewish: *Neuman.

V460. Clerical virtues and vices.

H1573.1.2. Loathly deed performed as evidence of Christian virtue.

V461. *Clerical virtue.* Irish myth: *Cross.

V461.1. *Obedient and industrious nun the worthiest in the convent.* Pauli (ed. Bolte) No. 690; Alphabet No. 322; Spanish Exempla: Keller.

V461.2. *Truthful monk refuses to cheat even for his order.* Pauli (ed. Bolte) No. 111.

V461.3. *Chastity as clerical virtue.* Irish myth: *Cross.

T300. Chastity and celibacy.

V461.4. *Submission as clerical virtue.* Irish myth: Cross.

V461.4.1. *Truthfulness as clerical virtue.* Irish myth: Cross.

V461.5. *Extended meditation as clerical virtue.* Irish myth: Cross.

V461.6. *Monk lives where people speak ill of him to avoid danger of flattery.* Spanish Exempla: Keller.

V461.7. *Clerical virtue of absolute faith.* Man captured by robbers is so confident that God will protect him that he is saved. Spanish Exempla: Keller.

V461.8. *Poverty as saintly virtue.* Irish myth: Cross.

V462. *Asceticism.* *Loomis White Magic 111f.; *Encyc. Rel. Ethics Index 42b; Irish myth: *Cross; Spanish Exempla: Keller; Jewish: *Neuman; India: *Thompson-Balys.

D1733.3. Magic power through ascetic practices. F932.3. Stream becomes hot in which saint performs his ascetic devotions. Q520. Penances. T330. Anchorites under temptation.

V462.0.1. *Kingship renounced to become an ascetic.* Irish myth: Cross; India: Thompson-Balys.

V462.0.2. *Since salvation is predestined, asceticism deemed useless.* Irish myth: Cross.

V462.0.3. *Husband abandons wife to become ascetic.* India: Thompson-Balys.

V462.0.4. *Murderer becomes ascetic.* India: Thompson-Balys.

V462.1. *Maintaining silence as ascetic practice.* Alphabet Nos. 709, 711, 712, 725; Swiss: Jegerlehner Oberwallis 310 No. 32; Spanish Exempla: Keller.

V462.2. *Ascetic fasting.* Alphabet Nos. 24, 145; Wesselski Mönchslatein 170 No. 135; Irish myth: *Cross; India: *Thompson-Balys.

C200. Tabu: eating. F1033. Person lives without food or drink for a year (or more).

V462.2.1. *Ascetic faster increases his sufferings by placing food and drink before himself.* Alphabet Nos. 22, 23; Scala Celi 4a No. 16; India: Thompson-Balys.

V462.2.2. *Person refuses to eat dainties.* Irish myth: *Cross.

V462.2.2.1. *Saint refuses pearls as alms and asks for food.* India: Thompson-Balys.

V462.2.3. *Death from ascetic devotions.* India: Thompson-Balys.

V462.3. *Ascetic weeping.* Irish myth: Cross.

V462.4. *Asceticism: allowing self no repose.* Irish myth: *Cross.

V462.4.1. *Asceticism: cleric practices continual genuflexion.* Irish myth: *Cross.

V462.4.2. *Cross vigil.* Cleric stands with hands extended in shape of cross. Irish myth: *Cross.

V462.4.3. *Saint always extends one hand toward heaven while performing such acts as eating or reaping.* Irish myth: *Cross.

V462.5. *Ascetic cleric tortures his flesh.* Irish myth: *Cross.

V462.5.0.1. *Ascetic cleric prays to become diseased.* Irish myth: *Cross.

V462.5.1. *Ascetic cleric wears hair garment.* Irish myth: *Cross.

V462.5.1.1. *Saint never wears woolen clothing, but skins of wolves and other beasts.* Irish myth: *Cross.

V462.5.1.2. *Ascetic cleric sleeps (prays) with wet sheet (mantle) about him.* Irish myth: *Cross.

V462.5.2. *Ascetic cleric sleeps on stone.* Irish myth: *Cross.

V462.5.2.1. *Saint takes but little sleep.* Irish myth: Cross.

V462.5.2.2. *Saint stands for seven years without sleep.* Irish myth: Cross.

V462.6. *Ascetic cleric avoids listening to music.* Irish myth: *Cross.

V462.7. *Ascetic cleric never smiles.* Irish myth: Cross.

V462.8. *Ascetic immersion.* Irish myth: *Cross.

V462.8.1. *Saint confines himself in narrow pen during Lent.* Irish myth: Cross.

V462.8.2. *Saint stands (asleep) while bird builds nest and hatches brood in his hand.* Irish myth: Cross.

V462.9. *Ascetic cleric leads mendicant life.* Irish myth: Cross.

V462.10. *Ascetic cleric lives for seven years on whale's back.* Irish myth: Cross.

B256.12. Whale raises back so that voyaging clerics can land to celebrate Easter.

V462.11. *Ascetic cleric renounces world (to become a herder).* Irish myth: *Cross.

V462.12. *Monk refuses chance of having temptation removed since he considers it strengthening to have it ever present to test him.* Spanish Exempla: Keller.

V462.13. *Evil ascetic misuses magic powers obtained through religious meditation.* India: Thompson-Balys.

V462.14. *Boy takes twelve years to wash off ascetic's dirt.* India: Thompson-Balys.

V463. *Religious martyrdom.* Irish myth: *Cross; Icelandic: *Boberg; Jewish: *Neuman

S263.5. Sacrificial suicide. Z141.2. Red as symbolic of martyrdom.

V463.1. *Cleric surrenders life that body may consecrate land.* Irish myth: Cross.

V463.2. *First martyr: John the Baptist.* Irish myth: Cross.

V464. *Self-torture to secure holiness.* India: *Thompson-Balys:

V465. *Clerical vices.*

J485. Three sins of the hermit. J1263. Repartee concerning clerical abuses.

V465.1. *Incontinence of clergy.* *Encyc. Rel. Ethics Index 113b, 136c; West Indies: Flowers 580.

J1264. Repartee concerning clerical incontinence. J1919.6. Simpleton's ignorance of anatomy leads him to share his wife with a priest. Q243. Incontinence punished—miscellaneous. Q414.0.3.1. Burning monastery and monks in it as punishment for incontinence.

V465.1.1. *Incontinent monk (priest).* Irish myth: *Cross; Italian Novella: Rotunda

E411.2.1. Priest's concubine cannot rest in grave. K1354.3.1. Trickster (friar) undertakes to awaken girl.

V465.1.1.1. *Monk seduces girl; then kills her; becomes infidel.* *Chauvin VIII 128 No. 118; Spanish Exempla: Keller.

V465.1.1.2. *Marriage of clerics.* Irish myth: *Cross.

V465.1.2. *Incontinent nun.* Irish myth: *Cross.

K1841. The Virgin Mary substitutes for a mortal. T401. Virgin Mary as protectress of illicit lovers. T640.1. Illegitimate child of nun. V254.5. Nun forgets to hail Mary and goes into the world of sin.

V465.1.2.1. *Nun hidden by abbess from pursuing knight betrays her own hiding place to him.* Is afterwards abandoned. *Pauli (ed. Bolte) No. 13; Crane Vitry 159 No. 58.

W136.1. Look! look! she cries from the barrel.

V465.1.2.2. *Nun tempted into sinning with man who tells her God can't see things that happen in the dark.* Spanish Exempla: Keller.

T331.4. No place secret enough for fornication.

V466. *Simony.* Italian Novella: Rotunda.

V466.1. *Pope guilty of simony.* Italian Novella: Rotunda.

V467. *Priest uses cook-book instead of breviary.* Italian Novella: Rotunda.

V468. *Priest is bribed into betraying the confessional.* Italian Novella: Rotunda.

K443.8. Priest induced to betray secrets of confessional: money then exacted from him for silence. Q224. Punishment for betraying confessional.

V470. Clerical vows. *Encyc. Rel. Ethics Index 634a.

M100. Vows and oaths.

V471. *Taking clerical vows heals disease.* Alphabet No. 783.

V472. *Clerical vows because of disappointment in love.*

V472.1. *Man becomes hermit when he realizes selfishness of his beloved's love.* (Cf. T93.2.) Heptameron No. 24.

V473. *Former monk refuses to take pay for his work, considering it as a religious act.* India: Thompson-Balys.

V475. *Renunciation of clerical vows.* Spanish Exempla: Keller.

K1841.1. The nun who saw the world (Sister Beatrice). Q226. Punishment for leaving holy orders. V265. Virgin miraculously prevents nun from leaving convent.

V475.1. *Monk who has left order punished (dies in torment).* Alphabet Nos. 73, 784.

V475.2. *Monk who has left his order forgiven and miraculously reinstated.* Alphabet No. 781.

V475.3. *Man who is disappointed with his religious order renounces his vow.* Italian Novella: Rotunda.

V475.4. *Saint leaves his order because he is fond of music.* India: Thompson-Balys.

V475.5. *Anchorite tempted by money to return to worldly life.* Buddhist myth: Malalasekera II 807.

V500—V599. Religious motifs—miscellaneous.

V510. Religious visions. *Encyc. Rel. Ethics Index 632b; Irish myth: *Cross; Jewish: *Neuman.

D1731.2. Marvels seen in dreams. D1812.3.3. Future revealed in dream. V222.0.1. Birth of saint predicted by visions of miracles. V235.0.1. Mortal visited by angel in vision.

V510.1. *God speaks in vision to devotee.* India: *Thompson-Balys.

V510.2. *Only man without sin can see God.* India: Thompson-Balys.

V511. *Visions of the other world.*

V511.1. *Visions of heaven.* **Becker Medieval Visions of Heaven and Hell (Baltimore, 1899); **Ward II 396ff. passim; Alphabet No. 622, 743; Dickson 265; Scala Celi 66a, 138b Nos. 362, 777. — Irish: *Cross, O'Suilleabhain 57, Beal XXI 322; English: Malory Morte D'Arthur XV 3; Finnish-Swedish: Wessman 105 No. 932; Spanish Exempla: Keller; Jewish: *Neuman.

A661. Heaven. A661.1.2. Saint sees vision of three cities in heaven. D1329.1. Putting head under saint's cloak reveals rewards of heaven. F10. Journey to upper world. F969.1. Skies open revealing heavenly company.

V511.1.1. *Saints have visions of heaven.* *Toldo IV 49.

V511.1.2. *Vision of angels defending road to heaven against devils.* Irish myth: Cross.

V511.2. *Visions of hell.* *Becker (see V511.1); Alphabet No. 610; Dickson 265; Herbert III 25; **Ward II 386ff.; *Crane Vitry 260f. No. 289; Scala Celi 34b, 74a, 85b Nos. 195, 422, 497. — Irish myth: *Cross; Icelandic: *Boberg; Spanish Exempla: Keller.

A671. Hell. F80. Journey to lower world.

V511.2.1. *Vision of fires of hell.* Irish myth: Cross.

V511.2.2. *Vision of gate of hell.* Irish myth: Cross.

V511.2.3. *Girl sees vision of her mother in hell.* She chooses to live the poor life of her father which leads to heaven. Spanish Exempla: Keller.

V511.3. *Visions of purgatory.* *Dickson 265 n. 87; *Loomis White Magic 116; Irish myth: *Cross.

A693. Intermediate future world. Residence for those whose good and evil deeds exactly counterbalance.

V511.4. *Visions of Land of the Saints.* Irish myth: *Cross.

A661.0.10. Land of the Saints surrounded by fiery circle.

V512. *Vision of judgment.* Man sees his own soul being judged.

V512.1. *His faith into the balance.* A clerk sees his good and evil deeds being weighed. He asks them to throw his faith in Christ (the Virgin) into the scale. He is saved. Ward II 651 No. 5; *Herbert III 471.

V512.2. *Man whose only good deed was unintentional sees this deed outweigh all his evil in the scales of judgment.* Spanish Exempla: Keller.

V513. *Saints have miraculous visions.* Irish myth: Cross.

V513.1. *Saint incited (instructed) through vision.* Irish myth: *Cross.

V513.2. *Vision of the earth in the devil's snares.* Saint sees earth in snares. Spanish Exempla: Keller.

V514. *Non-religious visions.* Irish myth: *Cross; Jewish: *Neuman.

D1731.2. Marvels seen in dreams. D1812.5.1.2.1. Vision as evil omen. D1813.1. Dream shows events in distant place.

V515. *Allegorical visions.* Irish myth: *Cross.

D1812.3.3.5. Prophetic dream allegorical. Z100. Symbolism.

V515.1. *Allegorical visions—religious.*

V515.1.1. *Vision of chairs (thrones) in heaven.* Chairs of gold, silver, crystal (glass) assigned to saints according to merit. (Cf. A661.0.3.) Irish myth: *Cross.

V515.1.2. *Wife sees moon enter mouth of husband; husband sees star enter mouth of wife: famous child (saint) will be born.* Irish myth: Cross.

V515.1.3. *Saint sees vision of flames covering Ireland quenched except for sparks;* then great light appears, dispelling darkness. Flames are those of the faith brought by St. Patrick; they become less until restored by St. Columkill. Irish myth: Cross.

V515.1.3.1. *When shower falls, small stone becomes larger, large stone wastes away.* Vision of present and future state of Irish church. Irish myth: Cross.

V515.1.3.2. *Vision in which swineherd sees yew tree upon a rock, with an oratory in front of it and angels ascending from it.* Vision interpreted by druid as symbolizing founding of Cashel and the royal line of Munster. Irish myth: *Cross.

V515.1.4. *Constantine's vision of the Cross.* Irish myth: *Cross.

V515.1.5. *Vision of dry bones.* Jewish: Neuman.

V515.2. *Allegorical visions—political.* Irish myth: Cross.

V515.2.1. *Vision in which chieftain sees pair of gray seals that sucked at his two breasts.* They are two of his allies who are being overpowered by invaders. Irish myth: Cross.

V515.2.1.1. *Vision in which king sees whelp reared by him gather dogs of Ireland and Britain against him but suffer death in battle at last.* The whelp is one of king's two foster sons. Irish myth: Cross.

V515.2.2. *Vision in which saint foresees allegorically the ramifications of king's family* Irish myth: Cross.

V515.2.3. *Vision in which king sees his four sons changed into lion, greyhound, beagle, cur,* which fight with alternating success, until lion subdues the other three. Irish myth: *Cross.

V516. *Vision of future.* Jewish: Neuman.

V520. Salvation. *Encyc. Rel. Ethics Index 517b; Irish myth: Cross.

A661. Heaven. A671. Hell. A693. Intermediate future world. Residence for those whose good and evil deeds exactly counterbalance. A1002. Doomsday. C741. Tabu: relieving souls in hell. D859.2. Quest to hell for magic object. E411. Dead cannot rest because of a sin. E411.0.4. Sinner wanders between heaven and earth. E501.3. Wild huntsmen wander because of sin. E750. Perils of the soul. E751. Souls at Judgment Day. E752. Lost souls. E754. Saved souls. E754.2. Saved soul goes to heaven. E755.1. Souls in heaven. E755.2. Souls in hell (Hades). E755.3. Souls in purgatory. E756.1. Devils and angels contest for man's soul. E757. The soul prays. F11. Journey to heaven (upper world paradise). F81. Descent to lower world of dead (Hell, Hades). H1261. Quest: a crown from heaven. H1262. Quest: god to be brought from heaven. H1270. Quest to lower world. K2371.1. Heaven entered by a trick. Q172. Reward: admission to heaven. Q545. Murderer's penance complete when he kills a greater murderer. V313. Last judgment.

V522. *Sinner reformed after visit to heaven and hell.* Irish myth: Cross.

V523. *The only king ever saved in spite of himself.* Irish myth: Cross.

V525. *Sinner who thinks of God saved; devotee who thinks of worldly things goes to hell.* India: Thompson-Balys.

V526. *Worship of particular deity brings reward of birth in Brahma-world.* Buddhist myth: Malalasekera I 13.

V530. Pilgrimages. Irish myth: Cross; India: *Thompson-Balys.

V531. *Pilgrimage to Holy Land.* Irish myth: Cross.

V531.1. *Pilgrimage to follow roads Christ walked.* Irish myth: Cross.

V532. *Pilgrimage to Mecca.* India: Thompson-Balys.

V533. *Pilgrimage to Benares.* India: Thompson-Balys.

V535. *Pilgrimage to Jerusalem.* Jewish: *Neuman.

V540. Intervention of Providence saves person's life. (Cf. R341.)

V541. *Man is prevented from taking passage on ship which later sinks.* U.S.: Baughman.

V542. *Man hears voice telling him to leave danger spot in mine.* U.S.: *Baughman.

W. TRAITS OF CHARACTER

DETAILED SYNOPSIS

W0—W99. Favorable traits of character
- W0. Favorable traits of character
- W10. Kindness
- W20. Other favorable traits of character

W100—W199. Unfavorable traits of character
- W100. Unfavorable traits of character
- W110. Unfavorable traits of character—personal
- W150. Unfavorable traits of character—social

W200—W299. Traits of character—miscellaneous
- W200. Traits of character—miscellaneous

W. TRAITS OF CHARACTER

W. Traits of character. *Hdwb. d. Märchens I 359b s.v. "Charaktermotive".

H1550. Tests of character.

W0—W99. Favorable traits of character.

W0. Favorable traits of character. Jewish: *Neuman.

W2. *Good inclinations enter body at puberty.* Jewish: Neuman.

W10. Kindness. (Cf. Q40.) Missouri French: Carrière; Icelandic: *Boberg; Jewish: *Neuman.

W10.1. *Saint never drives fly or gnat from his face.* Irish myth: *Cross.

W10.2. *Saint gives calf to wolf.* Irish myth: Cross.

W11. *Generosity.* Irish myth: *Cross; Spanish: Keller, Espinosa Jr. No. 200; Jewish: Neuman; India: Thompson-Balys.

H1552. Tests of generosity. H1552.2. Contest in generosity. Q42. Generosity rewarded.

W11.1. *Philanthropist will give his spurs if someone will drive his horse for him.* He has given away his coat, etc. to beggars. One finally asks for his spurs. Pauli (ed. Bolte) No. 330.

W11.2. *Munificent monarch.* India: Thompson-Balys; Icelandic: *Boberg.

W11.2.1. *Emperor thinks day lost when he gives no gifts.* Alphabet No. 443; Spanish Exempla: Keller.

W11.2.2. *King will not eat breakfast till gifts are given.* India: Thompson-Balys.

W11.3. *Man divides money into three parts:* (1) for the poor, (2) for pilgrims, (3) for himself and family. Scala Celi 164a No. 921.

H585.1. The four coins. What he does with the four coins he earns.

W11.4. *Man lets himself be sold as slave so as to practice generosity.* Wesselski Archiv Orientální II 429; Italian Novella: Rotunda.

W11.4.1. *Brahmin steals to feed guests (deities).* India: Thompson-Balys.

Q45.1. Angels entertained unawares.

W11.5. *Generosity toward enemy.* Italian Novella: Rotunda; Icelandic: Boberg.

W11.5.1. *Ruler pardons his enemies.* Italian Novella: *Rotunda.

W11.5.1.1. *Man pardons his assailants.* They attack again and are killed. Italian Novella: Rotunda.

W11.5.2. *Ruler pardons emissary who has come to murder him.* Italian Novella: *Rotunda.

W11.5.3. *Wronged knight conquers enemy and then pardons him.* Italian Novella: Rotunda.

W11.5.4. *Conqueror returns defeated man's wife and family to him.* Italian Novella: Rotunda.

W11.5.5. *Conqueror spares city.* Italian Novella: Rotunda.

W11.5.6. *Ruler reproaches son for bringing him the head of his fallen enemy.* Latter given honorable burial. Italian Novella: Rotunda.

W11.5.7. *Man saved through intercession of enemy.* Italian Novella: Rotunda.

W11.5.7.1. *Man pays fine for enemy who is falsely accused.* Italian Novella: *Rotunda.

K2100 False accusations.

W11.5.8. *Captor contributes to captive's ransom.* Italian Novella: Rotunda.

W11.5.9. *Warrior gives steed to his enemy.* Italian Novella: Rotunda.

W11.5.9.1. *Calumniated woman intercedes for accusers.* (Cf. K2112.) Italian Novella: Rotunda.

W11.5.9.2. *Man's life spared through the intercession of the daughter he has wronged.* He has ordered her killed. Italian Novella: Rotunda.

W11.5.10. *Champion grants requested boon of safe convoy to his enemies.* Irish myth: Cross.

W11.5.11. *Chieftain spares enemies whom he takes unawares (unarmed).* Irish myth: *Cross.

W11.5.11.1. *Chieftain who takes king unawares, spares him on condition that chieftain be called "lover" by women of king's tribe.* Irish myth: *Cross.

W11.5.12. *Hero in battle refuses to slay charioteers, women, or physicians.* (Cf. C867.1.) Irish myth: Cross.

W11.6. *Ruler generously settles quarrel between loser and finder of money.* Italian Novella: Rotunda.

W11.7. *Nobleman's generosity enables impoverished lover to entertain his lady.* Italian Novella: Rotunda.

W11.7.1. *Impoverished nobleman offers wife to ruler.* Latter spares her honor and aids the couple. Italian Novella: Rotunda.

W11.8. *General sends for king so that the latter may get credit for victory.* Italian Novella: Rotunda.

W11.9. *Prince donates all including a tooth.* When he has nothing left he is asked for a gift. He allows man to extract a tooth from his mouth. (Father had offered reward to anyone persuading his son to have it extracted.) Italian Novella: Rotunda.

W11.10. *Ruler protects thief.* Asks for the stolen plate and hides it so that it will not be found on the culprit. Italian Novella: Rotunda.

W11.11. *Ruler rewards man who would curb him.* Italian Novella: Rotunda.

W11.12. *The generous correction.* Ruler asks treasurer to give man 200 crowns. Treasurer makes error and puts down 300. Ruler raises sum to 400. "I can't allow your pen to be more liberal than I." Italian Novella: *Rotunda.

W11.12.1. *King rewards knight with large sum of money.* Chancellor: "If you saw such a sum it would seem large to you." King answers that it looks small and doubles it. Italian Novella: *Rotunda.

W11.13. *Novel sign of death.* It is the first time that what he has given away seems too much. Italian Novella: Rotunda.

W11.14. *Youngest brother shares wealth with older brothers who foolishly lost theirs.* (Cf. L31.) Africa (Jaunde): Heepe 262.

W11.15. *Generous person refuses no man anything.* (Cf. C871.) Irish myth: *Cross.

W11.16. *Generous king gives away his only eye.* Irish myth: *Cross.

W12. *Hospitality as a virtue.* (Cf. P320.) Irish myth: Cross.

W12.1. *Man (king) prefers death to loss of reputation for hospitality.* Irish myth: *Cross.

W12.2. *Man looks for strangers so as to bestow hospitality on them.* Jewish: Neuman.

W15. *Woman shelters son's murderer out of charity.* Spanish: Boggs FFC XC 86 No. 756D*; Italian Novella: *Rotunda.

W15.1. *Murderer goes to victim's son and asks to be killed.* The son aids him to escape. Italian Novella: Rotunda.

W16. *Bishop exchanges places with prisoner so as to have him return to his mother.* Italian Novella: Rotunda.

R121.6. Rescue from prison by saint, who enters and breaks fetters.

W18. *Envious man sets out to kill one who is noted for his generosity.* He is won over by the generosity of his intended victim. Italian Novella: *Rotunda.

W20. Other favorable traits of character.

W21. *Emperor friendly to everyone.* Would act as he should like an emperor to act toward him if he were a common man. Pauli (ed. Bolte) No. 166.

W23. *Man never listens to scandal.* Irish myth: *Cross.

W24. *Man speaks no evil.* Irish myth: Cross.

W25. *Equanimity of the comedian.* When he sees his house carried off by a flood, he fiddles the whole time. Type 944*.

W25.1. *Equanimity of the enslaved unfortunate.* Does not complain when beset by a series of misfortunes. (Cf. N251.1.) Italian Novella: Rotunda.

W25.2. *Minister always says, "It is for the best," when anything happens.* India: Thompson-Balys.

W26. *Patience.* Spanish Exempla: Keller; Jewish: Neuman.
H461. Test of wife's patience. Griselda. H1553. Tests of patience.

W27. *Gratitude.*
B350. Grateful animals. B361. Animals grateful for rescue from pit. B380. Animal grateful for relief from pain. D817. Magic object received from grateful person. D1658. Grateful objects. E341. The grateful dead. F420.4.4. Water-spirits are grateful. H1565. Tests of gratitude. R71. Captive prince joins captor out of gratitude for his freedom. V331.6. Conversion to Christianity out of gratitude.

W27.1. *Man weeps with gratitude to God because He did not make him hideous as toad.* Spanish Exempla: Keller.

W28. *Self-sacrifice.* Irish myth: Cross.

W28.1. *Woman drinks poison that son may be king.* Irish myth: Cross.
P231. Mother and son.

W28.2. *Woman sacrifices life for son's honor.* Irish myth: Cross.

W28.3. *Man leaps from vessel into jaws of sea-beast so as to save remaining passengers.* Irish myth: Cross.

W28.4. *Saint threatens to take place of homicide in hell unless soul is released.* Irish myth: Cross.

W31. *Obedience.*
H386. Bride test: obedience. H473. Test of wife's obedience. H1557. Tests of obedience. T251.2. Taming the shrew. By outdoing his wife in shrewishness the husband renders her obedient. W126. Disobedience.

W32. *Bravery.* Irish myth: *Cross.

W32.1. *King Richard leads host to victory by leaping his horse overboard.* Spanish Exempla: Keller.

W33. *Heroism.* Irish myth: *Cross; Icelandic: *Boberg.

W33.1. *Badly wounded warrior continues fighting.* Irish myth: *Cross; Icelandic: Boberg.

W33.2. *Warrior refuses to delay battle in return for promise of long, happy life.* Irish myth: Cross.

W34. *Loyalty.* Irish myth: Cross.

W34.1. *Man constrained to flee with leader's fiancée resists her blandishments.* Irish myth: *Cross.
T331. Man unsuccessfully tempted by woman.

W34.2. *Loyal friends refuse to fight against disgraced comrade.* (Cf. P310.) Irish myth: Cross.

W34.3. *Cowardly to leave battle while lord is alive.* Irish myth: *Cross.

W34.4. *Fakir rewarded by prince with a life of luxury in city chooses to return to his monkey friends in jungle.* India: Thompson-Balys.

W35. *Justice.* Irish myth: Cross; Jewish: *Neuman.
U10. Justice and injustice.

W35.1. *Man picked to judge bull-fight because he is "no fairer to his friend than to his foe."* Irish myth: Cross.

W35.2. *Upright judge refuses a bribe: he is responsible to a higher tribunal called Conscience.* India: Thompson-Balys.

J1192. The bribed judge.

W37. *Conscientiousness.*

W37.0.1. *Man never breaks his word.* Irish myth: *Cross.

W37.1. *Oil well digger runs out of money, leaves the country, forgetting to tell his driller.* He returns fifty years later, finds the driller still drilling away. U.S.: Baughman.

W37.2. *Man keeps promise to return to be eaten by tiger: let go without harm.* India: Thompson-Balys.

W37.3. *Rabbi returns jewel found with bought ass.* He had not paid for it. Jewish: Neuman.

W43. *Peacefulness.* Jewish: *Neuman.

W45. *Honor.*

W45.1. *Prostrate soldier asks his enemy to stab him in the chest instead of the back in order to save his honor.* The captor frees him and the two become friends. Spanish: Childers.

W100—W199. Unfavorable traits of character

W100. Unfavorable traits of character.

A1375. Origin of jealousy and selfishness. J455. Harm of association with flatterers. J2074. Twice the wish to the enemy. (The covetous and the envious.) K1637. Flattering foreman tricked by his master. L435. Self-righteousness punished.

W110. Unfavorable traits of character—personal.

W111. *Laziness.* Types 368*, 675, 822, 843*, 1370*, 1405, 1454*, 1561, 1950; *Chauvin IX 33f. Nos. 25, 26; *Krappe Bulletin Hispanique XXXIX 30; Missouri French: Carrière; S. A. Indian (Chiriguano): Métraux RMLP XXXIII 175; West Indies: Flowers 581.

H382. Bride test: industry. Q321. Laziness punished.

W111.1. *Contest in laziness.* Each cites instances of his laziness. *Type 1950; *BP III 207; Wesselski Märchen 213 No. 21; Pauli (ed. Bolte) No. 261; Oesterley No. 91; Fb "doven" IV 102b. — Spanish Exempla: Keller; India: Thompson-Balys.

J1486. Listening to the debate. L114.1 Lazy hero.

W111.1.1. *Man lets legs burn in fire rather than move them.* Wesselski Märchen 213 No. 21; Pauli (ed. Bolte) No. 261; India: Thompson-Balys.

W111.1.1.1. *Man is burned to death because he is too lazy to put out spark.* Italian Novella: Rotunda; India: Thompson-Balys.

W111.1.1.2. *Lazy man's belongings burn.* He is too lazy to stop rats from playing with lighted candle. Italian Novella: Rotunda.

W111.1.1.3. *Man too lazy to open eyes to see where fire is burning.* India: Thompson-Balys.

W111.1.1.4. *Three lazy beggars burn alive rather than run away from burning castle.* India: Thompson-Balys.

W111.1.1.5. *Mother calls to daughter to tell her that she (daughter) is standing on a live coal.* The daughter asks which foot the coal is under. U.S.: Baughman.

W111.1.2. *Man will not lift knife to cut rope about to hang him.* Wesselski Märchen 213 No. 21; Pauli (ed. Bolte) No. 261.

W111.1.3. *Man will not move in bed when water drops in his eyes.* Wesselski Märchen 213 No. 21; Spanish Exempla: Keller; Italian Novella: Rotunda.

W111.1.4. *Man so lazy that he will not wipe his running nose.* This causes him to lose prospective bride. Spanish Exempla: Keller.

W111.1.5. *Man floating in river too lazy to drink.* His voice is damaged. Spanish Exempla: Keller.

W111.1.6. *Man too lazy to pick up berries (dates).* India: *Thompson-Balys.

W111.2. *The lazy servant.* India: Thompson-Balys; West Indies: Flowers 581.

W111.2.0.1. *Lazy servant gets others to perform his duties*

W111.2.1. *Servant to call his master at daybreak:* looks into dark closet to see if it is yet light. They sleep till noon. Pauli (ed. Bolte) No. 263.

W111.2.2. *Servant to close door at night:* leaves it open so that he will not have to open it next morning. Wesselski Mönchslatein 54 No. 47; *Crane Vitry 216 No. 204.

W111.2.3. *"If it is day, give me food; if it is night, let me sleep."* The master has told the servant to go to work. Wesselski Mönchslatein 54 No. 47.

W111.2.4. *Boy to see whether it is raining:* calls dog (cat) in and feels of his paws. Wesselski Mönchslatein 54 No. 47; *Crane Vitry 216 No. 204; Spanish Exempla: Keller; India: *Thompson-Balys.

W111.2.5. *Boy to see whether there is fire in the house:* feels of cat to see if she is warm. Wesselski Mönchslatein 54 No. 47; *Crane Vitry 216 No. 204.

W111.2.6. *The boy eats breakfast, dinner, and supper one immediately after the other;* then lies down to sleep. *Type 1561.

W125.3. New son-in-law, given choice of meals, eats all.

W111.2.7. *Lazy boy always says that it is raining.* The peasant and the boy sleep during the rain in the hay barn. When the peasant asks, the boy always says that it is still raining. Type 1560**.

W111.2.8. *Lazy boy says he cannot walk.* Cheremis: Sebeok-Nyerges.

W111.2.9. *Servant tells master to cover his face: no need to put out lamp.* India: *Thompson-Balys.

W111.3. *The lazy wife.*

W111.3.1. *Lazy wife in soiled dress thinks husband is bringing her a new dress from market.* He is bringing a goose. Type 1371*.

W111.3.2. *Cat beaten for not working.* Lazy wife must hold cat and is scratched. Type 1370*; Russian: Andrejev No. 1370.

W111.3.3. *Lazy wife throws bread out of window instead of putting it back into oven.* Spanish: Boggs FFC XC 126 No. 1389.

W111.3.4. *Why he beats her.* Lazy wife beaten by husband maintains that she has done nothing. That is why he is beating her. Wesselski Bebel I 206 No 90.

W111.3.5. *Wife too lazy to spin.* Supposed dead husband comes back to life and gives his wife a beating, because there was no shirt even in the event of death. Lithuanian: Balys Index No. 1370B*; Russian: Andrejev No. 1370B*.

K1860. Deception by feigned death.

W111.3.6. *"Who will not work, shall not eat."* Idle daughter-in-law learns work. Lithuanian: Balys Index No. 1370A*.

W111.4. *Lazy husband.* Fansler MAFLS XII 236.

W111.5. *Other lazy persons.* Chinese: Graham.

W111.5.1. *Lazy mother given shoes of cotton; son knows that she will not wear them out.* *Wesselski Hodscha Nasreddin II 204 No. 406.

W111.5.2. *Lazy girl does not know where the spring is.* Type 1453*.

W111.5.3. *Lazy man asked direction only points with his foot.* *Dh II 115ff.; England: Baughman.

W111.5.4. *Lazy dog wakes only for his meals.* Wienert FFC LVI 73 (ET 381), 126 (ST 348); Halm Aesop No. 413.

W111.5.5. *Man in mud too lazy to take hand extended to help him up.* Scala Celi 5a No. 26.

W111.5.6. *Lazy son-in-law: afraid of a dog.* India: Thompson-Balys.

W111.5.7. *Ruler is too lazy to stop quarrels.* They lead to his death. Italian Novella: Rotunda (W111.6).

W111.5.8. *Man with stolen fig in his mouth submits to having cheek lanced rather than open his mouth* (Cf. J1842.2.) Italian Novella: Rotunda (W111.7).

W111.5.8.1. *Man is so lazy that he starves rather than open his mouth for food to fall in when it falls from trees.* U.S.: Baughman.

W111.5.9. *Learning a trade in bed.* Working independently, the lazy fellow spoils the materials received—starts making something big, which at the end turns to nothing. For example, begins with forging a plough: this becomes an axe, the axe a knife, and knife a needle, the needle —nothing. (Cf. J2080.) Lithuanian: Balys Index No. 2446*.

W111.5.10. *Lazy man asks if wood is split before he accepts it as a gift.* U.S.: Baughman.

W111.5.10.1. *Lazy man is being taken to poorhouse or out of town or to cemetery to be buried alive.* The group take pity on him, offer him various articles to help him get started again. One offers a bushel of corn. The lazy one rises up from the bottom of the wagon or coffin where he has been lying: "Is the corn shelled?" Canada, U.S.: *Baughman.

W111.5.11. *Lazy man misses seeing the sheriff's funeral;* he is facing the wrong way as the procession passes. U.S.: Baughman.

W111.5.12. *Man digs three potatoes in one day:* one dug, one being dug, one about to be dug. U.S.: Baughman.

W111.5.13. *Man weeds garden from cushioned rocking chair, using fire tongs to reach weeds.* U.S.: Baughman.

W115. *Slovenliness.* (Cf. Q322.)

W115.1. *The slovenly fiancée.* Type 1453**.

H383.1.1. Bride test: bread-making — dough under fingernails.

W115.2. *Woman becomes clean only after three washings and the use of three pounds of soap.* Type 1447*.

W115.3. *Rancher is not recognized by his wife and family after he has cleaned up in town at hotel.* U.S.: Baughman.

W116. *Vanity.* Irish myth: Cross; India: Thompson-Balys.

W116.1. *Old woman reaches town before vain fop who stops to adjust clothes.* India: Thompson-Balys.

W116.2. *Expenditure of money for vanity.* India: Thompson-Balys.

W116.3. *Plain people made rulers have vain display.* India: Thompson-Balys.

W116.4. *Peacock admires self in mirror.* India: Thompson-Balys.

W116.5. *Wasp seeking fame stings courtiers: killed.* India: Thompson-Balys.

W116.6. *Wealthy man pretends enjoyment of good music.* Told when to applaud. India: Thompson-Balys.

W116.7. *Use of strange language to show one's high education.* India: Thompson-Balys.

W116.8. *Jackal forces all animals who come to drink to praise him like a king.* India: *Thompson-Balys.

W117. *Boastfulness.*

W117.1. *Neglected wife given trifle boasts of it.* India: Thompson-Balys.

J2331. Numskull with unimportant office boasts of it.

W121. *Cowardice.* Irish myth: *Cross; Missouri French: Carrière; Icelandic: *Boberg.

J1488. What the bear whispered in his ear. J2600. Cowardly fool. K2320. Deception by frightening. T251.6. The browbeaten husband from under the table: "The man always has a man's heart."

W121.1. *Hunter wants to be shown lion tracks, not lion himself.* Wienert FFC LVI 67 (ET 314), 101 (ST 143); Halm Aesop No. 114.

W121.2. *Coward boasts when there is no danger.* (Cf. J974, J978.)

W121.2.1. *Ass insults dying lion.* Wienert FFC LVI 56 (ET 166), 112 (ST 233); Jacobs Aesop 202 No. 9; Spanish Exempla: Keller.

W121.2.2. *Fox insults caged lion.* Wienert FFC LVI 56 (ET 160), 112 (ST 232); Halm Aesop No. 40.

W121.2.3. *Crow sits on sheep's back; afraid to sit on dog's.* Wienert FFC LVI 55 (ET 154), 106 (ST 188).

W121.2.4. *Dogs tear up lion skin: fear living lion.* Wienert FFC LVI 55 (ET 153), 112 (ST 235); Halm Aesop No. 219.

W121.2.5. *Coward gloats over robber slain by another person.* Wienert FFC LVI 82 (ET 483), 101, 126 (ST 144, 350).

W121.2.6. *Monkey safe in tree insults gorilla as "broken face".* Africa (Fang): Nassau 233 No. 1.

W121.3. *Cowardly soldier turns back when he hears raven's croak.* Wienert FFC LVI 73 (ET 385), 137 (ST 425); Halm Aesop No. 379.

W121.4. *Queen mother shames cowardly son and companions.* "In truth, gentlemen, you do well in weeping; for since you didn't fight like men to defend your land, it is suitable that now you weep like women on leaving it." Spanish: Childers.

J87. Men shamed for their cowardice by women.

W121.5. *Cowardly spider rushes at fly but hides when wasp appears.* Spanish Exempla: Keller.

W121.6. *Coward gives his purse to thief with lame excuse.* India: Thompson-Balys.

W121.7. *Cowardly bridegroom flees elephant and loses bride.* India: Thompson-Balys.

J2462. Foolish bridegroom follows instructions literally.

W121.8. *Illness from fear.* India: Thompson-Balys.

F1041.1.11. Death from fear.

W121.8.1. *Swooning from cowardice.* India: Thompson-Balys.

W123. *Indecision.* (Cf. J1040.) West Indies: Flowers 581.

W123.1. *The man who only tasted wine.* Will not drink but gets drunk nevertheless by frequent tasting. Pauli (ed. Bolte) No. 246.

W125. *Gluttony.* Jewish: *Neuman; India: *Thompson-Balys; N. A. Indian (California): Gayton and Newman 67.

W125.1. *Greedy animal eats poisoned fruit in spite of warning.* India: Thompson-Balys.

W125.2. *Gluttonous wife eats all the meal while cooking it.* India: *Thompson-Balys.

W125.3. *New son-in-law given choice of meals eats all.* India: Thompson-Balys.

W111.2.6. Boy eats breakfast, dinner and supper, one immediately after the other.

W125.4. *Pupil eats cakes given as alms for his master.* India: Thompson-Balys.

W125.5. *Husband eats wife's share of food as well as his own.* India: *Thompson-Balys.

W126. *Disobedience.* Missouri French: Carriere; Spanish Exempla: Keller; Jewish: Neuman.

H473. Test of wife's obedience. H1557. Tests of obedience. Q325. Disobedience punished. T254. The disobedient wife. W31. Obedience.

W126.1. *Monk obedient only as long as work is agreeable.* Always says that unpleasant work is beneath his dignity. Pauli (ed. Bolte) No. 367.

W127. *Petulance.* Irish myth: Cross.

W128. *Dissatisfaction.* Irish myth: *Cross.

A2232. Animal characteristics: punishment for immoderate request. A2723.1. Discontented pine tree: cause of pine needles. J217.2. Discontented ass longs for death but changes mind when he sees skins of dead asses at fair. Q312. Fault-finding punished.

W128.1. *Hog tired of his daily food.* Goes to the judge and gets better food assigned to him, but the fox cheats him out of it. Type 211*.

W128.2. *Dissatisfied fox.* In kingdom of lions laments that he always gets the worst bits of food. *Wienert FFC LVI 34.

W128.3. *Dissatisfied rivers complain against sea.* Say that it makes their water unusable. Wienert FFC LVI *75 (ET 408), 125 (ST 344); Halm Aesop No 380.

W128.4. *Peacock dissatisfied with his voice.* Wienert FFC LVI 78 (ET 441), 133 (ST 388).

W128.5. *Monk dissatisfied with things as he has them is admonished to take what he receives from God.* Spanish Exempla: Keller.

W128.6. *Sparrow dissatisfied with pond water wants to go to sea.* India: Thompson-Balys.

W131. *Profligacy.* India: Thompson-Balys.

W131.1. *Profligate wastes entire fortune before beginning his own adventures.* *Chauvin V 77 No. 22 n. 1.

Q42.1. Spendthrift knight. Divides his last penny. He is later helped by the grateful person.

W133. *Inconsistency.*

W133.1. *Prince penalizes cursing, although he himself curses.* Wesselski Bebel I 167 No. 2.

W133.2. *Woman admires marvelous shot of hero which kills deer,* but angers him when she begs mercy for the deer. Fischer-Bolte 203ff.

W136. *False modesty.*

K2051. Adulteress feigns unusual sensitiveness. K2052. The oversensitive bride.

W136.1. *Look! look! she cries from the barrel.* A nobleman has arranged for a peasant girl to become his mistress. When he comes to take her away he cannot find her. Disappointed, he is about to depart when the girl, who has hidden in a barrel, calls out "Look!" She really wants to be found. Pauli (ed. Bolte) No. 13.

V465.1.2.1. Nun hidden by abbess from pursuing knight betrays her own hiding place to him.

W137. *Curiosity.* Missouri French: Carrière; Jewish: *Neuman; Icelandic: Boberg.

J1546. Overcurious wife learns of the senate's deliberations. Q341. Curiosity punished. T258. The curious wife.

W141. *Talkativeness.* Jewish: Neuman.

W150. Unfavorable traits of character—social.

W151. *Greed.* Irish myth: Cross; Jewish: *Neuman; Icelandic: *Boberg; West Indies: Flowers 582.

J514. One should not be too greedy. P446.2. Barbers are cunning and greedy.

W151.0.1. *Cauldron of greed.* Irish myth: *Cross

W151.1. *Harlot weeps when her impoverished lover leaves her to think that she has left him his coat.* *Crane Vitry 214 No. 200; Herbert III 16; *Pauli (ed. Bolte) No. 10; Scala Celi 87b No. 512; Italian Novella: Rotunda.

W151.2. *Visiting friends take everything from house of dying man.* Pauli (ed. Bolte) No. 496.

W151.2.1. *Visitors of sick stag eat up all his provisions so that he starves.* Wienert FFC LVI *60 (ET 227), 122 (ST 311); Halm Aesop No. 131.

W151.2.2. *Hospitable man impoverished by greedy guests.* Irish myth· *Cross.

W151.3. *Wolves devour an ox without leaving a share for the rightful owner.* Pauli (ed. Bolte) No. 495.

W151.4. *Snake and weasel stop fighting in order to catch mouse.* Wienert FFC LVI 49 (ET 80), 134 (ST 396); Halm Aesop No. 345.

W151.5. *Father-in-law sued for breach of contract because he does not die in two years as he has predicted.* Nouvelles Récréations No. 49.

W151.6. *Hog with broken leg refuses to tell another where peas are to be found.* "I intend to go there myself as soon as I get well again." Lithuanian: Balys Index No. 215*.

W151.7. *Eats up the money.* Old man before dying eats his money. In church, son wants to cut corpse open and get the money. The devil: "Don't spoil the skin." Shakes money out of the corpse's throat and takes the skin. Lithuanian: Balys Index No. 3621, Legends No. 638.

G303.18.3. Devil blows skin off man who belongs to him. Q272.3. Avaricious miser tries to eat his money.

W151.8. *Thieves quarrel over booty: owner comes.* (Cf. J2136.5.2.) India: Thompson-Balys.

W151.9. *Greedy person (animal) gets hand (head) stuck in food jar.* India: *Thompson-Balys.

W151.10. *Greedy man tries to stuff food into his nostrils as well as into his mouth.* Africa (Fang): Tessman 140.

W152. *Stinginess.* Irish myth: *Cross; Icelandic: *Boberg; India: *Thompson-Balys.

J1334. Beggar tells stingy to go beg. J1340. Retorts from hungry persons. J2199.4. Shortsighted economy. K341.13. Tailor throws piece of cloth out of window. K343.2.1. The stingy parson and the slaughtered pig. Q276. Stinginess punished.

W152.1. *Fox spoils his food rather than divide with ape.* Wienert FFC LVI 58 (ET 193), 133 (ST 393).

W152.2. *Man had rather be burned alive than to share food with a guest.* Penzer V 165ff.

W152.3. *Stingy dead woman raises her head to correct account of laundress,* who is overcharging her daughter. Spanish: Boggs FFC XC 128 No. 1482.

W152.4. *Stingy man forced to share his money* when he lies and says he has none. Pauli (ed. Bolte) No. 707.

W152.5. *Stingy woman will not give soup to man until she spills it.* Then she says he may have the soup. Pauli (ed. Bolte) No. 321.

W152.6. *Stingy king will not hire soldiers: defeated.* Pauli (ed. Bolte) No. 181.

W152.7. *Spider in stingy woman's house grows thin.* Type 286*.

W152.8. *Stingy horse refuses ass little feed, though he promises much for later time.* Wienert FFC LVI *58 (ET 196), 133 (ST 394); Hervieux II 142.

W152.9. *Stingy man cancels invitations to his guests.* "It is better that they speak ill of me on an empty stomach than on a full one." Italian Novella: Rotunda.

W152.10. *Drummer drums for own wedding so as to save expense.* Nouvelles Récréations No. 49.

T133.3. Drummer beats drums before bride on way to wedding.

W152.11. *Stingy men love possessions so much that they wear out their feet to save shoes.* Spanish Exempla: Keller.

W152.12. *Stingy man and his servants.* India: Thompson-Balys.

J1340. Retorts from hungry persons.

W152.12.1. *Farmer gets help up early in morning for a light breakfast:* a glass of water and a lantern. Canada: Baughman.

W152.12.2. *Stingy farmer encourages help by promise of hot lunch.* The servant discovers that the hot lunch is a mustard sandwich. Canada: Baughman.

W152.12.3. *Master insists that maid whistle when she brings in the dessert.* He is afraid she will eat the raisins out of the cakes. U.S.: Baughman.

W152.12.4. *Master insists that servants whistle as they pick strawberries so that they cannot eat any.* U.S.: Baughman.

W152.13. *The stingy man and his animals.*

W152.13.1. *A stranger notices that man's cows need feed, feeds them. They die of the shock of being fed.* U.S.: Baughman.

W152.14. *Man who insists on using everything that is useful.*

W152.14.1. *Man finds a bunghole lying around loose, has cooper build a barrel around it.* U.S.: Baughman.

W152.14.2. *Man saves sausage skins, sends them back for refilling.* U.S.: Baughman.

W152.15. *Stingy man does not eat butter; only looks at it and enjoys the thought.* India: Thompson-Balys.

W152.16. *Wife of stingy man prays that her husband become sick so that she can get better food.* India: Thompson-Balys.

W152.17. *Wife keeps half of the money she plans to give for a shrine.* India: Thompson-Balys.

W153. *Miserliness.* Spanish Exempla: Keller; India: *Thompson-Balys.

J1061.3. Foolish dog finds treasure and dies rather than leave it. J1061.4. Miser's treasure stolen. Advised to imagine that his treasure is still there: he will be as well off as before. Q272.0.1. Miserliness punished.

W153.1. *Miser's heart found in his strong-box.* Chauvin II 152 No. 14.

W153.2. *Miserly husband spies on wife to see that she does not eat too much.* Gets burned in the chimney and beaten in the bed where he hides. Type 1407; U.S.: Baughman.

W153.2.1. *Miserly husband spies on wife, lest she cook too much.* Italian Novella: Rotunda.

W153.3. *Miserly wife exposed to guests by her husband.* Russian: Andrejev No. 1454.

W153.4. *Man is so miserly that he never drinks wine until it becomes strong.* Gets full benefit from it. Italian Novella: Rotunda.

W153.5. *Friar so miserly that he stays in ditch three days before "lending" a hand to his rescuers.* Italian Novella: Rotunda.

W153.6. *Miser dreams that he spends some money.* Strangles himself in his sleep. Italian Novella: Rotunda.

W153.7. *Miser decides not to commit suicide.* Does not want the expense of a rope. Italian Novella: Rotunda.

W153.7.1. *Miser is given rope to hang himself.* Miser annoys merchant so much over the price of a rope that the latter gives it to him provided he will hang himself as he plans to do. Spanish: Childers.

W153.8. *Miser appoints himself as the sole heir of his own estate.* Italian Novella: Rotunda.

W153.9. *Miser decides to kill his pigs himself.* Refuses to pay fee. Chain of circumstances make it infinitely more expensive. Italian Novella: Rotunda.

W153.10. *Miser is rebuked by friend.* "You get no benefit from your wealth." Proves his folly. Italian Novella: Rotunda.

W153.11. *Miser dies because he will not buy a candle.* Italian Novella: Rotunda.

W153.11.1. *Dying miser tells son to extinguish candle just as soon as he dies.* Spanish: Childers.

W153.11.2. *Miser runs back home to put out lamp left burning.* India: Thompson-Balys.

W153.12. *Miser is kidnapped and held for ransom.* Italian Novella: Rotunda.

W153.13. *Wood dealer prays for raja's death so that he can sell sandal wood for funeral pyre.* India: Thompson-Balys.

W153.14. *Miser tries to reduce sacrifice promised to god.* India: *Thompson-Balys.

K171.3.1. Deceptive sacrifice of nuts and dates.

W153.15. *Miser prays to enter heaven with his clothes on: gold coins sewn into undergarments.* India: Thompson-Balys.

W154. *Ingratitude.* Jewish: *Neuman; India: *Thompson-Balys.

B336. Helpful animal killed (threatened) by ungrateful hero. H1565. Tests of gratitude. J121. Ungrateful son reproved by naive action of his own son: preparing for old age. J1172.3. Ungrateful animal returned to captivity. K231.3. Refusal to make sacrifice after need is past. K952.1. Ungrateful river passenger kills carrier from within. K2213.5. The faithless resuscitated wife. Q281. Ingratitude punished. Q281.1. Ungrateful children punished. T261. The ungrateful wife. W27. Gratitude.

W154.1. *Man dismissed after years of service with a pittance.* *Type 592; BP II 490ff.

W154.1.1. *Usurer's ingratitude toward servant.* Dismisses him and charges him for a rope which he had cut while saving the usurer from hanging. Spanish: Childers.

K231.9. Servant refused payment because of single mistake.

W154.2. *Monster ungrateful for rescue.* *Type 426; BP II 420; India: *Thompson-Balys.

W154.2.1. *Rescued animal threatens rescuer.* *Type 155; India: *Thompson-Balys.

W154.2.2. *Man ungrateful for rescue by animal.* India: *Thompson-Balys.

W154.3. *Crane pulls bone from wolf's throat: wolf refuses payment.* "That you were allowed to take your beak from my throat is payment enough." (Cf. B382.) *Type 76; *Crane Vitry 192 No. 136; *Wienert FFC LVI 54 n. 3 (ET 145), 147 (ST 517); Halm Aesop No. 276; Jacobs Aesop 200 No. 5. — Spanish Exempla: Keller; Italian Novella: Rotunda; Jewish: *Neuman; India: *Thompson-Balys.

W154.3.1. *Lion rescued from net by rat: eats rat.* Cf. Type 75. Italian Novella: Rotunda; Africa (Ibo, Nigeria): Thomas 86, (Kaffir): Kidd 243 No. 10 (lion and gazelle); West Indies: Flowers 582.

W154.3.2. *Tiger has thorn pulled by man: attacks man.* India: Thompson-Balys.

W154.4. *Hunter beats dog which has grown old in his service.* Wienert FFC LVI 73 (ET 380), 89 (ST 14); Spanish Exempla: Keller. Cf. Type 101.

W154.5. *Dog tries to bite man rescuing him from well.* Wienert FFC LVI 72 (ET 370), 147 (ST 523); Halm Aesop No. 192.

W154.5.1. *Ungrateful fox hits with tail the man who carries him across stream.* Spanish Exempla: Keller.

W154.5.1.1. *Man kills whale which carried him home across sea.* Tonga: Gifford 142.

K952.1. Ungrateful river passenger kills carrier from within.

W154.5.1.2. *Man who has been rescued from pit tries to kill his monkey rescuer for food.* Buddhist myth: Malalasekera II 472f.

W154.5.1.3. *Ungrateful ape plucks feathers from heron who has carried him across water.* Indonesia: DeVries's list No. 34.

W154.6. *Ungrateful wanderer pulls nut tree to pieces to get the nuts.* Wienert FFC LVI *74 (ET 394), 147 (ST 520); Halm Aesop No. 188.

W154.7. *Wanderers in shade of plane tree blame it for not bearing fruit.* Wienert FFC LVI *74 (ET 396), 147 (ST 519); Halm Aesop No. 313.

W154.8. *Grateful animals; ungrateful man.* A traveler saves a monkey, a snake, a tiger, and a jeweler from a pit. The monkey gives him fruit; the tiger a necklace of a princess he has killed. The jeweler accuses the rescuer before the king. The serpent saves him by biting the prince and then showing the man the proper remedy. *Type 160; Chauvin II 106 No. 71; *Penzer V 157 n. 1; Cosquin Études 22ff.; Moe Samlede Skrifter I 192ff.; *BP IV 139; *Wesselski Theorie 82ff.; *Oesterley No. 119; Fb "ulvgrav"; Bødker Exempler 304 No. 25. — Spanish Exempla: Keller; Jewish: bin Gorion Born Judas[2] IV 51, 277, Neuman; India: *Thompson-Balys; Africa: Frobenius Atlantis IX 385f. Nos. 103, 104, (Gold Coast): Barker and Sinclair 163 No. 32, (Zanzibar): Bateman 81ff. No. 6.

B361. Animals grateful for rescue from pit. B512. Medicine shown by animal. B522.1. Serpent shows condemned man how to save prince's life. K735. Capture in pitfall. R100. Rescues.

W154.9. *Man rescued from drowning kills rescuer.* Oceanic: Dixon 193 nn. 20—25.

W154.9.1. *Whales rescue drowning king who planned to kill them.* Polynesia: Beckwith Myth 502—05; Tuamotu: Stimson MS (T-G. 3/912).

W154.10. *Snake kills ungrateful tamer.* Chinese: Eberhard FFC CXX 33 No. 19.

W154.11. *Tiger returns rope to former captor: rewarded by having tail cut off.* India: Thompson-Balys.

W154.12. *Man kills his rescuer in order to collect reward.* Italian Novella: Rotunda.

W154.12.1. *Knight is ungrateful for rescue in battle.* Italian Novella: Rotunda.

W154.12.2. *Ungrateful Brahmin brings his wild goose rescuer to king as remedy against leprosy.* India: Thompson-Balys.

W154.12.3. *Ungrateful brothers plot against rescuer.* *Types 550, 551.

W154.13. *Benefactor falsely accused of theft by ungrateful youth.* Italian Novella: Rotunda.

W154.14. *Woman who saves suitor from death is later condemned to die by the ingrate.* Italian Novella: Rotunda.

K2112. Woman slandered as adulteress (prostitute).

W154.15. *Kind magistrate is victim of ingratitude.* Gives lawbreaker a light sentence. The latter seduces the magistrate's wife. Italian Novella: Rotunda.

W154.16. *Ruler persecutes his friends and is kind to his enemies.* Is killed. Italian Novella: Rotunda.

W154.17. *Man beheads rescuer for leaving him so long in pain.* Irish myth: Cross.

W154.18. *Man ungrateful for life saved because rescuer helped others also.* Irish myth: Cross.

W154.19. *Ungrateful Jew steals horse of Christian who has lent it to him.* Spanish Exempla: Keller.

W154.20. *Man beats people bearing him gifts.* Spanish Exempla: Keller.

W154.21. *Workers (builder) killed when secret building or grave is finished.* (Cf. W181.2.) Krappe "Les funérailles d'Alaric" Annuaire de l'institut de philologie et d'histoire orientales et slaves VII (1939—44) 229ff.

W154.22. *Person compared to nettle, which stings the hand that protects it.* Irish myth: *Cross.

W154.23. *Ingratitude from ignorance.* India: Thompson-Balys.

W154.24. *Man fails to feed his animal rescuer.* India: Thompson-Balys.

W154.25. *Man sets dogs onto bear after bear has carried him home to safety.* India: Thompson-Balys.

W154.26. *Man demands ever larger gifts.*

W154.26.1. *Man trades an egg for a needle, demands treat of a gill of rum, the traditional reward for traders.* The storekeeper gives him the rum; he asks for an egg in it. The storekeeper breaks an egg (the one he has just traded the needle for) into the rum. It has two yolks; the trader asks for two needles. U.S.: Baughman.

W154.27. *Man works his horses to death, then complains that borrowed horse overeats.* U.S.: Baughman.

W154.28. *Wizard makes pupil think himself Emperor and exposes pupil's ingratitude.* Herbert III 94, 431, 536; Chauvin II 150.

W155. *Hardness of heart.* England, U.S.: Baughman; West Indies: Flowers 583.

H491.1. In large family father unwilling but mother willing to sell children. H492.1. Husband refuses to murder his wife for high honors; wife agrees to murder husband. J56. Unscrupulous conduct of business learned from observation of usurer's own practice and used against him. Q291. Hard-heartedness punished.

W155.1. *Hardhearted horse allows ass to be overburdened until it is crushed.* Horse must then assume the load. Wienert FFC LVI *56 (ET 170), 144 (ST 397); Halm Aesop No. 177.

W155.1.1. *Old bullock deserted and left to die.* India: Thompson-Balys.

W155.1.2. *Man overloads and starves camel.* India: Thompson-Balys.

W155.2. *Man helping another across stream drops him* when he learns that he has lost his high position. Jaworskij Der Urquell II 195.

M205.1.1. Turtle carrying man through water upsets him because of a broken promise.

W155.3. *Man unable to weep for hardness of heart.* Irish myth: *Cross.

W155.4. *Hardhearted person refuses reprieve for father's murderers.* Irish myth: Cross.

W155.5. *Permission refused to drink from water tank.* India: Thompson-Balys.

W156. *The dog in the manger.* Has no use for the manger but refuses to give it up to the horse. Wienert FFC LVI 54, 58 (ET 142, 195), 132, 147 (ST 385, 518); Halm Aesop No. 228; Phaedrus I No. 19; Hervieux II 11; Herbert III 14; Crane Vitry 201 No. 161; Jacobs Aesop 209 No. 40.

W157. *Dishonesty.* Irish: Beal XXI 327, O'Suilleabhain 75; Icelandic: *Boberg; India: Thompson-Balys.

W157.1. *Priest uses fortune dishonestly made to erect monuments to himself.* Wesselski Bebel I 171 No. 10.

W158. *Inhospitality.* (Cf. Q292.) Irish myth: *Cross.

W161. *Love of publicity.*

J2162.1. Burning the temple to attain notoriety.

W161.1. *Three envoys debate as to which of them should be received with the greatest honor.* Italian Novella: Rotunda.

W165. *False pride.* Son ashamed of his peasant father who brings him money. Father disinherits him. (Cf. Q331.) *Pauli (ed. Bolte) No. 643; U.S.: Baughman.

W165.1. *Humble man after speaking to king disdains his own family.* India: Thompson-Balys.

W165.2. *Ass after associating with lion disdains his own family.* India: Thompson-Balys.

W167. *Stubbornness.* Grimm No. 3 (Type 710); U.S.: Baughman.

J2511. The silence wager.

W167.1. *Two stubborn goats meet each other on a bridge.* Neither will step aside; both fall into water. Type 202*; Wienert FFC LVI 56 (ET 171).

W167.2. *Woman's stubbornness causes loss of chance to go on pilgrimage.* Spanish Exempla: Keller.

J2060.1. Quarrel and fight over details of aircastles.

W171. *Two-facedness.*

W171.1. *Man winks both at buyer and seller.* He tries to appear friendly to both. Pauli (ed. Bolte) No. 491.

W175. *Changeableness.* Wienert FFC LVI 134.

W175.1. *Sister gives due honor and regard to brother only in times of his prosperity.* India: Thompson-Balys.

W181. *Jealousy.* Irish myth: *Cross; Missouri French: Carrière; Icelandic: *Boberg; Spanish: Espinosa Jr. Nos. 142—45.

A1375. Origin of jealousy and selfishness. Q301. Jealousy punished. T257. Jealous husband or wife.

W181.1. *Sheep jealous of dog because he does nothing.* Do not consider that he guards the flock. Wienert FFC LVI *58 (ET 197), 132 (ST 386); Halm Aesop No. 317.

W181.2. *King kills architect after completion of great building,* so that he may never again build one so great. (Cf. S161.0.1, W154.21.) Wesselski Theorie 15; Ireland, England: Baughman.

W181.2.1. *Architect kills pupil who has surpassed him in skill.* England: *Baughman.

W181.2.2. *Architect commits suicide when he discovers that his pupil has surpassed him in skill.* England: Baughman.

W181.3. *Raven wants to be as white as a swan.* Wienert FFC LVI *46 (ET 49), 90 (ST 26); Halm Aesop No. 206.

W181.4. *Jealous fox betrays wolf to peasant and then appropriates wolf's cave and food.* Peasant kills him in a few days. Wienert FFC LVI 58 (ET 194), 132, 139 (ST 383, 453).

W181.5. *Raven jealous of partridge's way of flying.* Wienert FFC LVI 46 (ET 50), 90 (ST 25).

W181.6. *Jealousy of Venus in the love of Psyche and Cupid.* Italian Novella: Rotunda.

W181.7. *Ruler who is jealous of his subjects' happiness prohibits their games.* Italian Novella: Rotunda.

W182. *The crying child.* He stops crying so that after a rest he can cry louder than ever. *Crane Vitry 265 No. 300; Herbert III 13 No. 85; *Pauli (ed. Bolte) No. 594; Scala Celi 158b No. 892.

W185. *Violence of temper.* Jewish: *Neuman.

W185.1. *Man demonstrates his violence of temper.* He overhears a man tell of his temper. In anger he enters and demands to know when he has ever lost his temper. Penzer V 90f.

W185.2. *Prayer that overbearing knight's illness be increased.* A little sickness has made him kind; more may make him kinder. Crane Vitry 48 No. 103; Mensa Philosophica No. 143.

T284. Frightened wife shows marks of affection for husband. That is so rare that he pardons the robber who has caused the fright.

W185.3. *Temper lost from reading history.* Man so angered that he refuses to pay his workmen. Italian Novella: Rotunda.

W185.4. *Monk loses temper at cup and breaks it.* Spanish Exempla: Keller.

W185.5. *Violence of judge's temper leads him to have men given death sentence unjustly.* Spanish Exempla: Keller.

W185.6. *Insult worse than wound.* The lion to the man: "The wound has healed, but the pain of harsh words still remains." Lithuanian: Balys Index No. 161*; Rumanian: Schullerus FFC LXXVIII No. 159IV*; India: Thompson-Balys.

W187. *Insolence.* Irish myth: Cross.

W188. *Contentiousness.* (Cf. Q300.) Irish myth: *Cross.

W193. *Extortion.*

W193.1. *Man extorts large price for betel leaf from addict.* India: Thompson-Balys.

W195. *Envy* (Cf. Q302.)

W195.1. *Goose and turkey envious of peacock point out its ugly legs and voice.* India: Thompson-Balys.

W196. *Lack of patience.* U.S.: Baughman.

W200—W299. Traits of character—miscellaneous.

W200. Traits of character—miscellaneous.

W211. *Active imagination.*

W211.1. *The boy: "If I had one and then got two more, I should have three."* Type 2411.

W211.2. *"I surely saw a hundred wolves (snakes)."* — "There weren't so many as that." — "Well, what made the noise in the bushes?" Type 2009*; Lithuanian: Balys Index No. 1863*; Estonian: Aarne FFC XXV No. 2009*; Russian: Andrejev No. 2009; India: *Thompson-Balys.

W211.3. *"I am not alone!"* Man travelling alone through the forest at night, is afraid of robbers. He hangs his cap on a stick and keeps repeating: "I am not travelling alone, there are two of us." Lithuanian: Balys Index No. 1862*.

W212. *Eagerness for combat.* Irish myth: Cross.

W212.1. *Eager warriors go through tent wall.* Warriors so eager for battle they do not take time to go out of tent door but go through the tent wall. Irish myth: *Cross.

W212.2. *Warriors contend with each other until battle starts.* When they agree to engage in battle, they cannot endure to be without combat. Irish myth: Cross.

W213. *Man will not allow food served to strangers until a man of them wrestles with him.* Irish myth: Cross.

W213.1. *Host requires deed of bravery before feast is eaten.* Irish myth: Cross.

M151. Vow not to eat before hearing of adventure.

W214. *Man will not do a woman's bidding.* Irish myth: Cross.

W215. *Extreme prudence.* Irish myth: Cross.

W215.1. *Magic help sent to enemy.* Hero sends fairy healing charms to his enemy so that when they resume fighting it cannot be said he wins because of superior care. Irish myth: Cross.

W215.2. *Refusal to fight wounded enemy.* Hero feels it dishonorable to fight with sorely wounded enemy, because it would be said he died of previous wounds rather than the ones hero might inflict. Irish myth: Cross.

W215.3. *Long life sacrificed that descendants may be kings as prophesied.* (Cf. M314.) Irish myth: Cross.

W216. *Thrift.*

W216.1. *Thrifty merchant tells son that even a snake laid by will be useful.* India: Thompson-Balys.

W225. *Taciturn man.*

W225.1. *Man is rebuked for loquaciousness when he speaks after thirty-seven days.* U.S.: Baughman.

W226. *Moving home simple for poor man.* Man is so poor that when he moves all he has to do is to put out the fire and whistle for the dog to follow him. U.S.: Baughman.

X. HUMOR

DETAILED SYNOPSIS

X900—X1899. HUMOR OF LIES AND EXAGGERATIONS

X910—X1099. Lie: the remarkable man
X910—X959. Lie: the remarkable man: his birth, growth, death, physical powers, strength
X910. Lie: the remarkable man
X920. Lie: the large man
X930. Lie: remarkable person's physical powers and habits
X940. Lie: remarkably strong man
X960—X1019. Lie: remarkable person's skills
X960. Lie: remarkable person's skills
X980. Lie: occupational or professional skills
X1010. Lie: remarkable mental skills
X1020—X1079. Remarkable man's extraordinary possessions
X1020. Lie: remarkable possessions of remarkable man
X1030. Lie: remarkable buildings
X1060. Lie: other possessions of remarkable man
X1070. Extraordinary man's family
X1080—X1099. Lie: occupations of remarkable man

X1100—X1199. Lie: great hunters and fishermen
X1100. Lie: the remarkable hunter
X1110. Lie: the wonderful hunt
X1120. Lie: the great marksman
X1130. Lie: hunter's unusual experiences
X1150. Lies about fishing

X1200—X1399. Lies about animals
X1200. Lie: remarkable animals
X1210. Lies about mammals
X1250. Lies about birds
X1280. Lies about insects
X1300. Lies about fish
X1320. Lies about reptiles
X1340. Lie: extraordinary amphibia and other animals
X1370. Lies about imaginary animals

X1400—X1499. Lies about plants, fruits, vegetables and trees
X1400. Lies about plants, fruits, vegetables and trees
X1410. Lies about fruits
X1420. Lies about vegetables
X1450. Lies about field crops
X1470. Lies about trees
X1480. Lies about flowers
X1490. Lie: miscellaneous plant motifs

X1500—X1599. Lies about geography and topography
X1500. Lies about geography and topography
X1510. Lies about land features
X1520. Lies about mountains and hills
X1530. Lies about remarkable soil
X1540. Lies about water features
X1550. Geography and topography—miscellaneous motifs
X1560. Lies about cities

X1600—X1699. Lies about weather and climate
X1600. Lies about weather and climate
X1610. Lies about winds and storms
X1620. Lies about cold weather
X1630. Lies about hot weather
X1640. Lies about dry weather

X. HUMOR

X0—X99. Humor of discomfiture

X0. Humor of discomfiture.

J1110. Clever persons. K800. Fatal deception. K1000. Deception into self-injury. K1200. Deception into humiliating position. K1300. Seduction. K1400. Dupe's property destroyed. K1500. Deception connected with adultery.

X11. *Red pepper for the slow ass: man tries it on himself.* When, on the advice of a friend, he gives the ass red pepper, the ass runs away. Then he tries it on himself. He runs so fast that he passes the ass. Arriving at home, he says to his wife, "Unload the ass when he comes. I must run through the village a couple of times more." Wesselski Hodscha Nasreddin I 224 No. 64.

X443.1 Chaplain on bucking mule.

X12. *Man interrupted each time he tries to eat something.* *Basset 1001 Contes I 273.

X12.1. *Man continually interrupted from eating answers in rhymed monosyllables.* Nouvelles Récréations.

X21. *Accidental cannibalism.* A man eats up the dried meat of a Jew on shipboard. It happens that the Jew is carrying his dead father back home for burial in this form. (Cf. G60.) *Wesselski Hodscha Nasreddin I 257 No. 193; Italian Novella: Rotunda. Cf. Japanese: Ikeda.

X31. *The dream of marking the treasure.* A man dreams that he finds treasure and that he marks the spot with his excrements. Only the latter part of the dream is true. *Wesselski Arlotto II 267 No. 216, Hodscha Nasreddin I 278 No. 314; Lithuanian: Balys Legends No. 788f.; Italian Novella: Rotunda.

N531. Treasure discovered through dream.

X31.1. *Man dreams that he is rich.* Finds cat's excrements. Italian Novella: Rotunda.

X31.2. *Pig licks sleeping man's lips: man thinks he is being kissed.* India: Thompson-Balys.

X32. *Wager with overdressed youths that servant can carry a large bucket of water upstairs.* They follow and are soaked when the servant purposely spills the dirty water. Italian Novella: *Rotunda.

X34. *Use of itch-producing ointment.* Italian Novella: Rotunda.

J2134.1. Trickster eats scratch-berries.

X52. *Ridiculous nakedness or exposure.*

X52.1. *Woman exposed to ridicule when her wig is snatched off by a monkey.* Spanish Exempla: Keller.

X53. *Man given ride on a hemp-dresser.* Cheremis: Sebeok-Nyerges.

X100—X199. Humor of disability.

X100. Humor of disability. Besides the motifs which follow, the entire series of motifs concerning fools (J1700—J2799) properly belongs here as well as where it is given.

X110. Humor of deafness.

K1981.1. Trickster feigns deafness and gets hospitality from miser.

X111. *Deaf men and their answers.* *Type 1698; **Aarne FFC XX; *Fb "tunghør"; India: Thompson-Balys.

X111.1. *Deaf persons: search for the lost animal.* A inquires for his lost animal. — B talks about his work and makes a gesture. — A follows the direction of the gesture and happens to find the animals. He returns and offers an injured animal to B in thanks. — B thinks that he is blamed for injuring the animals. Dispute. Taken to deaf judge. (Cf. X111.14.) *Type 1698A; Aarne FFC XX 16ff.; India: *Thompson-Balys.

X111.2. *Deaf peasant: travelers ask the way.* Travelers ask their direction. Peasant thinks they want to buy oxen. — Peasant's wife arrives; thinks they say her food is too salty. — Daughter-in-law and father-in-law misunderstand each other. *Type 1698B; Aarne FFC XX 28ff.; India: *Thompson-Balys.

X111.3. *Two persons believe each other deaf.* A trickster tells each of two persons before they meet that the other is hard of hearing and must be shouted at. A great shouting takes place, and each thinks the other out of his wits. *Type 1698C; *Aarne FFC XX 29ff.; Wesselski Gonnella 118 No. 16; Nouvelles Récréations No. 10; Nouvelles de Sens No. 4.

K1084. Liar brings about fight between dupes.

X111.4. *Deaf peasant: the wedding invitation.* Lord: Good morning, Peter. — Peasant: I come from Bingen. — L. What is the hog worth? — P. Two weeks from next Sunday (the wedding). — L. Shall I come to the wedding? — P. Three and a half gulden. *Type 1698D; *Aarne FFC XX 35ff.; *Pauli (ed. Bolte) No. 719.

X111.5. *Deaf man on the bridge.* Lord: Good day, Caspar. — Caspar: I am making a reel. — L. Good day, Caspar. — C. It is worth four pence. — L. Good day, Caspar. — C. Yes, my lord, whenever you wish. Type 1698E; *Aarne FFC XX 38ff.

X111.6. *The deaf man and the proud nobleman.* A nobleman amuses himself at the expense of the deaf man. Finally — Nobleman: I wish you a thousand gallows and ropes around your neck. — Peasant: My lord, I wish you twice as many. Type 1698F; *Aarne FFC XX 39ff.

X111.7. *Misunderstood words lead to comic results.* In some the people are not really deaf but fail to catch a word; in some they are deaf. Type 1698G; Aarne FFC XX 40, 76. — Spanish: Espinosa Jr. No. 189; India: Thompson-Balys; Indonesia: DeVries's list No. 296.

J1802. Words in foreign language thought to be insults. N275.2. Criminal confesses because of misunderstanding of a dialect.

X111.8. *The deaf man with the bird in the tree.* A traveler asks the way and the man keeps telling him about the bird he has caught. (The questions and answers often rime.) Type 1698H; Aarne FFC XX 41ff.

X111.9. *Deaf man visits the sick.* He plans the conversation with the expected answers. The answers turn out otherwise. — A. How are you?

— B. I am dead. — Thank God! What have you eaten? — Poison, I think. — I hope it agrees with you. *Type 1698I; Aarne FFC XX 50ff.; India: Thompson-Balys.

J1741.3. Prearranged answers in Latin not always successful.

X111.10. *"Good day." — "A woodchopper."* The workman answers the traveler's courtesies with remarks about his work. (Cf. X111.8.) Type 1698J; Aarne FFC XX 51ff., cf. 67ff., 72, 75 (Types 12, 13, 16, 18).

X111.11. *Buyer and deaf seller.* Type 1698K; Aarne FFC XX 60ff., 69ff. (Types 11, 14, 15).

X111.12. *The deaf parson.* The youth answers unintelligibly but is praised nevertheless. Type 1698L.

X111.13. *The deaf bishop.* The drunken priest says, "In the morning I take a drink of rum and afterwards four or five little drinks." Type 1698M.

X445.1. Parson takes a drink of liquor during the sermon.

X111.14. *Deaf litigants and deaf judge misunderstand one another.* (Cf. X111.1.) *Chauvin VII 113 No. 381; Italian Novella: Rotunda.

X111.15. *Travelers pass through Wesley.* One asks name of town; another replies, "This is Wesley." Another says, "I thought it was Thursday." Third says, "So am I; let's have a drink." U.S.: Baughman.

X112. *Deaf husband orders deaf wife to prepare a certain dish: misunderstanding.* India: Thompson-Balys.

X113. *Misunderstanding and quarrels in family of deaf.* India: Thompson-Balys.

X120. Humor of bad eyesight.

K1984.5. Blind fiancée betrays self. Mistakes one object for another. X413. One-eyed parson in dimly lighted church joins the wrong couples.

X121. *The wife who saw double.* Sees two plates where there are one, etc. Thinks two men are with her. Husband: "See everything double except your husband." Wesselski Hodscha Nasreddin II 186 No. 358.

X121.1. *The squint-eyed son and the bottle.* Sent by his father to get the only bottle of rare wine, he sees two. Not wishing to show his father to be a liar, he breaks one — really the only one. Chauvin II 196 No. 22.

J1623. Drunkard cured of seeing double.

X122. *One-eyed man as appraiser of horse.* Has appraised it at half a mark. "He saw only half a horse; otherwise he would have valued it at a mark." Bédier Fabliaux 123; Italian Novella: Rotunda.

X123. *Blind man and the bull.* Man asks bull if he is on the right road. Bull butts him and knocks him down. The man says that all that was not necessary, simply to say yes or no. Spanish: Boggs FFC XC 140 No. 1699.

J1761.10. Blind men and elephant.

X123.1. *Blind man reaches his home hanging on ox's tail* (or in other ridiculous situation). India: *Thompson-Balys.

X124. *Nearsighted knight mistakes own servant for one of the enemy.* Runs lance into his posterior. Italian Novella: Rotunda.

X124.1. *Blind man strikes woman thinking she is buffalo.* India: Thompson-Balys.

X124.2. *Blind son-in-law visits his wife's family: gets into difficulties.* India: Thompson-Balys.

X125. *Blind men trying to kill pigs with clubs strike one another.* (Cf. K1081.) Herbert III 71, 133, 572.

X128. *Blind man in awkward position pretends to see.* India: Thompson-Balys.

X130. Other physical disabilities.

X131. *The wry-mouthed family.* Each member has mouth turned in a different way. Unavailing attempts to blow out the light. U.S.: *Baughman; Danish: MS in Danske Folkemindesamling (Grundtvig No. 166).

X756. The mother trains the old maid to speak properly. Absurd results.

X133. *Man calls convention of all long noses.* Italian Novella: Rotunda.

X135. *The humor of stuttering.* U.S.: Baughman; Italian Novella: Rotunda.

X135.1. *Each of four stutterers thinks the others are ridiculing him.* Italian Novella: Rotunda.

X135.2. *Stutterer tries to give alarm.* Amusing results. U.S.: *Baughman.

X137. *Humor of ugliness.* U.S.: *Baughman.

X141. *Blind, lame, and deaf as witnesses in court.* Type 1673*.

X142. *The humor of small stature.* (Cf. F535.1.) Italian Novella: Rotunda.

X142.1. *Dwarf king falls into porridge-pot at court of human king.* Irish myth: *Cross.

X142.2. *Dwarf poet forced to swim in drinking-horn of human being.* Irish myth: *Cross.

X142.3. *Tiny ambassador put on horse with long stirrups.* Cannot say anything as he is too busy trying to keep his seat. Italian Novella: Rotunda.

X142.4. *Short magistrate wears a high helmet.* Italian Novella: Rotunda.

X143. *Humor of lameness.*

X143.1. *Lame man taken on hunt in wheel chair beats the dogs home when they tree a spook or when a bear gets after them.* (Cf. K1861.) U.S.: *Baughman.

X145. *Humor of bad singing.*

X145.1. *Audience of one hired to listen to egoistic dismal-voiced singer.* India: Thompson-Balys.

X151. *Humor of fatness.*

J1410. Repartee concerning fatness.

X151.1. *Six short, fat husbands married to six tall, fat wives try absurdly to kiss them at the threshold on their wedding day.* India: Thompson-Balys.

X151.2. *Fat man so unwieldly he fishes from his window in the street.* India: Thompson-Balys.

X200—X599. HUMOR OF SOCIAL CLASSES

X200—X299. Humor dealing with tradesmen

X200. Humor dealing with tradesmen.

X210. Jokes about millers. (Cf. P443.)

X211. *Millers as thieves.* Pauli (ed. Bolte) No. 785; Fb "møller" II 649; Italian Novella: *Rotunda.

X212. *The honest miller.* Baker cannot understand how a man who has been a miller can be a beggar. It is a wonder that the farmers are not beggars instead. Wesselski Bebel I 118 No. 3.

X212.1. *Priest commends the poor miller.* If he had been like the rest of the congregation he would have become rich. Pauli (ed. Bolte) No. 825.

X213. *Why no millers in hell.* A mad dog in place of a miller in a sack. Flemish: DeMeyer FFC XXXVII 84 No. 27b.

X214. *Monks get revenge on millers.* Drunken millers force monks to dance. Millers are enticed to monastery and beaten. Italian Novella: Rotunda.

X220. Jokes about tailors. (Cf. P441.)

H38.2.1. Tailor married to princess betrays trade by calling for needle and thread. J1401. The tailor's dream.

X221. *Oversight of the thievish tailor.* Sews the stolen piece of cloth on the outside of his coat, thinking that it is on the inside. Type 2005*.

X221.1. *Thievish tailor cuts a piece of his own coat.* Type 2005**; Nouvelles Récréations No. 46.

X221.2. *Thieving tailor can hide stolen cloth even in needle-and-thread tube.* India: Thompson-Balys.

X222. *Tailor always associated with goat.* **B. Salditt Hessische Blätter f. Vksk. XXX—XXXI 88.

X223. *Tailors cowards as warriors: go home to their needles.* (Cf. W121.) India: Thompson-Balys.

X230. Jokes about butchers.

X231. *Butcher wonders that man who has been buying his meat for seven years can still be alive.* Wesselski Mönchslatein 184 No. 142.

X240. Jokes about cobblers (shoemakers).

P453. Shoemaker.

X241. *Ugly cobbler continually threatens to throw his last at people.* The object of jokes. Spanish: Boggs FFC XC 98 No. 836D*.

X242. *Shoemaker drinks more than his portion of "drink of lies",* which has been prepared for all to partake of equally. Wienert FFC LVI 39; Halm Aesop No. 136.

X250. Jokes about other artisans and tradesmen.

X251. *Jokes on weavers.* (Cf. P445.) *Chauvin VIII 105 No. 81 n. 2.

X251.1. *Why no weavers in hell.* Devils annoyed at their noisy trade. Flemish: DeMeyer FFC XXXVII 84 No. 27a.

X252. *Jokes about barbers.* Italian Novella: Rotunda.

X252.1. *Client flees when cobwebs are brought in to medicate cuts.* Italian Novella: Rotunda.

X252.2. *Barber uses cut hair to staunch cuts.* Italian Novella: Rotunda.

X253. *Jokes on fishermen.* Nouvelles Récréations.

X253.1. *Talkativeness of the fishwives of Paris.* Anecdotes of their invective. Nouvelles Récréations No. 63.

X300—X499. Humor dealing with professions.

X300. Humor dealing with professions.

X310. Jokes on lawyers. (Cf. P422.)

X311. *What will happen when there are so many lawyers.* Woman sees the crowds of students in the law school. She knows that the one lawyer in her village has ruined nearly everyone. *Pauli (ed. Bolte) No. 787; *Wesselski Bebel I 216 No. 110.

X312. *Beggar frightens lawyer into giving by telling him of all the lawyers in hell.* Spanish: Boggs FFC XC 95 No. 819*; cf. U.S.: Baughman.

X313. *Dying like Christ—between two thieves.* The dying man has the lawyer and the notary stand on either side of him. U.S.: Baughman; Spanish: Boggs FFC XC 134 No. 1583*.

X314. *Lawyer who tries to practice without lying fails.* He enters religious order and tries to conduct the legal business without lying. *Pauli (ed. Bolte) No. 127; Crane Vitry 155 No. 52; Scala Celi 7b No. 47; Alphabet No. 483.

X315. *Dying lawyer says, "I appeal".* Crane Vitry 149f. No. 39; Scala Celi 7b No. 48; Herbert III 77 No. 200, 462 No. 94, 497 No. 238, 499 No. 262; Alphabet No. 41; Mensa Philosophica No. 147.

X315.1. *Dying lawyer asks delay.* Crane Vitry 150 No. 40; Scala Celi 7b No. 45; Mensa Philosophica No. 148.

X316. *Nero has reserved place in hell for lawyers.* Crane Vitry 148 No. 36; Spanish Exempla: Keller.

X317. *Lawyer thrown back into mud when rescuers learn that he is a lawyer.* Mensa Philosophica No. 37.

X318. *Lawyer loses tongue in death because he sold it in life.* Alphabet No. 40.

X319. *Miscellaneous jokes about lawyers.*

X319.1. *Eloquent lawyer makes obviously guilty client doubt his own guilt.* Canada, U.S.: *Baughman.

J2087. The persuasive auctioneer.

X330. Jokes on magistrates. (Cf. P421.)

X331. *Guilty of everything connected with the seven senses.* When the priest to whom he is confessing says there are but five senses, the magistrate says that he needs two more senses than other people. Pauli (ed. Bolte) No. 297.

X332. *Foreigner wonders why city with so many judges has not been destroyed.* Italian Novella: Rotunda.

X350. Jokes on teachers.

X351. *Music teacher charges double for those who have taken music before.* One fee for teaching and one for making them forget the old teaching. Pauli (ed. Bolte) No. 314.

X370. Jokes on scholars.

X371. *Master of seven liberal arts begs from wagoner.* With his one art latter supports his family. Pauli (ed. Bolte) No. 855.

J1662. The cat's only trick. She saves herself on a tree. The fox, who knows a hundred tricks, is captured.

X372. *Jokes on doctors.* U.S.: Baughman; Italian Novella: Rotunda.

D1500. Magic object controls disease. D2161. Magic healing power. F956. Extraordinary diagnosis. J1062. Cure yourself before doctoring others. J1513. Healed with his own medicine. J1734.1. Urine diagnosis to tell where a man comes from. J2412.3. Imitation of the prescription. J2469.2. Taking the prescription. K824. Sham doctor kills his patients. K1010. Deception through false doctoring. K1955.2. Sham physician pretends to diagnose entirely from urinalysis.

X372.1. *Doctor cures palpitation of heart: patient stops breathing.* India: Thompson-Balys.

X372.2. *Head cut off to cure snakebite.* India: Thompson-Balys.

X372.3. *Eyedrops prescribed for stomach ache so that patient can see what he eats.* India: *Thompson-Balys.

X372.4. *Foolish doctor performs useless operation.*

X372.4.1. *Man with cheeks stuffed with food operated on to remove swellings.* India: *Thompson-Balys.

X372.5. *Doctor called to attend sick man immediately gives orders for the funeral.* India: Thompson-Balys.

X410. Jokes on parsons. *Types 1725—1824; **Kristensen Vore Fædres Kirketjeneste (Aarhus, 1899); *Fb "præst" II 884a; West Indies: Flowers 583.

G303.3.1.8. Devil in form of priest. J1211.1. Peasant preaches about the bishop's amour. K262. The priest made sick of his bargain: three words at the grave. K343.2.1. The stingy parson and the slaughtered pig. K1961.1. Sham parson (priest). K1961.1.2.1. Parody sermon (mass). N5. Card-playing parson. N71. Wager: to begin sermon with illustration from card-playing. P120. Church dignitaries. P426.1. Parson (priest). V66.1. Witty funeral sermon.

X411. *Parson put to flight during his sermon.* Type 1785.

X411.1. *Sexton's dog steals sausage from parson's pocket: parson flees.* *Type 1785A.

X411.2. *Sexton puts needle in sacramental bread: parson sticks his hand.* *Type 1785B.

X411.3. *Sexton arranges wasp-nest so that parson sits on it.* Wasps chase him. *Type 1785C.

X412. *Tame bear tied to church bells.* Rings alarm. Italian Novella: Rotunda.

X413. *One-eyed parson in dimly lighted church joins the wrong couples.* Marries the old man to the girl and the old woman to the boy. Italian Novella: *Rotunda.

X120. Humor of bad eyesight.

X414. *Parson rides ox into church.* He wants to show how Christ rode into Jerusalem. Sexton sticks ox with needle. *Type 1786.

X415. *The hog in church.* Locked in church all week by mistake. When the congregation comes, the hog runs between the parson's legs and carries him out. *Type 1838; Fb "svin".

X416. *Parson preaches so that half the congregation weeps and half laughs.* Has clothes torn in the back. Those that see this laugh. He wins the wager. *Type 1828*; Wesselski Morlini 297 No. 44.

K1285. Rascals pull off judge's breeches and leave him exposed.

X417. *Parson smears his hand with butter.* Rascals have spread butter on the altarbread. The parson preaches, "What is the life of man?" and therewith brings his hand down on the altar-bread: "Pure butter!" Type 1836*.

X418. *Parson is to let a dove fly in the church.* It dies in his pocket. *Type 1837.

X421. *At the blessing of the grave the parson's ox breaks loose:* "Now the devil has him." *Type 1840; *Fb "tyr" III 908b.

X422. *The corpse with his feet cut off.* The coffin-maker has fitted him to the coffin. The parson: "On the last day he will arise." One of the coffin-makers: "Did I say that?" Type 1699*.

X424. *The devil in the cemetery.* A sexton hears thieves in the cemetery cracking nuts and thinks it is the devil cracking bones. With the gouty parson on his back he comes upon the thieves who, thinking it is their companion with the sheep, call out, "Is he fat?" The sexton: "Fat or lean, here he is!" *Type 1791; *BP III 395; *Pauli (ed. Bolte) No. 82; Scala Celi 101b No. 547; Alphabet No. 333; U.S., England: *Baughman; Lithuanian: Balys Index No. 1791, Legends No. 889.

X424.1. *Robbers mistake man for devil (the "sheep" speaks, "Gently, gently!").* India: Thompson-Balys.

G87. Cannibal crunching human bone says noise is only eating of peas.
J1765.2. Man taken to be sheep.

X425. *The parson who said there is no devil.* The bear-showman lets the bear climb up the pulpit. The parson thinks the bear is the devil. Type 1745*.

X426. *If his son were only a fool he would let him study to be a priest.* So says the innkeeper. Type 1865*.

X427. *A bad year for priests: few funerals.* All but the priest rejoice over the good health of the community. He bemoans his loss of income from burials. *Wesselski Arlotto II 248 No. 155.

X428. *Enmity between priests and monks: chickens and eggs.* Monks eat eggs and make chickens expensive; priests eat hens and make eggs high. Pauli (ed. Bolte) No. 69.

X431. *The hungry parson and the porridge-pot.* Overnight at the peasant's house. The hungry parson hunts the porridge in the dark, guided by a rope the sexton has given him. Series of accidents. *Type 1775; Fb "seng" III 187a.

J2541. Don't eat too greedily. Fool starves himself at table. Later hunts food in house and gets into trouble. K1240. Deception into humiliating position—miscellaneous.

X431.1. *Stupid man tries to take honey from jug at night while visiting.* Series of accidents. Chinese: Graham.

X434. *The parson put out of countenance.*

X434.1. *The large loaves need a large oven.* Parson says that the loaves with which Jesus fed the people in the wilderness were as large as the mountains. The mason asks what kind of oven they were baken in. Type 1834*.

X434.2. *Grace before meat.* The parson asks the boy: "What does your father say when you begin to eat?" Boy: "You young devil, etc." *Type 1841.

X435. *The boy applies the sermon.* Makes a present application of the words of the parson. *Type 1833; U.S.: Baughman.

X435.1. *"What says David?" — Boy: "Pay your old debts."* Variants: (a) What evil did Adam do? — He (shoemaker) made my shoes too small. (b) What kind of man was Moses? He was a day laborer. *Type 1833A; *Wesselski Arlotto II 233 No. 113.

X435.2. *Parson "Where did the father stay?" — "He stayed to hold the oxen."* *Type 1833B.

X435.3. *Parson: Where was Christ when he was neither in heaven nor on earth?* — He was in the willow-grove looking for a stick to beat those who ask foolish questions. *Type 1833C.

X435.4. *Names of persons in the Trinity.* The priest's example: the three cows. The boy: "The Holy Ghost has just had a calf." Type 1833D; England: Baughman.

X435.5. *Sermon about the rich man.* A boy rides with a rich man. Goes into church and leaves his coat lying on the sled. When the parson preaches about the rich man who went to hell, the boy calls out, "Then he took my coat along!" *Type 1832.

X436. *The parson sings like a goat.* The parson sees an old woman weeping and believes that she is touched by his singing. When spoken to she says that she has been reminded of her old goat which she has lost. *Type 1834; Wesselski Hodscha Nasreddin II 243 No. 539; *Crane Vitry 157 No. 56; *Pauli (ed. Bolte) No. 576; Fb "prædiken" II 882; Scala Celi 25a No. 164; — Italian Novella: Rotunda; India: Thompson-Balys.

X438. *The dream: all parsons in hell.* The smith tells the parson whom he has summoned that he has dreamed of going to heaven where St. Peter would not admit him before he saw a parson. There were no parsons in heaven, but all in hell. *Type 1738.

X438.1. *All devout women in hell.* Devout woman and a priest retell their dreams. The priest has dreamed that all the devout women are to be found in hell. Lithuanian: Balys Index No. 1847*.

X441. *Parson and sexton at mass.* Parson intones instructions to the sexton (cook) as a part of the mass. *Type 1831; Spanish: Boggs FFC XC 147 No. 1831A*.

K1546. Woman warns lover of husband by parody incantation. K1961.1.2.1. Parody sermon (mass).

X441.1. *"I can't hear you."* Rector confesses his sacristan: "Have you drunk the wine designated for the mass?" — "I can't hear you." Exchange of places. Sacristan asks rector: "Have you kissed my wife?" — "Really, I can't hear you." Lithuanian: Balys Index No. 2451*; Rumanian: Schullerus FFC LXXVIII No. 1777*.

X442. *Whistling at mass.* Bell breaks and priest's patron whistles in place of ringing the bell at mass. *Wesselski Arlotto I 187 No. 7.

X443. *Parson's poor horsemanship.*

X11. Red pepper for the slow ass: man tries it on himself.

X443.1. *Chaplain on bucking mule.* Nouvelles Récréations No. 27.

X445. *Parson refreshes himself during the sermon.*

X445.1. *Parson takes a drink of liquor during the sermon.* (Cf. X111.13.) *Type 1827.

X445.2. *Parson takes a chew of tobacco during the sermon.* Fb "kardus" II 91a.

X451. *Cock crows at church and the sexton awakes and begins to sing.* *Type 1828.

X452. *The parson has no need to preach.* Those who know may teach those who don't know. *Type 1826.

X452.1. *No need to give sermon about saint again.* "Last year I told you all about his life and works. He has performed no new miracles." *Wesselski Arlotto I 188 No. 8; Italian Novella: Rotunda.

X453. *The woman whose name was "Worthy."* Refuses to say, "I'm not worthy" at communion. Italian Novella: Rotunda.

X454. *Chapel endowed with fifty blows for the friar.* Italian Novella: Rotunda.

K187. Strokes shared.

X457. *Jokes on monks.*

X457.1. *Bishop willing to admit castrated man as monk:* wishes all were in the same condition. Nouvelles Récréations No. 15.

X459. *Jokes on parsons—miscellaneous.* England, U.S.: *Baughman.

X459.1. *Man heeds what he thinks to be call to the ministry.*

X459.1.1. *Young man plowing corn sees letters "P. C." formed by clouds.* He explains situation to minister, asks to be ordained. The minister explains that the letters mean "plow corn" instead of "preach Christ". U.S.: Baughman.

X460. Humor concerning other professions.

X461. *Jokes on fortune-tellers.*

X461.1. *Fortune-teller shows others how to get rich but remains poor himself.* (Cf. J1062.) Herbert III 22 No. 186; Crane Vitry 250 No. 266.

X500—X599. Humor concerning other social classes.

X500. Humor concerning other social classes.

X510. Jokes concerning usurers.

E411.4. Usurer cannot rest in grave. N277. Oxen bear dead usurer to gallows to be buried. P435. Usurer. Q273. Usury punished. W154.1.1. Usurer's ingratitude toward servant.

X511. *Barber alone praises usurer.* Custom not to bury dead until someone has something good to say about him. No one will praise a dead usurer until a barber is willing to say that he had a good beard. *Pauli (ed. Bolte) No. 195; Wesselski Mönchslatein 122 No. 105.

V66.1. Witty funeral sermon.

X512. *Usurers do not reply.* The parson asks the various trades and professions to rise one by one for a special blessing. When he calls for the usurers none reply. Pauli (ed. Bolte) Nos. 193, 194; Crane Vitry 207 No. 179; Scala Celi 168b No. 959; Alphabet No. 792.

X513. *Devil will not carry usurers to hell but will drag them by the legs.* So declares a youth paid by a usurer to protest against the priest's remarks that the devil would carry all usurers off. Pauli (ed. Bolte) No. 191; cf. Spanish: Espinosa Jr. No. 213.

X514. *Only usurers can carry the corpse of the usurer.* It refuses to be moved by anyone else. (Cf. X521.) Pauli (ed. Bolte) No. 190; Irish: Beal XXI 326, cf. O'Suilleabhain 74.

X516. *Usurer encourages sermons against usury,* so that his competitors will cease activity. Pauli (ed. Bolte) No. 192; Italian Novella: *Rotunda.

X520. Jokes concerning prostitutes.

X521. *Only prostitutes can carry the corpse of a prostitute.* (Cf. X514.) Pauli (ed. Bolte) No. 405.

X530. Jokes concerning beggars.

X531. *Begging cripples hurry away from shrine lest they be healed and lose their livelihood.* Wesselski Mönchslatein 183 No. 141.

X540. Jokes on madmen. Irish myth: Cross.

X541. *Cohabitation between lunatics brought about for sport.* Irish myth: Cross.

X550. Jokes on secret societies.

X551. *Jokes on freemasons.* *Fb "frimurer" I 371b; *Hdwb. d. Abergl. III 23ff.

G303.10.6. Devil in league with freemason.

X583. *Jokes about travelers.* U.S.: *Baughman.

X584. *Jokes about hunters.*

X584.1. *Man chased by bear to camp claims that he brought it in thus since he did not want to carry it.* (Cf. K1741.) U.S.: *Baughman.

X600—X699. Humor concerning races or nations.

X600. Humor concerning races or nations.

X610. Jokes concerning Jews.

A1662.1. Why Jews smell bad. A1681.2. Why Jews do not eat pork. A1689.6. Why Jews read and write from right to left. G303.16.19.3.3. Task for devil: washing a Jew, to rid him of his evil smell. J2336. Jewess makes parents believe she is to give birth to the Messiah. M211.4. Jews must repay devil's help. P715.1. Jews. V360. Christian and Jewish traditions concerning each other.

X611. *How the Jews were drawn from heaven.* Someone cries, "Clothes are being auctioned off in hell." *Type 2403; Lithuanian: Balys Index No. 1868*; cf. U.S.: Baughman (X597.1, X902).

X613. *Trickster breaks up Jewish marriage ceremony and seduces the bride.* (Cf. K1371.) Italian Novella: Rotunda.

X650. Jokes concerning other races or nations.

J652.4.2. Don't play tricks on Gascons.

X651. *Battle between lice of Strassburg and of Hungary.* Hungarians win. Wesselski Bebel II 149 No. 160.

X652. *Learning the Bavarian language.* A caretaker of an estate recently sold to a Bavarian sits among the swine so as to learn Bavarian. *Wesselski Bebel I 201 No. 80.

X661. *Why Arabians are liars.* Hermes and his wagon of lies break down in Arabia. Wienert FFC LVI 39; Halm Aesop No. 141.

X680. Jokes concerning various cities.

X681. *Blason populaire.* Despiteful names used by one city for another. P. Sébillot and H. Gaidoz Le Blason Populaire de la France.

X700—X799. Humor concerning sex.

X700. Humor concerning sex. [1]

A1313. Origins of sex organs. A1352. Origin of sexual intercourse. A1556.3. Origin of adultery. A2237.1. Animal reveals mistress's adultery: punished by master. C453. Tabu: boasting of love-conquest. D658. Transformation to seduce. D1355.5. Magic hair produces love. J1174. Clever decisions concerning kissing and rape. J1264. Repartee concerning clerical incontinence. J1351. Women call each other prostitutes. J1532. Adulteress's absurdity rebuked. J1551. Imagined intercourse, imagined payment. J1744. Ignorance of marriage relations. J2462. Foolish bridegroom follows instructions literally. K1210. Humiliated or baffled lovers. K1271. Amorous intrigue observed and exposed. K1300—K1399. Seduction or deceptive marriage. K1500—K1599. Deceptions connected with adultery. K1843. Wife deceives husband with substitute bedmate. K1910. Marital impostures. M130. Vows concerning sex. N131.1. Luck changing after cohabitation. T (entire chapter). Sex. T250. Characteristics of wives and husbands.

X750. Jokes on old maids. *Types 1475—1499; Hdwb. d. Abergl. I 334 s.v. "Alte Jungfer".

E613.0.3. Reincarnation of old maids as birds. J1811.1.1. Old maid answers owl's hoot, saying "Anybody, Lord!"

---

[1] Thousands of obscene motifs in which there is no point except the obscenity itself might logically come at this point, but they are entirely beyond the scope of the present work. They form a literature to themselves, with its own periodicals and collections. In view of the possibility that it might become desirable to classify these motifs and place them within the present index, space has been left from X700 to X749 for such motifs.

X751. *Marriage forbidden outside the parish.* An order is read in church forbidding the young people to marry girls from other parishes. *Type 1475.

X752. *The old maid in bed.* On one side is a bundle of straw (her husband) and on the other a dog (her child). She gives the straw bundle a push and thereupon falls on the floor herself. Type 1480*.

X753. *A youth promises to marry an old maid if she will sit all night on the roof.* She falls down. Type 1479*; Russian: Andrejev No. 1479*.

X754. *The meal of beans.* One of the old maid's three teeth breaks off. Type 1478.

X755. *The wolf steals the old maid.* She keeps him for a husband. Type 1477.

X756. *The mother trains the old maid to speak properly.* Absurd results. Types 1485*, 1486*.

H360. Bride test. K1984. Girls keep up appearances to deceive suitors as to their desirability. X131. The wry-mouthed family.

X760. Jokes on courtship.

H360. Bride test. K1984. Girls keep up appearances to deceive suitors as to their desirability. T50. Wooing.

X800—X899. Humor based on drunkenness.

X800. Humor based on drunkenness. Irish myth: *Cross; Icelandic: Boberg.

J1320. Repartee concerning drunkenness. J2311.10. Drunken man insists that he be beheaded.

X811. *Drunk man lying under his bed thinks he is lying in his shroud.* Is cured of drunkenness. Type 835*.

X812. *Drunk man goes to the king and wants to buy an island.* Type 1671*.

X813. *Drunk man at the wedding.* Goes to sleep and never reaches it, though at home he praises the wedding. Type 1705*.

X814. *Drunk men try to see one another home.* Absurd results. Pauli (ed. Bolte) No. 238.

X815. *Drunk man sees everything revolving and waits for his house to come to him.* *Wesselski Hodscha Nasreddin II 236 No. 520.

X816. *Drunk woman thinks she is in heaven.* Hears someone play the lyre. Italian Novella: Rotunda.

X818. *Drunk recruits make war on a haystack.* Italian Novella: Rotunda.

J2613. Surrender to the rake.

X821. *Drunken volunteer firemen bungle their work.* U.S.: Baughman.

X900—X1899. HUMOR OF LIES AND EXAGGERATION [1]

X900. Humor of lies and exaggeration. *Types 1875—1999; *Fb "løgn" II 513b; Irish myth: Cross.

F647. Marvelous sensitiveness. H342.1. Suitor test: forcing princess to say, "That is a lie."

X901. *One lie a year.* A man who tells but one lie a year is believed because of his general truthfulness. Amusing results. Chauvin V 278 No. 161; *BP II 371, 509; Köhler-Bolte I 322; India: Thompson-Balys; Africa (Vai): Ellis 239 No. 46.

---

[1] X900—X1099 has been reorganized as follows:

Old Number	New Number	Old Number	New Number
X900	X900	X961.7	X1235.4
X901	X901	X961.8	X1561
X905	X905	X961.9	X1547.2.1
X905.1	X905.1	X961.10	X1156.1
X910	X900	X961.11	X1267.2
X911	X1133.3	X961.12	X1855
X911.1	X1124.2	X961.13	X1244.1
X911.2	X1133.4	X961.14	X1252.1
X911.3	X1133.3.2	X961.15	X1294.1
X911.4	X1204.1	X961.16	X1226.1
X912	X1267.1	X961.17	X1727.1
X913	X1852	X961.18	X1856
X913.1	X1854.1	X961.19	X1215.12
X914	X1853	X961.20	X1241.2.3
X915	X1851	X961.21	X1244.2
X916	X1258.1	X961.22	X1235.5
X917	X1731.2.1	X961.23	X1208.2
X918	X1737.1.1	X961.24	X1741.4
X921	X1110	X961.25	X1342.3
X921.0.1	X1110.1	X961.26	X1857
X921.1	X1124.3	X961.27	X1472.1
X921.2	X1115.1	X961.28	X1858
X921.3	X1241.2.2	X961.29	X1739.2
X921.4	X1111	X961.30	X1856.1
X921.5	X1112	X961.31	X1856.2
X921.6	X1114.1	X961.32	X1242.0.1.1
X921.7	X1124.4	X961.33	X1791
X921.8	X1124.1	X961.34	X1344.1
X921.9	X1723.2	X961.35	X1345.1
X921.10	X1723.1.2	X961.36	X1211.1
X921.11	X1114	X961.37	X1256.1
X922	X1132.1	X1021	X1201
X923	X1130.2.1	X1021.1	X1237
X924	X1606.2.1	X1021.2	X1244.3
X925	X908	X1021.3	X1282.1
X926	X1204.2	X1021.4	X1233.1.2
X927	X1726.1	X1021.5	X1342.1.1
X927.1	X1726.2	X1021.6	X1241.1
X928	X1861	X1021.7	X1301
X931	X1233.4.1	X1022	X1150.1
X935	X1721.1	X1024	X1401
X936	X1216.1	X1024.1	X1423.1
X938	X1862	X1024.2	X1411.1
X941	J2349.4	X1024.3	X1424
X944	X1653.3	X1025	X1411
X950	X1503	X1025.1	X1411.4
X950.1	X1712	X1031	X1061.1
X950.2	X905.2	X1033	X1030.1
X950.3	X905.2	X1033.1	X1031
X951	X1506	X1033.2	X1036.1
X952	X1505	X1035	X1031.1.1
X953	X1863	X1036	X1813
X961.1	X1547.2	X1037	X1866
X961.2	X1757	X1038	X1811.1
X961.3	X1796.1	X1041	X920
X961.4	X1864	X1045	X1071
X961.5	X1528.1	X1049.1	X1296.1
X961.6	X1817.1	(Cross)	

X902. *Liar comes to believe his own lie.* He tells a lie so often that he believes it himself. (Cf. X611.) U.S.: Baughman.

X903. *Lie used as catch tale.* (Cf. Z13.) Type 2200; U.S.: Baughman.

X904. *The teller reduces the size of his lie.*

X904.1. *The liar reduces the size of his lie when his brother steps on his toes to remind him of his lying habits.* U.S.: *Baughman.

X904.2. *Liar reduces the size of his yarn when challenged.* U.S.: Baughman.

X905. *Lying contests.* Italian Novella: Rotunda; India: *Thompson-Balys; Japanese: Ikeda.

K455.7. Greatest liar to get his supper free. Wager. Each lie is corroborated by a confederate, who poses as a newly arrived stranger.

X905.1. *Master brought to say, "You lie!"* Type 1920C; Lithuanian: Balys Index No. 1920D*; Russian: Andrejev No. 1920D*; Prussian: Plenzat 78; Estonian: Aarne FFC XXV 119 No. 27; Livonian: Loorits FFC LXVI 51 No. 89; India: *Thompson-Balys.

H507.2. Test: making senseless remarks. K172. Anger bargain.

X905.2. *Greatest liar made king of Schlaraffenland.* (First ed. X950.3.) (Cf. X1503.) BP II 507.

X905.3. *Claim of property based on unusual lie.* India: Thompson-Balys.

X905.4. *The liar: "I have no time to lie today"; lies nevertheless.* Type 1920B; India: Thompson-Balys; Chinese: Eberhard FFC CXX 308ff. No. 18, FFC CXXVIII 260ff. No. 160.

X905.4.1. *Boy to deceive his uncle: induces uncle to climb tree before deception begins: this is the deception.* Chinese: Graham.

X905. *Would not lie for a trifle.* Liar tells of shooting large number of animals with one shot (an odd number, usually 99). When asked why he did not make it a round number (or an even hundred), he replies indignantly that he would not lie for one pigeon (rabbit). U.S.: *Baughman.

X907. *Man has servant corroborate his lies.* Rewards him poorly. Servant exposes him. Italian Novella: *Rotunda.

J2464. Servant to improve on master's statements.

X907.1. *The second liar corroborates the lie of the first.* Canada, U.S.: Baughman.

K451. Unjust umpire as trickster's confederate. K455.7. Greatest liar to get his supper free. M92. Decision left to first person to arrive.

X908. *Lie: sea has burned up.* (Often with answer: "Many fried fish.") (First ed. X925.) Type 1920A; *BP II 371; Fb "vesterhav" III 1042b, "å" III 1187b; Indonesian: DeVries Volksverhalen II 377.

X909. *Other stories about liars.*

X909.1. *The incorrigible liar.* U.S.: *Baughman.

X909.1.1. *Church member who has been called to task about his lying habits tells another lie in expressing his concern for his weakness.* He says he has shed barrels of tears because of his weakness. U.S.: *Baughman.

F1051.1. Barrel filled miraculously with penitent's tears.

X909.2. *The liar outdoes the tricksters who try to catch him in a lie.* He continues the lie the tricksters have made up to catch him. (Cf. K306, L142.1.) U.S.: Baughman.

X910—X1099. Lie: the remarkable man.

X910—X959. LIE: THE REMARKABLE MAN — HIS BIRTH, GROWTH, DEATH, PHYSICAL POWERS, STRENGTH

X910. Lie: the remarkable man. (Cf. F500—F599.) For bibliography of American hero material see Harold Felton Legends of Paul Bunyan (New York, 1947).

X911. *Lie concerning birth of hero.* U.S.: *Baughman.

X912. *Lie concerning babyhood and boyhood of hero.* England, U.S.: *Baughman.
F611.3.2. Hero's precocious strength.

X913. *Lie: death of extraordinary man.* U.S.: *Baughman.

X916. *Lie: persons with remarkable bodily parts.* U.S.: *Baughman.

X920. Lie: the large man. (First ed. X1041.) *Type 852; BP II 516.
F531. Giant. F610. Remarkably strong man.

X921. *Lie: remarkably tall person. England,* U.S.: *Baughman.
F533. Remarkably tall man. G152.1. Giant with tree for herding stick.

X922. *Lie: great weight of large person.* U.S.: *Baughman.

X923. *Lie: great girth of large person.* U.S.: *Baughman.

X924. *Lie: remarkably thin persons.* U.S.: *Baughman.

X930. Lie: remarkable person's physical powers and habits.

X931. *Lie: remarkable eater.* England, U.S.: *Baughman.
F531.3.4. Giant eats a prodigious amount. F632. Mighty eater. X1031. The great kitchen. X1032. The great dining quarters.

X932. *Lie: remarkable drinker.* (Cf. F633.) U.S.: *Baughman.

X933. *Lie: remarkable chewer.* U.S.: *Baughman.

X934. *Lie: remarkable spitter.* (Cf. F635.) Canada, U.S.: *Baughman.

X935. *Lie: remarkable blower.* (Cf. F622.) U.S.: *Baughman.

X936. *Lie: person with remarkable hearing.* (Cf. F641.) U.S.: *Baughman.

X937. *Lie: person with remarkable voice.* (Cf. F556.) U.S.: *Baughman.

X938. *Lie: person of remarkable sight.* (Cf. F642.) U.S.: *Baughman.

X939. *Lie: other motifs pertaining to extraordinary senses or bodily powers.* U.S.: *Baughman.

X940. Lie: remarkably strong man.

X941. *Remarkable lifter.* (Cf. F624.) Canada, England, U.S.: *Baughman.

X941.1. *Whole village lifted.* India: Thompson-Balys.

X941.2. *Fight on old woman's hand.* India: Thompson-Balys.

X941.3. *Elephant (camel) put in pocket as a curiosity to show friends.* India: Thompson-Balys.

X941.4. *Wind blows group of persons into woman's eye.* India: Thompson-Balys.

X942. *Lie: remarkable carrier.* (Cf. F631.) Canada, England, U.S.: *Baughman.

X942.1. *Lie: man ties up 700 camels in a corner of his sheet.* India: Thompson-Balys.

X943. *Lie: remarkable thrower.* (Cf. F636.) England, U.S.: *Baughman.

X943.1. *Beautiful girl seated on large lotus flower holding big elephant in each hand* which she devours and throws off alternately. India: Thompson-Balys.

X943.1.1. *Lie: child throws out elephant's carcass.* India: Thompson-Balys.

X944. *Lie: remarkable catcher.* U.S.: Baughman.

X945. *Lie: remarkable hitter or striker.* U.S.: *Baughman.

X946. *Lie: remarkable breaker.* (Cf. F625.) U.S.: *Baughman.

X947. *Lie: remarkable bender.* U.S.: *Baughman.

X948. *Lie: remarkable twister.* U.S.: *Baughman.

X951. *Lie: remarkable squeezer.* (Cf. X955.) U.S.: *Baughman.

X952. *Lie: remarkable pincher.* Hero marks logs by pinching a piece out of end of each one. U.S.: Baughman.

X953. *Lie: strong puller.* U.S.: *Baughman.

X953.1. *Man draws sixty (300) carts of wood.* India: Thompson-Balys.

X954. *Lie: remarkable pusher.* U.S.: *Baughman.

X955. *Lie: remarkable killer.* (Cf. X945.) U.S.: *Baughman.

X958. *Lie: hero responsible for topographical features (lakes, rivers, etc.).* (Cf. A901.) Canada, England, U.S.: *Baughman.

X959. *Lie: other strong physical reactions.*

X959.1. *Lie: hero breaking wen causes wall to fall down.* (Cf. D1562.3, F610.) Korean: Zong in-Sob 67 No. 37.

X960—X1019. LIE: REMARKABLE PERSON'S SKILLS

X960. Lie: remarkable person's skills.

X961. *Lie: extraordinary bodily skills.*

X964. *Lie: remarkable swimmer.* U.S.: *Baughman.

X965. *Lie: remarkable diver.* U.S.: Baughman.

X966. *Lie: remarkable jumper.* U.S.: Baughman.

X967. *Lie: remarkable kicker.* U.S.: *Baughman.

X971. *Lie: remarkable oarsman.* U.S.: *Baughman.

X972. *Lie: remarkable fighter.* U.S.: *Baughman.

X973. *Lie: remarkable wrestler.* U.S.: *Baughman.

X980. Lie: occupational or professional skill.

X1084. Lie: remarkable oil drilling operator. X1120. Lie: the great marksman.

X982. *Lie: remarkable smith.* (Cf. F663.) U.S.: *Baughman.

X983. *Lie: skillful flayer.* Man skins buffalo alive, turns them loose to grow new skins. (Cf. F664.1.) Type 654; U.S.: *Baughman.

X986. *Lie: skillful axe-man.* (Cf. F666.) Ireland, U.S.: *Baughman (X986 and X1796.3).

X986.1. *Axe of wax cuts jungle.* India: Thompson-Balys.

X987. *Lie: remarkable logger.* U.S.: *Baughman.

X991. *Lie: remarkable rock driller.* (John Henry.) Engages in contest with steam drill; he wins the contest but dies in the attempt. U.S.: *Baughman.

X994. *Lie: remarkable carpenter.* Ireland, U.S.: *Baughman.

X1001. *Lie: remarkable thresher.* U.S.: *Baughman.

X1002. *Lie: remarkable user of whip.* U.S.: Baughman.

X1003. *Lie: remarkable roper.* U.S.: *Baughman.

X1004. *Lie: remarkable rider.*

X1004.1. *Lie: man rides unusual riding animal (lion, deer, etc.).* (Cf. B557.) U.S.: *Baughman.

X1004.2. *Lie: man rides cyclone.* U.S.: *Baughman.

X1005. *Lie: remarkable cook.* U.S.: *Baughman.

X1031. The great kitchen.

X1010. Lie: remarkable mental skills.

X1011. *Lie: the great inventer.* U.S.: *Baughman.

X1012. *Lie: person displays remarkable ingenuity or resourcefulness.* U.S.: *Baughman.

X1012.1. *Lie: axes ground on boulders rolling down hill.* U.S.: *Baughman.

X1020—X1079. REMARKABLE MAN'S EXTRAORDINARY POSSESSIONS

X1020. Lie: remarkable possessions of remarkable man.

X1021. *Lie: remarkable clothing of remarkable man.* England, U.S.: *Baughman.

F820. Extraordinary clothing and ornaments.

X1021.1. *Lie: remarkable bouncing rubber boots (or the like).* U.S.: *Baughman.

X1022. *Lie: other extraordinary personal effects of remarkable person.* U.S.: *Baughman.

X1023. *Lie: extraordinary equipment of remarkable man.* U.S.: *Baughman.

X1024. *Lie: extraordinary tools of remarkable man.* U.S.: *Baughman.

X1025. *Lie: extraordinary machinery of remarkable man.* Canada, U.S.: *Baughman.

X1030. Lie: remarkable buildings. U.S.: *Baughman.

F770. Extraordinary buildings and furnishings.

X1030.1. *The great building.* (First ed. X1033.) Type 1960E.

X1031. *Lie: the great kitchen.* (First ed. X1033.1.) Chauvin VII 57 No. 77; U.S.: *Baughman, *Folk-Say I 62.

X1031.1. *Lie: remarkable equipment in big kitchen.* U.S.: *Baughman.

X1031.1.1. *Lie: The great kettle.* (First ed. X1035.) Type 1960F.

X1031.2. *Lie: help in big kitchen.* U.S.: *Baughman.

X1031.3. *Lie: remarkable cooking in big kitchen.* U.S.: *Baughman.

X1031.4. *Lie: remarkable baking in big kitchen.* Canada, U.S.: *Baughman.

X1031.4.1. *Lie: skating with bacon to grease griddle in big kitchen.* U.S.: *Baughman.

X1031.5. *Lie: other extraordinary foods from great kitchen.* U.S.: *Baughman.

X1031.6. *Lie: remarkable food preferences.* French loggers prefer pea soup for all three meals. U.S.: Baughman.

X1031.7. *Lie: extraordinary piles of garbage from great kitchen.* U.S.: *Baughman.

X1032. *Lie: the great dining quarters (Paul Bunyan tales).* U.S.: Baughman.

X1033. *Lie: the great bunkhouse.* U.S.: *Baughman.

X1035. *Lie: the great hotel.* U.S.: *Baughman.

X1036. *Lie: the great stable.* India: Thompson-Balys.

X1036.1. *Lie: the great stable: distance to stall.* Cow has calf and the calf grows up and has calf before it can reach its stall. (First ed. X1033.2.) Fb "stald" III 534a.

X1060. Lie: other possessions of remarkable man. (Cf. X1215 [dog], X1235 [cow], X1237 [ox]).

X1061. *Lie: great boat or ship of remarkable man.* (Cf. F861.)

X1061.1. *Remarkable size of great ship.* (First ed. X1031.) Type 1960H; BP II 516; U.S.: *Baughman.

X1070. Extraordinary man's family.

X1071. *The big wedding.* Giant with sixty daughters. (First ed. X1045.) Type 1961.

X1080. Lie: occupations of remarkable man. (Cf. X980.)

X1081. *Lie: remarkable logging operations.* U.S.: *Baughman.

X1082. *Lie: remarkable manufacturer.*

X1082.1. *Lie: remarkable sawmill operator.* U.S.: *Baughman.

X1082.2. *Lie: remarkable dairyman.* U.S.: Baughman.

X1083. *Lie: remarkable steel worker.* U.S.: Baughman.

X1084. *Lie: remarkable oil drilling operator.* U.S.: Baughman (X988 and X1084).

X1100—X1199. LIE: GREAT HUNTERS AND FISHERMEN

X1100. Lie: the remarkable hunter.

X1110. The wonderful hunt. (First ed. X921.) *Types 1890—1909; Wesselski Märchen 226f.; Indonesia: DeVries's list No. 312.

N620. Accidental success in hunting or fishing.

X1110.1. *The unlucky hunt.* (First ed. X921.0.1.) Indonesia: DeVries's list No. 313.

N300. Unlucky accidents.

X1111. *Hunter shoots ram-rod full of ducks.* (First ed. X921.4.) Type 1894.

X1112. *Hunter catches fish in boots while wading.* (First ed. X921.5.) Type 1895.

X1114. *Man lays bag by fencehole and all the hares run into it.* (First ed. X921.11.) Type 1893.

H1024.3. Task: chasing a hare into every trap in a high tree.

X1114.1. *Two hares run into each other and are caught.* (First ed. X921.6.) Type 1895*.

X1114.2. *Tiger lies in water with mouth open: cat drives fish in.* India: Thompson-Balys.

X1115. *Large bag of frozen raccoons taken by hunter.* (Cf. X1130.3.) U.S.: Baughman.

X1115.1. *The rabbit-catch: rabbits freeze feet fast to ice at night.* (First ed. X921.2.) Type 1891.

X1116. *The breathing tree.* Hunter cuts down tree packed full of animals. The tree is so full of animals that a crack in tree opens as animals inhale, closes when they exhale. U.S.: *Baughman.

X1119. *Miscellaneous stories of plentiful game.*

X1119.1. *Lie: thick flock of birds.* U.S.: Baughman.

X1119.2. *Lie: remarkable bag of deer.* U.S.: *Baughman.

X1120. Lie: the great marksman. (Cf. F661.) U.S.: Baughman (X1120 and X981).

X1121. *Lie: the great marksman's remarkable gun.* U.S.: *Baughman.

X1122. *Lie: hunter with remarkable marksmanship.*

X1122.1. *Lie: hunter shoots projectile great distance.* England: Baughman.

X1122.2. *Lie: person shoots many animals with one shot.* Canada, U.S.: *Baughman.

X1122.3. *Lie: ingenious person bends gun barrel to make spectacular shot.* Canada, U.S.: *Baughman.

X1124. *Lie: the hunter catches or kills game by ingenious or unorthodox method.* (Cf. X1132.) Canada, U.S.: *Baughman.

X1124.1. *Shooting off the leader's tail.* (First ed. X921.8.) An old blind bear is being led by a young bear, whose tail the old bear has in his mouth. The hunter shoots off the young bear's tail and seizes it. Thus leads the old bear home. Pauli (ed. Bolte) No. 748; U.S.: *Baughman.

X1124.2. *Hunter turns animal inside out.* He reaches down animal's throat, grasps his tail, and turns him inside out. (First ed. X911.1.) Wesselski Bebel II 137 No. 115; U.S.: *Baughman.

X1124.3. *Accidental discharge of gun kills much game.* Gun kills a bird which falls on loose limb of tree, which falls on bear, etc., etc. (First ed. X921.1.) Type 1890; American Negro (Georgia): Harris Friends 154 No. 21.

Z20. Cumulative tales.

X1124.3.1. *Gunshot splits limb and catches feet of birds.* Type 1890.

X1124.4. *Hunting wolves with rod and line.* (First ed. X921.7.) Type 1896*.

X1130. Lie: hunter's unusual experiences. Canada, U.S.: *Baughman.

X1130.1. *Game rolls down hill in snow;* snowball builds up around game, keeps it fresh and protected until used. U.S.: *Baughman.

X1130.2. *Fruit tree grows from head of deer shot with fruit pits.* Compare Münchhausen (1944) 32 (cherry tree). Canada, U.S.: *Baughman; India: Thompson-Balys.

X1130.2.1. *Tree grows out of horse and gives rider shade.* (First ed. X923.) Fb "træ" III 868a.

X1130.3. *Water of stream or lake freezes just as frogs jump into lake.* The frogs are caught in the ice. Canada, U.S.: *Baughman.

X1132. *Ingenious skinning of animal.*

X1132.1. *The nailed wolf's tail.* Wolf's tail nailed to tree. Wolf runs away and leaves his skin hanging. (First ed. X922.) Type 1896; U.S.: *Baughman.

X1133. *Lie: the hunter in danger.*

X1133.1. *Lie: man uses remarkable means of getting out of tree stump.* Type 1900; U.S.: *Baughman.

X1854. Man in hollow tree defends himself successfully from leopard and bear.

X1133.2. *Man escapes from bear by running for a long time, from summer to winter.* Bear chases man in July; he finally crosses a river on the ice. The bear falls in or stops following (in December). U.S.: *Baughman.

X1133.3. *Man in barrel grabs wolf by the tail and is drawn out of danger.* (First ed. X911.) *Type 1875; Köhler-Bolte I 410; *Fb "tønde" III 935a, "ræv" III 114a.

X1133.3.1. *Animal unwittingly puts tail into man's hands and is caught.* India: *Thompson-Balys.

X1133.3.2. *If the wolf's tail breaks.* Trickster and companion are wolf hunting. The companion goes into the wolf hole. The wolf comes. The other catches the wolf by the tail and the wolf scratches dust into the companion's eyes. "What a dust." — "If the wolf's tail breaks, you will see another kind of dust!" (First ed. X911.3.) Wesselski Hodscha Nasreddin I 216 No. 48; West Indies: Flowers 585.

X1133.4. *Man escapes from bee's nest on bear's tail.* (First ed. X911.2.) Type 1900.

X1133.5. *Tigers stand on each other's heads trying to reach man in tree.* His tears form a stream. India: Thompson-Balys.
J2133.6. Wolves climb on top of one another to tree.

X1150. Lies about fishing. (Cf. X1300.)

X1150.1. *The great catch of fish.* (First ed. X1022.) Type 1960C.

X1151. *Lie: large number of fishermen in one spot.* U.S.: Baughman.

X1153. *Lie: fish caught by remarkable trick.* U.S.: *Baughman.

X1154. *Lie: unusual catch by fisherman.*

X1154.1. *Fisherman catches fish with amazing contents.* Canada, U.S.: *Baughman.
N211.1. Lost ring found in fish.

X1154.1.1. *Man catches fish with larger fish inside.* U.S.: *Baughman.

X1156. *Lie: other unusual methods of catching fish.* U.S.: Baughman.

X1156.1. *Lie: fish caught with another's cries.* (First ed. X961.10.) Type 1930; BP III 244ff.

X1200—X1399. LIES ABOUT ANIMALS

X1200. Lie: remarkable animals. Types 1875—1910.

X1201. *Lie: the great animal.* (First ed. X1021.) Types 852, 1960A.
B31.6. Giant birds. B870. Giant animals.

X1202. *Lie: animals inherit acquired characteristics or conditions.* Canada, U.S.: *Baughman.

X1202.1. *Small cart serves as back legs for crippled sow.* Pigs also have these carts. U.S.: *Baughman.

X1203. *Lie: animal's food affects him in unusual way.* (E.g. Pine tops: milk good for cough syrup.) U.S.: *Baughman.

X1204. *Lie: animals eat one another up.* U.S.: *Baughman.

X1204.1. *Two wolves eat each other up so that only tails are left.* (First ed. X911.4.) *Fb "hale" IV 197b.

X1204.2. *Lie: two birds swallow each other.* (First ed. X926.) Africa (Vai): Ellis 239 No. 46.

X1205. *Lie: venom of animal (snake, hornet, bee) causes object to swell.* U.S.: *Baughman.

X1205.1. *Snake strikes object, causing it to swell.* Canada, U.S.: *Baughman.

B765.11. Snake's venom kills tree.

X1206. *Lies: animals trained to respond to certain sounds: absurd result.* U.S.: *Baughman.

X1208. *Animals already cooked for eating.*

X1208.1. *Roast pigs run around with knife and fork in back ready for eating.* U.S.: Baughman.

X1208.2. *Lie: roast hens fly, heads to sky, tails to ground.* (First ed. X961.23.) Type 1930; BP III 258.

X1210. Lies about mammals.

X1211. *Lies about cats.* U.S.: *Baughman.

X1211.1. *Lie: cat scratches out bear's tongue.* (First ed. X961.36.) Type 1930; BP III 244ff.

X1211.2. *Lie: crippled cat uses wooden leg to kill mice.* U.S.: *Baughman.

X1212. *Lies about wildcats.* U.S.: *Baughman.

X1213. *Lies about panthers.* U.S.: Baughman.

X1215. *Lies about dogs.* U.S.: *Baughman.

X1215.1. *Dog and other animal chase each other in hot weather.* Canada, U.S.: *Baughman.

X1215.2. *Lie: large dog.* U.S.: *Baughman.

X1215.3. *Lie: small dog.* U.S.: Baughman.

X1215.4. *Lie: weak dog.* U.S.: *Baughman.

X1215.5. *Lie: tough dog.* U.S.: Baughman.

X1215.6. *Lie: ferocious dog.* Canada, U.S.: *Baughman.

X1215.7. *Lie: fast dog.* U.S.: *Baughman.

X1215.8. *Lie: intelligent dog.* England, U.S.: *Baughman.

X1215.9. *Lie: obedient or dutiful dog.* U.S.: *Baughman.

X1215.10. *Lie: dog with remarkable scent.* U.S.: *Baughman.

X1215.11. *Lie: the split dog.* Put back together but back legs point upwards. Canada, England, U.S.: *Baughman.

X1215.12. *Lie: greyhounds drag mill out of water.* (First ed. X961.19.) Type 1930; BP III 244ff.

X1216. *Lies about wolves.* Canada, U.S.: *Baughman.

X1216.1. *The wolf harnessed.* Eats the horses, is harnessed and runs in the harness. (First ed. X936.) *Type 1910.

X1221. *Lies about bears.* Canada, U.S.: *Baughman.

X1224. *Lies about chipmunks.*

X1224.1. *Lie: the big chipmunk.* U.S.: *Baughman.

X1226. *Lies about mice.* U.S.: Baughman.

X1226.1. *Lie: mice consecrate bishop.* (First ed. X961.16.) Type 1930; BP III 244ff.

X1227. *Lies about rats.* U.S.: *Baughman.

X1233. *Lie: extraordinary hog.* Ireland, U.S.: *Baughman.

X1233.1. *Lie: large hog.*

X1233.1.1. *Lie: large boar has bristles as long as pitchfork tines.* England, Scotland: *Baughman; Lithuanian: Balys Index No. 1879*.

X1233.1.2. *The great wild-boar.* Tusks go through tree and come out on other side. (First ed. X1021.4.) *Wesselski Bebel II 137 No. 114.

X1233.2. *Lie: tough hog.*

X1233.2.1. *Hog finds dynamite supply, eats it, walks behind mule;* the mule kicks the hog. The explosion kills the mule, blows down the barn, breaks windows out of house. The hog is ill for several days. U.S.: *Baughman.

X1233.3. *Lies about thin hogs.* U.S.: *Baughman.

X1233.4. *Miscellaneous lies about hogs.*

X1233.4.1. *Lie: salesman guarantees sow to bear male, then female, then kid.* (First ed. X931.) Wienert FFC LVI 84 (ET 506), 104 (ST 167); Halm Aesop No. 11.

X1235. *Lie: remarkable cow.* U.S.: *Baughman.

X1235.1. *Large cow.* (Cf. B871.1.1.)

X1235.1.1. *Cow wears church bell for cowbell.* U.S.: *Baughman.

X1235.2. *Lie about cow's rich milk.* U.S.: *Baughman.

X1235.2.1. *Cow gives so much cream that several men do nothing but skim cream.* U.S.: *Baughman.

X1235.3. *Owner provides cow with green goggles, feeds her sawdust or snow.* U.S.: *Baughman.

X1235.4. *Lie: cow climbs to roof.* (First ed. X961.7.) Type 1930; BP III 258.

J1904. Absurd ignorance concerning place for animal to be kept.

X1235.5. *Lie: cow puts bread in oven.* (First ed. X961.22.) Type 1930; BP III 244ff.

X1237. *Lie: remarkable ox or steer.* (First ed. X1021.1.) U.S.: *Baughman, *Folk-Say I 62 (bibliography of "Paul Bunyan" stories).
B871.1.1.1. Giant ox.

X1237.1. *Lies about strong oxen.* U.S.: *Baughman.

X1237.1.1. *Man plows through stump which catches the back of his pants in cleft.* His oxen continue to pull; he holds onto the plow, pulls the stump out of the ground. U.S.: *Baughman.

X1237.2. *Lie: the remarkable blue ox.* U.S.: *Baughman.
B871.1.1.1. Giant ox.

X1241. *Lies about horses.* Canada, England, Scotland, U.S.: *Baughman.

X1241.1. *The great horse.* (First ed. X1021.6.) Fb "stud" III 619b.

X1241.2. *Well-trained horse.*

X1241.2.1. *Horse takes cattle out to pasture; brings them in by himself.* U.S.: Baughman.

X1241.2.2. *Trained horse as harvester and hunter.* He rolls in the field. Oats in his flanks; club in his tail kills birds. (First ed. X921.3.) (Cf. X1252.1.) Type 1892.

X1241.2.3. *Lie: horses knead dough.* (First ed. X961.20.) Type 1930; BP III 244ff.

X1242. *Lies about mules.* Canada, U.S.: *Baughman.

X1242.0.1. *Lies about asses.*

X1242.0.1.1. *Lie: ass with silver nose hunts hares.* (First ed. X961.32.) Type 1930; BP III 244ff.

X1243. *Lies about sheep.*

X1243.1. *Lie: the great Darby ram.* England: *Baughman.

X1244. *Lies about goats.*

X1244.1. *Lie: goat carries one hundred cartloads of grease.* (First ed. X961.13.) Type 1930; BP III 244ff.

X1244.2. *Lie: goats heat oven.* (First ed. X961.21.) Type 1930; BP III 244ff.

X1244.3. *The great he-goat.* (First ed. X1021.2.) BP II 515.

X1250. Lies about birds.

X1252. *Lies about crows.* U.S.: *Baughman.

X1252.1. *Lie: crows mow meadow.* (First ed. X961.14.) Type 1930; BP III 244ff.

X1256. *Lies about doves.* U.S.: Baughman.

X1256.1. *Lie: doves tear up wolf.* (First ed. X961.37.) Type 1930; BP III 244ff.

X1258. *Lies about geese.* U.S.: Baughman.

X1258.1. *Lie: man carried through air by geese.* (First ed. X916.) Type 1881; Japanese: Ikeda.

K1041. Borrowed feathers. Dupe lets himself be carried aloft by bird and dropped.

X1258.2. *Lie: the tough goose.* U.S.: Baughman.

X1261. *Remarkable ducks.* U.S.: *Baughman.

X1267. *Remarkable hawk.*

X1267.1. *Hawk flies away with geese on a line.* They have been tied together as a protection. (First ed. X912.) *Type 1876; BP III 337.

J681.1. Rat and frog tie paws together to cross marsh. Carried off by falcon.

X1267.2. *Lie: hawk swims.* (First ed. X961.11.) Type 1930; BP III 244ff.

X1280. Lies about insects.

X1280.1. *Lies about crossbreeding of insects.* U.S.: *Baughman.

X1280.1.1. *Bumblebees imported to rout mosquitoes; the two insects crossbreed and have stingers on both ends.* U.S.: *Baughman.

X1280.2. *Lies about ferocious insects.*

X1280.2.1. *Insects eat team of horses or mules, pitch horseshoes to see who gets what is left.* U.S.: *Baughman.

X1282. *Lies about bees.* Ireland, U.S.: *Baughman.

X1282.1. *Lie: the great bee.* Liar says that in a certain place bees are as big as sheep. — And the bee-hives? — The same as ours. — How do the bees get in? (Various answers.) (First ed. X1021.3.) BP II 515; *Wesselski Hodscha Nasreddin II 219.

X1285. *Lies about fleas.* U.S.: *Baughman.

X1286. *Remarkable mosquitoes.*

X1286.1. *Lie: the large mosquito.* North Carolina: Brown Collection I 703.

X1286.1.1. *Lie: wingspread of large mosquito.* U.S.: *Baughman.

X1286.1.2. *Lie: weight of large mosquito.* Canada, U.S.: *Baughman.

X1286.1.3. *Lie: mosquito's long bill.* U.S.: *Baughman.

X1286.1.4. *Large mosquitoes fly off with kettle.* They have drilled through kettle. Their bills are clinched inside like nails. U.S.: *Baughman.

X1286.1.5. *Large mosquitoes carry off prey.* U.S.: *Baughman.

X1286.1.6. *Big mosquito with golden palace in his mouth.* India: Thompson-Balys.

X1286.1.7. *Large mosquitoes—miscellaneous.* Canada, U.S.: *Baughman.

X1286.2. *Lies about ferocious mosquitoes.* U.S.: *Baughman.

X1287. *Lie: extraordinary fireflies.* U.S.: *Baughman.

X1288. *Lies about grasshoppers.* U.S.: *Baughman.

X1291. *Lies about bedbugs.* U.S.: *Baughman.

X1294. *Lies about flies.*

X1294.1. *Lie: flies build bridge.* (First ed. X961.15.) Type 1930; BP III 244ff.

X1295. *Lies about gnats.*

X1295.1. *The tragic death of the three gnats.* One of them meets his death between the horns of two struggling oxen, another because of two restless stallions, the third during a tussle between two giants. Lithuanian: Balys Index No. 291* (X1021.9).

X1296. *Lies about lice.*

X1296.1. *Rag so full of lice it can move.* Irish myth: *Cross (X1049.1).

X1300. Lies about fish. (Cf. X1150.)

X1301. *Lie: the great fish.* (First ed. X1021.7.) Type 1960B; England, U.S.: *Baughman.

B874. Giant fish.

X1303. *Lie: remarkable actions of big fish.*

X1303.1. *Big fish pulls man or boat.* (Cf. B551.1.) U.S.: *Baughman.

X1306. *Lie: tamed fish lives on dry land.* Canada, U.S.: *Baughman.

X1316. *Dogfish act like dogs.* U.S.: *Baughman.

X1317. *Crowded fish.* U.S.: *Baughman.

X1320. Lies about reptiles.

X1321. *Lies about snakes.*

B751.1. Snake swallows young. B752.2. Snake does not die before sunset. B765. Fanciful qualities of snakes. X1205.1. Snake strikes object, causing it to swell.

X1321.1. *Lie: the great snake.*

B875.1. Giant serpent. X1396.1. Sea serpent.

X1321.1.1. *Lie: remarkably long snake.* England, U.S.: *Baughman.

X1321.1.2. *Lie: great snake is thought to be a log.* U.S.: *Baughman.

J1761.1. Whale is thought to be an island.

X1321.2. *Lie: large number of snakes.* England, U.S.: *Baughman.

X1321.3. *Lies about remarkable kinds of snakes.*

X1321.3.1. *Lie: hoop snake.* Snake takes its tail in its mouth and rolls like a hoop toward its victim. (Cf. B765.1.) U.S.: *Baughman.

X1340. Lie: extraordinary amphibia and other animals.

X1342. *Lies about frogs.*

X1342.1. *Lie: the big frog.* U.S.: *Baughman.

X1342.1.1. *The great frog.* Eaten by one larger and this in turn by crow. (First ed. X1021.5.) *BP II 515.

X1342.2. *Ferocious frog.* U.S.: *Baughman.

X1342.3. *Lie: frog eats plowshare.* (First ed. X961.25.) (Cf. J1531.2.) Type 1930; BP III 258.

X1344. *Lies about crabs.* U.S.: *Baughman.

X1344.1. *Lie: crab hunts hare.* (First ed. X961.34.) Type 1930; BP III 258.

X1345. *Lies about snails.* U.S.: Baughman.

X1345.1. *Lie: snail kills lion.* (First ed. X961.35.) Type 1930; BP III 244ff.

X1346. *Lies about worms.* U.S.: *Baughman.

X1370. Lies about imaginary animals.

X1381. *Lie: the side-hill beast.* Animal with two short legs on one side for convenience in living on hillsides. It can walk around the hill in only one direction. U.S.: *Baughman; North Carolina: Brown Collection I 703.

B15.6. Animal with unusual legs or feet.

X1396. *Lie: imaginary snakes.* U.S.: *Baughman.

X1396.1. *Lie: seaserpent.* Canada, U.S.: *Baughman.

X1400—X1499. LIES ABOUT PLANTS, FRUITS, VEGETABLES, AND TREES

X1400. Lies about plants, fruits, vegetables, and trees.

F810. Extraordinary trees, plants, and fruits.

X1401. *Lie: the great vegetable.*

X1401.1. *Lie: animals live inside great vegetable, usually feeding from it.* Ireland, U.S.: *Baughman.

X1401.2. *Lie: harvesting great vegetable.* Canada, U.S.: *Baughman.

X1401.3. *Lie: hole from which great vegetable is removed.* U.S.: *Baughman.

X1402. *Lie about the fast-growing plants.*

D482.1. Transformation: stretching tree. F54.2. Plant grows to sky.

X1405. *Lie: plants produce fruit in remarkably short time after planting.* (Cf. F815.1, F811.13, F971.7.) U.S.: Baughman.

X1410. Lies about fruits. (Cf. X1402.1, X1405.)

X1411. *Lie: the large fruit.* U.S.: *Baughman.

X1411.1. *Lie: the great melon.* (First ed. X1024.2.) *BP II 516.

X1411.1.1. *Lie: large watermelon.* U.S.: *Baughman.

X1411.2. *Lies about large pumpkins.* U.S.: *Baughman.

X1411.3. *Lie: large pumpkin vine.* U.S.: *Baughman.

X1411.4. *Lie: the great pear.* (First ed. X1025.1.) Hdwb. d. Märchens I 256a n. 18.

X1420. Lies about vegetables.

X1423. *Lies about cabbages.* U.S.: *Baughman.

X1423.1. *Lie: the great cabbage.* (Usually matched by tale of great pot to put cabbage in.) (First ed. X1024.1.) *Type 1960D; *Wesselski Hodscha Nasreddin II 220 No. 454; Italian Novella: Rotunda. -

X1424. *The great mushroom.* (First ed. X1024.3.) Type 852; *BP II 516.

X1431. *Lies about turnips.* Type 1920A.

X1431.1. *Lies about big turnips.* U.S.: *Baughman.

X1435. *Lies about potatoes.* U.S.: Baughman.

X1435.1. *Lie: large potatoes.* Canada, U.S.: *Baughman.

X1450. Lies about field crops.

X1455. *Lies about corn (maise).*

X1455.1. *Lie: remarkable cornstalks.* U.S.: *Baughman.

X1455.2. *Lie: remarkable yield of corn.* U.S.: *Baughman.

X1470. Lies about trees.

F810. Extraordinary trees, plants, fruits, etc.

X1471. *Lies about large trees.* (Cf. F811.14.) U.S.: *Baughman.

X1472. *Lie: tree bears unusual fruit.*

X1472.1. *Lie: pancakes growing on lime-tree.* (First ed. X961.27.) Type 1930; BP III 244ff.

X1480. Lies about flowers.

X1481. *Lie: remarkable lilies.* U.S.: Baughman.

X1490. Lie: miscellaneous plant motifs. U.S.: *Baughman.

X1495. *Lie: man raises eggs from eggplant.* U.S.: *Baughman.

X1500—X1599. LIES ABOUT GEOGRAPHY AND TOPOGRAPHY

X1500. Lies about geography and topography.

A901. Topographical features caused by experiences of primitive hero.

X1503. *Schlaraffenland.* (Land of Cockaygne.) Land in which impossible things happen. (First ed. X950.) (Cf. X1712.) *Type 1930; *BP III 244ff.; Boccaccio Decameron VIII No. 3 (Lee 254); Irish myth: Cross; Italian Novella: *Rotunda; India: Thompson-Balys.

F0. Journey to other world. F111. Journey to earthly paradise. F701. Land of plenty. H1010. Impossible tasks.

X1503.1. *Land in which highest praise parents can earn is that they marry their children when they are babies.* India: Thompson-Balys.

X1503.2. *Blind town, its king fourfold blind.* India: Thompson-Balys.

X1503.3. *Lie: land where all things are sold for the same price.* India: Thompson-Balys.

X1503.4. *Mountain of grain to be eaten through on way to Schlaraffenland.* (First ed. X950.2.) (Cf. X1712.) BP III 250.

D791.1.2. Disenchantment when superhuman task is finished. Enchanted person appears every seven years in human form and puts one stitch in a smock. When it is finished, she will be delivered. H701. Riddle: how many seconds in eternity? H1583. Tests of time. Z61. Never. Various ways of expressing this idea. When black sheep turn white, when a dry branch sprouts, etc.

X1505. *Topsy-turvy land. Land where all is opposite from the usual.* (First ed. X952.) BP III 244ff., *254ff.; Wienert FFC LVI 44ff.

E489.2. Life in land of dead contrary to ours. F811.15. Upside-down tree. Branches in ground, roots in air. P617. People weep when child is born.

X1505.1. *House where omens go by contraries.* India: Thompson-Balys.

X1506. *The extraordinary names.* A place where animals and things are designated by senseless names. (First ed. X951.) (Cf. Z32.2.1.) Type 1940; BP IV 183; Bolte Zs. f. Vksk. XXVII 135; Wisser ibid. XXVIII 135; West Indies: Flowers 585.

X1510. Lies about land features.

X1520. Lies about mountains and hills.

X1521. *Remarkably narrow valleys.* U.S.: Baughman.

X1523. *Lies about steep slopes of mountains.* U.S.: *Baughman.

X1523.1. *Lie: country so steep that people look up chimney to see when the cows come home.* U.S.: *Baughman.

X1523.2. *Lies about farming on steep mountain.* U.S.: *Baughman.

X1526. *Lies about mountain roads.* U.S.: Baughman.

X1526.1. *Crooked railroads in mountains or hills.* (Cf. X1815.) U.S.: *Baughman.

X1528. *Mountain of unusual material.*

X1528.1. *Lie: mountain of cheese.* (First ed. X961.5.) Type 1930; BP III 258.

F771.1.10. Gingerbread house. House made of cake. X1503.4. Mountain of grain to be eaten through on way to Schlaraffenland. X1863. Why gypsies have no churches. They ate up their churches made of cheese and bacon.

X1530. Lies about remarkable soil.

X1532. *Rich soil produces remarkable crop.* U.S.: *Baughman.

X1532.1. *Rich land: corn grows so fast that it pulls up its own roots.* U.S.: *Baughman.

X1540. Lies about water features.

X1543. *Lies about hot springs.* U.S.: Baughman.

X1545. *Lies about remarkable underground channels.*

F715.3. Rivers with marvelous underground connections.

X1545.1. *Water passage through the earth.* U.S.: *Baughman.

X1546. *Remarkable pond.*

X1546.1. *Lie: fish pond supplies both fresh fish and cooked.* Italian Novella: Rotunda (X925.1).

X1547. *Lie: remarkable river.*

X1547.1. *Lie: round river: runs in circle without outlet.* U.S.: *Baughman.

X1547.2. *Lie: river of honey.* (First ed. X961.1). Type 852; BP II 515.

X1547.2.1. *Lie: honey flows up high mountain.* (First ed. X961.9.) Type 1930; BP III 244ff.

X1550. Geography and topography—miscellaneous motifs.

X1551. *Remarkable road.*

X1551.1. *Roads go over roofs of houses.* India: Thompson-Balys.

X1560. Lies about cities.

X1561. *Lie: Rome hanging by thread.* (First ed. X961.8.) Type 1930; BP III 244ff.

X1563. *City into which only married and mothers may enter.* India: Thompson-Balys.

X1564. *Village where rubies sell for four pice apiece.* India: Thompson-Balys.

X1600—X1699. LIES ABOUT WEATHER AND CLIMATE

X1600. Lies about weather and climate.

X1602. *Lie: year with two summers and no winter.* Canada: Baughman.
D2145.2.1. Summer magically lengthened.

X1603. *Lie: year with two winters and no summer.* It is winter all summer and in fall it gets colder. Canada, U.S.: *Baughman.

X1605. *Lie: mixed weather: summer in one spot and winter in another nearby.* Canada, U.S.: *Baughman.
D2145.1.1. Local winter.

X1606. *Lies about changes in weather.*

X1606.1. *Lies about quick change from cold to warm.* Canada, U.S.: *Baughman.

X1606.2. *Lies about quick change in weather from warm to cold.* U.S.: *Baughman.

X1606.2.1. *Man freezes to saddle.* Must be thawed out by the stove. (First ed. X924.) Pauli (ed. Bolte) No. 746.

X1610. Lies about winds and storms.

X1611. *Lies about the wind.* Canada, U.S.: *Baughman.

X1611.1. *Lies about big wind (cyclone, tornado).* Canada, U.S.: *Baughman.

X1620. Lies about cold weather. U.S.: *Baughman.

X1623. *Lies about freezing.* (Cf. X1606.2.1.) U.S.: *Baughman.

X1623.1. *Lie: shadow freezes.* Canada, U.S.: *Baughman.

X1623.2. *Lie: words freeze.* Canada, U.S.: *Baughman.

X1623.2.1. *Lie: frozen words thaw out in the spring.* Canada, U.S.: *Baughman.

X1623.3. *Lie: flame freezes: startling results.* U.S.: *Baughman.

X1630. Lies about hot weather. U.S.: *Baughman.

X1633. *Lie: effect of heat on animals.*

X1633.1. *Lie: weather so hot that corn pops in fields, animals freeze to death thinking it has snowed.* U.S.: *Baughman.

X1640. Lies about dry weather.

X1642. *Lie: clouds beaten by man until they promise to water his crops thrice daily.* India: Thompson-Balys.

X1643. *Lie: how dry weather affects animals.* Canada, U.S.: *Baughman.

X1643.1. *Lie: bullfrogs several years old cannot swim — have never had water to learn in.* Canada, U.S.: *Baughman.

X1650. Lies about precipitation and dampness.
F962. Extraordinary precipitation.

X1651. *Lies about fog.* U.S.: *Baughman.

X1651.1. *Lie: shingling the fog.* Man shingling building during thick fog shingles several feet of fog when he gets beyond the roof line. U.S.: *Baughman.

X1651.2. *Ship sails on thick fog.* U.S.: *Baughman.

X1653. *Lies about snow.*

X1653.1. *Lie: fast-melting snow leaves horse dangling in air.* U.S.: *Baughman.

X1653.2. *Lie: blue snow.* Canada, U.S.: *Baughman.

X1653.3. *The man who sold dried snow for salt.* (First ed. X944.) Pauli (ed. Bolte) No. 747.

X1654. *Lies about rain.*

X1654.1. *Lie: dry rain.* U.S.: *Baughman.

X1654.2. *Lie: extraordinary floods produced by heavy rain.* U.S.: *Baughman.

X1654.2.1. *Lie: heavy rain of boiling water melts palace.* India: Thompson-Balys.

X1655. *Lies about extraordinary mud.* Canada, U.S.: *Baughman.

X1655.1. *Lie: the man under the hat, which is the only thing seen above the mud.* England, U.S.: *Baughman.

X1660. Lies about climate.
J2214.12. False judgment of distance in clear atmosphere of mountain area.

X1663. *Lies about healthy atmosphere.*

X1663.1. *Lie: air from healthy climate revives dying person.* U.S.: *Baughman.

X1663.2. *Lie: place so healthful that residents shoot man to start cemetery.* Canada, U.S.: *Baughman.

X1700—X1799. LIES: LOGICAL ABSURDITIES

X1700. Lies: logical absurdities. (Cf. J2200.)

X1710. Lies about numbers.

J2213. Illogical use of numbers.

X1712. *Schlaraffenland lies three miles beyond Christmas.* (First ed. X950.1.) BP III 250.

X1720. Absurd disregard of anatomy. (Cf. X1202, X1203, X1204.)

J1910. Fatal disregard of anatomy.

X1721. *Lies about surgical operations.*

F668.1. Skillful surgeon removes and replaces vital organs.

X1721.1. *New backbone for the horse made from a stick.* (First ed. X935.) Type 1911**.

X1721.2. *Lie: man's organs replaced with animal's* (Cf. E782.) He acts like animal. Type 660; U.S.: *Baughman.

X1723. *Lies about swallowing.* (Cf. F910.)

X1723.1. *Swallowed person is discovered in animal's stomach still alive.* U.S.: *Baughman.

F913. Victim rescued from swallower's body.

X1723.1.1. *Fish swallows a gourd fruit where people have taken refuge during rain;* hawk swallows fish. India: Thompson-Balys.

X1723.1.2. *Lie: man swallowed by fish and later rescued alive.* (First ed. X921.10.) Wesselski Bebel II 137 No. 113.

F913. Victims rescued from swallower's belly.

X1723.2. *Falcon and heron eaten by wild boar recovered alive from his body.* (First ed. X921.9.) Wesselski Bebel II 138 No. 116.

X1723.3. *Person enters animal's body.* U.S.: Baughman.

X1723.3.1. *Man crawls into body of animal (after killing it) to escape cold.* The animal freezes back together; man must eat his way out. U.S.: *Baughman.

X1724. *Seeing without eyes.* India: Thompson-Balys.

X1725. *Digging without hands.* India: Thompson-Balys.

X1726. *Man cuts off own head.*

X1726.1. *Lie: man cuts off own head and eats it.* (First ed. X927.) Africa (Vai): Ellis 239 No. 46.

X1726.2. *Man cuts off own head, picks it up and replaces it.* (First ed. X927.1.) (Cf. E783.) Type 852; BP II 514; Missouri French: Carrière.

X1727. *Absurd stories about beards.*

X1727.1. *Lie: barber shaves wife's beard.* (First ed. X961.17.) Type 1930; BP III 244ff.

J2082. Squaring accounts by shaving the wife. A numskull has paid twice the regular amount for a shave. The barber shaves the wife.

X1731. *Lies about falling.*

X1731.1. *Person falls from great height without injury.* U.S.: *Baughman.

X1731.2. *Man falls from height, goes into solid rock up to knees.* Ireland, U.S.: *Baughman.

X1731.2.1. *Man falls and is buried in earth: goes for spade and digs self out.* (First ed. X917.) *Type 1882; Köhler-Bolte I 323; Gardner JAFL XXVII 305; U.S.: *Baughman.

X1733. *Lies about sinking.*

X1733.1. *Lie: man lifts heavy load, sinks into solid rock.* U.S.: *Baughman.

X1737. *Man stays under water for long time.*

X1737.1. *Man falls through ice, has to swim two miles to come out at an air hole.* U.S.: *Baughman.

X1737.1.1. *Man under the ice.* Falls through ice with his horse, wanders around on the river bottom, pushes his spear through ice from below and rises to the surface. (First ed. X918.) *Wesselski Bebel I 171 No. 8.

X1739. *Absurd disregard of anatomy—miscellaneous.* U.S.: *Baughman.

X1739.1. *Person swallows pin or needle; it later emerges through skin of relative.* England, U.S.: *Baughman.

X1739.2. *Lie: man makes drinking water from his own skull.* (First ed. X961.29.) Type 852; BP II 514.

X1740. Absurd disregard of natural laws.

X1741. *Lies about gravitation.*

X1741.1. *Person or animal rises into the air in defiance of gravity.* (Cf. D2135.0.1.) U.S.: *Baughman.

X1741.2. *Person or animal jumps back to starting place (from midair).* U.S.: *Baughman.

X1741.3. *Law of gravity is petrified in petrified forest.* U.S.: *Baughman.

X1741.4. *Lie: anvil swims river.* (First ed. X961.24.) Type 1930; BP III 258.

X1743. *Lies about occupying space.*

X1743.1. *Giants go through small hole where plant has been torn from earth.* India: Thompson-Balys.

X1743.2. *Lie: two bullocks go where one cannot.* India: Thompson-Balys.

X1743.3. *Lie: 900,000 roofs on point of needle.* India: Thompson-Balys.

X1750. Absurd disregard of the nature of objects. U.S.: *Baughman.

X1755. *Lies about watches.*

X1755.1. *Watch continues to run indefinitely when lost (swallowed).* Canada, U.S.: *Baughman.

X1756. *Disregard of nature of basketry.*

X1756.1. *Lie: people carry wine in baskets.* Italian Novella: Rotunda (X961.38).

X1757. *Rope of sand (chaff).* (First ed. X961.2.) (Cf. F843.) Type 852; BP II 513; Missouri French: Carrière.

H1021.2. Task: making a rope of chaff.

X1757.1. *Rope of dry dust.* India: *Thompson-Balys.

X1760. Absurd disregard of the nature of non-material things.

X1761. *Absurd disregard of the nature of holes.* U.S.: *Baughman.

X1761.1. *Person pulls up old oil wells and sells them for post holes after sawing them up into short lengths.* U.S.: *Baughman.

X1761.2. *Lie: people eat the bungholes from barrels.* Italian Novella: Rotunda (X961.39).

X1780. Absurdity based on the nature of the object.

X1781. *Lies about boats with light draft.* U.S.: *Baughman.

X1781.1. *Boat sailing over dry river bed (rice water).* India: *Thompson-Balys.

X1785. *Lies about stretching or shrinking.* U.S.: *Baughman.

X1785.1. *Lie: the stretching and shrinking harness.* Man driving team with wagon uphill in rain finds on arrival at the top of the hill that the tugs of rawhide or buckskin have stretched and that the loaded wagon is still at the bottom of the hill. He unhitches the horses and throws the harness across a stump. Sometime later, or the next morning, the sun comes out and shrinks the tugs, drawing the load to the top of the hill. Canada, U.S.: *Baughman.

X1787. *Man cures rheumatism: puts mosquito milk in a cat's horn, stirs it with duck's crotch.* U.S.: Baughman.

X1788. *Lie: the realistic painting.* (Cf. H504.1.) U.S.: *Baughman.

X1790. Other logical absurdities. U.S.: *Baughman.

X1791. *Lie: deaf, dumb, blind, and lame men catch hare.* (First ed. X961.33.) Type 1930; BP III 116, 258.

X1796. *Lies concerning speed.*

X1796.1. *Lie: footless man outruns swift horse.* (First ed. X961.3.) Type 1930; BP III 244ff.

X1800—X1899. MISCELLANEOUS LIES AND EXAGGERATIONS

X1800. Miscellaneous lies and exaggerations.

X1810. Tall tales about miscellaneous objects.

X1811. *Lies about loaves of bread.*

X1811.1. *Lie: the great loaf of bread.* (First ed. X1038.) Type 1960K.

X1813. *Lie: the great egg.* (First ed. X1036.) (Cf. B31.1.1.) *Fb "æg" III 1142a; U.S.: Baughman; India: Thompson-Balys.

X1815. *Lie: remarkable railroad.*
X1526.1. Crooked railroad.

X1815.1. *Lie about rough railroad.* U.S.: *Baughman.

X1815.2. *Lies about slow trains.* Canada, U.S.: *Baughman.

X1817. *Lies about bridges.* (Cf. F842.)

X1817.1. *Lie: razor-sharp sword as footbridge.* (First ed. X961.6.) Type 1930; BP III 244ff.

X1850. Other tall tales.

X1851. *Man in moon lets himself down.* (First ed. X915.) (Cf. A751.) Fb "måne" II 660a.

X1852. *Boy shot from a cannon.* (First ed. X913.) Type 1880; Fb "kanon" II 87.

X1853. *Boy with hat of butter, clothes of paper, etc.* (First ed. X914.) *Type 1880.

X1854. *Man in hollow tree defends himself successfully from leopard and bear.* India: Thompson-Balys.
X1133.1. Lie: man uses remarkable means of getting out of tree stump.

X1854.1. *The boy in the hollow tree.* He frightens the woodchopper who leaves behind his horse. (First ed. X913.1.) Type 1877*; Russian: Andrejev No. 1877*.

X1855. *Lie: plow without horse or wheels.* (First ed. X961.12.) Type 1930; BP III 244ff.

X1856. *Lie: suckling children rock mother in cradle.* (First ed. X961.18.) Type 1930; BP III 244ff.

X1856.1. *Lie: child throws down a kid.* (First ed. X961.30.) Type 1930; BP III 244ff.

X1856.2. *Lie: child throws down mill-wheels from one town to another.* (First ed. X961.31.) Type 1930; BP III 244ff.

X1857. *Lie: man drowned on mountain.* (First ed. X961.26.) Type 1930; BP III 258.

X1858. *Lie: man cuts ice with own head.* (First ed. X961.28.) Type 852; BP II 514.

X1861. *Lie: the hunt for the lost bee.* (First ed. X928.) Köhler-Bolte I 323.
H1371. Impossible quests.

X1862. *The over-hasty toad (beetle).* Is years ascending steps. On last step falls and curses haste. (First ed. X938.) Spanish: Boggs FFC XC 38 No. 288C*, Espinosa Jr. Nos. 59, 60; West Indies: Flowers 585.

X1863. *Why gypsies have no churches.* They ate up their churches made of cheese and bacon. (First ed. X953.) (Cf. X650.) Bolte Zs. f. Vksk. IX 85.

X1864. *Lie: warrior whose horse is cut in two continues to ride on the half horse.* (First ed. X961.4.) Wesselski Bebel II 108 No. 25.

X1866. *Lie: the great noise from the bass-viol.* (First ed. X1037.) BP II 516.

Z. MISCELLANEOUS GROUPS OF MOTIFS

DETAILED SYNOPSIS

Z. MISCELLANEOUS GROUPS OF MOTIFS

Z0—Z99. Formulas.

Z0. Formulas.

R255. Formula for girl fleeing: Behind me night, etc. "Behind me night and before me day that no one shall see where I go."

Z10. Formulistic framework for tales. *Hdwb. d. Märchens s.v. "Formel"; Irish myth: *Cross; India: *Thompson-Balys.

J1185.1. Sheherezade: story with indefinite sequels told to stave off execution. P331. Refusal to receive proffered help until series of stories has been told.

Z10.1. *Beginning formulas.* *Hdwb. d. Märchens II 161; *BP IV 14ff.; Korean: Zong in-Sob 14 No. 7.

Z10.2. *End formulas.* *BP IV 24ff.; Hdwb. d. Märchens II 164; *Petsch Formelhafte Schlüsse im Volksmärchen (1900); India: *Thompson-Balys.

Z10.3. *Transition formulas.* Hdwb. d. Märchens II 162; BP IV 20ff.

Z11. *Endless tales.* Hundreds of sheep to be carried over stream one at a time, etc. The wording of the tale so arranged as to continue indefinitely. *Type 2300; *BP II 209; Taylor Hdwb. d. Märchens II 190a; Irish myth: *Cross; Spanish Exempla: Keller; Italian Novella: *Rotunda; India: *Thompson-Balys.

H701.1. How many seconds in eternity? A bird carries a grain of sand from a mountain each century; when the whole mountain is gone, the first second of eternity has passed. H1111. Task: carrying hundreds of sheep across stream one at a time.

Z11.1. *Endless tale: corn carried away grain at a time.* England, U.S.: *Baughman.

Z11.2. *Endless tale: hundreds of birds in snare fly away one at a time.* India: Thompson-Balys.

Z12. *Unfinished tales.* Just as the interest is aroused the narrator quits. "If the bowl had been stronger my tale had been longer." *Types 2250, 2260; BP II 210, III 455; Taylor Hdwb. d. Märchens II 189b; Köhler-Bolte I 269.

Z13. *Catch tales.* The manner of the telling forces the hearer to ask a particular question, to which the teller returns a ridiculous answer. Type 2200; England, U.S., Canada: *Baughman; West Indies: Flowers 586.

Z13.1. *Tale-teller frightens listener: yells "Boo" at exciting point.* Type 366; Canada, England, U.S.: *Baughman.

Z13.2. *Catch tale: teller is killed in his own story.* Canada, U.S.: *Baughman.

Z14. *"Runs."* Conventional passages of set form within a tale, usually recited in a different voice from the rest. *Hdwb. d. Märchens II 163; *Campbell-McKay 233ff.; India: *Thompson-Balys.

Z15. *Tale avoiding all pronouns.* Lang English Fairy Tales 118.

Z16. *Tales ending with a question.* *Type 653; *BP III 45; Basset RTP VII 188; Cosquin Revue d'Ethnographie et des Traditions Populaires I 62, II 41; Africa: Werner African 359.

Z16.1. *Four brothers construct a woman.* Whose is she? India: Thompson-Balys.

Z17. *Rounds.* Stories which begin over and over again and repeat. Type 2350; Taylor JAFL XLVI 88, Hdwb. d. Märchens II 190; U.S.: Baughman; Lithuanian: Balys Index No. 2300; India: Thompson-Balys.

Z49.4. There was once a woman; the woman had a son; the son had red breeches; etc. — At last: "Shall I tell it again?"

Z18. *Formulistic conversations.*

Z18.1. *What makes your ears so big?* — To hear the better, my child, etc. Type 333.

Z19. *Formulistic frameworks—miscellaneous.*

Z19.1. *Game-tales.* (Used as game.) *BP II 210.

Z19.2. *Tales filled with contradictions.* West Indies: Flowers 587.

Z20—Z59. CUMULATIVE TALES

Z20. Cumulative tales.[1] Tales arranged in chains. (Kettenmärchen.) **Taylor JAFL XLVI 77ff.; *Types 2000—2199; Irish myth: *Cross; Spanish American: Boas JAFL XXV 219ff., 252f., Espinosa JAFL XXVII 222ff.; Indonesia: DeVries's list No. 316; cf. Nouvelles de Sens No. 31.

F571.2. Sending to the older. Old person refers enquirer to his father, who refers to his father, and so on for several generations. H602. Symbolic meaning of numbers one to seven (ten, twelve). E. g. one: sun; two: Moses'

1 Z20—Z59 has been reorganized as follows:

Old Number	New Number	Old Number	New Number
Z21	Z21	Z31.4	Z39
Z21.1	Z21.1	Z31.4.1	Z39.1
Z21.2	Z22	Z31.4.2	Z39.2
Z21.2.1	Z22.1	Z31.4.3	Z39.3
Z21.2.2	Z22.2	Z31.4.4	Z39.4
Z21.3	Z23	Z41	Z40
Z21.3.1	Z53	Z41.1	Z41
Z21.4	Z24	Z41.1.1	Z41.1
Z21.4.1	Z24.1	Z41.1.2	Z41.2
Z21.4.1.1	Z24.1.1	Z41.2	Z42
Z21.4.1.2	Z24.1.2	Z41.2.1	Z42.1
Z21.4.1.3	Z24.1.3	Z41.2.2	Z42.2
Z23	Z51	Z41.3	Z43
Z23.1	Z51.1	Z41.3.1	Z43.1
Z31	Z30	Z41.4	Z43.3
Z31.1	Z31	Z41.5	Z41.4
Z31.1.1	Z31.1	Z41.5.1	Z41.4.1
Z31.1.2	Z31.2	Z41.5.2	Z41.4.2
Z31.2	Z32	Z41.6	Z44
Z31.2.1	Z32.1	Z41.6.1	Z44.1
Z31.2.1.1	Z32.1.1	Z41.7	Z49.1
Z31.2.2	Z32.2	Z41.8	Z49.2
Z31.2.2.1	Z32.2.1	Z41.9	Z45
Z31.2.3	Z32.3	Z41.10	Z46
Z31.3	Z33	Z41.11	Z49.3
Z31.3.1	Z33.1	Z41.12	Z49.4
Z31.3.2	Z33.2	Z41.13	Z49.5
Z31.3.3	Z33.3	Z41.14	Z49.6
Z31.3.4	Z33.4		

tablets; three: three Marys; etc. H941. Cumulative tasks. Second assigned so that first can be done. H1235. Series of helpers on quest. One helper sends to another, who sends to another, etc. H1241. Series of quests. One quest can be accomplished when a second is finished, etc. J52. King observes retaliation among animals: becomes just. Dog breaks fox's foot; man breaks dog's; horse breaks man's leg; horse steps in hole and breaks his. J2233. Logically absurd defenses. Thief brought to judgment for breaking into house blames mason for building poor house. Mason blames maker of mortar, who blames potter, who blames pretty woman who diverted his attention. She blames goldsmith who caused her to go for her earrings. Goldsmith has no one to blame but he is too old to make a good execution. Hence a shopkeeper across the way is convicted. J1173. Series of clever unjust decisions. J2198. Bewailing a calamity that has not occurred. J2461. What should I have done (said)? The mother teaches the boy (the man his wife) what he should say (do) in this or that circumstance. He uses the words in the most impossible cases and is always punished. K1024. Beginning with the smallest. Animals are to eat one another up to avoid starvation. The fox persuades them to start with the smallest. N261. Train of troubles from sparrow's vengeance. N381. Drop of honey causes chain of accidents. Hunter drops honey in a grocery; weasel eats honey; cat chases weasel; dog chases cat; grocer kills dog; all the cause of a bloody feud between villages. Q401. Chain of punishments. X1124.3. Accidental discharge of gun kills much game. Gun kills a bird, which falls on loose limb of tree, which falls on bear, etc.

Z20.1. *Cumulative nonsense tales.* India: Thompson-Balys.

Z21. *Chains based on numbers.*

Z21.1. *Origin of chess.* Inventor asks one wheat-grain for first square, two for the second, four for the third, eight for the fourth, etc. The king cannot pay. **Taylor JAFL XLVI 79 No. 2009; *Livingston MLN XLV 246—51; Murray History of Chess (Oxford, 1913) 207—9, 755; India: Thompson-Balys.

F613.2. Strong man's labor contract: all the grain he can carry. K256. Deceptive wages. K1732. Wages: as much as he can carry.

Z21.1.1. *Wages: successive harvests from one grain of rice.* Master has no fields left. Chinese: Graham.

Z22. *Ehod mi yodea (One; who knows?);* Le dodici parole della verità, Las doce palabras retorneadas. The numbers from one to twelve are brought into relation with various objects, often of religious significance. **Espinosa Revista de Filologia Española XVII 390ff.; *Taylor JAFL XLVI 79 No. 2010; *Greenleaf Ballads and Sea-songs of Newfoundland (Cambridge, Mass., 1933) 93 No. 41; **Hdwb. d. Märchens II 171ff.; *Newell "The Carol of the Twelve Numbers" JAFL IV (1891) 215—220; Köhler-Bolte III 370 n. 2; BP III 15 n. — Lithuanian: Balys Index No. 2010*; Russian: Andrejev No. 812B*; Spanish: Boggs FFC XC 156 No. 2045*; Jewish: *Neuman.

H602. Symbolic meaning of numbers one to seven (ten, twelve).

Z22.1. *The Twelve Days (Gifts) of Christmas:* 1 partridge, 2 turtle-doves, 3 French hens, 4 colly birds, 5 gold rings, 6 geese, 7 swans, 8 maids, 9 drummers, 10 pipers, 11 ladies, 12 lords. **Taylor JAFL XLVI 79 No. 2010A, Hdwb. d. Märchens II 172b; Kristensen Danske Dyrefabler 146—60 Nos. 337—348; Fb "Juledagsgave" I 54, IV 248; T. Norlind Svenska Allmogens Liv^2 612.

Z22.2. *The Twelve kinds of Food:* 1 partridge, 2 turtledoves, 3 woodpigeons, 4 ducks, 5 rabbits, 6 hares, 7 hounds, 8 sheep, 9 oxen, 10 turkeys, 11 hams, 12 cheeses. **Taylor JAFL XLVI 80 No. 2010B, Hdwb. d. Märchens II 172b; Kristensen Danske Dyrefabler 150—54 Nos. 351—370.

Z23. *How the Rich Man paid his Servant* (Lönen hos den rike man). A farmer pays his servant in the first year a hen, in the second a cock, goose, goat, cow, horse, ... girl, farmstead. **Taylor JAFL

XLVI 80 No. 2010 I; Kristensen Danske Dyrefabler 168—78 Nos. 392—418; *T. Norlind Svenska Allmogens Liv[2] (Stockholm, 1925) 612. — Lithuanian: Balys Index No. 2010 I*.

Z24. *The forgetful man counts the days of the week.* On Monday they go to mill, etc. (First ed. Z21.4.) He thus discovers that it is Sunday. *Taylor JAFL XLVI 80 No. 2012, Hdwb. d. Märchens II 174b.

Z24.1. *Widower tells of his courtship, his marriage, and the death of his wife, all in a week.* (First ed. Z21.4.1.) *Taylor JAFL XLVI 80 No. 2012A.

Z24.1.1. *Life story in ten hours:* "At one I was born .... at ten my child's soul was crowned in heaven." *Taylor JAFL XLVI 80 No. 2012B.

Z24.1.2. *Bird advises man to treat his lazy children as she does her young:* "In March I make my nest .... in August I have nothing more to do with my young." *Taylor JAFL XLVI 80 No. 2012C.

Z24.1.3. *"Solomon Grundy, born on Monday .... buried on Sunday."* *Taylor JAFL XLVI 80 No. 2012D; Halliwell Nursery Rhymes of England 33 No. 49.

Z25. *Fly forgets her name; asks woodcutter, axe, tree, etc., in vain.* Finally foal in mare's belly says her name is "fly". India: Thompson-Balys.

Z30. Chains involving a single scene or event without interdependence among the individual actors.

Z31. *Chains involving a wedding.* Taylor JAFL XLVI 81 Nos. 2019—2020; Hdwb. d. Märchens II 176a.

Z31.1. *Pif Paf Poltrie.* The suitor sent from one relation to the other for consent to the wedding. *Type 2019; *BP III 71; *Taylor JAFL XLVI 81 No. 2019; India: Thompson-Balys.

T131.1.1. Brother's consent for sister's marriage needed.

Z31.2. *Louse and flea wish to marry.* Mosquito, toad, ant, etc. volunteer to supply the wedding feast. Spanish: Boggs FFC XC 154 No. 2020*.

B280. Animal wedding.

Z32. *Chains involving a death: animal actors.*

Z32.1. *The funeral procession of the hen.* Animals one by one join the procession. The funeral carriage breaks down or the procession drowns. *Type 2021; *BP II 147 n. 1; *Wesselski Hessische Blätter f. Vksk. XXXII 2ff.; *Taylor JAFL XLVI 82 No. 2021.

B257. Animal funeral. B295. Animal drives carriage.

Z32.1.1. *The death of the cock.* (Der Tod des Hühnchens.) The cock chokes and the hen seeks aid of objects and persons (stream, tree, pig, miller, baker, etc.). *Taylor JAFL XLVI 82 No. 2021A; BP II 146; **Haavio FFC XCIX; **Wesselski Hessische Blätter f. Vksk. XXXII 2ff.

Z32.2. *The death of the little hen.* She is characteristically mourned by objects and animals; e.g., flea, door, broom, cart, ashes, tree, girl. (First ed. Z31.2.2.) *Taylor JAFL XLVI 82 No. 2022A; *BP I 293; Parsons JAFL XXXIII 37; Missouri French: Carrière; India: *Thompson-Balys.

Z32.2.1. *The death of the little hen described with unusual words.* Each act of mourning described by a neologism: the table untables itself.

(First ed. Z31.2.2.1.) (Cf. X1506.) *Taylor JAFL XLVI 82 No. 2022A, Hdwb. d. Märchens II 177a; Tegethoff Französische Märchen II 78 No. 18; Rolland Rimes et jeux d'enfance (1881) 119f.; Kristensen Danske Dyrefabler 98ff. No. 171ff.

Z32.3. *Little ant finds a penny, buys new clothes with it, and sits in her doorway.* Various animals pass by and propose marriage. She asks what they do at night. Each one replies with its characteristic sound, and none pleases her but the quiet little mouse, whom she marries. She leaves him to tend the stew, and he falls in and drowns. She weeps and, on learning the reason, bird cuts off its beak, dove cuts off its tail, etc. (First ed. Z31.2.3.) *Taylor FFC XLVI 82 No. 2023; Spanish: Boggs FFC XC 154 No. 2023*; Italian: Crane Italian Popular Tales (1885) 376—77.

Z32.4. *Cumulative: master to kill hen.* She begs off; he goes to kill rooster .... goose, rabbit, toad, tiger. Chinese: Graham.

Z32.5. *Mourning about the dead ass (Tulsi Das):* from washerman to the queen. "But who is Tulsi Das?" The report is traced back to the washerman, who says: "He was my ass." India: *Thompson-Balys.

Z33. *Chains involving the eating of an object.* (Members of the chain not interrelated.) Taylor JAFL XLVI 83 Nos. 2025—2028, Hdwb. d. Märchens II 178b.

Z33.1. *The fleeing pancake.* A woman makes a pancake, which flees. Various animals try in vain to stop it. Finally the fox eats it up. (First ed. Z31.3.1.) *Taylor JAFL XLVI 82 No. 2025; *Dh III 272; Fb "pandekage" II 782b; Danish: Kristensen Danske Dyrefabler 58f. Nos. 113—18; Norwegian: Christensen Norske Eventyr 149; Lithuanian: Balys Index No. 2025; Russian: Andrejev Nos. 295, 296*.

Z33.2. *The fat cat.* While the mistress is away, the cat eats the porridge, the bowl, and the ladle. When the mistress returns she says, "How fat you are!" The cat: "I ate the porridge, the bowl, and the ladle, and I will eat you." The cat meets other animals and eats them after the same conversation. Finally eats too many. (First ed. Z31.3.2.) *Taylor JAFL XLVI 83 No. 2027; *Fb "kat" IV 255b; Danish: Kristensen Danske Dyrefabler 59ff. Nos. 119—130.

Z33.3. *Woman meets a pig.* "Good morning." "Why are you up so early?" "I am not up so early. I have drunk seven vats of milk and eaten seven plates of porridge and I shall eat you." She ate the pig. (First ed. Z31.3.3.) *Taylor JAFL XLVI 83 No. 2027A; Swedish: Norlander "Barnvisor och barnrim" Svenska Landsmålen V No. 5 n. 265.

Z33.4. *The fat troll (wolf).* A troll eats the watcher's five horses and finally the watcher himself. The master goes to investigate. The troll: "I ate the five horses, I ate the watcher, and I will eat you." Does so. Likewise the wife, servant, daughter, son, and dog. The cat scratches the troll open and rescues all. (First ed. Z31.3.4.) *Taylor JAFL XLVI 83 No. 2028; *Fb "ulv" III 970b, "æde" III 1139b, "bjørn" IV 43b; Danish: Kristensen Dyrefabler 68ff. Nos. 131—144; Swedish: T. Norlind Svenska Allmogens Liv[2] (Stockholm, 1925) 613; Russian: Andrejev No. 333B*.

F913. Victims rescued from swallower's belly.

Z33.4.1. *Louse and crow make covenant of friendship:* louse eats crow despite crow saying, "If I strike you once with my beak you will disappear; how then can you talk of eating me?" Likewise louse eats loaf of bread, she-goat, cow, buffalo, five sepoys, wedding procession with one lakh of people, elephant, tank of water. A sepoy cuts louse in two with his sword and rescues all. India: Thompson-Balys.

Z33.4.2. *The singing wolf.* By his singing the wolf compels the old man to surrender his cattle, his children and grandchildren, and finally his wife. The old woman goes in the wolf's service. She returns home bringing butter, etc. Lithuanian: Balys Index No. 162*; Russian: Andrejev No. 162*.

Z39. *Chains involving other events without interrelation of members.* (First ed. Z31.4.) Taylor JAFL XLVI 84 No. 2029.

Z39.1. *The goat who would not go home.* One animal after another tries in vain to persuade the goat to go home. Finally a wolf (bee) bites him and drives him home. (First ed. Z31.4.1.) *Taylor JAFL XLVI 81 No. 2015; *BP I 348 n. 1, II 100, 104; Fb "gjed" IV 178a; Swedish: T. Norlind Svenska Allmogens Liv[2] (Stockholm, 1925) 613.

Z39.1.1. *The goat who would not leave the hazel bush.* Final formula: The devil goes to strangle the Jew, the Jew to kill the ox, the ox to drink the water, the water to quench the fire, the fire to burn the stone, the stone to blunt the axe, the axe to cut the rope, the rope to tie the hunter, the hunter to shoot the goat — the goat leaves the hazel bush, the wee goat leaves the hazel bush. Lithuanian: Balys Index No. 2030.

Z39.2. *There was a wee wee woman who had a wee wee cow, etc.* (First ed. Z31.4.2.) *Taylor JAFL XLVI 81 No. 2016, Hdwb. d. Märchens II 176a; Jacobs English Fairy Tales 57; Danish: Kristensen Danske Dyrefabler 122ff. Nos. 230—37; Russian: Andrejev No. 2015 I*.

Z39.3. *The crow on the tarred bridge.* His beak and tail alternately stick. (Endless.) (First ed. Z31.4.3.) (Cf. Z11.) *Taylor JAFL XLVI 81 No. 2017, Hdwb. d. Märchens II 190a; Lithuanian: Balys Index No. 2017.

Z39.4. *Where have you been, goose? — In the fields. — What have you in your beak? — A knife. — etc.* (Tile, water, ox, firewood, old woman, friars, mass, shirt.) (First ed. Z31.4.4.) *Taylor JAFL XLVI 80 No. 2011, Hdwb. d. Märchens II 174a; Spanish: Boggs FFC XC 154 No. 2018A*.

Z39.4.1. *Titmouse, what are you eating? — A large turnip — etc.* Cheremis: Sebeok-Nyerges.

Z39.4.2. *Sparrow, where are you going? — To eat seed. — The owner will scold you. — I'll sit on a pine tree, etc.* Cheremis: Sebeok-Nyerges.

Z39.5. *The hen lays an egg, the mouse breaks it.* Sorrowing over this mishap, all show extraordinary behavior; the master puts an end to it. Final formula: hen strips off feathers, rubbish heap catches fire, oak falls to ground, hare drowns self, magpie twists leg, ox breaks horns, river flows blood, maid breaks pails, housewife scatters dough. Master locks up wife and maid, goes to seek people more foolish. Lithuanian: Balys Index No. 2022*; Russian: Andrejev No. 241 III*; Rumanian: Schullerus FFC LXXVIII No. 1963*.

Z39.6. *Mother ties bell on child; cat cuts it off.* "Why did you cut off the bell?" — "Why did you lay the block here, etc." Cheremis: Sebeok-Nyerges.

Z39.7. *Girl left in tree by sisters:* asks monkey, ape, bear, and tiger to put her down or else bite her. All refuse. Panther comes and devours her. India: Thompson-Balys.

Z39.8. *Small grain-measure runs away when her husband beats her:* succession of suitors. India: Thompson-Balys.

Z39.9. *Series of things acquired by mouse* — "You cannot have this but you may have that instead," etc. Clod—fish—cakes—kid—goat—drum —girl. Girl kills mouse accidentally. India: Thompson-Balys.

Z40. Chains with interdependent members.

N381. Drop of honey causes chain of accidents. Hunter drops honey in a grocery; weasel eats honey; cat chases weasel; dog chases cat; grocer kills dog: all the cause of a bloody feud between villages.

Z41. *The old woman and her pig.* Her pig will not jump over the stile so that she can go home. She appeals in vain for help until the cow gives her milk. The final formula is: cow give milk for cat; cat kill rat; rat gnaw rope; rope hang butcher; butcher kill ox; ox drink water; water quench fire; fire burn stick; stick beat dog; dog bite pig; pig jump over stile. (Various introductions.) (First ed. Z41.1.) *Taylor JAFL XLVI 84 No. 2030; *BP II 104, 108; **Goebel Hdwb. d. Märchens s.v. "Birnli" I 256ff.; *Emeneau JAFL LVI 272; Clouston Tales I 289; Köhler-Bolte I 136; Parsons JAFL XXXIII 34; Montet RTP VI 102; *Fb "and" IV 12; — Missouri French: Carrière; Spanish: Boggs FFC XC 155 Nos. 2030A, B, C, D; India: *Thompson-Balys; Indonesia: DeVries Volksverhalen I 364 No. 21; Africa (Benga): Nassau 200 No. 30, (Hottentot): Bleek 33 No. 17, (Gold Coast): Barker and Sinclair 177 No. 35, (Ila, Rhodesia): Smith and Dale II 392 No. 17, (Thonga): Junod 223; Jamaica: Beckwith MAFLS XVII 286 No. 138.

Z41.1. *Woman has meat (liver) stolen by bird.* Recovery chain (similar to Z41). *Wesselski Hessische Blätter f. Vksk. XXXII 25.

J1391.4. How he would act if he were a hawk. (Liver stolen by bird.)

Z41.2. *Crow must wash his bill in order to eat with other birds.* Asks water; water must first have horn from stag, who must first have milk from cow, etc. *Wesselski Hessische Blätter f. Vksk. XXXII 33; India: Thompson-Balys.

Z41.3. *Conflict between fowl and thistle.* Wind obeys and breaks the chain. India: *Thompson-Balys.

Z41.4. *The mouse regains its tail.* The cat bites off the mouse's tail and will return it in exchange for milk. The mouse goes to the cow for milk, the farmer for hay, the butcher for meat, the baker for bread. Other persons mentioned are the locksmith and the miner. *Taylor JAFL XLVI 86 No. 2034, Hdwb. d. Märchens II 185b; *Wesselski Hessische Blätter f. Vksk. XXXII 28; *Newell JAFL XVIII (1905) 34 n. 1; BP II 107—8; Basset Contes Berbères No. 45, Nouveaux Contes Berbères No. 168. — England, U.S.: *Baughman.

Z41.4.1. *Mouse bursts open when crossing a stream.* Series of helpers similar to Z41.4. *Taylor JAFL XLVI 86 No. 2034A; *Wesselski Hessische Blätter f. Vksk. XXXII 28; BP II 107—8.

Z41.4.2. *My dog picked up a string,* but did not wish to give it to me unless I gave her bread. Cupboard did not wish to give bread unless I gave it a key; smith, charcoal; charcoal-burner, calf's legbone; butcher, milk; cow, grass; meadow, water; clouds, dove's feather. Dove gave me a feather which I gave to clouds, etc. *Taylor JAFL XLVI 86 No. 2034B; Spanish: Boggs FFC XC 156 No. 2030D.

Z41.5. *Lending and repaying: progressively worse (or better) bargain.* Type 2034C*; Lithuanian: Balys Index No. 2009*; Africa (Tonga): Torrend Specimens of Bantu Folklore (New York, 1921) 169ff., (Ila): Smith and Dale II 392ff. No. 17, (Pende): Frobenius Atlantis XI 265 No. 4, (Bassari): ibid. 97ff. No. 12, (Ashanti): Rattray 268 No. 73.

J2081.1. Foolish bargain: horse for cow, cow for hog, etc. N421.1. Progressively lucky bargains.

Z41.6. *Bird's pea gets stuck in socket of mill-handle.* She goes to carpenter, king, queen, who refuse to help. She asks snake to bite queen, stick to beat snake, fire to burn stick, etc. Final formula: cat eats mouse, mouse cuts plant creeper, creeper snares elephant, elephant drinks up sea, sea quenches fire, fire burns stick, stick beats snake, snake bites queen, queen speaks to king, king chides carpenter, carpenter cuts mill handle, and pea is extracted. Questions in rhyme. India: Thompson-Balys.

Z41.6.1. *Gram (parched grain) sticks in post;* parrot goes to raja, etc., for help. Final formula: at last creeper took pity on birds, and elephant feared creeper, and ocean feared elephant, and fire feared ocean, and stick feared fire, and snake feared stick, and carpenter feared snake; and carpenter split post which gave up the grain to the birds, who went away. India: Thompson-Balys.

Z41.7. *The wormwood does not want to rock the sparrow.* Final formula: the worms begin to gnaw the rods, the rods to beat the oxen, the oxen to drink the water, the water to quench the fire, the fire to burn the hunters, the hunters to shoot the wolves, the wolves to kill the goats, the goats to gnaw the wormwood, the wormwood to rock me — it rocked and rocked me to sleep. Lithuanian: Balys Index No. 2003*.

Z41.7.1. *Boy dirties his shoe and asks the hay stack to wipe it clean.* Cheremis: Sebeok-Nyerges.

Z41.8. *Pulling the needle out of the seamstress's hand.* Final formula: That was just what the cat was waiting for — it sprang to devour the mouse, the mouse to tear the spider's web, the spider to entangle the dog, the dog to eat the goat, the goat to gnaw the rushes, the rushes to grow in the stream, the stream to quench the fire, the fire to burn the stone, the stone to beat the axe, the axe soon pulled out the needle that was stuck in the seamstress's hand. Lithuanian: Balys Index No. 2005*.

Z41.9. *The lazy servant and the grain.* "Lentils, lentils, get into my sack!" Final formula: the hungry hawk attacks the hens, the hens the worms, the worms the stick, the stick the ox, the ox runs to the water, the water attacks the fire, the fire the hunters, the hunters the wolf, the wolf the goat, the goat the willow, the willow the cat, the cat the mice, the mice the lentils, the lentils go whoosh whoosh into the sack. Lithuanian: Balys Index No. 2011*.

Z42. *Stronger and Strongest.* The frost-bitten foot. Mouse perforates wall, wall resists wind, wind dissolves cloud, cloud covers sun, sun thaws frost, frost breaks foot. *Taylor JAFL XLVI 84 No. 2031, Hdwb. d. Märchens II 182ff.; **DeCock Volkssage 22—36; BP I 148 n. 2; Haavio FFC LXXXVIII 20; Köhler-Bolte II 47; Stiefel Zs. f. Vksk. V 448—50; Benfey Panchatantra I 373—78, II 264; Chauvin II 97f.; DeVries Volksverhalen I 1—3 No. 1, 356; Voorhoeve 166 No. 176; Clouston Tales I 309. — India: Thompson-Balys; Africa (Ekoi): Talbot 384, (Zanzibar): Bateman 67 No. 5.

H631.4. What is strongest? — Woman. L392. Mouse stronger than wall, wind, mountain.

Z42.1. *The Esdras chain: stronger and strongest, wine, king, woman, truth.* *Taylor JAFL XLVI 85 No. 2031A, Hdwb. d. Märchens II 184b; DeCock Volkssage 35f.; Oesterley No. 258; Köhler-Bolte II 55. — Jewish: Neuman.

Z42.2. *Abraham learns to worship God.* At nightfall Abraham worships a star, then the moon, then the sun, and finally gives up idolatry. *Taylor JAFL XLVI 85 No. 2031B; Hdwb. d. Märchens II 184b; Köhler-Bolte I 578; Koran Surah 6, 75—78; *Basset RTP VII 397; Jewish: Neuman.

Z42.3. *Brahmin worships idol and sets sacrifices before it daily.* Rat devours offerings and he sets it up as his idol as a being more powerful than his idol. When cat devours rat, he worships it instead. His wife accidentally kills the cat, so he sets her up to worship. He happens to slap her and she loses consciousness. Thereafter he worships himself as most powerful after all. India: Thompson-Balys.

Z43. *The cock's whiskers.* A mouse throws a nut down and hits the cock on the head. He also steals the cock's whiskers. The cock goes to get an old woman to cure him. The final formula is: Fountain give up water for forest, forest give up wood for baker, baker give up bread for dog, dog give up hairs to cure the cock. (Variant: mouse loses tail.) *Taylor JAFL XLVI 85 No. 2032; *BP II 107; Norlind Svenska Allmogens Liv[2] (Stockholm, 1925) 613 "Tupen och hänen"; Haavio FFC LXXXVIII 89 n. 1; RTP XV 220. — Russian: Andrejev No. 241 I; N. A. Indian (Zuñi): Cushing 411.

Z43.1. *Toad asks magpie in tree to throw down a chestnut.* Magpie refuses, saying it might break its beak. Toad promises, if that happens, to get a horsehair to tie it up again. Magpie throws chestnut and breaks beak. Toad asks ass for hair, but ass first demands grass; mower demands sheep; shepherd, pup; mother dog, bread; baker, stumps. Toad cuts the stumps and gets the hair. *Wesselski Hessische Blätter f. Vksk XXXII 24; Spanish: Boggs FFC XC 156 No. 2032A*.

Z43.2. *The cock strikes out the hen's eye with a nut.* The cock blames the hazel bush for tearing its knickers, the hazel bush the goat for gnawing at it, the goat the shepherd-boy for not tending it, the boy his mistress for not baking him a bun, the mistress the pig for eating up the dough, the pig the wolf for killing its young. Lithuanian: Balys Index No. 2030G; Livonian: Looritz FFC LXVI No. 241[1]; Russian: Andrejev No. 241 II*.

Z43.3. *Nut hits cock in head: he thinks world is coming to an end.* He sends the hen to tell the duck, the duck to tell the goose, etc. Final formula: Fox, who told you? — Hare. — Hare, who told you? — Goose, etc. For sequel see Type 20C. Sometimes the animals have queer names (cf. Z53). Taylor JAFL XLVI 85 No. 2033, Hdwb. d. Märchens II 185a; *Wesselski Hessische Blätter XXXII 19; Cowell Jātaka III 49 No. 322; Fb "høne" I 750. — Danish: Danske Dyrefabler 103ff. Nos. 177—85; Lithuanian: Balys Index No. 2033; Africa (Kaffir): Kidd 240 No. 9; American Negro (Georgia): Harris Nights 108 No. 20.

Z43.4. *Fly frightens snake; snake frightens rats; rats frighten monkey, etc.* Africa (Cameroon): Mansfield 228, (Fang): Tessman 79ff., (Duala): Lederbogen Märchen 124, (Swahili): Steere 287ff.

Z43.5. *Boy changes self to nut; fowl eats nut; bush cat eats fowl; dog eats cat; dog swallowed by python.* Africa: Weeks Jungle 462.

Z43.6. *Man invites animals to come and work in his field.* Rooster kills beetle; cat kills rooster; dog kills cat; leopard kills dog; hyena kills leopard; buffalo kills hyena; elephant kills buffalo, and lion chases elephant so that both fall into trap. Man calls wives to see meat he has killed. Africa (Wute): Sieber 60ff.

Z44. *The house that Jack built.* Final formula: This is the farmer that sowed the corn that fed the cock that crowed in the morn, that waked the priest all shaven and shorn, that married the man all tattered and torn, that kissed the maiden all forlorn, that milked the cow with a crumpled horn, that tossed the dog, that worried the cat, that caught the rat, that ate the malt that lay in the house that Jack built. *Taylor JAFL XLVI 86 No. 2035; *BP II 108; Köhler-Bolte I 517f.; Kristensen Danske Dyrefabler 132ff. Nos 272, 295; *Fb "hus" I 687a, IV 229. — India: Thompson-Balys; Africa (Fang): Nassau 245ff. No. 11, (Zulu): Callaway 38.

Z44.1. *The house the old man was to build.* The woman for whom he is to build the house has some beans for him. The goat eats these up. Cumulative search. Final formula: Smith give me my iron, iron which belongs to the man, man who ate up my fish, fish which belongs to the sea .... sea — shirt — washerwoman — soap — woman — wood — press — grease — herder — cheese-frame — fig-tree — horn — goat — beans. *Taylor JAFL XLVI 86 No. 2035A; *Parsons JAFL XXV 219, XXVII 222, XXXIII 40, MAFLS XV (1) 207 n. 1.

Z45. *The Horseshoe Nail.* For want of a nail the shoe was lost, for want of a shoe the horse was lost, for the want of a horse the rider was lost .... and all for the want of a horseshoe nail. (First ed. Z41.9.) *Taylor JAFL XLVI 87 No. 2039; *BP III 335—37.

N258. Train of troubles from lost horseshoe nail.

Z46. *The climax of horrors.* The magpie is dead. Overate on horseflesh. — Horses dead? — Overworked at fire. — House burned down? — etc. (First ed. Z41.10.) *Taylor JAFL XLVI 87 No. 2040; Wesselski Hodscha Nasreddin II 203; Wesselski Mönchslatein 25 No. 20; **Zachariae Kleine Schriften 191ff.; *Crane Vitry 216ff. No. 205; *Bolte Zs. f. Vksk. VII 99 n. 5. — Lithuanian: Balys Index No. 2040*; Russian: Andrejev No. 2014 I*; Spanish Exempla: Keller; India: *Thompson-Balys.

Z47. *Series of trick exchanges.* India: *Thompson-Balys.

K251.1. The eaten grain and the cock as damages. N421. Lucky bargain.

Z47.1. *Series of trick exchanges: razor—pot—bride—drum by tricky fox.* Fox sings formula of exchanges. India: *Thompson-Balys.

Z49. *Miscellaneous interdependent chains.*

Z49.1. *"I killed my grandmother because she refused to cook a hare.* I killed a priest because he said my crime was bad. A friar absolved me to avoid being killed." (First ed. Z41.7.) *Taylor JAFL XLVI 87 No. 2037; Spanish: Boggs FFC XC 155 No. 2026*.

Z49.2. *Cumulative pursuit.* Boys get help. One of them injures the helper. Pursued. Hidden by kind hen. One injures the hen. Hen pursues, etc. (First ed. Z41.8.) *Taylor JAFL XLVI 87 No. 2038; Jamaica: Beckwith MAFLS XVII 264f. No. 70.

Z49.2.1. *Fat mouse cannot get into hole.* "Carpenter, please pare off a little flesh from my ribs." Refused. Final formula: the scythe cuts the creeper loose. India: Thompson-Balys.

Z49.3. *The bird indifferent to pain.* A man catches a mango-bird eating mangoes and strikes it against the roots of a mango-tree. The bird cannot be made to say it suffers from the blow. In turn, he puts it in water, strikes it on the ground, a stile, a door-frame, singes its feathers, cuts it up, cooks it, and eats it. The bird always expresses indifference in a cumulative rhyme. At last the bird asks him to look out of the window, whereupon it flies out of his nose and the man dies. (First ed. Z41.11.) *Taylor JAFL XLVI 87 No. 2041.

Z49.4. *There was once a woman; the woman had a son;* the son had red breeches; etc. — At last: "Shall I tell it again?" (First ed. Z41.12.) *Taylor JAFL XLVI 81 No. 2013.

Z17. Rounds. Stories which begin over and over again and repeat.

Z49.5. *Where is the warehouse?* — The fire burned it down. — Where is the fire? — The water quenched it. (First ed. Z41.13.) Type 2018.

Z49.5.1. *"Where is that grain?"* — "The cock snatched it." — "Where is that cock?" — "He drowned in the sea." — "Where is that sea?" — "It is grown over with reeds." — "Where are those reeds?" — "The maids have cut them down", etc. Lithuanian: Balys Index No. 2018.

Z49.5.2. *The wolf who wanted to make bread.* The farmer explained to him how bread is made. He keeps on asking: "Shall I then be able to eat?" Decides he will not have enough patience to make bread. (Cf. K555.1.2.) Lithuanian: Balys Index No. 164*.

Z49.6. *Trial among the animals.* Deer steps on kitten: cat investigates. Deer has been frightened by bird, this bird by another bird .... by crab's pointed claw, crab by mouse in his hole. Cat eats mouse. (Frog croaks because turtle carries his house on his head; turtle carries house because firefly is bringing fire; firefly brings fire because mosquito tries to bite him, etc.) (First ed. Z41.14.) India: Thompson-Balys; Indonesia, Malaya: Dixon 202; Philippine: Fansler MAFLS XII 390.

Z49.6.1. *Birds fight and cause series of accidents to other animals and people.* India: Thompson-Balys.

Z49.6.2. *Bite (prick) causes series of accidents.* India: *Thompson-Balys.

Z49.6.3. *Man sharpening his dao is bitten by a prawn.* He cuts down a big bamboo; a fruit falls from bamboo and strikes a bird on the nape of the neck; the bird scratches up an ant's nest with his feet; the ant bites a wild boar in the eye; and the boar bears down upon a plantain tree where a bat dwells under a leaf; the bat seeks refuge in the ear of an elephant, and the elephant kicks down the house on an old woman. She rushes out and falls into a well. India: *Thompson-Balys.

Z49.7. *Cumulative tale: bird who seeks carpenter to release young caught in closed tree.* Beetle bites calf, calf bites cow, cow hoofs carpenter, carpenter beats wife, hunters save carpenter's cow, carpenter releases birds. India: Thompson-Balys.

Z49.8. *Biting a grain in half.* Final formula: Forester attacks bear, the bear the wolf, the wolf the dog, the dog the cat, the cat the mouse, the mouse the grain — the grain is bitten in two. Lithuanian: Balys Index No. 2006*.

Z49.9. *Pulling up the turnip.* Final formula: The mouse holds onto the cat, the cat holds onto Mary, Mary holds onto Annie, Annie holds onto grandmother, grandmother holds onto grandfather, grandfather holds onto the turnip — they all pull and pull it out. Lithuanian: Balys Index No. 2008*; Russian: Andrejev No. 1960G*.

Z49.10. *Lizard eats cricket, frog eats lizard, snake eats frog, eagle eats snake, man shoots eagle;* animals escape except lizard. Man takes eagle home. U.S.: Baughman.

Z49.11. *Who is guilty of the accident.* (One person blames another who blames another, etc.) India: *Thompson-Balys.

Z49.11.1. *Wall in construction collapses.* Finally the king finds out that the sea is guilty. (The chain: mason—cement mixer—beautifully singing woman—pearl necklace—jeweller—diver—sea.) India: *Thompson-Balys.

Z49.11.2. *Thief breaks foot climbing wall to rob.* Suit against owner for dangerous wall. India: *Thompson-Balys.

J1173. Series of clever unjust decisions: plaintiff voluntarily withdraws.

Z49.12. *Hermit must get cat to kill rats in hunt, cow to give cat milk, etc.* India: Thompson-Balys.

Z49.13. *Chain of killings:* bulbul destroys flower and is killed by cat; cat shaken by dog; dog killed by boy; boy sentenced to death by king. India: Thompson-Balys.

Z49.14. *The little old lady who swallowed a fly.* She swallows a spider to eat up the fly, a bird to eat up the spider, a dog to eat the bird, a cow to eat the dog. "The little old lady swallowed a horse — she died, of course." U.S.: *Baughman.

Z50. Cumulative tales—miscellaneous.

Z51. *Chains involving contradictions or extremes.* (First ed. Z23.) *Taylor JAFL XLVI 81 No. 2014, Hdwb. d. Märchens II 175b.

Z51.1. *The house is burned down.* — That is too bad. — That is not bad at all, my wife burned it down. — That is good. — That is not good, etc. (First ed. Z23.1.) Type 2014; *Taylor JAFL XLVI 81 No. 2014; Nouvelles Récréations No. 75.

J2500. Foolish extreme.

Z52. *Bird avenges caged mate.* Builds cart, yokes frogs to it, arms himself with piece of reed, and proclaims war with king. Collects cat, ants, rope, club, and river. He is put by king into fowl house; cat eats up fowls. In stable rope and club beat up horses. In elephant-house ants get into their brains and kill them all. Tied to king's bed, river floods king in his bed. King gives bird back his mate. India: Thompson-Balys.

Z53. *The animals with queer names:* as hen (henny-penny), cock (cocky-locky), goose (goosey-poosey). (First ed. Z21.3.1.) (Cf. Z32.2.1.) *Wesselski Hessische Blätter f. Vksk. XXXII 55; *Taylor JAFL XLVI 80 No. 2010 IA; Jacobs English Fairy Tales 118; *T. Norlind Svenska Allmogens Liv[2] (Stockholm, 1925) 612; Kristensen Danske Dyrefabler 182 Nos. 431—32. — Antigua (British West Indies): Johnson JAFL XXXIV 68 No. 24.

X1506. The extraordinary names.

Z60. Other formulistic motifs.

Z61. *Never.* Various ways of expressing this idea. When black sheep turn white, when a dry branch sprouts, etc. *Fb "aldrig" IV 9a;

*Wehrhan 36; Hdwb. d. Märchens II 163a; *Gittee Zs. f. Vksk. III 442ff.; Weise Zs. f. hochdeutsche Mundarten III 47ff.; Stoett Nederlandsche Spreekwoorden, Spreekwijzen, Vitdrukkingen en Gezegden[4] (Zutphen, 1923) I 401ff. No. 1036; Berthold Nassauische Blätter V 199ff.; Treichel Der Urquell II 214; Heller Die Bedeutung des arabischen Antar-romans für die vergleichende Literaturkunde (Form und Geist XXI, Leipzig, 1931) 174ff.; Taylor English Riddles 54 No. 143; Muller-Fraureuth Die deutschen Lügendichtungen bis auf Münchhausen (Halle a. S., 1881) 19. — Irish myth: *Cross; Jewish: Neuman; India: Thompson-Balys; West Indies: Flowers 588.

D791.1.2. Disenchantment when superhuman task is finished. Enchanted person appears every seven years in human form and puts one stitch in a smock. When it is finished, she will be delivered. D1960.2.1. King asleep in mountain will awake when his horse's shoes are worn down. Every seven years the horse goes around the castle. He must wear his half-inch silver shoes to thinness of cat's ear before the king awakes. H701.1. How many seconds in eternity? H1583. Tests of time. M261. Chaste woman promises herself to her lover when the rocks leave the coast. Q521.1. Doing penance till green leaves grow on a dry branch. X1503.4. Mountain of grain to be eaten through on way to Schlaraffenland.

Z61.1. *Never. "Till Ogham and pillar be blent together,* till heaven and earth, till sun and moon be blent together." Irish myth: Cross.

Z61.2. *Forever. "A day and a night."* Irish myth: Cross.

Z61.3. *Butterby Church — no church at all.* If person says he has gone to Butterby Church, he has not gone to church. England: Baughman.

Z61.4. *"He struck him such a blow that he remembered the milk he drank on the sixth day after he was born."* India: Thompson-Balys.

Z62. *Proverbial simile.*

Z62.1. *The old and the new keys.* Hero marries his first sweetheart according to the proverb that the old key is better than the new. (Cf. L214.) *Type 313; *BP II 59, 246, 335, 516ff., III 40; *Fb "nøgle" II 511b; Rumanian: Schullerus FFC LXXVIII No. 906*.

Z62.2. *"Bridegroom like the sun and bride like the moon."* India: Thompson-Balys.

Z63. *Formulas signifying fruitlessness,* e.g. like putting a withe about sand, like mocking a beggar. Irish myth: Cross.

Z64. *Three explanations.* When explanation of phenomenon is asked, three explanations are offered of which the last is always the true one. (Cf. Z71.1.) Irish myth: Cross.

Z64. *Proverbs.*[1] India: Thompson-Balys.

Z64.1. *Proverb: one man for worship, two men for cultivation of a field, three men for a journey.* India: Thompson-Balys.

Z65. *Color formulas.* Hdwb. d. Märchens II 51a.

F873.1. Troops of black, white, and red soldiers. One third of an army of each. Z140. Color symbolism.

Z65.1. *Red as blood, white as snow.* Often from blood on snow as a suggestion, a wish is made for a child (wife) with skin like snow and cheeks like blood, etc. (Sometimes black as a raven.) Types 516, 709, 720; BP I 166, 450, *461, IV 245 n. 1; Rösch FFC LXXVII 100; *Böklen

[1] Though a place is found here for proverbs, this work makes no attempt to treat them.

62ff.; **Cosquin Contes indiens 218ff.; Italian: Basile Pentamerone V No. 9.

T11.6. Wish for wife red as blood, white as snow, black as raven.

Z65.1.1. *Red as blood, white as snow, (and black as a raven).* Usually applied to the cheeks, skin, and hair of a girl's lover. Irish myth: *Cross.

Z65.2. *Series: white cock, red cock, black cock.* These crow at dawn and scatter ghosts. (Cf. E452.) Köhler-Bolte III 581.

Z71. *Formulistic numbers.* *Hdwb. d. Abergl. s.v. "Zahl"; Penzer I 242 n. 3, 255 n. 2, VI 14 n. 1; Feilberg Dania II 185ff.

Z71.0.1. *Odd numbers — formulistic.* Roman: Pliny Natural History X 151, XXVIII 23; Hindu: Caland Verhandelingen der Koniglijke Akademie van Wetenschappen te Amsterdam XVII (4) 23 and NS I (6) 73, 103; Indonesian: Kruyt Het Animisme 514.

Z71.0.2. *Formulistic numbers: a number plus one* (101, 1001, etc.). R. M. Meyer Archiv f. Religionswissenschaft X (1907) 89ff.; *BP IV 397ff.; Irish myth: Cross; Jewish: Neuman.

J1185.1. Scheherezade. Z72.1. Year and a day.

Z71.1. *Formulistic number: three.* **R. Mueller Die Zahl Drei in Sage, Dichtung u. Kunst (Teschen, 1903); Wundt Völkerpsychologie VI 341; Diels Sibyllinische Blätter 40; Aly Volksmärchen bei Herodot 240: Hdwb. d. Märchens I 412ff.; *H. Usener "Dreiheit" Rheinisches Museum f. Philologie N. F. LVIII (1903) 1—47, 161—208; *Fb "tre". — Breton: Sébillot Incidents s.v. "trois"; Irish myth: *Cross; Icelandic: *Boberg; India: *Thompson-Balys; Chinese: Graham; Africa (Bulu): Krug 120f., (Luba): DeClerq ZsKS IV 201; S. A. Indian (Chiriguano): Métraux RMLP XXXIII 166.

Z71.1.0.1. *Triads.* Irish myth: *Cross; Icelandic: Boberg.

Z71.1.0.2. *Formulistic numbers: threefold* (e.g. three times thirty). Jewish: Neuman; Africa (Fang): Einstein 49.

Z71.1.1. *Formula: three days and three nights.* Irish myth: *Cross.

F1086. Saint preaches for three days and three nights. P634.1. Feast (hospitality) endures for three days and nights.

Z71.1.2. *Three chairs in heaven for three saints.* Irish myth: *Cross.

Z71.1.3. *Three strains of (fairy) music.* Irish myth: Cross.

Z71.1.4. *Three things that lead to hell (heaven).* Irish myth: Cross.

Z71.1.5. *Three innocent children:* Ananias, Zacharias, Misael. Irish myth: Cross.

Z71.1.6. *Three Lents.* Irish myth: Cross.

Z71.1.7. *Three Maries.* Irish myth: *Cross.

Z71.1.8. *Three orders of Irish saints.* Irish myth: Cross.

Z71.1.9. *Three seas surrounding the earth.* Irish myth: Cross.

Z71.1.10. *Three sods that none may escape:* "The sod of his birth, the sod of his death, the sod of his burying." Irish myth: *Cross.

Z71.1.11. *Three whom Christ raised from the dead.* Irish myth: Cross.

Z71.1.12. *Three spiritual gifts of God.* Irish myth: *Cross.

Z71.1.13. *Three persons who spoke immediately after birth.* Irish myth: Cross.

Z71.1.14. *Three weak things that are the strongest.* Irish myth: Cross.

Z71.1.15. *Three worst things in Ireland.* Irish myth: Cross.

Z71.1.16. *Three reasons why men should condemn wealth.* Irish myth: Cross.

Z71.1.17. *Three cries of the world.* Irish myth: *Cross.

Z71.1.18. *Three bad stories of the saints of Ireland.* Irish myth: Cross.

Z71.2. *Formulistic number: four.* Grimm Deutsche Rechtsalterthümer I 290ff.; Eisler Weltenmantel 337; Wundt Völkerpsychologie VI 354ff.; Brinton Myths of the New World 66ff.; India: Thompson-Balys; Icelandic: Boberg.

Z71.2.0.1. *Formulistic number: fourfold* (e.g. 400, 4000). Jewish: Neuman.

Z71.2.1. *Formula: north, south, east, west.* (The cardinal directions.) India: Thompson-Balys.

A417.1. Beast guardians of the four quarters.

Z71.2.2. *The four elements.* Irish myth: *Cross.

Z71.2.3. *The four humors.* Irish myth: Cross.

Z71.2.4. *Four places that cleanse the soul.* Irish myth: Cross.

Z71.2.5. *Four categories of souls at Judgment.* Irish myth: Cross.

Z71.2.6. *Four things that prevent the holy life.* Irish myth: Cross.

Z71.2.7. *Four things to which the glory of the world is compared.* Irish myth: Cross.

Z71.2.8. *Sending four messengers with four winds.* India: Thompson-Balys.

Z71.3. *Formulistic number: five.* Irish myth: Cross; English: Gawayne and the Green Knight lines 623ff.; Hdwb. d. Abergl. s.v. "Funf"; India: Thompson-Balys; N. A. Indian (Klikitat): Jacobs U Wash II 32ff.

Z71.3.0.1. *Formulistic numbers: fivefold* (e.g. 50, 500). Africa (Luba): De Clerq Zs KS IV 202.

Z71.3.1. *Five sighs we should vent over our sins.* Irish myth: Cross.

Z71.3.2. *Five wounds of Christ.* Irish myth: Cross.

Z71.4. *Formulistic number: six.* Hdwb. d. Märchens I 420a s.v. "Drie" nn. 408ff.

Z71.4.0.1. *Formulistic number: sixfold.* Jewish: Neuman.

Z71.5. *Formulistic number: seven.* *Nyrop Dania II 126; Grimm Deutsche Rechtsalterthümer I 292; Wundt Völkerpsychologie VI 349; *Roscher Die Sieben- und Neunzahl im Kultus und Mythus der Griechen (Leipzig, 1904); Aly Volksmärchen bei Herodot 241; *Fb "syv". — Irish: *Cross, O'Suilleabhain 45, 100, Beal XXI 316, 332; Breton: Sébillot Incidents s.v. "sept"; Icelandic: *Boberg; Spanish: Espinosa

Jr. Nos. 157, 178; India: *Thompson-Balys; Buddhist myth: Malalasekera I 457; Chinese: Eberhard FFC CXX 49, 162, Graham; N. A. Indian (Seneca): Curtin-Hewitt RBAE XXXII 93 No. 6, 149 No. 24, 154 No. 26; Africa (Cameroon): Mansfield 224, 236, (Togo): Einstein 7, (Congo): Weeks Cannibals 217.

P541.1. Heptads. Laws made in groups of sevens. T586.1.2. Seven children at a birth.

Z71.5.0.1. *Formulistic numbers: sevenfold* (e.g. 49, 70, 70,000, 7,777). (Cf. Z71.15.) Jewish: Neuman; India: Thompson-Balys; Buddhist myth: Malalasekera II 943; Chinese: Eberhard FFC CXX 78 No. 43, 80 No. 46.

Z71.5.1. *Seven brothers and one sister.* Type 451; *Gummere Kittredge Anniversary Volume 17; Italian: Basile Pentamerone IV No. 8; India: *Thompson-Balys; N. A. Indian (Seneca): Curtin-Hewitt RBAE XXXII 565 No. 116.

Z71.5.2. *Journey beyond seven seas.* India: Thompson-Balys.

Z71.5.3. *Seven year's peace with no killing of men.* Irish myth: *Cross.

Z71.5.4. *King for seven years.* Irish myth: Cross.

Z71.5.5. *Exile for seven years.* Irish myth: Cross.

Z71.5.6. *Seven as a number in religious and social records.* Irish myth: Cross.

Z71.5.6.1. *Seven causes of poverty.* Irish myth: Cross.

Z71.5.6.2. *Seven Deadly Sins.* Irish myth: Cross.

Z71.5.6.3. *Seven eclesiastical orders.* Irish myth: Cross.

Z71.5.6.4. *Seven grades of wisdom.* Irish myth: Cross.

Z71.5.6.5. *Seven joys of the Virgin Mary.* Irish myth: Cross.

Z71.5.6.6. *Seven masses necessary to free soul from hell.* Irish myth: *Cross.

Z71.5.6.7. *Seven orders of poets.* Irish myth: Cross.

Z71.5.6.8. *Seven gifts of God (Holy Spirit).* Irish myth: *Cross.

Z71.5.6.9. *Seven penitential psalms.* Irish myth: *Cross.

Z71.5.6.10. *Seven prayers of saint.* Irish myth: Cross.

Z71.5.6.11. *Seven to whom alms should be given.* Irish myth: Cross.

Z71.5.6.12. *Seven fair rivers in Inis Eidheand (Eden) in the East of Africa.* Irish myth: Cross.

Z71.5.6.13. *Seven daughters of Humility.* Irish myth: Cross.

Z71.5.7. *King with seven wives and seven mares.* The seven wives pregnant for seven years, the seven mares seven years in foal. India: Thompson-Balys.

B311. Congenital helpful animal.

Z71.5.8. *Seven brothers marry seven sisters.* India: Thompson-Balys.

Z71.6. *Formulistic number: nine* (99, 900, 999, 99,999, etc.). *Hdwb. d. Märchens I 419b, nn. 378—407; Grimm Deutsche Mythologie I 505f.;

Ohrt Danske Trylleformler I 196ff.; Agrell Runornas Talmystik 70ff.; Grimm Deutsche Rechtsalterthümer I 84, 295; Wundt Völkerpsychologie V 82, VI 350; Hdwb. d. Abergl. I 1397; Wuttke Volksaberglaube, register. — Irish myth: *Cross; Icelandic: *Boberg; Jewish: Neuman; Persian: Carnoy 342 (99,999); India: *Thompson-Balys; Chinese: Eberhard FFC CXX 56, 206 No. 154; Philippine (Tinguian): Cole 56ff.; Africa (Wakweli): Bender 76f.

Z71.6.1. *Three times nine.* Irish myth: *Cross.

Z71.6.2. *Nine whirlpools of the world.* Irish myth: Cross.

Z71.6.3. *(Nine) wonders of Ireland.* Irish myth: *Cross.

Z71.6.4. *Nine materials used in building Tower of Babel.* Irish myth: *Cross.

Z71.7. *Formulistic number: eleven.* Wuttke Volksaberglaube register s.v. "Elf"; Oldenberg Religion der Veda 514; Jewish: Neuman; Icelandic: Boberg.

Z71.8. *Formulistic number: twelve.* *Hdwb. d. Märchens I 420b nn. 416ff.; Wundt Völkerpsychologie VI 353; Hoops' Reallexikon I 496; Thien Motive 8f.; Fb "tolv". — Irish myth: Cross; Icelandic: *Boberg; India: *Thompson-Balys; Chinese: Eberhard FFC CXX 64.

Z71.8.1. *Twelve articles of faith.* Irish myth: Cross.

Z71.8.2. *Twelve abuses of the world.* Irish myth: Cross.

Z71.8.3. *Formulistic number: "twice twelve years".* India: Thompson-Balys.

Z71.8.4. *Formulistic number: twelve plus thirteen.* India: Thompson-Balys.

Z71.8.5. *Formulistic number: twelve score.* India: Thompson-Balys.

Z71.8.6. *Formulistic number: twenty-four.* India: Thompson-Balys.

Z71.8.7. *Formulistic number: thirty-six.* India: Thompson-Balys.

Z71.9. *Formulistic number: thirteen.* *Hdwb. d. Märchens I 424a; Grimm Rechtsalterthümer I 298; *Kyriakides To Dysoionon tou Arithmou 13 (Athenae, 1953); India: *Thompson-Balys.

D1273.1. Magic numbers. N135.1. Thirteen as unlucky number.

Z71.10. *Formulistic number: sixteen.* E. Skard Maal og Minne (1931) 106f.; India: Thompson-Balys.

Z71.11. *Formulistic number: thirty.* (Cf. Z71.1.0.1.) Hdwb. d. Märchens I 420b nn. 432ff.

Z71.12. *Formulistic number: forty.* *Clouston Eastern Romances 456 n. 1; Dh I 228, 283, 284; Grimm Deutsche Rechtsalterthümer I 301; Wundt Völkerpsychologie VI 341; *Roscher Die Zahl 40 im Glauben .. der Semiten (Leipzig, 1909). — India: Thompson-Balys.

Z71.13. *Formulistic number: sixty.* (Cf. Z71.4.) Hdwb. d. Märchens I 421a.

Z71.14. *Formulistic number: seventy-two.* (Cf. Z71.8.) Grimm Deutsche Rechtsalterthümer I 303, II 497; Hdwb. d. Abergl. III 989, 991; Schröder Germanentum u. Hellenismus 11f.; Thien Motive 2; Bojunga "Die 72 Völkerschalten in Widsith" Paul und Braune's Beiträge XVI

545ff.; R. Michel ibid. XV 377. — Chinese: Wilhelm Chinesische Märchen 364, 366, cf. 358, 363.

Z71.15. *Formulistic number: seventy-seven.* (Cf. Z71.5.0.1.) *Hdwb. d. Abergl. III 991; Wuttke Volksabergl. 525b s.v. "Sieben und Siebenzig"; Gaster Thespis 180, 192, 221.

Z71.16. *Formulistic numbers—miscellaneous.* Henry Ancient Tahiti (Honolulu, 1928) 430.

Z71.16.1. *Formulistic number: eight.* Irish myth: *Cross; Chinese: Eberhard FFC CXX 154, 210, 411 s.v. "acht"; Polynesia: *Beckwith Myth 209f.; Hawaii: ibid. 233; Tahiti: ibid. 209; Cook Islands: ibid. 256, Samoa: ibid. 256; Easter Island: Métraux Ethnology 80, 376.

Z71.16.1.1. *Eight deadly sins.* Irish myth: *Cross.

Z71.16.1.2. *Eight virtues.* Irish myth: *Cross.

Z71.16.1.3. *Eight miracles of Christ's body in the sacrament.* Irish myth: Cross.

Z71.16.1.4. *Eight unprofitable types of fasting.* Irish myth: Cross.

Z71.16.2. *Formulistic number: ten.* Irish myth: Cross; Society Islands: Henry Ancient Tahiti (Honolulu, 1928) 430; Africa (Fang): Trilles 186.

Z71.16.2.1. *Ten plagues.* Irish myth: Cross.

Z71.16.3. *Formulistic number: twenty-five.* India: Thompson-Balys.

Z71.16.4. *Formulistic number: twenty-six.* India: Thompson-Balys.

Z71.16.5. *Formulistic number: thirty-two.* India: Thompson-Balys.

Z71.16.6. *Formulistic number: eighty.* India: Thompson-Balys.

Z71.16.7. *Formulistic number: sixteen hundred.* India: Thompson-Balys.

Z71.16.8. *Formulistic number: eighty thousand.* India: Thompson-Balys.

Z71.16.9. *Formulistic number: fifty-two lakhs.* India: Thompson-Balys.

Z71.16.10. *Formulistic number: fourteen.* India: Thompson-Balys.

Z71.16.11. *Formulistic number: fifteen.* Irish myth: Cross.

Z71.16.11.1. *Fifteen characteristics of a good (bad) woman.* Irish myth: Cross.

Z71.16.11.2. *The fifteen Oes.* Irish myth: *Cross.

Z71.16.11.3. *Fifteen signs before Doomsday.* Irish myth: *Cross.

Z71.16.12. *Formulistic number: seventeen.* Irish myth: Cross.

Z71.16.13. *Formulistic number: twenty-one.* India: Thompson-Balys.

Z71.16.14. *Formulistic number: twenty-two.*

Z71.16.14.1. *Twenty-two rooms and twenty-two doors built by skillful carpenter.* India: Thompson-Balys.

Z71.16.15. *Formulistic number: fifty-three.* India: Thompson-Balys.

Z71.16.16. *Formulistic number: fifty-six.* India: Thompson-Balys.

Z72. *Formulas based on the year.* Irish myth: Cross.

Z72.1. *A year and a day.* (Cf. Z71.0.2.) *Fb "år" III 1195b; A Gobbe-Duval Essais de folklore juridique[2] (Paris, 1920) 178ff.; Schröder und v. Künssberg Lehrbuch d. dt. Rechtsgeschichte[6] (1922) 789 n.; Liebermann Herrig's Archiv (1916) 401f.; Köhler-Bolte I 6. — Irish myth: Cross; English: Malory X 36, 39 and passim; Breton: Sébillot Incidents s.v. "an", "congé"; French Canadian: Barbeau JAFL XXIX 18, 24.

Z72.2. *Seven years, seven months, sevcn days.* Type 451; BP I 431; Köhler-Bolte Zs. f. Vksk. VI 63.

Z72.3. *Seven (three) years between feasts.* Irish myth: *Cross.

Z72.4. *Seven years as length of course in school.* Irish myth: Cross.

Z72.5. *Every third year as period of tribute.* Irish myth: Cross.

Z72.6. *Three hundred and sixty-five.* Irish myth: Cross.

F782.1. Windows and doors for every day in the year. L435.2.1. Woman with 365 children.

Z72.7. *Twelve years and thirteen days.* India: Thompson-Balys.

Z73. *A day and a night.* Irish myth: Cross.

K232.2. One day and one night: object borrowed for a day and a night retained. K232.2.1. Fairy (god) loses stronghold by consenting to lend it for a day and a night. K2314. Saint has tribute remitted for a day and a night.

Z73.1. *After four days—another two days—another day.* India: Thompson-Balys.

Z75. *Formula: as many children as holes in a sieve.* Breton: Sébillot Incidents s.v. "enfants".

Z76. *Formulistic exaggerations.*

Z76.1. *Three-fourths of men of Ireland die in one night.* Irish myth: Cross.

Z78. *Testament willing rewards and punishments.* Conventional ending of a story. Child V 497 s.v. "testament".

Z80. Formulistic rimes.

F943. Sinking into mud in duel.

Z81. *Blowing the house in.* I'll huff and I'll puff till I blow your house in. Type 124; *Taylor JAFL XLVI 78; BP I 40f.; Jacobs English Fairy Tales 251 No. 14.

J741.1. Bear builds house of wood; fox of ice. Fox's house fails him in summer. K732. Intruder trapped in chimney.

Z90. Miscellaneous formulas.

Z91. *Formula for other world: "Where no man goes and no crow flies."* India: Thompson-Balys.

Z92. *Formulas of distance.*

Z92.1. *"A tree on island beyond the seven seas and the sixteen rivers."* India: Thompson-Balys.

Z100—Z199. Symbolism.

Z100. Symbolism. Jewish: *Neuman.

D1812.3.3.5.1. Allegorical dream: ripe and unripe ears, fat and lean kine. H601. Wise carving of the fowl. H602. Symbolic meaning of numbers one to seven (ten, twelve). H602.2. Symbolic interpretation of letters. H603. Symbolic interpretation of playing cards. H607. Discussion by symbols. H607.1. Discussion between priest and Jew carried on by symbols. H608. Symbolic interpretation of official robes. H608.1. Symbolic interpretation of points on a bishop's hat. H611. Youth asks for branch of tree; promised root. (Branch = youngest daughter; root = eldest.) H720. Metaphorical riddles.

Z100.1. *Names of giants (Fomorians) with sinister significance.* Irish myth: Cross.

Z110. Personifications.

A460. Gods of abstractions. D1731.2. Marvels seen in dreams. K2035. Personifications (in dreams) advise opposed kings how each can overcome the other.

Z111. *Death personified.* Hartland Science 192, 199; Lithuanian: Balys Index No. 3491; Spanish: Boggs FFC XC 47, 50 No. 332, Espinosa Jr. Nos. 86—90; Jewish: *Neuman; India: *Thompson-Balys; Buddhist myth: Malalasekera II 611; Africa (Togo): Einstein 16f.

A487. God of death. C11. Old man and Death. D1724. Magic power from Death. D1825.3.1. Magic power of seeing Death at head or foot of bed and thus forecasting progress of sickness. F492. Death on horseback. J486. Death preferred above God and Justice. K557. Death cheated by moving bed. K1851.1. Forged letter: god of death replaced by another. R185. Mortal fights with "Death".

Z111.1. *Death enclosed in a bottle.* Breton: Sébillot Incidents s.v. "bouteille"; India: Thompson-Balys.

K717. Deception into bottle (vessel).

Z111.1.1. *Death imprisoned by a soldier in a magic knapsack, bottle or nutshell.* Lithuanian: Balys Index No. 330C*; Estonian: Loorits Grundzüge I 531f.; Cheremis: Sebeok-Nyerges.

Z111.2. *Death magically bound to tree.* While he is bound no one can die. Wesselski Archiv Orientální I 301. Cf. Type 330; BP II 188.

D1413.1. Tree from which one cannot descend.

Z111.2.1. *Death stuck to tree.* Mason JAFL XXXV 55.

Z111.2.2. *Death (demons) glued to chair.* Espinosa JAFL XXVII 119—29.

Z111.3. *Death as eight-headed monster.* Africa: Werner African 177.

Z111.3.1. *Death allegorically personified as an animal made up of several different animals.* Spanish Exempla: Keller.

Z111.4. *Death excluded from sacred grove.* Penzer VI 92 n. 2.

Z111.5. *Death (fate) assumes various forms to destroy men.* India: *Thompson-Balys.

Z111.6. *Death's messengers.* India: Thompson-Balys.

J1051. Death's three messengers.

Z111.6.1. *Death's messengers bribed with food.* India: Thompson-Balys.

Z111.6.2. *Salt in food given Death's messengers renders them harmless.* India: Thompson-Balys.

F384.1.2. Salt sprinkled on fairy food renders it harmless.

Z112. *Sickness personified.* *Fb "sygdom" III 699a; India: *Thompson-Balys; Chinese: Eberhard FFC CXX 175 No. 117.
F493. Spirit of plague.

Z112.1. *Fever personified.* India: *Thompson-Balys.

Z113. *Life personified: old woman carrying healing potions and salves.* Italian Novella: *Rotunda.

Z114. *Old age personified.* Irish myth: *Cross; Icelandic: Boberg.
H1149.3. Task: defeating certain old woman. (She is Old Age.)

Z115. *Wind personified.* *Fb "vind" III 1059a; Lithuanian: Balys Index No. 3902; Estonian: Loorits Grundzüge I 521; Icelandic: Boberg; Jewish: *Neuman; India: Thompson-Balys.

Z115.1. *Man takes case against wind for damages.* Wanting to have nothing to do with a court, the wind generously makes good the damages, and punishes the judge guilty of bribery. Lithuanian: Balys Index No. 3901.

Z116. *Sovereignty personified.* Irish myth: *Cross.

Z116.1. *Empire personified.* India: Thompson-Balys.

Z117. *Poetry personified.* (Cf. A465.1.) Irish myth: *Cross.

Z118. *Sea personified.* Irish myth: Cross; Icelandic: *Boberg; Jewish: *Neuman; India: Thompson-Balys.

Z118.1. *Waves as tresses of sea-god's wife.* Irish myth: *Cross.
A421. Sea-god.

Z118.2. *Waves as sea-god's horses.* Irish myth: Cross.

Z118.3. *River personified (Mother Ganges).* India: Thompson-Balys.

Z121. *Truth personified.* Irish myth: Cross.

Z121.1. *Truth leaves city because there is no place left for her.* Wienert FFC LVI *81 (ET 471), 104 (ST 169); Halm Aesop No. 314.

Z122. *Time personified.* Italian: Basile Pentamerone IV No. 8; Jewish: Neuman.

Z122.1. *"Time" overpowered when weight is taken from his clock.* Italian: Basile Pentamerone IV No. 8.

Z122.2. *Mother of Time personified.* Italian: Basile Pentamerone IV No. 8.

Z122.3. *Twelve months as youths seated about fire.* *Roberts 122, 219; Italian: Basile Pentamerone V No. 2.

Z122.4. *The four seasons personified.* Roberts 122.

Z123. *Fury personified.* (Cf. A486.) Irish myth: Cross; Jewish: Neuman.

Z123.1. *Fury personified as demon which enters man's heart and counsels evil.* Irish myth: Cross.

Z124. *Valor personified.* Irish myth: Cross.

Z124.1. *Valor personified as bird which flutters over champion's head.* Irish myth: Cross.

Z125. *Virtue personified.* Jewish: Neuman; India: Thompson-Balys.

Z126. *Energy (strength) personified.* Irish myth: Cross; India: Thompson-Balys.

Z127. *Sin personified.* Jewish: Neuman; Buddhist myth: Malalasekera II 616.

Z127.1. *Sin personified as the goddess Venus with her train of nymphs.* Spanish Exempla: Keller.

Z127.2. *Lust personified.* India: Thompson-Balys; Buddhist myth: Malalasekera II 615.

Z128. *Wisdom personified.* Irish myth: Cross; Jewish: Neuman; India: *Thompson-Balys; Africa (Wakweli): Bender 99f.

Z128.1. *Intelligence personified.* India: Thompson-Balys.

Z131. *Falsehood personified.* Irish myth: Cross; Jewish: Neuman

Z132. *War personified.* (Cf. A485.1.) Irish myth: *Cross; Jewish: Neuman.

Z132.0.1. *Battle carnage personified.* Irish myth: Cross. (Z129.2.0.1.).

Z132.1. *Victory personified.* Irish myth: Cross.

Z132.2. *Defeat personified.* Irish myth: Cross.

Z133. *Poverty personified.*

Z133.1. *Poverty personified as diseased beggar woman.* Spanish Exempla: Keller.

Z134. *Fortune personified.* (Cf. N111.) India: *Thompson-Balys.

Z134.1. *Fortune personified as a matron in fine clothing.* Spanish Exempla: Keller.

Z135. *Adversity personified.* India: *Thompson-Balys.

Z136. *Civilization personified.* India: Thompson-Balys.

Z139. *Personifications—miscellaneous.* Jewish: *Neuman.

Z139.1. *Sloth personified.* Irish myth: Cross.

Z139.2. *Crime personified.* Irish myth: Cross.

Z139.3. *Wine personified.*

Z139.3.1. *Wine personified in person of the god Bacchus.* (Cf. A481.) Spanish Exempla: Keller.

Z139.4. *Cold personified.*

Z139.4.1. *Cold depreciated and praised.* Depreciated, takes revenge by becoming colder; praised, makes reward, gives clothing. Lithuanian: Balys Index No. 3904.

Z139.5. *Worry personified.* India: Thompson-Balys.

Z139.6. *Modesty personified.* India: Thompson-Balys.

Z139.7. *Ladder as symbol of upward progress.*

Z139.7.1. *Ladder to heaven as symbol of saint.* Irish myth: Cross.

Z139.8. *Virginity, Wisdom, and Prophecy personified as three beautiful maidens.* Irish myth: Cross.

Z140. Color symbolism. Hdwb. d. Märchens II 51a s.v. "Farben im Märchen".

T3.1. Blue fortunate in love matters. Z65. Color formulas.

Z140.1. *Color of flag (sails) on ship as message of good or bad news.* *Fb "sort" III 467; *Frazer Apollodorus II 134 n. 2, *Frazer Pausanias II 161; *Schoepperle 437f.; India: Thompson-Balys.

N344. Father kills self believing that son is dead. The son forgets to spread white sails, the prearranged signal of his safety. T595. Sign hung out informing brothers whether mother has borne boy or girl.

Z140.2. *Colors corresponding to the four world quarters.* Siberian: Holmberg Siberian 347; N. A. Indian: *Thompson Tales 317 n. 148.

Z140.2.1. *Color symbolism of the cardinal points.* Dixon JAFL XII 10—16.

Z140.3. *Symbolism of colors in mass vestments.* Irish myth: *Cross.

V40. Mass.

Z140.4. *Bridegroom inadvertently buys for bride cloth suitable only for widows.* She supposes he has died. India: Thompson-Balys.

Z141. *Symbolic color: red.* Irish myth: *Cross; Icelandic: Boberg; Jewish: Neuman.

Z141.1. *Red garment to show anger of king.* *Chauvin V 47 No. 18 n. 1.

Z141.2. *Red as symbolic of martyrdom.* Irish myth: *Cross.

Z141.2.1. *Martyrs called "red wheat"; saints,* "Dei triticum" (God's wheat). Irish myth: *Cross.

Z141.2.2. *Mill in which two men are slain said to grind "red wheat".* Irish myth: *Cross.

Z141.3. *Red as symbol of falsity.* Hdwb. d. Abergl. VII 802—3; Icelandic: *Boberg.

Z142. *Symbolic color: white.* Irish myth: *Cross; Jewish: Neuman.

Z142.1. *White rose the symbol of death.* BP III 460.

Z142.2. *White as symbolic of martyrdom.* Irish myth: *Cross.

Z143. *Symbolic color: black.* Irish myth: *Cross; Jewish: Neuman.

Z143.1. *Black as symbol of grief.* *Fb "sort" III 407a; *Dickson 94 n. 75.

Z144. *Symbolic color: blue.*

Z144.1. *Blue as symbolic of martyrdom.* Irish myth: Cross.

Z145. *Symbolic color: green.*

Z145.1. *Green as symbolic of martyrdom.* Irish myth: *Cross.

Z146. *Symbolic color: brown.*

Z146.1. *Brown hair as sign child is descended from goddess.* Hawaii: Beckwith Myth 285.

Z147. *Symbolic color: purple.*

Z147.1. *Purple is symbol of royalty.* Society Islands: Henry Ancient Tahiti (Honolulu, 1928) 384.

Z148. *Yellow a lucky color.* India: Thompson-Balys.
N135. Objects effect change of luck.

Z150. Other symbols. Jewish: *Neuman.

Z151. *Ring broken as token of broken engagement.* *Bolte Zs. f. Vksk. XX 69 n. 3.

Z153. *Princess crushes lotus-flower to show that she will be submissive.* India: Thompson-Balys.

Z155. *Gray hair the symbol of departed usefulness.* *Penzer I 121; *Bloomfield JAOS XXXVI 57.

Z156. *Cloud (mist) as symbol of misfortune.* Irish myth: Cross.

Z157. *Olive branch symbol of peace.* English: Malory XX 14.

Z161. *Symbolism: not to fight alone.* Various figures employed to show it is not good for one warrior alone to fight the battles of a host. Irish myth: Cross.

Z162. *Arthur's Round Table symbolic of round earth.* English: Malory XIV 2.

Z174. *Message or orders given symbolic action.* India: Thompson-Balys.

Z174.1. *Inverted shoes at doors to indicate banishment.* India: Thompson-Balys.

Z174.1.1. *Black dummy to indicate banishment.* India: Thompson-Balys.

Z175. *Sign language.* Message delivered by means of the fingers, etc. *Penzer I 80 n. 1; *Chauvin V 145, VIII 126 No. 112; Benfey Germania IV 482ff.; Köhler-Bolte I 513; India: *Thompson-Balys.
H607.1. Discussion between priest and Jew carried on by symbols.

Z175.1. *Language of flowers.* India: Thompson-Balys.

Z175.2. *Lovers' assignation by symbolic messages.* India: *Thompson-Balys.

Z176. *Symbolism of the mass.* Irish myth: Cross.

Z177. *Lamb as symbol of Christ.* Irish myth: Cross.

Z178. *Allegorical game.* Witch, aided by dragon (lion) is vanquished by maiden, aided by lamb (ram). Witch is devil; maiden, church of Christ. Irish myth: *Cross.

Z181. *Nudity as sign of anger.* Penzer Pentamerone I 12; Irish myth: Cross.
H341.3.1. Princess brought to laughter by indecent show made in quarrel with old woman at well.

Z181.1. *Nudity as sign of madness.* India: Thompson-Balys.

Z182. *Symbolic wounding of king.* Irish myth: *Cross.

Z183. *Symbolic names.*

Z183.1. *Three trees called "Grief," "Dark," and "Dumb-Mouthless Oak."* Irish myth: *Cross.

Z184. *Symbols of divinity.* Hawaii: Beckwith Myth 43, 65; Marquesas: Handy 106.

Z185. *Mill turned by the water of the grace of God as symbol of saint.* Irish myth: Cross.

Z186. *Symbolism: needle and thread—sexual intercourse.* Chinese: Graham.

Z200—Z299. Heroes.

Z200. Heroes. *Boggs "The Hero in the Folktales of Spain, Germany, and Russia" JAFL XLIV 27ff.; Dorson American Scholar X 389ff.

A500. Demigods and culture heroes. C566. Tabus of heroes. H41.5. Unknown prince shows his kingly qualities in dealing with his playmates. L0. Victorious youngest child. L100. Unpromising hero (heroine). L122. Unsophisticated hero. T682. Hero a posthumous son.

Z210. Brothers as heroes. Type 303; **A. Christensen "Trebrødre- og Tobrødre-Stamsagn" Danske Studier (1916) 45ff. — Irish: MacCulloch Celtic 158; India: *Thompson-Balys; N. A. Indian: *Alexander N. A. Myth 295 n. 44.

F601.5. Extraordinary companions are brothers (twins, triplets). P251. Brothers. P283.1. Stepbrothers kill devastating monsters. T685.1. Twin adventurers. T686. Quadruplet heroes.

Z210.0.1. *Warriors identically equipped (brothers).* Irish myth: Cross.

F577. Friends identical in appearance.

Z210.1. *Lodge-Boy and Thrown-Away as joint adventurers.* Of brothers (sometimes twins taken from body of slain mother) one is abandoned and becomes wild. Later he joins his brother. *Dickson passim; Krappe MLN XLVII 493ff.; Oceanic: Dixon 138 n. 12; N. A. Indian: *Thompson Tales 319 n. 152, (California): Gayton and Newman 91, 95; S. A. Indian (Bakuiri): Métraux RMLP XXXIII 145.

A511.2.1.1. Abandoned culture hero captured by use of net. F567. Wild man. Man lives alone in wood like a beast. L111.2.1. Future hero found in boat (basket, bushes). T572.2.3. Hero an abortion thrown into the bushes. T584.2. Child removed from body of dead mother. T612. Child born of slain mother cares for itself during infancy.

Z211. *Dreadnaughts.* Brothers deliberately seek dangers they have been warned against. Triumph. Greek: Fox 98; India: *Thompson-Balys; Oceanic: Dixon 131, 132 n. 2, 133; Tuamotu: Stimson MS (z-G. 3/1332; T-G. 3/818; z-G. 3/1122; z-G. 13/221); Marquesas: Handy 105; N. A. Indian: *Thompson Tales 320 n. 156, (California): Gayton and Newman 69.

C614. Forbidden road. All roads may be taken except one. H1212. Quest assigned because of feigned illness. Lion's milk (or the like) said to be necessary as cure; hero therefore sent on dangerous quest. H1220. Quests voluntarily undertaken. L111.4.1. Orphan hero lives with grandmother. Avenges slaughtered kin.

Z215. *Hero "son of seven mothers".* Seven mothers each with a child imprisoned. Six eat their children to keep from starving. Seventh does not. He rescues all the mothers and becomes hero. India: Thompson-Balys.

Z216. *Supernatural origin of hero: magic conception.* (Cf. T510.) India: Thompson-Balys.

Z221. *Eldest brother as hero.* India: Thompson-Balys.
L10. Victorious youngest son.

Z230. Extraordinary exploits of hero.

Z231. *Boyish exploits of hero.* Irish myth: *Cross; India: *Thompson-Balys.

Z235. *Hero with extraordinary animal companions* (cock, goat, cow, horse). India: Thompson-Balys.

Z251. *Boy hero.* Irish myth: *Cross; Jewish: Neuman.
A527.1. Culture hero precocious. F611.3.2. Hero's precocious strength. F611.3.3. Strong hero tests weapons. L112.2. Very small hero. L311. Weak (small) hero overcomes strong in conflict. T585. Precocious infant.

Z252. *Hero at first nameless.* Irish myth: *Cross.
A1281.6. Adam at first nameless.

Z253. *Fool as hero.* (Cf. L121.) Irish myth: Cross.

Z254. *Destined hero.* (Cf. M311, T22.) Irish myth: *Cross; Jewish: Neuman.

Z255. *Hero born out of wedlock.* (Cf. L111.2.) Irish myth: Cross.
A511.1.3.1. Demigod son of king's unmarried sister (daughter) by god.

Z257. *Beardless hero.* Irish myth: *Cross.

Z261. *Giant heroes.* Irish myth: Cross.

Z292. *Death of hero.* Irish myth: Cross; Jewish: Neuman.

Z293. *Return of the hero.* (Cf. L111.1.) Irish myth: Cross; Jewish: Neuman.

Z300—Z399. Unique exceptions

Z300. Unique exceptions.
C600. Unique prohibition. C650. The one compulsory thing. Unless one does this one thing, misfortune comes. C835.4. Tabu: fighting with certain person. D1651. Magic object obeys master alone. D2161.4.10.2. Wound healed only by person who gave it. E421.1.1. Ghost visible to one person alone. E421.1.2. Ghosts visible to horses alone. E765. Life dependent on external object or event. F235.2. Fairies visible only at certain times (to one person). H31. Recognition by unique ability. H1300. Quests for the unique. M431.5. Curse: wound not to heal.

Z310. Unique vulnerability. Chinese: Graham.
C742.1. Man must be killed with first blow: other blows will not harm him. D1651.1. Only master able to bend bow. D1651.1.1. Spear can be wielded by only one person. E714.8. Monster with life in his neck (one vulnerable place). M341.1. Prophecy: death at (before, within) certain time. M341.2.19. Prophecy: death at hands of certain person. M341.3. Prophecy: death in particular place. N335.5. Hound strikes unique vulnerable spot.

Z311. *Achilles heel.* Invulnerability except in one spot. **DeCock Studien 153ff. — Irish myth: *Cross; Welsh: MacCulloch Celtic 97; Icelandic: *Boberg; Norse: De la Saussaye 144, Von Sydow Fåvne 27ff.; French Canadian: Barbeau JAFL XXIX 11; Greek: *Basset RTP XXV 124 n. 1, Frazer Apollodorus II 60 n. 2, 214 n. 1; Jewish: *Neuman; Hindu: Keith 125, Penzer I 127; Siberian: Holmberg Siberian 389; Eskimo (Mackenzie Area): Jenness 67; N. A. Indian: *Thompson Tales 345 n. 246; Africa: Werner African 236, (Fang): Trilles 202.

Z311.1. *Left eye only vulnerable spot.* Irish myth: Cross.

Z311.2. *Spot below right ear only vulnerable one.* Irish myth: Cross.

Z311.3. *Leprosy cured by holy water except on thumb.* India: Thompson-Balys.

Z311.4. *Man can be injured only in armpits.* India: Thompson-Balys.

Z312. *Unique deadly weapon.* Only one thing will kill a certain man. *Dh II 211; *Wesselski Archiv Orientální II 430; Penzer VIII 109 n. 3; R. M. Meyer Archiv f. Religionsgeschichte (1907) 93ff. — Irish: MacCulloch Celtic 151, *Cross; Icelandic: De la Saussaye 154, 156, *Boberg; N. A. Indian: *Thompson Tales 357 n. 287g; Africa (Cameroon): Ittman 77, (Swahili): Steere 441.

D965.4. Magic mistletoe. G229.4.1. Witch can be killed only by certain lance. K362.0.1. Unique weapon got by misrepresenting to guardian use to which it is to be put. K581.1. Drowning punishment for turtle. K975.1. Pretended exchange of confidences as to the one thing that can kill.

Z312.1. *Person can be killed only by red-hot spits being thrust through soles of his feet.* Irish myth: *Cross.

Z312.2. *Giant ogre can be killed only with iron club he carries (with own sword).* Irish myth: *Cross; Icelandic: *Boberg.

C531. Tabu: touching with iron. D1254.2. Magic rod. D1840.3. Magic invulnerability of ogres. F531.6.12. Disappearance or death of giants. G100. Giant ogre.

Z312.3. *Unique source of weakness.* Hawaii: Beckwith Myth 204.

Z312.4. *Unique bait for fish.* Hawaii: Beckwith Myth 216.

Z313. *Vulnerability only by one person.* Irish myth: *Cross; Icelandic: *Boberg; India: Thompson-Balys; Hindu: Keith 153.

Z313.1. *Only one person can overtake hero.* Maori: Beckwith Myth 231.

Z314. *Sword which will break in only one peril:* this known only to the maker of the sword. Gaster FL II 57; Nutt Holy Grail 11.

Z315. *Ogre vulnerable only when his face is turned away when he is struck.* India: Thompson-Balys.

Z316. *Only one way to besiege certain city.* Jewish: Neuman.

Z320. Object will fit only one thing (or person). Irish myth: Cross.

H100. Identification by matching parts of divided token.

Z321. *Ring fits only one person.* Irish myth: Cross.

H36. Recognition by exact fitting of clothes. H94. Identification by ring.

Z322. *Only one ferule fits certain staff.* Irish myth: Cross.

Z323. *Vessel from which nothing can be drunk save through certain tube.* Irish myth: Cross.

Z350. Other unique exceptions.

Z351. *Only one person refuses to weep at hero's death.* Icelandic: Boberg.

A2231.2.1. Crane will not weep at crucifixion. Only exception.

Z352. *All trees except aspen refuse to make Christ's cross.* Dh II 209; North Carolina: Brown Collection I 635.

A2721.2.1. Tree cursed for serving as cross.

Z355. *All snakes but one placated by music.* In snake den prisoner fails to placate one snake and loses his life. Hdwb. d. Märchens I 437a.

Z356. *Unique survivor.* Only one person left from destruction of his community. India: *Thompson-Balys; Hawaii: Beckwith Myth 135, 443f., 449; Marquesas: Handy 77; Easter Island: Métraux Ethnology 71; Tuamotu: Stimson MS (z-G. 13/203); Tahiti: Henry Ancient Tahiti (Honolulu, 1928) 246.

A1006.1. New race from single pair (or several) after world calamity.

Z356.1. *Unique survivor from destruction of animals.* India: *Thompson-Balys.

Z357. *Unique exceptions from curse.* Irish myth: *Cross.

ADDITIONS AND CORRECTIONS

VOLUME 1.

P. 12, line 16.	*For* the present work *read* the first edition of the present work.
P. 16, line 25.	*For* Schimp *read* Schimpf.
P. 47, line 15.	Add ⊙Ikeda, Hiroko. Motif and Type Index of Japanese Folktales. (Indiana University dissertation). Ann Arbor, Michigan. Microfilm Service. 1955.
P. 156 (A762.1).	*For* Septenrionalia *read* Septentrionalia.
P. 184 (A1010).	*For* Melanesian: ibid. *read* Melanesian: Cole.
P. 186 (A1018).	*For* Stout CU IV 267 *read* Stewart BBAE CXLIII (4) 267.
P. 187 (A1021).	*For* (Objibwa) *read* (Ojibwa); *for* (Chochtaw) *read* (Choctaw).
P. 354 (B11.11.6).	*For* B11.6.6.1 *read* B11.6.8.1.
P. 405 (B242).	*For* Bødker Exempler 293.2 *read* Bødker Exempler 293 No. 52.
P. 439.	Delete B478 (see B495.1).
P. 542.	Delete C854.1 (see C833.8).

VOLUME 2.

P. 77, line 1.	*For* 670D *read* D670.
P. 102 (D876, line 8).	*For* D1901.1 *read* J1901.1.
P. 335 (D1821.3.5.1).	*For* Baly *read* Balys.
P. 394 (D2161.6.2).	*For* Messeanic *read* Messianic.